P9-CEE-672

Troubleshooting and Maintaining Cisco IP Networks (TSHOOT) Foundation Learning Guide

Foundation learning for the CCNP TSHOOT 642-832

Amir Ranjbar, CCIE No. 8669

Cisco Press

800 East 96th Street

Indianapolis, IN 46240

Troubleshooting and Maintaining Cisco IP Networks (TSHOOT) Foundation Learning Guide

Foundation learning for the CCNP TSHOOT 642-832

Amir Ranjbar, CCIE No. 8669

Published by:

Cisco Press

800 East 96th Street

Indianapolis, IN 46240 USA

Printed in the United States of America 1 2 3 4 5 6 7 8 9 0

First Printing March 2010

Library of Congress Cataloging-in-Publication Number is on file.

ISBN (10-digit): 1-58705-876-6

ISBN (13-digit): 978-1-58705-876-9

Warning and Disclaimer

This book is designed to provide information about the Troubleshooting and Maintaining Cisco IP Networks (TSHOOT) course as a reference in preparation for TSHOOT Exam 642-832 for the CCNP certification. Every effort has been made to make this book as complete and as accurate as possible, but no warranty or fitness is implied.

The information is provided on an "as is" basis. The authors, Cisco Press, and Cisco Systems, Inc., shall have neither liability nor responsibility to any person or entity with respect to any loss or damages arising from the information contained in this book or from the use of the discs or programs that may accompany it.

The opinions expressed in this book belong to the author and are not necessarily those of Cisco Systems, Inc.

Feedback Information

At Cisco Press, our goal is to create in-depth technical books of the highest quality and value. Each book is crafted with care and precision, undergoing rigorous development that involves the unique expertise of members from the professional technical community. Readers' feedback is a natural continuation of this process. If you have any comments regarding how we could improve the quality of this book or otherwise alter it to better suit your needs, you can contact us through e-mail at feedback@ciscopress.com. Please make sure to include the book title and ISBN in your message.

We greatly appreciate your assistance.

Trademark Acknowledgments

All terms mentioned in this book that are known to be trademarks or service marks have been appropriately capitalized. Cisco Press or Cisco Systems, Inc., cannot attest to the accuracy of this information. Use of a term in this book should not be regarded as affecting the validity of any trademark or service mark.

Corporate and Government Sales

Cisco Press offers excellent discounts on this book when ordered in quantity for bulk purchases or special sales. For more information, please contact: U.S. Corporate and Government Sales, 1-800-382-3419 or corpsales@pearsontechgroup.com.

For sales outside the U.S., please contact: International Sales, internatioal@pearsoned.com.

Publisher: Paul Boger

Associate Publisher: Dave Dusthimer

Executive Editor: Mary Beth Ray

Managing Editor: Patrick Kanouse

Copy Editor: Keith Cline

Editorial Assistant: Vanessa Evans

Cover Designer: Louisa Adair

Composition: Mark Shirar

Business Operation Manager, Cisco Press: Anand Sundaram

Manager Global Certification: Erik Ullanderson

Senior Development Editor: Christopher Cleveland

Project Editor: Jennifer Gallant

Technical Editors: Elan Beer, Sonya Coker, Jeremy Creech, Rick Graziani, David Kotfila, Wayne Lewis, Jim Lorenz, Snezhy Neshkova, Allan Reid, Bob Vachon

Proofreader: MPS Limited, A Macmillan Company

Indexer: WordWise Publishing Services

Americas Headquarters
Cisco Systems, Inc.
San Jose, CA

Asia Pacific Headquarters
Cisco Systems (USA) Pte. Ltd.
Singapore

Europe Headquarters
Cisco Systems International BV
Amsterdam, The Netherlands

Cisco has more than 200 offices worldwide. Addresses, phone numbers, and fax numbers are listed on the Cisco Website at **www.cisco.com/go/offices.**

About the Author

Amir Ranjbar, CCIE No. 8669, is a Certified Cisco Systems Instructor and an internetworking consultant. Operating under his own corporation, AMIRACAN Inc., Amir offers his training services to Global Knowledge Network, his consulting expertise to a variety of clients (mainly Internet service providers), and his technical writing skills to Cisco Press. Born in Tehran, Iran, Amir immigrated to Canada in 1983 at the age of 16 and completed his Master's degree in knowledge-based systems (a branch in AI) in 1991. He has been involved in training, consulting, and technical writing for the greater part of his career. Amir Ranjbar can be contacted through his e-mail address aranjbar@amiracan.com.

About the Technical Reviewers

Elan Beer, CCIE No. 1837, CCSI No. 94008, is a senior consultant and Certified Cisco Instructor. His internetworking expertise is recognized internationally through his global consulting and training engagements. As one of the industry's top internetworking consultants and Cisco instructors, Elan has used his expertise for the past 17 years to design, implement, and deploy multiprotocol networks for a wide international clientele. As a senior instructor and course developer, Elan has designed and presented public and implementation-specific technical courses spanning many of today's top technologies. Elan specializes in MPLS, BGP, QoS, and other internetworking technologies.

Sonya Coker has worked in the Cisco Networking Academy program since 1999 when she started a local academy. She has taught student and instructor classes locally and internationally in topics ranging from IT essentials to CCNP. As a member of the Cisco Networking Academy development team, she has provided subject matter expertise on both new courses and on course revisions.

Jeremy Creech is a Learning and Development Manager for Cisco Systems with more than 13 years of experience in researching, implementing, and managing data and voice networks. Currently, he is a curriculum development manager for the Cisco Networking Academy Program leveraging his experience as the Content Development Manager for CCNP Certification exams. He has recently completed curriculum development initiatives for ROUTE, SWITCH, TSHOOT, and CCNA Security.

Rick Graziani teaches computer science and computer networking courses at Cabrillo College in Aptos, California. Rick has worked and taught in the computer networking and information technology field for almost 30 years. Prior to teaching, Rick worked in IT for various companies, including Santa Cruz Operation, Tandem Computers, and Lockheed Missiles and Space Corporation. He holds an M.A. in computer science and systems theory from California State University Monterey Bay. Rick also does consulting work for Cisco Systems and other companies. When Rick is not working, he is most likely surfing one of his favorite Santa Cruz breaks.

David Kotfila, CCNA, CCDA, CCNP, CCDP, CCSP, CCVP, CCAI, teaches in the Computer Science department at Rensselaer Polytechnic Institute, Troy, New York. More than 550 of his students have received their CCNA, 200 have received their CCNP, and 14 have received their CCIE. David likes to spend time with his wife, Kate, his daughter, Charis, and his son, Chris. David enjoys hiking, kayaking, and reading.

Wayne Lewis has been a faculty member at Honolulu Community College since receiving a Ph.D. in math from the University of Hawaii at Manoa in 1992, specializing in finite rank torsion-free modules over a Dedekind domain. Since 1992, he served as a math instructor, as the state school-to-work coordinator, and as the legal main contact for the Cisco Academy Training Center (CATC). Dr. Lewis manages the CATC for CCNA, CCNP, and Security, based at Honolulu Community College, which serves Cisco Academies at universities, colleges, and high schools in Hawaii, Guam, and American Samoa. Since 1998, he has taught routing, multilayer switching, remote access, troubleshooting, network security, and wireless networking to instructors from universities, colleges, and high schools in Australia, Britain, Canada, Central America, China, Germany, Hong Kong, Hungary, Indonesia, Italy, Japan, Korea, Mexico, Poland, Singapore, Sweden, Taiwan, and South America, both onsite and at Honolulu Community College.

Jim Lorenz is an instructor and a curriculum developer for the Cisco Networking Academy Program. Jim has co-authored Lab Companions for the CCNA courses and the textbooks for the Fundamentals of UNIX course. He has more than 25 years of experience in information systems, ranging from programming and database administration to network design and project management. Jim has developed and taught computer and networking courses for both public and private institutions. As the Cisco Academy Manager at Chandler-Gilbert College in Arizona, he was instrumental in starting the Information Technology Institute (ITI) and developed a number of certificates and degree programs. Jim co-authored, with Allan Reid, the CCNA Discovery online academy courses Networking for Home and Small Businesses and Introducing Routing and Switching in the Enterprise. Most recently, he developed the hands-on labs for the CCNA Security course and the CCNPv6 Troubleshooting course.

Snezhy Neshkova, CCIE 11931, has more than 20 years of networking experience, including IT field services and support, management of information systems, and all aspects of networking education. Snezhy has developed and taught CCNA and CCNP networking courses to instructors from universities, colleges, and high schools in Canada, the United States, and Europe. Snezhy's passion is to empower students to become successful and lifelong learners. Snezhy holds a Master of Science degree in computer science from Technical University, Sofia (Bulgaria).

Allan Reid, CCNA, CCNA-W, CCDA, CCNP, CCDP, CCAI, MLS, is a professor in information and communications engineering technology and the lead instructor at the Centennial College CATC in Toronto, Canada. He has developed and taught networking courses for both private and public organizations and has been instrumental in the development and implementation of numerous certificate, diploma, and degree programs in networking. Outside of his academic responsibilities, Allan has been active in the computer and networking fields for more than 25 years and is currently a principal in a company specializing in the design, management, and security of network solutions for small and medium-sized companies. Allan is a curriculum and assessment developer for the Cisco Networking Academy program and has authored several Cisco Press titles.

Bob Vachon, CCNP, CCNA-S, CCAI, is a professor in the Computer Systems Technology program at Cambrian College and has more than 20 years of experience in the networking field. In 2001, he began collaborating with the Cisco Networking Academy on various curriculum development projects, including CCNA, CCNA Security, and CCNP courses. For 3 years, Bob was also part of an elite team authoring CCNP certification exam questions. In 2007, Bob co-authored the CCNA Exploration: Accessing the WAN Cisco Press book.

Dedication

I dedicate this book to my children Thalia, Ariana, and Armando, who are always in my cache no matter where I am or what I am doing (no timeouts!). I wish the best to all the children in the world.

Acknowledgments

This book is the result of the hard work of many individuals. I want to offer my sincere gratitude to all of them, whether we worked together directly or otherwise. The Executive Editor, Mary Beth Ray, had to do extraordinary work for this project to be completed successfully, and the Senior Development Editor, Christopher Cleveland, has done an excellent job correcting and cleaning up my work. I also want to thank all the technical editors for their efforts and feedback. Finally, I thank my wife, Elke, and my parents, Kavos and Batoul, for their continuous love, encouragement, and support.

Contents at a Glance

Table of Contents

Icons Used in This Book

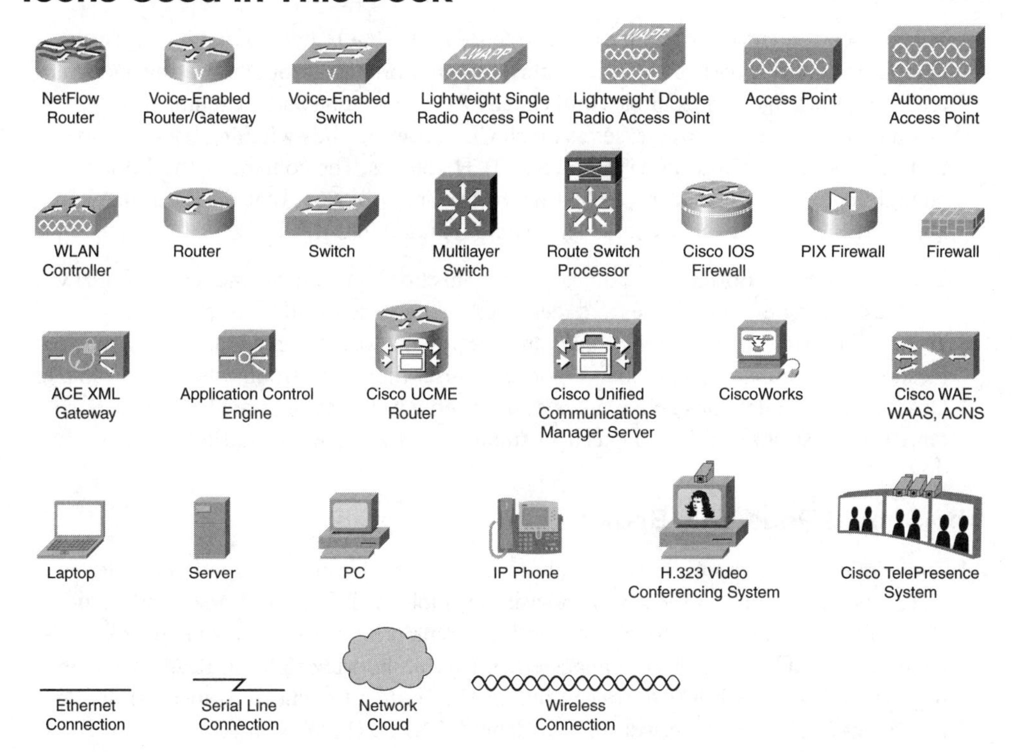

Command Syntax Conventions

The conventions used to present command syntax in this book are the same conventions used in the Cisco IOS Command Reference. The Command Reference describes these conventions as follows:

- **Boldface** indicates commands and keywords that are entered literally as shown. In actual configuration examples and output (not general command syntax), boldface indicates commands that are manually input by the user (such as a show command).
- *Italics* indicate arguments for which you supply actual values.
- Vertical bars (|) separate alternative, mutually exclusive elements.
- Square brackets ([ ]) indicate optional elements.
- Braces ({ }) indicate a required choice.
- Braces within brackets ([{ }]) indicate a required choice within an optional element.

Introduction

This book's content is based on the Cisco Systems TSHOOT course that has recently been introduced as part of the CCNP curriculum; it provides troubleshooting and maintenance knowledge and examples in the area of Cisco routing and switching. It is assumed that the reader possesses as much Cisco routing and switching background as that covered in the Cisco ROUTE and SWITCH courses. The content of this book is enough to prepare the reader for the TSHOOT exam, too. Note that the e-learning content of the Cisco TSHOOT course has been integrated into this book.

Teaching troubleshooting is not an easy task. This book introduces the reader to many troubleshooting methodologies and identifies the benefits of different techniques. Technical routing and switching topics are briefly reviewed, but the emphasis is on troubleshooting commands, and most important, presenting many troubleshooting examples. Chapter review questions help readers evaluate how well they absorbed the chapter content. The questions are also an excellent supplement for exam preparation.

Who Should Read This Book?

Those individuals who want to learn about modern troubleshooting methodologies and techniques and desire to see several relevant examples will find this book very useful. This book is most suitable for those who have some prior routing and switching knowledge but would like to learn or enhance their troubleshooting skill set. Readers who want to pass the Cisco TSHOOT exam can find all the content they need to successfully do so in this book. The Cisco Networking Academy CCNP TSHOOT course students will use this book as their official textbook.

Cisco Certifications and Exams

Cisco offers four levels of routing and switching certification, each with an increasing level of proficiency: Entry, Associate, Professional, and Expert. These are commonly known by their acronyms CCENT (Cisco Certified Entry Networking Technician), CCNA (Cisco Certified Network Associate), CCNP (Cisco Certified Network Professional), and CCIE (Cisco Certified Internetworking Expert). There are others, too, but this book focuses on the certifications for enterprise networks.

For the CCNP certification, you must pass exams on a series of CCNP topics, including the SWITCH, ROUTE, and TSHOOT exams. For most exams, Cisco does not publish the scores needed for passing. You need to take the exam to find that out for yourself.

To see the most current requirements for the CCNP certification, go to Cisco.com and click Training and Events. There you can find out other exam details such as exam topics and how to register for an exam.

The strategy you use to prepare for the TSHOOT exam might differ slightly from strategies used by other readers, mainly based on the skills, knowledge, and experience you have already obtained. For instance, if you have attended the TSHOOT course, you might take a different approach than someone who learned troubleshooting through on-the-job training. Regardless of the strategy you use or the background you have, this book is designed to help you get to the point where you can pass the exam with the least amount of time required.

How This Book Is Organized

Although this book can be read cover to cover, it is designed to be flexible and allow you to easily move between chapters to cover only the material with which you might need additional remediation. The chapters can be covered in any order, although some chapters are related and build upon each other. If you do intend to read them all, the order in the book is an excellent sequence to follow.

Each core chapter covers a subset of the topics on the CCNP TSHOOT exam. The chapters cover the following topics:

- **Chapter 1, "Planning Maintenance for Complex Networks":** This chapter presents and evaluates commonly practiced models and methodologies for network maintenance, introduces the processes and procedures that are fundamental parts of any network maintenance methodology, and identifies and evaluates tools, applications, and resources that support network maintenance processes.
- **Chapter 2, "Troubleshooting Processes for Complex Enterprise Networks":** This chapter explains the benefits of structured troubleshooting and how to implement troubleshooting procedures. Furthermore, the generic troubleshooting processes and their relation to network maintenance processes are analyzed, along with the role of change control and documentation.
- **Chapter 3, "Using Maintenance and Troubleshooting Tools and Applications":** This chapter reviews the built-in Cisco IOS tools and commands, plus some specialized tools and applications used for network troubleshooting and maintenance.
- **Chapter 4, "Maintaining and Troubleshooting Campus Switched Solutions":** This chapter reviews prominent campus multilayer switching technologies such as VLANs, Spanning Tree Protocol, inter-VLAN routing, and first-hop redundancy protocols, and it focuses on resolving problems related to these technologies.
- **Chapter 5, "Maintaining and Troubleshooting Routing Solutions":** This chapter's focus is on troubleshooting network layer connectivity. Troubleshooting EIGRP, OSPF, BGP, and route redistribution are presented in sequence.
- **Chapter 6, "Troubleshooting Addressing Services":** This chapter consists of two parts. The first part discusses how to identify and correct common IPv4 addressing service issues (NAT and DHCP specifically), and the second part does the same for common IPv6 routing issues.
- **Chapter 7, "Troubleshooting Network Performance Issues":** This chapter has three main sections. The first section presents troubleshooting network application services, and the second and third sections focus on troubleshooting performance issues on routers and switches.

- **Chapter 8, "Troubleshooting Converged Networks"**: This chapter discusses troubleshooting topics that relate to proper operation of wireless, unified communications, and video applications.
- **Chapter 9, "Maintaining and Troubleshooting Network Security Implementations"**: This chapter starts by explaining the troubleshooting challenges in secure networks. Next, troubleshooting the management plane, control plane, and data plane are discussed in sequence. Troubleshooting branch office connectivity is the final topic of this chapter.
- **Chapter 10, "Review and Preparation for Troubleshooting Complex Enterprise Networks"**: This chapter reviews the key maintenance and troubleshooting concepts and tools, and concludes with a brief discussion about applying maintenance and troubleshooting concepts and tools.

There is also an appendix that has answers to the "Review Questions" questions found at the end of each chapter.

Chapter 1

Planning Maintenance for Complex Networks

This chapter covers the following topics:

- Applying maintenance methodologies
- Maintenance processes and procedures
- Network maintenance tools, applications, and resources

Many modern business processes and transactions depend on high availability and reliability of an organization's computer network and computing resources. Downtime can cause significant loss of reputation/revenue. Planning the network maintenance processes and procedures facilitates high availability and cost control. This chapter presents and evaluates commonly practiced models and methodologies for network maintenance, introduces the processes and procedures that are fundamental parts of any network maintenance methodology, and identifies and evaluates tools, applications, and resources that support network maintenance processes.

Applying Maintenance Methodologies

Support and maintenance are two of the core tasks that network engineers perform. The objective of network maintenance is to keep the network available with minimum service disruption and at acceptable performance levels. Network maintenance includes regularly scheduled tasks such as making backups and upgrading devices or software. Structured network maintenance provides a guideline that you can follow to maximize network uptime and minimize unplanned outages, but the exact techniques you should use are governed by your company's policies and procedures and your experience and preferences. Network support includes following up on interrupt-driven tasks, such as responding to device and link failures and to users who need help. You must evaluate the commonly practiced models and methodologies used for network maintenance and identify the benefits that these models bring to your organization. You must also select generalized maintenance models and planning tools that fit your organization the best.

Maintenance Models and Methodologies

A typical network engineer's job description usually includes elements such as installing, implementing, maintaining, and supporting network equipment. The exact set of tasks performed by network engineers might differ between organizations. Depending on the size and type of organization, some or all of the following are likely to be included in that set:

- **Tasks related to device installation and maintenance:** Includes tasks such as installing devices and software, and creating and backing up configurations and software
- **Tasks related to failure response:** Includes tasks such as supporting users that experience network problems, troubleshooting device or link failures, replacing equipment, and restoring backups
- **Tasks related to network performance:** Includes tasks such as capacity planning, performance tuning, and usage monitoring
- **Tasks related to business procedures:** Includes tasks such as documenting, compliance auditing, and service level agreement (SLA) management
- **Tasks related to security:** Includes tasks such as following and implementing security procedures and security auditing

Network engineers must not only understand their own organization's definition of network maintenance and the tasks it includes, but they must also comprehend the policies and procedures that govern how those tasks are performed. In many smaller networks, the process is largely *interrupt driven*. For example, when users have problems, you start helping them, or when applications experience performance problems, you upgrade links or equipment. Another example is that a company's network engineer reviews and improves the security of the network only when security concerns or incidents are reported. Although this is obviously the most basic method of performing network maintenance, it clearly has some disadvantages, including the following:

- Tasks that are beneficial to the long-term health of the network might be ignored, postponed, or forgotten.
- Tasks might not be executed in order of priority or urgency, but instead in the order they were requested.
- The network might experience more downtime than necessary because problems are not prevented.

You cannot avoid interrupt-driven work entirely because failures will happen and you cannot plan them. However, you can reduce the amount of incident-driven (interrupt-driven) work by proactively monitoring and managing systems.

The alternative to the interrupt-driven model of maintenance is *structured* network maintenance. Structured network maintenance predefines and plans much of the processes and procedures. This proactive approach not only reduces the frequency and quantity of user, application, and business problems, it also renders the responses to incidents more efficiently. The structured approach to network maintenance has some clear benefits over the interrupt-driven approach, including the following:

- **Reduced network downtime:** By discovering and preventing problems before they happen, you can prevent or at least minimize network downtime. You should strive to maximize mean time between failures (MTBF). Even if you cannot prevent problems, you can reduce the amount of time it takes to fix them by following proper procedures and using adequate tools. You should strive to minimize mean time to repair (MTTR). Maximizing MTBF and minimizing MTTR translates to lower financial damage and higher user satisfaction.
- **More cost-effectiveness:** Performance monitoring and capacity planning allows you to make adequate budgeting decisions for current and future networking needs. Choosing proper equipment and using it to capacity means better price/performance ratio over the lifetime of your equipment. Lower maintenance costs and network downtime also help to reduce the price/performance ratio.
- **Better alignment with business objectives:** Within the structured network maintenance framework, instead of prioritizing tasks and assigning budgets based on incidents, time and resources are allocated to processes based on their importance to the business. For example, upgrades and major maintenance jobs are not scheduled during critical business hours.
- **Higher network security:** Attention to network security is part of structured network maintenance. If prevention techniques do not stop a breach or attack, detection mechanisms will contain them, and support staff will be notified through logs and alarms. Monitoring allows you to observe network vulnerabilities and needs and to justify plans for strengthening network security.

Several well-known network maintenance methodologies have been defined by a variety of organizations, including the International Organization for Standardization (ISO), International Telecommunication Union Telecommunication Standardization sector (ITU-T), and Cisco Systems. Network support engineers must study these and incorporate the elements of these models as per their environment needs. Four examples of well-known network maintenance and methodologies are as follows:

- **IT Infrastructure Library (ITIL):** This framework for IT service management describes best practices that help in providing high-quality IT services that are aligned with business needs and processes.
- **FCAPS:** This model, defined by ISO, divides network management tasks into five different categories:
  - Fault management
  - Configuration management
  - Accounting management

- Performance management
- Security management.

Note that the term *FCAPS* is driven from the first letter of each management category.

- **Telecommunications Management Network (TMN):** The ITU-T integrated and refined the FCAPS model to define a conceptual framework for the management of telecommunications networks and describes establishing a management network that interfaces with a telecommunications network at several different points for the purpose of manual and automated maintenance tasks.
- **Cisco Lifecycle Services:** This approach is a model that helps businesses to successfully deploy, operate, and optimize Cisco technologies in their network. This model is sometimes also referenced to as the Prepare, Plan, Design, Implement, Operate, and Optimize (PPDIOO) model, based on the names of the six phases of the network lifecycle. Network maintenance tasks are usually considered part of the operate and optimize phases of the cycle.

Determining Procedures and Tools to Support Maintenance Models

Those who decide to perform structured network maintenance either select one of the recommended network maintenance models or build a custom model that meets their particular needs by taking elements from different models. For example, if a company chooses the FCAPS model, they will have five main management tasks on their hands:

- **Fault management:** Fault management is the domain where network problems are discovered and corrected. Although some of this effort is inevitably event driven, the focus here is on preventive maintenance. Proper steps are taken to prevent breakdowns and past incidents from recurring; hence, network downtime is minimized.
- **Configuration management:** Configuration management is concerned with tasks such as installation, identification, and configuration of hardware (including components such a line cards, modules, memory, and power supplies) and services. Configuration management also includes software and firmware management, change control, inventory management, plus monitoring and managing the deployment status of devices.
- **Accounting management:** Accounting management focuses on how to optimally distribute resources among enterprise subscribers. This helps to minimize the cost of operations by making the most effective use of the systems available. Cost distribution and billing of departments/users are also accounting management tasks.
- **Performance management:** Performance management is about managing the overall performance of the enterprise network. The focus here is on maximizing throughput, identifying bottlenecks, and forming plans to enhance performance.
- **Security management:** Security management is responsible for ensuring confidentiality, integrity, and availability (CIA). The network must be protected against unauthorized access and physical and electronic sabotage. Security management ensures CIA

through authentication, authorization, and accounting (AAA), plus other techniques such as encryption, network perimeter protection, intrusion detection/prevention, and security monitoring and reporting.

Upon selection of a network maintenance *model*, you must translate the theoretical model to practical *procedures* that structure the network maintenance processes for your network. Figure 1-1 shows an example where four procedures are defined for the configuration management element of the FCAPS model.

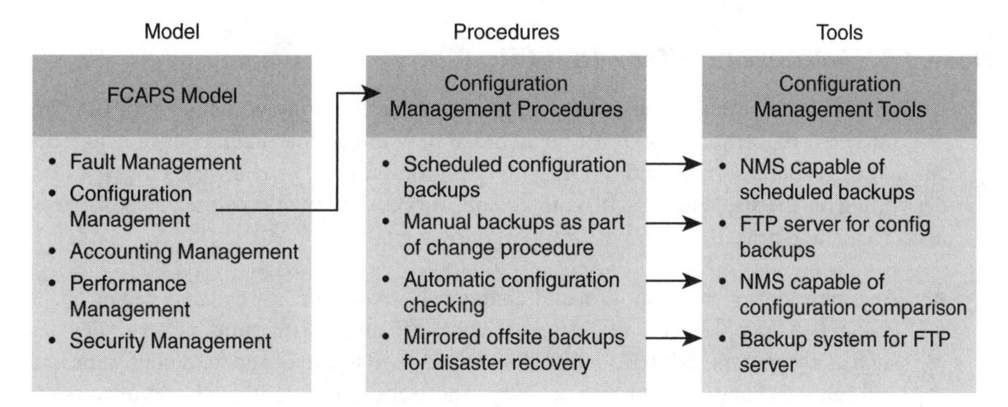

Figure 1-1 *Models, Procedures, and Tools*

After you have defined your processes and procedures, it becomes much easier to see what functionalities and *tools* you need to have in your network management toolkit to support these processes. As a result, you can select an efficient and cost-effective network management and support toolkit that offers those tools and hopefully meets your budgetary constraints. Figure 1-1 shows a network management toolkit (in the rightmost column) that offers four tools, one for each of the defined procedures (in the middle column). It is noteworthy that an interrupt-driven network maintenance approach usually leads to a fragmented network management toolkit. The reason is that tools are acquired on an on-demand basis to deal with a particular need, instead of considering the toolkit as a whole and building it to support all the network maintenance processes.

Maintenance Processes and Procedures

Network maintenance involves many tasks. Some of these tasks are nearly universal, whereas others might be deployed by only some organizations or performed in unique ways. Processes such as maintenance planning, change control, documentation, disaster recovery, and network monitoring are common elements of all network maintenance plans. To establish procedures that fit an organization's needs best, network engineers need to do the following:

- Identify essential network maintenance tasks.

- Recognize and describe the advantages of scheduled maintenance.
- Evaluate the key decision factors that affect change control procedures to create procedures that fit organization's needs.
- Describe the essential elements of network documentation and its function.
- Plan for efficient disaster recovery.
- Describe the importance of network monitoring and performance measurement as an integral element of a proactive network maintenance strategy.

Network Maintenance Task Identification

Regardless of the network maintenance model and methodology you choose or the size of your network, certain tasks must be included in your network maintenance plan. The amount of resources, time, and money you spend on these tasks will vary, however, depending on the size and type of your organization. All network maintenance plans need to include procedures to perform the following tasks:

- **Accommodating adds, moves, and changes:** Networks are always undergoing changes. As people move and offices are changed and restructured, network devices such as computers, printers, and servers might need to be moved, and configuration and cabling changes might be necessary. These adds, moves, and changes are a normal part of network maintenance.
- **Installation and configuration of new devices:** This task includes adding ports, link capacity, network devices, and so on. Implementation of new technologies or installation and configuration of new devices is either handled by a different group within your organization, by an external party, or handled by internal staff.
- **Replacement of failed devices:** Whether replacement of failed devices is done through service contracts or done in house by support engineers, it is an important network maintenance task.
- **Backup of device configurations and software:** This task is linked to the task of replacing failed devices. Without good backups of both software and configurations, the time to replace failed equipment or recover from severe device failures will not be trouble free and might take a long time.
- **Troubleshooting link and device failures:** Failures are inevitable; diagnosing and resolving failures related to network components, links, or service provider connections are essential tasks within a network engineer's job.
- **Software upgrading or patching:** Network maintenance requires that you stay informed of available software upgrades or patches and use them if necessary. Critical performance or security vulnerabilities are often addressed by the software upgrades or patches.
- **Network monitoring:** Monitoring operation of the devices and user activity on the network is also part of a network maintenance plan. Network monitoring can be

performed using simple mechanisms such as collection of router and firewall logs or by using sophisticated network monitoring applications.

- **Performance measurement and capacity planning:** Because the demand for bandwidth is continually increasing, another network maintenance task is to perform at least some basic measurements to decide when it is time to upgrade links or equipment and to justify the cost of the corresponding investments. This proactive approach allows one to plan for upgrades (capacity planning) before bottlenecks are formed, congestions are experienced, or failures occur.
- **Writing and updating documentation:** Preparing proper network documentation that describes the current state of the network for reference during implementation, administration, and troubleshooting is a mandatory network maintenance task within most organizations. Network documentation must be kept current.

Network Maintenance Planning

You must build processes and procedures for performing your network maintenance tasks; this is called network maintenance planning. Network maintenance planning includes the following:

- Scheduling maintenance
- Formalizing change-control procedures
- Establishing network documentation procedures
- Establishing effective communication
- Defining templates/procedures/conventions
- Planning for disaster recovery

Scheduling Maintenance

After you have determined the tasks and processes that are part of network maintenance, you can assign priorities to them. You can also determine which of these tasks will be interrupt driven by nature (hardware failures, outages, and so on) and which tasks are parts of a long-term maintenance cycle (software patching, backups, and so on). For the long-term tasks, you will have to work out a schedule that guarantees that these tasks will be done regularly and will not get lost in the busy day-to-day work schedule. For some tasks such as moves and changes, you can adopt a procedure that is partly interrupt driven (incoming change requests) and partly scheduled: Change requests need not be handled immediately, but during the next scheduled timeframe. This allows you to properly prioritize tasks but still have a predictable lead time that the requesting party knows they can count on for a change to be executed. With scheduled maintenance, tasks that are disruptive to the network are scheduled during off-hours. You can select maintenance windows during evenings or weekends where outages will be acceptable, thereby reducing unnecessary outages during office hours. The uptime of the network will increase as both the number of unplanned outages and their duration will be reduced. To summarize, the benefits of scheduled maintenance include the following:

- Network downtime is reduced.
- Long-term maintenance tasks will not be neglected or forgotten.
- You have predictable lead times for change requests.
- Disruptive maintenance tasks can be scheduled during assigned maintenance windows, reducing downtime during production hours.

Formalizing Change-Control Procedures

Sometimes it is necessary to make changes to configuration, software, or hardware. Any change that you make has an associated risk due to possible mistakes, conflicts, or bugs. Before making any change, you must first determine the impact of the change on the network and balance this against the urgency of the change. If the anticipated impact is high, you might need to justify the need for the change and obtain authorization to proceed. High-impact changes are usually made during maintenance windows specifically scheduled for this purpose. On the other hand, there will also have to be a process for emergency changes. For example, if a broadcast storm occurs in your network and a link needs to be disconnected to break the loop and allow the network to stabilize, you might not be able to wait for authorization and the next maintenance window. In many companies, change control is formalized and answers the following types of questions:

- Which types of change require authorization and who is responsible for authorizing them?
- Which changes have to be done during a maintenance window and which changes can be done immediately?
- What kind of preparation needs to be done before executing a change?
- What kind of verification needs to be done to confirm that the change was effective?
- What other actions (such as updating documentation) need to be taken after a successful change?
- What actions should be taken when a change has unexpected results or causes problems?
- What conditions allow skipping some of the normal change procedures and which elements of the procedures should still be followed?

Establishing Network Documentation Procedures

An essential part of any network maintenance is building and keeping up-to-date network documentation. Without up-to-date network documentation, it is difficult to correctly plan and implement changes, and troubleshooting is tedious and time-consuming. Usually, documentation is created as part of network design and implementation, but keeping it up-to-date is part of network maintenance. Therefore, any good change-control procedure will include updating the relevant documentation after the change is made. Documentation can be as simple as a few network drawings, equipment and software lists, and the current configurations of all devices. On the other hand, documentation can be extensive, describing all implemented features, design choices that were made, service contract numbers, change procedures, and so on. Typical elements of network documentation include the following:

- **Network drawings:** Diagrams of the physical and logical structure of the network
- **Connection documentation:** Lists of all relevant physical connections, such as patches, connections to service providers, and power circuits
- **Equipment lists:** Lists of all devices, part numbers, serial numbers, installed software versions, (if applicable) software licenses, warranty/service information
- **IP address administration:** Lists of the IP subnets scheme and all IP addresses in use
- **Configurations:** A set of all current device configurations or even an archive that contains all previous configurations
- **Design documentation:** This is a document describing the motivation behind certain implementation choices.

Establishing Effective Communication

Network maintenance is usually performed by a team of people and cannot easily be divided into exclusive sets of tasks that do not affect each other. Even if you have specialists who are responsible for particular technologies or set of devices, they will always have to communicate with team members who are responsible for different technologies or other devices. The best means of communication depends on the situation and organization, but a major consideration for choosing a communication method is how easily it is logged and shared with the network maintenance team.

Communication is vital both during troubleshooting and technical support and afterward. During troubleshooting, certain questions must be answered, such as the following:

- Who is making changes and when?
- How does the change affect others?
- What are the results of tests that were done, and what conclusions can be drawn?

If actions, test results, and conclusions are not communicated between team members, the process in the hands of one team member can be disruptive to the process handled by another team member. You don't want to create new problems while solving others.

In many cases, diagnosis and resolution must be done by several persons or during multiple sessions. In those cases, it is important to have a log of actions, tests, communication, and conclusions. These must be distributed among all those involved. With proper communication, one team member should comfortably take over where another team member has left off. Communication is also required after completion of troubleshooting or making changes.

Defining Templates/Procedures/Conventions (Standardization)

When a team of people execute the same or related tasks, it is important that those tasks be performed consistently. Because people might inherently have different working methods, styles, and backgrounds, standardization makes sure work performed by different people remain consistent. Even if two different approaches to the same task are both valid, they might yield inconsistent results. One of the ways to streamline processes and make sure that tasks are executed in a consistent manner is to define and document procedures; this is called *standardization*. Defining and using templates is an effective method of network documentation, and it helps in creating a consistent network maintenance process. The following are some of the types of questions answered by network conventions, templates, and best practices (standardization) documentation:

- Are logging and debug time stamps set to local time or coordinated universal time (UTC)?
- Should access lists end with an explicit "deny any"?
- In an IP subnet, is the first or the last valid IP address allocated to the local gateway?

In many cases, you can configure a device in several different ways to achieve the same results. However, using different methods of achieving the same results in the same network can easily lead to confusion, especially during troubleshooting. Under pressure, valuable time can be wasted in verifying configurations that are assumed incorrect simply because they are configured differently.

Planning for Disaster Recovery

Although the modern MTBF for certain network devices is claimed to be 5, 7, or 10 years or more, you must always consider the possibility of device failure. By having a plan for such occasions and knowing what to do, you can significantly reduce the amount of downtime. One way to reduce the impact of failure is to build redundancy into the network at critical points and eliminate single points of failure. A single point of failure means that a single device or link does not have a backup and its failure can cause major damage to your network operation. However, mainly because of budgetary limitations, it is not always possible to make every single link, component, and device redundant. Disasters, natural and otherwise, must also be taken into account. For example, you could be struck by a disaster such as a flood or fire in the server room. The quicker you can replace failed devices and restore functionality, the quicker your network will be running again. To replace a failed device, you need the following items:

- Replacement hardware
- The current software version for the device
- The current configuration for the device

- The tools to transfer the software and configuration to the device
- Licenses (if applicable)
- Knowledge of the procedures to install software, configurations, and licenses

Missing any of the listed items severely affects the time it takes to replace the device. To make sure that you have these items available when you need them, follow the following guidelines:

- **Replacement hardware:** You either need to have spare devices or a service contract with a distributor or vendor that will replace the failed hardware. Typically, this means that you need documentation of the exact hardware part numbers, serial numbers, and service contract numbers for the devices.
- **Current software:** Usually devices are delivered with a particular version of software, which is not necessarily the same as the version that you were running on the device. Therefore, you should have a repository where you store all current software versions in use on your network.
- **Current configuration:** In addition to creating backups of your configurations any time you make a change, you need to have a clear versioning system so that you know which configuration is the most recent.
- **Tools:** You need to have the appropriate tools to transfer software and configurations to the new device, which you should be able to do even if the network is unavailable.
- **Licenses:** If your software requires a license, you need to have that license or know the procedure to obtain a new license.
- **Knowledge:** Because these procedures are used infrequently, you might not have them committed to memory. Having all necessary documentation ready, however, will save time in executing the necessary procedures and will also decrease the risk of making mistakes.

In short, the key factors to a successful disaster recovery are defining and documenting recovery procedures and making sure you always have the necessary elements available in case a disaster strikes.

Network Monitoring and Performance Measurement

Another process that helps you transform your network maintenance process to a less interrupt-driven, more methodical approach is the implementation of network and performance monitoring. Ideally, you want to be able to spot potential issues before they develop into problems, and to be able to isolate problems faster when they occur. Gathering performance data enables you to upgrade before a lack of resource situation develops into a performance problem. Gathering performance data also helps in building a business case for investing in network upgrades. When you are committed to meeting the SLAs for the performance of your network, or if your service provider is guaranteeing you a certain level of service, monitoring network performance can assist you in determining whether those SLAs are met.

One essential step in network performance measurement and monitoring is choosing the variables to be monitored and measured, including interface status, interface load, CPU load, and memory usage of your devices. Also, the more sophisticated metrics such as measurements of network delay, jitter, or packet loss can be included in a network monitoring and performance measurement policy. The network performance measurement and monitoring policy and the corresponding choices of metrics will differ for each organization and need to be aligned to the business requirements.

Network Maintenance Tools, Applications, and Resources

After you determine and define the network maintenance methods, processes, and procedures to be implemented in your organization, you can choose the tools, applications, and resources for executing your network maintenance tasks in an efficient manner. These tools must be adequate and affordable. Ideally, all the tasks that are part of your maintenance plan should be supported by the products and applications that you choose, with the initial and ongoing costs within your budget. To determine the suitability of a network maintenance toolkit, you must learn to perform the following tasks:

- Identify, evaluate, and implement the elements of a basic network maintenance toolkit.
- Evaluate tools that support the documentation process and select the tools appropriate to your organization.
- Describe how configuration, software, and hardware resource management can improve disaster recovery procedures.
- Describe how network monitoring software benefits the maintenance process.
- Analyze the metrics that could be used to measure network performance and the key elements of the performance measurement process to create a performance measurement plan appropriate to your organization.

Fundamental Tools, Applications, and Resources

You have many tools, applications, and resources from which to choose to support network maintenance processes. These tools and applications vary based on price, complexity, capability, and scalability. Figure 1-2 shows the fundamental tools and applications that belong to network maintenance toolkits.

The basic components of a network maintenance toolkit are as follows:

- **Command-line device management:** Cisco IOS Software includes a powerful command-line interface (CLI) that you can use to configure and monitor individual routers and switches. This includes commands such as the **show** commands, the

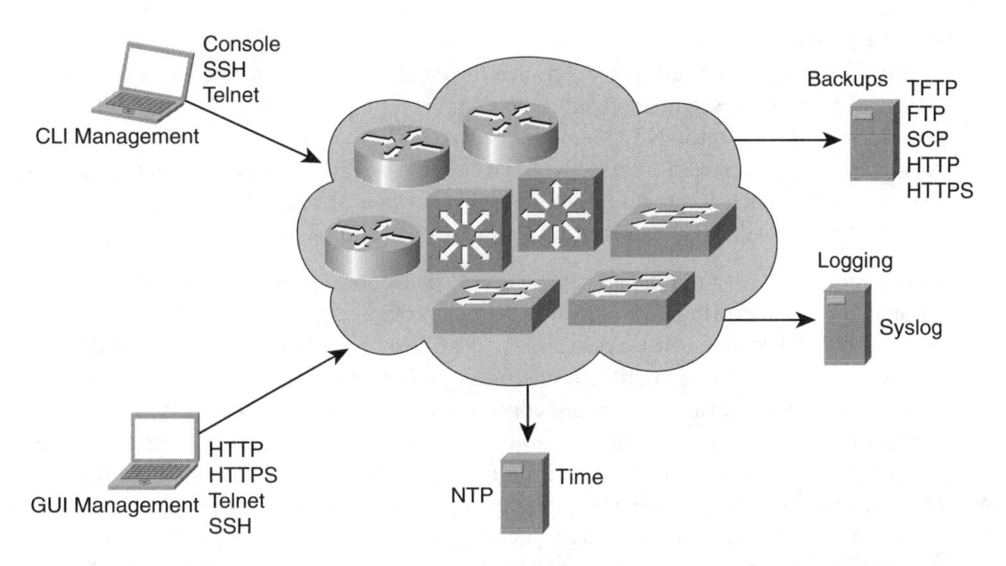

Figure 1-2 *Fundamental Tools and Applications of Network Maintenance Toolkits*

debug commands, Embedded Event Manager (EEM) commands, and IP SLA commands. After an initial configuration through the serial console of the device, the CLI is commonly accessed remotely through use of the Telnet or Secure Shell (SSH) protocols. To be able to manage the devices during network outages, an out-of-band management solution can be implemented to allow access to the CLI using the serial console at all times.

- **Graphical user interface (GUI)-based device management:** Cisco provides free GUI-based device management tools for many Cisco routers and switches. Examples of such tools include Cisco Configuration Professional (CCP), Secure Device Manager (SDM), Cisco Configuration Assistant (CCA), and Cisco Network Assistant (CNA).
- **Backup server:** To create backups of the software and configurations of your routers and switches, you need to provide a TFTP, FTP, HTTP, or Secure Copy Protocol (SCP) server. Many operating systems include these services as optional add-ons, and many software packages offer those services, too.
- **Log server:** Basic logging functionality can be provided by sending the router's or switch's log messages to a syslog server using the syslog protocol. Syslog is a standard service on most UNIX-based operating systems or could be provided by installing additional software on the operating system of your choice.
- **Time server:** To synchronize clocks on all your network devices, it is useful to have a Network Time Protocol (NTP) server on your network. You could even synchronize your router and switch clocks to one of the many public time servers available on the Internet.

To ensure correct time stamps on **logging** and **debug** output and to support other time-based features such as the use of certificates or time-based access, it is vital that the clocks of the network devices be properly set and synchronized. The Network Time Protocol (NTP) can be used to synchronize the clock of a device to the clock of an NTP server, which in turn is synchronized to another server higher up the NTP hierarchy. The position of a device in the NTP hierarchy is determined by its stratum, which serves as an NTP hop count. A stratum 1 server is a server that is directly connected to an authoritative time source such as a radio or atomic clock. A server that synchronizes its clock to a stratum 1 server will become a stratum 2 time source, and so on.

It is common to have a redundant set of servers in the core of the network that are synchronized to an authoritative source or a service provider server, and to configure other devices to synchronize their clocks to these central sources. In large networks, this hierarchy could even consist of multiple levels. You configure time servers using the **ntp server** command. If multiple time servers are configured for redundancy, the NTP protocol decides which server is most reliable and will synchronize to that server. Alternatively, a preferred server can be appointed by use of the **prefer** command option on the **ntp server** command. In addition to defining timeservers, you can define your local time zone and configure the devices to adapt to daylight savings time. Finally, after you have the time synchronized and the correct time zone has been configured, you configure the router or switch to time stamp its log and debug entries.

Example 1-1 shows the clock of a device that is synchronized to a single time server with IP address 10.1.220.3. The time zone is configured to Pacific standard time (PST), which has an –8 hour offset to universal time coordinated (UTC). The clock is configured to change to daylight savings time on the second Sunday in March at 2:00 a.m. and back to standard time on the first Sunday in November at 2:00 a.m. The logging for system logging is configured to use the local date and time in the time stamps and to include the time zone in the time stamp. For log entries generated by debugs, the settings are similar, but milliseconds are included in the time stamps for greater accuracy.

Example 1-1 *NTP Example*

```
service time stamps debug datetime msec localtime show-timezone
service time stamps log datetime localtime show-timezone
!
clock timezone PST -8
clock summer-time PDT recurring 2 Sun Mar 2:00 1 Sun Nov 2:00
!
ntp server 10.1.220.3
```

For more details about the configuration of NTP, consult the "Configuring NTP" section of the *Cisco IOS Network Management Configuration Guide:*

http://tinyurl.com/yezfkr3

Configuration and Documentation Tools

Many web-based (online) maintenance tools and resources can prove helpful during the planning and implementation of network maintenance procedures. Cisco.com provides numerous tools to support your network maintenance processes. Many of the tools are available only to registered users with a valid Cisco service contract or to Cisco Channel Partners, however. Some useful and freely available tools are as follows:

- **Dynamic Configuration Tool:** This tool aids you in creating hardware configurations. It verifies compatibility of the hardware and software you select, and it gives you a complete bill of materials (BoM) that lists all the necessary part numbers. For more information, see https://apps.cisco.com/qtc/config/html/configureHomeGuest.html.
- **Cisco Feature Navigator:** This tool enables you to quickly find the right Cisco IOS Software release for the features you want to run on your network. For more information, see http://tools.cisco.com/ITDIT/CFN/
- **SNMP Object Navigator:** The Simple Network Management Protocol (SNMP) Navigator translates SNMP object identifiers (OIDs) into object names. This tool also enables you to download SNMP Management Information Base (MIB) files and to verify the supported MIBs in a particular Cisco IOS Software version. For more information, see http://tools.cisco.com/Support/SNMP/do/BrowseOID.do?local=en.
- **Cisco Power Calculator:** This tool calculates the power-supply requirements for a particular Power over Ethernet (PoE) hardware configuration. Access to this tool requires a Cisco.com account.

Good documentation is mostly the result of a good process. Good tools can prove extremely helpful in supporting the documentation process, but it is most important that creating and updating documentation be an integral part of your maintenance processes. The value of documentation heavily depends on how accessible it is and how up-to-date it is. If you cannot find or cannot access the documentation when you need it or if you cannot trust its information, the documentation has almost no value. Therefore, you must ensure that any tool or application you use to support creation, retrieval, and updating of documentation must be easy to access and easy to use. Examples of tools that can be used to access, create, and maintain documentation include the following:

- **Wiki:** A wiki combines easy web-based access with intuitive editing capabilities. It is suitable as a base documentation system. You can use a wiki as a framework to link various other existing documentation systems.
- **Issue tracking system:** Other names for issue tracking systems include trouble ticket, support ticket, or incident ticket system. An issue tracking system allows incoming support requests, problems, or other incidents to be logged, tracked, and documented. By documenting progress, communication, and escalation of incidents, an issue tracking system enables a team of people to work on the same incidents in an efficient manner. You can also build a historical database of problems, their treatments, and the resolutions.

Logging Services

Events that happen on a networking device such as router can be logged. There are different types of events, and different events have different levels of significance or severity. Examples of events include interfaces going up and down, configuration events, and routing protocol adjacencies being established. By default, events are usually logged only to the device's console; however, because the console is usually not easily accessible, let alone monitored, it is worthwhile to collect and store the logs on a server, or at least in a separate piece of memory of the router, to facilitate access to them during troubleshooting procedures.

Logging the messages to buffers on the router or switch is a minimal step that guarantees that logs are available on the device, as long as it is not rebooted. On some devices and Cisco IOS Software versions, logging to buffers is turned on by default. To enable buffer logging manually, you can use the **logging buffered** command to specify that messages should be logged to a buffer in the device's RAM. As an option, you can specify the amount of RAM that should be allocated to this buffer. The buffer is circular, meaning that when the buffer has reached its maximum capacity, the oldest messages will be discarded to allow the logging of new messages. You can display the content of this logging buffer via the **show logging** command. Logging severity levels on Cisco Systems devices are as follows:

- (0) Emergencies
- (1) Alerts
- (2) Critical
- (3) Errors
- (4) Warnings
- (5) Notifications
- (6) Informational
- (7) Debugging

When logging is enabled, the severity level can be specified as an option. This causes the device to only log messages with a severity at the configured level or lower numeric value. By default, messages of all severity levels are logged to buffer.

You can also adjust the logging severity level of the console. By default, all messages from level 0 to 7 are logged to the console; however, similar to buffer logging, you can configure the severity level as an optional parameter on the **logging console** command.

Logging messages are best to be sent to a syslog server. Doing so allows you to store the logs of all your network devices centrally. When logging messages are sent to a syslog server, logs are no longer lost when the networking device crashes or reboots. You can configure one or more syslog servers by entering the **logging** *host* command. By default, only messages of severity level 6 or lower are logged to the syslog server. This can be changed, similar to buffer or console logging, but unlike these other commands, the severity is configured by entering the **logging trap** *level* command. This command applies to all configured syslog hosts. Figure 1-3 shows three logging commands configured on a device and an explanation for each command.

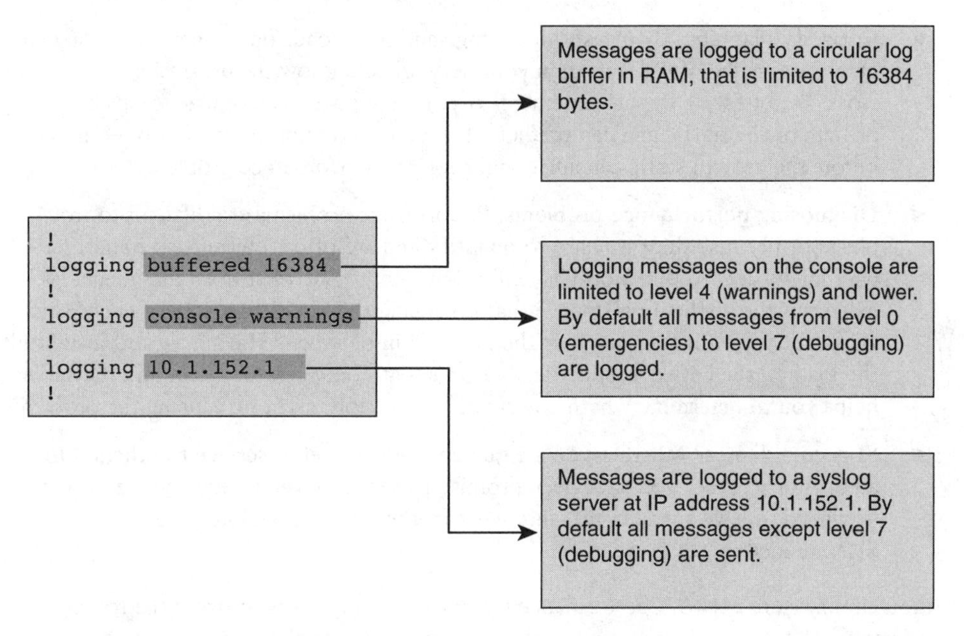

Figure 1-3 *A Logging Command Example with Explanation*

For more detail about the configuration of logging and syslog services, consult the "Logging System Messages" section of the *Cisco IOS Network Management Configuration Guide:*

http://tinyurl.com/yc8ftr6

Network Monitoring and Performance Measurement Tools

GUI- and CLI-based device management tools are used to examine individual devices, for example, at a time you suspect a problem exists. However, the problem might not be noticed until a user complains. At that point, when users have already noticed the failure, the problem has most likely had some impact on the business. A network monitoring system continuously checks your network devices' availability and status. This enables you to detect possible problems as soon as they occur, and it might even allow you to diagnose and resolve these problems before they even become apparent to end users. Most network monitoring software incorporates various protocols such as SNMP, ICMP, and syslog so that you can monitor devices and network events. In addition, Cisco IOS NetFlow technology can be leveraged, not just to monitor the devices, but also to monitor the actual traffic on the network. Some network monitoring tools also incorporate performance monitoring capabilities. There is a gray area between network monitoring and performance measurement. While you monitor the network's performance and look for faults and problems, you can also use your data as input for capacity planning, SLA compliance measurements, or accounting purposes.

The three main motivations for measuring network performance are as follows:

- **Capacity planning:** By measuring average and peak loads on the network, you can create a baseline of the traffic on your network and know the utilization of your network. By repeating the measurements over time, you also recognize trends in the growth of the traffic and can predict when you need to upgrade links or equipment before the growth starts causing congestion and performance problems.
- **Diagnosing performance problems:** Performance problems are difficult to troubleshoot because they are hard to quantify and are often intermittent in nature. A user might say, "Application *x* is really slow lately." But what does that mean? When exactly is the application slow? What is causing this problem? Is it the client software faulty, or is it the server, or the network in between? Having a good insight into the load on the network, specifically on the path between the client and the server, helps you to determine whether network congestion might be causing the problems.
- **SLA compliance:** Whether you are guaranteeing a level of service to others through an SLA or whether you have been promised a certain level of service by a provider, you need to have a way to measure whether the service guarantees defined in the SLA are met.

You can measure network performance by first gathering statistics from the routers and switches. The gathered statistics can then be stored in a database, graphed over time, and analyzed. This information can be very useful for capacity planning and performance troubleshooting. Typical statistics to gather are the packet and byte counters on interfaces and device CPU and memory utilization. For SLA compliance, on the other hand, it is most useful to measure key indicators such as round-trip time (RTT), jitter, and packet loss. The IP SLA feature that is available on many Cisco routers enables you to set up probes that measure these key indicators along particular paths through your network. The statistics can then be read using Cisco IOS commands or collected using SNMP. The raw data is stored in a database and can then be analyzed or graphed. Cisco Internetwork Performance Monitor (IPM), which is part of the CiscoWorks LAN Management Solution, can leverage the IP SLA functionality in the routers to provide detailed performance graphs. In addition, various other network management software have the capability to collect statistics using SNMP and graph the results. The open source Multi Router Traffic Grapher (MRTG) and other products based on it are examples of this type of software.

Implementing Backup and Restore Services

An essential element of any network maintenance toolkit is a backup server from which device configurations and Cisco IOS Software can be copied to and restored. The simplest and most commonly implemented service is TFTP, which does not require any configuration on the network devices. The server is set up to serve and receive files without any need for authentication or identification, other than specifying the name of the configuration or software file itself. The fact that the protocol does not require any authentication and that all content is sent across the network in clear text makes it a relatively unsecure mechanism. More secure protocols such as FTP, SCP, and HTTP or HTTPS can also be used as a means of transferring configurations and software. To use any of these more-secure protocols, you must specify the username and password that are used to authenticate to the server. For all of these protocols, the credentials can be specified as part of the Uniform Resource Locator (URL) that is used with the **copy** command. The username and password are specified by placing the username and password as username:password@ before the server name or IP address in the URL. Example 1-3 shows how to copy the startup configuration using FTP to a server with the IP address 10.1.152.1 and a file named RO1-test.cfg using the user name backup and password san-fran.

Example 1-3 *Performing Backup Using FTP with Username and Password*

```
RO1# copy startup-config ftp://backup:san-fran@10.1.152.1/RO1-test.cfg
Address or name of remote host [10.1.152.1]?
Destination filename [RO1-test.cfg]?
Writing RO1-test.cfg !
2323 bytes copied in 0.268 secs (8668 bytes/sec)
```

For SCP, HTTP and HTTPS you would use a similar syntax, replacing the URL prefix ftp:// with scp://, http:// or https://, respectively. Specifying the username and password on the command line is somewhat cumbersome and suffers from the fact that the password is displayed in clear text on the screen, which is less desirable from a security standpoint. To circumvent this issue, the username and password can be specified in the configuration, instead of on the command line, for the FTP, HTTP, and HTTPS protocols. Example 1-4 shows how to store FTP and HTTP username and passwords in the configuration and perform an FTP backup without having to type the username and password.

Example 1-4 *Storing FTP, HTTP Usernames and Passwords in Configuration*

```
RO1(config)# ip ftp username backup
RO1(config)# ip ftp password san-fran
RO1(config)# ip http client username backup
RO1(config)# ip http client password 0 san-fran
RO1(config)# exit
RO1# copy startup-config ftp://10.1.152.1/RO1-test.cfg
Address or name of remote host [10.1.152.1]?
Destination filename [RO1-test.cfg]?
Writing RO1-test.cfg !
2323 bytes copied in 0.304 secs (7641 bytes/sec)
```

The same configuration commands are used for both HTTP and HTTPS. The only difference is the protocol identifier in the URL. It is important to know that even though FTP and HTTP require authentication, these protocols send credentials in clear text. HTTPS and SCP use encryption to ensure confidentiality of both the transmitted credentials and the content of the transferred file. When possible, use secure protocols such as HTTPS and SCP.

Creating backups of configurations should be an integral part of your network maintenance routines. After any change, you should create backups, copying the configuration file to NVRAM on the device and to a network server. If you have sufficient flash storage space on the device, you might find it useful to not only build a configuration archive on the server, but in the flash memory of the device, too. A feature that can be helpful in the creation of configuration archives, either locally on the device or remotely on a server, is the configuration archiving feature that is part of the *Configuration Replace and Configuration Rollback* feature that was introduced in Cisco IOS Software Release 12.3(7)T. Example 1-5 shows how to set up the configuration archive.

Example 1-5 *Setting Up the Configuration Archive*

```
Router(config)# archive
Router(config-archive)# path flash:/config-archive/$h-config
Router(config-archive)# write-memory
Router(config-archive)# time-period 10080
```

The configuration archive is set up by entering the **archive** command in global configuration mode, which gets you into the config-archive configuration mode. In this configuration submode, you can specify the parameters for the archive. The only mandatory parameter is the base file path. This path will be used as the base filename and is appended with a number for each subsequent archived configuration. The path is specified in URL notation and can either be a local or a networked path supported by the Cisco IOS file system. Not all types of local flash storage are supported, so check your device's flash type for support of this feature if you want to store your configuration archive locally on a device instead of on a server. The configuration path can include the variables **$h** for the device's hostname and **$t** to include a time and date stamp in the filename.

After you specify the location of the archive, it is ready to be used, and archive copies of the configuration can be created manually by issuing the **archive config** command. However, the biggest advantage of this feature is the way you can use it to create and update a configuration archive automatically. By adding the **write-memory** option to the archive configuration section, you can trigger an archive copy of the running configuration to be created any time the running configuration is copied to NVRAM. It is also possible to generate archive copies of the configuration periodically by specifying the **time-period** option followed by a time period, specified in minutes. Each time the configured time period elapses, a copy of the running configuration will be archived.

You can verify the presence of the archived configuration files by using the **show archive** command. In addition to the files themselves, this command displays the most recent archived file and the filename for the next archive to be created, as demonstrated in Example 1-6.

Example 1-6 show archive *Command Output*

```
R01# show archive
There are currently 5 archive configurations saved.
The next archive file will be named flash:/config-archive/R01-config-6
 Archive #  Name
   0
   1        flash:/config-archive/R01-config-1
   2        flash:/config-archive/R01-config-2
   3        flash:/config-archive/R01-config-3
   4        flash:/config-archive/R01-config-4
   5        flash:/config-archive/R01-config-5 <- Most Recent
```

By creating backups, either by manually copying the files or through use of configuration archiving, you have something to fall back to when disaster strikes. If the configuration of a device is lost through human error, hardware failure, or when a device needs to be replaced, you can copy the last archived configuration to the NVRAM of the device and boot it to restore it to the exact same configuration that you had stored in your archive. Another common event when you might want to restore the device to its last archived configuration is when you have made a change or a series of changes and they did not work out as expected. If these changes were made during a regularly scheduled maintenance window, you can often perform the same procedure as if you have lost a configuration entirely. You copy the last archived known-good configuration to the NVRAM of the device and reload it. However, if you made these changes during normal network operation (for example, while troubleshooting a problem), reloading the device could be a disruptive operation and not acceptable unless you have no other option.

This situation is what the configuration replace feature was designed to deal with. The **configure replace** command enables you to replace the currently running configuration on the router with a saved configuration. It does so by comparing the running configuration with the configuration file appointed by the **configure replace** command and then creates a list of differences between the files. Based on the discovered differences, various Cisco IOS configuration commands are generated that will change the existing running configuration to the replacement configuration. Example 1-7 makes a simple demonstration of this command. The advantage of this method is that only parts of the configuration that differ will be changed. The device does not need to be reloaded, and existing commands are not reapplied. This manner of rolling back to an existing archived configuration is the least-disruptive method you can use. Within the documentation at Cisco.com, the **configure replace** command is sometimes referred to as *configuration rollback*, although the command itself does not include *rollback* as a keyword.

Example 1-7 *A Simple Demonstration of the* **configure replace** *Command*

```
R01# configure terminal
Enter configuration commands, one per line.  End with CNTL/Z.
R01(config)# hostname TEST
TEST(config)# ^Z
TEST# configure replace flash:config-archive/R01-config-5 list
This will apply all necessary additions and deletions
to replace the current running configuration with the
contents of the specified configuration file, which is
assumed to be a complete configuration, not a partial
configuration. Enter Y if you are sure you want to proceed. ? [no]: yes
!Pass 1

!List of Commands:
no hostname TEST
hostname R01
end


Total number of passes: 1
Rollback Done

R01#
```

Example 1-7 shows that the hostname of a device is changed and then the configuration is rolled back to the most current archived configuration. The command option **list** is added to the **configure replace** command to show the configuration commands that are being applied by the configuration replacement. As you can see from the example, the change that was made is undone, without affecting any other parts of the configuration. Although this command was designed to complement the configuration archiving feature, you can use the **configure replace** command with any complete Cisco IOS configuration file.

Disaster Recovery Tools

To successfully recover from a disaster, you need the following:

- Up-to-date configuration backups
- Up-to-date software backups
- Up-to-date hardware inventories
- Configuration and software provisioning tools

As parts of the fundamental network maintenance toolkit, TFTP, FTP, SCP, HTTP, and HTTPS servers are useful for creating backups of the configuration and operating system of a router or switch. Additional software can be used to extend the functionality of the toolkit and perform the following tasks:

- Automatic backup scheduling
- Configuration file comparison and change tracking
- Template creation and editing
- Pushing configurations to multiple devices
- Hardware inventory tracking

CiscoWorks Resource Manager Essentials (RME), which is part of the CiscoWorks LAN Management Solutions (LMS), is a prime example of software that provides these functions. For more on LMS and other network management utilities offered by Cisco, see http://www.cisco.com/en/US/products/sw/netmgtsw/index.html.

Summary

There are two network maintenance models: interrupt driven and structured. The structured network maintenance model has the following advantages over its interrupt-driven counterpart:

- Reduced network downtime
- More cost-effectiveness
- Better alignment with business objectives
- Higher network security

Examples of structured network maintenance methodologies include the following:

- IT Infrastructure Library (ITIL)
- FCAPS (Fault, Configuration, Accounting, Performance, and Security Management; by ISO)
- TMN (Telecommunications Management Network; By ITU-T)
- Cisco Lifecycle Services

Upon selection of a network maintenance model/methodology, you must translate the theoretical model to practical procedures that structure the network maintenance processes for your network. After you have defined your processes and procedures, it becomes much easier to see what functionalities and tools you need to have in your network management toolkit to support these processes. As a result, you can select an efficient and cost-effective network management and support toolkit that offers those tools and hopefully meets your budgetary constraints.

All network maintenance plans need to include procedures to perform the following tasks:

- Accommodating adds, moves, and changes
- Installing and configuring new devices
- Replacing failed devices
- Backing up device configurations and software
- Troubleshooting link and device failures
- Upgrading or patching software
- Monitoring the network
- Performance measurement and capacity planning
- Writing and updating documentation

Network maintenance planning includes the following:

- Scheduling maintenance
- Change-control procedures
- Network documentation
- Effective communication
- Defining templates/procedures/conventions
- Disaster recovery.

Benefits of scheduled maintenance include the following:

- You reduce network downtime.
- Long-term maintenance tasks will not be neglected or forgotten.
- You have predictable lead times for change requests.
- Disruptive maintenance tasks can be scheduled during assigned maintenance windows, reducing downtime during production hours.

Typical elements of network documentation include the following:

- Network drawings
- Connection documentation
- Equipment lists
- IP address administration
- Configurations
- Design documentation

To perform successful disaster recovery when a device fails, you need to have the following saved and available:

- Replacement hardware
- The current software version for the device
- The current configuration for the device
- The tools to transfer the software and configuration to the device
- Licenses (if applicable)
- Knowledge of the procedures to install software, configurations, and licenses

To determine the suitability of a network maintenance toolkit, you must learn to perform the following tasks:

- Identify, evaluate, and implement the elements of a basic network maintenance toolkit.
- Evaluate tools that support the documentation process and select the tools appropriate to your organization.
- Describe how configuration, software, and hardware resource management can improve disaster recovery procedures.
- Describe how network monitoring software benefits the maintenance process.
- Analyze the metrics that could be used to measure network performance and the key elements of the performance measurement process to create a performance measurement plan that is appropriate to your organization.

The basic components of a network maintenance toolkit are as follows:

- CLI-based device management
- GUI-based device management
- Backup server
- Log server
- Time server

Examples of Cisco Systems web-based (online) maintenance tools and resources that can prove helpful during the planning and implementation of network maintenance procedures are as follows:

- **Dynamic Configuration Tool:** This tool aids you in creating hardware configurations. It verifies compatibility of the hardware and software you select, and it gives you a complete bill of materials (BoM) that lists all the necessary part numbers.

- **Cisco Feature Navigator:** This tool enables you to quickly find the right Cisco IOS Software release for the features you want to run on your network. At the time of this writing, Cisco Feature Navigator does not support Cisco IOS Software Release 15.0.
- **SNMP Object Navigator:** The Simple Network Management Protocol (SNMP) Navigator translates SNMP object identifiers (OIDs) into object names. This tool also enables you to download SNMP Management Information Base (MIB) files and to verify the supported MIBs in a particular Cisco IOS Software version.
- **Cisco Power Calculator:** This tool calculates the power supply requirements for a particular Power over Ethernet (PoE) hardware configuration.

Examples of tools that can be used to access, create, and maintain documentation are as follows:

- Wiki
- Issue tracking system

The three main motivations for measuring network performance are as follows:

- Capacity planning
- Diagnosing performance problems
- SLA compliance

TFTP, FTP, SCP, HTTP, and HTTPS can all be used to transfer files between your network and backup devices. FTP, SCP, HTTP, and HTTPS are more secure than TFTP because they require authentication. SCP and HTTPS are most secure because they also incorporate encryption.

A feature that can prove helpful in the creation of configuration archives, either locally on the device or remotely on a server, is the configuration archiving feature that is part of the Configuration Replace and Configuration Rollback feature that was introduced in Cisco IOS Software Release 12.3(7)T.

To successfully recover from a disaster, you need the following:

- Up-to-date configuration backups
- Up-to-date software backups
- Up-to-date hardware inventories
- Configuration and software provisioning tools

Review Questions

1. Which three of the following are benefits of a structured approach to network maintenance?
   a. Maintenance processes are better aligned to business needs.
   b. Hardware discounts can be negotiated with the reseller.
   c. The overall security of the network will be higher.
   d. The total unplanned network downtime will be lower.
   e. Users will never have to wait to get support.
   f. Network maintenance can be outsourced to lower the cost.
2. Which three of the following is a methodology that can be applied to network maintenance?
   a. Fault management, Configuration management, Accounting management, Performance management, and Security management (FCAPS)
   b. IT Infrastructure Library (ITIL)
   c. Optimization and Maintenance (OaM)
   d. Telecommunications Management Network (TMN)
3. Which two of the following are common network maintenance processes?
   a. Disaster recovery
   b. Network design
   c. Budget approval
   d. Documentation
4. Which two of the following are benefits of scheduled maintenance?
   a. Network engineers will not have to work outside regular work hours.
   b. Lead times for change requests will be more predictable.
   c. Disruptive maintenance tasks can be scheduled during assigned maintenance windows.
5. Which factors should be considered during the implementation of change procedures?

6. Which three of the following items do you need to have to replace a failed device?
   a. Replacement hardware for the failed device
   b. Proof of purchase of the failed device
   c. TAC support for the failed device
   d. The current configuration of the failed device
   e. The current software version of the failed device
   f. The original box that the failed device was shipped in
7. Network monitoring is a fundamental aspect of a proactive network management strategy. True or False?
   a. True
   b. False
8. Which five of the following protocols can be used to transfer a configuration file from a router to a server to create a configuration backup?
   a. HTTPS
   b. HTTP
   c. FTP
   d. SNMP
   e. TFTP
   f. SCP
9. Which of the following commands is the correct command to copy the running configuration of a router to a file named test.cfg residing on an FTP server with IP address 10.1.1.1, using the username admin and password cisco?
   a. **copy running-config ftp://10.1.1.1/test.cfg user admin password cisco**
   b. **copy running-config ftp://10.1.1.1/test.cfg /user:admin /password:cisco**
   c. **copy running-config ftp://admin:cisco@10.1.1.1/test.cfg**
   d. **archive running-config ftp://10.1.1.1/test.cfg user admin password cisco**
   e. None of these are correct; FTP does not require authentication.
10. What command enables you to manually create an archive copy of the running configuration?

11. Which of the following commands is the correct command to restore the current configuration to the archived configuration file RO1-archive-config-5 residing in flash?

    a. **archive rollback flash:/RO1-archive-config-5**

    b. **configure replace flash:/RO1-archive-config-5**

    c. **copy flash:/RO1-archive-config-5 running-config**

    d. **archive restore flash:/RO1-archive-config-5**

12. What command enables you to configure a switch to log system messages to a syslog server at IP address 10.1.1.1?

13. What is the functionality delivered by the online Dynamic Configuration Tool?

    a. It interprets router configurations and recommends changes based on a set of best current practices.

    b. It converts Cisco IOS firewall configurations to PIX or ASA configurations and vice versa.

    c. It converts CatOS switch configurations to Cisco IOS configurations.

    d. It validates hardware configurations and creates a bill of materials from it.

14. Which two of the following are processes that benefit from the implementation of a network performance measurement system?

    a. Disaster recovery

    b. Change management

    c. Capacity planning

    d. SLA compliance

Chapter 2

Troubleshooting Processes for Complex Enterprise Networks

This chapter covers the following topics:

- Troubleshooting principles and approaches
- Implementing troubleshooting processes
- Integrating troubleshooting into the network maintenance process

Most modern enterprises depend heavily on the smooth operation of their network infrastructure. Network downtime usually translates to loss of productivity, revenue, and reputation. Network troubleshooting is therefore one of the essential responsibilities of the network support group. The more efficiently and effectively the network support personnel diagnose and resolve problems, the lower impact and damages will be to business. In complex environments, troubleshooting can be a daunting task, and the recommended way to diagnose and resolve problems quickly and effectively is by following a structured approach. Structured network troubleshooting requires well-defined and documented troubleshooting procedures.

This chapter explains the benefits of structured troubleshooting and identifies the leading principles that are at the core of all troubleshooting methodologies. Implementing troubleshooting procedures is the next topic, with a discussion on gathering and analyzing information and solving the problem. Finally, the generic troubleshooting processes and their relation to network maintenance processes are analyzed along with the role of change control and documentation.

Troubleshooting Methodologies

Troubleshooting is not an exact science, and a particular problem can be diagnosed and sometimes even solved in many different ways. However, when you perform structured troubleshooting, you make continuous progress, and usually solve the problems faster than it would take using an ad hoc approach. There are many different structured troubleshooting approaches. For some problems, one method might work better, whereas for others, another method might be more suitable. Therefore, it is beneficial for the troubleshooter to be familiar with a variety of structured approaches and select the best method or combination of methods to solve a particular problem.

Troubleshooting Principles

Troubleshooting is the process that leads to the diagnosis and, if possible, resolution of a problem. Troubleshooting is usually triggered when a person reports a problem. Some people say that a problem does not exist until it is noticed, perceived as a problem, and reported as a problem. This implies that you need to differentiate between a problem, as experienced by the user, and the actual cause of that problem. The time a problem is reported is not necessarily the same time at which the event causing the problem happened. Also, the reporting user generally equates the problem to the symptoms, whereas the troubleshooter often equates the problem to the root cause. For example, if the Internet connection fails on Saturday in a small company, it is usually not a problem, but you can be sure that it will turn into a problem on Monday morning if it is not fixed before then. Although this distinction between symptoms and cause of a problem might seem philosophical, you need to be aware of the potential communication issues that might arise from it.

Generally, reporting of a problem triggers the troubleshooting process. Troubleshooting starts by defining the problem. The second step is diagnosing the problem during which information is gathered, the problem definition is refined, and possible causes for the problem are proposed. Eventually this process should lead to a hypothesis for the root cause of the problem. At this time, possible solutions need to be proposed and evaluated. Next, the best solution is selected and implemented. Figure 2-1 illustrates the main elements of a structured troubleshooting approach and the transition possibilities from one step to the next.

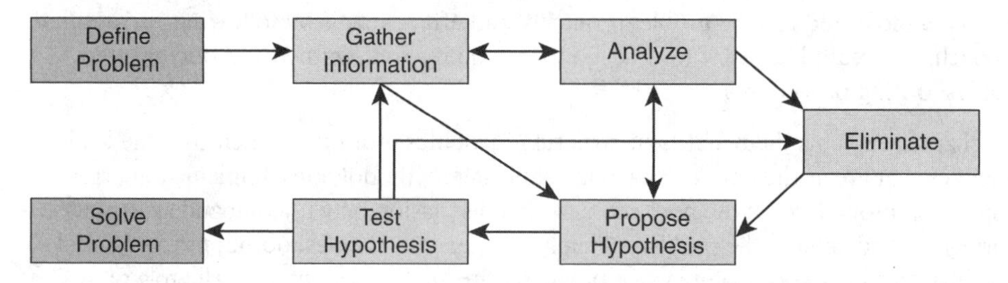

Figure 2-1 *Flow Chart of a Structured Troubleshooting Approach*

It is noteworthy, however, that the solution to a network problem cannot always be readily implemented and an interim workaround might have to be proposed. The difference between a solution and a workaround is that a solution resolves the root cause of the problem, whereas a workaround only alleviates the symptoms of the problem.

Although problem reporting and resolution are definitely essential elements of the troubleshooting process, most of the time is spent in the diagnostic phase. One might even believe that diagnosis is all troubleshooting is about. Nevertheless, within the context of network maintenance, problem reporting and resolution are indeed essential parts of troubleshooting. Diagnosis is the process of identifying the nature and cause of a problem. The main elements of this process are as follows:

- **Gathering information:** Gathering information happens after the problem has been reported by the user (or anyone). This might include interviewing all parties (user) involved, plus any other means to gather relevant information. Usually, the problem report does not contain enough information to formulate a good hypothesis without first gathering more information. Information and symptoms can be gathered directly, by observing processes, or indirectly, by executing tests.
- **Analyzing information:** After the gathered information has been analyzed, the troubleshooter compares the symptoms against his knowledge of the system, processes, and baselines to separate normal behavior from abnormal behavior.
- **Eliminating possible causes:** By comparing the observed behavior against expected behavior, some of the possible problems causes are eliminated.
- **Formulating a hypothesis:** After gathering and analyzing information and eliminating the possible causes, one or more potential problem causes remain. The probability of each of these causes will have to be assessed and the most likely cause proposed as the hypothetical cause of the problem.
- **Testing the hypothesis:** The hypothesis must be tested to confirm or deny that it is the actual cause of the problem. The simplest way to do this is by proposing a solution based on this hypothesis, implementing that solution, and verifying whether this solved the problem. If this method is impossible or disruptive, the hypothesis can be strengthened or invalidated by gathering and analyzing more information.

All troubleshooting methods include the elements of gathering and analyzing information, eliminating possible causes, and formulating and testing hypotheses. Each of these steps has its merits and requires some time and effort; how and when one moves from one step to the next is a key factor in the success level of a troubleshooting exercise. In a scenario where you are troubleshooting a complex problem, you might go back and forth between different stages of troubleshooting: Gather some information, analyze the information, eliminate some of the possibilities, gather more information, analyze again, formulate a hypothesis, test it, reject it, eliminate some more possibilities, gather more information, and so on.

If you do not take a structured approach to troubleshooting and go through its steps back and forth in an ad hoc fashion, you might eventually find the solution; however, the process in general will be very inefficient. Another drawback of this approach is that handing the job over to someone else is very hard to do; the progress results are mainly lost. This can happen even if the troubleshooter wants to resume his own task after he has stopped for a while, perhaps to take care of another matter. A structured approach to troubleshooting, regardless of the exact method adopted, yields more predictable results in the long run. It also makes it easier to pick up where you left off or hand the job over to someone else without losing any effort or results. A troubleshooting method that is commonly deployed both by inexperienced and experienced troubleshooters is the shoot-from-the-hip method. Using this method, after a very short period of gathering information, the troubleshooter quickly makes a change to see if it solves the problem. Even though it may seem like random troubleshooting on the surface, it is not. The reason is that the guiding principle for this method is knowledge of common symptoms and their corresponding causes, or simply extensive relevant experience in a particular environment or application. This technique might be quite effective for the experienced troubleshooter most times, but it usually does not yield the same results for the inexperienced troubleshooter. Figure 2-2 shows how the "shoot from the hip" goes about solving a problem, spending almost no effort in analyzing the gathered information and eliminating possibilities.

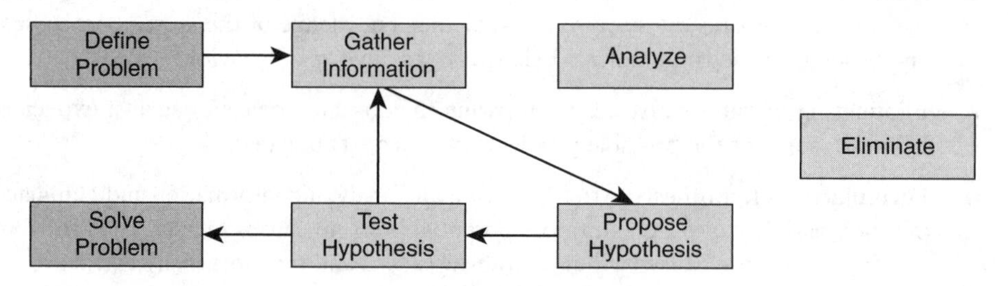

Figure 2-2 *The Shoot-from-the-Hip Troubleshooting Method*

Assume that a user reports a LAN performance problem and in 90 percent of the past cases with similar symptoms, the problem has been caused by duplex mismatch between users' workstation (PC or laptop) and the corresponding access switch port. The solution has been to configure the switch port for 100-Mbps full duplex. Therefore, it sounds reasonable to quickly verify the duplex setting of the switch port to which the user connects and change it to 100-Mbps full duplex to see whether that fixes the problem. When it works, this method can be very effective because it takes very little time. Unfortunately, the downside of this method is that if it does not work, you have not come any closer to a possible solution, you have wasted some time (both yours and users'), and you might possibly have caused a bit of frustration. Experienced troubleshooters use this method to great effect. The key factor in using this method effectively is knowing when to stop and switch to a more methodical (structured) approach.

Structured Troubleshooting Approaches

A structured troubleshooting method is used as a guideline through a troubleshooting process. The key to all structured troubleshooting methods is systematic elimination of hypothetical causes and narrowing down on the possible causes. By systematically eliminating possible problem causes, you can reduce the scope of the problem until you manage to isolate and solve the problem. If at some point you decide to seek help or hand the task over to someone else, your findings can be of help to that person and your efforts are not wasted.

Commonly used troubleshooting approaches include the following:

- **Top down:** Using this approach, you work from the Open Systems Interconnection (OSI) model's application layer down to the physical layer.
- **Bottom up:** The bottom-up approach starts from the OSI model's physical layer and moves up to the application layer.
- **Divide and conquer:** Using this approach, you start in the middle of the OSI model's stack (usually the network layer) and then, based on your findings, you move up or down the OSI stack.
- **Follow the path:** This approach is based on the path that packets take through the network from source to destination.
- **Spot the differences:** As the name implies, this approach compares network devices or processes that are operating correctly to devices or processes that are not operating as expected and gathers clues by spotting significant differences. In case the problem occurred after a change on a single device was implemented, the spot-the-differences approach can pinpoint the problem cause by focusing on the difference between the device configurations, before and after the problem was reported.
- **Move the problem:** The strategy of this troubleshooting approach is to physically move components and observe whether the problem moves with the components.

The sections that follow describe each of these methods in greater detail.

Top-Down Troubleshooting Method

The top-down troubleshooting method uses the OSI model as a guiding principle. One of the most important characteristics of the OSI model is that each layer depends on the underlying layers for its operation. This implies that if you find a layer to be operational, you can safely assume that all underlying layers are fully operational as well. So for instance, if you are researching a problem of a user that cannot browse a particular website and you find that you can establish a TCP connection on port 80 from this host to the server and get a response from the server, you can typically draw the conclusion that the transport layer and all layers below must be fully functional between the client and the server and that this is most likely a client or server problem and not a network problem. Be aware that in this example it is reasonable to conclude that Layers 1 through 4 must be fully operational, but it does not definitively prove this. For instance, non-fragmented packets might be routed correctly, while fragmented packets are dropped. The TCP connection to port 80 might not uncover such a problem. Essentially, the goal of this method is to find the highest OSI layer that is still working. All devices and processes that work on that layer or layers below are then eliminated from the scope of the problem. It might be clear that this method is most effective if the problem is on one of the higher OSI layers. This approach is also one of the most straightforward troubleshooting methods, because problems reported by users are typically defined as application layer problems, so starting the troubleshooting process at that layer is an obvious thing to do. A drawback or impediment to this method is that you need to have access to the client's application layer software to initiate the troubleshooting process, and if the software is only installed on a small number of machines, your troubleshooting options might be limited.

Bottom-Up Troubleshooting Method

The bottom-up troubleshooting approach also uses the OSI model as its guiding principle with the physical layer (bottom layer of the OSI stack) as the starting point. In this approach you work your way layer by layer up toward the application layer, and verify that relevant network elements are operating correctly. You try to eliminate more and more potential problem causes so that you can narrow down the scope of the potential problems. A benefit of this method is that all of the initial troubleshooting takes place on the network, so access to clients, servers, or applications is not necessary until a very late stage in the troubleshooting process. Based on experience, you will find that most network problems are hardware related. If this is applicable to your environment, the bottom-up approach will be most suitable for you. A disadvantage of this method is that, in large networks, it can be a time-consuming process, because a lot of effort will be spent on gathering and analyzing data and you always start from the bottom layer. The best bottom-up approach is to first reduce the scope of the problem using a different strategy and then switch to the bottom-up approach for clearly bounded parts of the network topology.

Divide-and-Conquer Troubleshooting Method

The divide-and-conquer troubleshooting method strikes a balance between the top-down and bottom-up troubleshooting approaches. If it is not clear which of the top-down or bottom-up approaches will be more effective for a particular problem, an alternative is to start in the middle (typically the network layer) and perform some tests such as ping. Ping is an excellent connectivity testing tool. If the test is successful, you can assume that all lower layers are functional, and so you can start a bottom-up troubleshooting starting from this layer. However, if the test fails, you can start a top-down troubleshooting starting from this layer. Whether the result of the initial test is positive or negative, this method will usually result in a faster elimination of potential problems than what you would achieve by implementing a full top-down or bottom-up approach. Therefore, the divide-and-conquer method is considered a highly effective troubleshooting approach.

Follow-the-Path Troubleshooting Method

The follow-the-path approach is one of the most basic troubleshooting techniques, and it usually complements one of the other troubleshooting methods such as the top-down or the bottom-up approach. The follow-the-path approach first discovers the actual traffic path all the way from source to destination. Next, the scope of troubleshooting is reduced to just the links and devices that are actually in the forwarding path. The principle of this approach is to eliminate the links and devices that are irrelevant to the troubleshooting task at hand.

Spot-the-Differences Troubleshooting Method

Another common troubleshooting approach is called spotting the differences. By comparing configurations, software versions, hardware, or other device properties, links, or processes between working and nonworking situations and spotting significant differences between them, this approach attempts to resolve the problem by changing the non-operational elements to be consistent with the working ones. The weakness of this method is that it might lead to a working situation, without clearly revealing the root cause of the problem. In some cases, you are not sure whether you have implemented a solution or a workaround. Example 2-1 shows two routing tables; one belongs to Branch2, experiencing problems, and the other belongs to Branch1, with no problems. If you compare the content of these routing tables, as per the spotting-the-differences approach, a natural deduction is that the branch with problems is missing a static entry. The static entry can be added to see whether it solves the problem.

Example 2-1 *Spot the Differences: One Malfunctioning and One Working Router*

```
-------------- Branch1 is in good working order -----------
Branch1# show ip route
<...output omitted...>
     10.0.0.0/24 is subnetted, 1 subnets
C       10.132.125.0 is directly connected, FastEthernet4
C    192.168.36.0/24 is directly connected, BVI1
S*   0.0.0.0/0 [254/0] via 10.132.125.1
-------------- Branch2 has connectivity problems -----------
Branch2# show ip route
<...output omitted...>
     10.0.0.0/24 is subnetted, 1 subnets
C       10.132.126.0 is directly connected, FastEthernet4
C    192.168.37.0/24 is directly connected, BVI1
```

To further illustrate the spotting-the-differences approach and highlight its shortcomings, assume that you are troubleshooting a connectivity problem with a branch office router and you have managed to narrow down the problem to some issue with the DSL link. You have not discovered the real culprit, but you notice that this branch's router is an older type that was phased out in most of the other branch offices. In the trunk of your car, you have a newer type of router that must be installed at another branch office next week. You decide to copy the configuration of the existing malfunctioning branch router to the new router and use the new router at this branch. Now everything works to your satisfaction, but unfortunately, the following questions remain unanswered:

- Is the problem actually fixed?
- What was the root cause of the problem?
- What should you do with the old router?

- What will you do for the branch that was supposed to receive the new router you just used?

In a case like this, the default settings (and behavior) of the old and the newer operating systems (IOS) could be different, and that explains why using the newer router solves the problem at hand. Unless those differences are analyzed, explained, and documented (that is, communicated to others), merely changing the routers is not considered a solution to the problem, and the questions in the preceding list remain unanswered.

Obviously, the spotting-the-differences method has a number of drawbacks, but what still makes it useful is that you can use it even when you lack the proper technological and troubleshooting knowledge and background. The effectiveness of this method depends heavily on how easy it is to compare working and nonworking device, situations, or processes. Having a good baseline of what constitutes normal behavior on the network makes it easier to spot abnormal behavior. Also, the use of consistent configuration templates makes it easier to spot the significant differences between functioning and malfunctioning devices. Consequently, the effectiveness of this method depends on the quality of the overall network maintenance process. Similar to the follow the path approach, spot the differences is best used as a supporting method in combination with other troubleshooting approaches.

Move-the-Problem Troubleshooting Method

Move the problem is a very elementary troubleshooting technique that can be used for problem isolation: You physically swap components and observe whether the problem stays in place, moves with the component, or disappears entirely. Figure 2-3 shows two PCs and three laptops connected to a LAN switch, among which laptop B has connectivity problems. Assuming that hardware failure is suspected, you must discover if the problem is on the switch, the cable, or the laptop. One approach is to start gathering data by checking the settings on the laptop with problems, examining the settings on the switch, comparing the settings of all the laptops, and the switch ports, and so on. However, you might not have the required administrative passwords for the PCs, laptops, and the switch. The only data that you can gather is the status of the link LEDs on the switch and the laptops and PCs. What you can do is obviously limited. A common way to at least isolate the problem (if it is not solved outright) is cable or port swapping. Swap the cable between a working device and laptop B (the one that is having problems). Move the laptop from one port to another using a cable that you know for sure is good. Based on these simple moves, you can isolate whether the problem is cable, switch, or laptop related.

Just by executing simple tests in a methodical way, the move-the-problem approach enables you to isolate the problem even if the information that you can gather is minimal. Even if you do not solve the problem, you have scoped it to a single element, and you can now focus further troubleshooting on that element. Note that in the previous example if you determine that the problem is cable related, it is unnecessary to obtain the administrative password for the switch, PCs, and laptops. The drawbacks of this method is that you are isolating the problem to only a limited set of physical elements and not gaining

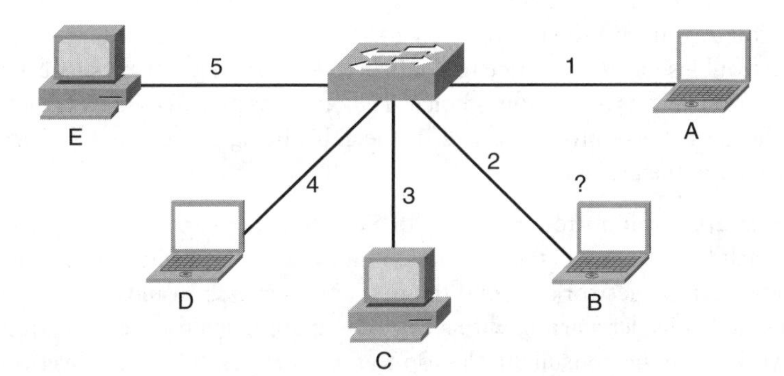

Figure 2-3 *Move the Problem: Laptop B Is Having Network Problems*

any real insight in what is happening, because you are gathering only very limited indirect information. This method assumes that the problem is with a single component. If the problem lies within multiple devices, you might not be able to isolate the problem correctly.

Troubleshooting Example: Methodologies

An external financial consultant has come in to help your company's controller with an accounting problem. He needs access to the finance server. An account has been created for him on the server, and the client software has been installed on the consultant's laptop. You happen to walk past the controller's office and are called in and told that the consultant can't connect to the finance server. You are a network support engineer and have access to all network devices, but not to the servers. Think about how you would handle this problem, what your troubleshooting plan would be, and which method or combination of methods you would use.

What possible approaches can you take for this troubleshooting task? This case lends itself to many different approaches, but some specific characteristics can help you decide an appropriate approach:

- You have access to the network devices, but not to the server. This implies that you will likely be able to handle Layer 1–4 problems by yourself; however, for Layer 5–7, you will probably have to escalate to a different person.
- You have access to the client device, so it is possible to start your troubleshooting from it.
- The controller has the same software and access rights on his machine, so it is possible to compare between the two devices.

What are the benefits and drawbacks of each possible troubleshooting approach for this case?

- **Top down:** You have the opportunity to start testing at the application layer. It is good troubleshooting practice to confirm the reported problem, so starting from the application layer is an obvious choice. The only possible drawback is that you will not discover simple problems, such as the cable being plugged in to a wrong outlet, until later in the process.
- **Bottom up:** A full bottom-up check of the whole network is not a very useful approach because it will take too much time and at this point, there is no reason to assume that the network beyond the first access switch would be causing the issue. You could consider starting with a bottom-up approach for the first stretch of the network, from the consultant's laptop to the access switch, to uncover potential cabling problems.
- **Divide and conquer:** This is a viable approach. You can ping from the consultant's laptop to the finance server. If that succeeds, you know that the problem is more likely to be with the application (although you have to consider potential firewall problems, too). If the ping fails, you are definitely dealing with a network issue, and you are responsible for fixing it. The advantage of this method is that you can quickly decide on the scope of the problem and whether escalation is necessary.
- **Follow the path:** Similar to the bottom-up approach, a full follow-the-path approach is not efficient under the circumstances, but tracing the cabling to the first switch can be a good start if it turns out that the link LED is off on the consultant's PC. This method might come into play after other techniques have been used to narrow the scope of the problem.
- **Spot the differences:** You have access to both the controller's PC and the consultant's laptop; therefore, spot the differences is a possible strategy. However, because these machines are not under the control of a single IT department, you might find many differences, and it might therefore be hard to spot the significant and relevant differences. Spot the differences might prove useful later, after it has been determined that the problem is likely to be on the client.
- **Move the problem:** Using this approach alone is not likely to be enough to solve the problem, but if following any of the other methods indicates a potential hardware issue between the consultant's PC and the access switch, this method might come into play. However, merely as a first step, you could consider swapping the cable and the jack connected to the consultant's laptop and the controller's PC, in turn, to see whether the problem is cable, PC, or switch related.

Many combinations of these different methods could be considered here. The most promising methods are top down or divide and conquer. You will possibly switch to follow-the-path or spot-the-differences approach after the scope of the problem has been properly reduced. As an initial step in any approach, the move-the-problem method could be used to quickly separate client-related issues from network-related issues. The bottom-up approach could be used as the first step to verify the first stretch of cabling.

Implementing Troubleshooting Procedures

The troubleshooting process can be guided by structured methods, but it is not static, and its steps are not always the same and may not be executed in the exact same order every time. Each network is different, each problem is different, and the skill set and experience of the engineer involved in a troubleshooting process is different. However, to guarantee a certain level of consistency in the way that problems are diagnosed and solved in an organization, it is still important to evaluate the common subprocesses that are part of troubleshooting and define procedures that outline how they should be handled. The generic troubleshooting process consists of the following tasks:

Step 1. Defining the problem

Step 2. Gathering information

Step 3. Analyzing the information

Step 4. Eliminating possible problem causes

Step 5. Formulating a hypothesis about the likely cause of the problem

Step 6. Testing that hypothesis

Step 7. Solving the problem

It is important to analyze the typical actions and decisions that are taken during each of these processes and how these could be planned and implemented as troubleshooting procedures.

The Troubleshooting Process

A network troubleshooting process can be reduced to a number of elementary subprocesses, as outlined in the preceding list. These subprocesses are not strictly sequential in nature, and many times you will go back and forth through many of these subprocesses repeatedly until you eventually reach the solving-the-problem phase. A troubleshooting method provides a guiding principle that helps you move through these processes in a structured way. There is no exact recipe for troubleshooting. Every problem is different, and it is impossible to create a script that will solve all possible problem scenarios. Troubleshooting is a skill that requires relevant knowledge and experience. After using different methods several times, you will become more effective at selecting the right method for a particular problem, gathering the most relevant information, and analyzing problems quickly and efficiently. As you gain more experience, you will find that you can skip some steps and adopt more of a shoot-from-the-hip approach, resolving problems more quickly. Regardless, to execute a successful troubleshooting exercise, you must be able to answer the following questions:

- What is the action plan for each of the elementary subprocesses or phases?
- What is it that you actually do during each of those subprocesses?

- What decisions do you need to make?
- What kind of support or resources do you need?
- What kind of communication needs to take place?
- How do you assign proper responsibilities?

Although the answers to these questions will differ for each individual organization, by planning, documenting, and implementing troubleshooting procedures, the consistency and effectiveness of the troubleshooting processes in your organization will improve.

Defining the Problem

All troubleshooting tasks begin with defining the problem. However, what triggers a troubleshooting exercise is a failure experienced by someone who reports it to the support group. Figure 2-4 illustrates reporting of the problem (done by the user) as the trigger action, followed by verification and defining the problem (done by support group). Unless an organization has a strict policy on how problems are reported, the reported problem can unfortunately be vague or even misleading. Problem reports can look like the following: "When I try to go to this location on the intranet, I get a page that says I don't have permission," "The mail server isn't working," or "I can't file my expense report." As you might have noticed, the second statement is merely a conclusion a user has drawn perhaps merely because he cannot send or receive e-mail. To prevent wasting a lot of time during the troubleshooting process based on false assumptions and claims, the first step of troubleshooting is always verifying and defining the problem. The problem has to be first verified, and then defined by you (the support engineer, not the user), and it has to be defined clearly.

A good problem description consists of accurate descriptions of symptoms and not of interpretations or conclusions. Consequences for the user are strictly not part of the problem description itself, but *can* be helpful to assess the urgency of the issue. When a problem is reported as "The mail server isn't working," you must perhaps contact the user and find out exactly what he has experienced. You will probably define the problem as "When user *X* starts his e-mail client, he gets an error message saying that the client can not connect to the server. The user can still access his network drives and browse the Internet."

After you have clearly defined the problem, you have one more step to take before starting the actual troubleshooting process. You must determine whether this problem is your responsibility or if it needs to be escalated to another department or person. For example, assume the reported problem is this: "When user *Y* tries to access the corporate directory on the company intranet, she gets a message that says permission is denied. She can access all other intranet pages." You are a network engineer, and you do not have access to the servers. A separate department in your company manages the intranet servers. Therefore, you must know what to do when this type of problem is reported to you as a network problem. You must know whether to start troubleshooting or to escalate it to the server department. It is important that you know which type of problems is

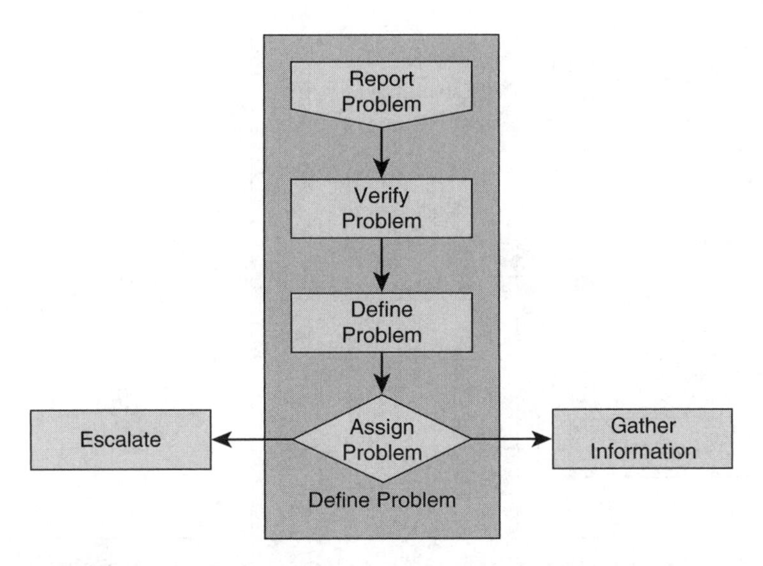

Figure 2-4 *A Reported Problem Must First Be Verified and Then Defined by Support Staff*

your responsibility to act on, what minimal actions you need to take before you escalate a problem, and how you escalate a problem. As Figure 2-4 illustrates, after defining the problem, you assign the problem: The problem is either escalated to another group or department, or it is network support's responsibility to solve it. In the latter case, the next step is gathering and analyzing information.

Gathering and Analyzing Information

Before gathering information, you should select your initial troubleshooting method and develop an information-gathering plan. As part of this plan, you need to identify what the targets are for the information-gathering process. In other words, you must decide which devices, clients, or servers you want to collect information from, and what tools you intend to use to gather that information (assemble a toolkit). Next, you have to acquire access to the identified targets. In many cases, you might have access to these systems as a normal part of your job role, but in some cases, you might need to get information from systems that you cannot normally access. In this case, you might have to escalate the issue to a different department or person, either to obtain access or to get someone else to gather the information for you. If the escalation process would slow the procedure down and the problem is urgent, you might want to reconsider the troubleshooting method that you selected and first try a method that uses different targets and would not require you to escalate. As you can see in Figure 2-5, whether you can access and examine the devices you identified will either lead to problems escalation to another group or department or to the gathering and analyzing information step.

The example that follows demonstrates how information gathering can be influenced by factors out of your control, and consequently, force you to alter your troubleshooting

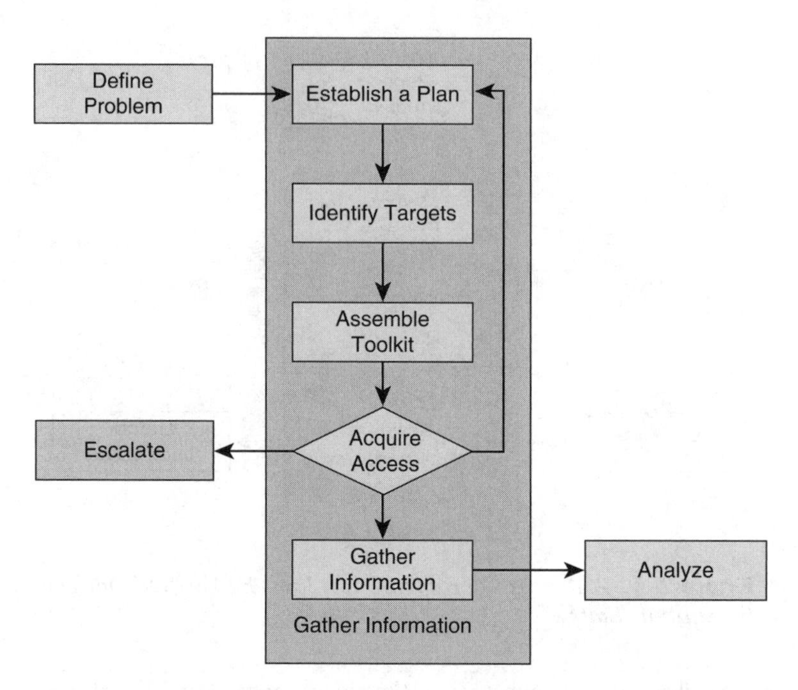

Figure 2-5 *Lack of Access to Devices Might Lead to Problem Escalation to Another Group*

approach. Imagine that it is 1.00 p.m. now and your company's sales manager has reported that he cannot send or receive e-mail from the branch office where he is working. The matter is quite urgent because he has to send out a response to an important request for proposal (RFP) later this afternoon. Your first reaction might be to start a top-down troubleshooting method by calling him up and running through a series of tests. However, the sales manager is not available because he is in a meeting until 4:30 p.m. One of your colleagues from that same branch office confirms that the sales manager is in a meeting, but left his laptop on his desk. The RFP response needs to be received by the customer before 5:00 p.m. Even though a top-down troubleshooting approach might seem like the best choice, because you will not be able to access the sales manager's laptop, you will have to wait until 4:30 before you can start troubleshooting. Having to perform an entire troubleshooting exercise successfully in about 30 minutes is risky, and it will put you under a lot of pressure. In this case, it is best if you used a combination of the "bottom-up" and "follow-the-path" approaches. You can verify whether there are any Layer 1–3 problems between the manager's laptop and the company's mail server. Even if you do not find an issue, you can eliminate many potential problem causes, and when you start a top-down approach at 4:30, you will be able to work more efficiently.

Eliminating Possible Problem Causes

After gathering information from various devices, you must interpret and analyze the information. In a way, this process is similar to detective work. You must use the facts and evidence to progressively eliminate possible causes and eventually identify the root of the problem. To interpret the raw information that you have gathered, for example, the output of **show** and **debug** commands, or packet captures and device logs, you might need to research commands, protocols, and technologies. You might also need to consult network documentation to be able to interpret the information in the context of the actual network's implementation. During the analysis of the gathered information, you are typically trying to determine two things: What is happening on the network and what should be happening. If you discover differences between these two, you can collect clues for what is wrong or at least a direction to take for further information gathering. Figure 2-6 shows that the gathered information, network documentation, baseline information, plus your research results and past experience are all used as input while you interpret and analyze the gathered information to eliminate possibilities and identify the source of the problem.

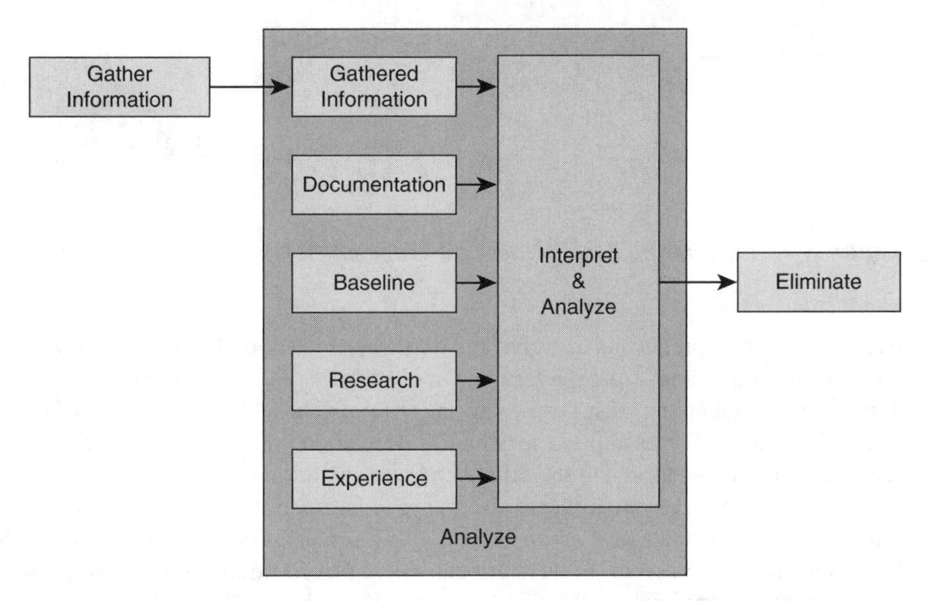

Figure 2-6 *Useful Factors That Can Feed and Support the Interpret and Analyze Task*

Your perception of what is actually happening is usually formed based on interpretation of the raw data, supported by research and documentation; however, your understanding of the underlying protocols and technologies also plays a role in your success level. If you are troubleshooting protocols and technologies that you are not very familiar with, you will have to invest some time in researching how they operate. Furthermore, a good baseline of the behavior of your network can prove quite useful at the analysis stage. If you know how your network performs and how things work under normal conditions, you can spot anomalies in the behavior of the network and derive clues from those deviations. The benefit of vast relevant past experience cannot be undermined. An experienced network engineer will spend significantly less time on researching processes, interpreting raw data, and distilling the relevant information from the raw data than an inexperienced engineer.

Formulating/Testing a Hypothesis

Figure 2-7 shows that based on your continuous information analysis and the assumptions you make, you eliminate possible problem causes from the pool of proposed causes until you have a final proposal that takes you to the next step of the troubleshooting process: formulating and proposing a hypothesis.

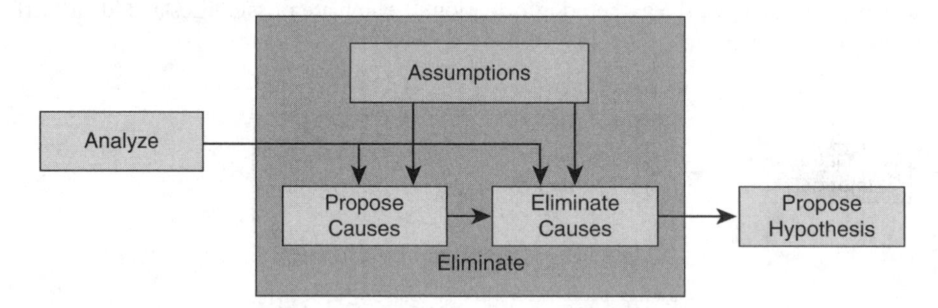

Figure 2-7 *Eliminating Possibilities and Proposing a Hypothesis Based on*

After you have interpreted and analyzed the information that you have gathered, you start drawing conclusions from the results. On one hand, some of the discovered clues point toward certain issues that can be causing the problem, adding to your list of potential problem causes. For example, a very high CPU load on your multilayer switches can be a sign of a bridging loop. On the other hand, you might rule out some of the potential problem causes based on the gathered and analyzed facts. For example, a successful ping from a client to its default gateway rules out Layer 2 problems between them. Although the elimination process seems to be a rational, scientific procedure, you have to be aware that assumptions play a role in this process, too, and you have to be willing to go back and reexamine and verify your assumptions. If you do not, you might sometimes mistakenly eliminate the actual root cause of a problem as a nonprobable cause, and that means you will never be able to solve the problem.

An Example on Elimination and Assumptions

You are examining a connectivity problem between a client and a server. As part of a follow-the-path troubleshooting approach, you decide to verify the Layer 2 connectivity between the client and the access switch to which it connects. You log on to the access switch and using the **show interface** command, you verify that the port connecting the client is up, input and output packets are recorded on the port, and that no errors are displayed in the packet statistics. Next, you verify that the client's MAC address was correctly learned on the port according to the switch's MAC address table using the **show mac-address-table** command. Therefore, you conclude that Layer 2 is operational between the client and the switch, and you continue your troubleshooting approach examining links further up the path.

You must always keep in mind which of the assumptions you have made might need to be reexamined later. The first assumption made in this example is that the MAC address table entry and port statistics were current. Because this information might not be quite fresh, you might need to first clear the counters and the MAC address table and then verify that the counters are still increasing and that the MAC address is learned again. The second assumption is hidden in the conclusion: Layer 2 is operational, which implies that the client and the switch are sending and receiving frames to each other successfully in both directions. The only thing that you can really prove is that Layer 2 is operational from the client to the switch, because the switch has received frames from the client.

The fact that the interface is up and that frames were recorded as being sent by the switch does not give you definitive proof that the client has correctly received those frames. So even though it is reasonable to assume that, if a link is operational on Layer 2 in one direction it will also be operational in the other direction, this is still an assumption that you might need to come back to later.

Spotting faulty assumptions is one of the tricky aspects of troubleshooting, because usually you are not consciously making those assumptions. Making assumptions is part of the normal thought process. One helpful way to uncover hidden assumptions is to explain your reasoning to one of your colleagues or peers. Because people think differently, a peer might be able to spot the hidden assumptions that you are making and help you uncover them.

Solving the Problem

After the process of proposing and eliminating some of the potential problem causes, you end up with a short list of remaining possible causes. Based on experience, you might even be able to assign a certain measure of probability to each of the remaining potential causes. If this list still has many different possible problem causes and none of them clearly stands out as the most likely cause, you might have to go back and gather more information first and eliminate more problem causes before you can propose a good hypothesis. After you have reduced the list of potential causes to just a few (ideally just one), select one of them as your problem hypothesis. Before you start to test your proposal, however, you have to reassess whether the proposed problem cause is within your area of responsibilities. In other words, if the issue that you just proposed as your hypothesis causes the problem, you have to determine whether it is your responsibility to solve it or you have to escalate it to some other person or department. Figure 2-8 shows the steps that you take to reach a hypothesis followed by escalating it to another group, or by testing your hypothesis.

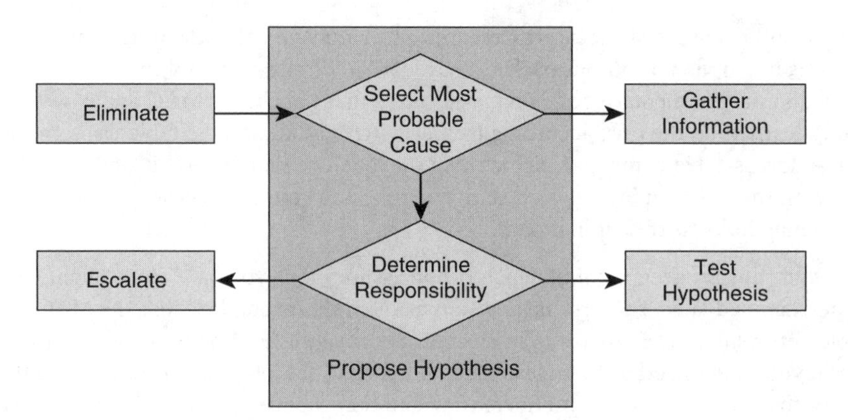

Figure 2-8 *Formulating a Hypothesis Is Followed by Escalation or Testing the Hypothesis*

If you decide to escalate the problem, ask yourself if this ends your involvement in the process. Note that escalating the problem is not the same as solving the problem. You have to think about how long it will take the other party to solve the problem and how urgent is the problem to them. Users affected by the problem might not be able to afford to wait long for the other group to fix the problem. If you cannot solve the problem, but it is too urgent to wait for the problem to be solved through an escalation, you might need to come up with a workaround. A temporary fix alleviates the symptoms experienced by the user, even if it does not address the root cause of the problem.

After a hypothesis is proposed identifying the cause of a problem, the next step is to come up with a possible solution (or workaround) to that problem, and plan an implementation scheme. Usually, implementing a possible solution involves making changes to the network. Therefore, if your organization has defined procedures for regular network maintenance, you must follow your organization's regular change procedures. The next step is to assess the impact of the change on the network and balance that against the urgency of the problem. If the urgency outweighs the impact and you decide to go ahead with the change, it is important to make sure that you have a way to revert to the original situation after you make the change. Even though you have determined that your hypothesis is the most likely cause of the problem and your solution is intended to fix it, you can never be entirely sure that your proposed solution will actually solve the problem. If the problem is not solved, you need to have a way to undo your changes and revert to the original situation. Upon creation of a rollback plan, you can implement your proposed solution according to your organization's change procedures. Verify that the problem is solved and that the change you made did what you expected it to do. In other words, make sure the root cause of the problem and its symptoms are eliminated, and that your solution has not introduced any new problems. If all results are positive and desirable, you move on to the final stage of troubleshooting, which is integrating the solution and documenting your work. Figure 2-9 shows the flow of tasks while you implement and test your proposed hypothesis and either solve the problem or end up rolling back your changes.

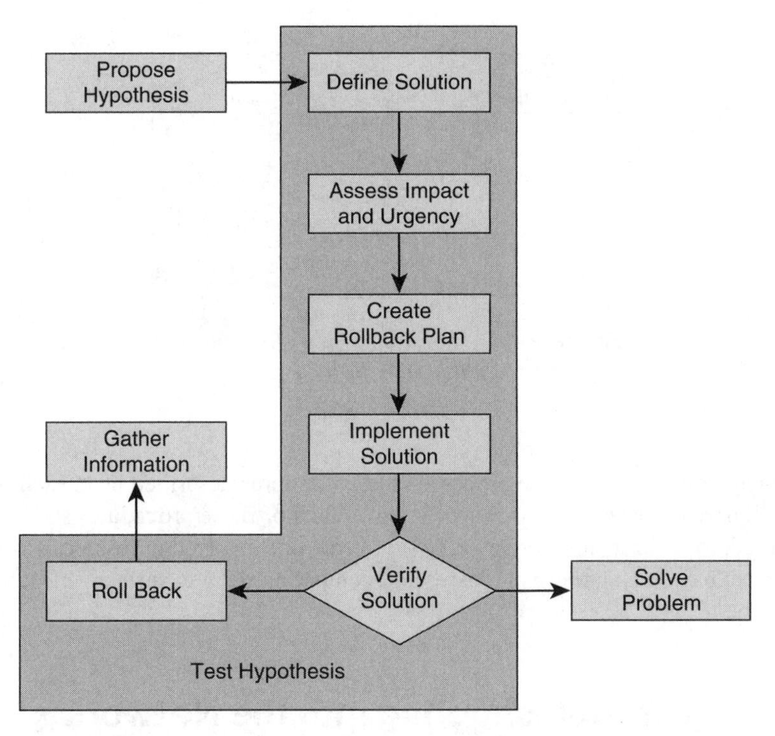

Figure 2-9 *Testing a Proposed Hypothesis*

You must have a plan for the situation if it turns out that the problem was not fixed, the symptoms have not disappeared, or new problems have been introduced by the change that you have made. In this case, you should execute your rollback plan, revert to the original situation, and resume the troubleshooting process. It is important to determine if the root cause hypothesis was invalid or whether it was simply the proposed solution that did not work.

After you have confirmed your hypothesis and verified that the symptoms have disappeared, you have essentially solved the problem. All you need to do then is to make sure that the changes you made are integrated into the regular implementation of the network and that any maintenance procedures associated with those changes are executed. You will have to create backups of any changed configurations or upgraded software. You will have to document all changes to make sure that the network documentation still accurately describes the current state of the network. In addition, you must perform any other actions that are prescribed by your organization's change control procedures. Figure 2-10 shows that upon receiving successful results from testing your hypothesis, you incorporate your solution and perform the final tasks such as backup, documentation, and communication, before you report the problem as solved.

The last thing you do is to communicate that the problem has been solved. At a minimum, you will have to communicate back to the original user that reported the problem, but if you have involved others as part of an escalation process, you should communicate

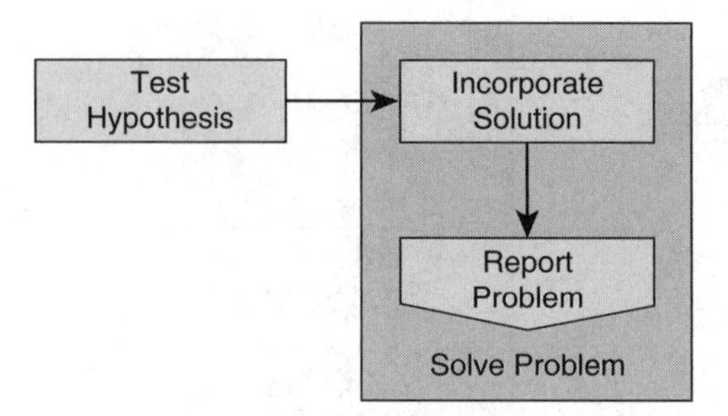

Figure 2-10 *The Final Step: Incorporate the Solution and Report the Problem as Solved*

with them, too. For any of the processes and procedures described here, each organization will have to make its own choices in how much of these procedures should be described, formalized, and followed. However, anyone involved in troubleshooting will benefit from reviewing these processes and comparing them to their own troubleshooting habits.

Integrating Troubleshooting into the Network Maintenance Process

Troubleshooting is a process that takes place as part of many different network maintenance tasks. For example, it might be necessary to troubleshoot issues arisen after implementation of new devices. Similarly, it could be necessary to troubleshoot after a network maintenance task such as a software upgrade. Consequently, troubleshooting processes should be integrated into network maintenance procedures and vice versa. When troubleshooting procedures and maintenance procedures are properly aligned, the overall network maintenance process will be more effective.

Troubleshooting and Network Maintenance

Network maintenance involves many different tasks, some of which are listed within Figure 2-11. For some of these tasks, such as supporting users, responding to network failures, or disaster recovery, troubleshooting is a major component of the tasks. Tasks that do not revolve around fault management, such as adding or replacing equipment, moving servers and users, and performing software upgrades, will regularly include troubleshooting processes, too. Hence, troubleshooting should not be seen as a standalone process, but as an essential skill that plays an important role in many different types of network maintenance tasks.

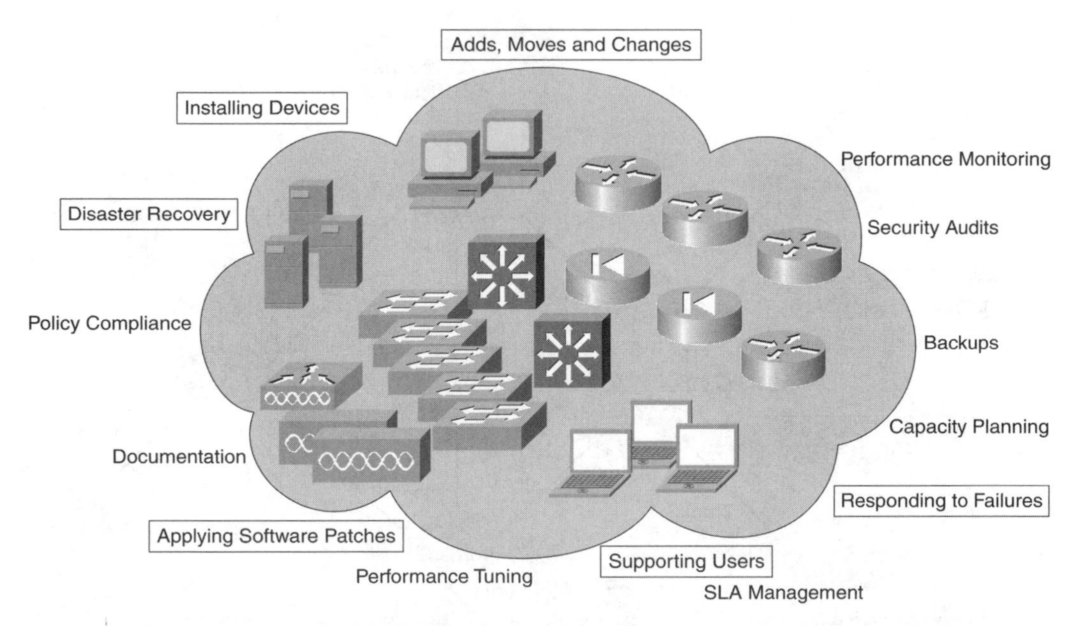

Figure 2-11 *Troubleshooting Plays an Important Role in Many Network Maintenance Tasks*

To troubleshoot effectively, you must rely on many processes and resources that are part of the network maintenance process. You need to have access to up-to-date and accurate documentation. You rely on good backup and restore procedures to be able to roll back changes if they do not resolve the problem that you are troubleshooting. You need to have a good baseline of the network so that you know which conditions are supposed to be normal on your network and what kind of behavior is considered abnormal. Also, you need to have access to logs that are properly time stamped to find out when particular events have happened. So in many ways, the quality of your troubleshooting processes depends significantly on the quality of your network maintenance processes. Therefore, it makes sense to plan and implement troubleshooting activities as part of the overall network maintenance process and to make sure that troubleshooting processes and maintenance processes are aligned and support each other, making both processes more effective.

Documentation

Having accurate and current network documentation can tremendously increase the speed and effectiveness of troubleshooting processes. Having good network diagrams can especially help in quickly isolating problems to a particular part of the network, tracing the flow of traffic, and verifying connections between devices. Having a good IP address schematic and patching administration is invaluable, too, and can save a lot of time while trying to locate devices and IP addresses. Figure 2-12 shows some network documentation that is always valuable to have.

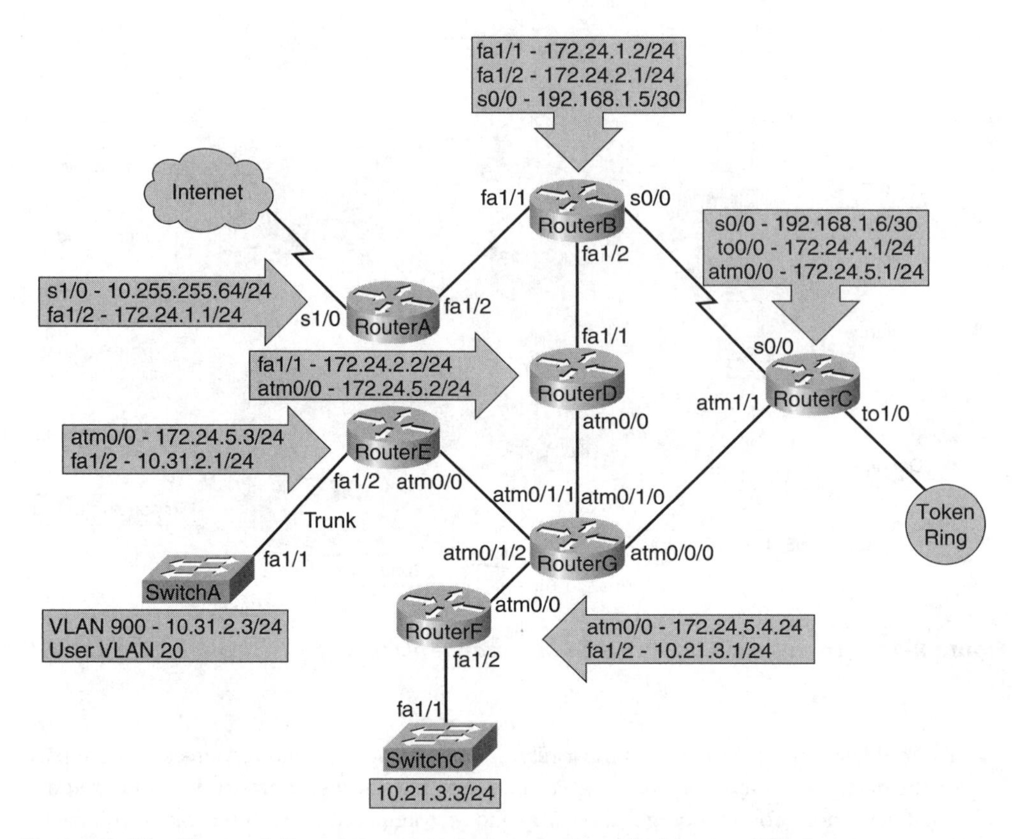

Figure 2-12 *Network Documentation Increases Troubleshooting Efficiency*

On the other hand, documentation that is wrong or outdated is often worse than having no documentation at all. If the documentation that you have is inaccurate or out-of-date, you might start working with information that is wrong and you might end up drawing the wrong conclusions and potentially lose a lot of time before you discover that the documentation is incorrect and cannot be relied upon.

Although everyone who is involved in network maintenance will agree that updating documentation is an essential part of network maintenance tasks, they will all recognize that in the heat of the moment, when you are troubleshooting a problem that is affecting network connectivity for many users, documenting the process and any changes that you are making is one of the last things on your mind. There are several ways to alleviate this problem. First, make sure that any changes you make during troubleshooting are handled in accordance with normal change procedures (if not during the troubleshooting process itself, then at least after the fact). You might loosen the requirements concerning authorization and scheduling of changes during major failures, but you have to make sure that after the problem has been solved or a workaround has been implemented to restore connectivity, you always go through any of the standard administrative processes like updating the documentation. Because you know that you will have to update the documentation afterward, there is an incentive to keep at least a minimal log of the changes that you make while troubleshooting.

One good policy to keep your documentation accurate, assuming that people will forget to update the documentation, is to schedule regular checks of the documentation. However, verifying documentation manually is tedious work, so you will probably prefer to implement an automated system for that. For configuration changes, you could implement a system that downloads all device configurations on a regular basis and compares the configuration to the last version to spot any differences. There are also various IOS features such as the Configuration Archive, Rollback feature, and the Embedded Event Manager that can be leveraged to create automatic configuration backups, to log configuration commands to a syslog server, or to even send out configuration differences via e-mail.

Creating a Baseline

An essential troubleshooting technique is to compare what is happening on the network to what is expected or to what is normal on the network. Whenever you spot abnormal behavior in an area of the network that is experiencing problems, there is a good chance that it is related to the problems. It could be the cause of the problem, or it could be another symptom that might help point toward the underlying root cause. Either way, it is always worth investigating abnormal behavior to find out whether it is related to the problem. For example, suppose you are troubleshooting an application problem, and while you are following the path between the client and the server, you notice that one of the routers is also a bit slow in its responses to your commands. You execute the **show processes cpu** command and notice that the average CPU load over the past 5 seconds was 97 percent and over the last 1 minute was around 39 percent. You might wonder if this router's high CPU utilization might be the cause of the problem you are troubleshooting. On one hand, this could be an important clue that is worth investigating, but on the other hand, it could be that your router regularly runs at 40 percent to 50 percent CPU and it is not related to this problem at all. In this case, you could potentially waste a lot of time trying to find the cause for the high CPU load, while it is entirely unrelated to the problem at hand.

The only way to know what is normal for your network is to measure the network's behavior continuously. Knowing what to measure is different for each network. In general, the more you know, the better it is, but obviously this has to be balanced against the effort and cost involved in implementing and maintaining a performance management system. The following list describes some useful data to gather and create a baseline:

- **Basic performance statistics such as the interface load for critical network links and the CPU load and memory usage of routers and switches:** These values can be polled and collected on a regular basis using SNMP and graphed for visual inspection.

- **Accounting of network traffic:** Remote Monitoring (RMON), Network Based Application Recognition (NBAR), or NetFlow statistics can be used to profile different types of traffic on the network.

- **Measurements of network performance characteristics:** The IP SLA feature in Cisco IOS can be used to measure critical performance indicators such as delay and jitter across the network infrastructure.

These baseline measurements are useful for troubleshooting, but they are also useful inputs for capacity planning, network usage accounting, and SLA monitoring. Clearly, a synergy exists between gathering traffic and performance statistics as part of regular network maintenance and using those statistics as a baseline during troubleshooting. Moreover, once you have the infrastructure in place to collect, analyze, and graph network statistics, you can also leverage this infrastructure to troubleshoot specific performance problems. For example, if you notice that a router crashes once a week and you suspect a memory leak as the cause of this issue, you could decide to graph the router's memory usage for a certain period of time to see whether you can find a correlation between the crashes and the memory usage.

Communication and Change Control

Communication is an essential part of the troubleshooting process. To review, the main phases of structured troubleshooting are as follows:

Step 1. Defining the problem

Step 2. Gathering facts

Step 3. Analyzing information

Step 4. Eliminating possibilities

Step 5. Proposing a hypothesis

Step 6. Testing the hypothesis

Step 7. Solving the problem

Figure 2-13 shows several spots where, while performing structured troubleshooting, communication is necessary if not inevitable.

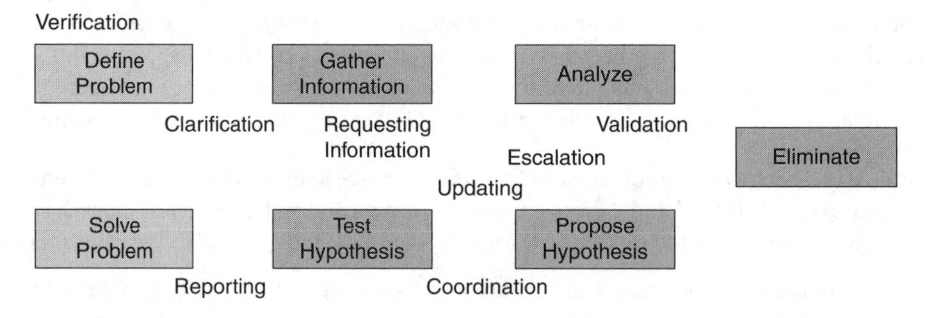

Figure 2-13 *Communication Plays a Role in All Phases of Structured Troubleshooting*

Within each phase of the troubleshooting process, communication plays a role:

- **Defining the problem:** Even though this is the first step of the structured troubleshooting, it is triggered by the user reporting the problem. Reporting the problem and defining the problem are not the same. When someone reports a problem, it is often too vague to act on it immediately. You have to verify the problem and gather as much information as you can about the symptoms from the person who reported the problem. Asking good questions and carefully listening to the answers is essential in this phase. You might ask questions such as these: "What do you mean exactly when you say that something is failing? Did you make any changes before the problem started? Did you notice anything special before this problem started? When did it last work? Has it ever worked?" After you communicate with the users and perhaps see the problems for yourself, and so on, you make a precise and clear problem definition. Clearly, this step is all about communication.
- **Gathering facts:** During this phase of the process, you will often depend on other engineers or users to gather information for you. You might need to obtain information contained in server or application logs, configurations of devices that you do not manage, information about outages from a service provider, or information from users in different locations, to compare against the location that is experiencing the problem. Clearly, communicating what information you need and how that information can be obtained determines how successfully you can acquire the information you really need.
- **Analyzing information and eliminate possibilities:** In itself, interpretation and analysis is mostly a solitary process, but there are still some communication aspects to this phase. First of all, you cannot be experienced in every aspect of networking, so if you find that you are having trouble interpreting certain results or if you lack knowledge about certain processes, you can ask specialists on your team to help you out. Also, there is always a chance that you are misinterpreting results, misreading information, making wrong assumptions, or are having other flaws in your interpretation and analysis. A different viewpoint can often help in these situations, so discussing your reasoning and results with teammates to validate your assumptions and conclusions can be very helpful, especially when you are stuck.
- **Proposing and testing a hypothesis:** Most of the time, testing a hypothesis involves making changes to the network. These changes may be disruptive, and users may be impacted. Even if you have decided that the urgency of the problem outweighs the impact and the change will have to be made, you should still communicate clearly what you are doing and why you are doing it. Even if your changes will not have a major impact on the users or the business, you should still coordinate and communicate any changes that you are making. When other team members are working on the same problem, you have to make sure that you are not both making changes. Any results from the elimination process might be rendered invalid if a change was made during the information-gathering phase and you were not aware of it. Also, if two changes are made in quick succession and it turns out that the problem was resolved, you will not know which of the two changes actually fixed it. This does not mean

that you cannot be working on the same problem as a team, but you have to adhere to certain rules. Having multiple people working on different parts of the network, gathering information in parallel or pursuing different strategies, can help in finding the cause faster. During a major disaster, when every minute counts, the extra speed that you can gain by working in parallel may prove valuable. However, any changes or other disruptive actions should be carefully coordinated and communicated.

- **Solving the problem:** Clearly, this phase also involves some communication. You must report back to the person who originally reported the problem that the problem has been solved. Also, you must communicate this to any other people who were involved during the process. Finally, you will have to go through any communication that is involved in the normal change processes, to make sure that the changes that you made are properly integrated in the standard network maintenance processes.

Sometimes it is necessary to escalate the problem to another person or another group. Common reasons for this could be that you do not have sufficient knowledge and skills and you want to escalate the problem to a specialist or to a more senior engineer, or that you are working in shifts and you need to hand over the problem as your shift ends. Handing the troubleshooting task over to someone else does not only require clear communication of the results of your process, such as gathered information and conclusions that you have drawn, but it also includes any communication that has been going on up to this point. This is where an issue-tracking or trouble-ticketing system can be of tremendous value, especially if it integrates well with other means of communication such as e-mail.

Finally, another communication process that requires some attention is how to communicate the progress of your troubleshooting process to the business (management or otherwise). When you are experiencing a major outage, there will usually be a barrage of questions from business managers and users such as "What are you doing to repair this issue? How long will it take before it is solved? Can you implement any workarounds? What do you need to fix this?" Although these are all reasonable questions, the truth is that many of these questions cannot be answered until the cause of the problem is found. At the same time, all the time spent communicating about the process is taken away from the actual troubleshooting effort itself. Therefore, it is worthwhile to streamline this process, for instance by having one of the senior team members act as a conduit for all communication. All questions are routed to this person, and any updates and changes are communicated to him; this person will then update the key stakeholders. This way, the engineers who are actually working on the problem can work with a minimal amount of distraction.

Change Control

Change control is one of the most fundamental processes in network maintenance. By strictly controlling when changes are made, defining what type of authorization is required and what actions need to be taken as part of that process, you can reduce the frequency and duration of unplanned outages and thereby increase the overall uptime of your network. You must therefore understand how the changes made as part of troubleshooting fit into the overall change processes. Essentially, there is not anything different between making a change as part of the maintenance process or as part of troubleshooting. Most of the actions that you take are the same. You implement the change, verify that it achieved the desired results, roll back if it did not achieve the desired results, back up the changed configurations or software, and document/communicate your changes. The biggest difference between regular changes and emergency changes is the authorization required to make a change and the scheduling of the change. Within change-control procedures, there is always an aspect of balancing urgency, necessity, impact, and risk. The outcome of this assessment will determine whether a change can be executed immediately or if it will have to be scheduled at a later time.

The troubleshooting process can benefit tremendously from having well-defined and well-documented change processes. It is uncommon for devices or links just to fail from one moment to the next. In many cases, problems are triggered or caused by some sort of change. This can be a simple change, such as changing a cable or reconfiguring a setting, but it may also be more subtle, like a change in traffic patterns due to the outbreak of a new worm or virus. A problem can also be caused by a combination of changes, where the first change is the root cause of the problem, but the problem is not triggered until you make another change. For example, imagine a situation where somebody accidentally erases the router software from its flash. This will not cause the router to fail immediately, because it is running IOS from its RAM. However, if that router reboots because of a short power failure a month later, it will not boot, because it is missing the IOS in its flash memory. In this example, the root cause of the failure is the erased software, but the trigger is the power failure. This type of problem is harder to catch, and only in tightly controlled environments will you be able to find the root cause or prevent this type of problem. In the previous example, a log of all privileged EXEC commands executed on this router can reveal that the software had been erased at a previous date. You can conclude that one of the useful questions you can ask during fact gathering is "Has anything been changed?" The answer to this question can very likely be found in the network documentation or change logs if network policies enforce rigid documentation and change-control procedures.

Summary

The fundamental elements of a troubleshooting process are as following:

- Gathering of information and symptoms
- Analyzing information
- Eliminating possible causes
- Formulating a hypothesis
- Testing the hypothesis

Some commonly used troubleshooting approaches are as follows:

- Top down
- Bottom up
- Divide and conquer
- Follow the path
- Spot the differences
- Move the problem

A structured approach to troubleshooting (no matter what the exact method is) will yield more predictable results in the long run and will make it easier to pick up the process where you left off in a later stage or to hand it over to someone else.

The structured troubleshooting begins with problem definition followed by fact gathering. The gathered information, network documentation, baseline information, plus your research results and past experience are all used as input while you interpret and analyze the gathered information to eliminate possibilities and identify the source of the problem. Based on your continuous information analysis and the assumptions you make, you eliminate possible problem causes from the pool of proposed causes until you have a final proposal that takes you to the next step of the troubleshooting process: formulating and proposing a hypothesis. Based on your hypothesis, the problem might or might not fall within your area of responsibility, so proposing a hypothesis is either followed by escalating it to another group or by testing your hypothesis. If your test results are positive, you have to plan and implement a solution. The solution entails changes that must follow the change-control procedures within your organization. The results and all the changes you make must be clearly documented and communicated with all the relevant parties.

Having accurate and current network documentation can tremendously increase the speed and effectiveness of troubleshooting processes. Documentation that is wrong or outdated is often worse than having no documentation at all.

To gather and create a network baseline, the following data proves useful:

- Basic performance statistics obtain by running **show** commands
- Accounting of network traffic using RMON, NBAR, or NetFlow statistics
- Measurements of network performance characteristics using the IP SLA feature in IOS

Communication is an essential part of the troubleshooting process, and it happens in all of the following stages of troubleshooting:

- Reporting the problem
- Gathering information

- Analyzing and eliminating possible causes
- Proposing and testing a hypothesis
- Solving the problem

Change control is one of the most fundamental processes in network maintenance. By strictly controlling when changes are made, defining what type of authorization is required and what actions need to be taken as part of that process, you can reduce the frequency and duration of unplanned outages and thereby increase the overall uptime of your network. Essentially, there is not much difference between making a change as part of the maintenance process or as part of troubleshooting.

Review Questions

1. Which three of the following processes are subprocesses or phases of a troubleshooting process? (Choose three.)
   a. Elimination
   b. Testing
   c. Termination
   d. Problem definition
   e. Calculation
   f. Compilation
2. Which four of the following approaches are valid troubleshooting methods? (Choose four.)
   a. Top down
   b. Bottom up
   c. Follow the path
   d. Seek-and-destroy
   e. Divide and conquer
3. Which three of the following troubleshooting approaches use the OSI reference model as a guiding principle? (Choose three.)
   a. Top down
   b. Bottom up
   c. Follow the path
   d. Spot the differences
   e. Move the problem
   f. Divide and conquer

4. Which of the following troubleshooting methods is most appropriate to find a bad cable?

a. Top down

b. Bottom up

c. Follow the path

d. Spot the differences

e. Move the problem

f. Divide and conquer

5. Which conditions make troubleshooting by spotting the differences more effective?

6. Which of the following has a clear problem definition?

a. I cannot order printer cartridges because the Internet is down.

b. My e-mail does not work.

c. I cannot log on to the network because the server is down.

d. When I try to access http://www.cisco.com, my Internet Explorer says that it cannot display the web page.

7. Which two of the following resources will help in interpreting and analyzing information gathered during troubleshooting? (Choose two.)

a. Documentation

b. Network baseline

c. Packet sniffers

d. Assumptions

8. Which of the following steps are parts of testing a hypothesis? (Choose four.)

a. Defining a solution

b. Creating a rollback plan

c. Implementing the solution

d. Defining the problem

e. Assessing impact and urgency

9. During which three of the troubleshooting phases could it be necessary to escalate a problem to a different department? (Choose three.)

   a. Defining the problem

   b. Gathering information

   c. Analyzing the facts

   d. Eliminating possible causes

   e. Formulating a hypothesis

   f. Solving the problem

10. Which of the following technologies can be deployed to measure critical network performance indicators such as delay and jitter?

    a. NetFlow

    b. RMON

    c. IP SLA

    d. NBAR

11. Which of the following phases of the troubleshooting process does not have communication as a major component?

    a. Defining the problem

    b. Solving the problem

    c. Eliminating causes

    d. Gathering information

Chapter 3

Using Maintenance and Troubleshooting Tools and Applications

This chapter covers the following topics:

- Using the Cisco IOS commands to selectively gather information in support of basic diagnostic processes
- Identifying the tools commonly used for specific maintenance and troubleshooting processes and preparing the infrastructure for their use

Troubleshooting can be a time-consuming process. While the network is down, productivity and revenue are lost, and reputations can be ruined. Tools that enable you to diagnose and resolve problems quickly recoup their acquisition and maintenance costs. Some diagnostic tools are built in to Cisco IOS Software, and therefore learning and optimizing the use of those tools should be a top priority for any engineer that performs troubleshooting. Furthermore, Cisco IOS Software supports many technologies and protocols that can be used in combination with other specialized tools and applications to support troubleshooting and maintenance processes such as fault notification and baseline creation. This chapter reviews the built-in Cisco IOS tools and commands and specialized tools and applications.

Using Cisco IOS Software for Maintenance and Troubleshooting

As covered previously in Chapter 2, "Troubleshooting Processes for Complex Enterprise Networks," much of the total time spent on troubleshooting processes is usually spent on the information-gathering stage. One of the challenges during this process is how to gather only the relevant information. Collecting and processing a lot of irrelevant information is distracting and a waste of time. Learning how to efficiently and effectively apply the basic tools that support the elementary diagnostic processes that you repeatedly exercise is worthwhile. Learning the Cisco IOS **show** commands used for collecting and filtering information and the commands used to test connectivity problems is vital to the support staff's troubleshooting strength. Other relevant and beneficial skills are collecting real-time information using Cisco IOS **debug** commands and diagnosing basic hardware-related problems.

Collecting and Filtering Information Using Cisco IOS show Commands

You must learn how to apply filtering to Cisco IOS **show** commands to optimize your information gathering. During troubleshooting, you are often looking for specific information. For example, you might be looking for a particular prefix in the routing table, or you might want to verify whether a specific MAC address has been learned on an interface. Sometimes you need to find out the percentage of CPU time that is being used by a process such as the IP Input process. Using the **show ip route** command and the **show mac-address-table** command, you can display the IP routing table and the MAC address table, and using the **show processes cpu** command, you can check the CPU utilization for all processes on a Cisco router or switch. However, because the routing table and MAC address table can contain thousands to tens of thousands of entries, scanning through these tables to find a particular entry is neither viable nor realistic. Also, if you cannot find the entry that you are searching for, does it really mean that it is not in the table or that you simply did not spot it? Repeating the command and not seeing what you are looking for again still does not guarantee that you did not simply miss it. The list of processes on a router or switch is not hundreds or thousands of entries long; you could indeed just look through the full list and find a single process such as the IP Input process. But if you want to repeat the command every minute to see how the CPU usage for the IP Input process changes over time, displaying the whole table might not be desirable. In all these cases, you are interested in only a small subset of the information that the commands can provide. Cisco IOS Software provides options to limit or filter the output that displays.

To limit the output of the **show ip route** command, you can optionally enter a specific IP address on the command line. Doing so causes the router to execute a routing table lookup for that specific IP address and see whether it finds a match. If the router finds a match in the routing table, it displays the corresponding entry with all its details. If the router does not find a match in the routing table, it displays the **% Subnet not in table** message (see Example 3-1). Keep in mind that if gateway of last resort (default route) is present in the IP routing table, but no entry matches the IP address you entered, the router again responds with the **% Subnet not in table** message even though packets for that destination are forwarded using the gateway of last resort.

Example 3-1 *Filtering Output of the* **show ip route** *Command*

```
RO1# show ip route 10.1.193.3
Routing entry for 10.1.193.0/30
  Known via "connected", distance 0, metric 0 (connected, via interface)
  Redistributing via eigrp 1
  Routing Descriptor Blocks:
  * directly connected, via Serial0/0/1
      Route metric is 0, traffic share count is 1

RO1# show ip route 10.1.193.10
% Subnet not in table
```

Another option to limit the output of the **show ip route** command to a particular subset of routing information that you are interested in is typing a prefix followed by the optional **longer-prefixes** keyword, as demonstrated in Example 3-2. The router will then list all subnets that fall within the prefix that you have specified (including that prefix itself, if it is present in the routing table). If the network that you are troubleshooting has a good hierarchical IP numbering plan, the **longer-prefixes** command option can prove useful for displaying addresses from a particular part of the network. You can display all subnets of a particular branch office or data center, for example, using the summary address for these blocks and the **longer–prefixes** keyword.

Example 3-2 *Using the* **longer-prefixes** *Keyword with* **show ip route**

```
CRO1# show ip route 10.1.193.0 255.255.255.0 longer-prefixes
Codes: C - connected, S - static, R - RIP, M - mobile, B - BGP
       D - EIGRP, EX - EIGRP external, O - OSPF, IA - OSPF inter area
       N1 - OSPF NSSA external type 1, N2 - OSPF NSSA external type 2
       E1 - OSPF external type 1, E2 - OSPF external type 2
       i - IS-IS, su - IS-IS summary, L1 - IS-IS level-1, L2 - IS-IS level-2
       ia - IS-IS inter area, * - candidate default, U - per-user static route
       o - ODR, P - periodic downloaded static route
Gateway of last resort is not set
     10.0.0.0/8 is variably subnetted, 46 subnets, 6 masks
C       10.1.193.2/32 is directly connected, Serial0/0/1
C       10.1.193.0/30 is directly connected, Serial0/0/1
D       10.1.193.6/32 [90/20517120] via 10.1.192.9, 2d01h, FastEthernet0/1
                      [90/20517120] via 10.1.192.1, 2d01h, FastEthernet0/0
D       10.1.193.4/30 [90/20517120] via 10.1.192.9, 2d01h, FastEthernet0/1
                      [90/20517120] via 10.1.192.1, 2d01h, FastEthernet0/0
D       10.1.193.5/32 [90/41024000] via 10.1.194.6, 2d01h, Serial0/0/0.122
```

Unfortunately, **show** commands do not always have the option that allows you filter the output down to exactly what you need. You can still perform a more generic way of filtering. The output of Cisco IOS **show** commands can be filtered by appending a pipe character (|) to the **show** command followed by one of the keywords **include**, **exclude**, or **begin**, and then a regular expression. Regular expressions are patterns that can be used to match strings in a piece of text. In its simplest form, you can use it to match words or text fragments in a line of text, but full use of the regular expression syntax allow you to build complex expressions that match specific text patterns. Example 3-3 shows usage of the **include**, **exclude**, and **begin** keywords with the **show processes cpu**, **show ip interface brief**, and the **show running-config** commands correspondingly.

Example 3-3 *Using* **include, exclude,** *and* **begin** *Keywords with* **show** *Commands*

```
RO1# show processes cpu | include IP Input
  71      3149172    7922812         397  0.24%  0.15%  0.05%   0 IP Input

SW1# show ip interface brief | exclude unassigned
Interface                  IP-Address       OK? Method Status                Protocol
Vlan128                    10.1.156.1       YES NVRAM  up                    up

SW1# show running-config | begin line vty
line vty 0 4
 transport input telnet ssh
line vty 5 15
 transport input telnet ssh
!
end
```

In Example 3-3 you are only interested in the IP Input process in the output of the **show processes cpu** command, so you select only the lines that contain the string "IP Input" by using the command **show processes cpu | include IP Input.**

You can exclude lines from the output through use of the **| exclude** option, which, for example, can be useful on a switch where you are trying to obtain all of the IP addresses on the interfaces with the **show ip interface brief** command. On a switch that has many interfaces (ports), the output of this command will also list all the interfaces that have no IP address assigned. If you are looking for the interfaces that have an IP address only, these lines obscure the output. If you know that all interfaces without an IP address have the string "unassigned" in place of the IP address, as you can see in Example 3-3, you can exclude those lines from the output by issuing the command **show ip interface brief | exclude unassigned.**

Finally, using **| begin** allows you to skip all command output up to the first occurrence of the regular expression pattern. In Example 3-3, you are only interested in checking the configuration for the vty lines and you know that the vty configuration commands are at the bottom of the router's running configuration file. So, you jump straight to the vty configuration point by issuing the command **show running-config | begin line vty.**

Cisco IOS Software Release (12.3(2)T) introduced the **section** option, which allows you to select and display a specific section or lines from the configuration that match a particular regular expression and any following associated lines. For example, Example 3-4 demonstrates using the command **show running-config | section router eigrp** to display the EIGRP configuration section only.

Example 3-4 *Using the* **| section** *and* ^ *Options to Filter Output of* **show** *Commands*

```
RO1# show running-config | section router eigrp
router eigrp 1
```

```
 network 10.1.192.2 0.0.0.0
 network 10.1.192.10 0.0.0.0
 network 10.1.193.1 0.0.0.0
 no auto-summary

R01# show processes cpu | include ^CPU|IP Input
CPU utilization for five seconds: 1%/0%; one minute: 1%; five minutes: 1%

  71     3149424   7923898         397  0.24%  0.04%  0.00%   0 IP Input
```

If you used **show running-config | section router** however, all lines that include the expression **router** and the configuration section that follows that line would be displayed. In other words, all routing protocol configuration sections would be displayed and the rest of the configuration wouldn't. This makes **| section** more restrictive than the **| begin** option, but more useful than the **| include** option when you want to select sections instead of only lines that contain a specific expression. Although, the **show running-config** command is the most obvious candidate for the use of the **| section** option, this option can also be applied to any **show** command that separates its output in sections. For example, if you want to display only the standard access lists in the output of the **show access-lists** command, you could achieve that by issuing the command **show access-lists | section standard.**

The **include**, **exclude**, **begin**, and **section** options are usually followed by just a word or text fragment, but it is possible to use regular expressions for more granular filtering. For example, the second command used in Example 3-4 uses the caret (^) character, which is used to denote that a particular string will be matched only if it occurs at the beginning of a line. The expression **^CPU** will therefore only match lines that start with the characters "CPU" and not any line that contains the string "CPU". The same line uses the pipe character (|) (without a preceding and following space) as part of a regular expression to signify a logical OR. As a result, the **show processes cpu | include ^CPU|IP Input** command displays only the lines that start with the string "CPU" or contain the string "IP Input".

Other useful options that can be used with the pipe character after the **show** command are **redirect**, **tee**, and **append**. The output of a **show** command can be redirected, copied or appended to a file by using the pipe character, followed by the options **redirect**, **tee**, or **append** and a URL that denotes the file. Example 3-5 depicts sample usage of these options with the **show tech-support**, **show ip interface brief** and the **show version commands.**

Example 3-5 *Using the* **redirect**, **append**, *and* **tee** *options with* **show** *Commands*

```
R01# show tech-support | redirect tftp://192.168.37.2/show-tech.txt
! The redirect option does not display the output on the console
R01# show ip interface brief | tee flash:show-int-brief.txt
! The tee option displays the output on the console and send it to the file
```

```
Interface                  IP-Address      OK? Method Status
Protocol
FastEthernet0/0            10.1.192.2      YES manual up                    up
FastEthernet0/1            10.1.192.10     YES manual up                    up
Loopback0                  10.1.220.1      YES manual up                    up

R01# dir flash:
Directory of flash:/
  1  -rw-    23361156   Mar 2 2009 16:25:54 -08:00  c1841-
advipservicesk9mz.1243.bin
  2  -rw-         680   Mar 7 2009 02:16:56 -08:00  show-int-brief.txt

R01# show version | append flash:show-commands.txt
R01# show ip interface brief | append flash:show-commands.txt
! The append option allows you to add the command output to an existing file
R01# more flash:show-commands.txt
Cisco IOS Software, 1841 Software (C1841-ADVIPSERVICESK9-M), Version 12.4(23),
RELEASE SOFTWARE (fc1)
Technical Support: http://www.cisco.com/techsupport
Copyright (c) 1986-2008 by Cisco Systems, Inc.
Compiled Sat 08-Nov-08 20:07 by prod_rel_team
ROM: System Bootstrap, Version 12.3(8r)T9, RELEASE SOFTWARE (fc1)
R01 uptime is 3 days, 1 hour, 22 minutes
<...output omitted...>
Interface                  IP-Address      OK? Method Status
Protocol
FastEthernet0/0            10.1.192.2      YES manual up                    up
FastEthernet0/1            10.1.192.10     YES manual up                    up
Loopback0                  10.1.220.1      YES manual up                    up
```

When you use the **| redirect** option on a **show** command, the output will not display on the screen, but will be redirected to a text file instead. This file can be stored locally on the device's flash memory or it can be stored on a network server such as a TFTP or FTP server. The **| tee** option is similar to the **| redirect** option, but this command both displays the output on your screen and copies it to a text file. Finally, the **| append** option is analogous to the **| redirect** option, but it allows you to append the output to a file instead of replacing that file. The use of this command option makes it easy to collect the output of several **show** commands in a text file. A prerequisite for this option is that the file system that you are writing to must support "append" operations; so for instance, a TFTP server cannot be used in this case.

Testing Network Connectivity Using ping and Telnet

The ping utility is a popular network connectivity testing tool that has been part of Cisco IOS Software since the first version of IOS. The ping utility has some extended options that are useful for testing specific conditions, including the following:

- **repeat** *repeat-count*: By default, he Cisco IOS **ping** command sends out five ICMP echo-request packets. The **repeat** option allows you to specify how many echo-request packets are sent. This proves particularly useful when you are troubleshooting a packet-loss situation. The **repeat** option enables you to send out hundreds to thousands of packets to help pinpoint a pattern in the occurrence of the packet loss. For example, if you see a pattern where every other packet is lost, resulting in exactly 50 percent packet loss, you might have a load-balancing situation with packet loss on one path.
- **size** *datagram-size*: This option allows you to specify the total size of the ping packet (including headers) in bytes that will be sent. In combination with the **repeat** option, you can send a steady stream of large packets and generate some load. The quickest way to generate a heavy load using the **ping** command is to combine a very large repeat number, a size set to 1500 bytes, and the timeout option set to 0 seconds. When used with the Don't Fragment (**df-bit**) option (discussed after Example 3-6), the **size** option allows you to determine the maximum transmission unit (MTU) along the path to a particular destination IP address.
- **source** [*address* | *interface*]: This option allows you to set the source IP address or interface of the ping packet. The IP address has to be one of the local device's own IP addresses. If this option is not used, the router will select the IP address of the egress interface as the source of the ping packets.
- Example 3-6 shows a case where a simple **ping** succeeds, but the ping with the source IP address set to the IP address of the FastEthernet 0/0 interface fails. You can conclude from the successful initial ping that the local router has a working path to the destination IP address 10.1.156.1. For the second ping, because a different source address is used, the return packets will have a different destination IP address. The most likely explanation for the failure of the second ping is that at least one of the routers on the return path does not have a route to the address/subnet of the FastEthernet 0/0 interface (used as source in the second ping). There might be several other reasons for this, too. For example, an access list on one of the transit routers might be blocking the IP address of the Fa 0/0 interface. Specifying the source IP address or interface proves useful when you want to check two-way reachability to/from a network/address other than the router's egress interface's IP address/network.

Example 3-6 **ping** *Extended Option: Source*

```
RO1# ping 10.1.156.1
Type escape sequence to abort.
```

```
Sending 5, 100-byte ICMP Echos to 10.1.156.1, timeout is 2 seconds:
!!!!!
Success rate is 100 percent (5/5), round-trip min/avg/max = 1/2/4 ms

RO1# ping 10.1.156.1 source FastEthernet 0/0
Type escape sequence to abort.
Sending 5, 100-byte ICMP Echos to 10.1.156.1, timeout is 2 seconds:
Packet sent with a source address of 10.1.192.2
.....
Success rate is 0 percent (0/5)
```

- **df-bit:** This option sets the Don't Fragment bit in the IP header to indicate that routers should not fragment this packet. If it is larger than the MTU of the outbound interface, the router should drop the packet and send an ICMP **Fragmentation needed and DF bit set** message back to the source. This option can be very useful when you are troubleshooting MTU-related problems. By setting the **df-bit** option and combining it with the **size** option, you can force routers along the path to drop the packets if they would have to fragment them. By varying the size and looking at which point the packets start being dropped, you can determine the MTU.

Example 3-7 shows successful **ping** results when packet size of 1476 bytes is used; however, ping packets with a size of 1477 bytes are not successful. The *M* in the output of the **ping** command signifies that an ICMP **Fragmentation needed and DF bit set** message was received. From this, you can conclude that somewhere along the path to the destination there must be a host that has an MTU of 1476 bytes. A possible explanation for this could be usage of a generic routing encapsulation (GRE) tunnel, which typically has an MTU of 1476 bytes (1500 bytes default MTU minus 24 bytes for the GRE and IP headers).

Example 3-7 ping *Extended Option:* df-bit

```
RO1# ping 10.1.221.1 size 1476 df-bit
Type escape sequence to abort.
Sending 5, 1476-byte ICMP Echos to 10.1.221.1, timeout is 2 seconds:
Packet sent with the DF bit set
!!!!!
Success rate is 100 percent (5/5), round-trip min/avg/max = 184/189/193 ms

RO1# ping 10.1.221.1 size 1477 df-bit
Type escape sequence to abort.
```

```
Sending 5, 1477-byte ICMP Echos to 10.1.221.1, timeout is 2 seconds:
Packet sent with the DF bit set
M.M.M
Success rate is 0 percent (0/5)
```

There are more extended options available for ping through the interactive dialog. If you type **ping** without any additional options and press **Enter**, you will be prompted with a series of questions regarding the source and destination and all the ping options. In Example 3-8, the **Sweep range of sizes** option is highlighted. This option allows you to send a series of packets that increase in size and can be useful to determine the MTU along a path, similar to the previous example.

Example 3-8 ping *Option: Sweep Range of Sizes*

```
R01# ping
Protocol [ip]:
Target IP address: 10.1.221.1
Repeat count [5]: 1
Datagram size [100]:
Timeout in seconds [2]:
Extended commands [n]: y
Source address or interface:
Type of service [0]:
Set DF bit in IP header? [no]: yes
Validate reply data? [no]:
Data pattern [0xABCD]:
Loose, Strict, Record, Time stamp, Verbose[none]:
Sweep range of sizes [n]: y
Sweep min size [36]: 1400
Sweep max size [18024]: 1500
Sweep interval [1]:
Type escape sequence to abort.
Sending 101, [1400..1500]-byte ICMP Echos to 10.1.221.1, timeout is 2 seconds:
Packet sent with the DF bit set
!!!!!!!!!!!!!!!!!!!!!!!!!!!!!!!!!!!!!!!!!!!!!!!!!!!!!!!!!!!!!!!!!!!!!!
!!!!!!!M.M.M.M.M.M.M.M.M.M.M.M.
Success rate is 76 percent (77/101), round-trip min/avg/max = 176/184/193 ms
```

When you want to determine the MTU of a particular path, a lot of times you do not really have a good initial guess, and it might take you many tries to find the exact MTU. In Example 3-8, the router is instructed to send packets starting at a size of 1400 bytes, sending a single packet per size and increasing the size one byte at a time until a size of 1500 bytes is reached. Again, the DF bit is set on the packets. The result is that the router sent out 101 consecutive packets, the first one was 1400 bytes, the last one was 1500 bytes, 77 of the pings were successful, and 24 failed. Again, this means that there must be a link along the path that has an MTU of 1476 bytes.

Note Because some applications cannot reassemble fragmented packets, if the network fragments that application's packet, the application will fail. Sometimes by discovering the MTU of a path, the application can be configured to not send packets larger than the MTU so that fragmentation does not happen. That is why it is sometimes necessary to find out the MTU of a path.

Note The various symbols generated in ping output are described as follows:

- !: Each exclamation point indicates receipt of a reply.
- .: Each period indicates the network server timed out while waiting for a reply.
- U: A destination unreachable error PDU was received.
- Q: Source quench (destination too busy).
- M: Could not fragment.
- ?: Unknown packet type.
- &: Packet lifetime exceeded

Telnet is an excellent companion to ping for testing transport layer connections from the command line. Assume that you are troubleshooting a problem where someone has trouble sending e-mail through a particular SMTP server. Taking a divide-and-conquer approach, you ping the server, and it is successful. This means that the network layer between your device and the server is operational. Now you have to investigate the transport layer. You could configure a client and start a top-down troubleshooting procedure, but it is more convenient if you first establish whether Layer 4 is operational. The Telnet protocol can prove useful in this situation. If you want to determine whether a particular TCP-based application is active on a server, you can attempt a Telnet connection to the TCP port of that application. In Example 3-9, a Telnet connection to port 80 (HTTP) on a server shows success, and a Telnet connection to port 25 (SMTP) is unsuccessful.

Example 3-9 *Using Telnet to Test the Transport Layer*

```
R01# telnet 192.168.37.2 80
Trying 192.168.37.2, 80 ... Open
GET
<html><body><h1>It works!</h1></body></html>
[Connection to 192.168.37.2 closed by foreign host]


R01# telnet 192.168.37.2 25
Trying 192.168.37.2, 25 ...
% Connection refused by remote host
```

Even though the Telnet server application uses the TCP well-known port number 23 and Telnet clients connect to that port by default, you can specify a specific port number on the client and connect to any TCP port that you want to test. The connection is either accepted (as indicated by the word **Open** in Example 3-9), or it is refused, or times out. The **Open** response indicates that the port (application) you attempted is active, and the other results require further investigation. For applications that use an ASCII-based session protocol, you might even see an application banner or you might be able to trigger some responses from the server by typing in some keywords (as in Example 3-9). Good examples of these types of protocols are SMTP, FTP, and HTTP.

Collecting Real-time Information Using Cisco IOS debug Commands

First, it is important to caution readers that because debugging output is assigned high priority in the CPU process, it can render the system unusable. For this reason, use **debug** commands only to troubleshoot specific problems or during troubleshooting sessions with Cisco technical support staff. Moreover, it is best to use **debug** commands during periods of lower network traffic and fewer users.

All **debug** commands are entered in privileged EXEC mode, and most **debug** commands take no arguments. All **debug** commands can be turned off by retyping the command and preceding it with a **no**. To display the state of each debugging option, enter the **show debugging** command in the Cisco IOS privileged EXEC mode. The **no debug all** command turns off all diagnostic output. Using the **no debug all** command is a convenient way to ensure that you have not accidentally left any **debug** commands turned on. To list and see a brief description of all the debugging command options, enter the **debug?** command. Because there are numerous useful Cisco IOS debug commands, only two of **debug ip** options are discussed here.

debug ip packet [*access-list-number*][detail]

To display general IP debugging information and IP security option (IPSO) security transactions, use the **debug ip packet** command. The option to use an access list with the **debug ip packet** command enables you to limit the scope of the **debug ip packet** command to those packets that match the access list. The **detail** option of this debug displays detailed IP packet-debugging information. This information includes the packet types and codes and source and destination port numbers.

If a communication session is closing when it should not be, an end-to-end connection problem may be the cause. The **debug ip packet** command is useful for analyzing the messages traveling between the local and remote hosts. IP packet debugging captures the packets that are process switched including received, generated, and forwarded packets. Example 3-10 shows sample output from the **debug ip packet** command.

Example 3-10 debug ip packet *Sample Output*

```
IP: s=172.69.13.44 (Fddi0), d=10.125.254.1 (Serial2), g=172.69.16.2, forward
IP: s=172.69.1.57 (Ethernet4), d=10.36.125.2 (Serial2), g=172.69.16.2, forward
IP: s=172.69.1.6 (Ethernet4), d=255.255.255.255, rcvd 2
IP: s=172.69.1.55 (Ethernet4), d=172.69.2.42 (Fddi0), g=172.69.13.6, forward
IP: s=172.69.89.33 (Ethernet2), d=10.130.2.156 (Serial2), g=172.69.16.2, forward
IP: s=172.69.1.27 (Ethernet4), d=172.69.43.126 (Fddi1), g=172.69.23.5, forward
IP: s=172.69.1.27 (Ethernet4), d=172.69.43.126 (Fddi0), g=172.69.13.6, forward
IP: s=172.69.20.32 (Ethernet2), d=255.255.255.255, rcvd 2
IP: s=172.69.1.57 (Ethernet4), d=10.36.125.2 (Serial2), g=172.69.16.2, access denied
```

debug ip rip

To display information on Routing Information Protocol (RIP) routing transactions, use the **debug ip rip** command. Example 3-11 shows a sample output from the **debug ip rip** command.

Example 3-11 debug ip rip *Sample Output*

```
RIP: received v2 update from 10.1.1.2 on Serial0/0/0
     30.0.0.0/8 via 0.0.0.0 in 1 hops
RIP: sending  v2 update to 224.0.0.9 via FastEthernet0/0 (20.1.1.1)
RIP: build update entries
     10.0.0.0/8 via 0.0.0.0, metric 1, tag 0
     30.0.0.0/8 via 0.0.0.0, metric 2, tag 0
RIP: sending  v2 update to 224.0.0.9 via Serial0/0/0 (10.1.1.1)
RIP: build update entries
     20.0.0.0/8 via 0.0.0.0, metric 1, tag 0
RIP: received v2 update from 10.1.1.2 on Serial0/0/0
     30.0.0.0/8 via 0.0.0.0 in 1 hops
RIP: sending  v2 update to 224.0.0.9 via FastEthernet0/0 (20.1.1.1)
```

Example 3-11 shows that the router being debugged has received a RIPv2 update from a router with the address 10.1.2.2. That router sent an update about network 30.0.0.0/8 being one hop away from it. If a destination is reported as more than 15 hops away, it is considered inaccessible. The router being debugged also sent updates to the multicast address 224.0.0.9, as opposed to RIP, which sends updates to the broadcast address 255.255.255.255.

Diagnosing Hardware Issues Using Cisco IOS Commands

The three main categories of failure causes in a network are as follows: hardware failures, software failures (bugs), and configuration errors. One could argue that performance problems form a fourth category, but performance problems are symptoms rather than failure causes. Having a performance problem means that there is a difference between the expected behavior and the observed behavior of a system. Sometimes the system is functioning as it should, but the results are not what were expected or promised. In this case, the problem is not technical, but organizational in nature and cannot be resolved through technical means. On the other hand, there are situations where the system is not functioning as it should. In this case, the system behaves differently than expected, but the underlying cause is a hardware failure, a software failure, or a configuration error. The focus here is on diagnosing and resolving configuration errors. There are a number of reasons for this focus. Hardware and software can really be swapped out only if they are suspected to be the cause of the problem, so the actions that can be taken to resolve the problem are limited.

The detailed information necessary to pinpoint a specific hardware or software problem is often not publicly available, and therefore hardware and software troubleshooting are processes that are generally executed as a joint effort with a vendor (or a reseller or partner for that vendor). Documentation of the configuration and operation of software features is generally publicly available, and therefore configuration problems can often be diagnosed without the need for direct assistance from the vendor or reseller. However, even if you decide to focus your troubleshooting effort on configuration errors initially, as your work progresses and you eliminate common configuration problems from the equation, you might pick up clues that hardware components are the root cause of the problem. You will then need to do an initial analysis and diagnosis of the problem, before it is escalated to the vendor. The move the problem method is an obvious candidate to approach suspected hardware problems, but this method works well only if the problem is strictly due to a broken piece of hardware. Performance problems that might be caused by hardware failures generally require a more subtle approach and require more detailed information gathering. When hardware problems are intermittent, they are harder to diagnose and isolate.

Due to its nature, diagnosing hardware problems is highly product and platform dependent. However, you can use a number of generic commands to diagnose performance-related hardware issues on all Cisco IOS platforms. Essentially, a network device is a specialized computer, with a CPU, RAM, and storage, to say the least. This allows the network devise to boot and run the operating system. Next, interfaces are initialized and started, which allows for reception and transmission of network traffic. Therefore, when you decide that a problem you are observing on a given device may be hardware related, it is important that you verify the operation of these generic components. The most commonly used Cisco IOS commands used for this purpose are the **show processes cpu**, **show memory**, and **show interface** commands, as covered in the sections that follow.

Checking CPU Utilization

Both routers and switches have a main CPU that executes the processes that constitute Cisco IOS Software. Processes are scheduled to share the available CPU cycles and take turns executing their code. The **show processes cpu** command provides you with an overview of all processes currently running on the router, including a display of the total CPU time that the processes have consumed over their lifetime; plus their CPU usage over the last 5 seconds, 1 minute, and 5 minutes. The first line of output from the **show**

processes cpu command displays the percentages of the CPU cycles. From this information, you can see whether the total CPU usage is high or low and which processes might be causing the CPU load. By default, the processes are sorted by process ID, but they can be sorted based on the 5-second, 1-minute, and 5-minute averages. Figure 3-1 shows a sample output of the **show processes cpu** command entered with the 1-minute sort option.

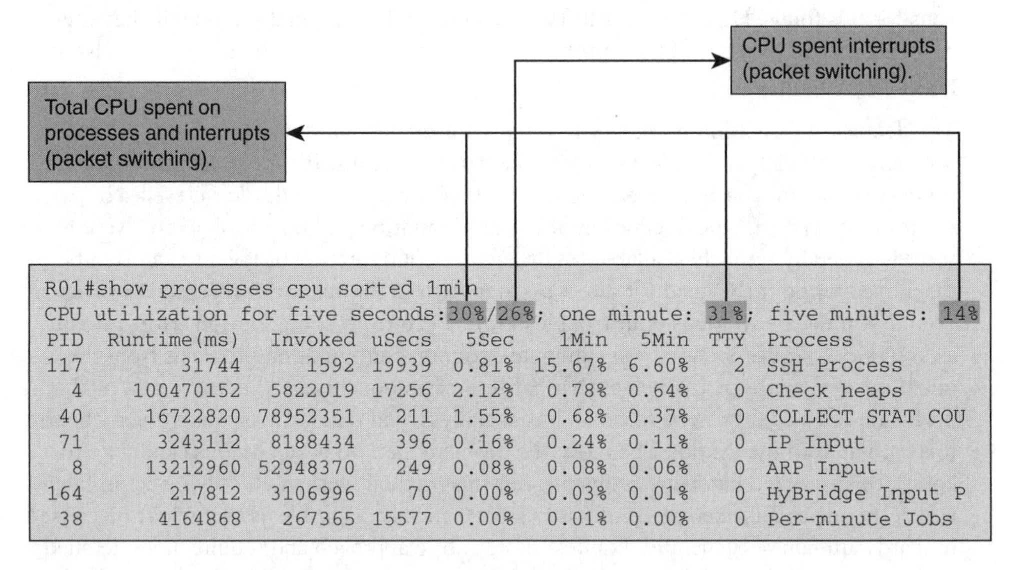

Figure 3-1 *The* **show processes cpu** *Command Output Example*

The example depicted in Figure 3-1 shows that over the past minute 31 percent of the available CPU has been used and the "SSH Process" was responsible for roughly half of these CPU cycles (15.67 percent) over that period. However, the next process in this sorted list is the "Check heaps" process, which has consumed only 0.78 percent of the total available CPU time over the last minute and the list quickly drops off after that. You might wonder what the remaining 15 percent CPU cycles recorded over the last minute were spent on. On the router used to generate the output depicted in Figure 3-1, the same CPU that is used to run the operating system processes is also responsible for packet switching. The CPU is interrupted to suspend the current process that it is executing, switch one or more packets, and resume the execution of scheduled processes. The CPU time spent on interrupt-driven tasks can be calculated by adding the CPU percentages for all processes and then subtracting that total from the total CPU percentage listed at the top. For the 5-second CPU usage, this figure is actually even listed separately behind the slash. This means that in the example shown in Figure 3-1, 30 percent of the total available CPU cycles over the past 5 seconds were used, out of which 26 percent were spent in interrupt mode and 4 percent for the execution of scheduled processes.

Because of this, it is quite normal for routers to be running at high CPU loads during peaks in network traffic. In those cases, most of the CPU cycles will be consumed in interrupt mode. If particular processes consistently use large chunks of the available CPU time, however, this could be a clue that a problem exists associated with that particular process. However, to be able to draw any definitive conclusions, you need to have a baseline of the CPU usage over time. Keep in mind that the better caching mechanisms reduce the number of CPU interrupts and, consequently, the CPU utilization attributable to interrupts. For example, Cisco Express Forwarding (CEF) in distributed mode allows most packet switching to happen on the line card without causing any CPU interrupts.

On LAN switches, the essential elements of the **show processes cpu** command output are the same as routers, but the interpretation of the numbers tends to be a bit different. Switches have specialized hardware that handle the switching task, so the main CPU should in general not be involved in this. When you see a high percentage of the CPU time being spent in interrupt mode, this usually indicates that the forwarded traffic is being forwarded in software instead of by the ternary content-addressable memory (TCAM). Punted traffic is the traffic that is processed and forwarded through less-efficient means for a reason, such as tunneling or encryption. Once you have determined that the CPU load is abnormally high and you decide to investigate further, you generally have to resort to platform-specific troubleshooting commands to gain more insight into what is happening.

Checking Memory Utilization

Similar to CPU cycles, memory is a finite resource shared by the various processes that togetheform the Cisco IOS operating system. Memory is divided into different pools and used for different purposes: the processor pool contains memory that can be used by the scheduled processes, and the I/O pool is used to temporarily buffer packets during packet switching. Processes allocate and release memory, as needed, from the processor pool, and generally there is more than enough of free memory for all the processes to share. Example 3-12 shows sample output from the **show memory** command. In this example, the processor memory is shown on the first line, and the I/O memory is shown on the second line. Each row shows the total memory available, used memory, and free memory. The least amount of free memory and the most amount of free memory over the measurement interval (device dependent, but usually 5 minutes) are also displayed at each row.

Example 3-12 show memory *Command Output*

```
R01# show memory
                    Head      Total(b)       Used(b)       Free(b)    Lowest(b)
Largest(b)
Processor    820B1DB4     26534476      19686964      6847512      6288260       6712884
      I/O     3A00000      6291456       3702900      2588556      2511168       2577468
```

Typically, the memory on routers and switches is more than enough to do what they were designed for. However, in particular deployment scenarios, for example if you decide to run Border Gateway Protocol (BGP) on your router and carry the full Internet routing table, you might need more memory than the typical amount recommended for the router. Also, whenever you decide to upgrade Cisco IOS Software on your router, you should verify the recommended amount of memory for the new software version.

As with CPU usage, it is useful to create a baseline of the memory usage on your routers and switches and graph the utilization over time. You should monitor memory utilization over time and be able to anticipate when your devices need memory upgrade or a complete system upgrade. If a router or switch does not have enough free memory to satisfy the request of a process, it will log a memory allocation failure, signified by a **%SYS-2-MALLOCFAIL** message. The result of this is that the process cannot get the memory that it requires, and this might result in unpredictable disruptions or failures. Apart from the processes using up the memory through normal use, there is a possibility for memory leak. Caused by a software defect, a process that does not properly release memory (making memory to "leak" away) eventually leads to memory exhaustion and memory-allocation failures. Creating a baseline and graphing memory usage over time allows us monitor for these types of failures, too.

Checking Interfaces

Checking the performance of the device interfaces while troubleshooting, especially while hardware faults are suspected, is as important as checking your device's CPU and memory utilization. The **show interfaces** command is a valuable Cisco IOS troubleshooting command. Example 3-13 shows sample output from the **show interfaces** command for a FastEthernet interface.

Example 3-13 show interfaces *Command Output*

```
RO1# show interfaces FastEthernet 0/0
FastEthernet0/0 is up, line protocol is up
<...output omitted...>
  Last input 00:00:00, output 00:00:01, output hang never
  Last clearing of "show interface" counters never
  Input queue: 0/75/1120/0 (size/max/drops/flushes); Total output drops: 0

  Queueing strategy: fifo
  Output queue: 0/40 (size/max)
  5 minute input rate 2000 bits/sec, 3 packets/sec
  5 minute output rate 0 bits/sec, 1 packets/sec
     110834589 packets input, 1698341767 bytes

     Received 61734527 broadcasts, 0 runts, 0 giants, 565 throttles
     30 input errors, 5 CRC, 1 frame, 0 overrun, 25 ignored

     0 watchdog
     0 input packets with dribble condition detected
     35616938 packets output, 526385834 bytes, 0 underruns
```

```
0 output errors, 0 collisions, 1 interface resets

0 babbles, 0 late collision, 0 deferred
0 lost carrier, 0 no carrier
0 output buffer failures, 0 output buffers swapped out
```

The output of this command lists a number of key statistics, which are briefly described as follows:

- **Input queue drops:** Input queue drops (and the related ignored and throttle counters) signify that at some point more traffic was delivered to the router than it could process. This does not necessarily indicate a problem, as it could be normal during traffic peaks. However, it may indicate that the CPU cannot process packets in time. If this number is consistently high and the dropped packets are causing application failures, the reasons must be detected and resolved.
- **Output queue drops:** Input packet drops indicate congestion on the interface. Seeing output drops is normal when the aggregate input traffic rate is higher than the output traffic rate on an interface. However, even if this is considered normal behavior, it leads to packet drops and queuing delays. Applications that are sensitive to delay and packet loss, such as Voice over IP, will have serious quality issues in those situations. This counter is a good indicator that you need to implement a congestion management mechanism to provide good quality of service (QoS) to your applications.
- **Input errors:** This counter indicates the number of errors such as cyclic redundancy check (CRC) errors, experienced during reception of frames. High numbers of CRC errors could indicate cabling problems, interface hardware problems, or in an Ethernet-based network, duplex mismatches.
- **Output errors:** This counter indicates the number of errors, such as collisions, during the transmission of frames. In most Ethernet-based networks today, full-duplex transmission is the norm, and half-duplex is the exception. In full-duplex operation, collisions cannot occur, and therefore collisions, and especially late collisions, often indicate duplex mismatches.

The absolute number of drops or errors in the output of the **show interfaces** command is not very significant. The error counters should be evaluated against the total number of input and output packets. For example, a total of 25 CRC errors in relation to 123 input packets is reason for concern, whereas 25 CRC errors for 1,458,349 packets is not a problem at all. Furthermore, note that these counters accumulate from the time the router boots, so the numbers displayed on the output might be accumulated over months. Therefore, it is difficult to diagnose a problem that has been happening over 2 days based on these statistics. After you have decided that you need to investigate the interface counters in more detail, it is good practice to reset the interface counters by using the **clear counters** command, let it accumulate statistics for a specific period, and then reevaluate the outcome. If you repeatedly want to display selected statistics to see how the counters are increasing, it is useful to filter the output. Using a regular expression to include only the lines in which you are interested can prove quite useful in this case. In Example 3-14, the output is limited to the lines that start with the word *Fast*, include the word *errors* or include the word *packets*.

Example 3-14 *Filtering the Output of the* **show interfaces** *Command*

```
RO1# show interfaces FastEthernet 0/0 | include ^Fast|errors|packets
FastEthernet0/0 is up, line protocol is up
  5 minute input rate 3000 bits/sec, 5 packets/sec
  5 minute output rate 2000 bits/sec, 1 packets/sec
     2548 packets input, 257209 bytes
     0 input errors, 0 CRC, 0 frame, 0 overrun, 0 ignored
     0 input packets with dribble condition detected
     610 packets output, 73509 bytes, 0 underruns
     0 output errors, 0 collisions, 0 interface resets
```

The **show processes cpu**, **show memory**, and **show interfaces** commands form a limited toolkit of hardware troubleshooting commands, but they are a good starting point to collect some initial clues to either confirm that the problem may be hardware related or to eliminate hardware problems from the list of potential problem causes. Once you have decided that the cause of the problem might be hardware related, you should research the more specific hardware troubleshooting tools that are available for the platform that you are working with. Many additional hardware troubleshooting features and commands are supported in the Cisco IOS Software, including the following:

- **show controllers:** The output of this command varies based on interface hardware type. In general, this command provides more detailed packet and error statistics for each type of hardware and interface.
- **show platform:** On many of Cisco LAN switches, this command can be used to examine the TCAM and other specialized switch hardware components.
- **show inventory:** This command lists the hardware components of a router or switch. The output includes the product code and serial number for each component. This is very useful for documenting your device and for ordering replacement or spare parts.
- **show diag:** On routers, you can use this command to gather even more detailed information about the hardware than the output provided by the **show inventory command.** For example, the output of this command includes the hardware revision of the individual components. In case of known hardware issues, this command can be used to determine whether the component is susceptible to a particular hardware fault.
- **Generic Online Diagnostics (GOLD):** GOLD is a platform-independent framework for runtime diagnostics. It includes command-line interface (CLI)-based access to boot and health monitoring, plus on-demand and scheduled diagnostics. GOLD is available on many of the mid-range and high-end Catalyst LAN switches and high-end routers such as the 7600 series and CRS-1 routers.

- **Time Domain Reflectometer.** Some of the Catalyst LAN switches support the TDR feature. This feature enables you to detect cabling problems such as open or shorted UTP wire pairs.

Using Specialized Maintenance and Troubleshooting Tools

Information gathering is essential to both troubleshooting and maintenance. Information is either gathered on a need basis, such as during a troubleshooting effort, or continuously as part of baseline creation. Sometimes network events trigger information gathering. In addition to the tools available in the Cisco IOS CLI, many specialized network maintenance and troubleshooting tools support information gathering processes. These tools and applications typically require communication with the network devices, and several different underlying technologies can govern this communication. Network support professionals must familiarize themselves with the commonly used network management platforms and troubleshooting tools and learn to perform the following tasks:

- Identify the tools and their underlying technologies to support the troubleshooting process.
- Enable Switched Port Analyzer (SPAN) and Remote SPAN (RSPAN) to facilitate the use of packet sniffers.
- Configure routers and switches for communication with Simple Network Management Protocol (SNMP) or NetFlow-based network management systems to facilitate the collection of device and traffic statistics that are part of a network baseline.
- Configure routers and switches to send SNMP traps to provide fault notification to SNMP-based network management systems.

Categories of Troubleshooting Tools

A generic troubleshooting process consists of several phases or subprocesses. Some of these are primarily mental; an example is the elimination process. Some of these processes are administrative in nature, such as documenting and reporting the changes and solutions. Finally, some of these are more technical in nature, such as the gathering and analysis of information. The processes that benefit the most from the deployment of network maintenance and troubleshooting tools are the processes that are technical in nature:

- **Defining the problem:** One of the main objectives of deploying a proactive network management strategy is to learn about potential problems before users report that they are experiencing outages or performance degradation. Network monitoring and event reporting systems can notify the network support team of events as they happen, giving them lead time to battle the problem before the users notice and report them.

- **Gathering information:** This is one of the most essential steps in the troubleshooting process, and it is incident driven and targeted. It is beneficial to be able to leverage any tool to obtain detailed information about events in an effective way.
- **Analyzing:** A major aspect of interpreting and analyzing the gathered information is comparing them against the network baseline. The ability to differentiate between normal and abnormal behavior can yield important clues about the potential problem cause. Collecting statistics about network behavior and network traffic is therefore a key process to support troubleshooting data analysis.
- **Testing the hypothesis:** Testing a hypothesis commonly involves making changes to the network. This might entail the need to roll back these changes if they do not resolve the problem or cause new ones. Tools that enable easy rollback of changes are therefore important to an efficient troubleshooting process.

With the exception of configuration rollback, which is more a generic change management tool than a specific troubleshooting tool, the mechanisms mentioned fall into one of the following three categories:

- **Collection of information on demand, driven by incidents:** This is the typical information gathering that you do during the troubleshooting process itself. Information is gathered, interpreted, and analyzed, and based on the outcome of this process, more information is gathered. Examples of this are capturing of network traffic or debugging output of device processes.
- **Continuous collection of information to establish a baseline:** This operation entails establishing a set of key network performance indicators. Based on these indicators, statistics about the network behavior over a long period of time are collected. These statistics form a baseline that you can use to judge whether the network behavior that you observe is normal. This process also provides historical data that you can correlate to events. Examples of this are collection of statistics through use of the SNMP and traffic accounting by use of NetFlow technology.
- **Notification of network events:** This method, instead of continuously collecting information, is based on events triggering devices to report specific information. Examples of this are the reporting of events through syslog messages or SNMP traps and the definition and the reporting of specific events through the use of the Embedded Event Manager (EEM) that is part of Cisco IOS Software.

What these categories all have in common is that their functionality depends on interaction between a tool or an application running on a host and the network devices. In the first two categories, the information is pulled from the network elements to the application or tool, whereas in the last category the information is pushed to the application or tool by the network devices. A broad spectrum of tools and applications can perform the processes mentioned, but it is unfeasible to mention them all, let alone compare and contrast them. However, many of these tools depend on the same underlying technologies and protocols for the communication between the application and the network devices. Examples of such technologies and protocols are syslog, SNMP, and NetFlow, plus network event notification technologies. Apart from understanding the main benefits that a particular tool or application brings to the network troubleshooting process, it is therefore also important for an engineer to know how to enable the necessary communication between the network devices and the tools and applications.

Using Traffic-Capturing Tools

Packet sniffers, also called network or protocol analyzers, are important and useful tools for network engineers. Using these tools, you can look for and observe protocol errors like retransmissions or session resets. Captured traffic can also be helpful when diagnosing communication problems between two hosts. If you can spot where packets start to go missing, for example, this will help in pinpointing the problem. Packet sniffers are powerful tools because they capture large amounts of very detailed data, but that can also be a drawback. Unless you know exactly what you are looking for and you know how to set up a filter so that only the traffic you are interested in is displayed, it can be very hard to analyze packet captures. Figure 3-2 displays a sample screen from a protocol analyzer. The first four packets shown on the screen are the four-way DHCP exchange resulting in an IP address lease from a DHCP server to a DHCP client. The next three packets are gratuitous ARP from an IP device.

File Edit View Go Capture Analyze Statistics Help

Filter: Expression... Clear Apply

No.	Time	Source	Destination	Protocol	Info
1	0.000000	0.0.0.0	255.255.255.255	DHCP	DHCP Discover - Transaction ID 0x611ca31b
2	0.007990	192.168.37.1	192.168.37.3	DHCP	DHCP Offer - Transaction ID 0x611ca31b
3	0.023609	0.0.0.0	255.255.255.255	DHCP	DHCP Request - Transaction ID 0x611ca31b
4	0.031527	192.168.37.1	192.168.37.3	DHCP	DHCP ACK - Transaction ID 0x611ca31b
5	0.036872	00:0d:54:9c:4d:5d	ff:ff:ff:ff:ff:ff	ARP	Gratuitous ARP for 192.168.37.3 (Request)
6	0.684875	00:0d:54:9c:4d:5d	ff:ff:ff:ff:ff:ff	ARP	Gratuitous ARP for 192.168.37.3 (Request)
7	1.686321	00:0d:54:9c:4d:5d	ff:ff:ff:ff:ff:ff	ARP	Gratuitous ARP for 192.168.37.3 (Request)

Figure 3-2 *Sample Screenshot from a Protocol Analyzer*

Various tools on the market (some free and some for a fee) enable packet capturing and packet analysis. These tools can be either software based and installed on a regular computer or they can be appliance-style devices (with specialized hardware) that can capture vast amounts of data in real time. Whichever tool you select, it is always important to learn the filtering capabilities of the product so that can select just the information that you are interested in. Furthermore, one of the issues that you generally run into is that it is not always practical or even possible to install the software on the device that is the subject of your troubleshooting. On servers, and even on certain clients, the installation of software is often tightly controlled (and in many cases, prohibited). Sometimes it is the capturing of large amount of data that is not possible or allowed on the server or client. Fortunately, a solution to this problem exists. If you cannot perform packet capturing on a particular device itself, then from the switch that the device is connected to, you can transport the traffic that you want to capture to another device that has the software installed.

SPAN and RSPAN

The Switched Port Analyzer (SPAN) feature of Cisco Catalyst switches allows copying the traffic from one or more switch interfaces or VLANs to another interface on the same switch. You connect the system with the protocol analyzer capability to an interface on the switch; this will be the destination interface of SPAN. Next, you configure the switch to send a copy of the traffic from one or more interfaces or VLANs to the SPAN destination interface, where the protocol analyzer can capture and analyze the traffic. The traffic that is copied and sent to the SPAN destination interface can be the incoming traffic, outgoing traffic, or both, from the source interfaces. The source and destination interfaces (or VLANs) all reside on the same switch.

Figure 3-3 shows a switch that is configured to send traffic from the source interface Fa0/7 to the destination interface Fa0/8 using the SPAN feature. The objective is to capture all the traffic sent or received by the server connected to interface Fa0/7, to troubleshoot a problem with that server. A packet sniffer is connected to interface Fa0/8. The switch is instructed to copy all the traffic that it sends and receives on interface Fa0/7 to interface Fa0/8. This is done using the **monitor session** *session#* commands shown on the top of Figure 3-3. Each SPAN session has a unique session identifier; in this particular case, the configured SPAN session number is 1. The source ports or VLANs are identified by use of the **monitor session** *session#* **source** command, and the destination port is identified by use of the **monitor session** *session#* **destination** command. The session number is what binds the commands together to form a single session. On the bottom of Figure 3-3, the configuration of the SPAN session is verified using the **show monitor** command. The output of this command shows that both incoming and outgoing traffic are sent from Fa0/7 to Fa0/8. Also, the frame type of native indicates Ethernet frames rather than 802.1Q frames. The last line indicating ingress as disabled means that on the destination interface Fa0/8 (where the sniffer is connected) ingress traffic is not accepted as per the current configuration.

Using the Remote Switched Port Analyzer (RSPAN) feature, however, you can copy traffic from ports or VLANs on one switch (let's call it the source switch) to a port on a different switch (destination switch). A VLAN must be designated as the RSPAN VLAN and not be used for any other purposes. The RSPAN VLAN receives traffic from the ports or VLANs on the source switch. The RSPAN VLAN then transports the traffic through one or more switches all the way to the destination switch. On the destination switch, the traffic is then copied from the RSPAN VLAN to the destination port. Be aware that each switching platform has certain capabilities and imposes certain restrictions on the usage of RSPAN/SPAN. You can discover these limitations and capabilities of such in the corresponding device documentation. Figure 3-4 shows an example of RSPAN configuration on two LAN switches connected by an 802.1Q trunk.

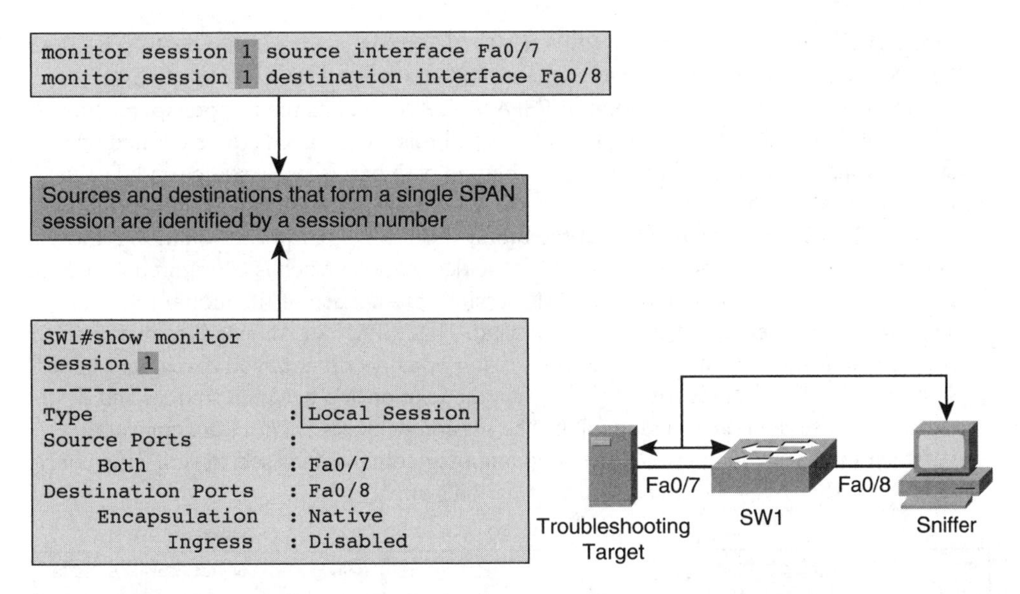

Figure 3-3 *SPAN Configuration Example*

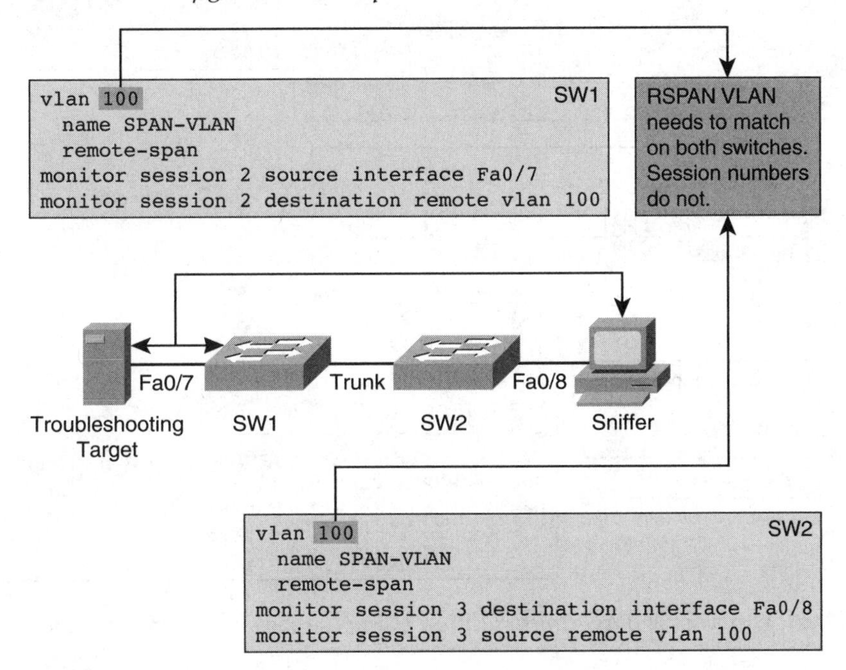

Figure 3-4 *RSPAN Configuration Example*

The configuration of RSPAN is similar to the configuration of SPAN in the sense that it uses the **monitor session** *session#* **source** and **monitor session** *session#* **destination** commands to define the interface that traffic is captured from and the interface that traffic is copied to. However, because the source and destination interface are now on two different switches, a medium is needed to transport the traffic from one switch to the other. This is done using a special RSPAN VLAN. As you can see in Figure 3-4, the SPAN VLAN number 100 is used for this purpose, and it is created similarly to any other VLAN. However, the configuration of RSPAN VLAN requires the **remote-span** command within the VLAN configuration mode, and this VLAN needs to be defined on all switches and allowed on all the trunks within the path between the source and destination switches. On the source switch, the RSPAN VLAN is configured as the destination for the SPAN session through use of the **monitor session** *session#* **destination remote vlan** *vlan#* command, and in a similar way the destination switch is configured to use the RSPAN VLAN as the source of the SPAN session through use of the **monitor session** *session#* **source remote vlan** *vlan#* command. The RSPAN VLAN needs to match on the source and destination switches, but the session numbers do not need to match. The session numbers are local identifiers that define the relationship between sources and destinations for a session on a single switch. The session numbers are not communicated between switches. In Figure 3-5, the **show monitor** command is used to verify the configuration of RSPAN on the source and destination switches.

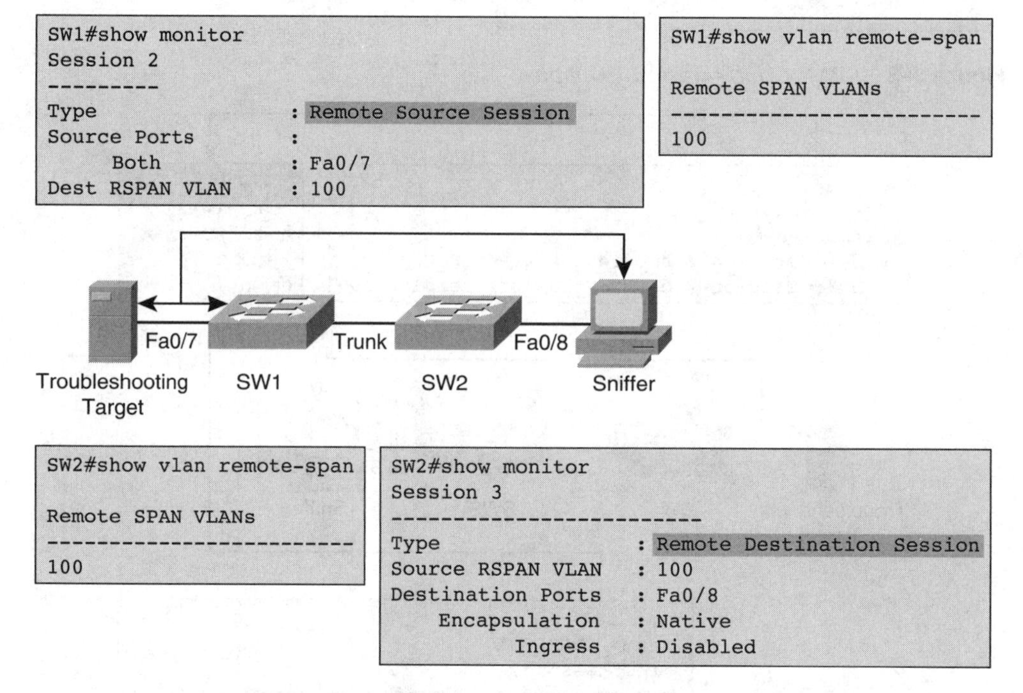

Figure 3-5 *Verifying RSPAN Configuration Using the* **show monitor** *Command*

From the output of the **show monitor** command in Figure 3-5, notice that on the source switch (SW1), the session is identified as a Remote Source Session, whereas on the destination switch (SW2), it is marked as a Remote Destination Session. In addition to verifying the correct configuration of the RSPAN session, it is important that you verify the fact that the VLAN is configured correctly as a RSPAN VLAN on both switches. The **show vlan remote-span** command enables you to verify this. Finally, if pruning is enabled on the trunks within the path between source and destination switches, you should verify that the RSPAN VLAN is allowed on those trunks.

Gathering Information with SNMP

Simple Network Management Protocol (SNMP) and NetFlow are two main technologies that are used to gather statistics from Cisco switches and routers. Although there is a certain amount of overlap between the types of data they can collect, SNMP and NetFlow each have a different focus. SNMP's focus is primarily on the collection of various statistics from network devices. Routers and switches (and other network devices) keep statistics about the operation of their processes and interfaces locally. These statistics can be viewed through the CLI or graphical user interface (GUI), which is enough if all you need is a snapshot view of particular statistics or parameters at a single moment of time. However, if you want to collect and analyze these statistics over time, you can take advantage of SNMP.

SNMP makes use of an SNMP network management station (NMS) and one or more SNMP agents. Agents are special processes running on the devices we would like to monitor and collect information about. You can query the SNMP Agent by use of the SNMP protocol and obtain the values for the parameters or counters of interest. By periodically querying (polling) the SNMP agent, the SNMP NMS can collect valuable ongoing information and statistics and store them. This data can then be processed and analyzed in various ways. Averages, minimums, maximums, and so on can be calculated, the data can be graphed, and thresholds can be set to trigger a notification process when they are exceeded. Statistics gathering with SNMP is considered a pull-based system because the NMS polls devices periodically to obtain the values of the objects that it is set up to collect. An NMS can query about numerous objects. These objects are organized and identified in a hierarchical model called a Management Information Base (MIB).

To configure a router for SNMP-based access is fairly simple. Although SNMP Version 3 is the official current standard, Version 2c is still the most widely used version. SNMP Version 3 offers enhanced security, through authentication and encryption. In SNMP Version 2c, access to the SNMP agent is granted based on an SNMP community string. An SNMP community string is comparable to a shared password; it must match between the NMS and the agent. Two different SNMP community strings are usually defined, one for read-only access and another one for read-write access. For statistics gathering, only read access is required, and therefore a read-write community is optional and does not need to be defined. Although it is not strictly necessary, it is also beneficial to define the SNMP contact and location. Because these parameters can be collected using SNMP, the support contact and physical location of a device can be retrieved. Another useful configuration, especially when creating a baseline or graphing interface-related variables, is the **snmp-server ifindex persist** command. This command guarantees that the SNMP interface index for each interface will stay the same, even if the device is rebooted. Without this command, you could run into a situation where the interface's ifindex changes after a reboot and counters for that interface are no longer correctly graphed. Figure 3-6 displays a simple set of SNMP configuration commands on a router.

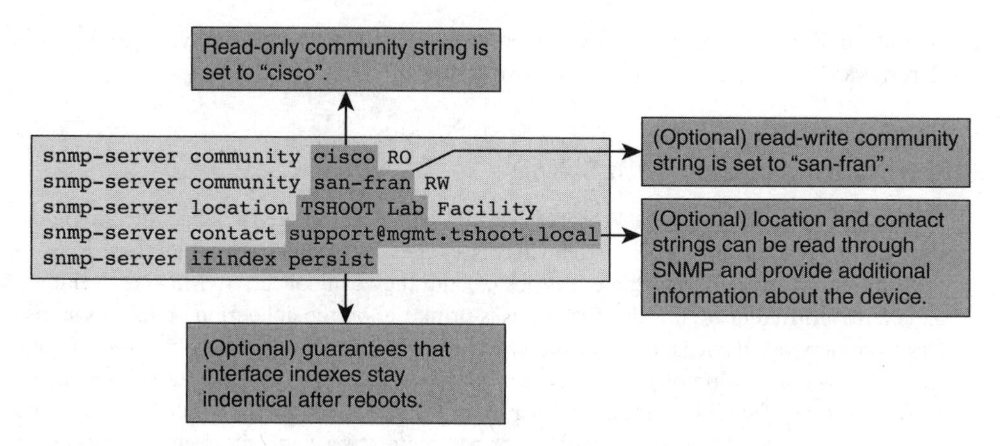

Figure 3-6 *A Simple SNMP Configuration Example*

In the example shown in Figure 3-6, the read-only community string is set to cisco, and the read-write community is set to san-fran. Furthermore, the location is set to TSHOOT Lab Facility, the contact is set to support@mgmt.tshoot.local, and ifindex is set to persistent.

For increased security, you can define access lists to allow only SNMP access from certain subnets. Finally, in scenarios where access needs to be granted for only a small collection of MIB objects, an SNMP view can be defined together with a specific community string. Then, access to those MIBs will be granted only if the requestor has a matching community.

Gathering Information with NetFlow

NetFlow has a different focus and uses different underlying mechanisms. A NetFlow-enabled device, such as a router or Layer 3 switch, will collect information about the IP traffic that is flowing through (transit through) the device. The NetFlow feature classifies traffic by flow. A flow is identified as a collection of packets that have the same essential header fields, such as source IP address, destination IP address, protocol number, Type of Service (TOS) field, port number (if applicable), plus the ingress interface. For each individual flow, the number of packets and bytes is tracked and accounted. This information is kept in a flow cache. Flows are expired from the cache when the flows are terminated or time out.

Among Cisco LAN switches, NetFlow is currently supported on most router platforms. Regarding the Catalyst switches, currently only 4500 and 6500 series support the NetFlow. You can enable this feature as a standalone feature on a router (interfaces) and examine the NetFlow cache using the proper CLI commands. This can be a useful tool during troubleshooting, because it enables you to see the flow entries being created as packets enter the router. In that sense, you could utilize NetFlow as a diagnostic tool. However, the biggest strength of the NetFlow technology is that in addition to keeping a local cache and temporary accounting of the flows on the device itself, the flow information can be exported to a NetFlow collector. Before entries are expired from the cache, the flow information, consisting of the key packet headers and additional information such as packet counts, byte counts, egress interface, flow start, and flow duration, is sent to the flow collector. The collector receives the flow information and records it in a database. Although the content of the packet payloads is not recorded, the flow information transferred to the collector by the router essentially contains a full view of all the traffic that has transited through the router. Enabling NetFlow and exporting the flows from a number of key routers can yield a fairly complete view of all the traffic on the network. After collection, the NetFlow data can be processed and graphed.

To export NetFlow information to a collector, you must first enable NetFlow accounting (collection) on the desired router interfaces. This is done using the **ip flow ingress** interface configuration mode IOS command. You also need to configure three more items:

Step 1. Configure the version of the NetFlow protocol. The most commonly used and supported version is NetFlow Version 5. The most current and flexible version is NetFlow Version 9, which is the recommended version only if your collector supports it. Consult the documentation of your collector to find out which versions of NetFlow are supported.

Step 2. Configure the IP address and UDP port number of the collector. There is no default port number for NetFlow, so check the documentation of your collector to make sure that the port number on your collector and the exporting router match.

Step 3. Because the collector is configured with and verifies the source IP address of the incoming packets, it is important that the NetFlow packets are always sourced from the same router interface. Using a loopback interface as the source interface for NetFlow ensures that the packets will always be sourced from the same address, regardless of the interface used to transmit the NetFlow packets.

Figure 3-7 shows a router with its Fa0/0 and Fa0/1 interfaces enabled to collect NetFlow information for ingress traffic. The definition of a flow is unidirectional, so if you want to account for both inbound and outbound traffic, the feature needs to be turned on for both interfaces. The Cisco IOS router command **ip flow ingress** replaces the old **ip route-cache flow** command. The NetFlow information is exported to a collector with the IP address 10.1.152.1 (at UDP port 9996), the packet format version is 5, and interface loopback 0's IP address is used as the source of the outgoing IP packet.

After the router starts caching and accounting flow information locally in its memory, you can display the NetFlow cache content by issuing the **show ip cache flow** command. This command can prove very useful when troubleshooting connection problems because it shows the active flows that are sending packets through the router. Example 3-15 shows partial output of the **show ip cache flow** command on a router.

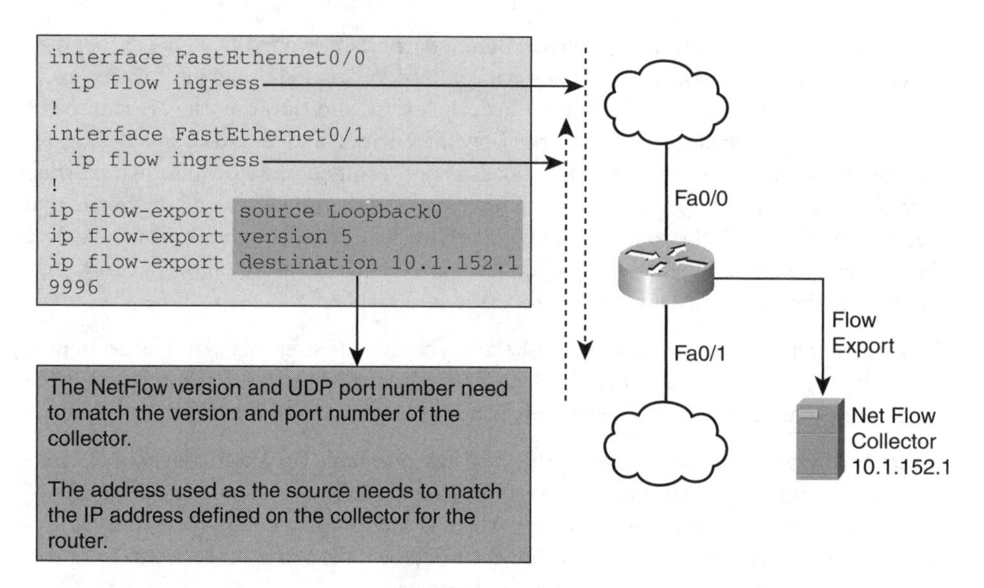

Figure 3-7 *A Simple NetFlow Configuration Example*

Example 3-15 show ip cache flow *Command Output*

```
R01# show ip cache flow
<...output omitted>
SrcIf          SrcIPaddress    DstIF     DstIPaddress     Pr  SrcP  DstP  Pkts
Se0/0/0.121    10.1.194.10     Null      224.0.0.10       58  0000  0000  27
Se0/0/0.121    10.1.194.14     Null      224.0.0.10       58  0000  0000  28
Fa0/0          10.1.192.5      Null      224.0.0.10       58  0000  0000  28
Fa0/1          10.1.192.13     Null      224.0.0.10       58  0000  0000  27
Fa0/1          10.1.152.1      Local     10.1.220.2       01  0000  0303   1
Se0/0/1        10.1.193.6      Null      224.0.0.10       58  0000  0000  28
Fa0/1          10.1.152.1      Se0/0/1   10.1.163.193     11  0666  E75E  1906
Se0/0/1        10.1.163.193    Fa0/0     10.1.152.1       11  E75E  0666  1905
```

The output filtering options for **show** commands can be used to select only those IP addresses that you are interested in. For example, for the sample output in Example 3-15, the command **show ip cache flow | include 10.1.163.193** could have been used to limit the output to only those flows that have 10.1.163.193 as the source or destination IP address.

In contrast to SNMP, NetFlow uses a “push”-based model. The collector will simply be listening to NetFlow traffic, and the routers will be in charge of sending NetFlow data to the collector, based on changes in their flow cache. Another difference between NetFlow and SNMP is that NetFlow only gathers traffic statistics, whereas SNMP can also collect many other performance indicators, such as interface errors, CPU usage, and memory usage. On the other hand, the traffic statistics collected using NetFlow have a lot more granularity than the traffic statistics that can be collected using SNMP.

Enabling Network Event Notification

A key element of a proactive network management strategy is fault notification. When a significant event such as a failure or intrusion happens on a network, the support group should not be notified of it through user reports or complaints. It is best if network devices report that event to a central system and the support group becomes aware of the issue before problems associated with the event are noticed and reported by users. In addition to learning about the event earlier, the support group will also have the advantage of getting a report of the underlying event rather than a mere description of symptoms. Two popular protocols that are used for this purpose are syslog and SNMP. In addition, the EEM feature in Cisco IOS provides an advanced method to create custom events and define actions to be taken in response to those events.

Syslog is a simple protocol used by an IP device (syslog client) to send text-based log messages to another IP device (syslog server). These messages are the same messages that are displayed on the console of Cisco routers and switches. The syslog protocol allows these messages to be forwarded across the network to a central log server that collects and stores the messages from all the devices. By itself, this constitutes only a very basic form of event notification and collection: The network device notifies the log server, and the log message is stored. However, the network support team must be notified of significant events. Fortunately, syslog capabilities are included as a component of many network management systems, and these systems often include advanced mechanisms to notify network support engineers of significant events.

SNMP allows an agent running on a network device to be queried by an SNMP manager for various matters, including configuration settings, counters, and statistics. In addition to responding to polling, the agent can be configured to send messages to the SNMP manager based on the occurrence of events, such as an interface going down or device configuration change. These messages are called *traps* and do not contain user-readable text; instead, they include SNMP MIB objects and the associated variables. Consequently, traps must always be processed by an SNMP-based network management system that can interpret and process the MIB object information contained in the trap.

Both syslog messages and SNMP traps use predefined messages that are embedded in Cisco IOS Software. These messages can be triggered on predefined conditions, and the content of each message is fixed. The number and variety of defined syslog messages and SNMP traps is extensive, and as a result, they will fulfill the fault-notification needs of most organizations. However, special cases arise at times when you would like to be notified of a particular condition or event that is not part of the standard set of log messages and events included in Cisco IOS. For these special cases, Cisco IOS Software has a feature called Embedded Event Manager (EEM), which enables you to define custom events and corresponding actions.

Figure 3-8 shows a router configured with the commands that enable SNMP trap notification. This task is performed in two steps. In the first step, one or more trap receivers are defined, and in the second step, sending traps is enabled.

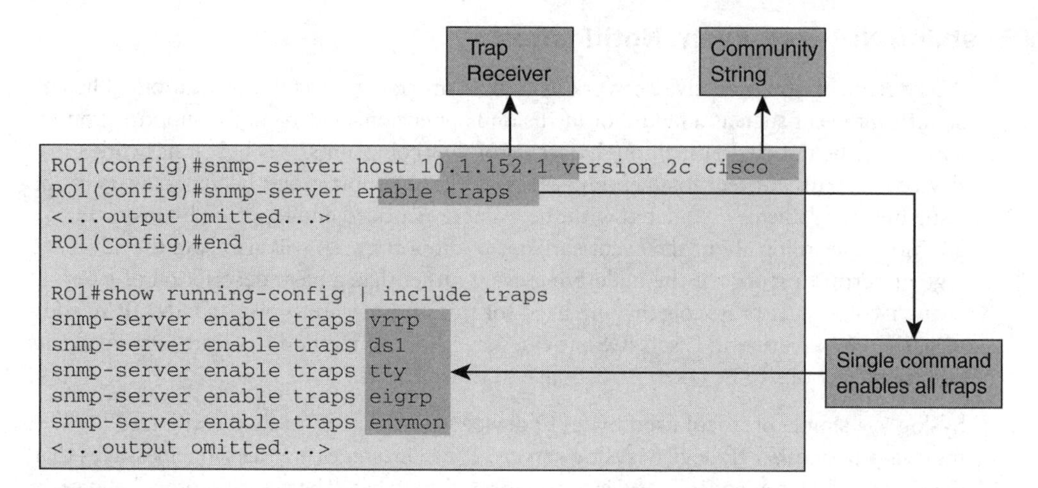

Figure 3-8 *Sample Configuration for Enabling SNMP Traps on a Router*

Trap receivers are configured using the **snmp-server host** *host* **traps** [**version** {**1** | **2c** | **3**}] **community-string** command. By default, Cisco routers send SNMP Version 1 traps, but higher versions can be configured explicitly. If you want a router to send specific traps, each desired trap must be encoded with the **snmp-server enable traps** *notification-type* command. On the other hand, to enable all trap types with a single command, you must use the **snmp-server enable traps** command. This command will not appear in the configuration as a command because it executes a macro that enables all available categories of traps. This effect is visible in the output of the **show running-config | include traps** command in Figure 3-8. SNMP and syslog both act on predefined triggers and send predefined messages. Both protocols allow for a limited amount of filtering, but it is not possible to define entirely new event triggers or messages.

The EEM framework enables the creation of custom policies that trigger actions based on events. Events can be triggered based on various Cisco IOS subsystems such as syslog messages, Cisco IOS counter changes, SNMP MIB object changes, SNMP traps, CLI command execution, timers, and many other options. Actions can consist of sending SNMP traps or syslog messages, executing CLI commands, sending e-mail, or even running tool command language (TCL) scripts. Thus, EEM allows you to create very powerful and complex policies.

Example 3-16 shows how to implement a policy using the Cisco IOS EEM feature. Assume that all network engineers within an organization are granted privileged access to the routers and switches and can make changes if necessary. The rule is that only Level 3 support engineers are allowed to make emergency changes if required, but Level 1 and 2 engineers always need to obtain authorization before making any change to the system. Whenever an engineer configures a router or switch, a %SYS-5-CONFIG_I message is logged to the syslog server. However, this message is logged as a syslog level five "notification" message and does not show up in the logs as a high-priority item. There is a requirement that a message must be logged as soon as anybody enters configuration mode; that is in addition to the %SYS-5-CONFIG_I message that is logged after configuration mode is exited. This message should be logged as a critical message and an informational message should be logged reminding the engineer of the existing change-control policies.

Example 3-16 *A Sample EEM Configuration*

```
Router(config)#event manager applet CONFIG-STARTED
Router(config-applet)#event cli pattern "configure terminal" sync no skip no
occurs 1
Router(config-applet)#action 1.0 syslog priority critical msg "Configuration mode
was entered"
Router(config-applet)#action 2.0 syslog priority informational msg "Change control
policies apply. Authorized access only."
```

The simple EEM applet shown in Example 3-16 accomplishes the policy requirements using the following four command lines:

- The **event manager applet CONFIG-STARTED** command creates an applet called CONFIG-STARTED.
- The event that should trigger this applet is defined on the second line using the command **event cli pattern "configure terminal" sync no skip no occurs 1**. This line effectively says that the policy should be triggered if a command that includes "configure terminal" is entered. The **occurs 1** option forces the event to be triggered on a single occurrence of the CLI pattern.
- The **action 1.0 syslog priority critical msg "Configuration mode was entered"** command defines an action named 1.0 (actions are sorted in alphabetic order) and instructs the router to log a critical message containing the text "Configuration mode was entered."
- The **action 2.0 syslog priority informational msg "Change control policies apply. Authorized access only."** command defines an action named 2.0 and instructs the router to log an informational message containing the text "Change control policies apply. Authorized access only."

Example 3-17 shows the effect and result of the EEM policy discussed in Example 3-16. As soon as a user enters the IOS global configuration mode, two messages appear. The first message is a critical message (syslog level 2) stating "%HA_EM-2-LOG: CONFIG-STARTED: Configuration mode was entered," and the second message is an informational message (syslog level 6) stating "%HA_EM-6-LOG: CONFIG-STARTED: Change control policies apply. Authorized access only."

Example 3-17 *A Sample EEM Policy Result*

```
RO1# conf t
Enter configuration commands, one per line.  End with CNTL/Z.
```

```
R01(config)#
Mar 13 03:24:41.473 PDT: %HA_EM-2-LOG: CONFIG-STARTED: Configuration mode was
entered
Mar 13 03:24:41.473 PDT: %HA_EM-6-LOG: CONFIG-STARTED: Change control policies
apply. Authorized access only.
```

Examples 3-16 and 3-17 demonstrated a simple implementation of EEM and its policy results. Bear in mind, however, that the EEM is a very powerful tool, and by incorporating the use of the TCL scripting language tool, you can implement a complete distributed notification system.

Note Complete coverage of EEM is beyond the scope of this chapter. However, you can find more information about the latest version and features of EEM at Cisco.com or at http://tinyurl.com/3hrdm7.

Summary

You can apply filtering to the Cisco IOS **show ip route** command. For example:

- To limit the output of the **show ip route** command, you can enter a specific IP address on the command line as an option. Doing so causes the router to execute a routing table lookup for that specific IP address and see whether it finds a match. If it finds a match in the routing table, it displays the corresponding entry with all its details. If it does not find a match in the routing table, it displays a message saying **% Subnet not in table.**
- Another way to limit the output from the **show ip route** command to a particular subset of routing information that you are interested in is to specify a prefix followed by the **longer-prefixes** keyword. The router will then list all subnets that fall within the prefix that you have specified (including that prefix itself, if it is listed in the routing table).

The output of Cisco IOS **show** commands can be filtered by appending a pipe character (|) to the **show** command followed by one of the keywords **include**, **exclude**, or **begin** and then a regular expression.

For selecting pieces of the configuration file, there is an option that allows you to select lines from the configuration that match a particular regular expression and any following associated lines. For example, the command **show running-config | section router** will select all lines that include the expression *router* and the configuration section that follows that line.

Instead of filtering the output of a **show** command, the output can also be redirected, copied or appended to a file by using the pipe character followed by the options **redirect**, **tee**, or **append** and a URL that denotes the file.

When you use the **| redirect** option on a **show** command, the output will not be displayed on the screen, but redirected to a text file instead. This file can be stored locally on the device's flash memory or it can be stored on a network server such as a TFTP or FTP server. The **| tee** option is similar to the **| redirect** option, but the difference is that this command both displays the output on your screen and copies it to a text file. Finally, the **| append** option is analogous to the **| redirect** option, but it allows you to append the output to a file instead of replacing that file.

Ping is an excellent connectivity-testing tool, especially when used with its options such as **repeat**, **size**, **source**, and **df-bit**. The **repeat** option enables you to specify the number of echo requests sent out. The **size** option enables you to specify the size of the packets sent out, and the **source** option enables you to specify which local interface IP address should be used as the source IP address on the packets sent out. The Don't Fragment option (**df-bit**) instructs the routers on the path not to fragment the packet sent; this option proves useful for path MTU testing. If you type **ping** with no IP address and press **Enter**, the extended ping dialog allows you to choose more options such as sweep sizes.

The Telnet application on Cisco IOS enables you to do transport layer testing by attempting to build a Telnet session to any TCP port of an IP device. If the port is active, you will get a response such as Open. A no response or refusal indicates that either the port is not active on the target IP device or that security features do not allow you to connect to that port.

Cisco IOS Software includes many commands to diagnose hardware operation. Due to their nature, many of those commands and features are product and platform specific. Essential commands common to both routers and switches include the following:

- **show processes cpu**
- **show memory**
- **show interfaces**

The **show processes cpu** command gives you an overview of all processes currently running on the router, the total amount of CPU time that they have consumed over their lifetime, and their CPU usage over the last 5 seconds. This command also displays a 1-minute and a 5-minute weighted average of CPU utilization for all processes

Both routers and switches have an amount of generic RAM memory, used by processes and for temporary packet buffering. Not having sufficient free memory can cause memory-allocation problems. Establishing a baseline can help discover these issues before they cause disruption.

The output of the **show interfaces** command include statistics such as input and output errors, CRC errors, collisions, and queue drops. Error statistics should be related to total packet statistics. Use the **clear counters** command to reset the interface counters and ensure that you are observing recent data. Use output filtering to limit the output to the fields that you are interested in viewing.

Other commands that can be useful in troubleshooting hardware related problems include the following:

- **show controllers**
- **show platform**
- **show inventory**
- **show diag**

You can use the following features, among others, to diagnose interface hardware or cabling issues:

- Generic Online Diagnostics (GOLD)
- Time Domain Reflectometer (TDR)

Different phases of the troubleshooting process can benefit from specific types of troubleshooting tools:

- **Defining the problem:** Network monitoring and event reporting tools
- **Gathering information:** Incident driven, targeted information-gathering tools
- **Analyzing:** Baseline creation and traffic-accounting tools
- **Testing the hypothesis:** Configuration rollback tools

Examples of network monitoring and event reporting tools include the following:

- Logging system messages to syslog
- Event notification using SNMP
- Event notification using the Embedded Event Manager (EEM)

Examples of incident-related information gathering are SPAN and RSPAN (used for traffic capturing).

The following are examples of baseline creation and traffic-accounting tools:

- Statistics gathering using SNMP
- Traffic accounting using NetFlow

Packet sniffers can be used to capture packets to allow detailed analysis of packet flows. Taking packet captures at various points in the network allows you to spot potential differences.

The SPAN feature allows traffic to be copied from one or more source ports or source VLANs to a port on the same switch for capture and analysis.

The RSPAN feature allows traffic to be copied from one or more source ports or source VLANs on one switch to a port on another switch by use of a special RSPAN VLAN. The RSPAN VLAN needs to be carried between the source and destination switches by use of trunks. RSPAN cannot cross Layer 3 boundaries.

Two main technologies that can be used to create a baseline of network usage and performance are SNMP and NetFlow.

SNMP is a standard protocol and is a pull model where the NMS polls devices for specific information. Cisco IOS NetFlow is based on the collection of detailed traffic profiles, and it is considered a push model. The NetFlow-enabled device pushes flow information to a collector, as traffic flows through the device. NetFlow is a Cisco router-specific feature.

Routers and switches can notify network management stations of significant events using two common methods: syslog and SNMP. In addition, you can use the EEM feature in Cisco IOS to create custom events and define actions to be taken in response to the event.

Review Questions

Use the questions here to review what you learned in this chapter. The correct answers are found in Appendix A, "Answers to Chapter Review Questions."

1. Which of the following commands will display all subnets contained in the prefix 10.1.32.0/19?

   a. **show ip route 10.1.32.0 /19 longer-prefixes**

   b. **show ip route 10.1.32.0 255.255.224.0 subnets**

   c. **show ip route 10.1.32.0 /19 subnets**

   d. **show ip route 10.1.32.0 255.255.224.0 longer-prefixes**

2. You execute the command **show ip route 10.1.1.1**, and the response of the router is **% Subnet not in table.** Which of the following is the most accurate conclusion you can draw from this response? (Select the best answer)

   a. The host entry 10.1.1.1/32 is not in the routing table.

   b. There is no route in the routing table that matches IP address 10.1.1.1. All packets to that destination will be dropped.

   c. There is no specific route in the routing table that matches IP address 10.1.1.1. Packets to that destination may be forwarded by the default route, if it is present.

   d. The classful network 10.0.0.0 is not present in the routing table.

3. Which of the following commands will display the part of the running configuration that contains all statements for the EIGRP routing protocol?

   a. **show running-config | section router eigrp**

   b. **show running-config | include router eigrp**

   c. **show running-config | exclude router eigrp**

   d. **show running-config | start router eigrp**

   e. None of these options are correct; this requires using a regular expression.

4. Which of the following commands will display the output of the command **show ip interface brief** onscreen and copy the output of the command to the file show-output.txt on TFTP server 10.1.1.1?

   a. **show ip interface brief | tee tftp://10.1.1.1/show-output.txt**

   b. **show ip interface brief | append tftp://10.1.1.1/show-output.txt**

   c. **show ip interface brief | redirect tftp://10.1.1.1/show-output.txt**

   d. **show ip interface brief | copy tftp://10.1.1.1/show-output.txt**

   e. None of these options are correct; **show** command output can be copied only to a file in the flash memory of the device.

5. Which of the following Cisco IOS commands will send 154 ICMP request packets of 1400 bytes each with the Don't Fragment bit set to IP address 10.1.1.1?

   a. **ping 10.1.1.1 –l 1400 –r 154 -f**

   b. **ping 10.1.1.1 size 1400 repeat 154 df-bit**

   c. **ping 10.1.1.1 repeat 154 size 1400 df 1**

   d. None of these options are correct; this can be accomplished only by use of the extended ping interactive dialog.

6. You execute the command **telnet 192.168.37.2 80**, and the response of the router is **Trying 192.168.37.2, 80 ... Open**. Which conclusion can you draw from this response?

   a. The web server on host 192.168.37.2 is running and serving files.

   b. There is a service running on TCP port 80 on host 192.168.37.2, and it accepts connections.

   c. The server on 192.168.37.2 is accepting Telnet connections.

   d. No conclusions can be drawn about the server. The word *Open* just means that the IP address could be found in the routing table.

7. You execute the command **show processes cpu**, and the output includes CPU utilization for 5 seconds: 30%/26%. Which two of the following statements are correct?

   a. The total CPU load over the past 5 seconds was 56 percent.

   b. The total CPU load over the past 5 seconds was 30 percent.

   c. The percentage of CPU time spent on scheduled processes was 26 percent.

   d. The percentage of CPU time spent on scheduled processes was 30 percent.

   e. The percentage of CPU time spent on scheduled processes was 4 percent.

8. Which two of the following technologies can be implemented to create a baseline of network usage?

   a. SPAN

   b. SNMP

   c. EEM

   d. Syslog

   e. NetFlow

9. SPAN traffic is carried in a RSPAN VLAN over which of the following?

   a. An access connection

   b. An EtherChannel connection

   c. An uplink connection

   d. A trunk connection

   e. An optical connection

10. Which two of the following commands are necessary to configure a switch to copy all traffic from interface Fa0/1 to a packet sniffer on interface Fa0/5?

    a. **monitor session 1 source interface Fa0/1**

    b. **span session 1 destination interface Fa0/5**

    c. **span session 1 destination remote interface Fa0/5**

    d. **monitor session 1 destination interface Fa0/5**

    e. **span session 1 source interface Fa0/1**

    f. **span session 1 destination remote interface Fa0/5**

11. Cisco IOS NetFlow technology enables you to gather detailed traffic profiles and performance statistics such as CPU and memory usage. True or False?

  a. True

  b. False

12. Which two of the following commands are necessary to configure a router to send SNMP traps to an SNMP manager at IP address 10.2.2.2 using community string cisco?

  a. **snmp-server community cisco RW**

  b. **snmp-server ifindex persist**

  c. **snmp-server contact 10.2.2.2 community cisco**

  d. **snmp-server enable traps**

  e. **snmp-server host 10.2.2.2 cisco**

  f. **snmp-server trap-host 10.2.2.2**

13. Which of the following best describes EEM?

  a. It is a framework that allows for the creation of custom events and corresponding actions.

  b. It is a technology that allows traffic to be copied from one switch port to another to allow it to be captured.

  c. It is a protocol that allows statistics to be gathered from a device and notifications to be sent by that same device.

  d. It is a technology that enables the collection of detailed traffic profiles.

14. Which of the following best describes SNMP?

  a. It is a framework that allows for the creation of custom events and corresponding actions.

  b. It is a technology that allows traffic to be copied from one switch port to another to allow it to be captured.

  c. It is a protocol that allows statistics to be gathered from a device and notifications to be sent by that same device.

  d. It is a technology that enables the collection of detailed traffic profiles.

15. Which of the following best describes NetFlow?

a. It is a framework that allows for the creation of custom events and corresponding actions.

b. It is a technology that allows traffic to be copied from one switch port to another to allow it to be captured.

c. It is a protocol that allows statistics to be gathered from a device and notifications to be sent by that same device.

d. It is a technology that enables the collection of detailed traffic profiles.

16. Which of the following best describes SPAN?

a. It is a framework that allows for the creation of custom events and corresponding actions.

b. It is a technology that allows traffic to be copied from one switch port to another so that the traffic can be captured.

c. It is a protocol that allows statistics to be gathered from a device and notifications to be sent by that same device.

d. It is a technology that enables the collection of detailed traffic profiles.

Chapter 4

Maintaining and Troubleshooting Campus Switched Solutions

This chapter covers the following topics:

- Troubleshooting VLANs
- Troubleshooting Spanning Tree
- Troubleshooting Switched Virtual Interfaces and Inter-VLAN Routing
- Troubleshooting First-Hop Redundancy Protocols

Ethernet LAN switching is a commonly used technology in current enterprise networks. Layer 2 and Layer 3 switching are a major part of campus networks, and they can also be found in data centers and some WAN solutions. It is therefore essential to have a good understanding of campus switching technologies, such as virtual local-area networks (VLANs), trunks, Spanning Tree Protocol (STP), multilayer switching, and first-hop redundancy protocols. It is also important for a network engineer to be able to diagnose and resolve problems associated with these technologies. This chapter reviews prominent campus multilayer switching technologies and focuses on resolving problems related to these technologies.

Troubleshooting VLANs

Switched Ethernet has been the dominant LAN technology for more than a decade. This is why a good understanding of the processes involved in Layer 2 switching is essential to any engineer who is involved in network troubleshooting. VLAN-based switched infrastructures are at the core of every campus network and being able to diagnose and resolve Layer 2 switching problems in these environments is a fundamental skill that any network engineer should have. This section first reviews the Layer 2 switching process and the associated switch data structures. Next, you will learn how to gather information from these data structures using Cisco IOS Software commands. Finally, you will learn how to interpret and analyze the gathered information in order to verify the proper operation of the Layer 2 switching process or to pinpoint and resolve problems.

LAN Switch Operation

As a network engineer, you must have an in-depth knowledge of the core processes performed by hosts and network devices. When things break down and devices do not function as they should, a good understanding of processes helps you determine where exactly a process breaks down. In addition, you will be able to determine which parts of the network are functioning correctly and which parts are not functioning correctly. This section examines the processes that take place when two IP hosts communicate over a switched LAN. The focus here is at the IP and lower layers; this means that the host application is in working condition and matters such as name to IP address resolution are functional. To limit the scope of the discussion to the processes involved in Layer 2 switching, assume that the two hosts reside on a common subnet (VLAN). Because the actual application being used is irrelevant to this discussion, imagine that the user of Host A would like to test connectivity to Host B using ping as per the network shown in Figure 4-1.

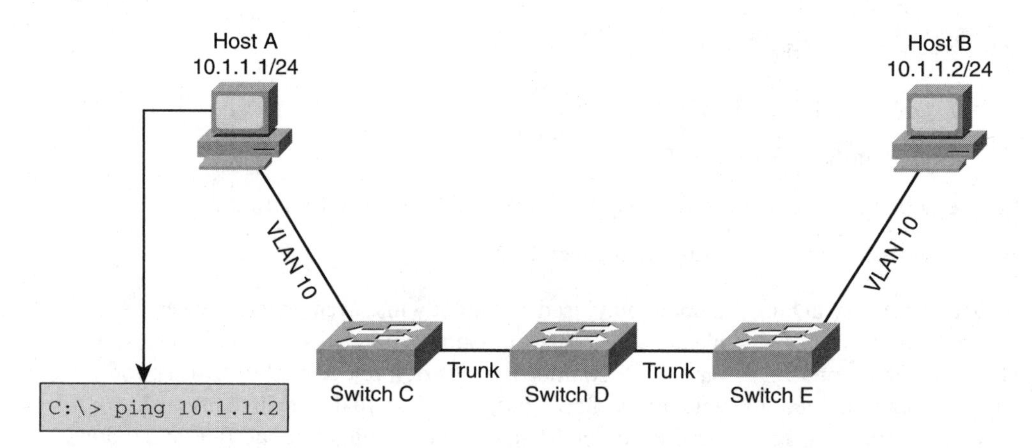

Figure 4-1 *Host A Tests Connectivity to Host B on the Same VLAN (Subnet)*

This process can be broken down into the following steps:

Step 1. Host A will look up the destination (Host B) IP address in its routing table and determine that it is on a directly connected network.

Step 2. Because Host B is directly reachable, Host A will consult its Address Resolution Protocol (ARP) cache to the find the MAC address of Hose B.

Step 3. If the ARP cache on Host A does not contain an entry for the IP address of Host B, it will send out an ARP request as a broadcast to obtain the MAC address of Host B (see Figure 4-2).

Step 4. Switch C checks the VLAN of the port upon which it receives the frame, records the source MAC address in its MAC address table, and associates it to that port and VLAN. Switch C will perform a lookup in its MAC address table to try to find the port that is associated to the broadcast MAC address.

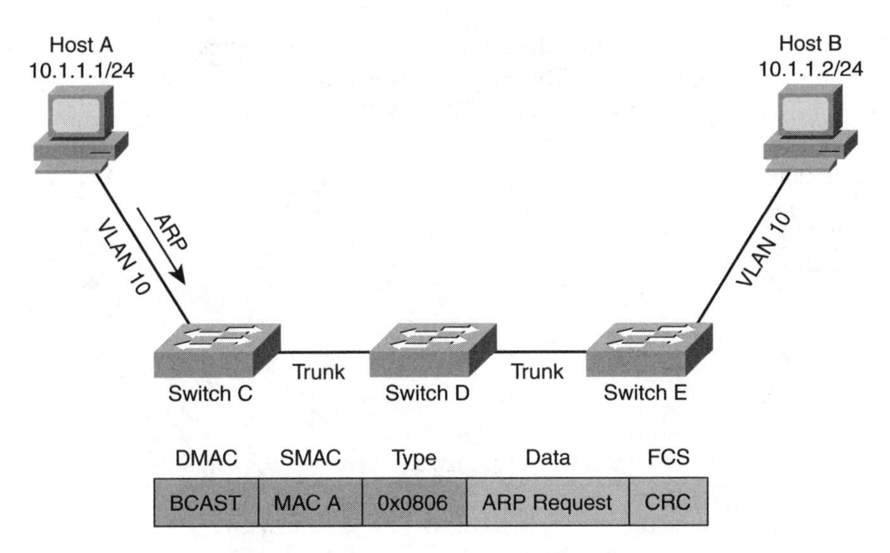

Figure 4-2 *Host A Sends a Broadcast ARP Request to Obtain Host B's MAC Address*

The MAC address table never contains an entry for the broadcast MAC address (FFFF:FFFF:FFFF). Therefore, Switch C will flood the frame on all ports in that VLAN, including all trunks that this VLAN is allowed, that are active, and that are not pruned on (except the port it came in from). Switches D and E repeat this process as they receive the frame (see Figure 4-3).

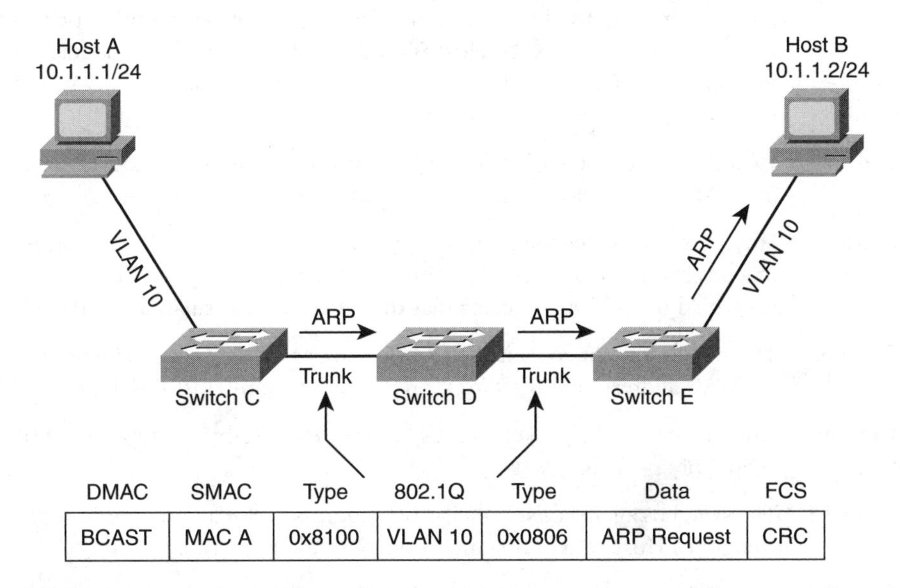

Figure 4-3 *Switches Flood Broadcast Frames*

Step 5. Host B receives the ARP request, records the IP address and MAC address of Host A in its own ARP cache, and then proceeds to send an ARP reply as a unicast back to Host A (see Figure 4-4).

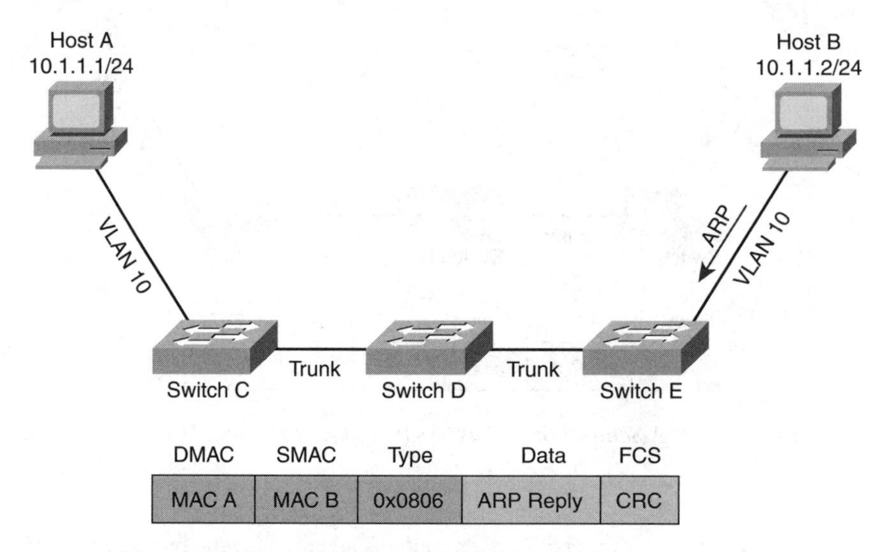

Figure 4-4 *Host B Sends a Unicast ARP Reply Back to Host A*

Step 6. The switches will check the VLAN of the port they received the frame on, and because all switches now have an entry in their MAC address table for the MAC address of Host A, they will forward the frame containing the ARP reply on the path to Host A only, not flooding it out on any other port. At the same time, they will record Host B's MAC address and corresponding interface and VLAN in their MAC address table if they did not already have that entry (see Figure 4-5).

Step 7. Host A receives the ARP reply and records the IP and MAC address of Host B in its ARP cache. Now it is ready to send the original IP packet.

Step 8. Host A encapsulates the IP packet (which encapsulates an ICMP echo request) in a unicast frame destined for Host B and sends it out. Note that the Ethernet type field of 0x0800 indicates that the frame is encapsulating an IP packet.

Step 9. The switches again consult their MAC address tables, find an entry for Host B's MAC address, and forward it on the path toward Host B (see Figure 4-6).

Step 10. Host B receives the packet and responds to Host A (by sending an ICMP echo-reply packet).

Step 11. The switches again consult their MAC address tables and forward the frame straight to Host A, without any flooding (see Figure 4-7).

Step 12. Host A receives the packet, and this concludes this simple packet exchange (see Figure 4-8).

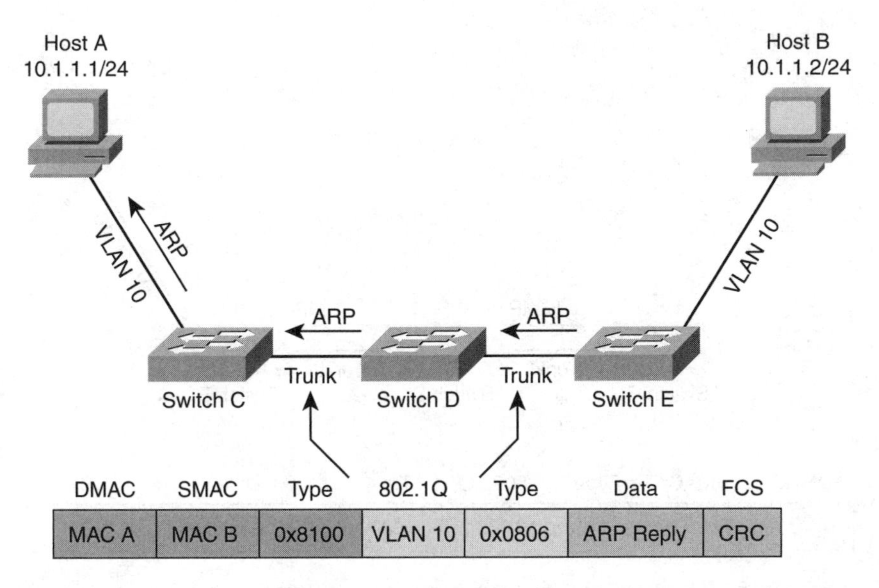

Figure 4-5 *Switches Forward the ARP Reply Unicast Frame Toward Host A*

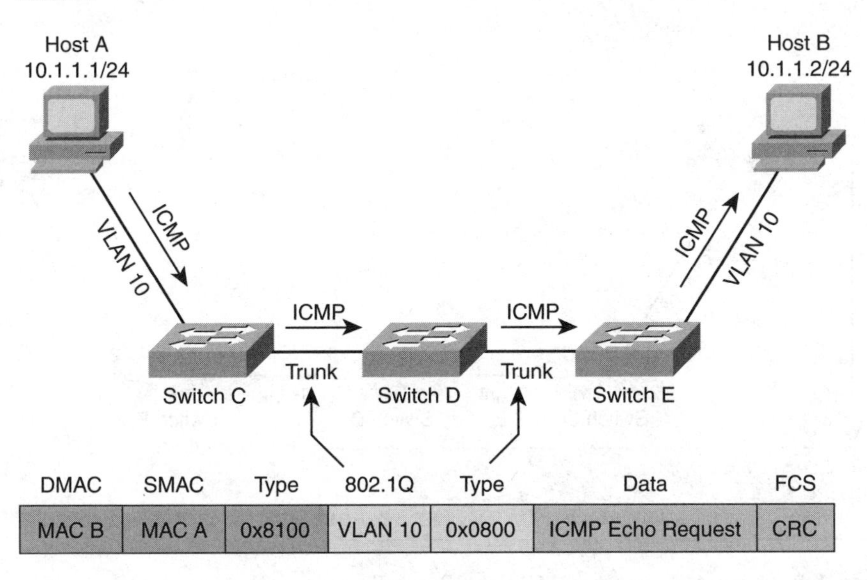

Figure 4-6 *Switches Forward ICMP Echo-Request Unicast Frame Toward Host B*

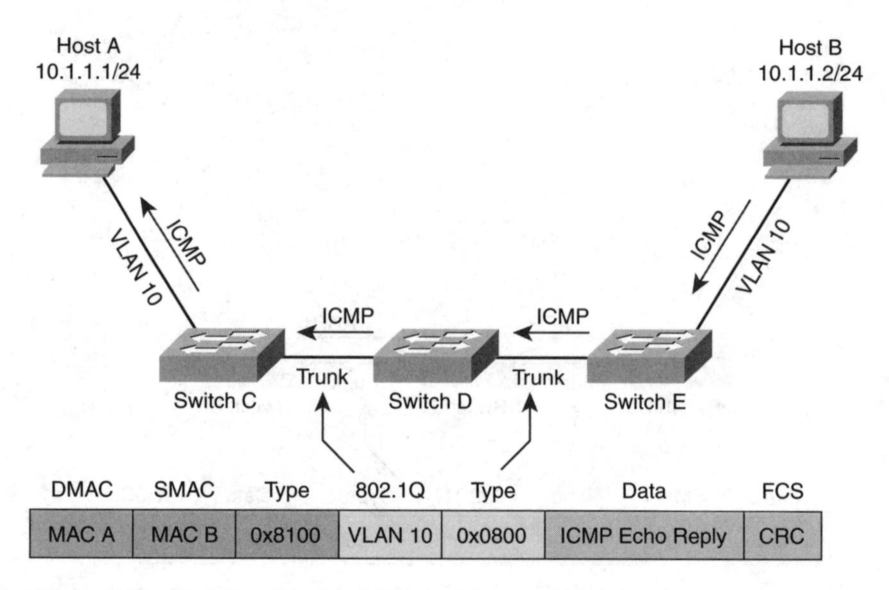

Figure 4-7 *Switches Forward ICMP Echo-Reply Unicast Frames Toward Host A*

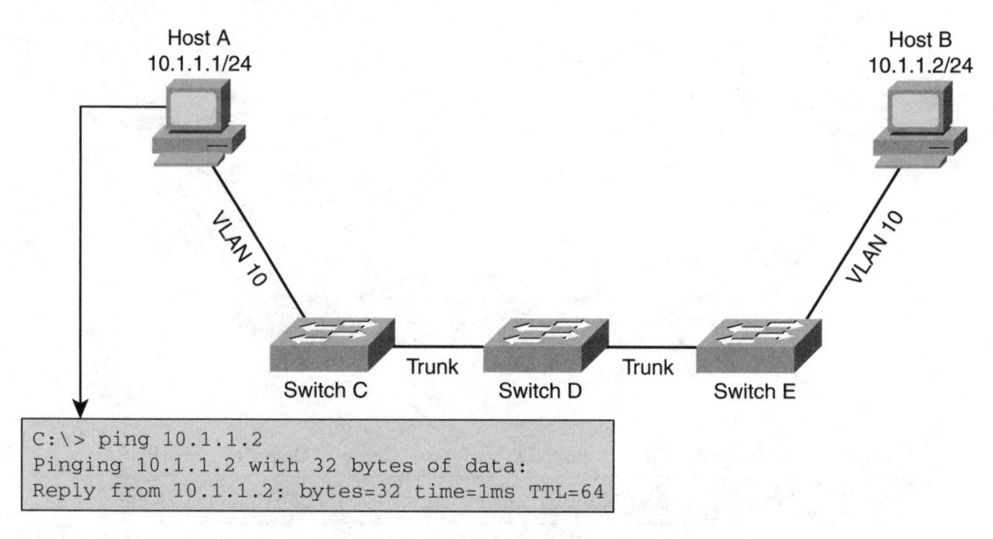

Figure 4-8 *Host A Receives ICMP Echo Reply Back from Host B*

Although this process might seem trivial, listing the steps clearly shows that even for the simplest communication, an elaborate chain of events take place. If at any point this chain is broken due to faulty cabling, failing devices, or misconfiguration, the communication will fail. Therefore, you must leverage your knowledge of these processes to diagnose and solve problems in a switched environment. Possible issues that could cause the communication to fail include the following:

- Physical problems
- Bad, missing, or miswired cables
- Bad ports
- Power failure
- Device problems
- Software bugs
- Performance problems
- Misconfiguration
- Missing or wrong VLANs
- Misconfigured VLAN Trunking Protocol (VTP) settings
- Wrong VLAN setting on access ports
- Missing or misconfigured trunks
- Native VLAN mismatch
- VLANs not allowed on trunk

Note Note that this list is not complete, and is focused on Layer 1 and Layer 2 issues. For example, a firewall may stop the Internet Control Message Protocol (ICMP) packets. Sometimes the very first ICMP echo request times out because of the requirement for an ARP request, which is not necessary on the following ICMP echo requests.

To keep the focus specifically on LAN switching, this chapter does not discuss any generic physical problems. However, you will learn how specific commands available on the Cisco Catalyst LAN switches could supplement your troubleshooting toolkit to help troubleshoot data link and physical layer problems.

Verifying Layer 2 Forwarding

A common method to troubleshoot Layer 2 switching problems is to follow the path of the frames through the switches. Following the actual frames themselves in real time takes a lot of time and effort because it requires packet captures at various points in the network; that is neither practical nor feasible. Instead of trying to follow the frame in real time, you must follow the trail of the frame. The objective is to confirm that frames have passed through the switches and to verify how each switch made its forwarding decisions. If you find a point where the trail suddenly stops or if you find that the information that the switch uses to forward frames does not match our expectations, you will gain important clues. These clues will help in reducing the scope of the possible problem areas, and it helps in formulating a hypothesis on the cause of the problem; it may even outright point at the cause of the problem. Consequently, a troubleshooter needs to learn how to follow the trail of the frame, and know which data structure proves whether frames have passed through the switch.

One key data structure that you can consult is the switch's MAC address table. In this table, the switch registers the source MAC address of each frame that it receives, and records the port and VLAN on which the frame was received. When you see an entry for a particular MAC address in this table, it proves that at some point, usually up to five minutes ago, this switch received frames from that source. This does not necessarily tell you anything about a particular frame or how long ago the last frame was received. Therefore, it might be a good practice to clear the MAC entry from the table by using the **clear mac-address-table dynamic** command and verify that the MAC address is learned again when you reinitiate the connection. Second, the MAC address table enables you to verify that frames are received on the port and VLAN where they are expected. If the output does not match your expectations and assumptions, use it as a clue in forming a hypothesis about the cause of the problem. Because there are many possible findings and conclusions that you might draw from, the following is a short list of some common findings and plausible conclusions:

- **Frames are not received on the correct VLAN:** This could point to VLAN or trunk misconfiguration as the cause of the problem.
- **Frames are received on a different port than you expected:** This could point to a physical problem, spanning-tree issues, or duplicate MAC addresses.
- **The MAC address is not registered in the MAC address table:** This tells you that the problem is most likely upstream from this switch. You should retrace your steps and investigate between the last point where you know that frames were received and this switch.

The next step is to use your knowledge of the forwarding process combined with the information you can gather using the switch's diagnostic commands output to determine what the next step in the process must be. Again, you should validate the facts that you gather about the switch's forwarding behavior against your expectations and assumptions. After you have confirmed that the behavior of the switch matches your expectations, you have successfully reduced the possible scope of the problem: You have confirmed that everything works as expected up to this point.

You must definitely have a good grasp of the switch diagnostic commands and use them effectively. You will use these commands to gather the information from the switch that is needed to validate your assumptions. Some commonly used diagnostic commands that help you obtain information about the Layer 2 switching process, VLANs, and trunks are as follows:

- **show mac-address-table:** This is the main command to verify Layer 2 forwarding. It shows you the MAC addresses learned by the switch and their corresponding port and VLAN associations. This command gives you an indication if frames sourced by a particular host have succeeded in reaching this switch. It will also help you verify whether these frames were received on the correct inbound interface. Note that if the MAC address table becomes full, no more learning can happen. During troubleshooting, always check to see whether the table is full.

- **show vlan:** This command enables you to verify VLAN existence and port-to-VLAN associations. This command lists all VLANS that were created on the switch (either manually or through VTP). It will also list the ports that are associated to each of the VLANs. Note that trunks are not listed because they do not belong to any particular VLAN.
- **show interfaces trunk:** This command displays all interfaces that are configured as trunks. It will also display on each trunk which VLANs are allowed and what the native VLAN is.
- **show interfaces switchport:** This command combines some of the information found in **show vlan** and **show interfaces trunk** commands. It is most useful if you are not looking for a switch-wide overview of trunk or VLAN related information, but if you would rather have a quick summary of all VLAN-related information for a single interface.
- **show platform forward** ***interface*****:** You can use many parameters with this command and find out how the hardware would forward a frame that matches the specified parameters, on the specified interface.
- **traceroute mac:** You specify a source and destination MAC address with this command to see the list of switch hops that a frame from that source MAC address to that destination MAC address passes through. Use this command to discover the Layer 2 path frames take from the specified source MAC address to the specified destination MAC address. This command requires that Cisco Discovery Protocol (CDP) be enabled on all the switches in the network (or at least within the path).

Based on the information they provide, the commands listed can be categorized. To display the MAC address table, use the **show mac-address-table** command. To display VLAN database and port-to-VLAN mapping, use the **show vlan** command. To see the trunk port settings and port-to-VLAN associations, use the **show interfaces switchport** and **show interfaces trunk** commands. To directly verify frame forwarding, use the **show platform forward** and the **traceroute mac** commands.

Troubleshooting Spanning Tree

High availability is an important requirement for today's campus LANs. The more dependent enterprises have become on their networks to support their business, the more important it is that those networks are highly available and have minimized downtime. One primary way to build highly available networks is through usage of redundant devices and links. However, when you introduce redundancy in a Layer 2 switched network, you can introduce bridging loops, resulting in broadcast storms that render the network unusable. The IEEE 802.1D Spanning Tree Protocol eliminates active bridging loops and thereby prevents broadcast storms. This is why a good understanding of the operation of STP is essential to any network engineer. It is important to know how to predict the spanning-tree topology or, in the absence of spanning-tree documentation, determine the spanning-tree topology using the appropriate Cisco IOS commands. Spanning-tree failures can be catastrophic when they happen. Therefore, recognizing the symptoms and having an action plan for these types of failures is an essential skill in reducing network downtime.

Spanning-Tree Operation

The IEEE 802.1D Spanning Tree Protocol is one of the most important protocols within a LAN switching environment, such as a campus network. A LAN that does not run this protocol in some form or another is not common. If you hear someone say that they do not use STP in their LAN, what they probably mean is that in their network spanning tree is not actively blocking ports or involved in the reconvergence process when a failure occurs. In most of those instances, STP is running in the background, in case a topological loop is created. The main purpose of STP is to prevent bridging loops and packet storms that might stem from loop conditions. Figure 4-9 shows a LAN with four LAN switches and many topological loops. Anyone who has been involved in a situation where loops were introduced in the switching topology while STP was not running, or not functioning correctly, knows how badly this type of failure can affect the network. The LAN can become fully saturated, and switches might become entirely unresponsive until the loops are eliminated. Therefore, it is crucial for any engineer who implements or supports switched LANs understand STP, recognize the symptoms of a spanning-tree failure, and know how to resolve those issues.

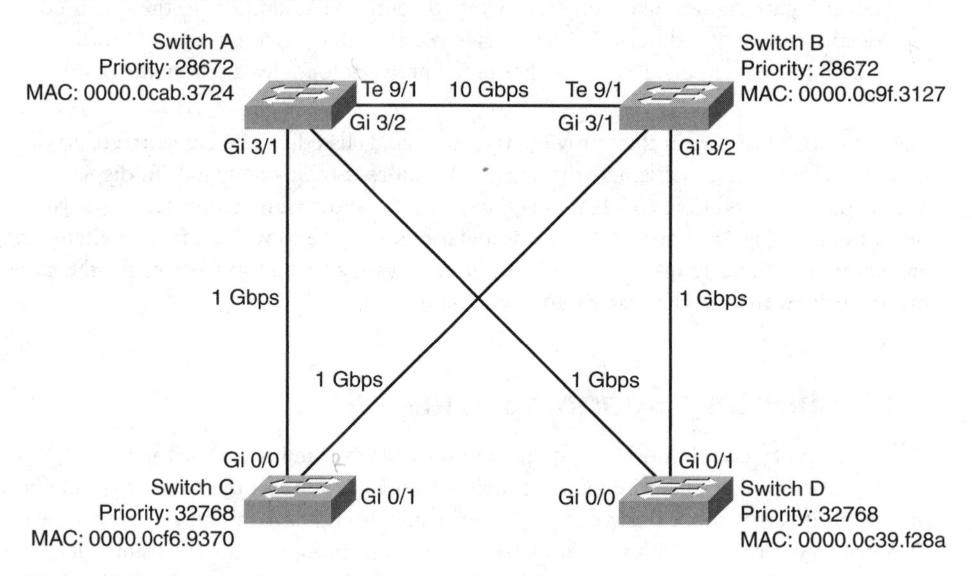

Figure 4-9 *A Switched LAN with Topological Loops*

The text that follows reviews spanning-tree operation making use of the topology depicted in Figure 4-9. Building the spanning tree requires the following four main steps:

Step 1. Elect a root bridge/switch.

This is based on lowest bridge ID (Bridge ID consists of the bridge/switch priority and lowest MAC address).

Step 2. Select a root port on each bridge/switch (except on the root bridge/switch).

This is based on least cost to root.

Ties are broken based on lowest upstream bridge ID.

Further ties are broken based on lowest port ID.

Step 3. Elect a designated device/port on each network segment.

This is based on least cost to root.

Ties are broken based on bridge ID.

Further ties are broken based on lowest port ID.

Step 4. Ports that ended up as neither a root port nor a designated port go into blocking state, and the root ports and designated ports go into learning, and then into forwarding state.

Electing a Root Bridge

The first step in the spanning-tree algorithm is the election of a root bridge. Initially, all switches assume that they are the root. They transmit bridge protocol data units (BPDUs) with the Root ID field containing the same value as the Bridge ID field. This implies that each switch nominates itself as the root bridge on the network. As soon as the switches start receiving BPDUs from the other switches, each switch compares the root ID in the received BPDUs against the value that it currently has recorded as the root ID. If the received value is lower than the recorded value (which was originally the switch's own bridge ID), the switch replaces the recorded value with the received value and starts transmitting this in the Root ID field in its own BPDUs. As a result, shortly, all switches will have learned and recorded the bridge ID of the switch that has the lowest bridge ID of all switches, and they will all be transmitting this ID in the Root ID field of their BPDUs. The root bridge is elected. Based on this method, in Figure 4-10 it is shown that Switch B is elected as the root bridge.

Electing a Root Port

As soon as a switch receives BPDUs that show a root ID different from its own bridge ID, the switch recognizes that it is not the root, and it will mark the port on which it is receiving those BPDUs as its root port. If these types of BPDUs are received on multiple ports, the switch selects the port that has the lowest cost path to the root as its root port. If two ports have an equal path cost to the root, the switch will look at the bridge ID values in the received BPDUs and selects the port that is receiving the BPDU with lower bridge ID. If the root path cost and the bridge ID in the received BPDUs are the same (because both ports are connected to the same upstream switch), the switch selects the port that is receiving the BPDU with the lower port ID to be the root port. Note that the port ID

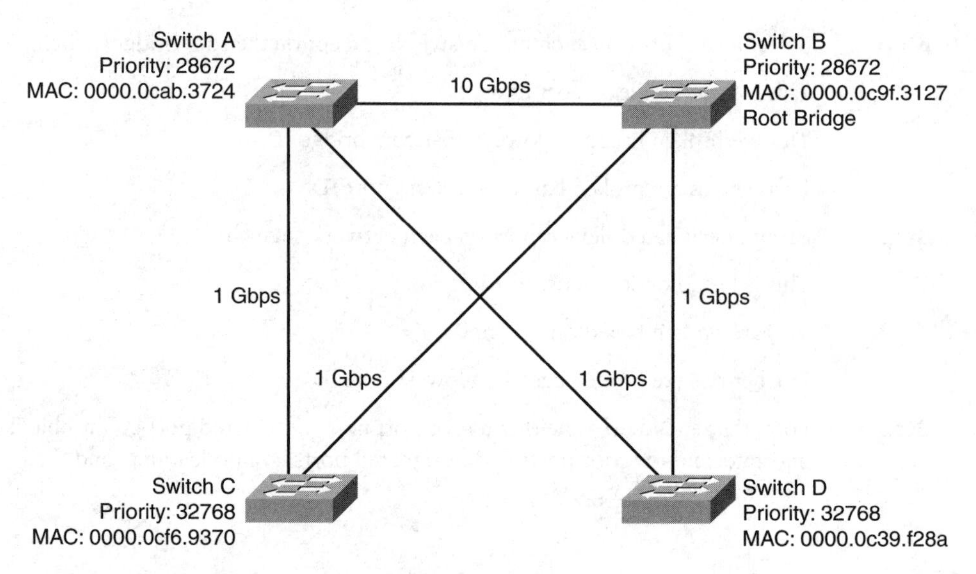

Figure 4-10 *Spanning Tree Protocol: Elect Root Bridge*

consists of two parts: port priority and port index (number). The port ID on the received BPDU is the port ID of the sending (upstream) switch. Based on these steps, Figure 4-11 shows the ports selected as root ports on each switch (except the root bridge).

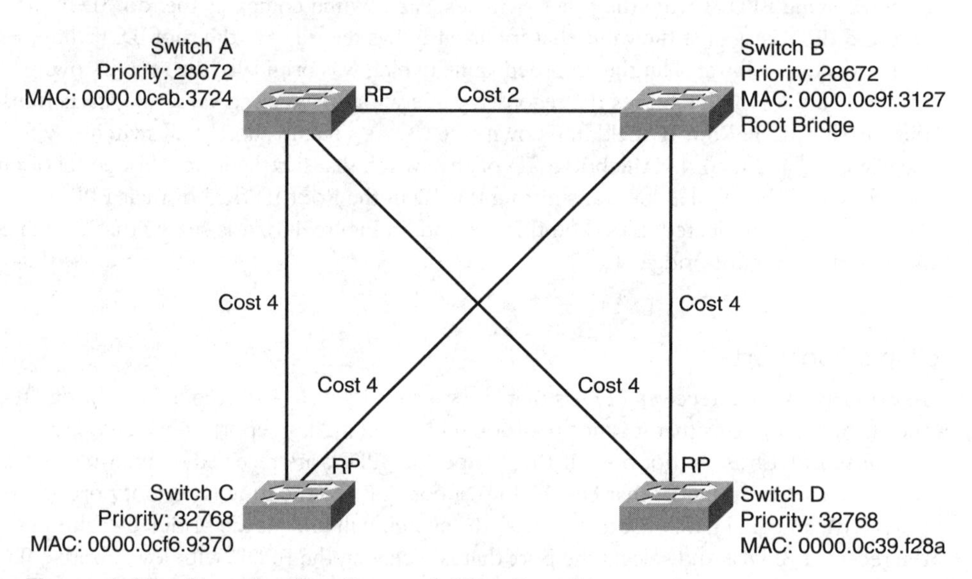

Figure 4-11 *Spanning Tree Protocol: Elect Root Port*

The way a switch determines the path cost is by adding the cost associated to the port on which it receives the BPDU to the value in the Root Path Cost field of the received BPDU.

The lowest value determines the switch's root port, and this value in turn is transmitted in the switch's own BPDUs. In short, this means that the root bridge starts sending BPDUs with the root path cost set to zero, and then each switch adds the cost of its root port to the received cost when it sends BPDUs to neighboring switches. The cost associated to each port is, by default, inversely related to its speed, but can be manually changed.

Electing Designated Ports

After electing the root bridge and root ports, the switches determine which interface/port in each Ethernet segment must be the designated port. This process has similarities to both root bridge and root port elections. Each switch connected to a segment will send BPDUs out of its port connected to that segment, essentially claiming that port to be the designated port for that segment. At this point, each switch considers its port to be the designated port for that Ethernet segment. However, as soon as a switch starts receiving BPDUs from other switches on that segment, it compares the received values of the Root Path Cost, Bridge ID, and Port ID fields (in that order) against the values in its own BPDUs that it is sending out that port. If it turns out that the other switch has lower values than this switch, it stops transmitting BPDUs on the port and marks it as a nondesignated port (in modern spanning-tree protocols, this port can be either an alternative or a backup port). In a rare case that a switch has multiple ports on the same Ethernet segment, the tie is broken using the local port ID. Note that a single port is designated for an Ethernet segment. This is emphasized because it is theoretically possible for two ports of the same switch to be connected to the same Ethernet segment. Figure 4-12 shows the designated ports on each Ethernet segment marked as DP.

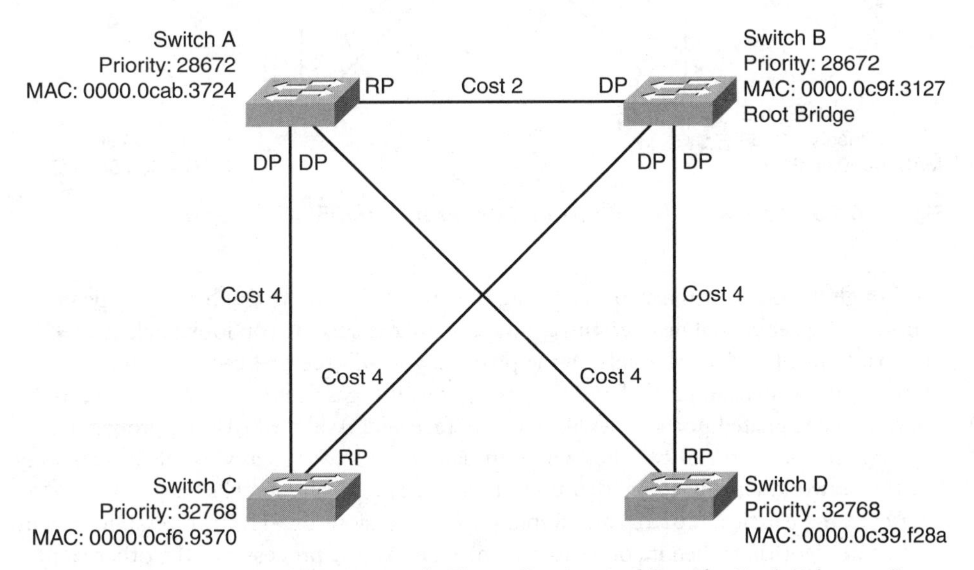

Figure 4-12 *Spanning Tree Protocol: Elect a Designated Port for Each Ethernet Segment*

Ports Going into Blocking, or Learning, and Forwarding State

To prevent bridging loops during the time it takes the STP to execute its algorithm, all ports are in a state called listening. While in the listening state, the port is busy building the spanning tree, and it does not forward any traffic. After forward_delay seconds, if the switch marks a port as either a root port or a designated port, that port transitions to the learning state. The port learns MAC addresses and records them in the MAC address table for a period called forwarding delay, and then the port proceeds to the forwarding state and starts to forward traffic. The ports that ended up as neither designated nor root ports transition into the blocking state. Figure 4-13 shows the ports in the blocking state with the letter *B* and an X marker. The designated or root ports that have completed the learning state and are now in the forwarding state have the letter *F*. From this moment going forward, the designated ports release a BPDU periodically based on a timer called the hello timer.

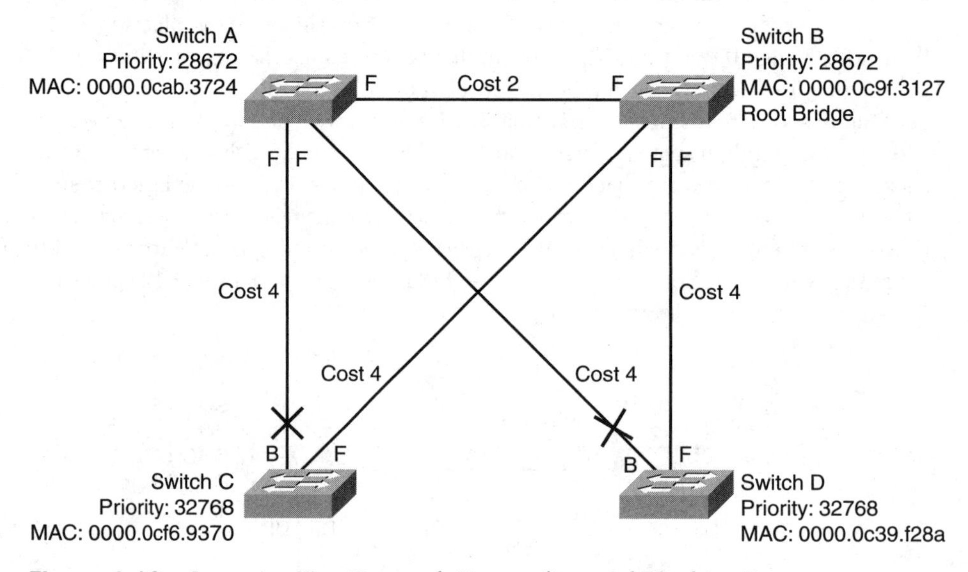

Figure 4-13 *Spanning Tree Protocol: Forwarding and Blocking Ports*

Although the order of the steps listed suggests that STP goes through these steps in a coordinated sequential manner, this is not actually the case. If you look back at the descriptions of each of the steps in the process, you will see that each switch is going through these steps in parallel and that it might adapt its selection of root bridge, root port, and designated ports as new BPDUs are received. As the BPDUs are propagated through the network, all switches will eventually have a consistent view of the topology of the network. Finally, notice that up to this point no distinction has been made between the classical (802.1D) and Rapid (802.1w) versions of STP. Both versions execute the same algorithm when it comes to the decision-making process. On the other hand, when it comes to the process of transitioning a port from the blocking (or *discarding* in RSTP terms) to the forwarding state, a significant difference exists between these two

STP versions. Classical 802.1D can take up to 50 seconds to transition a port to forwarding, whereas RSTP can leverage additional mechanisms to transition a port in blocking state to the forwarding state in less than a second.

Analyzing the Spanning-Tree Topology

In many networks, the optimal spanning-tree topology is determined as part of the network design and then implemented through manipulation of spanning-tree priority and cost values. Sometimes you might run into situations where spanning tree was not considered in the initial design and implementation. In other situations, the spanning-tree topology might have been considered initially, but the network has undergone significant growth and changes since then. In these types of situations, it is important that an engineer know how to analyze the actual spanning-tree topology in the operational network. Troubleshooting includes comparing the actual state of the network against the expected state of the network and spotting the differences to gather clues about the problem. To do that, you should be able to examine the switches and determine the actual topology and compare that with the spanning-tree topology as per design. Important commands for gathering information about the status of STP and the corresponding topology include the following:

Note The original spanning-tree timers are based on the assumption that the network diameter is up to seven bridges/switches long.

- **show spanning-tree** [**vlan** *vlan-id*]: This command, without specifying any additional options, is useful if you want a quick overview of the status of STP for all VLANs that are defined on a switch. If you are interested in only a particular VLAN, you can limit the scope of this command by specifying the VLAN number as an option. Figure 4-14 shows sample output from this command.
- **show spanning-tree interface** *interface-id* **detail:** This command is useful if you need to see the status of an interface plus all the STP-related parameters on that interface and the BPDUs on this interface. It will either give you the BPDU content of the BPDUs received from the upstream switch (if that switch's port is the designated port) or the content of the BPDUs that are sent out by this switch (if this switch's port is the designated port for the segment connected to the interface). Figure 4-15 shows sample output from this command.

In the example shown in Figure 4-15, you can see that port 88 (TenGigabitEthernet9/1) is a root port and the upstream switch's port is the designated port. This is also reflected by the fact that this switch is receiving BPDUs (it received 670 BPDUs), but not transmitting them (it sent 10 BPDUs during initial spanning-tree convergence and stopped after that). You can also see that the upstream switch is the root bridge. This can be concluded from the fact that the designated bridge ID and the root bridge ID are the same. This is further confirmed by the fact that the designated path cost is reported as a cost of 0.

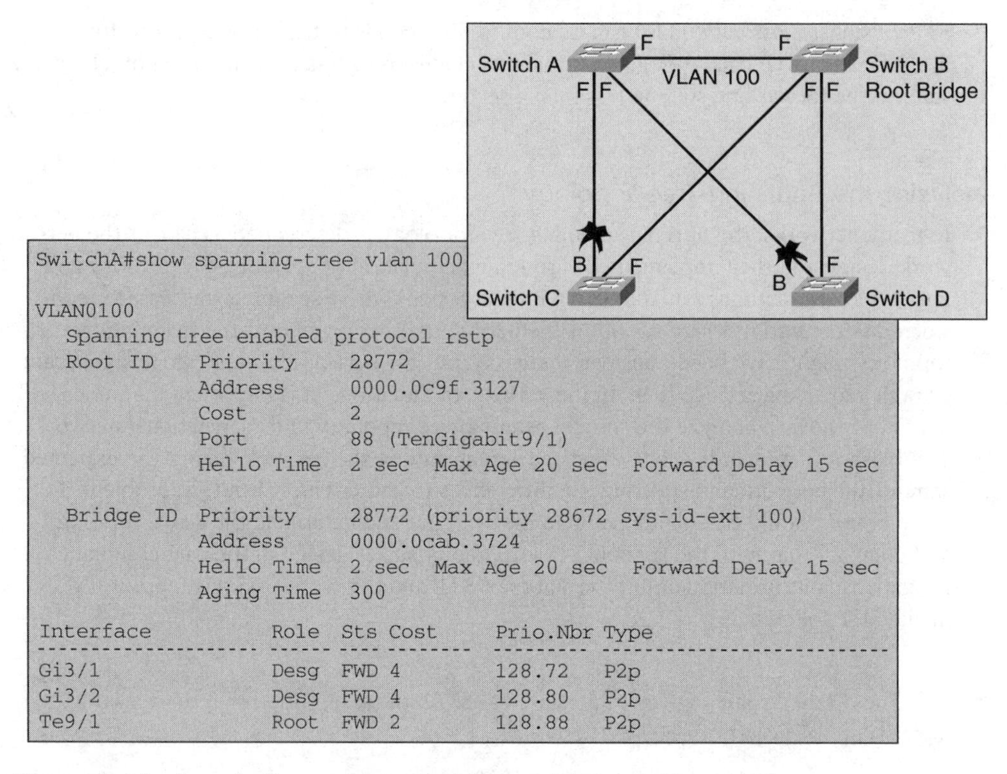

Figure 4-14 *Sample Output from the* **show spanning-tree** *Command*

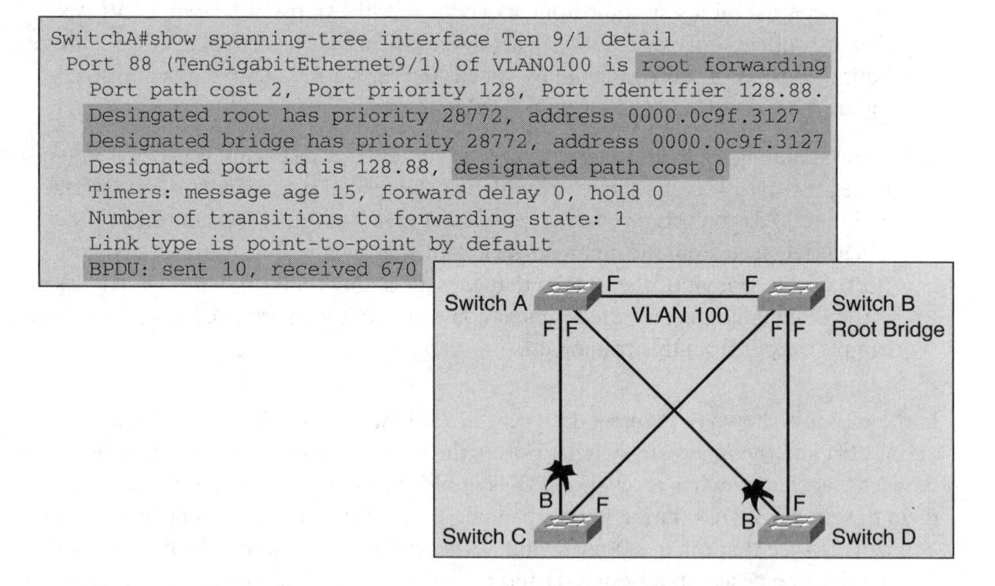

Figure 4-15 *Sample Output from the* **show spanning-tree interface** *Command*

Spanning-Tree Failures

The biggest problem with STP is not the fact that it can fail, as any protocol can. In fact, STP is one of the most reliable protocols available. The main concern is that when a problem related to STP exists, there are usually major negative consequences. For many protocols, when they malfunction, all that happens is that you lose some of the functionality that was gained through this protocol. For instance, if Open Shortest Path First (OSPF) Protocol is malfunctioning on one of your routers, you might lose connectivity to networks that are reachable through that particular router. However, this generally does not affect the rest of your OSPF network. If you have some way to connect to that router, you can still perform your troubleshooting routines to diagnose and fix the problem.

With STP, there are two different types of failures. The first one is similar to the OSPF problem just described. STP may erroneously block certain ports that should have gone to the forwarding state. This will cause problems that are similar to the OSPF problem: You might lose connectivity to certain parts of your network, but the rest of the network is unaffected. If you are able to access the switch, you can perform some troubleshooting, and even fix the problem. The second type of failure is a lot more disruptive, and it happens when STP erroneously moves one or more ports to the forwarding state.

An Ethernet frame header does not include a Time To Live (TTL) field; therefore, any frame that enters a bridging loop will continue to be forwarded by the switches indefinitely. The only exceptions are the frames that have their destination address recorded in the MAC address table of the switches. These frames will simply be forwarded to the port that the MAC address is associated with and will not go into an endless loop. However, any frame that is flooded by a switch, such as broadcasts, multicasts, and unicasts with an unknown destination MAC address, will go into an endless loop and start circling. The consequences and corresponding symptoms of this behavior are as follows:

- The load on all links in the switched LAN will quickly start increasing as more and more frames enter the loop. Note that this is not limited to just the links that form the loop, but also any other links in the switched domain, because some frames are flooded on all links. Naturally, when the spanning-tree failure is limited to a single VLAN, then only links in that VLAN will be affected and switches and trunks that do not carry that VLAN will operate normally.
- If the spanning-tree failure has caused more than one bridging loop to form, traffic will increase exponentially (because frames will not only start circling, but will also start getting duplicated). This happens because, in the case of multiple loops, there will be switches that receive a frame on a port and then flood it out on multiple ports, essentially creating a copy of the frame every time they forward it.
- When control plane traffic, such as Hot Standby Router Protocol (HSRP), OSPF, or Enhanced Interior Gateway Routing Protocol (EIGRP) hellos, starts entering the loop, the devices that are running these protocols will quickly start getting overloaded. Their CPU will approach 100 percent utilization while they are trying to process an ever-increasing load of control plane traffic. In many cases, the earliest

indication of a broadcast storm in progress is that routers or Layer 3 switches are reporting control plane failures, such as continual HSRP state changes, or that they are running at a very high CPU utilization load.

- Switches will experience very frequent MAC address table changes. This happens because frames might loop in both directions, causing a switch to see a frame with a certain source MAC address enter through one port and then see a frame with the same source MAC address enter through a different port shortly later.
- Because of the combination of very high load on all links and the CPU running at maximum load on Layer 3 switches or routers, these devices typically become unreachable, making it nearly impossible to diagnose the problem while it is in progress.

Spanning-tree problems, especially when they result in bridging loops and broadcast storms, are severe. During these periods, execution of proper troubleshooting methods is severely hindered by the fact that some links and devices are overloaded. One intrusive but effective way to start tackling severe spanning-tree problems is eliminating topological loops by either physically disconnecting links or by shutting down interfaces if that is still possible. Once the loops are broken, the traffic and CPU loads should quickly drop to normal levels, and you should regain connectivity to your devices. Although this restores connectivity to the network, you cannot consider this the end of your troubleshooting process. You have removed all redundancy from your switched network, and you need to restore the redundant links. Redundancy is a common way to provide fault tolerance and load sharing within a network. Naturally, if the underlying cause for the spanning-tree failure has not been fixed, restoring the redundant links will trigger a new broadcast storm. To find the root cause of the failure, you should identify and correct the cause of the problem, before you restore the redundant links. An example of a failure that causes spanning-tree problems is a unidirectional link. If you identify and remove a faulty cable that caused the unidirectional link, you can use a new cable to replace the old faulty one. After restoring the redundant links, always carefully monitor the network and have an emergency plan to fall back on if you see a new broadcast storm developing.

EtherChannel Operation

EtherChannel is a technology that bundles multiple physical Ethernet links (100 Mbps,1 Gbps,10 Gbps) into a single logical link and distributes the traffic across these links. This logical link is represented in Cisco IOS syntax as a *port-channel* interface. Control protocols like STP or routing protocols will only interact with this single port-channel interface and not with the associated physical interfaces. Packets and frames are routed or switched to the port-channel interface, and then a hashing mechanism determines which physical link will be used to transmit them. There are three common EtherChannel problems:

- **Inconsistencies between the physical ports that are members of the channel:** The physical links in an EtherChannel must have the same operational characteristics. For example, they must have the same speed, duplex, trunk, or access port status, native VLAN when trunking, and same access VLAN when they are access ports. As a rule, it is therefore recommended that the configuration of all physical links in the channel be identical. If at a certain point in time (usually due to misconfiguration), one of the physical links changes its operational status in such a way that a mismatch with the other physical links is created, this port will be suspended and removed from the EtherChannel bundle until consistency is restored. When the switch suspends a physical link in the channel because of incompatibilities, it generates a %EC-5-CANNOT_BUNDLE2 log message.

- **Inconsistencies between the ports on the opposite sides of the EtherChannel link:** If the switch on one side of a few links is configured to bundle these links into an EtherChannel and the switch on the other side is not, the switch that is configured for EtherChannel will detect this (by detecting inconsistencies in the spanning-tree behavior) and move the port to an error-disabled state. The switch will generate a %SPANTREE-2-CHNL_MISCFG message when it "error disables" the port. The use of an EtherChannel negotiation protocol like the 802.3ad Link Aggregation Control Protocol (LACP) or the Port Aggregation Protocol (PAgP) prevents this situation from happening because both sides must first agree to form the channel.
- **Uneven distribution of traffic between EtherChannel bundle members:** Some people expect that when EtherChannel is used, the traffic is equally balanced across all physical links in the bundle. You must realize, however, that the method used to distribute traffic over the physical links is to calculate a hash of a combination of fields in the Ethernet and IP headers of a frame and then send the frame to a physical interface based on the hash result. Therefore, the distribution of traffic depends on two things: The distribution of hash values over the physical links, and the header fields that are used as a key into the hash calculation. The Cisco EtherChannel hash algorithm results in a value between 0 and 7. This means that in case of an eight-port EtherChannel, one hash value is assigned to each of the links, and (assuming a random traffic mix) traffic is equally balanced across all eight links. However, if the channel consists of six links, the distribution will be 2:2:1:1:1:1 instead, meaning that the first two links in the channel will each handle twice as much traffic as the other links. The second factor in EtherChannel load balancing is which header fields are used as the base of the hash value. If you could assume those fields in the traffic to be entirely random, it would not matter what hashing mechanism were used; however, because header fields are typically not random, the choice of header fields to be hashed does affect the distribution. For example, when only the destination MAC address is used as the input for the hash calculation, if 90 percent of all frames are destined for a single MAC address (for instance, the MAC address of the default gateway), all of that traffic would end up on the same physical link. Therefore, if you see an uneven distribution of traffic over the links in the channel, you should examine the hashing method and the traffic mix to determine the cause.

Troubleshooting Example: Switch Replacement Gone Bad

A broken access switch has been replaced by a new access switch ASW1 (see Figure 4-16). The junior support staff has configured ASW1 to the best of his knowledge and using the documentation that exists. After the switch booted and its physical connections to the

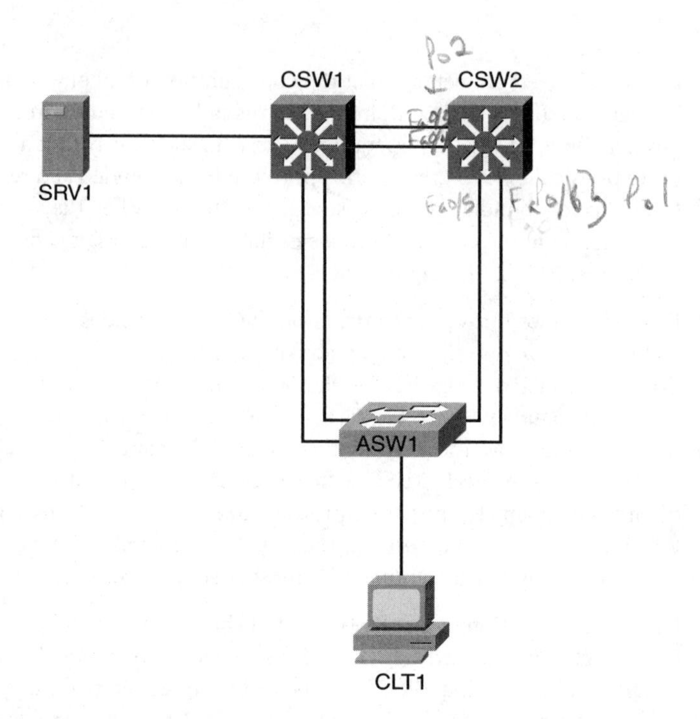

Figure 4-16 *ASW1 Has Introduced Three Problems on the Network to Solve*

two other switches (CSW1 and CSW2) were restored, the junior support staff reported three problems that he could not solve:

- On CSW2, port channel 1, which connects to ASW1, is down.
- On ASW1, the following log message on the console indicates a spanning-tree problem on Po2, which connects to CSW1: %SPANTREE-2-PVSTSIM_FAIL: Blocking designated port Po2: Inconsistent superior PVST BPDU received on VLAN 17, claiming root 24593:001f.2721.8400
- On ASW1, interface VLAN 128 is down.

A key command used to troubleshoot problems with EtherChannel bundles is the **show etherchannel summary** command. The output from this command presents a concise overview of all links that are configured for EtherChannel, the status of the individual physical interfaces, and the logical port-channel interfaces. Starting with the first problem, you would use the **show etherchannel summary** command (see results in Example 4-1) and see the letters *SD* beside the Po1 interface. *S* means that it is configured as a Layer 2 interface, but *D* means that Po1 is down, as reported by the junior staff. Also, the small letter s is present beside the physical interfaces Fa0/5 and Fa0/6. Small *s*, marking the physical interfaces, indicates that those interfaces have been suspended.

Example 4-1 *Using the* **show etherchannel summary** *Command*

```
CSW2# show etherchannel summary
Flags:  D - down        P - bundled in port-channel
        I - stand-alone s - suspended
        H - Hot-standby (LACP only)
        R - Layer3      S - Layer2
        U - in use      f - failed to allocate aggregator

        M - not in use, minimum links not met
        u - unsuitable for bundling
        w - waiting to be aggregated
        d - default port

Number of channel-groups in use: 2
Number of aggregators:           2

Group  Port-channel  Protocol    Ports
------+-------------+-----------+-----------------------------------------------
1      Po1(SD)          -        Fa0/5(s)    Fa0/6(s)
2      Po2(SU)          -        Fa0/3(P)    Fa0/4(P)
```

When you see physical interfaces in an EtherChannel that are marked as suspended, this usually indicates that a configuration mismatch, either between interfaces in the channel itself or between the configuration on this end of the EtherChannel and the configuration at the other end. To find more detail about what exactly caused the problem, you can use the **show etherchannel** *number* **detail** command, or search the log for a message that tells you why the links were suspended. Issuing the **show etherchannel 1 detail** command provides the output shown in Example 4-2.

Example 4-2 **show etherchannel 1 detail** *Command Output*

```
CSW2# show etherchannel 1 detail
Group state = L2
Ports: 2   Maxports = 8
Port-channels: 1 Max Port-channels = 1
Protocol:    -
Minimum Links: 0
Ports in the group:
-------------------
Port: Fa0/5
------------


Port state    = Up Cnt-bndl Suspend Not-in-Bndl
Channel group = 1           Mode = On              Gcchange = -
Port-channel  = null        GC   =   -             Pseudo port-channel = Po1
```

```
Port index     = 0              Load = 0x00              Protocol =    -

Age of the port in the current state: 0d:00h:25m:13s

Probable reason: vlan mask is different
Port: Fa0/6
------

Port state     = Up Cnt-bndl Suspend Not-in-Bndl
Channel group = 1              Mode = On                Gcchange = -
Port-channel  = null           GC   =    -              Pseudo port-channel = Po1
Port index     = 0              Load = 0x00              Protocol =    -

Age of the port in the current state: 0d:00h:25m:14s

Probable reason: vlan mask is different
Port-channels in the group:
---------------.

Port-channel: Po1
------
Age of the Port-channel   = 0d:00h:24m:48s
Logical slot/port   = 2/1          Number of ports = 0
GC                    = 0x00000000       HotStandBy port = null
Port state           = Port-channel Ag-Not-Inuse
Protocol             =   -
Port security        = Disabled
```

The output shown in Example 4-2 indicates that the cause of the problem is the VLAN mask, which means that there must be a mismatch between the VLANs allowed on the port channel versus the VLANs allowed on the physical interfaces. You could also find the problem indication from the log, which contains the messages shown in Example 4-3.

Example 4-3 *Log Messages Indicate Etherchannel Incompatibility*

```
Mar 20 08:12:39 PDT: %EC-5-CANNOT_BUNDLE2: Fa0/5 is not compatible with Po1 and
will be suspended (vlan mask is different)
Mar 20 08:12:39 PDT: %EC-5-CANNOT_BUNDLE2: Fa0/6 is not compatible with Po1 and
will be suspended (vlan mask is different)
```

These findings lead you to compare the port-channel interface to the physical interfaces to find out that the VLAN allowed list is missing on physical interfaces Fa0/5 and Fa0/6 of ASW1. You notify the junior staff member of the problem, and he changes the configuration by adding allowed VLAN list to physical interfaces Fa0/5 and Fa0/6. He then saves both pre- and post-change configurations in flash on the switch and communicates the change and the results to other team members.

To investigate the second problem, use the **show spanning-tree** command on VLAN 17, as demonstrated in Example 4-4.

Example 4-4 *Use the* **show spanning-tree** *Command to Examine SPT Issues*

```
ASW1# show spanning-tree vlan 17

MST0
  Spanning tree enabled protocol mstp
  Root ID     Priority    32768
              Address     001e.79a9.b580
              This bridge is the root
              Hello Time   2 sec  Max Age 20 sec  Forward Delay 15 sec

  Bridge ID   Priority    32768  (priority 32768 sys-id-ext 0)
              Address     001e.79a9.b580
              Hello Time   2 sec  Max Age 20 sec  Forward Delay 15 sec

Interface            Role Sts Cost      Prio.Nbr Type
-------------------- ---- --- --------- -------- --------------------------------
Fa0/7                Desg FWD 200000    128.9    P2p Edge
Po1                  Desg BLK 100000    128.56   P2p
Po2                  Desg BKN*100000    128.64   P2p Bound(PVST) *PVST_Inc
```

The output of this command has two elements that clearly point to a spanning-tree configuration issue. The BKN* and *PVST_Inc elements in the output point toward a spanning-tree inconsistency, while the Bound (PVST) element points toward a boundary between two different spanning-tree varieties. Because all other switches run Rapid Per-VLAN Spanning Tree (R-PVST+), it is reasonably safe to assume that switch ASW1 should not be running Multiple Spanning Tree (MST), but should be running R-PVST+. Note that the third line in Example 4-4 clearly indicates that ASW1 is running MST.

After verifying that CSW2 uses R-PVST+, and ASW1 uses MST, you check the baseline documentation and confirm that all switches should run R-PVST+. You notify the junior staff, and he makes the required configuration change on ASW1 by entering the command **spanning-tree mode rapid-pvst**. He also saves both pre- and post-change configurations in flash on the switch and communicates the problem and the resolution to team members.

Before starting to troubleshoot the third problem as reported, you check the status of the VLAN interface VLAN128, and based on the results shown in Example 4-5, you notice that the VLAN interface 128 is indeed down (and not administratively down).

Example 4-5 *Use the* **show ip interfaces brief** *Command to Check an Interface Status*

```
ASW1# show ip interfaces brief | exclude unassigned
Interface              IP-Address      OK? Method Status                Protocol
Vlan128                10.1.156.1      YES NVRAM  up                    down
```

A VLAN interface is up as long as the VLAN exists and there is an active port in that VLAN that is in spanning-tree forwarding state. Therefore, when you discover that a VLAN interface is down, it is a good idea to first check the spanning-tree status for that VLAN. You enter the **show spanning tree vlan 128** and the **show vlan id 128** commands and discover, as shown in the output of Example 4-6, that spanning tree is not running for VLAN 128. That leads to the hypothesis that VLAN 128 does not exist on ASW1, which is confirmed immediately.

Example 4-6 *Verifying the Status of a VLAN*

```
ASW1# show spanning-tree vlan 128
Spanning tree instance(s) for vlan 128 does not exist.




ASW1# show vlan id 128
VLAN id 128 not found in current VLAN database
```

You notify the junior staff, and he adds VLAN 128 to the configuration of ASW1. He then saves pre- and post-change configurations in flash on the switch and communicates both the problem and the solution to the other team members.

Troubleshooting Switched Virtual Interfaces and Inter-VLAN Routing

The traditional distinction between routers and switches has become blurred over the past decade. Multilayer switches have taken over the role of the router in the campus LAN environment and are even being used in other Ethernet-based environments as a replacement for the traditional router. It is important that network engineers understand the differences between hardware-accelerated Layer 3 switching and software-based routing architectures and how these differences translate to the troubleshooting process that you would use to troubleshoot Layer 3 problems on a multilayer switch versus troubleshooting Layer 3 problems on a router. This section reviews multilayer switching concepts first. Diagnosing specific problems related to multilayer switching and switched virtual interfaces (SVIs) is discussed next.

Inter-VLAN Routing and Multilayer Switching

To further clarify the increasingly blurry distinction between a router and a switch, a multilayer switch is a "switch that can route." On the other hand, you could create a "router that can switch" by inserting an Ethernet switching module in a modular router. Therefore, as far as troubleshooting is concerned, there is not that much difference between troubleshooting IP routing on a multilayer switch compared to troubleshooting IP routing on a router. Table 4-1 summarizes the similarities and differences between multilayer switches and routers.

Table 4-1 *Similarities and Differences Between Multilayer Switches and Routers*

Similarities	Differences
Both routers and multilayer switches use routing protocols or static routes to maintain information about the reachability and direction to network destinations (prefixes) and record this information in a routing table.	Routers connect heterogeneous networks and support a wide variety of media and interfaces. Multilayer switches typically connect homogenous networks. Nowadays LAN switches are mostly Ethernet only.
Both routers and multilayer switches perform the same functional packet switching actions: **1.** They receive a frame and strip off the Layer 2 header. **2.** They perform a Layer 3 lookup to determine the outbound interface and next hop. **3.** They encapsulate the packet in a new Layer 2 frame and transmit the frame.	Multilayer switches use specialized hardware to achieve wire-speed Ethernet-to-Ethernet packet switching. Low- to mid-range routers use multipurpose hardware to perform the packet-switching process. On average, the packet-switching throughput of routers is lower than the packet-switching throughput of multilayer switches.
	Routers usually support a wider range of features, mainly because switches need specialized hardware to be able to support certain data plane features or protocols. On routers, you can often add features through a software update.

From a troubleshooting perspective, the process of troubleshooting the control plane is exactly the same for routers and multilayer switches. There is no difference between troubleshooting OSPF or EIGRP on a multilayer switch compared to troubleshooting OSPF or EIGRP on a router. Therefore, you can use exactly the same toolkit of Cisco IOS commands on both routers and multilayer switches. Troubleshooting of data plane problems (like performance problems) is different, however, mainly because of the differences in the implementation of packet-switching process. Figure 4-17 depicts a Catalyst 6504 LAN switch and a Cisco 7206 router with some sample control and data plane commands.

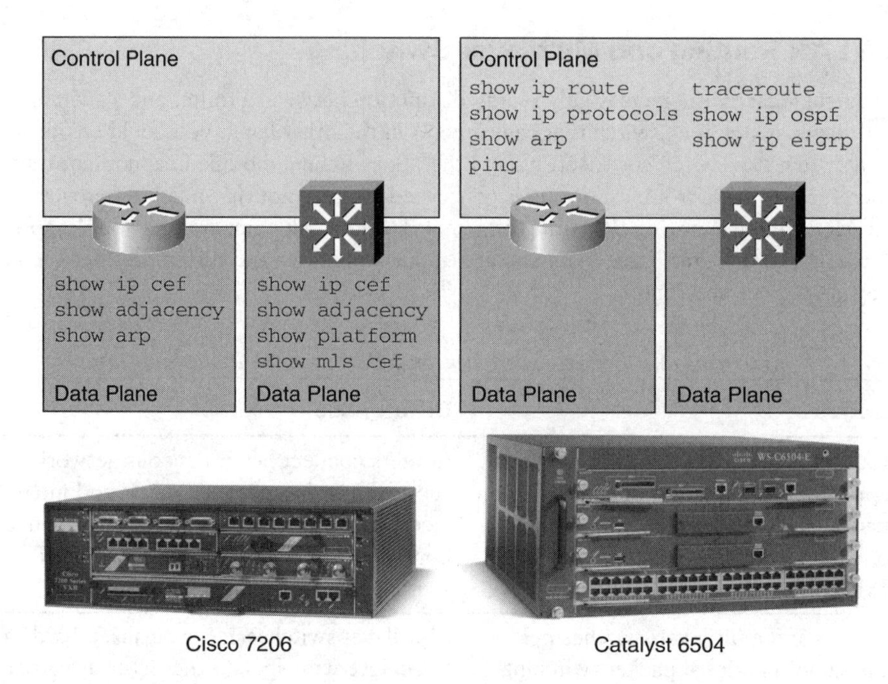

Figure 4-17 *Router, Multilayer Switch, Control Plane, and Data Plane*

Routers use Cisco Express Forwarding (CEF) as the main packet-switching mechanism. The CEF Forwarding Information Base (FIB) and adjacency table are both stored in the router's main memory and are consulted by the router to forward packets using the CEF switching method. The router builds the CEF data structures by combining information from a number of control plane data structures (the routing table and ARP cache, for example). Therefore, the information in the CEF data structures should accurately reflect the information in the control plane data structures. Under normal circumstances, checking the control plane data structures should suffice when you are troubleshooting IP routing. However, if you run into a situation where control plane information is correct, but packets are not being forwarded as expected, you might need to check the CEF data structures and verify that they are in line with the control plane information.

There are two main commands to check the CEF data structures:

- **show ip cef:** This command displays the content of the CEF FIB. The FIB reflects the content of the routing table with all the recursive lookups resolved already, and the output interface determined for each destination prefix. The FIB also holds additional entries for directly connected hosts, the router's own IP addresses, and multicast and broadcast addresses.
- **show adjacency:** This command displays the content of the CEF adjacency table. This table contains the Layer 2 frame information, such as destination MAC address, that is used to encapsulate the egress packets forwarded using CEF FIB.

Multilayer switches also use CEF for Layer 3 packet switching. Just like routers, they build the CEF FIB and adjacency table in the main memory of the Route Processor (if an RP is present). In contrast to routers, however, multilayer switches do not just use these tables for packet forwarding, but they compile and download the information contained in the CEF (FIB) into the ternary content-addressable memory (TCAM). Using specialized hardware, multilayer switches forward packets at high speeds based on the information **looked up by the TCAM.** Using specialized hardware, multilayer switches forward packets at high speeds based on the information contained in the TCAM. The term often used for the specialized hardware used by switches is *ASIC*, which is an acronym for application-specific integrated circuit.

Although the exact process and the way information is stored in the TCAMs depends on the switch hardware architecture, it is generally possible to gather information about the state of the content of the TCAMs using Cisco IOS commands. To extract information about the forwarding behavior of switches from the TCAMs on some of the common Cisco Catalyst series switches, you can use the following commands:

- **show platform:** On the Catalyst 3560, 3750 and 4500 platforms, the **show platform** family of commands can be used to obtain detailed information about the forwarding behavior of the hardware.
- **show mls cef:** On the Catalyst 6500 platform, the **show mls cef** family of commands can be used to obtain detailed information about the forwarding behavior of the hardware.

Switched Virtual Interfaces and Routed Ports

The logical operation of a multilayer switch is easier to explain using a diagram similar to the one depicted in Figure 4-18. In Figure 4-18, a Catalyst 6504 is shown and its operation is logically compared to a pair of Layer 2 switches and a router in the middle section of the figure, combined.

Figure 4-18 depicts that the multilayer switch performs the plain switching function within a VLAN, such as VLAN 10 and VLAN 20. Interfaces (ports) Fa4/1 and Fa4/2 are in VLAN 10, and interface Gi3/1 is in VLAN 20; these interfaces are regular switch ports. For each of VLANs 10 and 20, the multilayer switch has a switched virtual interface (SVI) that the devices within each VLAN can use as their default gateway. Interface Fa4/3 is configured as a routed port, so it is not in a VLAN, and it has its own IP address. The multilayer switch routes between the two SVIs and the routed interface once IP routing is enabled.

A multilayer switch provides three different core functions in a single device:

- **Layer 2 switching within each VLAN:** The traffic is switched between the ports that belong to the same VLAN. This includes traffic associated to the same VLAN transiting through a trunk connection. The MAC address tables for different VLANS are logically separated. No IP or Layer 3 configuration is necessary for this task.

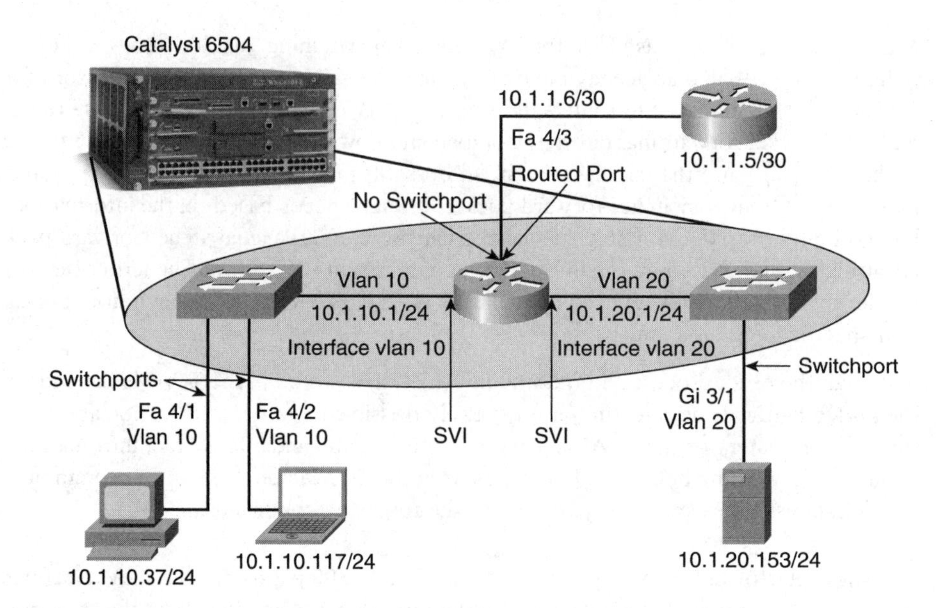

Figure 4-18 *A Logical Demonstration of a Multilayer Switch*

- **Routing and multilayer switching between the local VLANs:** To provide Layer 3 switching between VLANs connected to a switch, SVIs need to be configured. Using Cisco IOS CLI these interfaces are created using the **interface vlan** *vlan-id* command. You need to configure each of these SVIs with an appropriate IP address and subnet mask. Hosts on this subnet (VLAN) can use the SVI's IP address as their default gateway. IP routing is not enabled by default; you must enable it using the global configuration mode **ip routing** command.

- **Routing and multilayer switching between the local VLANs and one or more routed interfaces:** Modern multilayer switches allow you to change the behavior of a regular physical switched port and make it a routed port using the **no switchport** command. When you do that, the port no longer belongs to any VLAN. In other words, the traffic on this port is not bridged (switched) to any other port, and there is no logical MAC address table associated to it. This port acts like a regular router interface and needs its own IP address and subnet mask. In the absence of this feature or because of a lack of interest, you can always connect a switch port or a trunk port to an external router. The features and tools available to and applicable to routed interfaces and SVIs are not identical at this moment; this is the main motivation behind converting a switched port to a routed interface rather than just using SVIs. For example, because an SVI is associated to a VLAN, its status depends on the status of that VLAN (not active, pruned, and so on); however, a routed interface has no dependency on any VLAN's status.

Note Traditionally on Layer 2 switches, the term *port* has been used, and on routers the term *interface* has been used. With the invention of multilayer switches (Layer 3 switches), Cisco IOS merely uses the term *interface* (in multilayer switches). However, in writings and speeches, many still refer to interfaces that only do switching as *ports* and refer to the interfaces that do not do switching and route instead as *interfaces*.

The main differences between SVIs and routed interfaces are as follows:

- A routed interface is not a Layer 2 port. This means that on a routed interface typical Layer 2 protocols that are enabled by default, such as STP and Dynamic Trunking Protocol (DTP), are not active.
- A direct relationship exists between the status of a routed interface and the availability of the corresponding directly connected subnet. When/if the interface goes down, the corresponding connected route is immediately removed from the routing table.

An SVI is not a physical interface, and so it generally does not fail, but its status directly depends on the status of the VLAN with which it is associated. The rule that Catalyst LAN switches use to determine the status of an SVI is that an SVI stays up as long as there is at least one port associated to the corresponding VLAN; that port has to be up and in the spanning-tree forwarding state. Note that this rule includes both access ports and trunks that have this VLAN in their allowed VLAN list. As a result, an SVI can only go down (and the corresponding connected subnet will be removed from the routing table) when the last active port in the VLAN goes down or loses its spanning-tree forwarding status.

Troubleshooting First-Hop Redundancy Protocols

One of the important elements in building highly available networks is implementing a first-hop redundancy protocol (FHRP). Even if you have multiple routers or multilayer switches on a subnet, the clients and servers will still point to a single default gateway, and they lose connectivity to other subnets if their gateway fails. FHRPs such as the Hot Standby Router Protocol (HSRP), Virtual Router Redundancy Protocol (VRRP), and Gateway Load Balancing Protocol (GLBP) can solve this issue by providing redundant default gateway functionality in a way that is transparent to the end hosts. This section reviews the operation of common FHRPs and shows you how to use Cisco IOS commands to diagnose and resolve problems that might occur while using these protocols.

Using First-Hop Redundancy

FHRPs such as HSRP, VRRP, and GLBP all serve the same purpose: They provide a redundant default gateway on a subnet and do this in such a way that actions such as failover and load balancing remain entirely transparent to the hosts. These protocols provide a virtual IP address (and the corresponding virtual MAC address) that can be used as the default gateway by the hosts on the subnet. This virtual IP address is not bound to any particular router, but can be controlled by a router within a group of routers participating in the protocol's scheme. Under normal circumstances, at any given moment, only one router, the active router, has control over the virtual IP address. Consequently, most of the mechanisms of these protocols revolve around the following functions:

- Electing a single router that controls the virtual IP address
- Tracking availability of the active router
- Determining whether control of the virtual IP address should be handed over to another router

The example shown in Figure 4-19 shows two routers R1 and R2 with IP addresses 10.1.1.1 and 10.1.1.2 on their FastEthernet interfaces, respectively, configured with HSRP. Routers R1 and R2 have been configured for the same HSRP group (group 1) and virtual IP address (10.1.1.254). Both routers have been configured for preemption. This will allow either of them to take over the role of active router when its priority is the highest of the routers in the group. R1 has been configured with a priority of 110, which is higher than the default priority of 100. This will cause R1 to be elected as the active router, while R2 will be elected as the standby router. This means that R1 will be in control of the virtual IP address and will forward packets sent to the virtual router's IP and MAC address.

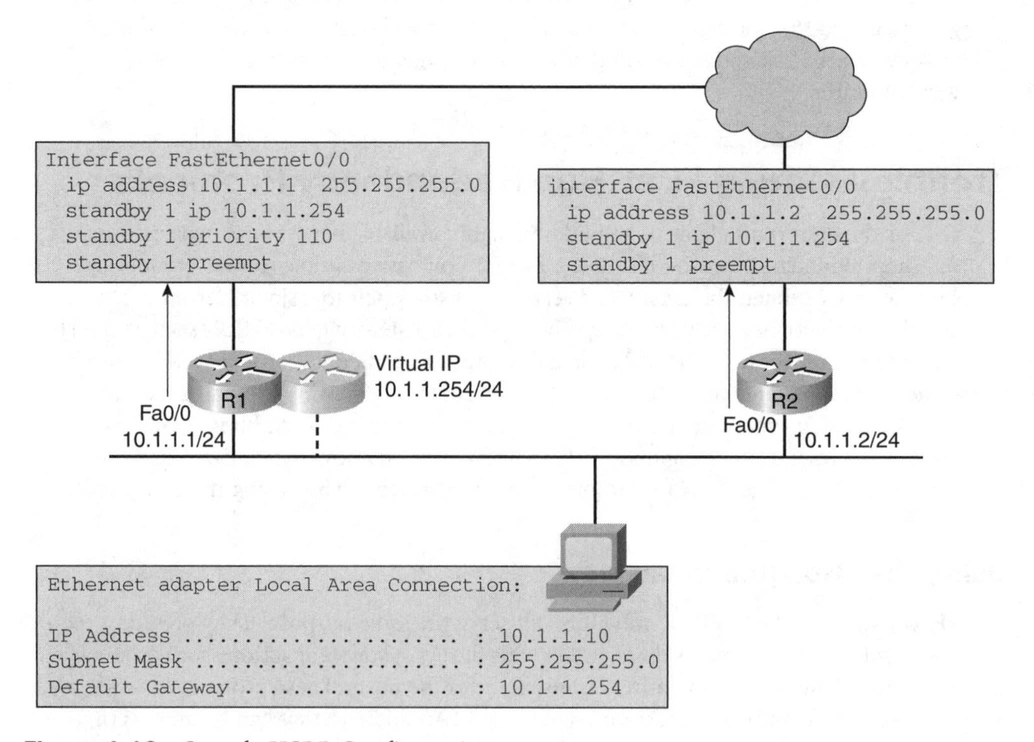

Figure 4-19 *Sample HSRP Configuration*

When a failure occurs (for example, if the Fast Ethernet interface of R1 goes down), the end hosts that are using the virtual router IP address as their default gateway lose connectivity to destinations outside of their own subnet. For a short period of time, there is no active router and, as a consequence, traffic destined for the virtual router's IP or MAC address is dropped. After detecting the loss of hello packets from R1, router R2 assumes the active role and ownership of the virtual IP and MAC addresses. At this time, the default gateway on this subnet is functioning again, and hosts within this subnet can resume communication with IP devices outside their subnet. The following types of questions are often raised about the convergence of this type of protocol and the effect on active applications:

- What effect does this process have on the network connectivity of the hosts on the subnets?
- How long does it take R2 to discover that R1 is not active any longer?
- How long before R2 takes over the packet-forwarding role?
- What will happen when R1 comes back? Will R1 take over the active router role?
- If R1 comes up, how long will it take for it to take over the active role? Will any packets be dropped during this transition?

Depending on whether the active router has failed, or if the administrator has made configuration changes, the time it takes for the backup (standby) router to take over varies. In case of a physical failure, the only way for the standby router to detect failure of the active router is through the loss of hello packets. By default, both the active and the standby router send hello packets every 3 seconds. If hellos are not received for 10 seconds (the default hold time), the standby router assumes that the active router has disappeared and takes on the active role. This means that for a period of 10 seconds (based on the default timer values), the hosts will lose connectivity because of lack of an active router to forward packets. If the failure is caused by administrative actions such as a shutdown of an interface, reload of the router, or modification of the priority value, the active HSRP router sends a "resign" message, causing the standby router to assume the active role immediately. This means that the 10-second hold time does not come into play.

The convergence for the return traffic plays a role in the overall convergence. HSRP is only involved in the convergence of outbound packets that the host sends through the default gateway. Convergence for packets returning to the host is governed by the used routing protocol's convergence, not HSRP. Therefore, the overall convergence is as fast as the protocol that is the slowest to converge, which could be either HSRP or the routing protocol.

Each router participating in the HSRP process has a priority value, and this value is 100 by default. The router with the higher priority is elected as the active HSRP router, and a tie is broken using the IP address of the contenders. When a router with a higher priority than the active HSRP router loads up or is added, the behavior depends on whether the preempt option has been configured on the added device. When a router with a higher priority **or with the same priority but a higher IP address** than the **current** active HSRP router loads up or is added, the behavior depends on what role are we looking at and whether the preempt option has been configured on the added device. An important fact to consider is that the standby role can be preempted at any time and its preemption is not influenced by the preempt option. Assuming that the preempt option has not been configured, the new router will not preempt the current active router. The router that is currently active will stay active. However, if the new router has a higher priority than the current standby router, or the same priority but a higher IP address, it will become the new standby router. It will also become a standby router if there is no standby router currently present.

If the new router has a higher priority or the same priority but a higher IP address than the current active router, and has been configured with the preempt option, however, it takes over the active role immediately. Overthrowing the standby router does not depend on the configuration of the preempt option. If no standby router is present, the new router simply takes on the standby role. If the new router has a higher priority and has been configured with the **preempt** option, however, it takes over the active role immediately. It sends out a "coup" message, telling the current active router that it will take over the active role due to its higher priority. You might wonder whether this action will cause any packet loss. The HSRP coup mechanism, in itself, does not cause packet loss because there is an active HSRP router on the segment continuously. Nevertheless, the role that the routing protocol plays cannot be ignored. If the new active router which preempted the previous one has not completed its routing convergence, it might not have a complete forwarding table yet, causing it to drop packets for a period. Therefore, it is important that the new router not assume the active role until it has fully built its routing and forwarding table. The HSRP configuration has a delay option that is used precisely for this reason.

Verifying FHRP Operation

The best way to get a quick overview of the actual HSRP status on the network is to use the **show standby brief** command. Figure 4-20 shows a sample output from this command for routers R1 and R2 that participate in HSRP group 1. For each interface, this command shows the configured HSRP group, the IP addresses for the active and standby router, the virtual IP address, configured priority, and the preemption option.

You can obtain more detailed information such as configured timers, the virtual MAC-address for the HSRP group, and information about recent HSRP state changes by using the **show standby** *interface-id* command. Figure 4-21 shows the output from this command on R1 for interface Fa0/0. This figure also shows the content of a workstation's ARP cache, which includes the virtual IP address and MAC address of the HSRP group provided by R1 and R2.

When you are troubleshooting HSRP-related problems, it is useful to know the virtual MAC address used for the standby group because it can be used to verify the correct operation of ARP and the Layer 2 connectivity between the end host and the active HSRP router. In many cases, HSRP-related problems are not really, at the root, caused by HSRP itself, but by problems in the underlying switched network. For example, a typical

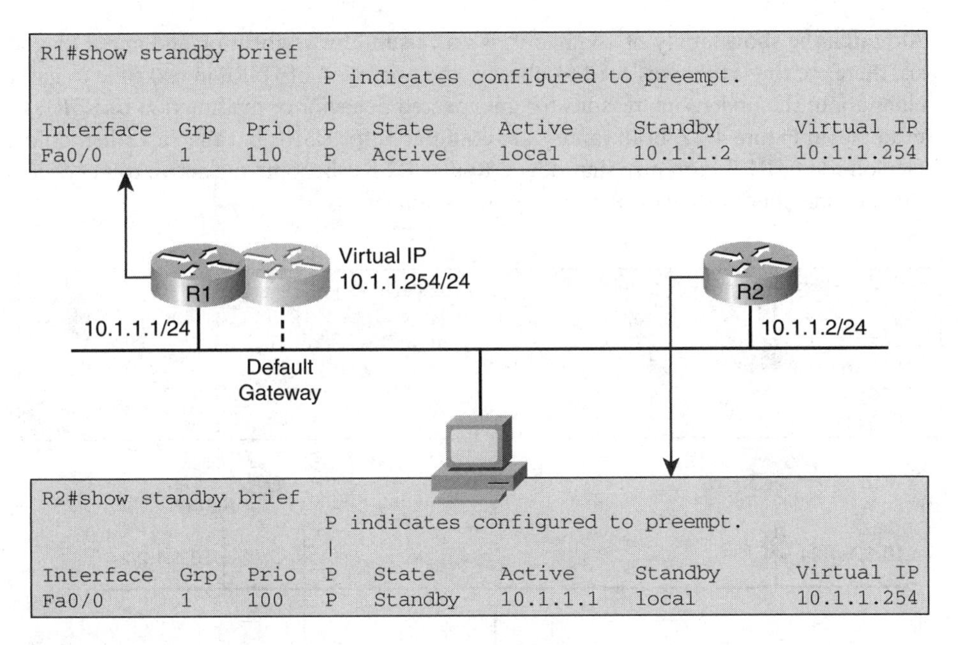

Figure 4-20 *Sample Output from the* **show standby brief** *Command*

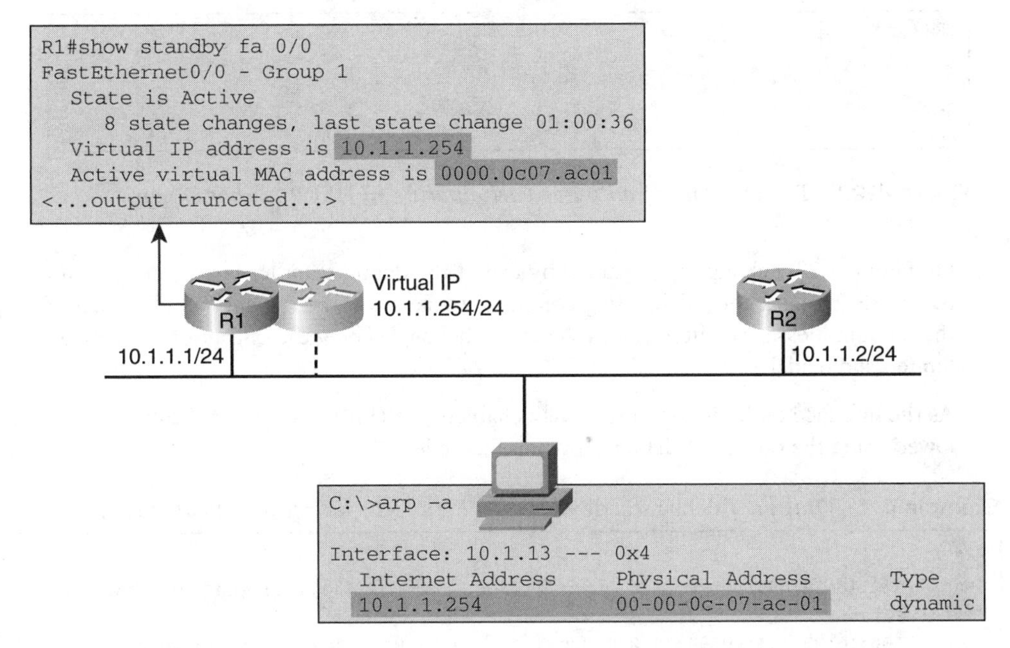

Figure 4-21 *Sample Output from the* **show standby** *interface-id Command*

symptom of a broadcast storm is that you start seeing frequent HSRP state changes on the Layer 3 switches that are connected to the affected VLANs.

Although the **show** family of commands is very useful for verification and initial diagnosis, there are times that you need to observe the operation of HSRP in real time to gather clues about the underlying reasons for unexpected behavior or malfunction of HSRP. For example, in Figure 4-22, both routers are configured for HSRP, but the FastEthernet interface on router R1 is currently shut down. Router R2 has become the active router as it is the only member of the HSRP group on that segment.

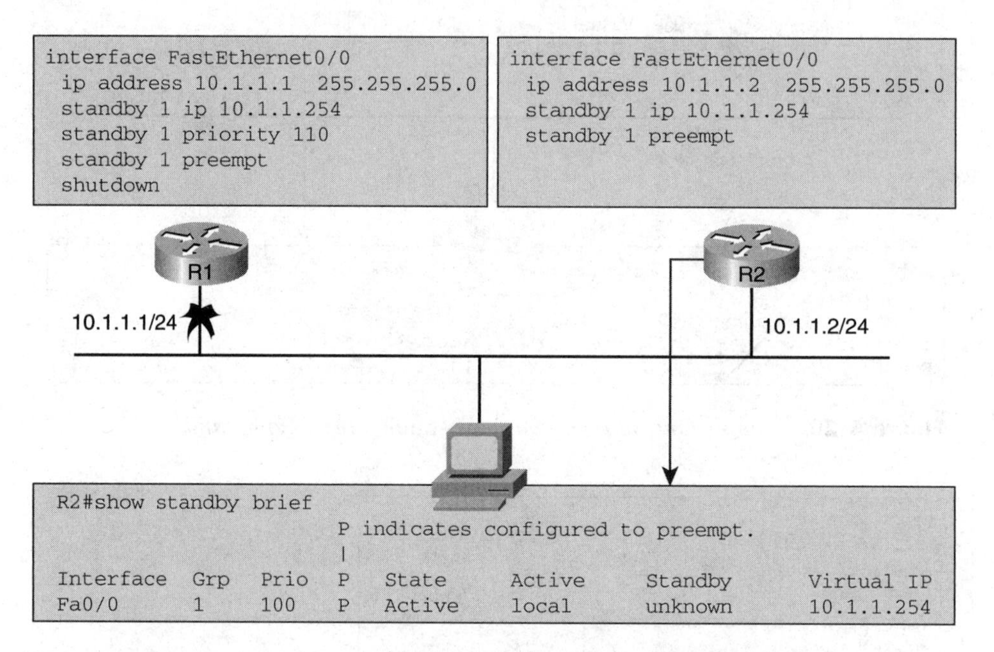

Figure 4-22 *The Interface of a Router Participating in HSRP Is Shut Down*

On Figure 4-23, debugging is enabled by use of the **debug standby terse** command for router R2. This is a good debugging command to start with because it includes most of the relevant messages, but excludes the HSRP hellos, keeping the output of the debug limited and readable.

As the interface on R1 is administratively enabled, the HSRP process on R2 can be followed using the output of **debug** shown in Example 4-7.

Example 4-7 *Output of* debug standby terse *on R2 as R1's Interface Is Enabled*

```
R2#
*Mar  1 00:16:23.555: HSRP: Fa0/0 Grp 1 Coup   in  10.1.1.1 Listen  pri 110 vIP
10.1.1.254
*Mar  1 00:16:23.555: HSRP: Fa0/0 Grp 1 Active: j/Coup rcvd from higher pri
router (110/10.1.1.1)
*Mar  1 00:16:23.555: HSRP: Fa0/0 Grp 1 Active router is 10.1.1.1, was local
*Mar  1 00:16:23.555: HSRP: Fa0/0 Grp 1 Active -> Speak
```

```
*Mar  1 00:16:23.555: %HSRP-5-STATECHANGE: FastEthernet0/0 Grp 1 state Active ->
Speak
*Mar  1 00:16:23.555: HSRP: Fa0/0 Grp 1 Redundancy "hsrp-Fa0/0-1" state Active ->
Speak
*Mar  1 00:16:33.555: HSRP: Fa0/0 Grp 1 Speak: d/Standby timer expired (unknown)
*Mar  1 00:16:33.555: HSRP: Fa0/0 Grp 1 Standby router is local
*Mar  1 00:16:33.555: HSRP: Fa0/0 Grp 1 Speak -> Standby

*Mar  1 00:16:33.555: %HSRP-5-STATECHANGE: FastEthernet0/0 Grp 1 state Speak ->
Standby
*Mar  1 00:16:33.559: HSRP: Fa0/0 Grp 1 Redundancy "hsrp-Fa0/0-1" state Speak ->
Standby
R2#
```

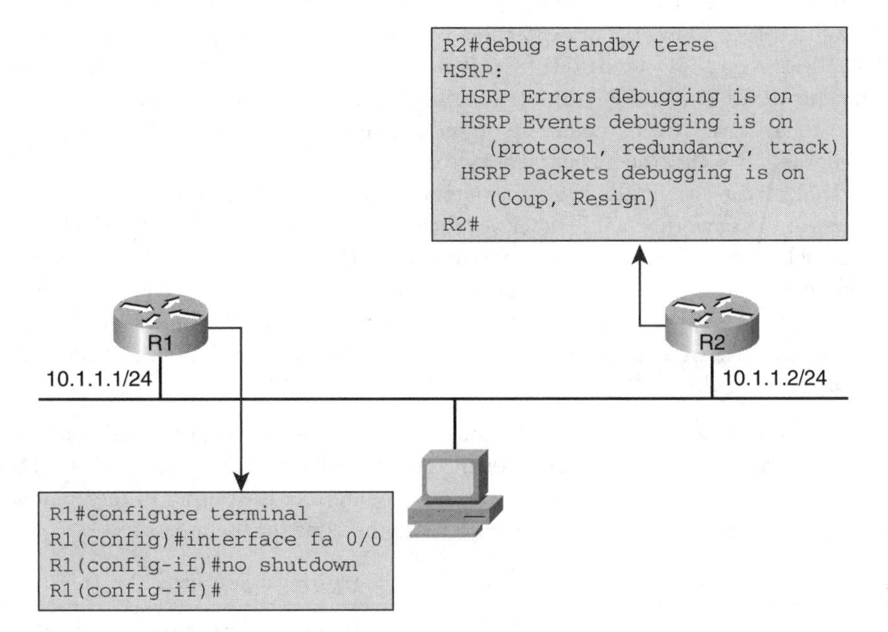

Figure 4-23 *As* **debug standby terse** *Is Enabled on R2, R1's Interface Is Enabled*

The debugging command output shown in Example 4-7 clearly shows the following actions taking place:

- When R1 comes up on the segment, because it has a higher priority than the current active router and it is configured with the **preempt** option, it sends out a "coup" message to take over the active role.
- R2 loses its active role, causing it to step back to the role of a nonactive, nonstandby HSRP router. Because there is no standby router on the segment, R2 moves to the "speak" state to announce its eligibility for the standby role.

- R2 does not see another (better) candidate for the role of standby router for 10 seconds and, thus, promotes itself to the standby role.

Alternatives to HSRP

Besides HSRP, two other protocols also provide first-hop redundancy: VRRP and GLBP. From a troubleshooting perspective, the methods that you use to troubleshoot these protocols are almost identical. The Cisco IOS commands used to troubleshoot these protocols are also similar in style to the HSRP commands. For VRRP and GLBP troubleshooting commands, you just have to replace the keyword **standby** with **vrrp** or **glbp.**

With respect to operation, some differences exist between these protocols. HSRP and GLBP always require an additional IP address to function as the virtual IP address. Consequently, this router will always be the master router for that IP address when it is up because it will automatically claim a priority of 255 that cannot be configured manually. Note that VRRP allows the priority value be manually set to a number between 1 and 254. VRRP is an IETF standard (RFC 3768), which makes it suitable for multivendor environments. HSRP and GLBP do not preempt by default. If you want a higher priority router to take over when it comes up on the segment, you have to configure the preemption option. In VRRP, the higher-priority router preempts by default, but it can be disabled. GLBP can have multiple active routers forwarding traffic for a single virtual IP address at the same time. GLBP achieves this by using multiple virtual MAC addresses for a single virtual IP address. There is still a single router that is in control of the virtual IP address and responds to ARP requests for that IP address. This router effectively balances the load over the different forwarding routers. Default hello timers are also varied: 3 seconds for HSRP, 1 second for VRRP, and 3 seconds for GLBP. Table 4-2 summarizes these differences.

Example 4-8 shows the output of the **show standby brief**, **show vrrp brief**, and **show glbp brief** commands. The structure of the major troubleshooting commands for HSRP, VRRP, and GLBP are similar. If you know how to interpret the output of the commands for one of these protocols, it is quite easy to do the same for the others.

Table 4-2 *Operational Differences Between HSRP, VRRP, and GLBP*

Feature	HSRP	VRRP	GLBP
Transparent default gateway redundancy.	Yes	Yes	Yes
Virtual IP address can also be a real address.	No	Yes	No
IETF standard.	No	Yes	No
Preempt is enabled by default.	No	Yes	No
Multiple active forwarding gateways per group.	No	No	Yes
Default hello timer (seconds).	3	1	3

Example 4-8 *The Output of the* **show** *Commands for HSRP, VRRP, and GLBP Are Similar*

```
R1# show standby brief
                     P indicates configured to preempt.
                     |
Interface   Grp Prio P State    Active          Standby         Virtual IP
Fa0/0       1   110  P Active   local           10.1.1.2        10.1.1.254
...
R1# show vrrp brief
Interface          Grp Pri Time  Own Pre State   Master addr     Group addr
Fa0/0               1   110 3570      Y  Master  10.1.1.1        10.1.1.254
...
R1# show glbp brief
Interface   Grp  Fwd Pri State    Address         Active router   Standby router
Fa0/0       1    -   110 Active   10.1.1.254      local           10.1.1.2
Fa0/0       1    1   -   Active   0007.b400.0101  local           -
Fa0/0       1    2   -   Listen   0007.b400.0102  10.1.1.2        -
```

Table 4-3 lists the typical troubleshooting commands for HSRP, VRRP, and GLBP. Note that there is no **debug terse** option for VRRP. This means that each **debug** option that you are interested in must be entered manually.

Table 4-3 *Main Troubleshooting Commands for HSRP, VRRP, and GLBP*

HSRP	VRRP	GLBP
show standby brief	show vrrp brief	show glbp brief
show standby *interface-id*	show vrrp interface *interface-id*	show glbp *interface-id*
debug standby terse	No real equivalent option exits. Multiple debug options must be used simultaneously.	debug glbp terse

Summary

Some commonly used diagnostic commands that help you obtain information about the Layer 2 switching process, VLANs, and trunks are as follows:

- **show mac address-table**
- **show vlan**
- **show interfaces trunk**
- **show interfaces switchport**
- **show platform forward interface**
- **traceroute mac**

Building the spanning tree requires the following four main steps:

Step 1. Elect a root bridge/switch.

This is based on lowest bridge ID.

Step 2. Select a root port on each nonroot bridge/switch.

This is based on least cost to root.

Ties are broken based on lowest upstream bridge ID.

Further ties are broken based on lowest port ID.

Step 3. Elect a designated port on each network segment.

This is based on least cost to root.

Ties are broken based on bridge ID.

Further ties are broken based on lowest port ID.

Step 4. Ports that ended up as neither a root port nor a designated port go into blocking state, and the root ports and designated ports go into learning, and then into forwarding state.

Important commands for gathering information about the status of STP and the corresponding topology include the following:

- **show spanning-tree** [**vlan** *vlan-id*]
- **show spanning-tree interface** *interface-id* **detail**

The consequences and corresponding symptoms of broadcast (or unknown MAC) storms include the following:

- The load on all links in the switched LAN will quickly start increasing as more and more frames enter the loop.
- If the spanning-tree failure has caused more than one bridging loop to form, traffic will increase exponentially.
- When control plane traffic start entering the loop, the devices that are running these protocols will quickly start getting overloaded, and their CPU will approach 100 percent utilization.
- Switches will experience frequent MAC address table changes.
- Because of the combination of very high load on all links and the CPU running at maximum load on Layer 3 switches or routers, these devices typically become unreachable, making it nearly impossible to diagnose the problem while it is in progress.

Three common EtherChannel problems are as follows:

- Inconsistencies between the physical ports that are members of the channel (a %EC-5-CANNOT_BUNDLE2 log message is generated)
- Inconsistencies between the ports on the opposite sides of the EtherChannel link (The switch will generate a %SPANTREE-2-CHNL_MISCFG message)
- Uneven distribution of traffic between EtherChannel bundle members

The similarities between multilayer switches and routers are as follows:

- Both routers and multilayer switches use routing protocols or static routes to maintain information about the reachability and direction to network destinations (prefixes) and record this information in a routing table.
- Both routers and multilayer switches perform the same functional packet switching actions:

Step 1. They receive a frame and strip off the Layer 2 header.

Step 2. They perform a Layer 3 lookup to determine the outbound interface and next hop.

Step 3. They encapsulate the packet in a new Layer 2 frame and transmit the frame.

The differences between multilayer switches and routers are as follows:

- Routers connect heterogeneous networks and support a wide variety of media and inter-faces. Multilayer switches typically connect homogenous networks. Nowadays, LAN switches are mostly Ethernet only.
- Multilayer switches use specialized hardware to achieve wire-speed Ethernet-to-Ethernet packet switching. Low- to mid-range routers use multipurpose hardware to perform the packet-switching process. On average, the packet-switching throughput of routers is lower than the packet-switching throughput of multilayer switches.
- Routers usually support a wider range of features, mainly because switches need specialized hardware to be able to support certain data plane features or protocols. On routers, you can often add features through a software update.

There are two main commands to check the CEF data structures:

- **show ip cef**
- **show adjacency**

To extract information about the forwarding behavior of switches from the TCAMs on some of the common Cisco Catalyst series switches, you can use the following commands:

- **show platform**
- **show mls cef**

A multilayer switch provides three different core functions in a single device:

- Layer 2 switching within each VLAN
- Routing and multilayer switching between the local VLANs
- Routing and multilayer switching between the local VLANs and one or more routed interfaces

The main differences between SVIs and router interfaces are as follows:

- A routed port is not a Layer 2 port. This means that on a routed port typical Layer 2 protocols that are enabled by default, such as STP and DTP, are not active.
- A direct relationship exists between the status of a routed port and the availability of the corresponding directly connected subnet. When/if the port goes down, the corresponding connected route is immediately removed from the routing table.

Among first-hop redundancy protocols, VRRP is the only standards-based protocol, the only one that has the **preempt** option enabled by default, and the only one that allows the virtual IP address to also be a real address assigned to one of the participating routers. VRRP's default hello timer is 1 second, as opposed to HSRP's and GLBP's 3-second default hello timer. Among HSRP, VRRP, and GLBP, only GLBP makes use of multiple routers in the group to do simultaneous forwarding (load balancing). With respect to **debug**, VRRP does not have the **terse** option, but HSRP and GLBP do.

Review Questions

Use the questions here to review what you learned in this chapter. The correct answers are found in Appendix A, "Answers to Chapter Review Questions."

1. Figure 4-24 shows a frame containing an ARP reply from Host B in response to a request from Host A as it traverses the 802.1Q trunk between the switches. What is the destination MAC address for that frame?

   a. The MAC address of Host A

   b. The MAC address of Host B

   c. The broadcast MAC address ffff.ffff.ffff

   d. The 801.1Q multicast MAC address 0180.C200.0000

2. Figure 4-25 shows a frame encapsulating an ARP reply from Host B in response to a request from Host A as it traverses the 802.1Q trunk between the switches. Which two items do the values 0x0806 and 0x8100 in the type fields represent?

   a. The value 0x0806 indicates that this frame is an 802.1Q frame.

   b. The value 0x8100 indicates that this frame is an 802.1Q frame.

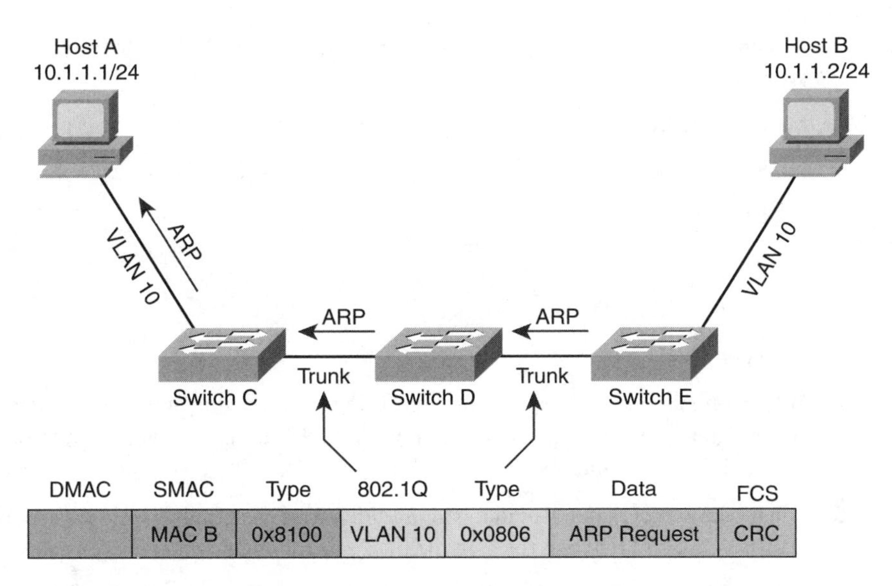

Figure 4-24 *What Is the Destination MAC Address for the Frame?*

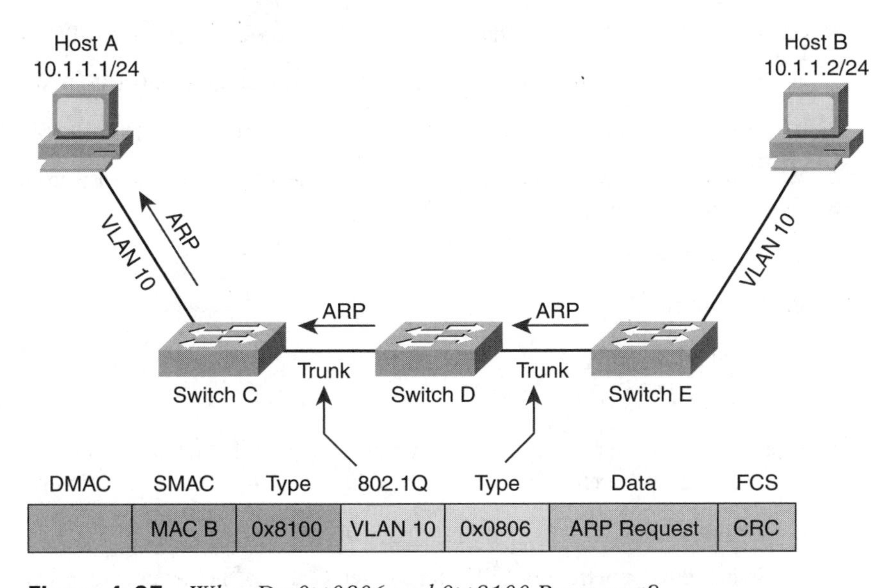

Figure 4-25 *What Do 0×0806 and 0×8100 Represent?*

c. The value 0x0806 indicates that the data inside this frame belongs to the ARP protocol.

d. The value 0x8100 indicates that the data inside this frame belongs to the ARP protocol.

3. Which three of the following items are recorded in the MAC address table of a switch?

   a. MAC address
   b. Switch port
   c. IP address
   d. VLAN
   e. Trunk or access port status
   f. Type

4. What command combines information from the **show vlan** and **show interfaces trunk** commands, in addition to other VLAN-related information, such as the voice VLAN of an interface?

5. What data structure of a switch can provide proof that frames from a particular host have passed through the switch?

6. What is the correct order in which the IEEE 802.1D Spanning Tree Protocol evaluates the following criteria to select a root port?

   a. The lowest bridge ID in the received bridge protocol data units (BPDUs)
   b. The lowest port ID in the received bridge protocol data units (BPDUs)
   c. The lowest root path cost in the received bridge protocol data units (BPDUs)

7. Which two of the following port roles will be transitioned to the forwarding state by the Spanning Tree Protocol?

   a. Alternate port
   b. Root port
   c. Backup port
   d. Designated port

8. Based on the output of the **show** command in Figure 4-26, what was the reason that Switch B was preferred over Switch A during the root bridge election process?

   a. Switch B has a better (lower) priority than switch A.
   b. Switch B has a better port value for the Ten Gigabit Ethernet port than switch A.
   c. Switch B has a better (lower) bridge ID than switch A.
   d. Switch B has a better (lower) cost for the Ten Gigabit Ethernet port than switch A.

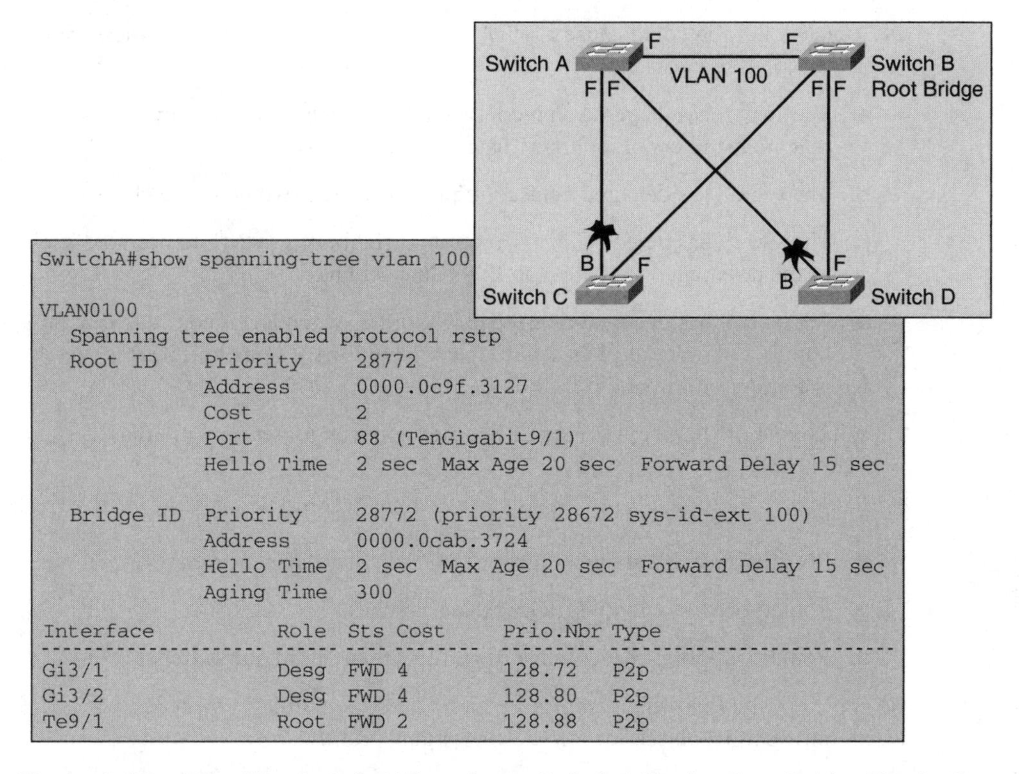

```
SwitchA#show spanning-tree vlan 100

VLAN0100
  Spanning tree enabled protocol rstp
  Root ID    Priority    28772
             Address     0000.0c9f.3127
             Cost        2
             Port        88 (TenGigabit9/1)
             Hello Time  2 sec  Max Age 20 sec  Forward Delay 15 sec

  Bridge ID  Priority    28772 (priority 28672 sys-id-ext 100)
             Address     0000.0cab.3724
             Hello Time  2 sec  Max Age 20 sec  Forward Delay 15 sec
             Aging Time  300

Interface           Role  Sts Cost      Prio.Nbr Type
------------------- ----- --- --------- -------- --------------------------
Gi3/1               Desg  FWD 4         128.72   P2p
Gi3/2               Desg  FWD 4         128.80   P2p
Te9/1               Root  FWD 2         128.88   P2p
```


Figure 4-26 *Why Was Switch B Elected over Switch A During Root Bridge Election?*

9. Which three of the following symptoms indicate that a bridging loop might exist in the network?

a. The CPU load of the switches approaches 100 percent utilization.

b. MAC addresses flap frequently between ports of the switch.

c. Time To Live (TTL) expired messages are received by the hosts.

d. The load on the WAN links in the network approaches 100 percent utilization.

e. Layer 3 switches report frequent HSRP state changes.

10. What can you do to restore the network to a stable condition, when you have determined that a broadcast storm might be happening on the network and you have lost all remote connectivity to the switches?

11. Which condition could cause a %SPANTREE-2-CHNL_MISCFG log message to be generated by a switch?

- **a.** The switch has detected an inconsistency between two of its physical ports that are members of an EtherChannel.
- **b.** The switch has detected a misconfiguration of the spanning-tree channel.
- **c.** The switch has detected an attempt of a neighboring switch to promote itself to the designated switch on an EtherChannel link.
- **d.** The switch has detected that the neighboring switch is not configured to bundle a number of physical interfaces in an EtherChannel, while this switch is configured to bundle the links.

12. Which two of the following are differences between routers and multilayer switches?

- **a.** Routers support a wider variety of media than multilayer switches.
- **b.** Routers can achieve higher throughput than multilayer switches.
- **c.** Routers are less energy efficient than switches.
- **d.** Routers support a wider range of features than multilayer switches.

13. Which of the following commands can be used on multilayer switches, but not on routers to troubleshoot Layer 3 forwarding problems?

- **a.** **show ip cef**
- **b.** **show ip route**
- **c.** **show adjacency**
- **d.** **show platform**
- **e.** None of these options are correct. All commands necessary to troubleshoot Layer 3 forwarding are available on both routers and multilayer switches.

14. SVIs and routed ports are both capable of running DTP. True or False?

- **a.** True
- **b.** False

15. Which two of the following conditions need to be met for an SVI to be up?

- **a.** The VLAN corresponding to the SVI must exist in the VLAN database of the switch.
- **b.** There must be at least one access port assigned to the VLAN corresponding to the SVI.
- **c.** There must be at least one interface in the spanning-tree forwarding state for the VLAN corresponding to the SVI.
- **d.** The VLAN corresponding to the SVI must have been advertised by VTP.

16. Based on the configurations shown in Figure 4-27, which router do you predict will be the active router for standby group 1 and for which reason?

a. Router R1, because it has the lowest IP address.

b. Router R2, because it has the highest IP address.

c. Router R1, because it has the highest priority.

d. Router R2, because it has the highest priority, the default priority of 200.

e. There is not enough information to answer the question. It will depend on the order in which the routers are enabled.

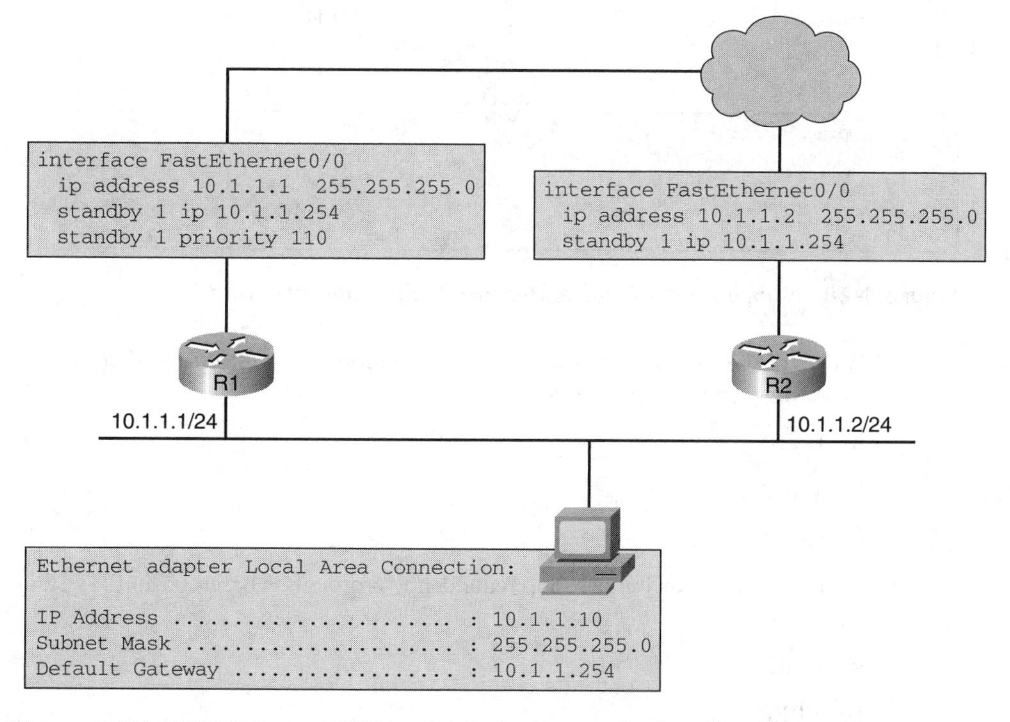

Figure 4-27 *Which Router Will Be the Active Router for Standby Group 1?*

17. Based on the output of the commands displayed in Figure 4-28, which router is the active router for standby group 1 and for what reason?

a. Router R1, because it has the lowest IP address

b. Router R2, because it has the highest IP address

c. Router R1, because it has the highest priority

d. Router R2, because it has the lowest priority

e. Router R1, because it was enabled first

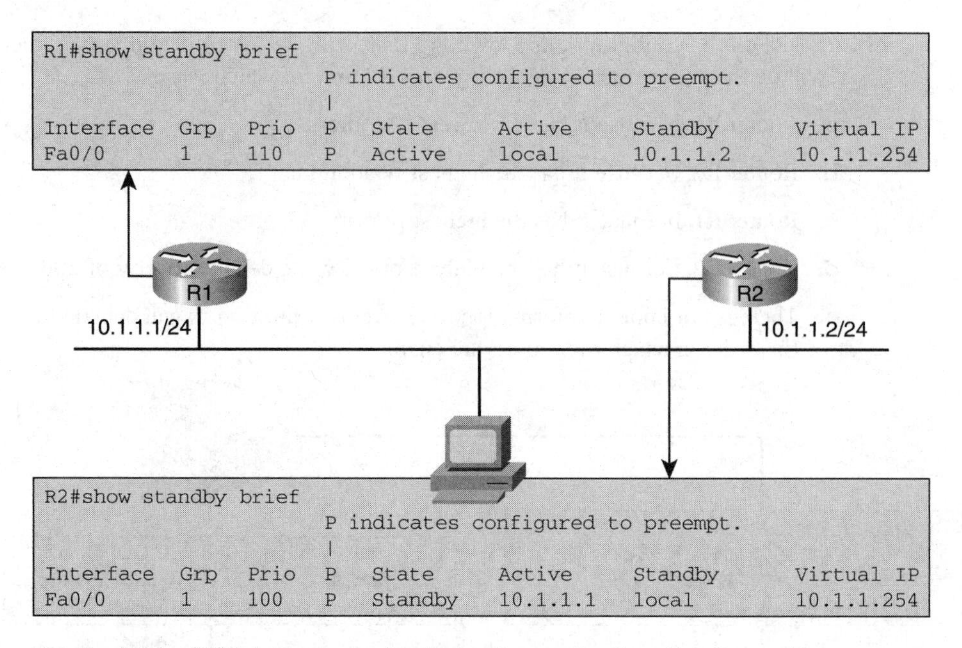

Figure 4-28 *Which Router Is the Active Router for Standby Group 1?*

18. Which of the following first-hop redundancy protocols supports multiple active forwarding gateways per group?

a. HSRP

b. VRRP

c. GLBP

19. Which of the following first-hop redundancy protocols is based on an IETF standard?

a. HSRP

b. VRRP

c. GLBP

20. For which of the following first-hop redundancy protocols is preemption the default behavior?

a. HSRP

b. VRRP

c. GLBP

Chapter 5

Maintaining and Troubleshooting Routing Solutions

This chapter covers the following topics:

- Troubleshooting network layer connectivity
- Troubleshooting EIGRP
- Troubleshooting OSPF
- Troubleshooting route redistribution
- Troubleshooting BGP

TCP/IP is the dominant networking protocol suite within modern networks. Internet Protocol (IP) routing takes place in almost all parts of an enterprise network, and it facilitates communication within a campus network, between branch and headquarter offices, to and from the Internet, and among virtual private network (VPN) sites. Border Gateway Protocol (BGP) is the only routing protocol capable of inter-autonomous system (liner-AS) or interdomain routing. Enhanced Interior Gateway Routing Protocol (EIGRP) or Open Shortest Path First (OSPF) Protocol, are the most preferred intra-autonomous system (intra-AS) or interior routing protocols. A good understanding of EIGRP, OSPF, BGP, route redistribution mechanisms, network layer connectivity in general, and the ability to diagnose and resolve problems associated with these technologies is therefore essential to any network engineer.

Troubleshooting Network Layer Connectivity

For most connectivity problems in IP networks, the network layer is the point where troubleshooting processes start. Examining network layer connectivity between two hosts helps determine whether the problem cause is at the same, lower, or higher layer than the network layer of the Open Systems Interconnection (OSI) model. If network layer connectivity between two hosts is functional, the problem is more likely to be caused by application issues or security-related problems. On the other hand, lack of network layer connectivity indicates that the problem is at or below network layer. A network engineer should have the skills and knowledge to diagnose and resolve these problems in an efficient manner. This can be accomplished by comprehending the processes and data structures used by routers to forward IP packets and the Cisco IOS tools that can be used to diagnose those types of problems.

Routing and Routing Data Structures

To troubleshoot Layer 3 connectivity, you need to have a good understanding of the processes involved in routing a packet from a host through multiple routers to the final destination. Figure 5-1 shows an IP network with IP Hosts A and B on the opposite ends of the network, interconnected by two networks and Routers C, D, and E.

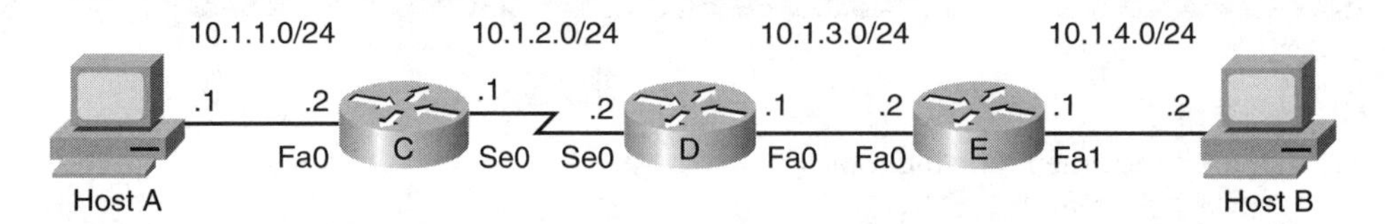

Figure 5-1 *Which Processes and Data Structures Are Involved in Sending Packets from Host A to Host B and Back?*

As a network support and troubleshooting professional, you need to be able to answer the following questions about the data structures used and the processes involved in the packet exchange process between Hosts A and B, on all the devices:

Step 1. Which decisions does host A make, what information does it need, and which actions does it perform to successfully send a packet destined for host B to the first hop Router C?

Step 2. Which decisions does Router C make, what information does it need, and which actions does it perform to successfully send the packet from Host A destined for Host B to the next hop Router D?

Step 3. Which decisions does Router D make, what information does it need, and which actions does it perform to successfully send the packet from Host A destined for Host B to the next hop Router E? Is the answer to this question the same as the answer to the previous question or are there any differences?

Step 4. Which decisions does Router E make, what information does it need, and which actions does it perform to successfully send the packet from Host A destined for Host B to its final destination, Host B?

Step 5. Are there any differences in the processes and information required to successfully transmit return packets from Host B back to Host A?

If the source host or any of the routers in the path are not capable of forwarding packets, because of the lack of proper configuration or the required forwarding information, the packets are dropped, and Layer 3 connectivity is lost.

The sequence of the major processes, decisions, and actions that take place on the end devices and the intermediate devices (routers) is as follows:

Step 1. When Host A starts the process to send a packet to Host B, it first determines whether the destination network is the same or different from its own local subnet. This is done by comparing the destination IP address (10.1.4.2) to its own IP address and subnet mask (10.1.1.1/24). Host A concludes that the destination is not local, and therefore it attempts to forward the packet to its default gateway, which is known through manual configuration or learned through Dynamic Host Configuration Protocol (DHCP). To encapsulate the packet in an Ethernet frame, Host A needs the MAC address of the default gateway. This can be resolved using the Address Resolution Protocol (ARP). Host A will either already have an entry in its ARP cache for the default gateway IP address or, alternatively, it will send out an ARP request to obtain the information and populate the cache.

Step 2. Router C de-encapsulates the IP packet from the received Ethernet frame and examines the destination IP address of the IP packet. Router C decrements the Time To Live (TTL) field in the IP header of the packet by one. If this causes the TTL field to be set to zero, Router C will discard the packet and send an Internet Control Message Protocol (ICMP) "time exceeded" message back to the source, Host A. If the TTL of the packet is not reduced to zero the router performs a forwarding table lookup to find the longest prefix that matches the destination IP address of the packet being processed. In this example, Router C finds the entry 10.1.4.0/24 as the best match for the destination address of the packet (10.1.4.2). Two important parameters are associated with this entry: the next-hop IP address 10.1.2.2 and the egress interface Serial 0. This serial interface uses the High-Level Data Link Control (HDLC) protocol on Layer 2. Because this protocol does not require a MAC address or other form of Layer 2 address for the next-hop IP address, no further lookups are necessary. Router C encapsulates the packet (datagram) in a HDLC frame and transmits it out of interface Serial 0.

Step 3. Router D goes through the same general process as Router C. It also finds an entry for prefix 10.1.4.0/24 in its forwarding table. In this case, the next hop is 10.1.3.2, and the egress interface is FastEthernet 0. The biggest difference with the previous step is the Layer 2 protocol of the egress interface. Because this is a Fast Ethernet interface, the router might have to make use of ARP to resolve the next-hop IP address 10.1.3.2 to a MAC address. Normally, Router D has this address recorded in its Cisco Express Forwarding (CEF) adjacency table and need not use ARP. Router D encapsulates the packet in an Ethernet frame and forwards it to the next hop, Router E.

Step 4. The process on Router E is similar to the process on Router C and Router D. The most important difference is that the entry for prefix 10.1.4.0/24 that Router E finds in the routing table is listed as being directly connected to interface FastEthernet 1. Therefore, instead of forwarding the packet to a next-hop router, Router E forwards the packet directly to the destination Host

B on the connected network. Because the Layer 2 protocol in this example is again Ethernet, Router E consults its ARP cache to find the MAC address for Host B (10.1.4.2). Host B's MAC address might or might not be present in Router E's ARP cache. Therefore, Router E might have to send an ARP request out and obtain Host B's MAC address. Router E encapsulates the packet in an Ethernet frame destined for Host B and transmits the frame out of its FastEthernet 1 interface. When Host B receives the packet, this concludes the transmission of a packet from Host A to Host B.

Step 5. The process in sending return packets from Host B to Host A is similar. However, the information used in the lookups in the routing table and Layer 3 to Layer 2 mapping tables, such as the ARP cache, is different. For the return packets, the destination IP address is 10.1.1.1, so instead of entries for subnet 10.1.4.0/24, entries for subnet 10.1.1.0/24 will have to be present in all router forwarding tables. These entries will have different associated egress interfaces and next-hop IP addresses. As a result, the corresponding ARP cache entries for those next hops need to be present, and these differ from the entries that were used on the path from Host A to Host B. Consequently, you cannot conclude that if packets are successfully forwarded from Host A to Host B, return packets from Host B to Host A will automatically be successful, too. This is a wrong assumption made by many people.

When you find that there is no network layer connectivity between two hosts, a good method to troubleshoot the problem is to track the path of the packet from router to router, similar to the method of tracking the path of a frame from switch to switch to diagnose Layer 2 problems. Along the way, you have to verify the availability of a matching route in the forwarding table for the destination of the packet and, subsequently, the availability of a Layer 3 to Layer 2 address mapping for the next hop for those technologies that require a Layer 2 address, such as Ethernet. For any type of application that requires two-way communication, you have to track the packets in both directions. Availability of the correct routing information and Layer 3 to Layer 2 mappings for packets traveling in one direction does not imply that the correct information is available for packets traveling in the opposite direction, too.

Based on the processes that take place in the example presented in Figure 5-1, as packets from Host A are forwarded across multiple router hops (Routers C, D, and E) to Host B, the correct values for the packet and frame header address fields are shown in Table 5-1.

To forward packets, a router combines information from various control plane data structures. The most important of these data structures is the routing table. Unlike switches, which flood a frame to all ports if its destination MAC address is not known by the MAC address table, routers drop any packet for which they cannot find a matching entry in the routing table. When a packet has to be forwarded, the routing table is searched for the longest possible prefix that matches the destination IP address of the packet. Associated with this entry is an egress interface and, in most cases, a next-hop IP address.

For point-to-point egress interfaces, such as a serial interface running PPP or HDLC, a point-to-point Frame Relay or point-to-point Asynchronous Transfer Mode (ATM)

Table 5-1 *Packet and Frame Header Address Fields on the Packet in Transit*

Packet Position	Source IP Address	Destination IP Address	Source MAC Address	Destination MAC Address
From Host A to Router C	10.1.1.1	10.1.4.2	Host A's MAC address	MAC address of interface Fa0 on router C
From Router C to Router D	10.1.1.1	10.1.4.2	Not applicable	Not Applicable
From Router D to Router E	10.1.1.1	10.1.4.2	MAC address of Router D's Fa0 interface	MAC address of router E's Fa0 interface
From Router E to Host B	10.1.1.1	10.1.4.2	MAC address of router E's Fa1 interface	Host B's MAC Address

subinterface, a next-hop IP address is not mandatory, because all the information that is necessary to construct the frame and encapsulate the packet can be derived from the egress interface itself. For example, in the case of Frame Relay, a point-to-point subinterface has a single associated data-link connection identifier (DLCI), so there is no need to map the next-hop IP address to a DLCI to be able to construct the Frame Relay frame header and encapsulate the packet. For multipoint egress interfaces, such as Ethernet interfaces or multipoint Frame Relay or ATM subinterfaces, the next-hop IP address is a mandatory element because it is used to find the correct Layer 2 destination address or other Layer 2 identifier to construct the frame and encapsulate the packet. The mapping between the next hop-IP address and the Layer 2 address or identifier is stored in a data structure specific for that Layer 2 protocol. For example, in the case of Ethernet, this information is stored in the ARP cache, and in the case of Frame Relay, the information is stored in the Frame Relay map table. Consequently, a routing table lookup may need to be followed up by a lookup in a Layer 3 to Layer 2 mapping table to gather all the necessary information required to construct a frame, encapsulate the packet, and transmit it.

Executing different table lookups and combining the information to construct a frame every time a packet needs to be routed is an inefficient approach to forwarding IP packets. To improve this process and increase the performance of IP packet-switching operations on routers, Cisco has developed Cisco Express Forwarding (CEF). This advanced Layer 3 IP switching mechanism can be used on all routers, and is at the core of the Layer 3 switching technology used in Cisco Catalyst multilayer switches. On most platforms, the CEF switching method is enabled by default.

CEF combines the information from the routing table and other data structures, such as Layer 3 to Layer 2 mapping tables, into two new data structures: the Forwarding Information Base (FIB) and the CEF adjacency table. The FIB mostly reflects the routing table with all the recursive lookups resolved. A lookup in the FIB results in a pointer to an adjacency entry in the CEF adjacency table. Similar to an entry from the routing table, an adjacency table entry can consist of an egress interface only for a point-to-point interface or an egress interface and next-hop IP address for a multipoint interface.

Using IOS Commands to Verify Routing Functions

To determine the information that is used to forward packets, you can verify the availability of specific routing entry (prefix) in the routing table or the CEF FIB table.

Note Since the release of RFC 3222 in 2001, the routing table is also called Routing Information Base (RIB) by many. Note that during discussions about protocols such as BGP and OSPF, the collection of the best paths to different destinations are referred to as BGP RIB or OSPF RIB, too. However, you must remember that BGP, OSPF, or any protocol's best path to any destination might or might not be installed in the IP routing table (or the generic IP RIB). The reason is that when there are multiple alternatives, the IP process installs paths with the smallest administrative distance in the IP routing table (or the generic IP RIB).

The choice of whether to check the IP routing table or the FIB depends on what you are exactly trying to diagnose. To diagnose control plane problems, such as the exchange of routing information by routing protocols, the **show ip route** command is a clear choice because it contains all the control plane details for a route, such as the advertising routing protocol, routing source, administrative distance, and routing protocol metrics. To diagnose problems more closely related to the data plane, for example by tracking the exact traffic flow between two hosts through the network, the FIB is often the best choice because it contains all the details that are necessary to make packet-switching decisions.

To display the content of the IP routing table, you can use the following commands:

- **show ip route** *ip-address*: Supplying the destination IP address as an option to the **show ip route** command causes the router to perform a routing table lookup for that IP address and display the best route that matches the address and all associated control plane details. (Note that the default route will never be displayed as a match for an IP address.)
- **show ip route** *network mask*: The provided network and mask as options to this command request the routing table to be searched for an exact match (for that network and mask). If an exact match is found, this entry is displayed with all of its associated control plane details.
- **show ip route** *network mask* **longer-prefixes:** The **longer-prefixes** option causes the router to display all prefixes in the routing table that fall within the prefix specified by the *network* and *mask* parameters. This command can prove useful to diagnose problems related to route summarization.

To display the content of the CEF FIB table, you can use the following commands:

- **show ip cef** *ip-address*: This command is similar to the **show ip route** *ip-address* command, but it searches the FIB rather than the routing table. Therefore, the displayed results do not include any routing protocol-related information, but only the information necessary to forward packets. (Note that this command will display the default route if it is the best match for a particular IP address.)

- **show ip cef** *network mask*: This is similar to the **show ip route** *network mask* command, but it displays information from the FIB rather than the routing table (RIB).
- **show ip cef exact-route** *source destination*: This command displays the exact adjacency that will be used to forward a packet with source and destination IP addresses, as specified by the source and destination parameters. The main reason to use this command is in a situation when you are tracking a packet flow across the routed network but the routing table and FIB contain two or more equal routes for a particular prefix. In this case, the CEF mechanisms will balance the traffic load across the multiple adjacencies associated with that prefix. By use of this command, you can determine which of the possible adjacencies is used to forward packets for a specific source and destination IP address pair.

After the egress interface and, in case of multipoint interfaces, a next-hop IP address for the destination of a packet has been determined by the routing table or FIB, the router needs to construct a frame for the data link layer protocol associated with the egress interface. Depending on the data link layer used on the egress interface, the header of this frame will require some connection specific parameters, such as source and destination MAC addresses for Ethernet, DLCI for Frame Relay, or virtual path identifier/virtual channel identifier (VPI/VCI) for ATM. These data link layer parameters are stored in various different data structures. For point-to-point (sub-) interfaces, the relation between the interface and data link identifier or address is usually statically configured. For multipoint (sub-) interfaces, the relation between the next-hop IP address and the data link identifier and address can be manually configured or dynamically resolved through some form of an address resolution protocol. The commands to display the statically configured or dynamically obtained mappings are unique for each data link layer technology. Research the command references for the data link layer protocol that you are troubleshooting to find the appropriate commands. Commands that enable you to verify the Layer 3 to Layer 2 mappings include the following:

- **show ip arp:** You can use this command to verify the dynamic IP address to Ethernet MAC address mappings that were resolved by ARP. Routers cache this information for four hours by default. If you need to refresh the content of the ARP cache, you can enter the **clear ip arp** command to clear all or a particular entry from the ARP cache.
- **show frame-relay map:** This command lists all the mappings of next-hop IP addresses on multipoint (sub-) interfaces to the DLCI of the corresponding permanent virtual circuit (PVC). These mappings may have been manually configured or dynamically resolved using Frame Relay inverse ARP. In addition, this command lists any DLCIs that were manually associated to specific point-to-point subinterfaces.

When CEF is used as the switching method, the information from the various Layer 2 data structures is used to construct a frame header for each adjacency that is listed in the adjacency table. You can display the full frame header that will be used to encapsulate the packet via the **show adjacency detail** command. In addition, this command displays packet and byte counters for all traffic that was forwarded using this particular adjacency entry. Certain troubleshooting cases require verifying the Layer 3 to Layer 2 mappings. If the routing table or the FIB lists the correct next-hop IP address and egress interface for a particular destination, but packets do not arrive at that next hop, you should verify the Layer 3 to Layer 2 mappings for the data link protocol that is used on the egress interface. Specifically, verify that a correct frame header is constructed to encapsulate the packets and forward them to the next hop.

Troubleshooting EIGRP

The Enhanced Interior Gateway Routing Protocol (EIGRP) is a Cisco Systems proprietary interior gateway or intra-autonomous system routing protocol. This means that EIGRP is used inside an enterprise network for computing best paths and exchange of routing information among the routers. EIGRP is one of the routing protocols commonly used in any size, even large, enterprise networks. Troubleshooting problems related to the exchange of routing information is one of the most essential skills for a network engineer who is involved in the implementation and maintenance of enterprise networks. To diagnose and resolve problems related to EIGRP, you must be able to do the following:

- Apply your knowledge of EIGRP data structures to plan the gathering of necessary information as part of a structured approach to troubleshooting EIGRP routing problems.
- Apply your knowledge of the processes that EIGRP uses to exchange routing information to interpret and analyze the information that is gathered during an EIGRP troubleshooting process.
- Use Cisco IOS commands to gather information from the EIGRP data structures and track the flow of EIGRP routing information to troubleshoot EIGRP operation.

EIGRP Routing Review

Network layer connectivity depends on having correct, consistent, and up-to-date routing information available in all routers. To forward packets correctly between hosts across a routed network, all routing tables in the path between the source and the destination need to have an entry for the destination network in their routing tables. The information used to select the best path needs to be consistent, to ensure that no routing loops occur. The information also needs to be up-to-date, to ensure that traffic will not be forwarded toward a broken link or a failed router. Although static routing can be efficiently deployed in relatively small environments or in networks that do not incorporate a lot of redundant elements at the network layer, many large routed enterprise networks deploy a routing protocol to exchange routing information in a highly scalable manner and to ensure that routing information accurately reflects changes in the state of the network. At a high level, each routing protocol consists of the following elements and processes:

- **Reception of routing information from neighbors:** Through routing protocol updates, each router learns about the availability of paths to other (nonconnected) subnets. Interior gateway protocol (IGP) updates are exchanged among routers that are Layer 2 adjacent, commonly called *neighbors*. Some protocols, such as EIGRP, OSPF, or Intermediate System-to-Intermediate System (IS-IS), have a process to establish a neighbor relationship before exchanging routing information. Other protocols, such as Routing Information Protocol (RIPv2) simply accept routes that they receive without building a neighbor session first.
- **Routing protocol data structures:** Most modern routing protocols have their own data structures where they store the routing updates that they receive from their neighbors, the locally connected or injected routes (static), or the routes redistributed from other routing protocols. Some older routing protocols, such as RIP (Version 1), do not have data structures of their own, but install and store their routing information directly in the routing table.
- **Route injection or redistribution:** All routing information originates at a certain device in the network. All IGPs inject directly connected routes, which are associated with the interfaces that the routing protocol is activated for, into their data structures, and advertise them out to their neighbors. Routes from other sources can also be specifically redistributed into the protocol's data structures and advertised out to the neighbors.
- **Route selection and installation:** For each prefix stored in its data structures, a routing protocol selects one or more paths as the best for that particular prefix from all the available alternatives. Different routing protocols use different algorithms to calculate the best path. Best path selection is based on the routing protocol's metric. Multiple paths for the same prefix will only be selected (as best) if their metrics are identical (unless the protocol, such as EIGRP, supports unequal cost load balancing). The routing protocol offers its best paths to each prefix to the IP routing table. If multiple routing protocols offer paths for the same prefix to the IP routing table, the administrative distance of the routing protocols involved will determine which routing protocol succeeds in installing its path. The path with lower administrative distance is preferred and will be installed in the IP routing table.
- **Transmission of routing information to neighbors:** Routing information learned from other routers, plus those injected or redistributed into the routing protocol data structures, are forwarded to neighboring routers that run the same protocol. As stated about the reception of routing information, some routing protocols, such as EIGRP, OSPF, or IS-IS, require a neighbor relationship to be established before any exchange of routing information, whereas other protocols such as RIP just broadcast or multicast their information to any adjacent router that is listening.

These generic elements, behaviors, and processes help us understand the flow of information among neighboring routers, inside the router, and between the routing protocol data structures and the routing table. A main trigger that makes us start troubleshooting routing protocol operation is discovering a router that is missing routing information or has incorrect information in the routing table. That router will drop packets or send traffic out of the wrong egress interface or to the wrong next hop. Understanding these generic processes helps us establish a troubleshooting plan and track the flow of routing information as it is propagated by the routing protocol. Most of the principles used to troubleshoot one routing protocol apply to other routing protocols, too.

EIGRP stores its operational data, configured parameters, and statistics in three main data structures:

- **Interface table:** This table lists all interfaces that have been enabled for the processing of EIGRP packets, such as hellos, updates, queries, replies, and acknowledgments. Passive interfaces are not listed in this table.
- **Neighbor table:** This table is used to keep track of all active EIGRP neighbors. Neighbors are added to this table based on the reception of hello packets, and they are removed when a neighbors hold-time expires or when the associated interface goes down or is removed from the interface table. This table is also used to keep track of the status of any routing information exchanges between the router and its neighbors.
- **Topology table:** This table holds all the routes that were received from neighboring routers, locally injected, or redistributed into EIGRP. For each prefix, EIGRP selects the best path from among the available possible paths stored in this table to be offered to the IP routing table. EIGRP's best path selection is based on the diffusing update algorithm (DUAL). If multiple paths have the exact same metric, all entries that share that same metric are selected for installation in the routing table. Routes with a higher metric are not selected for installation in the routing table, unless unequal-cost load balancing has been enabled.

EIGRP uses an incremental update process. When the adjacency is first established, each router sends a full update to its neighbor (adjacent) router, sending all prefixes that it has a successor for in the topology table (Note that only the successor route entries will be sent, not feasible successors or possible successors). After the initial updates have been exchanged, routing updates will be exchanged only as a result of changes on the networks. Changes can be caused by changes in connectivity, such as loss of a link or neighbor, or they can be caused by configuration events, such as the addition of new interfaces to EIGRP, implementation of route summarization, or implementation of route filtering. All routes received from neighbors are stored in the topology table. From the routes in the topology table, the router selects the best path (or paths) for each prefix and attempts to install these entries in the routing table. Entries marked as a successor in the topology table are offered to the IP routing table and advertised to neighbors.

Monitoring EIGRP

You can use the following commands to gather information from the EIGRP data structures:

- **show ip eigrp interfaces:** This command is used to display the list of interfaces that have been activated for EIGRP processing. This list contains all the interfaces that have an IP address that is covered by one of the network statements under the EIGRP configuration, and have not been marked as a passive interface within the EIGRP process.
- **show ip eigrp neighbors:** This command lists all neighbors that have been discovered by this router on its active EIGRP interfaces.
- **show ip eigrp topology:** This command displays the content of the EIGRP topology table. To select a specific entry from the table, the network and mask of the selected prefix can be provided as an option to the command.

The following **debug** commands enable you to observe the transmission and reception of packets and the exchange of routing information:

- **debug ip routing:** This command is not specific to EIGRP, but displays any changes that are made to the routing table, such as installation or removal of routes. This can be useful to diagnose routing protocol instabilities.
- **debug eigrp packets:** This command displays the transmission and reception of EIGRP packets. Either all packets can be displayed, or packets of a particular type, such as hellos, updates, queries, and replies, can be selected.
- **debug ip eigrp:** This command displays EIGRP routing events, such as updates, queries, and replies, sent to or received from neighbors. Whereas the **debug eigrp packets** command shows the transmission and reception of the packets themselves, **debug ip eigrp** focuses on the routing information contained in the packets and the actions that EIGRP takes as a result of the information received.

debug commands can generate a large amount of output, so you must take proper care to prevent the execution of **debug** commands from affecting the router's performance. Logging **debug** output to buffers on the router instead of to the console can limit the impact of these commands. The output of the **debug eigrp neighbor** and **debug ip eigrp** commands can be further limited by use of two additional **debug** commands:

- **debug ip eigrp neighbor** *as-number ip-address*: By imposing this extra condition, the output of the **debug eigrp packets** and **debug ip eigrp** commands will be limited to information associated with the specified neighbor.
- **debug ip eigrp** *as-number network mask*: By imposing this extra condition, the output of the **debug eigrp packets** and **debug ip eigrp** commands will be limited to information associated with the network specified by the network and mask options.

Troubleshooting Example: Routing Problem in an EIGRP Network

This example illustrates how you can leverage knowledge of EIGRP data structures, update processes, and Cisco IOS commands to troubleshoot a routing problem. The network depicted in Figure 5-2 is using EIGRP as its routing protocol.

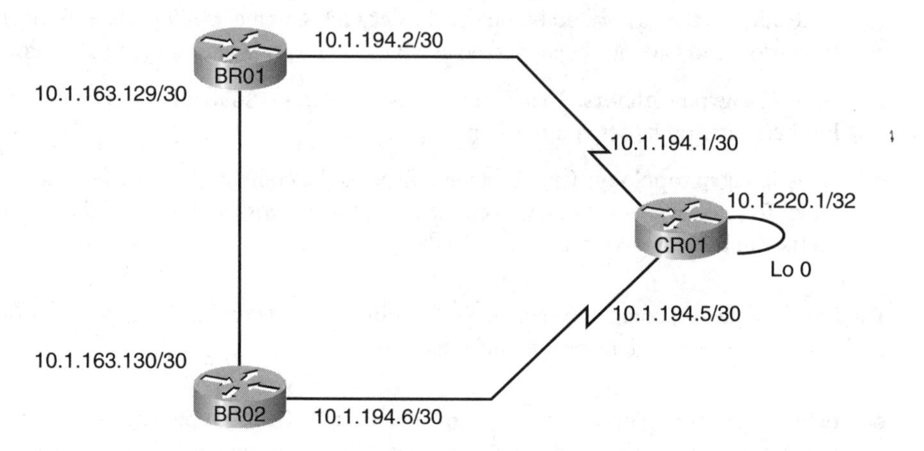

Figure 5-2 *Network Diagram for the EIGRP Troubleshooting Example*

When a **traceroute** command is executed on the BRO1 router to determine the path used to reach the loopback of router CRO1, as shown in Example 5-1, it turns out that the traffic path goes through BRO2.

Example 5-1 *Result of* **traceroute** *from BRO1 to CRO1's Loopback Interface*

```
BR01# traceroute 10.1.220.1

Type escape sequence to abort.
Tracing the route to cro1.mgmt.tshoot.local (10.1.220.1)

  1 10.1.163.130 0 msec 0 msec 0 msec
  2 10.1.194.5 12 msec 12 msec *
```

This is not the expected behavior because the path across the WAN link is the better path (both WAN links have the same bandwidth). To verify whether this problem is caused by an underlying Layer 1, Layer 2, or Layer 3 problem, as shown in Example 5-2, a **ping** command is executed to test the Layer 3 connectivity to the other side of the WAN link.

Example 5-2 *Result of* **ping** *from BRO1 to CRO1's WAN (Serial) Interface*

```
BRO1# ping 10.1.194.1

Type escape sequence to abort.
Sending 5, 100-byte ICMP Echos to 10.1.194.1, timeout is 2 seconds:
!!!!!
Success rate is 100 percent (5/5), round-trip min/avg/max = 28/29/32 ms
```

From the fact that the ping from BRO1 to CRO1 succeeds, you can conclude that the WAN link is operational at Layers 3 and below. Given that the link is functional, but is not used to route the packets across, makes this a routing problem and calls for investigation of the operation of EIGRP. Note that you can troubleshoot this problem in various ways. The objective is to find out why the direct route across the WAN is not used to route packets to the loopback interface of router CRO1, but the packets are routed through router BRO2 instead. There are two likely reasons why the traffic is routed through router BRO2 instead of directly across the WAN to router CRO1. The first reason could be that router BRO1 has not learned about the direct route to router CRO1. The second reason could be that the router has learned about the route but incorrectly selects the route through router BRO2 as the best route. To find out which of these two possible scenarios fits the situation, you should look at the EIGRP topology table. The topology table lists all routes that were received, so you can see whether the direct route to CRO1 is missing. On the other hand, if both routes were learned, but the wrong route was selected, you will see both routes listed in the topology table, together with their metrics and this might yield a clue as to why the wrong path was selected. Example 5-3 shows the output of the **show ip eigrp topology** for the 10.1.220.1 prefix.

Example 5-3 *How Many Paths to 10.1.220.1 in BRO1's EIGRP Topology Table?*

```
BRO1# show ip eigrp topology 10.1.220.1 255.255.255.255
IP-EIGRP (AS 1): Topology entry for 10.1.220.1/32
  State is Passive, Query origin flag is 1, 1 Successor(s), FD is 40642560
  Routing Descriptor Blocks:
  10.1.163.130 (FastEthernet0/1.30), from 10.1.163.130, Send flag is 0x0
      Composite metric is (40642560/40640000), Route is Internal
      Vector metric:
        Minimum bandwidth is 64 Kbit
        Total delay is 25100 microseconds
        Reliability is 255/255
        Load is 1/255
        Minimum MTU is 1500
        Hop count is 2
```

The output of Example 5-3 shows that only one entry is listed in BRO1's topology table. Therefore, you can conclude that the direct route through router CRO1 was not learned by BRO1. Because EIGRP learns all its routes from neighbors that were first discovered using hello packets, you must now determine whether the route was not learned because a neighbor relationship with CRO1 was never established or if the relationship was established but the specific route was not exchanged. Therefore, a good next step is to display the neighbor table to find out if a neighbor relationship was established between router BRO1 and router CRO1, and if so, determine what the status is. Example 5-4 displays the output of the **show ip eigrp neighbors** command on router BRO1.

Example 5-4 *Have BRO1 and CRO1 Built an EIGRP Neighbor Relation?*

```
BRO1# show ip eigrp neighbors
IP-EIGRP neighbors for process 1
H    Address                    Interface         Hold Uptime     SRTT    RTO  Q    Seq
                                                  (sec)           (ms)         Cnt  Num
0    10.1.163.130               Fa0/1.30          12 00:09:56     4       200  0    585
```

As you can see from the output of Example 5-4, router CRO1 is not listed as a neighbor on router BRO1. There can be two different reasons why router BRO1 does not list router CRO1 in its neighbor table. The trigger to add a neighbor to the neighbor list is the reception of hello packets from that neighbor. So one reason that could explain why router CRO1 is not listed is that router BRO1 has not received any hello packets from router CRO1. Another explanation could be that the packets were received, but ignored, because router BRO1 is not processing EIGRP packets on that interface. The interface table will allow you to see which interfaces are enabled for EIGRP processing. Example 5-5 shows the output of the **show ip eigrp interfaces** command on router BRO1.

Example 5-5 *Is EIGRP Enabled on the WAN (Serial) Interface of the BRO1 Router?*

```
BRO1# show ip eigrp interfaces
IP-EIGRP interfaces for process 1

                          Xmit Queue   Mean   Pacing Time   Multicast    Pending
Interface          Peers  Un/Reliable  SRTT   Un/Reliable   Flow Timer   Routes
Fa0/1.30             1        0/0        4        0/1           50            0
```

Output from the **show ip eigrp interfaces** command shown in Example 5-5 does not list the serial interface of router BRO1. Consequently, even if hello packets are received on the serial interface, router BRO1 does not process them. Two conditions need to be met for an interface to be added to the EIGRP interface table:

- The interface has to be up, and its IP address must match one of the configured network statements.
- The interface should not be configured as a passive interface.

These two conditions are both controlled by configuration commands, so at this point the configuration needs to be checked to see whether one of these two conditions is not met. Example 5-6 shows the EIGRP section of BRO1's running configuration.

Example 5-6 *On BRO1, Is EIGRP Configured to Operate over the WAN (Serial) Interface?*

```
BRO1# show running-config ¦ section router eigrp
router eigrp 1
 network 10.1.163.129 0.0.0.0
 network 10.1.194.1 0.0.0.0
 no auto-summary
```

As you can see in the output of Example 5-6, a problem exists with one of the network statements. The statement **network 10.1.194.1 0.0.0.0** matches IP address 10.1.194.1, which is not one of router BRO1's IP addresses, but an IP address of router CRO1. This is clearly a configuration mistake, and the **network** statement needs to be replaced with the statement **network 10.1.194.2 0.0.0.0** or some other **network** statement that matches IP address 10.1.194.2, which is the IP address of router BRO1 for the WAN link. The **network** statement must be replaced to test the hypothesis that the misconfigured network statement was the cause of the problem. Next, the results of the change need to be verified to confirm that the problem was solved. Strictly speaking, the only test that needs to be performed to confirm that the problem was solved is to execute the **traceroute** command again to confirm that packets traveling to the loopback IP address of router CRO1 are now sent directly across the WAN instead of making a detour through router BRO2. However, to show the impact of the change on all the EIGRP data structures, the changes in the output of the **show** commands that were earlier used to diagnose the problem can be tested next. Example 5-7 shows the output of **show ip eigrp interfaces** and the **show ip eigrp neighbors** commands on router BRO1 after the erroneous EIGRP **network** statement was replaced by the correct one. Example 5-7 shows that the interface table now lists subinterface Serial 0/0/0.111 in addition to subinterface FastEthernet 0/1.30. This means that EIGRP packets are now processed on interface Serial 0/0/0.111. Also, the IP address of router CRO1 (10.1.194.2) is now listed in the neighbor table on the WAN interface.

Example 5-7 *Results of* **show** *Commands After Correcting the EIGRP* **network** *Statement*

```
BRO1# show ip eigrp interfaces
IP-EIGRP interfaces for process 1

                          Xmit Queue   Mean   Pacing Time   Multicast    Pending
Interface          Peers  Un/Reliable  SRTT   Un/Reliable   Flow Timer   Routes
Fa0/1.30             1        0/0         1       0/1           50            0
Se0/0/0.111          1        0/0       707      10/380        4592           0

BRO1# show ip eigrp neighbors
IP-EIGRP neighbors for process 1
H   Address                 Interface          Hold Uptime   SRTT   RTO  Q  Seq
                                               (sec)         (ms)   Cnt     Num
1   10.1.194.1              Se0/0/0.111          14 00:10:10  707  4242  0  783
0   10.1.163.130            Fa0/1.30             12 01:34:49    1   200  0  587
```

Next, the EIGRP topology table must be examined. Example 5-8 shows the output from the **show ip eigrp topology** command with 10.1.220.1 as the parameter. The EIGRP topology table now lists two entries for network 10.1.220.1/32. It lists the entry through router BRO2 (10.1.163.130), which was present before the change was made, but it also lists an entry through router CRO1 (10.1.194.1). The entry through router CRO1 was selected as the best route because its metric of 40640000 is better than the metric through router BRO1, which equals 40642560. Based on the metric difference, the successor for network 10.1.220.1 is CRO1, and this path must be offered to the IP routing table.

Example 5-8 *The New EIGRP Topology Table After Corrections Were Made*

```
BRO1# show ip eigrp topology 10.1.220.1 255.255.255.255
IP-EIGRP (AS 1): Topology entry for 10.1.220.1/32
  State is Passive, Query origin flag is 1, 1 Successor(s), FD is 40640000
  Routing Descriptor Blocks:
  10.1.194.1 (Serial0/0/0.111), from 10.1.194.1, Send flag is 0x0
      Composite metric is (40640000/128256), Route is Internal
      Vector metric:
        Minimum bandwidth is 64 Kbit
        Total delay is 25000 microseconds
        Reliability is 255/255
        Load is 1/255
        Minimum MTU is 1500
        Hop count is 1
  10.1.163.130 (FastEthernet0/1.30), from 10.1.163.130, Send flag is 0x0
      Composite metric is (40642560/40640000), Route is Internal
      Vector metric:
        Minimum bandwidth is 64 Kbit
        Total delay is 25100 microseconds
        Reliability is 255/255
        Load is 1/255
        Minimum MTU is 1500
        Hop count is 2
```

Example 5-9 shows the output of the **show ip route** command with network 10.1.220.1 as the parameter. The output confirms that the path through router CRO1 has been installed in the routing table, and the result of the **traceroute** command, also shown in Example 5-9, confirms that this path is now used to forward packets to the loopback of CRO1.

Example 5-9 *The IP Routing Table After the EIGRP Corrections Were Made*

```
BR01# show ip route 10.1.220.1 255.255.255.255
Routing entry for 10.1.220.1/32
  Known via "eigrp 1", distance 90, metric 40640000, type internal
  Redistributing via eigrp 1
  Last update from 10.1.194.1 on Serial0/0/0.111, 00:20:55 ago
  Routing Descriptor Blocks:
  * 10.1.194.1, from 10.1.194.1, 00:20:55 ago, via Serial0/0/0.111
      Route metric is 40640000, traffic share count is 1
      Total delay is 25000 microseconds, minimum bandwidth is 64 Kbit
      Reliability 255/255, minimum MTU 1500 bytes
      Loading 1/255, Hops 1

BR01# traceroute 10.1.220.1

Type escape sequence to abort.
Tracing the route to cro1.mgmt.tshoot.local (10.1.220.1)
  1 10.1.194.1 16 msec 12 msec *
```

This troubleshooting example illustrates the use of the Cisco IOS **show** commands to display the content of the EIGRP data structures. It also illustrates how you can leverage knowledge of these data structures and the flow of EIGRP routing information to diagnose and resolve EIGRP routing problems.

Troubleshooting OSPF

OSPF is arguably the most popular routing protocol used in large enterprise networks and in service provider networks. Troubleshooting problems related to the exchange of routing information is an essential skill for a network engineer who is involved in the implementation and maintenance of large networks that use OSPF as the IGP. To diagnose and resolve problems related to the exchange of routing information by use of the OSPF routing protocol, you must do the following:

- Apply your knowledge of OSPF data structures to plan the gathering of necessary information as part of a structured approach to troubleshooting OSPF routing problems.
- Apply your knowledge of the processes that OSPF uses to exchange network topology information within an area, to interpret and analyze the information that is gathered during an OSPF troubleshooting process.
- Apply your knowledge of the processes that OSPF uses to exchange network topology information between areas to interpret and analyze the information that is gathered during an OSPF troubleshooting process.
- Use Cisco IOS commands to gather information from the OSPF data structures and track the flow of OSPF routing information to troubleshoot OSPF operation.

OSPF Data Structures

To troubleshoot IP connectivity problems caused by missing or incorrect routes in a network that uses OSPF as the routing protocol, you need to have a good understanding of the processes and data structures that OSPF uses to distribute, store and select routing information. For any routing protocol, the following high-level elements and processes can be discerned:

- **Reception of routing information from neighbors:** With OSPF, routing information is not exchanged in the form of routes, but in the form of link-state advertisements (LSAs), which contain information about elements of the network topology, such as routers, neighbor relationships, connected subnets, subnets available in different areas, redistributing routers, and redistributed subnets.
- **Routing protocol data structures:** OSPF stores the LSAs that it receives in a link-state database. Dijkstra's shortest path first (SPF) algorithm is used to compute the shortest path in terms of cost, which is the OSPF metric, to each network, based on the information in the link-state database. In addition, several other data structures, such as an interface table, a neighbor table, and a Routing Information Base (RIB) are maintained.
- **Route injection or redistribution:** Directly connected networks that are enabled for OSPF are advertised in the router's LSA. Routes from other sources, such as other routing protocols or static routes, can also be imported into the link-state database and advertised by use of special LSAs.
- **Route selection and installation:** OSPF will attempt to install the best routes that are computed using the SPF algorithm in the routing table. OSPF discerns three different types of routes: intra-area routes, interarea routes, and external routes. If two routes of different types for the same prefix are available for installation in the routing table, OSPF will prefer intra-area routes over interarea routes, and both these types will be preferred over external routes, regardless of the cost of the paths. If two equal-cost routes of the same type are available, they will both be selected for installation in the routing table.
- **Transmission of routing information to neighbors:** Routing information is flooded to all routers in an area by passing LSAs from neighbor to neighbor using a reliable transport mechanism. Area Border Routers (ABRs) inject routing information from an area into the backbone area or, conversely, from the backbone area into the other areas that it is connected to.

OSPF stores its operational data, configured parameters, and statistics in four main data structures:

- **Interface table:** This table lists all interfaces that have been enabled for OSPF. The directly connected subnets associated with these interfaces are included in the type 1 router LSA that the router injects into the OSPF link-state database for its area. When an interface is configured as a passive interface, it is still listed in the OSPF interface table, but no neighbor relationships are established on this interface.

- **Neighbor table:** This table is used to keep track of all active OSPF neighbors. Neighbors are added to this table based on the reception of Hello packets, and they are removed when the OSPF dead time for a neighbor expires or when the associated interface goes down. OSPF goes through a number of states while establishing a neighbor relationship (also known as adjacency), and the neighbor table lists the current state for each individual neighbor.
- **Link-state database:** This is the main data structure that OSPF uses to store all its network topology information. This database contains full topology information for the areas that a router connects to, and information about the paths available to reach networks and subnets in other areas or other autonomous systems. Because this database contains a wealth of network topology information, it is one of the most important data structures to gather information from when troubleshooting OSPF problems.
- **Routing Information Base:** After executing the SPF algorithm, the results of this calculation are stored in the RIB. This information includes the best routes to each individual prefix in the OSPF network with their associated path costs. When the information in the link-state database changes, only a partial recalculation might be necessary (depending on the nature of the change), and routes might be added to or deleted from the RIB without the need for a full SPF recalculation. From the RIB, OSPF offers its routes to the IP routing table.

Note Within the OSPF link-state database, the best path to each destination is determined based on the SPF (Dijkstra) algorithm. The collection of these best paths is referred to as the *OSPF RIB*. There is no separate *physical* data structure called the OSPF RIB. The best path to each destination is offered to be installed in the IP routing table. When there are alternatives, the IP process selects the path with the smallest administrative distance and installs it in the IP routing table. As of year 2001 and after the release of RFC 3222, many writings have referred to the IP routing table as the RIB (generic RIB rather than OSPF or BGP RIB). This term is easier to use than IP routing table, and it allows us to distinguish it from the FIB that CEF creates. Although the FIB is created based on RIB, it is indeed a separate data structure, and IP packet forwarding (a data plane task) in a Cisco router is performed using FIB and the FIB adjacency table.

The OSPF link-state database is used to store all the network topology information a router receives. There are separate (logical) databases for each OSPF area. In a stable situation, the database for each area will be identical on all routers in that area. An ABR has a database for each of the areas that it participates in and is responsible for exchanging network topology information between the databases of its connected areas and the backbone area. External routing information that was redistributed into OSPF from a different source is maintained in a separate section of the database that is not specific to any area. Figure 5-3 shows a network using OSPF and consisting of areas 0, 1, and 2. Table 5-2 lists the LSA types present in the database of each of the routers and the number of each LSA

Table 5-2 *Number and Type of LSAs in OSPF Database of the Routers in Figure 5-3*

Router	Type 1	Type 2	Type 3
Router A	2	1	5
Router B	5	2	9
Router C	3	1	4
Router D	5	1	9
Router E	2	0	5

type. These numbers are based on the fact the no redistribution or summarization has been configured and each link represents a single subnet.

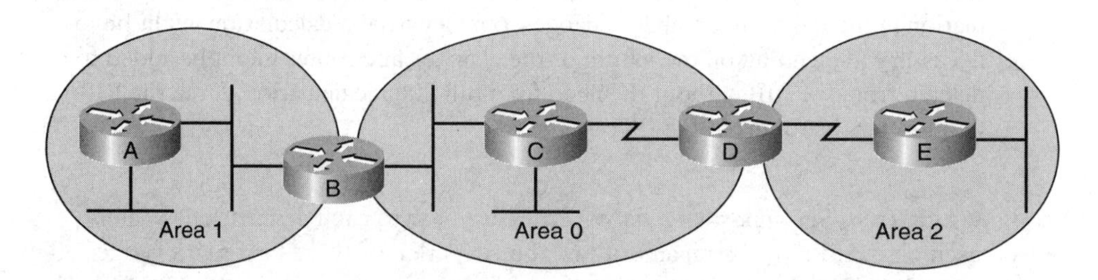

Figure 5-3 *A Multi-Area OSPF Network with Five Routers Performing No Route Redistribution*

In a multi-area OSPF network without any redistribution, only LSA type 1, type 2, and type 3 are used. They serve the following purposes:

- Each router in an area generates a type 1 LSA that describes that router's link state, including its directly connected subnets, connection types, and neighbors. Type 1 LSAs are not passed between areas.
- By default, for each multiaccess (broadcast or nonbroadcast) type network, OSPF elects a designated router. If the network is a transit network (more than one router is connected to it), the designated router generates a type 2 LSA that describes the link state for that link, including its subnet and connected routers. Type 2 LSAs are not passed between areas.
- For each subnet that an ABR can reach in a connected area, it will generate a type 3 LSA in the database of the backbone area 0, listing the subnet and its associated cost. For each subnet that it can reach in the backbone area, either directly or through another ABR, it will generate a type 3 LSA in the database of each connected area listing the subnet and its cost.

Based on these rules for the network depicted in Figure 5-3, you can calculate the number of elements in each area's database:

- **Type 1:** Area 1 contains two routers (A and B), and therefore its database will contain two type 1 entries. Area 0 contains three routers (B, C, and D), and therefore its database will contain three type 1 entries. Area 2 contains two routers, and its database will therefore contain two type 1 entries.
- **Type 2:** Area 1 contains one transit Ethernet (broadcast) network, and therefore its database will contain one type 2 entry. There is a second Ethernet network in area 1, but this is a stub network and not a transit network. Area 0 also contains one transit Ethernet link, and therefore it will also contain one type 2 entry. A designated router is not elected for a point-to-point link. Area 2 has no transit broadcast or nonbroadcast type networks, and therefore no type 2 entries are generated.
- **Type 3:** Area 1 contains two subnets. For each of these subnets, a type 3 entry will be generated in the area 0 database by Router B. Subsequently, Router D will generate a type 3 entry for each of these subnets in the area 2 database. Area 0 contains three subnets. Router B will generate a type 3 entry for each of those subnets in the area 1 database, and Router D will also generate three entries in the area 2 database. Area 2 contains two subnets, and therefore Router D will generate two type 3 entries in the area 0 database, and Router B will generate two type 3 entries in the area 1 database. In total, this means that the area 1 database contains 3 + 2 = 5 type 3 entries, the area 0 database contains 2 + 2 = 4 type 3 entries, and the area 2 database contains 2 + 3 = 5 type 3 entries. For each area database, the total equals the number of subnets available outside its area.

Therefore, the totals for each area database are the following:

- **Area 1:** Two type 1, one type 2, and five type 3 entries
- **Area 0:** Three type 1, one type 2, and four type 3 entries
- **Area 2:** Two type 1, zero type 2, and five type 3 entries

The final step is to add the numbers for each individual router:

- **Router A:** Router A carries only the area 1 database, and as a result, it has two type 1, one type 2, and five type 3 entries.
- **Router B:** Router B is an ABR and carries the databases for both area 1 and area 0. Therefore, it has 2 + 3 = 5 type 1 entries, 1 + 1 = 2 type 2 entries, and 5 + 4 = 9 type 3 entries.
- **Router C:** Router C carries only the area 0 database, which contains three type 1, one type 2, and four type 3 entries.
- **Router D:** Router D is an ABR and carries the databases for area 0 and area 2. Therefore, it has 3 + 2 = 5 type 1, 1 + 0 = 1 type 2 and 4 + 5 = 9 type 3 entries.

- **Router E:** Router E carries only the area 2 database, which contains two type 1, zero type 2, and five type 3 entries.

To troubleshoot, you often need to compare observed behavior against expected behavior, and when troubleshooting OSPF this means that you must predict which different types of LSAs you can expect each router to generate. Understanding the role and content of the most fundamental OSPF LSA types (type 1, type 2, and type 3) is essential to troubleshoot OSPF effectively.

OSPF Information Flow Within an Area

OSPF discovers neighbors through the transmission of periodic Hello packets. Two routers will become neighbors only if the following parameters match in the Hello packets:

- **Hello and dead timers:** Two routers will only become neighbors if they use the same Hello and dead time. The default values for broadcast and point-to-point type networks are 10-second Hello and 40-second dead time. If these timers are changed on an interface of a router, the timers should be configured to match on all neighboring routers on that interface.
- **OSPF area number:** Two routers will become neighbors on a link only if they both consider that link to be in the same area.
- **OSPF area type:** Two routers will become neighbors only if they both consider the area to be the same type of area (normal, stub, or not-so-stubby area [NSSA]).
- **IP subnet and subnet mask:** Two routers will not become neighbors if they are not on the same subnet. The exception to this rule is on a point-to-point link, where the subnet mask is not verified.
- **Authentication type and authentication data:** Two routers will become neighbors only if they both use the same authentication type (null, clear text, or message digest 5 [MD5]). If they use authentication, the authentication data (password or hash value) also needs to match.

If two routers do not list each other as neighbors on a link and the interfaces have been activated for OSPF on both sides, you must verify the parameters in the preceding list. A mismatch in any of these parameters will also show in the output of the **debug ip ospf event** command. After a router has received a Hello packet and registered the neighbor in its neighbor table, it will attempt to build a neighbor relationship or adjacency with the neighboring router and exchange topology information to synchronize their link-state databases. This process consists of several stages:

- **Attempt:** This state is encountered only when unicast Hellos are used and a neighbor has been explicitly configured. When the router has sent a Hello to the configured neighbor but not received any Hello from the neighbor yet, the neighbor relationship is in the attempt state. This state is not used on point-to-point or broadcast type networks, which use multicast Hellos rather than unicast Hellos.

- **Init:** This is the state that a neighbor is in if a Hello has been received from the neighbor but the neighbor is not listing this router in its neighbor list yet. This is a transitory state, and if a router is stuck in this state, this usually indicates that the neighbor is not receiving this router's Hello packets correctly.
- **2-way:** This is the state that a neighbor relationship is in when the router sees its own router ID listed in the active neighbor list in the Hello packets received from that neighbor. This is usually a transitory state. The only time when this is considered the normal state is on broadcast or non-broadcast networks, between two routers that both are neither the designated router (DR) nor the backup designated router (BDR) for the segment.
- **Exstart:** This stage indicates that the routers are starting the database exchange state by establishing a master and slave relationship and determining the initial sequence number for the database description (DBD) packets.
- **Exchange:** During the exchange stage, neighboring routers exchange database description packets to list the content of their link-state database to discover which entries each neighbor is missing. Exstart and exchange are transitory states, and if a neighbor is stuck in exstart or exchange state, this could indicate a mismatch in the maximum transmission unit (MTU) between the neighbors or a duplicate router ID.
- **Loading:** During this stage, each of the two routers can request missing LSAs from the other router. This is a transitory state. If routers are stuck in this state, this could indicate packet or memory corruption, or in certain scenarios, an MTU mismatch between the neighbors.
- **Full:** This is the normal final stage of OSPF adjacency establishment. This state indicates that the router and its neighbor have successfully synchronized their link-state databases.

Full is the normal state after establishing a neighbor relationship and indicates that the routers have synchronized their databases. 2-way is an acceptable final state for certain types of neighbor relationships (two non-DR, non-BDR routers on a broadcast or non-broadcast network). Any other state is a transitory state, and if a router is stuck in one of these states for an extended period of time, this calls for further investigation. During this adjacency building process, two routers in the same area synchronize their link-state databases for that area, and when they have reached the "full" state, their databases for the area are identical.

OSPF Information Flow Between Areas

ABRs play a key role in exchanging routing information between OSPF areas. Two routers can become neighbors on a link only if they are in the same area. When they exchange their databases during the initial database exchange, LSAs that belong to different areas are not exchanged. To distribute information about subnets that are available in a particular area to other areas, the ABR generates type 3 LSA to inject the information into the area 0 database. Other ABRs use these type 3 LSAs to compute the best path to these subnets and then in turn inject the information into their connected areas by use of type 3 LSAs. The diagram in Figure 5-4 illustrates this process.

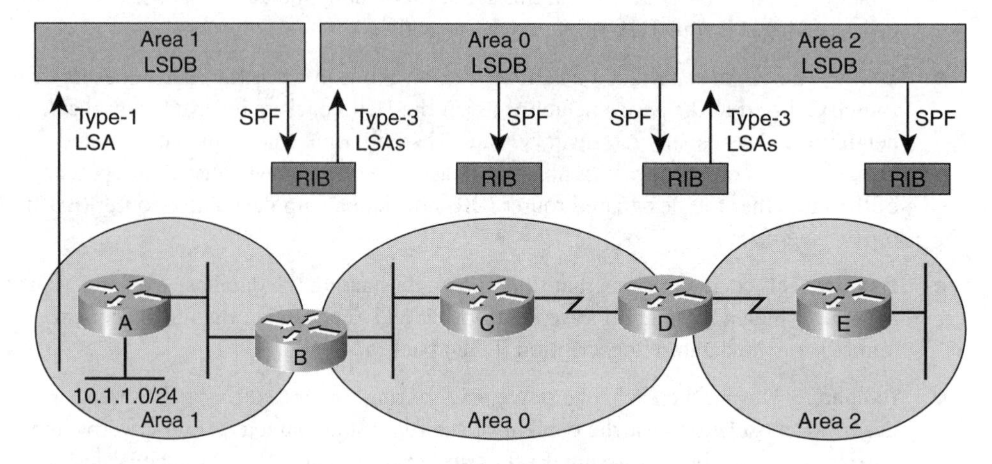

Figure 5-4 *Role of LSA Type 3 in OSPF Interarea Routing*

In the network shown in Figure 5-4, Router B, which is an ABR, executes the SPF algorithm using the area 1 database to compute the best path for each subnet that is available in area 1. Based on this computation, Router B will generate a type 3 LSA, which is then injected into the area 0 database. These type 3 LSAs include the cost that Router B has computed for each of these prefixes. Any other router in area 0, such as Router C or D, executes its own SPF algorithm based on the area 0 database. They then add the cost in the type 3 LSAs to their computed cost to Router B to find their total cost to the prefixes in area 1. After Router D has computed these costs, it generates type 3 LSAs for the prefixes from area 1 and injects these into the area 2 database. Any router in area 2, such as Router E, can now compute its own best path to Router D and add this cost to the cost advertised by Router D in the type 3 LSAs to find the total path cost to each prefix in area 1. When you are troubleshooting OSPF and tracking the advertisement of routes and their associated costs, it is important to understand this process. It will enable you to know which routers are expected to generate the necessary type 3 LSAs and how the cost of the total path is calculated. Understanding this process helps you to track the flow of routing information from a router in one area to routers in different areas.

Cisco IOS OSPF Commands

The following commands enable you to gather information from the OSPF data structures:

- **show ip ospf interface:** This command is used to display the interfaces that have been activated for OSPF. This list contains all the interfaces that have an IP address that is covered by one of the network statements under the OSPF configuration. This command displays a lot of detailed information for each interface. For a brief overview, issue the command **show ip ospf interface brief**.

Note Current releases of IOS allow an interface to be activated for a particular OSPF process using the interface configuration mode command: **ip ospf** *process-number* **area** *area-number*.

This is an alternative to the **network** statement used within the OSPF process configuration mode. This alternative was first created to be used for unnumbered interfaces. It is interesting to note that in IPv6, this is the normal way of activating an OSPFv3 process on an interface.

- **show ip ospf neighbor:** This command lists all neighbors that have been discovered by this router on its active OSPF interfaces and shows their current state.
- **show ip ospf database:** This command displays the content of the OSPF link-state database. When the command is issued without any additional options, it will display a summary of the database, listing only the LSA headers. Using additional command options, specific LSAs can be selected, and the actual LSA content can be inspected.
- **show ip ospf statistics:** This command can be used to view how often and when the SPF algorithm was last executed. This command can be helpful when diagnosing routing instability.

The following **debug** commands enable you to observe the transmission and reception of packets and the exchange of routing information:

- **debug ip routing:** This command is not specific to the OSPF protocol, but displays any changes that are made to the routing table, such as installation or removal of routes. This can prove useful when troubleshooting routing protocol instabilities.
- **debug ip ospf packet:** This command displays the transmission and reception of OSPF packets. Only the packet headers are displayed, not the content of the packets. This command is useful to verify whether Hellos are sent and received as expected.
- **debug ip ospf events:** This command displays OSPF events. This includes reception and transmission of Hellos, but also the establishment of neighbor relationships and the reception or transmission of LSAs. This command can also provide clues (mismatched parameters such as timers, area number, and so on) as to why neighbor Hellos might be ignored.
- **debug ip ospf adj:** This command displays events related to the adjacency building process and enables you to see a neighbor relationship transition from one state to the next. During troubleshooting, you can observe the transitions from one state to another, and possibly the state at which the relation gets stuck.
- **debug ip ospf monitor:** This command monitors when the SPF algorithm is scheduled to run and displays the triggering LSA and a summary of the results after the SPF algorithm has completed. During troubleshooting, this command enables you to

discover which LSA was received and triggered an SPF computation. For example, you can easily discover a flapping link.

These **debug** commands can generate a large amount of output, and proper care needs to be taken to prevent this from affecting the router's performance. Logging **debug** output to buffers on the router rather than to the console can limit the impact of these commands.

Troubleshooting Example: Routing Problem in an OSPF Network

The network shown in Figure 5-5 is using OSPF as the routing protocol and is configured for multiple areas. When you examine the routing table on router CRO1, you only find a single entry, the path through router CSW1.

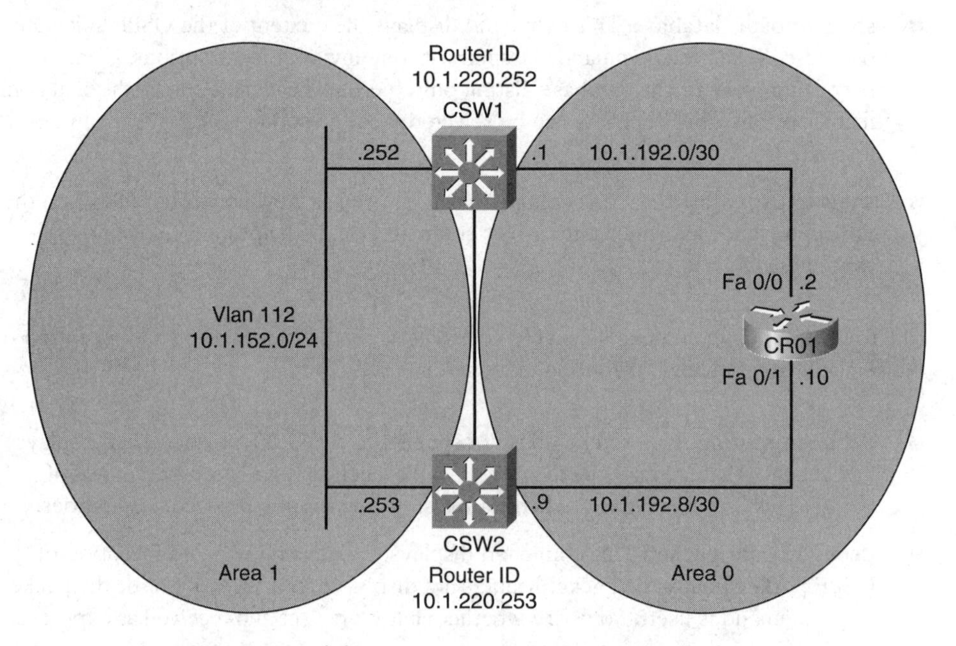

Figure 5-5 *The Output of* **show ip route** *on CRO1 for the Prefix 10.1.152.0*

Example 5-10 displays the output of the **show ip route** command on router CRO1 for prefix 10.1.152.0.

Example 5-10 **show ip route** *Command Output on CR01 for Prefix 10.1.152.0*

```
Routing entry for 10.1.152.0/24
  Known via "ospf 100", distance 110, metric 2, type inter area
  Last update from 10.1.192.1 on FastEthernet0/0, 00:00:11 ago
  Routing Descriptor Blocks:
  * 10.1.192.1, from 10.1.220.252, 00:00:11 ago, via FastEthernet0/0
      Route metric is 2, traffic share count is 1
```

This result is unexpected because Figure 5-5 shows that two equal-cost paths are available to CRO1, one through CSW1 and one through CSW2. To verify whether this problem is caused by an underlying Layer 1, Layer 2, or Layer 3 problem, execute a **ping** command to test the Layer 3 connectivity to router CSW2 using the FastEthernet 0/1 interface, as demonstrated in Example 5-11.

Example 5-11 *Result of the* **ping** *Command on CR01 to 10.1.192.9*

```
CRO1# ping 10.1.192.9

Type escape sequence to abort.
Sending 5, 100-byte ICMP Echos to 10.1.192.9, timeout is 2 seconds:
!!!!!
Success rate is 100 percent (5/5), round-trip min/avg/max = 1/2/4 ms
```

Because this ping succeeds, you can conclude that the Fast Ethernet link between router CRO1 and router CSW2 is operational at Layers 3 and below. Given that the link is functional, but is not used to route the packets across, this is a routing problem and calls for an investigation of the operation of OSPF. There are various different methods to troubleshoot this problem. The objective is to find out why the second, equal-cost path through router CSW2 is not installed in the routing table in addition to the entry through router CSW1. There are two main reasons why this could be happening. Either router CSW2 is not advertising subnet 10.1.152.0/24 to area 0, or it might be advertising the route, but the cost to reach subnet 10.1.152.0/24 through router CSW2 from router CRO1 is considered to be worse than the cost through router CSW1. To find out whether router CSW2 is advertising subnet 10.1.152.0/24 to area 0, you can consult the OSPF database in router CRO1. It is expected that both routers CSW1 and CSW2 advertise a type 3 summary LSA for subnet 10.1.152.0/24. Example 5-12 shows the output from the **show ip ospf database summary** command for the lsa-id 10.1.152.0 on CRO1. For type 3 LSAs, the link-state identifier is the subnet part of the associated prefix.

Example 5-12 **show ip ospf database summary** *Command Output on CR01*

```
CRO1# show ip ospf database summary 10.1.152.0
            OSPF Router with ID (10.1.220.1) (Process ID 100)
            Summary Net Link States (Area 0)
Routing Bit Set on this LSA
  LS age: 201
  Options: (No TOS-capability, DC, Upward)
  LS Type: Summary Links(Network)
  Link State ID: 10.1.152.0 (summary Network Number)
  Advertising Router: 10.1.220.252
  LS Seq Number: 80000001
  Checksum: 0x1C97
  Length: 28
```

```
Network Mask: /24    TOS: 0    Metric: 1

LS age: 136
Options: (No TOS-capability, DC, Upward)
LS Type: Summary Links(Network)
Link State ID: 10.1.152.0 (summary Network Number)
Advertising Router: 10.1.220.253
LS Seq Number: 80000001
Checksum: 0x169C
Length: 28
Network Mask: /24    TOS: 0    Metric: 1
```

The result of the **show ip ospf database summary** command for the lsa-id 10.1.152.0 on CRO1 shows two entries. One entry was generated by the router with router ID 10.1.220.252 (CSW1). The second entry is generated by the router with router ID 10.1.220.253 (CSW2). Both entries are advertised with an OSPF cost of 1. Therefore, the preference for the path to 10.1.152.0/24 via CSW1 must be based on the topology within area 0. Given that router CRO1 has a direct connection in area 0 to both router CSW1 and CSW2, there are only two plausible explanations for the fact that router CRO1 is not using the path via router CSW2. Either the direct path to router CSW2 is not used because routers CSW2 and CRO1 have not become neighbors, or the path is not used because the cost for interface FastEthernet 0/1 is higher than the cost for interface FastEthernet 0/0. The second option is less likely because the interfaces are of the same type and by default the OSPF cost is related to the interface bandwidth. To verify whether router CRO1 has established a proper neighbor relationship with router CSW1, the **show ip ospf neighbor** command was executed on CR01, and Example 5-13 shows the results.

Example 5-13 show ip ospf neighbor *Command Output on Router CR01*

```
CRO1# show ip ospf neighbor

Neighbor ID     Pri   State           Dead Time   Address         Interface
10.1.220.252      1   FULL/DR         00:00:33    10.1.192.1      FastEthernet0/0
```

The output in Example 5-13 shows only one neighbor listed as a neighbor of Router CSW1. Note that in the output of the command the first address is the router ID of the neighbor, whereas the second IP address in the Address column is the interface IP address of the neighbor. There could be several reasons why router CSW2 is not listed as a neighbor of CRO1. One reason could be that it is not sending Hellos. Another reason could be that the Hellos are received but ignored because of mismatched Hello parameters. A third explanation could be that the Hellos are sent but not received because interface FastEthernet 0/1 has not been activated for OSPF and therefore does not listen to the OSPF multicast group 224.0.0.5. To verify whether interface FastEthernet 0/1 has been enabled for OSPF, you would issue the **show ip ospf interface brief** command on CRO1, as demonstrated in Example 5-14.

Example 5-14 show ip ospf interface brief *Command Output on CR01*

```
CRO1# sh ip ospf interface brief
Interface     PID   Area            IP Address/Mask    Cost  State Nbrs F/C
Lo0            100   0               10.1.220.1/32      1     LOOP  0/0
Fa0/0          100   0               10.1.192.2/30      1     BDR   1/1
```

Because the interface FastEthernet 0/1 is not listed in output shown in Example 5-14, one can conclude that it has not been activated for OSPF. Unlike the **show ip eigrp interfaces** command, the **show ip ospf interface** command will display interfaces that are enabled for OSPF, but configured as passive interfaces. Therefore, the only possible explanation is that the interface Fa0/1 has not been enabled for OSPF on router CRO1. Whether an interface is enabled for OSPF is controlled by configuration commands. Therefore, you would need to check the configuration to see why interface FastEthernet 0/1 has not been enabled. This is done using the **show running-config** command for the OSPF section, as demonstrated in Example 5-15.

Example 5-15 *The OSPF Section of Router CRO1's Running Configuration*

```
CRO1# show running-config | section router ospf
router ospf 100
 log-adjacency-changes
 network 10.1.192.2 0.0.0.0 area 0
 network 10.1.192.9 0.0.0.0 area 0
 network 10.1.220.1 0.0.0.0 area 0
```

From the output shown in Example 5-15, it is obvious that a problem exists with one of the **network** statements. The statement **network 10.1.192.9 0.0.0.0 area 0** matches IP address 10.1.192.9, which is not one of router CRO1's IP addresses, but an IP address of router CSW2. This is clearly a configuration mistake, and the **network** statement needs to be replaced with the statement **network 10.1.192.10 0.0.0.0 area 0** or some other network statement that matches IP address 10.1.192.10 (which is the IP address of router CRO1 on interface FastEthernet 0/1). The **network** statement is replaced to test the hypothesis that the misconfigured **network** statement was the cause of the problem. Next, you must verify the results of the change to confirm that the problem was solved. Strictly speaking, the only test that needs to be performed to confirm that the problem was solved is to execute the **show ip route 10.1.152.0 255.255.255.0** command again to confirm that both paths through routers CSW1 and CSW2 now show up in the IP routing table. However, to demonstrate the impact of the changes on the OSPF data structures, the changes in the OSPF interface table and OSPF neighbor table are displayed in Example 5-16.

Example 5-16 *Result of Correcting CRO1's OSPF* **network** *Statement*

```
CRO1# show ip ospf interface brief
Interface     PID    Area            IP Address/Mask     Cost   State Nbrs F/C
Lo0           100     0              10.1.220.1/32        1     LOOP  0/0
Fa0/1         100     0              10.1.192.10/30       1     BDR    1/1
Fa0/0         100     0              10.1.192.2/30        1     BDR    1/1

CRO1# show ip ospf neighbor

Neighbor ID     Pri    State          Dead Time    Address          Interface
10.1.220.253      1    FULL/DR        00:00:39     10.1.192.9       FastEthernet0/1
10.1.220.252      1    FULL/DR        00:00:31     10.1.192.1       FastEthernet0/0
```

After we make the change to the OSPF **network** statement in router CRO1, as shown in Example 5-16, the interface table lists interface FastEthernet 0/1. This means that OSPF has now been enabled for the interface and OSPF packets are processed on interface FastEthernet 0/1. The router ID (10.1.220.253) and interface IP address (10.1.192.9) of router CSW2 are now listed in the neighbor table on the FastEthernet 0/1 interface. Finally, the output shown in Example 5-17 confirms that the path through router CSW2 has been installed in the routing table in addition to the path through router CSW1.

Example 5-17 *Two Paths to 10.1.152.0/24 Are Now Installed in CRO1's Routing Table*

```
CRO1# show ip route 10.1.152.0 255.255.255.0
Routing entry for 10.1.152.0/24
  Known via "ospf 100", distance 110, metric 2, type inter area
  Last update from 10.1.192.9 on FastEthernet0/1, 00:00:29 ago
  Routing Descriptor Blocks:
    10.1.192.9, from 10.1.220.253, 00:00:29 ago, via FastEthernet0/1
      Route metric is 2, traffic share count is 1
  * 10.1.192.1, from 10.1.220.252, 00:00:29 ago, via FastEthernet0/0
      Route metric is 2, traffic share count is 1
```

Note that the routing source for the entries (the address behind the word *from*) in the routing table lists the router IDs of routers CSW2 (10.1.220.253) and CSW1 (10.1.220.252), respectively. These routers are listed as the source of the route, because they generated the type 3 LSA entries from which these routes were calculated. This OSPF troubleshooting example illustrates the use of the Cisco IOS **show** commands to display the content of the OSPF data structures and how to leverage knowledge of these data structures and OSPF routing information flow to diagnose and resolve OSPF routing problems.

Troubleshooting Route Redistribution

Ideally, no more than one interior (intra-autonomous system) routing protocol is used within an organization. However, organizational requirements such as partnerships, mergers, technology migrations, and changes in policy might impose usage of multiple routing protocols in a single enterprise network. In such situations, route redistribution between the different routing protocols is often necessary to achieve IP connectivity between the different parts of the network. Route redistribution adds an extra layer of complexity to a routed network. In addition to understanding each of the routing protocols involved, it is also important to understand the interactions between them. This understanding is vital to be able to diagnose and resolve problems such as suboptimal routing and routing feedback that can occur when route redistribution is implemented. As a network support engineer, you must know the data structures and processes that play a part in the exchange of routing information between different routing protocols. You must also master the Cisco IOS commands to gather information about the operation of a route redistribution process.

Route Injection and Redistribution Process

The most common way to distribute routing information is to select a single routing protocol and use this throughout the network. On each of the participating routers, interfaces are activated for the routing protocol, and the directly connected subnets associated with these interfaces are injected into the routing protocol data structures and distributed via the routing protocol update mechanisms. However, in some situations, you might have routes that are not local to the part of the network where the routing protocol operates, and you want to distribute these routes using the routing protocol. For instance, you have a number of static routes that point to routers that are not using the same routing protocol and you want to distribute the information about these subnets using your routing protocol.

Alternatively, you might have a situation where two different routing protocols are used for two different parts of the network and you want to take the routes from the part of the network that are learned through one routing protocol and distribute that information by means of the other protocol to all routers that participate in the second routing protocol. You can implement these scenarios by use of redistribution. There are two ways for routes to be injected in a routing protocol:

- **Directly connected:** These subnets can be injected by enabling the routing protocol on an interface. These routes are considered internal by the routing protocol.
- **External:** These are subnets from a different source that are present in the routing table and can be redistributed by using the routing protocol's update mechanisms. Because these routes were not originated by the routing protocol, they are considered external.

Older routing protocols, such as RIP do not have the capability to mark routes as external in their routing update messages. Newer routing protocols, such as EIGRP, OSPF, and

IS-IS, can mark routes as external and prefer internal routes over external routes. This is an important mechanism in the prevention of routing loops caused by route feedback.

The redistribution process takes routes from the routing table. As a result, only routes that are installed in the routing table can be redistributed. Routes are not transferred directly between the data structures of different routing protocols. As an example of this process, consider a router that is running two routing protocols, OSPF and EIGRP. EIGRP has been configured to redistribute the routes learned from OSPF. OSPF receives network topology information in the form of LSAs from its neighbor OSPF routers, places these in its link-state database, and executes the SPF algorithm to calculate the best routes to the subnets in the OSPF network. After calculating the best path for each prefix, OSPF offers these prefixes to the IP routing table. If no competing routes with a lower administrative distance are present for a prefix, the OSPF route is installed in the routing table. EIGRP, which is configured to redistribute OSPF, scans the routing table and takes any route that was installed in the routing table by OSPF, imports these routes in its topology table, marking them as external, and advertises them using its own update mechanisms. In addition to routes that are marked as OSPF routes in the routing table, EIGRP takes any connected routes from the routing table that are enabled for OSPF (either by use of a **network** statement under the router OSPF configuration or by use of the **ip ospf** *process-id* **area** *area-number* command on the interface). Although these routes are not marked as OSPF routes, but as directly connected routes in the routing table, EIGRP treats these routes as OSPF routes.

Note that the redistribution process is the process that takes the routes from the routing table, not the process that installs the routes in the routing table. Therefore, redistribution is always configured under the "destination" protocol for the routing information. For example, when OSPF routes are redistributed into EIGRP, this is configured under the EIGRP process. When the route is taken from the routing table and imported into the other protocol's data structures, a metric for the redistributing protocol needs to be attached to that route. This metric is not computed from the metric of the original protocol through the use of some formula. A starting metric, or seed metric, should be configured, which will then be attached to all redistributed routes by the router. If no seed metric is configured, a default value for the redistributing protocol is used. For some protocols, such as RIP and EIGRP, the default metric is the maximum possible value, which represents "infinity" or "unreachable." This is important to know when troubleshooting redistribution issues because redistribution into these protocols will fail without explicit configuration of a seed metric. The seed metric can be configured using the **default-metric** command or along with each redistribution statement (as a parameter or within a route map).

Two important conditions must be met for a prefix learned from one protocol (using redistribution) to be successfully advertised through another protocol:

- **The route needs to be installed in the routing table:** The route needs to be selected as the best route by the source protocol and, if routes from competing sources are present, the route will need to have a lower administrative distance than the competing routes.

- **A proper seed metric is assigned to the redistributed route:** The route needs to be redistributed in the destination protocol data structures with a valid metric for the destination protocol.

Access lists and route maps can be used to influence the redistribution process further by filtering routes, manipulating the seed metric, or setting additional parameters, such as route type or tags for specific routes.

Verifying and Troubleshooting Route Propagation

When troubleshooting problems in a network that uses route redistribution, troubleshooting the actual redistribution process itself is often only a small part of the process. The main challenge is usually troubleshooting IP connectivity problems caused by redistribution, which involves the following elements:

- **Troubleshooting the source routing protocol:** Routes can be redistributed only if they are present in the routing table of the redistributing router. If routes are not redistributed as expected, you first need to confirm that they are learned on the redistributing router via the source protocol. Next, you have to check that the route is installed in the routing table.
- **Troubleshooting route selection and installation:** To redistribute a route, it needs to be selected and successfully installed in the routing table by the source protocol. When routes are redistributed between routing protocols in two directions (to and from one protocol to another), it is possible that routing information that originates in one of the routing domains is redistributed into the other routing domain and eventually propagates back to a router that is also connected to the source domain. This happens when there is a topological loop in the network scheme. If the route is subsequently accepted as a better route than the original source route, suboptimal routing can happen. However, if that route is subsequently redistributed back into the source protocol, it might cause routing loops and routing instability. After diagnosing a suboptimal routing problem or routing loop, changing the administrative distance or filtering routes to influence the route selection and installation process can often solve the problem.
- **Troubleshooting the redistribution process:** If routes are learned and installed in the routing table of the redistributing router, but not inserted into the data structures and advertisements of the redistributing protocol, you should verify the configuration of the redistribution process. Bad seed metrics, route filtering, or misconfigured routing protocol process or autonomous system numbers are common causes for the redistribution process to fail.
- **Troubleshooting the destination routing protocol:** After the routing information is inserted into the destination protocol's data structures, the routing information is propagated using that protocol's routing update mechanisms. If the routing information is not properly distributed to all routers in the destination routing domain, you should troubleshoot the routing exchange mechanisms for the destination protocol.

Each routing protocol has its own methods of exchanging routing information, including external routing information. Research the specific protocol that you are working with to find out if external routes are handled differently than internal routes. For example, OSPF external routes do not propagate into stub areas.

Diagnosing route redistribution problems mostly involves troubleshooting routing protocols and routing information exchange in general. To troubleshoot redistribution from one routing protocol to another, you need to be proficient with the troubleshooting toolkit for both the source and destination protocols. The redistribution process itself consists of interaction between the data structures of the involved routing protocols and the routing table. To troubleshoot, you have to use the commands to gather information from the routing protocol data structures, such as **show ip ospf database** to display the content of OSPF link-state database or **show ip eigrp topology** to display the content of the EIGRP topology table. Detailed information about specific routes installed in the routing table can be gathered by use of the **show ip route** *network mask* command.

The **debug ip routing** command displays routes being installed or removed from the routing table in real time. This command can be very powerful when you are troubleshooting routing loops or flapping routes caused by route redistribution. Another feature that can prove helpful in diagnosing suspected route instability is the route-profiling feature. Using the **ip route profile** command in global configuration mode enables this feature. After enabling this feature, the router tracks the number of routing table changes that occurred over 5-second sampling intervals. This can give you an indication of the overall stability of the routing table, without the need to enable a **debug** command. However, to find out which particular route or routes are causing the instability, enabling the **debug ip routing** command might be necessary. The output of the **show ip route profile** command might not be self-explanatory without researching the command references. Example 5-18 displays the output of the **show ip route profile** command after the feature has been enabled in global configuration mode using the **ip route profile** command. This example shows the frequency of routing table changes in a 5-second sampling interval. In Example 5-18, number 2 under the Prefix add column and row 20 indicates that there have been two 5-second intervals during which 20 or more (but less than 25) Prefix adds have happened. Note that the number of changes in the forwarding path is the accumulation of prefix-add, next-hop change, and pathcount change statistics.

Example 5-18 show ip route profile *Command Output*

```
Router# show ip route profile
-------------------------------------
Change/    Fwd-path    Prefix    Nexthop    Pathcount    Prefix
interval   change       add        Change      Change          refresh
-------------------------------------
0             87          87         89          89             89
1             0           0          0           0              0
2             0           0          0           0              0
3             0           0          0           0              0
```

```
4          0          0          0          0          0
5          0          0          0          0          0
10         0          0          0          0          0
15         0          0          0          0          0
20         2          2          0          0          0
25         0          0          0          0          0
```

Within the table drawn as the output of the **show ip route profile** command, the numeric value under each column is interpreted as follows:

- **Change/interval:** Represents the frequency buckets. A Change/interval of 20, for example, represents the bucket that is incremented when a particular event occurs 20 times in a sampling interval. It is common to see high counters for the Change/interval bucket for 0. This counter represents the number of sampling intervals in which there were no changes to the routing table. Route removals are not counted in the statistics, only route additions.
- **Fwd-path change:** Number of changes in the forwarding path. This value represents the accumulation of Prefix add, Nexthop change, and Pathcount change.
- **Prefix add:** A new prefix was added to the routing table.
- **Nexthop change:** A prefix is not added or removed, but the next hop changes. This statistic is seen only with recursive routes that are installed in the routing table.
- **Pathcount change:** The number of paths in the routing table has changed. This change is the result of an increase in the number of paths for an IGP.
- **Prefix refresh:** Indicates standard routing table maintenance. The forwarding behavior was not changed.

When the network is stable, only the counters in the first row should increase, because this row represents the number of intervals during which no changes to the routing occurred. When rows other than the first row increase in a situation that you thought to be stable, this could indicate a routing loop.

Troubleshooting Example: Redistribution from OSPF to EIGRP

The example presented here has been designed to illustrate the redistribution process and the commands that you can use to verify it. The case does not revolve around a problem that needs to be diagnosed and resolved; it simply tracks a route originating from an OSPF network being redistributed into EIGRP. The output of various **show** commands are presented to demonstrate how a route can be tracked in a situation where redistribution is working correctly. To troubleshoot effectively, it is important to know the behavior of processes and protocols when everything is working correctly, so it can be compared and contrasted against the behavior when it is malfunctioning. The situation is based on the network shown in Figure 5-6. Network 10.1.152.0/24 resides in area 1 of the OSPF network and is connected to the multilayer switches CSW1 and CSW2. Router CRO1 is participating in OSPF in area 0 to communicate with switches CSW1 and CSW2. Router CRO1 is also connected to router BRO1, and these two routers use EIGRP to exchange routing information. Redistribution has been configured as the commands shown in Figure 5-6.

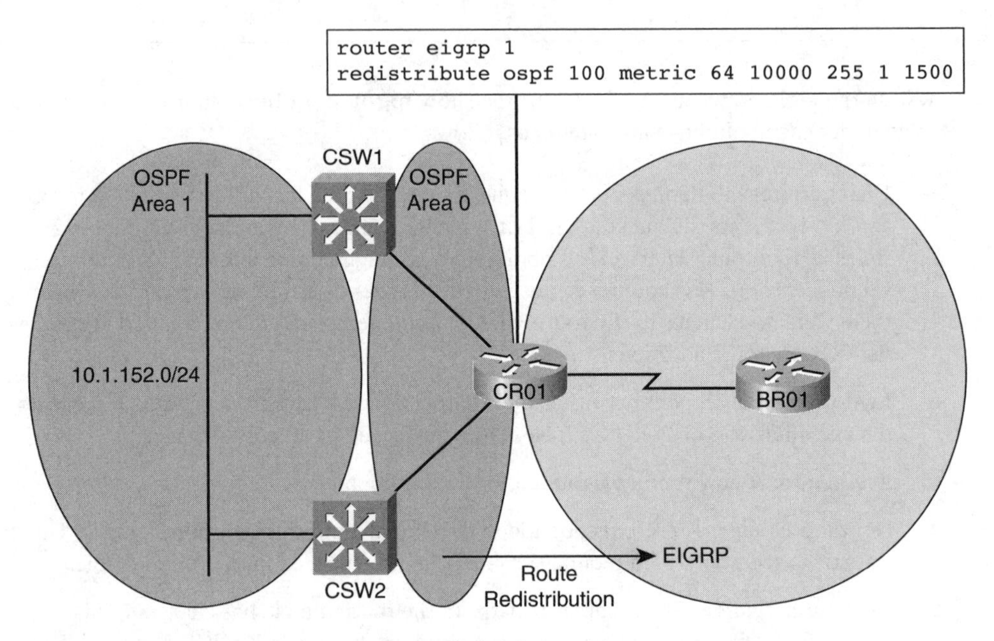

Figure 5-6 *Tracking Routes Redistributed from OSPF into EIGRP*

To follow the routing information as it is passed between the various routing protocol data structures, Example 5-19 shows the main data structure of the source protocol, the OSPF database. Two type 3 summary LSAs have been received and stored in the database for network 10.1.152.0/24, one from switch CSW1 and one from switch CSW2.

Example 5-19 *Router CRO1's OSPF Database Is Displayed Looking for LSA Type 3*

```
CRO1# show ip ospf database ¦ begin Summary
        Summary Net Link States (Area 0)

Link ID         ADV Router      Age         Seq#         Checksum
10.1.152.0      10.1.220.252    472         0x8000003B   0x00A7D1
10.1.152.0      10.1.220.253    558         0x8000003B   0x00A1D6
<... further output omitted ...>
```

OSPF executes the SPF algorithm and calculates the cost of the path to 10.1.152.0 through switches CSW1 and CSW2. After computing the results, the lowest-cost path is selected for installation into the routing table if no competing routes with a lower administrative distance are present. Next, Example 5-20 shows the routing table for network 10.1.152.0/24 on router CRO1. Both paths through switch CSW1 and switch CSW2 have been installed in the routing table because their costs are identical. The routing table also shows that this route has been marked for redistribution by EIGRP, and the configured EIGRP seed metric is also listed.

Example 5-20 *The IP Routing Table Includes Two OSPF Paths to 10.1.152.0/24*

```
CRO1# show ip route 10.1.152.0 255.255.255.0
Routing entry for 10.1.152.0/24
  Known via "ospf 100", distance 110, metric 2, type inter area
  Redistributing via eigrp 1
  Advertised by eigrp 1 metric 64 10000 255 1 1500
  Last update from 10.1.192.9 on FastEthernet0/1, 00:28:24 ago
  Routing Descriptor Blocks:
    10.1.192.9, from 10.1.220.253, 00:28:24 ago, via FastEthernet0/1
      Route metric is 2, traffic share count is 1
  * 10.1.192.1, from 10.1.220.252, 00:28:24 ago, via FastEthernet0/0
      Route metric is 2, traffic share count is 1
```

The output in Example 5-21 shows the EIGRP topology table for network 10.1.152.0/24 on router CRO1, verifying that the route is being redistributed. Here, you can clearly see that the route was taken from the routing table and inserted into the topology table as an external route. The five components of the configured seed metric are listed. In addition, some extra parameters were attached to the route to mark that the route was originated by the OSPF protocol with process number 100 and was injected into EIGRP by the router with EIGRP router ID 10.1.220.1 (which is the local router, CRO1).

Example 5-21 *The EIGRP Topology Table Information About 10.1.152.0/24 on CRO1*

```
CRO1# show ip eigrp topology 10.1.152.0 255.255.255.0
IP-EIGRP (AS 1): Topology entry for 10.1.152.0/24
  State is Passive, Query origin flag is 1, 1 Successor(s), FD is 42560000
  Routing Descriptor Blocks:
  10.1.192.9, from Redistributed, Send flag is 0x0
      Composite metric is (42560000/0), Route is External
      Vector metric:
        Minimum bandwidth is 64 Kbit
        Total delay is 100000 microseconds
        Reliability is 255/255
        Load is 1/255
        Minimum MTU is 1500
        Hop count is 0
```

```
    External data:
      Originating router is 10.1.220.1 (this system)
      AS number of route is 100
      External protocol is OSPF, external metric is 2
      Administrator tag is 0 (0x00000000)
```

The external information that router CRO1 added to the route during redistribution is passed along to router BRO1 within the EIGRP routing updates. When you display the EIGRP topology table on router BRO1, as demonstrated in Example 5-22, the originating router and routing protocol are still visible. Clearly, this information can be useful when you are troubleshooting redistribution into EIGRP because it makes it easy to see which router is the source when you are seeing unexpected routes. The information that is attached to and exchanged along with the external routes is different for each routing protocol.

Example 5-22 *The EIGRP Topology Table Information About 10.1.152.0/24 on BRO1*

```
BRO1# show ip eigrp topology 10.1.152.0 255.255.255.0
IP-EIGRP (AS 1): Topology entry for 10.1.152.0/24
  State is Passive, Query origin flag is 1, 1 Successor(s), FD is 43072000
  Routing Descriptor Blocks:
  10.1.193.1 (Serial0/0/1), from 10.1.193.1, Send flag is 0x0
      Composite metric is (43072000/42560000), Route is External
      Vector metric:
        Minimum bandwidth is 64 Kbit
        Total delay is 120000 microseconds
        Reliability is 255/255
        Load is 1/255
        Minimum MTU is 1500
        Hop count is 1
      External data:
        Originating router is 10.1.220.1
        AS number of route is 100
        External protocol is OSPF, external metric is 2
        Administrator tag is 0 (0x00000000)
```

Finally, on router BRO1, EIGRP selects 10.1.152./24 as the best route. The route is then installed in the IP routing table. The route is marked as an EIGRP external route and has a corresponding administrative distance of 170, as shown in Example 5-23. However, the external information that was present in the EIGRP topology table, such as the originating router and protocol, is not carried into the routing table.

Example 5-23 *BRO1's Routing Table Has the EIGRP External Route 10.1.152.0/24 Installed*

```
BRO1# show ip route 10.1.152.0 255.255.255.0
Routing entry for 10.1.152.0/24
  Known via "eigrp 1", distance 170, metric 43072000, type external
  Redistributing via eigrp 1
  Last update from 10.1.193.1 on Serial0/0/1, 00:00:35 ago
  Routing Descriptor Blocks:
  * 10.1.193.1, from 10.1.193.1, 00:00:35 ago, via Serial0/0/1
      Route metric is 43072000, traffic share count is 1
      Total delay is 120000 microseconds, minimum bandwidth is 64 Kbit
      Reliability 255/255, minimum MTU 1500 bytes
      Loading 3/255, Hops 1
```

This case illustrated the process that you can use to verify the various data structures that play a role in redistribution processes. It also shows that it is important to practice the use of these commands as part of the creation of a baseline of your network to know the expected results in a working situation.

Troubleshooting BGP

Enterprise networks might use the Border Gateway Protocol (BGP) to exchange routing information in a controlled fashion with external parties such as Internet service providers or other providers of IP-based services. BGP can also be used to exchange routing information between different regions (within the enterprise network) that are managed and administered by different organizational groups. BGP offers a toolkit to implement routing policies and control the flow of traffic to and from external parties such as service providers, or between the different regions of the network. BGP is an inter-autonomous (inter-AS) or exterior gateway protocol (EGP) ofter used in combination with an intra-autonomous system (intra-AS) or interior gateway protocol (IGP) such as EIGRP, IS-IS, or the OSPF routing protocol. Understanding the mechanics of BGP and its interaction with IGPs is essential for troubleshooting complex networks that deploy BGP. A network support engineer must know the data structures used by BGP and the flow of routing information between routers running the BGP protocol. Network support engineers must also be familiar with the processing of routing information inside the router. Finally, a support staff must know the Cisco IOS commands to gather information from the BGP data structures and routing processes to perform structured troubleshooting.

BGP Route Processing and Data Structures

BGP is classified as an EGP or an inter-autonomous-system routing protocol. BGP fulfills a different role in enterprise networks when compared to IGPs, such as EIGRP or the OSPF routing protocols. BGP is not used to find the best paths within the enterprise network based on metrics such as bandwidth, delay, or path cost, but it is used to exchange routing information with external networks (other autonomous systems), such as Internet service providers, and to implement routing policies to control the flow of traffic to and from those external networks. Although its purpose is different from IGPs, BGP is still a routing protocol in the sense that it exchanges information about reachability of prefixes with other BGP routers, selects the best path for each of the prefixes that it has learned about, and offers the best paths to the routing table.

Similar to other routing protocols, the following elements must be discerned about BGP:

- **Reception of routing information from neighbors:** One of the major differences between BGP and IGPs is that for BGP, its neighbors need not be directly connected. Neighbors are manually configured, not automatically discovered through a hello protocol. A TCP session is established between the predefined neighbors to exchange routing information, and this TCP session can span multiple router hops if necessary. Because the term *neighbor* inherently implies a sense of close proximity, an alternative commonly used term for two BGP routers that exchange information is *peer*. The terms *peer* and *neighbor* are used interchangeably within the BGP context. Cisco IOS command outputs use the term *neighbor*.
- **Routing protocol data structures:** BGP has two main data structures. The first one is a neighbor table to keep track of the state of configured neighbors. The second is BGP's main data structure, the BGP table, which BGP uses to store all the prefixes, including those received from the neighbors.
- **Route injection or redistribution:** BGP does not automatically inject any routes into the BGP table. Routes learned from neighbors are placed in the BGP table and can be advertised out to other BGP neighbors. Routes learned from internal (IBGP) neighbors are subject to the synchronization rule, unless synchronization is off. There are two methods to inject prefixes into the BGP table and advertise them to BGP neighbors:
  - The prefixes must be specifically configured under the BGP routing process (using the **network** statement).
  - The prefixes must be redistributed into BGP (from connected, static, or another interior routing protocol).

  In both cases, a prefix needs to be present in the IP routing table before it can be advertised to BGP neighbors. Because conditional route injection is beyond the scope of this book, it is not discussed here.
- **Route selection and installation:** BGP has a complex decision algorithm to compare paths received from different neighbors and select the best one for each prefix. Similar to other routing protocols, BGP offers the paths that it selects as best to the IP routing table. On Cisco routers, BGP routes have an administrative distance of 200, unless they are learned from external BGP neighbors (those with different autonomous system numbers); in which case, the administrative distance is 20.

- **Transmission of routing information to neighbors:** Paths that are selected as best in the BGP table can be advertised to other BGP routers. Several rules, such as the one commonly referred to as IBGP split-horizon rule, govern the advertisement of BGP routes to neighbors. Also, access lists, prefix lists, and route maps may be applied to filter and manipulate the prefixes and their attributes before exchanging them with a neighbor. This type of filtering and manipulation can be performed either before transmitting the information to a neighbor or when receiving information from a neighbor.

BGP uses two main data structures to store its operational data, configured parameters, and statistics:

- **Neighbor table:** This table lists all neighbors that have been configured on a router. This table stores valuable information such as the configured autonomous system number of the neighbor, whether the neighbor is an internal or an external peer, the state of the session, how long the neighbor has been up/down for (uptime), and how many prefixes were exchanged with the neighbor.
- **BGP table:** This table, sometimes called the BGP Routing Information Base (RIB), stores all the locally injected routes, plus all routes that were received from all the router's peers, together with all the BGP attributes that are associated with each route, such as the next hop, autonomous system path, local preference, origin, multi-exit discriminator (MED) or metric, origin code, and community attributes. For each prefix, the BGP best path selection algorithm assesses the usability of the available paths and, if one or more usable paths exist, selects one of the paths as the best path. The best path is subsequently advertised to other BGP peers, and BGP attempts to install this route in the routing table (offers it to the IP routing table). One of the tests that the BGP best path selection algorithm performs is validating the reachability of the next-hop attribute of a path. If the next-hop IP address is reachable as per the IP routing table's content, the path may be considered as a best path candidate. If no match can be found in the routing table for the next-hop address, the path is not considered usable, and it will not be considered as a best path candidate. By default, BGP will select only one best path for each prefix. The BGP Multipath feature allows additional paths to be installed in the IP routing table.

BGP Routing Information Flow

Unlike interior routing protocols, BGP neighbors are explicitly configured, not automatically discovered based on a hello protocol. A BGP neighbor is configured manually by specifying its IP address and autonomous system number within BGP router configuration. A BGP router attempts to establish a TCP session to the neighbor IP address on TCP port 179. Alternatively, it will accept incoming TCP sessions to port 179, as long as the source IP address matches one of its configured neighbor IP addresses. After a TCP session has been successfully established with the neighbor, the two routers send BGP OPEN messages to exchange basic parameters and capabilities, such as autonomous system number, router ID, hold time, and supported address families. During this phase, each router compares the neighbor's claimed autonomous system number to the autonomous system number its administrator has entered for the neighbor. If these numbers do not match, the session is reset, and the relation is not established.

As a result of this process, the following issues are common causes for failure of BGP peering establishment:

- There is no IP connectivity between the local BGP router and the configured peer's IP addresses. Because BGP peers are not necessarily directly connected, both routers need to have an IP path to the configured neighbor IP address in their routing table.
- The source IP address used by the router that initiates the session does not match the configured neighbor IP address on the receiving router.
- The autonomous system number of a BGP router (specified in its HELLO or OPEN message) does not match the autonomous system number its neighbor has configured for it (and expects from it).

After the TCP session has been established and OPEN messages have been successfully exchange and accepted, BGP starts exchanging update messages over the established TCP session. BGP uses an incremental update process. When a BGP peer relationship is first established, each of the peers advertises its best route for each prefix to its peer. Both peers subsequently install the received routes in the BGP table and execute the BGP best path selection algorithm to select the best path for each prefix based on the newly received information. Each time a new best path for a prefix is selected in the BGP table, an update for that prefix is sent to all relevant peers. When a prefix is removed from the BGP table, a WITHDRAW message for the prefix is sent to all relevant peers. To determine which peers need to be updated, the router applies rules such as the IBGP split-horizon rule or any administratively configured filters. BGP updates are commonly filtered or manipulated by use of access lists, prefix lists, or route maps. These tools can either be applied at the time updates are received, before the prefixes are installed in the BGP table, or at the time updates are transmitted to a peer.

Cisco IOS BGP Commands

The following commands enable you to gather information from the BGP data structures:

- **show ip bgp summary:** This command displays essential BGP parameters, such as the router ID and autonomous system number of the router, statistics on the memory usage of the BGP process, and a brief overview of the configured neighbors and the state of the relationship with each of the configured neighbors. This command is often used to quickly check the status of the relationship with one or more neighbors or how long the relation has been down/up.
- **show ip bgp neighbors:** This command lists all configured neighbors and their current operational state, configured parameters, and extensive statistics for each neighbor. The output of this command can be limited to a specific neighbor by using the **show ip bgp neighbors** *ip-address* command. This command provides more detail about the neighbor than the **show ip bgp summary** command.

- **show ip bgp:** This command displays the content of the BGP table. To select a specific entry from the table, the network and mask of the selected prefix can be provided as an option to the command. This command is useful during troubleshooting to see which paths are present, what their attributes are, and why certain paths are selected as best. Note that this command does not reveal all the attributes of the BGP paths. To see all the attributes, you must display one BGP prefix at a time using the **show ip bgp** *prefix* command.

The following debugs can be used to observe the transmission and reception of BGP packets and the exchange of routing information:

- **debug ip bgp:** This debug displays significant BGP-related events, most notably the subsequent phases of establishing a BGP peering relationship. This command does not display the content of the BGP updates and is a relatively safe to use. This command is useful during fact gathering.
- **debug ip bgp updates:** This debug displays the transmission and reception of BGP updates. The output of this debug can be limited to a specific neighbor and specific prefixes by use of extra options. Issuing the command **debug ip bgp ip-address updates** *access-list* limits the output of the command to only updates received from or sent to the neighbor specified by the **ip-address** option and only for those networks that match the access list specified by the *access-list* option. If no restrictions are imposed by use of the *access-list* or **neighbor** options, this command can generate a large amount of output and affect the router's performance. During troubleshooting, this proves useful because you can see which router is or is not sending which updates.

Troubleshooting Example: Routing Problem in a BGP Network

The purpose of this troubleshooting example is to illustrate how you can leverage knowledge of BGP data structures, update processes, and Cisco IOS commands for BGP troubleshooting. The enterprise network shown in Figure 5-7 uses BGP to exchange routing information with two different Internet service providers (ISPs). When a **traceroute** command is executed on router IRO1 to determine the path that is used to reach IP address 192.168.224.1, which belongs to an IP address block that is owned by ISP1, it turns out that the traffic path goes through router IRO2, as shown in Example 5-24.

Example 5-24 traceroute *Results Show Packets Going Through IRO1 Toward ISP1*

```
IRO1# trace 192.168.224.1
Type escape sequence to abort.
Tracing the route to 192.168.224.1
  1 10.1.192.20 4 msec 0 msec 0 msec
  2 172.24.244.86 [AS 64566] 4 msec 0 msec 4 msec
  3 192.168.100.1 [AS 65486] 0 msec 4 msec 0 msec
  4 192.168.224.1 [AS 65525] 0 msec *  0 msec
```

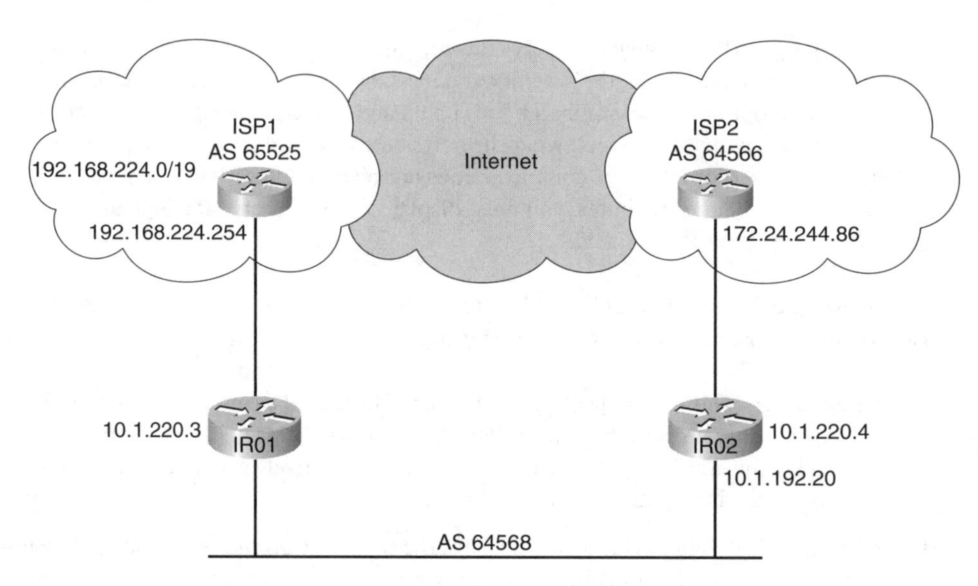

Figure 5-7 *Troubleshooting a BGP Routing Problem*

This behavior is worth investigating because it is expected that traffic destined for a network that is advertised by Internet service provider 1 would go directly to ISP1 and not through Internet service provider 2. To verify whether this problem is caused by an underlying Layer 1, Layer 2, or Layer 3 problem, a **ping** command is executed to test the Layer 3 connectivity to the access router of ISP1, as demonstrated in Example 5-25.

Example 5-25 **ping** *Command Results Show That the Link to ISP1 Access Router Is Up*

```
IRO1# ping 192.168.224.254

Type escape sequence to abort.
Sending 5, 100-byte ICMP Echos to 192.168.224.254, timeout is 2 seconds:
!!!!!
Success rate is 100 percent (5/5), round-trip min/avg/max = 1/1/4 ms
```

The successful ping to ISP1's access router verifies that the link between router IRO1 and ISP1 access router is operational at Layers 3 and below. Given that the link to ISP1 is functional, but is not used to route the packets to ISP1, this is a routing problem. Because BGP is used for external routing, investigation of the BGP operation is in order. There are various different methods to troubleshoot this problem. The objective is to find out why the direct path to Internet service provider 1 is not being used to route traffic to IP address 192.168.224.1. There are two likely reasons why the traffic is routed through router IRO2 instead of directly to Internet service provider 1:

- Router IRO1 has not learned about the prefix directly from ISP1 at all.

- Router IRO1 router has learned about the route, but it incorrectly prefers the path through router IRO2.

To start the investigation, a good first step is to confirm that the path used to route the traffic to 192.168.224.1 is indeed the BGP route learned from router IRO2 and not a route obtained from some other source. The output of Example 5-26 shows that the route to network 192.168.224.0/19 is the best match for destination IP address 192.168.224.1 and that this route is an internal BGP path and its source is the router with IP address 10.1.220.4, which is IRO2.

Example 5-26 *Within IP Routing Table, What Protocol Is the Source of the Path to 192.168.224.0/19?*

```
IRO1# show ip route 192.168.224.1
Routing entry for 192.168.224.0/19, supernet
  Known via "bgp 64568", distance 200, metric 0
  Tag 64566, type internal
  Redistributing via eigrp 1
  Last update from 172.24.244.86 00:24:22 ago
  Routing Descriptor Blocks:
  * 172.24.244.86, from 10.1.220.4, 00:24:22 ago
      Route metric is 0, traffic share count is 1
      AS Hops 2
      Route tag 64566
```

After verifying the routing table, it is clear that prefix 192.168.224.0/19 was learned through BGP and installed in the IP routing table. However, the IP routing table does not show whether the path through IRO2 is used because no other path is available or simply because the path through IRO2 was selected as the best path. This information can be obtained from the BGP table. The output of Example 5-27 shows that only the path through router IRO2 is present in the BGP table and no other BGP-learned paths are available.

Example 5-27 *BGP Table Shows Only One Path to 192.168.224.0/19*

```
IRO1# show ip bgp 192.168.224.1
BGP routing table entry for 192.168.224.0/19, version 12
Paths: (1 available, best #1, table Default-IP-Routing-Table)
  Not advertised to any peer
  64566 65525
    172.24.244.86 (metric 30720) from 10.1.220.4 (10.1.220.4)
      Origin IGP, metric 0, localpref 100, valid, internal, best
```

The fact that the path through Internet service provider 1 is not present in the BGP table can have several different causes. ISP1 might not advertise the route, or ISP1 advertises it, but router IRO1 rejects or ignores the advertisement, or possibly router IRO1 and ISP1 have not successfully established a peering relationship and no routes have been exchanged at all. At this point, a good next step is to start with the third option and investigate whether a neighbor relationship has been established between routers IRO1 and the ISP1 router. Example 5-28 displays the output of the **show ip bgp summary** command executed on IRO1 router.

Example 5-28 *BGP Neighbor 192.168.224.244 (ISP1 Access Router) Is in Active State*

```
IRO1# show ip bgp summary
BGP router identifier 10.1.220.3, local AS number 64568
BGP table version is 14, main routing table version 14
6 network entries using 702 bytes of memory
7 path entries using 364 bytes of memory
6/4 BGP path/bestpath attribute entries using 744 bytes of memory
3 BGP AS-PATH entries using 72 bytes of memory
0 BGP route-map cache entries using 0 bytes of memory
0 BGP filter-list cache entries using 0 bytes of memory
BGP using 1882 total bytes of memory
BGP activity 6/0 prefixes, 13/6 paths, scan interval 60 secs

Neighbor        V    AS MsgRcvd MsgSent   TblVer  InQ OutQ Up/Down  State/PfxRcd
10.1.220.4      4 64568      82      80       14    0    0 01:12:02            6
192.168.224.244 4 65525       0       0        0    0    0 never    Active
```

The output shown on Example 5-28 reveals that the peering to IP address 10.1.220.4 (IRO2) has been established and six prefixes have been received from the neighbor, while the peering to IP address 192.168.224.244 is in the Active state. This means that this router is trying to establish a TCP session to neighbor 192.168.224.244, but has not succeeded yet. Executing a **ping** command to IP address 192.168.224.244 yields the result shown in Example 5-29.

Example 5-29 ***ping*** *Command to the Configured Neighbor's Address Fails*

```
IRO1# ping 192.168.224.244
Type escape sequence to abort.
Sending 5, 100-byte ICMP Echos to 192.168.224.244, timeout is 2 seconds:
.....
Success rate is 0 percent (0/5)
```

The earlier ping to the directly connected interface of ISP1 (192.168.224.254) was successful, yet the ping to the IP address 192.168.224.244, which is the configured neighbor address for ISP1, fails. This might lead to the conjecture that IP address 192.168.224.244 is not the correct IP address and IP address 192.168.224.254 should have been used for the peering to ISP1 instead. After the IP address in the **neighbor** statement is changed to

IP address 192.168.224.254 to test the hypothesis that the misconfigured IP address was the cause of the problem, the results must be examined. Strictly speaking, the only test that you need to perform to confirm you have solved the problem is to execute the **traceroute** command again to confirm that packets traveling to IP address 192.168.224.1 are now sent directly to ISP1, instead of taking the longer path through router IRO2 and ISP2. However, to show the impact of the change on all the BGP data structures, the changes in the output of the **show** commands that were used earlier to diagnose the problem are displayed in Example 5-30.

Example 5-30 *After the Correction Was Made, the Neighbor State for 192.168.224.254 Is Established, and a Path to 192.168.224.0/19 Is Received from This Neighbor*

```
IR01(config)# router bgp 64568
IR01(config-router)# no neighbor 192.168.224.244
IR01(config-router)# neighbor 192.168.224.254 remote-as 65525
IR01(config-router)# end
IRO1# show ip bgp summary | begin Neighbor
Neighbor        V    AS MsgRcvd MsgSent  TblVer  InQ  OutQ Up/Down   State/PfxRcd
10.1.220.4      4 64568     146     146      19    0     0 02:15:17        5
192.168.224.254 4 65525      14      12      19    0     0 00:03:23        5

IRO1# show ip bgp 192.168.224.0
BGP routing table entry for 192.168.224.0/19, version 17
Paths: (1 available, best #1, table Default-IP-Routing-Table)
  Advertised to update-groups:
     2
  65525
    192.168.224.254 from 192.168.224.254 (192.168.100.1)
      Origin IGP, metric 0, localpref 100, valid, external, best
```

As the output in Example 5-30 shows, the peering to ISP1 router has now been successfully established, and five prefixes were received from neighbor 192.168.224.254. Verification of the BGP table on router IRO1 shows that the path to prefix 192.168.224.0/19 via neighbor 192.168.224.254 to autonomous system 65525 has now been selected as the best path. It is interesting to note that the path to 192.168.224.0/19 through router IRO2 is no longer displayed in IRO1's BGP table. You might expect to see that path displayed as an alternative path to reach prefix 192.168.224.0/19, but it is not present in IRO's BGP table at all.

To answer this question, you need to examine the BGP table on router IRO2, as shown in Example 5-31.

Example 5-31 *IRO2's BGP Table Shows Two Paths to 192.168.224.0/19*

```
IRO2# show ip bgp 192.168.224.0
BGP routing table entry for 192.168.224.0/19, version 24
```

```
Paths: (2 available, best #1, table Default-IP-Routing-Table)
  Advertised to update-groups:
     1
  65525

    192.168.224.254 (metric 30720) from 10.1.220.3 (10.1.220.3)
      Origin IGP, metric 0, localpref 100, valid, internal, best
  64566 65525

    172.24.244.86 from 172.24.244.86 (172.24.240.1)
      Origin IGP, localpref 100, valid, external
```

Example 5-31 shows that router IRO2 has received a path to 192.168.224.0/19 from router IRO1 and installed it in its BGP table. After executing the BGP best path selection algorithm for prefix 192.168.224.0/19, IRO2 selects the path through (learned from) IRO1 as the best path to prefix 192.168.22.0/19 in autonomous system 65525. The less-attractive alternative is through ISP2 with two items in the AS-Path. Because BGP on IRO2 has changed its best path to this prefix, it now withdraws the old path that it has previously advertised, and subsequently it advertises the new best path to prefix 192.168.224.0/19 to all relevant neighbors. After IRO2 withdraws its old path from its neighbors, IRO1 remains with a single path to 192.168.224.0/19, which is through ISP1. You can see this in the output shown in Example 5-32. You should also notice that IRO1 is now showing five prefixes received from IRO2 as shown in Example 5-30 instead of six as shown in Example 5-28.

Example 5-32 *IRO1's BGP Table Has One Path to 192.168.224.0/19, Through ISP1*

```
IRO1# show ip route 192.168.224.1
Routing entry for 192.168.224.0/19, supernet
  Known via "bgp 64568", distance 20, metric 0
  Tag 65525, type external
  Redistributing via eigrp 1
  Last update from 192.168.224.254 00:49:55 ago
  Routing Descriptor Blocks:
  * 192.168.224.254, from 192.168.224.254, 00:49:55 ago
      Route metric is 0, traffic share count is 1
      AS Hops 1
      Route tag 65525

IRO1# traceroute 192.168.224.1
Type escape sequence to abort.
Tracing the route to 192.168.224.1

  1 192.168.224.254 [AS 65525] 0 msec 0 msec 4 msec
  2 192.168.224.1 [AS 65525] 0 msec 0 msec *
```

The output shown in Example 5-32 confirms that the path through neighbor 192.168.224.254 (ISP1) has been installed in the routing table, and the result of the **traceroute** command, also shown in Example 5-32, confirms that this path is now used to route packets to IP address 192.168.224.1. This troubleshooting example illustrates the use of the Cisco IOS **show** commands to display the content of the BGP data structures. It also illustrates how you can leverage knowledge of these data structures and the flow of BGP routing information to diagnose and resolve BGP routing problems.

Note At Cisco.com, you can find an extremely helpful flowchart for troubleshooting BGP issues. Assuming you have a Cisco.com login, you can find this information at http://www.cisco.com/en/US/customer/tech/tk365/technologies_tech_note09186a008009478a.shtml.

Summary

There are several variations of the **show ip route** command, with different options. These variations reveal different amounts of information. During troubleshooting, you might find one or more of these options more useful than the generic command:

- **show ip route** *ip-address*: Causes the router to perform a routing table lookup for that IP address and display the best route that matches the address and all associated control plane details.
- **show ip route** *network mask*: Searches the routing table for an exact match for that network and mask, and if it is found, this entry is displayed with all of its associated control plane details.
- **show ip route** *network mask* **longer-prefixes**: Using the **longer-prefixes** option will cause the router to display all prefixes in the routing table that fall within the prefix specified by the network and mask parameters. This command can be very useful to diagnose problems related to route summarization.

There are several variations of the **show ip cef** command, with different options. These variations reveal different amounts of information. During troubleshooting, you might find one or more of these options more useful than the generic command:

- **show ip cef** *ip-address*: Searches the FIB for the prefix and displays no routing protocol related information, but only the information that is necessary to forward packets
- **show ip cef** *network mask*: Searches the FIB table for an exact match for that network and mask, and if it is found, displays the entry
- **show ip cef exact-route** *source destination*: Displays the exact adjacency that will be used to forward a packet with source and destination IP addresses as specified by the *source* and *destination* parameters

Two examples of commands that can be used to verify the Layer 3 to Layer 2 mappings are as follows:

- **show ip arp:** Verifies the dynamic IP address to Ethernet MAC address mappings that were resolved by the Address Resolution Protocol.
- **show frame-relay map:** Lists all the mappings of next-hop IP addresses on multipoint (sub-) interfaces to the DLCI of the corresponding PVC. It also lists any DLCIs that were manually associated to specific point-to-point subinterfaces.

Virtually all routing protocols include the following elements and processes:

- Reception of routing information from neighbors
- Routing protocol data structures
- Route injection or redistribution
- Route selection and installation
- Transmission of routing information to neighbors

EIGRP stores its operational data, configured parameters, and statistics in three main data structures:

- Interface table
- Neighbor table
- Topology table

You can use the following commands to gather information from the EIGRP data structures:

- **show ip eigrp interfaces:** Displays the list of interfaces that have been activated for EIGRP
- **show ip eigrp neighbors:** Lists all neighbors that have been discovered by the local router
- **show ip eigrp topology:** Displays the content of the EIGRP topology table

The following **debug** commands enable you to observe the transmission and reception of packets and the exchange of EIGRP routing information:

- **debug ip routing**

  (This is a generic IP debugging command that displays any changes that are made to the routing table, such as installation or removal of routes. This can be useful to diagnose routing protocol instabilities)
- **debug eigrp packets**
- **debug ip eigrp**

- **debug ip eigrp neighbor** *as-number ip-address*
- **debug ip eigrp** *as-number network mask*

OSPF stores its operational data, configured parameters, and statistics in four main data structures:

- **Interface table:** This table lists all interfaces that have been enabled for OSPF.
- **Neighbor table:** This table is used to keep track of all active OSPF neighbors.
- **Link-state database:** This is the main data structure that OSPF uses to store all its network topology information. This database contains full topology information for the areas that a router connects to, and information about the paths that are available to reach networks and subnets in other areas or other autonomous systems.
- **Routing Information Base:** After executing the SPF algorithm, the results of this calculation are stored in the RIB. This information includes the best routes to each individual prefix in the OSPF network and their associated path costs.

Two routers will become neighbors only if the following parameters match in the Hello packets:

- Hello and dead timers
- OSPF area number
- OSPF area type
- IP subnet and subnet mask
- Authentication type and authentication data

Once two OSPF routers are enabled to operated on a network, their neighbor relationship state goes through the following states: init, 2-way, exstart, exchange, loading, and full. Attempt state is only encountered when unicast Hellos are used and a neighbor has been explicitly configured. When the router has sent a Hello to the configured neighbor, but not received any Hello from the neighbor yet, the neighbor relationship is in the attempt state. This state is not used on point-to-point or broadcast type networks, which use multicast Hellos instead of unicast Hellos.

The following commands can be used to gather information from the OSPF data structures:

- **show ip ospf interface:** Displays the interfaces that have been activated for OSPF.
- **show ip ospf neighbor:** Lists all neighbors that have been discovered by this router on its active OSPF interfaces and shows their current state.
- **show ip ospf database:** Displays the content of the OSPF link-state database.

- **show ip ospf statistics:** Shows how often and when the SPF algorithm was last executed. This command can be helpful when diagnosing routing instability.

The following **debug** commands enable you to observe the transmission and reception of packets and the exchange of routing information:

- **debug ip routing:** Displays any changes that are made to the routing table
- **debug ip ospf packet:** Displays the transmission and reception of OSPF packets
- **debug ip ospf events:** Displays OSPF events
- **debug ip ospf adj:** Displays events that are related to the adjacency building process
- **debug ip ospf monitor:** Monitors when the SPF algorithm is scheduled to run and displays the triggering LSA and a summary of the results after the SPF algorithm has completed

There are two ways for routes to be injected in a routing protocol:

- **Directly connected:** These subnets can be injected by enabling the routing protocol on an interface. These routes are considered internal by the routing protocol.
- **External:** These are subnets from a different source and can be redistributed into the routing protocol's data structure. Because these routes were not originated by the routing protocol, they are considered external.

Two important conditions must be met for a prefix learned from one protocol (using redistribution) to be successfully advertised through another protocol:

- The route needs to be installed in the routing table.
- A proper seed metric is assigned to the redistributed route.

A feature that can be helpful in diagnosing suspected route instability is the route-profiling feature. Entering the **ip route profile** command in global configuration mode enables this feature. After you enable this feature, the router tracks the number of routing table changes that occur over 5-second sampling intervals. The **show ip route profile** command displays the results gathered by this feature. The output can give you an indication of the overall stability of the routing table, without the need to enable a **debug** command.

BGP uses two main data structures to store its operational data, configured parameters, and statistics:

- **Neighbor table:** This table lists all neighbors that have been configured on a router. This table stores valuable information such as the configured autonomous system number of the neighbor, whether the neighbor is an internal or an external peer, the state of the session, how long the neighbor has been up/down for (uptime), and how many prefixes were exchanged with the neighbor.

- **BGP table:** This table, sometimes called the BGP Routing Information Base (RIB), stores all the locally injected routes, plus all routes that were received from all the router's peers, together with all the BGP attributes that are associated with each route, such as the next hop, autonomous system path, local preference, origin, multi-exit discriminator (MED) or metric, origin code, and community attributes. For each prefix, the BGP best path selection algorithm assesses the usability of the available paths and, if one or more usable paths exist, selects one of the paths as the best path. The best path is subsequently advertised to other BGP peers, and BGP attempts to install this route in the IP routing table (offers it to the IP routing table).

The following issues are common causes for failure of BGP peering establishment:

- There is no IP connectivity between the local BGP router and the configured peer's IP addresses. Because BGP peers are not necessarily directly connected, both routers need to have an IP path to the configured neighbor IP address in their routing table.
- The source IP address used by the router that initiates the session does not match the configured neighbor IP address on the receiving router.
- The autonomous system number of a BGP router (specified in its HELLO or OPEN message) does not match the autonomous system number its neighbor has configured for it (and expects from it).

The following commands can be used to gather information from the BGP data structures:

- **show ip bgp summary:** Displays essential BGP parameters, such as the router ID and autonomous system number of the router, statistics on the memory usage of the BGP process, and a brief overview of the configured neighbors and the state of the relationship with each of the configured neighbors.
- **show ip bgp neighbors:** Lists all configured neighbors and their current operational state, configured parameters, and extensive statistics for each neighbor. The output of this command can be limited to a specific neighbor by using the **show ip bgp neighbors** *ip-address* command.
- **show ip bgp:** Displays the content of the BGP table. To select a specific entry from the table, the network and mask of the selected prefix can be provided as an option to the command.

The following **debug** commands enable you to observe the transmission and reception of BGP packets and the exchange of routing information:

- **debug ip bgp:** Displays significant BGP-related events, most notably the subsequent phases of establishing a BGP peering relationship. This command does not display the content of the BGP updates and is a relatively safe to use.

- **debug ip bgp updates:** Displays the transmission and reception of BGP updates. The output of this debug can be limited to a specific neighbor and specific prefixes by use of extra options.

Review Questions

Use the questions here to review what you learned in this chapter. The correct answers are found in Appendix A, "Answers to Chapter Review Questions."

1. Which two of the following items are recorded in the routing table for a prefix?
   a. VLAN
   b. Next-hop IP address
   c. Egress interface
   d. Ingress interface
   e. Next-hop MAC address
2. After consulting the routing table to route a packet, which other data structure on a router needs to be consulted to encapsulate the packet in an Ethernet frame (assuming the packet is not CEF switched)?
   a. MAC address table
   b. Link-state database
   c. Topology table
   d. Address Resolution Protocol (ARP) cache
   e. None of the answers are correct. All information necessary to route a packet and encapsulate it is contained in the routing table.
3. For a route that has a point-to-point interface as the egress interface, a next-hop IP address is not mandatory.
   a. True
   b. False
4. Which two of the following data structures contain similar information when using CEF? (Choose two.)
   a. The routing table and the FIB.
   b. The routing table and the adjacency table contain similar information.
   c. The FIB and the Layer 3 to Layer 2 mapping tables, such as the ARP cache contain similar information.
   d. The adjacency table and the Layer 3 to Layer 2 mapping tables, such as the ARP cache.

5. Figure 5-8 shows an IP packet that is in transit from Host A to Host B as it traverses the Ethernet LAN between Router E and host B. Which two addresses are contained in the two fields marked with? in the figure?

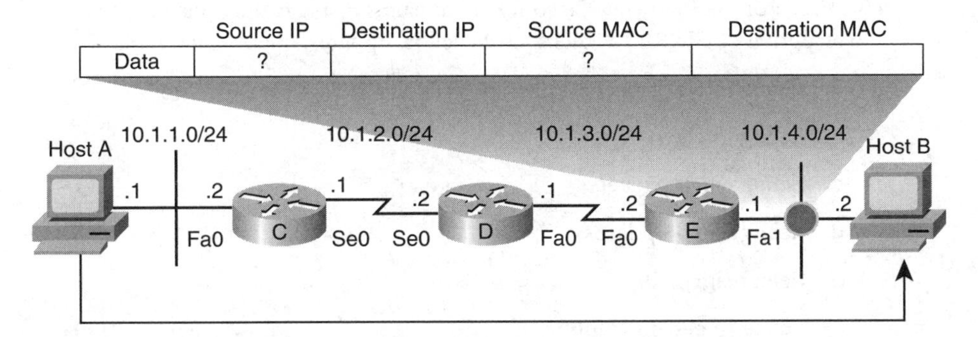

Figure 5-8 *An IP Packet from Host A to Host B in Transit*

a. IP address 10.1.4.1 and MAC address of Host B

b. IP address 10.1.4.1 and MAC address of Router E (Fa0)

c. IP address 10.1.4.2 and MAC address of Host B

d. IP address 10.1.1.1 and MAC address of Host A

e. IP address 10.1.1.1 and MAC address of Router E (Fa1)

f. IP address 10.1.4.1 and MAC address of Host A

6. Which Cisco IOS command displays the exact adjacency used to forward a packet from a specific source IP address to a specific destination IP address on a router that is using CEF?

7. Which Cisco IOS command displays the full Layer 2 header that will be used to forward frames to an adjacency on a router that is using CEF?

8. Which three of the following data structures does EIGRP use?

a. Link-state database

b. Topology table

c. ARP cache

d. Interface table

e. Adjacency table

f. Neighbor table

9. The EIGRP topology table contains all the routes that were received from all EIGRP routers in the autonomous system.

a. True

b. False

10. Which of the following Cisco IOS commands displays the transmission and reception of EIGRP packets such as hellos, updates, queries, and replies?

a. **debug ip eigrp packets**

b. **debug ip eigrp**

c. **debug eigrp packets**

d. **debug eigrp updates**

e. **debug eigrp adj**

f. **debug ip eigrp neighbor**

11. When you issue the **show ip eigrp interfaces** command on a router, it lists interface FastEthernet 0/1, but it does not list interface FastEthernet 0/0. Which two of the following statements could be a possible explanation for the absence of interface FastEthernet 0/0?

a. Interface FastEthernet 0/0 has been configured as a passive interface.

b. EIGRP is not enabled on the router.

c. The command **ip eigrp** *as-number* is not configured on interface FastEthernet 0/0.

d. None of the configured network statements matches the IP address of FastEthernet 0/0.

e. There are no active EIGRP neighbors on interface FastEthernet 0/0.

f. Interface FastEthernet 0/0 is not a feasible successor.

12. Based on the command output shown in Example 5-33, which route is the successor?

Example 5-33 *Which EIGRP Path to 10.1.220.1/32 Is Better?*

```
BRO1# show ip eigrp topology 10.1.220.1 255.255.255.255
IP-EIGRP (AS 1): Topology entry for 10.1.220.1/32
  State is Passive, Query origin flag is 1, 1 Successor(s), FD is 40640000
  Routing Descriptor Blocks:
  10.1.194.1 (Serial0/0/0.111), from 10.1.194.1, Send flag is 0x0
      Composite metric is (40640000/128256), Route is Internal
      Vector metric:
        Minimum bandwidth is 64 Kbit
```

```
          Total delay is 25000 microseconds
          Reliability is 255/255
          Load is 1/255
          Minimum MTU is 1500
          Hop count is 1
  10.1.163.130 (FastEthernet0/1.30), from 10.1.163.130, Send flag is 0x0
        Composite metric is (40642560/40640000), Route is Internal
        Vector metric:
          Minimum bandwidth is 64 Kbit
          Total delay is 25100 microseconds
          Reliability is 255/255
          Load is 1/255
          Minimum MTU is 1500
          Hop count is 2
```

- **a.** The route via 10.1.194.1, because it has the lowest hop count.
- **b.** The route via 10.1.163.130, because a Fast Ethernet interface has a higher bandwidth than a Serial interface.
- **c.** The route via 10.1.163, because its feasible distance (40642560) is better than the composite feasible distance (40640000).
- **d.** The route via 10.1.194.1, because its metric (40640000) is better than the metric via 10.1.163.1 (40642560).
- **e.** The route via 10.1.194.1, because its metric (128256) is better than the metric via 10.1.163.1 (40640000).

13. Which three of the following data structures does the OSPF protocol use?

- **a.** Link-state database
- **b.** Topology table
- **c.** ARP cache
- **d.** Interface table
- **e.** Adjacency table
- **f.** Neighbor table

14. Figure 5-9 displays an OSPF network consisting of three areas. No redistribution or summarization has been configured, and each link represents a single subnet. How many type 1 and type 2 LSAs are contained in the OSPF link-state database on router A?

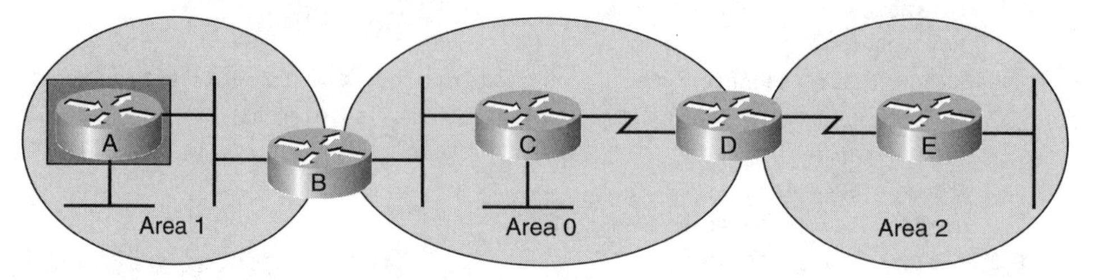

Figure 5-9 *How Many LSA Type 1 and 2 Are Stored in Router A?*

a. Two type 1 LSAs and two type 2 LSAs

b. Five type 1 LSAs and five type 2 LSAs

c. One type 1 LSA and one type 2 LSA

d. Two type 1 LSAs and one type 2 LSA

e. Two type 1 LSAs and five type 2 LSAs

15. Which three of the following parameters need to match in the Hello packets for two OSPF routers to become neighbors?

a. Hello and dead timer

b. Autonomous system number

c. Area number

d. Subnet mask on a point-to-point link

e. Area type

f. Router type

16. Figure 5-10 displays an OSPF network consisting of three areas. No redistribution or summarization has been configured and each link represents a single subnet. How many type 3 LSAs are contained in the OSPF link-state database on Router D?

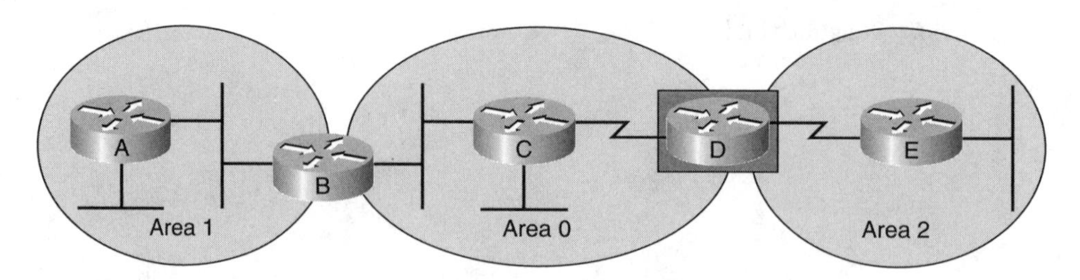

Figure 5-10 *How Many Type 3 LSAs Are Stored in Router D?*

17. Which of the following statements best describes the subsequent stages of the establishment of an OSPF adjacency? Fill in the blanks with init, 2-way, exstart, loading.

a. __________: This state indicates that the routers are starting the database exchange by establishing a master and slave relationship and determining the initial sequence number for the database description (DBD) packets.

b. __________: A neighbor is in this state if a Hello has been received from the neighbor, but the neighbor is not listing this router in its neighbor list yet.

c. __________: During this stage, each of the two routers can request missing LSAs from the other router.

d. __________: This is the state that a neighbor relationship is in when the router sees its own router ID listed in the active neighbor list in the Hello packets received from that neighbor.

18. Which four of the following OSPF neighbor states are transitory states?

a. Init

b. 2-way

c. Exstart

d. Exchange

e. Loading

f. Full

19. What Cisco IOS **debug** command for OSPF displays events related to the adjacency building process and allows you to see a neighbor relationship transition from one state to the next?

20. Which of the following Cisco IOS commands can be used to display the content of the OSPF link-state database?

a. **show ip ospf lsdb**

b. **show ip ospf link-states**

c. **show ip ospf database**

d. **show ip route ospf**

e. None of the answers are correct. Only the results of the shortest path first (SPF) calculation can be displayed, not the content of the database itself.

21. When you issue the **show ip ospf interface** command on a router, it lists interface FastEthernet 0/1, but it does not list interface FastEthernet 0/0. Which of the following statements could be a possible explanation for the absence of interface FastEthernet 0/0?

- **a.** Interface Fast Ethernet 0/0 has been configured as a passive interface.
- **b.** OSPF is not enabled on the router.
- **c.** None of the configured network statements matches the IP address of FastEthernet 0/0.
- **d.** There are no active OSPF neighbors on interface FastEthernet 0/0.
- **e.** The router is not a designated router for interface FastEthernet 0/0.

22. Which type of OSPF LSA is displayed in the output of Example 5-34?

Example 5-34 *Verifying OSPF LSAs*

```
CRO1# show ip ospf database summary 10.1.152.0
              OSPF Router with ID (10.1.220.1) (Process ID 100)
              Summary Net Link States (Area 0)
Routing Bit Set on this LSA
  LS age: 201
  Options: (No TOS-capability, DC, Upward)
  LS Type: Summary Links(Network)
  Link State ID: 10.1.152.0 (summary Network Number)
  Advertising Router: 10.1.220.252
  LS Seq Number: 80000001
  Checksum: 0x1C97
  Length: 28
  Network Mask: /24
  TOS: 0      Metric: 1
```

- **a.** Type 1 LSA
- **b.** Type 2 LSA
- **c.** Type 3 LSA
- **d.** Type 4 LSA
- **e.** Type 5 LSA

23. How does a router determine which route to install in the routing table if two routes for the same prefix from different routing protocols are available?

- **a.** It compares the metrics of the two protocols and installs the route with the lowest metric.
- **b.** It compares the administrative distance of the two protocols and installs the route with the lowest administrative distance.

c. It converts the metric of each of the routing protocols to the universal route metric (URM) and then installs the route with the lowest URM.

d. It installs both routes in the routing table and load balances the traffic across the two paths.

24. Which two of the following routing protocols have their default seed metric for redistribution set to infinity or unreachable?

a. RIP

b. IS-IS

c. OSPF

d. EIGRP

e. BGP

25. What Cisco IOS **debug** command displays routes being installed or removed from the routing table in real time?

26. Which two of the following information elements are exchanged by EIGRP for an external route that was redistributed from OSPF?

a. Originating OSPF area number

b. EIGRP router ID of the redistributing router

c. OSPF router ID of the originating router

d. Source routing protocol (OSPF)

27. Which two of the following data structures does Border Gateway Protocol (BGP) use?

a. Link-state database

b. Topology table

c. BGP table

d. Address Resolution Protocol (ARP) cache

e. Interface table

f. Adjacency table

g. Neighbor table

28. The BGP table on a router contains all the routes that were received from all its BGP peers. True or False?

a. True

b. False

29. BGP neighbors are discovered by use of a hello protocol. True or False?

a. True

b. False

30. Which two of the following reasons could cause the establishment of a BGP session to fail?

a. The source IP address used by the router that initiates the session does not match the configured IP address on the receiving router.

b. The TCP source port used by the router that initiates the session is not set to 179.

c. The autonomous system number of the router that initiates the session does not match the configured autonomous system number for the peer router on the receiving router.

d. The BGP keepalive and hold timer of the peers do not match.

31. Which of the following Cisco IOS commands displays the subsequent phases of establishing a BGP peering relationship?

a. **debug ip bgp**

b. **debug ip bgp adj**

c. **debug ip bgp peer**

d. **debug ip bgp updates**

e. **debug ip bgp events**

32. The output of the **show ip bgp summary** command displays Active as the state of a neighbor. What does this mean?

a. The peering session has been established and the routers are actively exchanging routes.

b. BGP has lost the best route in the BGP table for a prefix and is attempting to find a backup route via a query and reply process.

c. BGP is attempting to establish a TCP session to the neighbor, but has not succeeded yet.

d. This is the state that a peering relationship is in when the router sees its own router ID listed in the active peer list in the hello packets received from that peer.

Chapter 6

Troubleshooting Addressing Services

This chapter covers the following topics:

- Identify common IPv4 addressing service issues
- Identify common IPv6 routing issues

Network Address Translation (NAT) is a widely used tool by organizations that use private IP addresses on the inside and have global or registered addresses for Internet connectivity. This tool provides some level of privacy and security to the organization network, too. Along with its advantages, NAT has some disadvantages and conflicts with certain protocols and applications. Troubleshooting NAT requires knowledge of its operation, its conflicts, and appropriate troubleshooting tools and commands.

Dynamic Host Configuration Protocol (DHCP) is widely used technique for configuring the IP address and other parameters of IP devices. Usage of this protocol involves servers, relay agents, routers, and clients. Troubleshooting DHCP requires knowledge of this protocol, common configuration errors with respect to this protocol, and the relevant troubleshooting tools and commands.

IPv6 deployment has started in many parts of the world at different extents. Most vendor devices support all aspects of IP Version 6 (IPv6), including addressing, routing, filtering, and translations. Understanding IPv6 and troubleshooting IPv6 are progressively becoming more important and more in demand.

Identify Common IPv4 Addressing Service Issues

This section reviews NAT and DHCP and highlights common troubleshooting issues with respect to each one. For both of these topics, a troubleshooting example is provided as a case study practice.

NAT/PAT Operation

NAT was designed for IP Version 4 (IPv4) address conservation. Today, NAT is also used for address hiding, with security implications. NAT usually operates at the border of a network and translates the source address of the exiting IP packets that are private addresses to public addresses before packets are forwarded out, as illustrated in Figure 6-1. The packet header information and the corresponding translated IP address are kept in a NAT table. NAT does the reverse for the destination address of the responding IP packets based on the content of the NAT table. NAT can be used in multiple scenarios, not just in the classic situation of connecting to the public Internet. For example, NAT can be used to renumber your global address space when you switch between service providers. Also, in virtual private network (VPN) connectivity situations, you frequently find remote locations that have overlapping address spaces and NAT can overcome the connectivity issues that arise by translating the overlapping address spaces to nonoverlapping addresses.

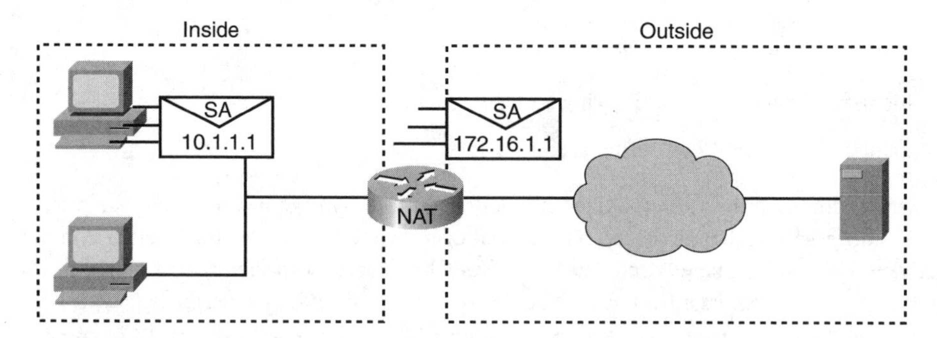

Figure 6-1 *NAT Operates at the Border of the Network, and It Generally Translates the Source IP Address of the Outgoing Packets and the Destination IP Address of the Incoming IP Packets*

In troubleshooting NAT, you need to be aware that NAT is used in different ways, each of which uses different resources and has its own limitations and barriers. Over the years, there have been multiple semantics and terminologies applied to these NAT types by different vendors, but in their simplest and most popular forms they fall within these three categories:

- **Static NAT:** In this case, inside local (locally significant) and inside global (globally significant) addresses are mapped one to one. This mapping is particularly useful when an inside device must be accessible from the outside network, such as the case of web servers in an Internet data center. In troubleshooting this type of NAT, you must be aware of its static nature, and how IP address changes might affect an existing static configuration. If the server changes inside or outside addresses, the static NAT entry will have the wrong settings and there will be connectivity problems.

  - **Dynamic NAT:** Dynamic NAT also translates addresses following the same underlying technology as static NAT; however, local addresses are translated to a group or pool of global addresses. This way of translating opens the door to issues related to the size of that global pool, because you are still dealing with one-to-one translation once a global address has been selected. You might leave some inside hosts without a valid global address, thus causing connectivity problems. This also opens the door to management, tracking, and audit issues, because of the dynamic nature of the translation: one time the host obeys a certain translation entry, and the next time it could be translating to a different address.

- **NAT overloading:** This type of NAT is a special type of dynamic NAT in which addresses are translated in a many-to-many fashion. This type is also known as Port Address Translation (PAT) because global addresses can be reused and the differentiator between many inside local addresses sharing the same global address is the port number. NAT overloading suffers from some application support issues.

The NAT types have slight design variations and each has its own benefits and limitations. Understanding the specific implementation method of each NAT type and its unique limitations is very useful during troubleshooting cases involving NAT. The main advantages of NAT are well known. Examples of that are keeping IP addresses from being depleted and providing some security by concealing the actual addresses of internal resources. However, the limitations of NAT add several issues that you need to consider. Examples of those issues are incompatibility of certain protocols and applications to NAT's address or port translation. In some cases, end-to-end traceability is lost and you must make changes to, or at least clear translations at the NAT device, which requires you to have administrative access and know the translation rules. You must also consider the performance degradation caused by NAT. Packets are assembled and disassembled to carry out the address translations, affecting device resources to a certain extent. Table 6-1 summarizes the main advantages and disadvantages of implementing NAT.

Table 6-1 *Advantages and Disadvantages of NAT Implementation*

Advantage	Disadvantages
Conserves registered addresses	Translation introduces processing delays
Hides the actual address of internal hosts and services	Loss of end-to-end IP reachability
Increases flexibility when connecting to Internet	Certain applications will not function with NAT enabled
Eliminates address renumbering as the network changes from one ISP to another	Considerations are needed when working with VPNs

Some applications or protocols have direct conflict with NAT or PAT. For example, imagine a case involving IPsec VPN. IPsec protocols encapsulate the original IP packet, and therefore the protocol type on the IP header changes (to Encapsulating Security Payload [ESP] or Authentication Header [AH]) and there is no TCP or UDP header next to the IP header. A lack of TCP or UDP header means that there is no port number for NAT/PAT to translate. If IPsec is not used in tunnel mode, meaning that the original IP header is not encapsulated in a new one, there is a chance that NAT/PAT will conflict with the integrity checks of IPsec protocols (ESP or AH). Some mechanisms have been invented to allow IPsec and NAT to coexist. Those mechanisms include NAT Transparency or NAT Traversal, IPsec over TCP, and IPsec over UDP. In certain cases, however, you might still be required to disable NAT for VPN traffic, or create exceptions for it. For some protocols, the reason of the conflict with NAT is the way those protocols function at the application layer. For example, some Internet Control Message Protocol (ICMP) packets make a reference to the IP address, which might not match the IP packet's header due to NAT's translation. Other applications related to multimedia traffic, such as voice and video, negotiate ports at the moment of connection, or have IP addresses embedded in the payload of the packets, forcing NAT to be application aware and be capable of changing its traditional behavior to allow those applications function with no problems. Applications and protocols as such might be labeled as NAT sensitive; examples of those protocols and applications include Kerberos, X Window System (remote-access application), remote shell (rsh), Session Initiation Protocol (SIP), Simple Network Management Protocol (SNMP), File Transfer Protocol (FTP), and Domain Name System (DNS). Table 6-2 lists some well-known NAT-sensitive protocols and explains why they conflict with NAT.

Note For more information about conflicts with NAT, see the Cisco.com article "The Trouble with NAT," which you can at http://tinyurl.com/re2g7.

In many cases, NAT is implemented on a device that has several other services active, too. This makes the troubleshooting task more complicated. Figure 6-2 lists several features that can be enabled for inbound and outbound traffic on each router interface. Note that as Figure 6-2 shows, the features are enforced in specific order as per the IOS rules, and the order makes a significant difference in the outcome.

Some of the features and services shown in Figure 6-2 are as follows:

- Security through access control lists (ACLs)
- Quality of service (QoS) through rate limiting and queuing
- Encryption through VPN technologies

Table 6-2 *NAT-Sensitive Protocols and Their NAT-Sensitive Behavior*

Protocol	Behavior
IPsec	NAT changes certain IP header fields such as the IP address and the IP header checksum, and this can conflict with IPsec integrity.
ICMP	Many ICMP packets, such as Destination Unreachable, carry embedded IP header information inside the ICMP message payload, not matching IP packet's translated address.
Session Initiation Protocol (SIP)	Protocols such as SIP negotiate address and ports numbers at the application layer, which can become invalid through a NAT device.

Inside to Outside

- IPsec decryption
- Input access list
- Input rate limits
- Input accounting
- Policy routing
- IP routing
- Redirect to web cache
- NAT inside to outside (local to global)
- Crypto (check map and mark for encryption)
- Check output access list
- Inspect (Cisco IOS Firewall)
- TCP intercept
- Encryption

Outside to Inside

- IPsec decryption
- Input access list
- Input rate limits
- Input accounting
- NAT outside to inside (global to local)
- Policy routing
- IP routing
- Redirect to web cache
- Crypto (check map and mark for encryption)
- Check output access list
- Inspect (Cisco IOS Firewall)
- TCP intercept
- Encryption

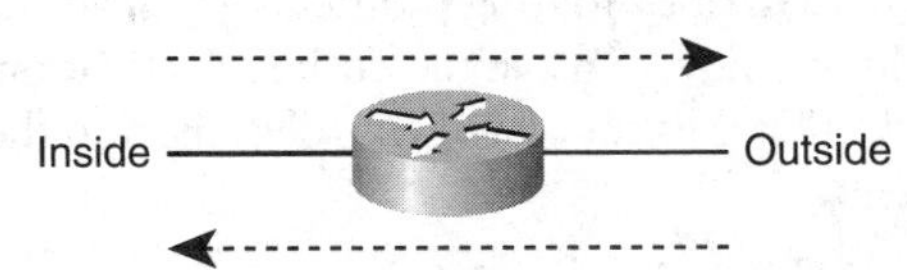

Figure 6-2 *Order of Operations with Reference to NAT for Incoming and Outgoing Traffic*

It is important to understand the impact of NAT on all those services. You must also think about the order in which the enabled services are enforced before you begin troubleshooting. Furthermore, you must note that this order changes depending on the direction of the traffic flow, whether it is entering an interface or leaving the interface. Notice, for example, that for outbound traffic (inside to outside), address translation occurs before output access lists are evaluated. This changing order means that in building your output access policy, you must consider "post-NAT" addresses.

Troubleshooting Common NAT/PAT Issues

Similar to any other troubleshooting case, NAT troubleshooting requires you to be familiar with the relevant tools and commands to help at different steps of troubleshooting. This includes useful **show** commands for information gathering and specific considerations when analyzing symptoms and eliminating possible hypothesis. One important consideration, for example, is the impact of routing in NAT configurations. Global addresses are not usually applied to the inside physical network segments, but they must be advertised to the outside world so that outsiders know where and how to send (respond) packets back. Another consideration must be given to the size of the NAT pools because they have a critical effect on specific troubleshooting scenarios where dynamic NAT is involved. Finally, during every stage of the troubleshooting process, you must consider configuration errors of all sorts.

Some of the important NAT issues and considerations to keep in mind are as follows:

- Having a diagram for the NAT configuration is always helpful and should be a standard practice. Do not just start configuring without a good drawing or diagram that shows or explains each item involved.
    - ACLs are used to tell the NAT device "what source IP addresses are to be translated," and IP NAT pools are used to specify "to what those addresses translate," as packets go from IP NAT inside to IP NAT outside.
    - Marking the IP NAT inside interfaces and the IP NAT outside interfaces correctly is very important; otherwise, NAT could have unpredictable and undesirable effects.
- NAT packets still have to obey routing protocols and reachability rules, so make sure that every router knows how to reach the desired destinations. Make sure the public addresses to which addresses translated, are advertised to the outside neighbors and autonomous systems.

Some helpful commands that enable you to determine the correct or incorrect functioning of NAT are as follows:

- **clear ip nat translation:** In the case of a change or inaccuracy, this command enables you can specify exactly which entries you want to clear by specifying more parameters. Clearing all translations might cause a disruption until new translations are re-created.
    - **show ip nat translations:** Allows you to see all the translations that are currently installed and active on the router.
    - **show ip nat statistics:** This command displays NAT statistics such as number of translations (static, dynamic, extended), number of expired translations, number of hits (matches), number of misses (no matches), and so on.
    - **debug ip nat:** Use this command to verify the operation of the NAT feature by displaying information about each packet that the router translates. The **debug ip nat detailed** command generates a description of each packet considered for translation. This command also displays information about certain errors or exception conditions, such as the failure to allocate a global address.
    - **debug ip packet [*access-list*]:** Use this command to display general IP debugging information and IP security option (IPSO) security transactions. If a communication session is closing when it should not be, an end-to-end connection problem can be the cause. The **debug ip packet** command is useful for analyzing the messages traveling between the local and remote hosts. IP packet debugging captures the packets that are process switched including received, generated, and forwarded packets. IP packets that are switched in the fast path are not captured. The access-list option allows you to narrow down the scope of your debugging.

- **debug condition interface** *interface*: This is called conditionally triggered debugging. When this feature is enabled, the router generates debugging messages for packets entering or leaving the router on the specified interface; the router will not generate debugging output for packets entering or leaving through a different interface.

Always be careful when running **debug** commands on a production or critical network; the more specific your **debug** statement, the better. Extensive **debug** commands typically impair or overload resources in the routers. Again, you can further scope the **debug** command with additional keywords and access lists.

For example, the **debug ip packet** command is fairly dangerous because it generates a lot of information that might clutter your console and even cause critical performance degradation to the router. You can, however, use access lists to filter the output. For example, you can use access list 100 to narrow down the scope of the **debug ip packet** by typing **debug ip packet 100**, and filter the output to what access list 100 permits. Some commands do not have the *access-list* option, so a more recent approach is to use conditionally triggered debugs. To use a conditionally triggered debug, first define your condition with the **debug condition** command. For example, you can define a condition of interface serial 0/0 by typing **debug condition interface serial 0/0**. This definition means that all **debug** output will be limited only to that particular interface. The condition remains there until it is removed. You can check the active **debug** conditions using the **show debug condition** command.

Troubleshooting Example: NAT/PAT Problem Caused by a Routing Issue

The first NAT troubleshooting example to be discussed here is based on the diagram shown in Figure 6-3. In this case, router R1 can ping R4, but router R1 cannot ping R3. You do not have much more information, except that there are no routing protocols running in any of the routers and R1 uses R2 as its gateway of last resort. Your objective is to restore end-to-end connectivity from R1 to all destinations.

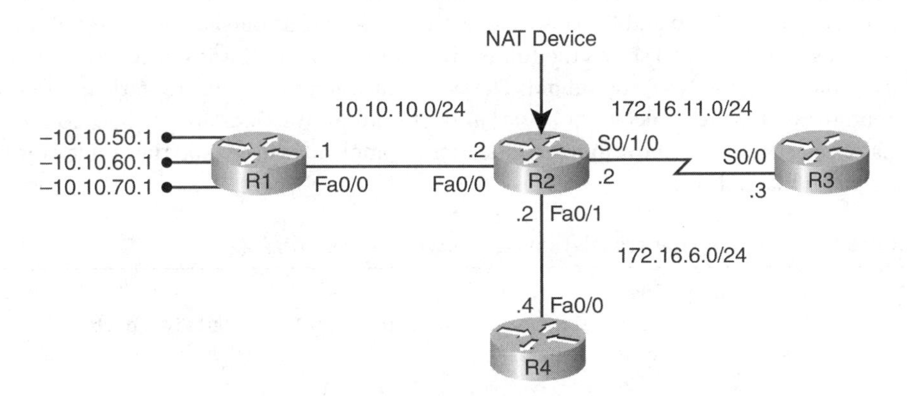

Figure 6-3 *NAT Troubleshooting Example Diagram*

When troubleshooting NAT, the structured approach can begin with learning where the NAT boundaries are located. Among the very few commands used for NAT monitoring and verification, the **show ip nat statistics** command is informative about all basic components of a NAT configuration. Using this command on router R2 generated the output shown in Example 6-1.

Example 6-1 show ip nat statistics *Command Output on R2*

```
R2# sh ip nat statistics
Total active translations: 1 (1 static, 0 dynamic, 0 extended)
Outside interfaces:

  FastEthernet0/1, Serial0/1/0, Loopback0
Inside interfaces:

  FastEthernet0/0

Hits: 39  Misses: 6
CEF Translated packets: 45, CEF Punted packets: 49
Expired translations: 6
Dynamic mappings:
-- Inside Source
[Id: 1] access-list 10 pool NAT_OUT refcount 0
 pool NAT_OUT: netmask 255.255.255.0
        start 172.16.6.129 end 172.16.6.240
        type generic, total addresses 112, allocated 0 (0%), misses 0
Appl doors: 0
Normal doors: 0
Queued Packets: 0
R2#
```

On the top lines of the output shown in Example 6-1, the outside and inside NAT interfaces are listed as per R2's current configuration: Fa0/0 is correctly configured as inside interface, while s0/1/0 and Fa0/1 are correctly configured as outside interfaces. Notice that this command also shows the full NAT configuration. In this instance, you have both dynamic and static NAT configured. The only indication that there are static translations configured is the reference to "1 static" in the "Total Active Translations" line. To see the static translation, the **show ip nat translations** command is used, and the result of it is shown in Example 6-2.

Example 6-2 show ip nat translations *Command Output on R2*

```
R2# sh ip nat translations
Pro  Inside global     Inside local       Outside local      Outside global
---  172.16.6.1        10.10.10.1         ---                ---
R2#
```

The only entry in the NAT translation table is the static translation for 10.10.10.1 into 172.16.6.1. The address 10.10.10.1 is the IP address of R1's Fast Ethernet interface (fa0/0). This translation might be causing the problem. Typical issues with static translations occur when there is no route back to the statically translated address, or when the statically selected global address overlaps with an available address in the dynamic address pool. Hence, as the next step, you can verify whether packets leaving R1 actually reach R3. This can help you discover whether the problem is with NAT or if it is a routing problem. To find out if packets reach R3 and do not return, or whether they never reach R3, you can make use of ICMP debugging on R3; accomplished by typing the **debug ip icmp** command. Next, ping R3 from R1 and observe the **debug** output on R3. The results are shown in the output of Example 6-3.

Example 6-3 debug ip icmp *Output on R3*

```
R3# debug ip icmp
ICMP packet debugging is on
R2#
*Aug 23 13:54:00.556:  ICMP:  echo reply sent, src 172.16.11.3,  dst 172.16.6.1
*Aug 23 13:54:02.552:  ICMP:  echo reply sent, src 172.16.11.3,  dst 172.16.6.1
*Aug 23 13:54:04.552:  ICMP:  echo reply sent, src 172.16.11.3,  dst 172.16.6.1
*Aug 23 13:54:06.552:  ICMP:  echo reply sent, src 172.16.11.3,  dst 172.16.6.1
*Aug 23 13:54:07.552:  ICMP:  echo reply sent, src 172.16.11.3,  dst 172.16.6.1
```

Based on the output of the **debug ip icmp** command shown in Example 6-3, the ICMP echo requests reach R3, but R3's ICMP echo replies do not reach R1. Notice that the **debug** output shown in Example 6-3 is R3's echo reply that is not reaching R1. You can conclude that the NAT translation is working but there is a routing issue on R3 toward the 172.16.6.0 destination, which you can verify with the **show ip route** command on R3 as demonstrated in Example 6-4.

Example 6-4 *R3's Routing Table Has No Path to 172.16.6.0*

```
R3#
R3# show ip route 172.16.6.0
% Subnet not in table
R3#
R3# configure terminal
R3(config)# ip route 172.16.6.0 255.255.255.0 172.16.11.2
R3(config)# exit
```

Because there are no routing protocols in use, you can only fix the routing problem by entering a static route in R3's routing table, so that it sends packets destined to 172.16.6.0/24 to R2 (also shown in Example 6-4). Following the addition of the static route to R3's routing table, you can check to see whether the connectivity problem between R1 and R3 has been corrected. Example 6-5 shows the ping result from R1 to R2.

Example 6-5 *After the Routing Correction on R3, R1 Can Now Reach R3 Through NAT*

```
R1# ping 172.16.11.3
Type escape sequence to abort.
Sending 5, 100-byte ICMP Echos to 172.16.11.3, timeout is 2 seconds:
!!!!!
Success rate is 100 percent (5/5), round-trip min/avg/max = 1/2/4 ms
R1#
```

The source of problem has been discovered, and it has been corrected. The problem was not directly a NAT problem; it was a routing issue. When NAT is deployed, a set of inside local addresses are normally translated to a set of inside global addresses. The inside global addresses might not be assigned to any physical networks, yet they need to be advertised so that outside devices know about those addresses and know how to forward packets to those networks. In this example, because no routing protocols were used, a static route was added to router R3's routing table so that it can send packets to the devices such as R1 that are behind the NAT device (R2).

Troubleshooting Example: NAT Problem Caused by an Inaccurate Access List

The second NAT troubleshooting example is based on the diagram shown on Figure 6-4. In this scenario, administrators are reporting that they are unable to use Secure Shell (SSH) from the 10.10.10.0/24 network to routers R3 or R4, but they can accomplish connectivity from the R1 loopbacks. In addition, the risk management team recently performed an upgrade to router and firewall security policies, and some of the changes might have affected the NAT configuration and operations. The routing protocol used is the Open Shortest Path First (OSPF) Protocol, single-area model. Your mission is to restore end-to-end connectivity and make sure SSH is operational to support management processes.

The indication of an upgrade in security policies draws attention to some sort of blocking or filtering as the problem source. You definitely need to consider if SSH traffic is being filtered and if the answer is yes, you need to determine which devices it is being filtered. On the other hand, the problem could just be a routing problem (traffic is either not reaching the destination, or it is not coming back). There might be other problems, too, so the best course of action is to apply a structured approach. With the security filter possibility in mind, you can start with a follow-the-path approach, testing connectivity from R1 to R3. Using R1 console, you try to verify the symptoms by pinging the destination 172.16.11.3 (R3's serial 0/1/0 interface) from the loopback interfaces using extended ping. This ping is successful as expected. Next, you do a ping from R1, but this time sourcing it from the fa0/0 interface, and the result is 100 percent success again. The results are shown in the output of Example 6-6. You can conclude that connectivity is not an issue and no routing problems exist. Next, try SSH from R1 to R3 using the command **ssh –l user 172.16.11.3**. The username is just the word user, which has already

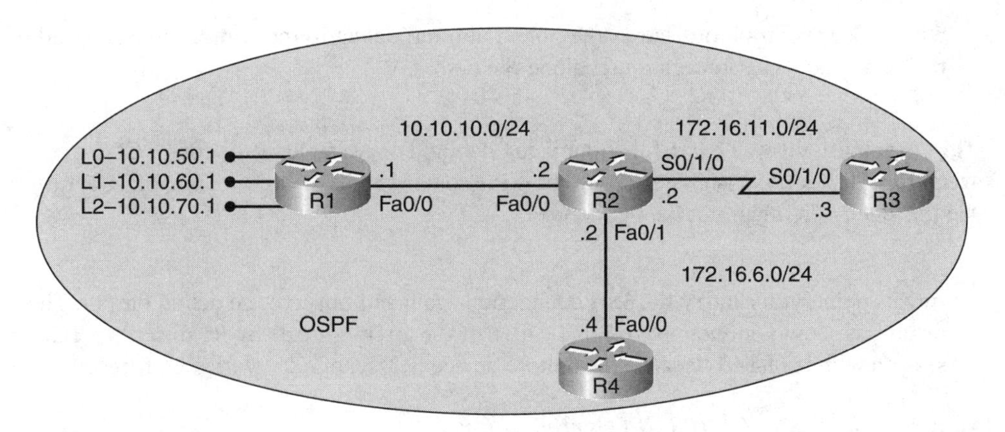

Figure 6-4 *NAT Troubleshooting Case: SSH Problems in the Single-Area OSPF Network*

been created on R3. The SSH connection fails as reported. The results are shown in the third section of Example 6-6.

Example 6-6 *Extended Ping and SSH Results from R1 to R3*

```
R1# ping 172.16.11.3 source 10.10.50.1
Type escape sequence to abort.
Sending 5, 100-byte ICMP Echos to 172.16.11.3, timeout is 2 seconds:
Packet sent with a source address of 10.10.50.1
!!!!!
Success rate is 100 percent (5/5), round-trip min/avg/max = 1/1/4 ms
R1#

R1# ping 172.16.11.3 source 10.10.10.1
Type escape sequence to abort.
Sending 5, 100-byte ICMP Echos to 172.16.11.3, timeout is 2 seconds:
Packet sent with a source address of 10.10.10.1
!!!!!
Success rate is 100 percent (5/5), round-trip min/avg/max = 1/1/4 ms
R1#
R1# ssh -l user 172.16.11.3
% Connection refused by remote host

R1#
```

Given the recent security policy updates, the next logical step is to review possible access lists or security controls. The follow-the-path strategy points to looking at the intermediate routers all the way up to the destination (R3). In this instance, however, you will use a clever tool to discover the potential filter: **debug ip tcp transactions**, instead of trying to find ACLs in each router along the path.

Tip You must always be careful about using **debug.** For example, if the router CPU or memory utilization is sustained at high, or if the router handles a high volume of TCP, turning this **debug** on might not be a good idea.

At this point, you can try the SSH connection again and observe the **debug** output. The results, as shown on Example 6-7, indicate that the attempt made by R1 to setup a TCP session with R3 failed because the remote device (R3) responded with a RST (reset).

Example 6-7 *Cisco IOS IPS CLI Configuration*

```
R1# debug ip tcp transactions
TCP special event debugging is on
R1# ssh -l user 172.16.11.3
% Connection refused by remote host

R1#
*Aug 23 14:59:42.636: TCP: Random local port generated 42115, network 1
*Aug 23 14:59:42.636: TCB63BF854C created
*Aug 23 14:59:42.636: TCB63BF854C bound to UNKNOWN.42115
*Aug 23 14:59:42.636: TCB63BF854C setting property TCP_TOS (11) 62AAF6D55
*Aug 23 14:59:42.636: Reserved port 42115 in Transport Port Agent for TCP IP type 1
*Aug 23 14:59:42.640: TCP: sending SYN, seq 1491927624, ack 0
*Aug 23 14:59:42.640: TCP0: Connection to 172.16.11.3:22, advertising MSS 536
*Aug 23 14:59:42.640: TCP0: state was CLOSED -> SYNSENT [42115 ->
  172.16.11.3(22)]
*Aug 23 14:59:42.640: TCP0: state was SYNSENT -> CLOSED [42115 ->
  172.16.11.3(22)]
*Aug 23 14:59:42.640: Released port 42115 in Transport Port Agent for TCP IP
  type 1 delay 240000
*Aug 23 14:59:42.640: TCP0: bad seg from 172.16.11.3 — closing connection:
  port 42115 seq 0 ack 1491927625 rcvnxt 0 rcvwnd 0 len 0
*Aug 23 14:59:42.640: TCP0: connection closed - remote sent RST

*Aug 23 14:59:42.640: TCB 0x63BF854C destroyed
```

Now you have to focus on R3. The output of **show ip int serial 0/1/0** shows that an access list called FIREWALL-INBOUND is applied to serial 0/1/0 interface on the inbound direction. Next, you look at the content of the FIREWALL-INBOUND access list using the **show access-lists** command, and the access list looks correct: statement number 30 permits TCP connection to 172.16.11.3 TCP port number 22 (SSH). Example 6-8 shows the output from these two commands.

Example 6-8 *Checking the Access List Applied to the Serial Interface on R3*

```
R3# sh ip int s0/1/0
Serial 0/1/0 is up, line protocol is up
  Internet address is 172.16.11.3/24
  Broadcast address is 255.255.255.255
  Address determined by nonvolatile memory
  MTU is 1500 bytes
  Helper address is not set
  Directed broadcat forwarding is disabled
  Multicast reserved groups joined: 224.0.0.5
  Outgoing access list is not set
  Inbound access list is FIREWALL-INBOUND
  Proxy ARP is enabled
  Local Proxy ARP is disabled
  Security level is default
  Split horizon is enabled
  ICMP redirects are always sent
  ICMP unreachables are always sent
  ICMP mask replies are never sent
  IP fast switching is enabled
  IP fast switching on the same interface is enabled
  IP Flow switching is disabled
  IP CEF switching is enabled
  IP CEF Feature Fast switching turbo vector
  IP multicast fast switching is enabled
R3# sh access-lists
Standard IP access list 11
    10 permit any
Extended IP access list FIREWALL-INBOUND
    10 permit tcp any host 172.16.11.3 eq www
    20 permit tcp any host 172.16.11.3 eq telent
    30 permit tcp any host 172.16.11.3 eq 22
    40 permit tcp any host 172.16.11.3 eq ftp
    50 permit tcp any host 172.16.11.3 eq ftp-data
    60 permit ospf any any (20 matches)
    70 deny ip any any (1 match)
R3#
```

As an attempt to find out why the SSH packets from R1 are rejected by R3, you cautiously make use of **debug ip packet** on R3. You re-attempt the SSH session from R1 to R3 and observe the **debug** output on R3, as shown in the output of Example 6-9.

Example 6-9 *The Output of* **debug ip packet** *While SSH Is Attempted from R1*

```
R1# ssh -l user 172.16.11.3
% Connection refused by remote host

R1#
R3# debug ip packet
IP packet debugging is on
R3#
R3#
*Aug 23 16:32:42.711: IP: s=172.16.11.2 (Serial0/1/0), d=224.0.0.5, len 80,
  rcvd 0
*Aug 23 16:32:49.883: %SEC-6-IPACCESSLOGP: list FIREWALL-INBOUND denied tcp
  10.10.10.1(29832) -> 172.16.11.3(2222), 1 packet
*Aug 23 16:32:49.883: IP: s=10.10.10.1 (Serial0/1/0), d-172.16.11.3, len 44,
  access denied
*Aug 23 16:32:49.883: IP: tableid=0, s-172.16.11.3 (local), d=10.10.10.1
  (Serial0/1/0), routed via FIB
*Aug 23 16:32:49.883: IP: s=172.16.11.3 (local), d=10.10.10.1 (Serial0/1/0),
  len 56, sending
*Aug 23 16:32:50.067: IP: s=172.16.11.3 (local), d=224.0.0.5 (Serial0/1/0),
  len 80, sending broad/multicast
```

The SSH attempt from R1 fails again, but the security message (**%SEC-6-IPACCESS-LOGP**) in the output of **debug** on R3 states that the denied TCP has the source IP address 10.10.10.1 and port number 29832 and destination IP address 172.16.11.3 and port number 2222! The destination port number is 2222 instead of 22, which is the allowed port (SSH) in access list FIREWALL-INBOUND that is applied inbound to R3's serial 0/1/0 interface. Now you know why the packet is denied, but you have to find out why the destination port number is 2222 rather than 22. In other words, you have to determine which device has translated the port number from 22 to 2222. Based on the network topology, the prime suspect is NAT on R2. Once again, cautiously, you use **debug ip nat** on R2 and observe the results as you re-attempt SSH from R1 to R3. To confirm your findings, you would also enter the **show ip nat translations** command on R2. Example 6-10 shows the results.

Example 6-10 *Investigating NAT on R2 While SSH Is Attempted from R1 to R3*

```
R2# debug ip nat
IP NAT debugging is on
R2#
R2#
R2#
R2#
*Aug 23 16:28:31.731: NAT*: TCP s=55587, d=22->2222
```

```
R1# ssh -l user 172.16.11.3
% Destination unreachable; gateway or host down

R1#

R2# sh ip nat translations
Pro Inside global        Inside local        Outside local      Outside global
tcp ---                  ---                 172.16.11.3:22     172.16.11.3:2222
tcp 10.10.10.1:29832     10.10.10.1:29832    172.16.11.3:22     172.16.11.3:2222
tcp 10.10.10.1:43907     10.10.10.1:43907    172.16.11.3:22     172.16.11.3:2222
tcp 10.10.10.1:55587     10.10.10.1:55587    172.16.11.3:22     172.16.11.3:2222
tcp 10.10.10.1:60089     10.10.10.1:60089    172.16.11.3:22     172.16.11.3:2222
tcp 10.10.10.1:62936     10.10.10.1:62936    172.16.11.3:22     172.16.11.3:2222
R2#
```

The output shown on Example 6-10 clearly shows that R2 is port mapping. It is translating port 22 to port 2222, and that is the problem. It seems that the risk management team updated the security policies, but did not update the access lists for the custom ports being used. You are using TCP 2222; but the access list on R3 is permitting TCP 22. The next step is to correct the FIREWALL-INBOUND on R3 and re-attempt SSH from R1 to R3. The results are shown in the output shown in Example 6-11.

Example 6-11 *The Access List on R3 Is Corrected and SSH Is Retried to See the Results*

```
R3# conf t
Enter configuration commands, one per line. End with CNTL/Z.
R3(config)# ip access-list exten FIREWALL-INBOUND
R3(config-ext-nacl)# permit tcp any ho 172.16.11.3 eq 2222
R3(config-ext-nacl)# end
R3#

R1# ssh -l user 172.16.11.3

Password:
*Aug 23 16:30:42.604: TCP: Random local port generated 43884, network 1
*Aug 23 16:30:26.604: TCB63BF854C created
*Aug 23 16:30:26.604: TCB63BF854C bound to UNKNOWN.43884
*Aug 23 16:30:26.604: TCB63BF854C setting property TCP_TOS (11) 62AF6D55
*Aug 23 16:30:26.604: Reserved port 43884 in Transport Port Agent for TCP IP type 1
*Aug 23 16:30:26.604: TCP: sending SYN, seq 1505095793, ack 0
*Aug 23 16:30:26.604: TCP0: Connection to 172.16.11.3:22, advertising MSS 536
*Aug 23 16:30:26.608: TCP0: state was CLOSED -> SYNSENT [43884 ->
  172.16.11.3(22)]
```

```
*Aug 23 16:30:26.608: TCP0: state was SYNSENT -> ESTAB [43884 ->
  172.16.11.3(22)]

*Aug 23 16:30:26.608: TCP: tcb 63BF854C connection to 172.16.11.3:22, peer MSS
  536, MSS is 536
*Aug 23 16:30:26.608: TCB63BF854C connected to 172.16.11.3.22
```

As shown in Example 6-11, the SSH attempt is successful now. In summary, the problem was not the NAT configuration, but a lack of synchronization between the configuration teams: The configuration on R2 is doing port mapping to a custom port (2222), but the access list configuration on R3 did not consider or account for the custom port.

Reviewing DHCP Operation

DHCP is a client/server protocol. The DHCP client acquires IP configuration parameters, such as IP address, subnet mask, and default gateway, from a DHCP server. The DHCP server is typically centrally located and operated by the network administrator; therefore, DHCP clients can be reliably and dynamically configured with parameters appropriate to the current network architecture. Because the DHCP client initially does not have IP configuration, it must find a DHCP server and obtain its IP configuration based on broadcast communication.

Most enterprise networks are divided into sub-networks (subnets). Each subnet usually maps to a virtual LAN (VLAN) and routers or multilayer switches route between the subnets. Because routers do not pass broadcasts by default, a DHCP server would be needed on each subnet. To address this issue, you can configure a router's interface with a feature called DHCP relay agent, using the **ip helper-address** *server-address* command. When configured with this command, the router interface will forward the clients DHCP messages to the configured *server-address*. When the server sends its reply back to the router interface, the router interface forwards it to the client subnet.

DHCP has historically been used for automatic provisioning of IP parameters. Increased mobility and usage of laptop computers have made DHCP even more popular. The DHCP server offers more than just the IP address, subnet mask, and the default gateway. Cisco IP phones, for example, require a TFTP server address to download their configuration files and become active in the network. IP phones obtain the TFTP server's IP address from the DHCP server through DHCP options and extensions. These options allow the protocol to expand the number and nature of parameters that can be delivered to hosts, including vendor specific parameters.

To troubleshoot DHCP, it is important to understand the nature and semantics of the various transactions that happen between servers and clients. Figure 6-5 illustrates the first set of actions that must complete so that a client with no IP configuration finds a DHCP server and obtains its IP configuration.

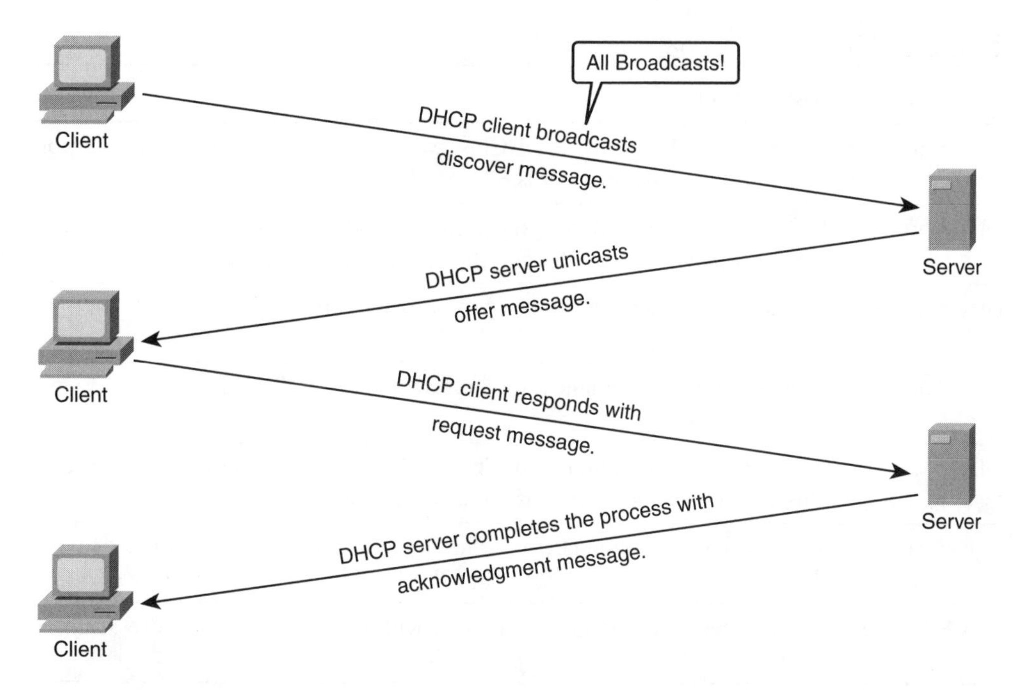

Figure 6-5 *The Four-Way DHCP Communication Through Which the Client Obtains Its Configuration*

As shown in Figure 6-5, the client starts with a DHCP discover message with the source IP address 0.0.0.0; this address is referred to as the alien address! One or more servers reply with a DHCP offer. The client responds, typically to the first offer, using the DHCP request message. Multiple offer messages could be sent, but only one will be accepted by the client, indicated by the request message. The request message is a broadcast, and reaches all offering servers. The servers whose offers are not selected withdraw their offer by putting the offered IP address back into the pool of available addresses. The selected server responds with a DHCP ack, and confirms the transaction by delivering all configured parameters. Table 6-3 lists these and other DHCP packets (message types) involved in DHCP transactions, some issued by servers, and some issued by clients.

The DHCP messages listed in Table 6-3 are most helpful to know during the troubleshooting process. For example, the DHCP decline message, which is a client-to-server message, indicates that the IP address is already in use. The DHCP nak message is useful in determining whether the DHCP server refuses the request for a certain configuration parameter.

Common DHCP Troubleshooting Issues

For troubleshooting purposes, the DHCP problems can be divided into three categories with relation to the router's role in the DHCP process. As Figure 6-6 displays, a router can play three roles: DHCP server, DHCP client, or DHCP relay agent.

Table 6-3 *DHCP Packets (Messages)*

Packet Type	Description
DHCP discover	Client looking for available DHCP servers. It is a UDP broadcast (source port is 68, and the destination port is 67).
DHCP offer	This is the server's response to the client's discover message. This is also a UDP broadcast (source port is 67, and the destination port is 68).
DHCP request	This is client's response to one specific DHCP offer.
DHCP decline	Client-to-server communication, indicating that the IP address is already in use.
DHCP ack	Server-to-client communication. This is the server's response to a client request. This message includes all configuration parameters.
DHCP nack	Server-to-client communication. This is the server's negative response to a client's request, indicating the original offer is no longer available.
DHCP release	Client-to-server communication. The client relinquishes its IP address and other parameters.
DHCP inform	Client-to-server communication. Using this message, the client asks for local configuration parameters such as DNS server's IP address, but it has its IP address externally configured.

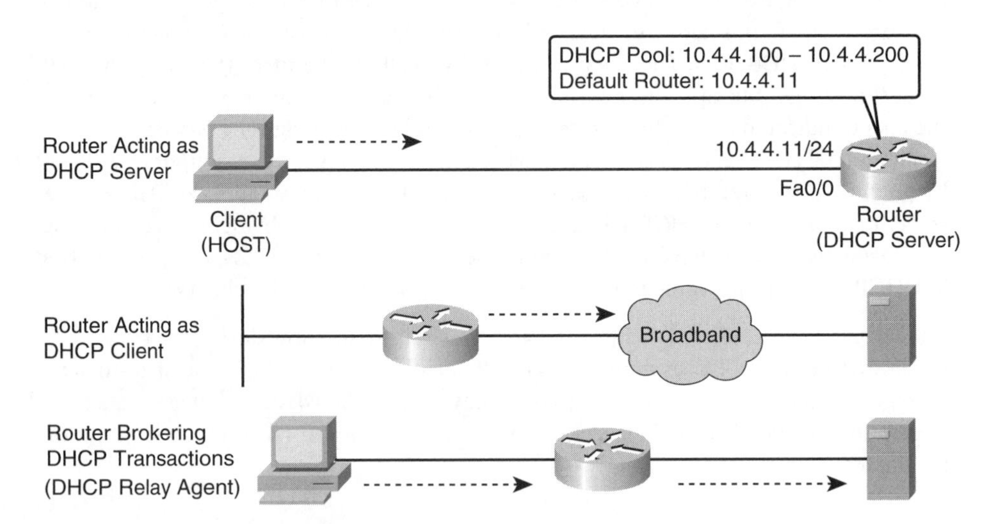

Figure 6-6 *The Three Roles a Router May Take with Respect to DHCP*

In branch office scenarios, it is typical to have Cisco IOS routers or firewalls acting as the DHCP server. In that case, troubleshooting DHCP is critical because it will affect the operations of all hosts in the branch, including IP phones and video devices.

In some other scenarios, routers can act as DHCP clients. An example of this is a branch or home office router using broadband connectivity such as digital subscriber line (DSL) or cable and obtaining IP address and IP parameters from the service provider's DHCP server.

The router can also act as a broker for DHCP transactions, located in the path of DHCP requests. This is a typical scenario in networks where DHCP servers are centralized and serve multiple network segments and the router acts as a DHCP relay agent.

In all three scenarios, your typical DHCP issues can come from multiple sources. It is crucial to apply a structured troubleshooting method and to know the inner workings of the protocol.

The most common reasons for problems are configuration issues. This can result in a multitude of symptoms, such as clients not obtaining IP information from the server, client requests not reaching the server across a DHCP relay agent, or clients failing to obtain DHCP options and extensions. Poor capacity planning and security issues might also be a source of problems. For example, DHCP scope exhaustion is becoming increasingly common, in part due to malicious attacks. In some scenarios, the infrastructure and requirements lead to a combination of static and dynamic IP address assignments. In those scenarios, it is possible that a DHCP server grants an IP address that is already in use. Different implementations of servers and clients react differently to this and that is important to know for troubleshooting purposes. Furthermore, if you have multiple DHCP servers, or even rogue DHCP servers in your network, because there is no stateful communication between DHCP servers, there is a chance that duplicate IP addresses will be assigned to hosts. Other management issues arise due to the "pull" nature of DHCP. There are no provisions in the protocol to allow the DHCP server to push configuration parameters or control messages to DHCP clients. A good example, with critical implications in IP address renumbering, is that IP addresses must be renewed from the client side. There is no server-side, push-type renewal process. This means that during renumbering, all clients would need to reboot or manually renew their IP addresses. Otherwise, you need to wait until the clients leases expire, which might not be a viable option.

Note The phrase "no stateful communication between the DHCP servers" means that the servers do not communicate about the addresses they have assigned and have not assigned. In other words, they do not exchange state information.

Problems related to the DHCP relay agent require special consideration. The Cisco IOS command that makes a router a DHCP relay agent is the **ip helper-address** command. This is an interface configuration command that makes the router forward the BOOTP/DHCP requests from clients to the DHCP server. However, if the DHCP server's IP address changes, you must reconfigure all the interfaces of all the routers with the new IP helper address (DHCP server's new IP address). Another issue related to DHCP relay agent is that enabling a router interface with the **ip helper-address** command makes the interface forward UDP broadcasts for six protocols (not just DHCP) to the IP address configured using the **ip helper-address** command. Those protocols are as follows:

- TFTP (port 69)
- DNS (port 53)
- Time Service (port 37)
- NetBIOS Name Service and Datagram Service (ports 137 and 138)
- TACACS (port 49)
- DHCP/BOOTP client and server (ports 67 and 68)

If other protocols do not require this service, forwarding their requests must be disabled manually on all routers using the Cisco IOS **no ip forward-protocol udp** *port-number* global configuration mode command.

Another area of DHCP troubleshooting is the vendor-specific and function-specific DHCP options.

DHCP options have historically been an integral part of the protocol, because they are used to deliver parameters in addition to the traditional IP address, subnet mask, default gateway, and DNS server address. Some options aim at tuning the DHCP operation, or even the TCP/IP operation. Table 6-4 lists some important DHCP configured parameters and options.

Some DHCP options are required for certain other protocols or applications to function properly. For example, the relay agent information option number 82 makes DHCP relay agents add source port (or interface or circuit) information to the forwarded DHCP

Table 6-4 *DHCP Parameters and Options*

DHCP Option	Code	Description
Subnet mask	1	Specifies the subnet mask for the client to use (as per RFC 950)
Router	3	The list of routers the client can use (usually, in order of preference)
Domain name server	6	The list of DNS servers the client can use (usually, in order of preference)
ARP cache timeout	35	Specifies the timeout (seconds) for ARP cache entries
IP address lease time	51	Specifies the period over which the IP address is leased for (it must be renewed)
Relay agent information	82	Information about the port from which the DHCP request originates
TFTP server IP address	150	Typically used by devices such as IP phones to download their configuration files

requests. The DHCP server obtains and stores that information which can be used to identify the physical location of a DHCP client. For enhanced 911 purposes, for example, it is important to know the switch port that an IP phone connects to, to determine the 911 caller's location. Another example of DHCP options field is number 150, which is used by IP phones requesting DHCP information from the network. Option 150 provides the IP address of the TFTP server to the IP phones so that they can download their firmware and configuration files, which is a critical step in the IP phone boot process. The bottom line is that you need to ensure that the DHCP servers support and are configured with the needed options. Unfortunately, sometimes those options are vendor-specific and might not be supported by all devices. In that case, options as such would have to be entered manually, provided in a configuration file (through TFTP, for example), or using another method.

Other troubleshooting scenarios might be related to DHCP security efforts. This is a perfect example of how multiple services act in an integrated fashion: Automatic addressing is accomplished through DHCP, and security is accomplished through DHCP snooping. A misconfigured service can and will affect other services. The following are some specific issues related to DHCP snooping:

- Improper configuration of the DHCP snooping trust boundaries
- Failure to configure DHCP snooping on certain VLANs
- Improper configuration of the DHCP snooping rate limits
- Performance degradation

These issues illustrate the impact of poor planning of DHCP snooping, which can result in DHCP transactions being blocked or affected. Improper location of DHCP snooping boundaries, low DHCP snooping rate limits, and other configurations related to security must be part of your considerations during the DHCP troubleshooting process.

DHCP Troubleshooting Tips and Commands

For troubleshooting purposes, it is important that you can answer the following questions:

- Where are the DHCP servers and clients located? Are they co-located in the same IP subnet, or do you need to configure relay agents?
- Are DHCP relay agents configured? (They are most likely necessary.)
- What are the DHCP pool sizes? Are they sufficient? (Otherwise you'll run out of addresses.)
- Are there any DHCP option compatibility issues? (Some applications will fail if all necessary options are not supplied.)

You must also investigate the following possibilities:

- Are there any ACLs or firewalls filtering UDP port 67 or UDP port 68?

    - Are there any active DHCP denial-of-service (DoS) attacks?
    - Is forwarding disabled on the router acting as DHCP Relay Agent for any UDP ports (using the Cisco IOS **no ip forward-protocol udp** *port* command)?
- Is the **ip helper-address** command applied to correct router interfaces?

Some of the Cisco IOS commands that can prove helpful for DHCP troubleshooting are as follows:

- **show ip dhcp server statistics:** Because this command displays count information about server statistics and messages sent and received, it can be very helpful during troubleshooting of an IOS-based DHCP server.
- **show ip dhcp binding:** This command is used to display DHCP binding information for IP address assignment and subnet allocation.
- **show ip dhcp conflict:** Use this command to display address conflicts found by a Cisco IOS DHCP server when addresses are offered to the client. The server uses ping to detect conflicts. The client uses gratuitous Address Resolution Protocol (ARP) to detect clients. If an address conflict is detected, the address is removed from the pool and the address is not assigned until an administrator resolves the conflict.
- **show ip dhcp database:** This command is used to display Cisco IOS DHCP server database agent information, such as the following:
    - **URL:** Specifies the remote file used to store automatic DHCP bindings
    - **Read/written:** The last date and time bindings were read/written from the file server
    - **Status:** Indication of whether the last read or write of host bindings was successful
    - **Delay:** The amount of time (in seconds) to wait before updating the database
    - **Timeout:** The amount of time (in seconds) before the file transfer is aborted
    - **Failures/Successes:** The number of failed/successful file transfers
- **show ip dhcp pool:** This command is used to determine the subnets allocated and to examine the current utilization level for the pool or all the pools if the name argument is not used.
- **debug ip udp:** This debug displays all UDP packets sent and received and it can use considerable CPU cycles on the device.
- **debug ip dhcp server [packets | events]:** It is evident that this command enables DHCP server debugging, which can be helpful during relevant troubleshooting exercises. The events option reports server events such as address assignments and database updates and the packets option decodes DHCP receptions and transmissions.
- **clear ip dhcp binding {* |** ***address*****}:** Use this command to delete an address binding from the Cisco IOS DHCP server database. The address denotes the IP address of

the client. If the asterisk (*) character is used as the address parameter, DHCP clears all automatic bindings.

- **clear ip dhcp conflict {* | *address*}:** Use this command to clear an address conflict (or all address conflicts, with the * option) from the Cisco IOS DHCP server database.

DHCP Troubleshooting Example: Problems After a Security Audit

This troubleshooting example is based on the diagram depicted in Figure 6-7. Router R1 provides DHCP services to the clients in the 10.1.1.0 subnet. The DHCP clients in this example are routers R2 and R3. A security audit has been recently performed in router R1, and you receive reports that R1 is no longer providing reliable DHCP services: The clients are unable to renew their IP addresses.

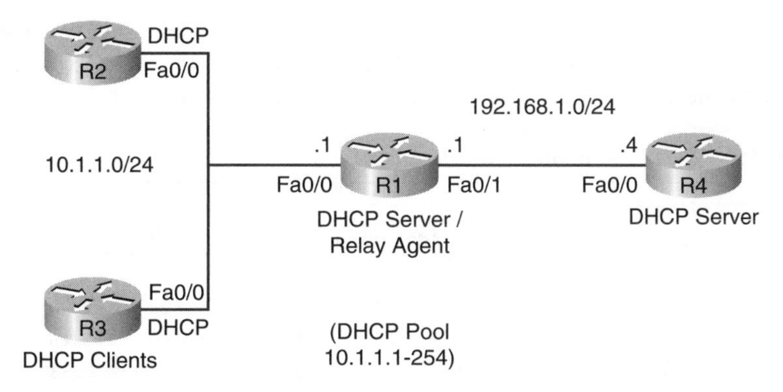

Figure 6-7 *The DHCP Server (R1) Is Not Properly Serving Its Clients (R2 and R3)*

As the first step in fact gathering, you can try to determine whether the problem affects all clients in the LAN, or if only some clients are experiencing the reported symptoms. You check R2 to make sure that it is configured as a DHCP client. The output of the **show ip interfaces brief** command, displayed in Example 6-12, shows that interface fa0/0 is configured as a DHCP client and it shows an "unassigned" IP address. Next, you check router R3 and find the same situation (also displayed in Example 6-12). Because multiple clients are having the same problem, it is reasonable to suspect the problem originates elsewhere. You can check the configuration of the DHCP server next.

Example 6-12 *Output of* **show ip int brief** *on R2 and R3 (DHCP Clients)*

```
R2# show ip int brief
Interface          IP-Address   OK?  Method  Status                 Protocol
FastEthernet0/0    unassigned   YES  DHCP    up                     up
FastEthernet0/1    unassigned   YES  NVRAM   administratively down  down
Serial0/0/0        unassigned   YES  NVRAM   administratively down  down
R2#
```

```
R3# show ip int brief
Interface          IP-Address    OK?  Method  Status                 Protocol
FastEthernet0/0    unassigned    YES  DHCP    up                     up
FastEthernet0/1    unassigned    YES  unset   administratively down  down
Serial0/0/0        unassigned    YES  unset   administratively down  down
Serial0/1/0        unassigned    YES  unset   administratively down  down
R3#
```

To investigate the interaction between the clients and server, you can check whether the clients are issuing DHCP discovery messages. Using the **debug dhcp detail** command on R3, you find that the DHCP discovery messages are generated out of interface fa0/0, but no DHCP offers are received back from the DHCP server. Also, this client is making multiple requests, and after three attempts, it times out with the **Timed out selecting state** message, followed by **No allocation possible.** The results are shown in Example 6-13. Using the same **debug** command on the second client, R2, provides the exact same results.

Example 6-13 *Results of* **debug dhcp detail**

```
R3# debug dhcp detail
DHCP client activity debugging is on (detailed)
R3#
R3#
*Aug 23 17:32:37.107:    Retry count: 1  Client-ID: cisco-0019.5592.a442-Fa0/0
*Aug 23 17:32:37.107:    Client-ID hex dump: 636973636F2D303031392E353539322E
*Aug 23 17:32:37.107:                        613434322D4551302F30
*Aug 23 17:32:37.107:    Hostname: R3
*Aug 23 17:32:37.107:  DHCP: SDiscover: sending 291 byte length DHCP packet
*Aug 23 17:32:37.107:  DHCP: SDiscover 291 bytes
*Aug 23 17:32:37.107:            B cast on FastEthernet0/0 interface
  from 0.0.0.0
*Aug 23 17:32:40.395:  DHCP: SDiscover attempt #2 for entry:
*Aug 23 17:32:40.395:  Temp IP addr: 0.0.0.0 for peer on Interface:
  FastEthernet0/0
*Aug 23 17:32:40.395:  Temp sub net mask: 0.0.0.0
*Aug 23 17:32:40.395:    DHCP Lease server: 0.0.0.0, state: 1 Selecting
*Aug 23 17:32:40.395:    DHCP transaction id: 13BA
*Aug 23 17:32:40.395:    Lease: 0 secs,  Renewal: 0 secs,  Rebind: 0 secs
*Aug 23 17:32:40.395:    Next timer fires after: 00:00:04
*Aug 23 17:32:40.395:    Retry count: 2  Client-ID: cisco-0019.5592.a442-Fa0/0
*Aug 23 17:32:40.395:    Client-ID hex dump: 636973636F2D303031392E353539322E
*Aug 23 17:32:40.395:                        613434322D4551302F30
*Aug 23 17:32:40.395:    Hostname: R3
*Aug 23 17:32:40.395:  DHCP: SDiscover: sending 291 byte length DHCP packet
*Aug 23 17:32:40.395:  DHCP: SDiscover 291 bytes
```

```
*Aug 23 17:32:40.395:             B cast on FastEthernet0/0 interface
  from 0.0.0.0
*Aug 23 17:32:44.395:  DHCP: SDiscover attempt #3 for entry:
*Aug 23 17:32:44.395:  Temp IP addr: 0.0.0.0 for peer on Interface:
  FastEthernet0/0
*Aug 23 17:32:44.395:  Temp sub net mask: 0.0.0.0
*Aug 23 17:32:44.395:    DHCP Lease server: 0.0.0.0, state: 1 Selecting
*Aug 23 17:32:44.395:    DHCP transaction id: 13BA
*Aug 23 17:32:44.395:    Lease: 0 secs,  Renewal: 0 secs,  Rebind: 0 secs
*Aug 23 17:32:44.395:    Next timer fires after: 00:00:04
*Aug 23 17:32:44.395:    Retry count: 3  Client-ID: cisco-0019.5592.a442-Fa0/0
*Aug 23 17:32:44.395:    Client-ID hex dump: 636973636F2D303031392E353539322E
*Aug 23 17:32:44.395:                        613434322D4551302F30
*Aug 23 17:32:44.395:    Hostname: R3
*Aug 23 17:32:44.395:  DHCP: SDiscover: sending 291 byte length DHCP packet
*Aug 23 17:32:44.395:  DHCP: SDiscover 291 bytes
*Aug 23 17:32:44.395:             B cast on FastEthernet0/0 interface
  from 0.0.0.0
*Aug 23 17:32:48.395:  DHCP: Qscan: Timed out Selecting state%Unknown
  DHCP problem... No allocation possible
*Aug 23 17:32:57.587:  DHCP: waiting for 60 seconds on interface FastEthernet0/0
```

Now you can start to check router R1, the DHCP server. Applying a bottom-up approach and using the **show ip int brief** command to verify that Layers 1 and 2 are operational on the documented DHCP server, you find that R1's fa0/0 interface is up, with the IP address 10.1.1.1/24. Next, you would check the DHCP server information. Two commands are useful: The first command, **show ip dhcp server statistics**, displays useful counters. Changes on those counters are a signal of good operation. The output of this command on R1 is shown in Example 6-14, which displays that one address pool configured as part of the service and very few DHCP messages sent and received. So it looks to be in good shape, just not very active. You must verify the address pool configuration. In case the IP address scope, known as the address pool in Cisco IOS DHCP, is either misconfigured or exhausted, you check the DHCP address pool using the **show ip dhcp pool** command. The results, also displayed in Example 6-14, show one address pool, vlan10. You see that the number of leased addresses are zero, meaning that there are no leased addresses. You still have 254 addresses in this pool, but none are allocated at the moment.

Example 6-14 *Results of* **show ip dhcp server statistics** *and* **show ip dhcp pool**

```
R1# show ip dhcp server statistics
Memory usage          9106
Address pools         1
Database agents       0
Automatic bindings    0
```

```
Manual bindings        0
Expired bindings       0
Malformed messages     0
Secure arp entries     0

Message                Received
BOOTREQUEST            0
DHCPDISCOVER           1
DHCPREQUEST            1
DHCPDECLINE            0
DHCPRELEASE            0
DHCPINFORM             0

Message                Semt
BOOTREPLY              0
DHCPOFFER              1
DHCPACK                1
DHCPNAK                0
R1#
R1# sh ip dhcp pool

Pool vlan10 :

 Utilization mark (high/low)        : 100/0
 Subnet size (first/next)           : 0/0
 Total addresses                    : 254
 Leased addresses                   : 0

 Pending event                      : none
 1 subnet is currently in the pool  :
 Current index        IP address range                 Leased addresses
 10.1.1.12            10.1.1.1         -10.1.1.254      0
R1#
```

Now you know both the DHCP server and the DHCP clients have the correct configurations, and are operationally UP at physical and data link layers. Remembering that there has been a security audit recently (including one on R1), it is a good idea to verify whether any changes were made by security auditors that affect DHCP. One hardening method that security experts use to make a device less vulnerable to security incidents is shutting down unused services. It is possible that the auditors have shut down the DHCP service on R1. This sounds like a plausible conjecture because the rest of the configuration looks fine. The output of the **show ip sockets** command in Example 6-15 displays the active ports on R1, the DHCP server. The **show ip sockets** command is not frequently used by network administrators, but it is handy in monitoring the open ports on a router.

Example 6-15 show ip sockets *Command Output on R1*

```
R1# show ip sockets
Proto    Remote       Port      Local       Port  In  Out   Stat  TTY  OutputIF
 88   --listen--            10.1.1.1         10   0    0      0    0
 17   --listen--            10.1.1.1        161   0    0   1001    0
 17   --listen--            10.1.1.1        162   0    0   1011    0
 17   --listen--            10.1.1.1      57767   0    0   1011    0
 17   --listen--            --any--         161   0    0  20001    0
 17   --listen--            --any--         162   0    0  20011    0
 17   --listen--            --any--       60739   0    0  20011    0
R1#
```

In the output of the **show ip sockets** command, you see a series of services functioning on certain open ports; however, DHCP/BOOTP is nowhere to be found. You would need to see UDP 67 if the DHCP service was running. This is certainly a problem, so you would enable the DHCP service using the **service dhcp** command. After enabling this service, you must wait a few seconds, because DHCP clients retry at different intervals. Meanwhile, you would use the **show ip sockets** command again and now see port 67 as an active port on R1. The results are shown in Example 6-16.

Note The **show ip sockets** command has been replaced by the **show udp** and **show sockets** commands as of Cisco IOS Software Release 12.4(11)T.

Example 6-16 *Results of* show ip socket, *After Enabling the DHCP Service on R1 Using the* service dhcp *Command*

```
R1# conf t
Enter configuration commands, one per line. End with CNTL/Z.
R1(config)# service dhcp
R1(config)#
R1(config)# end
R1#
R1#
R1# show ip socket
Proto    Remote       Port      Local       Port  In  Out   Stat  TTY  OutputIF
 88   --listen--            10.1.1.1         10   0    0      0    0
 17   --listen--            10.1.1.1        161   0    0   1001    0
 17   --listen--            10.1.1.1        162   0    0   1011    0
 17   --listen--            10.1.1.1      57767   0    0   1011    0
 17   --listen--            --any--         161   0    0  20001    0
 17   --listen--            --any--         162   0    0  20011    0
 17   --listen--            --any--       60739   0    0  20011    0
 17 0.0.0.0               0 10.1.1.1         67   0    0   2211    0
R1#
```

Finally, you would check routers R2 and R3 (the DHCP clients) and see that they successfully obtained IP addresses. The problem was that the security auditors have shut down the DHCP service on the DHCP server!

DHCP Troubleshooting Example: Duplicate Client IP Addresses

The second DHCP troubleshooting example is based on the topology shown in Figure 6-8. The IP address of router R1 on the Fast Ethernet interface was changed from 10.1.1.100 to 10.1.1.1 to comply with the new addressing scheme and policies of the network. This policy states that all branch routers will have the first IP address on any subnet that is being assigned to a network segment. After the change, some DHCP clients are reporting duplicated IP addresses. Clients state that this happens sporadically, a few times a week.

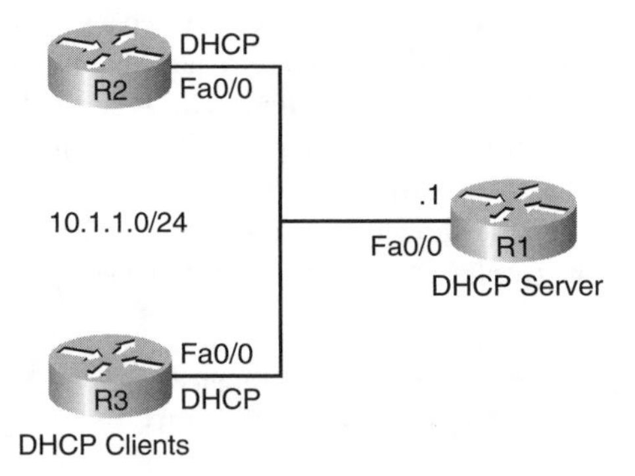

Figure 6-8 *R2 and R3 Are DHCP Clients and Report Sporadic Address Conflicts*

Because you know that the change happened at the router acting as the DHCP server (R1), it is good to get the troubleshooting process started there, while you ask the questions and try to gather more information on what the exact symptoms are. One piece of information that you have is that the IP address duplication happens sporadically, and one host at a time. Knowing that, perhaps your first order of business is to look at the lease times, and see whether they match the frequency of the symptoms. If the lease time of a Cisco IOS DHCP server is set to default values, there is really no command to display it other than **show running-config | begin ip dhcp pool**. The output of this command, displayed in Example 6-17, shows the vlan10 DHCP pool with a lease time of 3 days.

Example 6-17 *The DHCP Pool Named vlan10 on R1 Has a Lease Period of 3 Days*

```
R1# show running-config | beg ip dhcp pool
```

```
ip dhcp pool vlan10
   network 10.1.1.0  255.255.255.0
   default-router 10.1.1.1
   lease 3
```

The DHCP pool seems to be correct. Based on the reported symptoms, it seems logical to check whether there are statically assigned IP addresses conflicting with some of the addresses that are being delivered to the clients as part of the DHCP dynamic address pool. The **show ip dhcp conflict** command will verify whether the DHCP server has found overlap or duplication in the IP addresses that it has assigned. Example 6-18 shows the output of this command, entered on R1. One of the many conflicting addresses is 10.1.1.1, which is the new IP address of router R1 (the DHCP server itself) on interface fa0/0. However, you know that the DHCP server will not provide its own IP address to its clients.

Example 6-18 *The* **show ip dhcp conflict** *Command Displays Many Conflicts*

```
R1# show ip dhcp conflict
IP address          Detection method    Detection time           VRF
10.1.1.1            Gratuitous ARP      Aug 23 2009 06:28 PM
10.1.1.3            Gratuitous ARP      Aug 23 2009 06:29 PM
10.1.1.3            Gratuitous ARP      Aug 23 2009 06:29 PM
10.1.1.4            Gratuitous ARP      Aug 23 2009 06:29 PM
10.1.1.5            Gratuitous ARP      Aug 23 2009 06:29 PM
10.1.1.6            Gratuitous ARP      Aug 23 2009 06:29 PM
10.1.1.7            Gratuitous ARP      Aug 23 2009 06:29 PM
10.1.1.8            Gratuitous ARP      Aug 23 2009 06:29 PM
10.1.1.9            Gratuitous ARP      Aug 23 2009 06:29 PM
10.1.1.10           Gratuitous ARP      Aug 23 2009 06:29 PM
10.1.1.11           Gratuitous ARP      Aug 23 2009 06:29 PM
10.1.1.12           Gratuitous ARP      Aug 23 2009 06:29 PM
10.1.1.13           Gratuitous ARP      Aug 23 2009 06:29 PM
--More--
```

Many devices such as servers and printers are usually configured as DHCP clients and have static IP addresses. If their addresses are not excluded from the DHCP dynamic pool, there will definitely be conflict problems. You must check and verify which IP addresses are being excluded on R1, the DHCP server. You do that using the **show running-config | include excluded** command as demonstrated in Example 6-19.

Example 6-19 *On R1, the Only DHCP Excluded Address is 10.1.1.100*

```
R1# show running-config | inc excluded
ip dhcp excluded-address 10.1.1.100
R1#
R1#
```

As per the output shown in Example 6-19, the only IP address excluded from the DHCP dynamic pool is 10.1.1.100, which is R1's old address. The static addresses assigned to devices such as printers and servers are not excluded and are handed out to DHCP clients. The result is the address conflicts the users are experiencing. What you need to do is put the 10.1.1.100 back in the pool, because it need not be excluded any more. You also need to exclude the range of addresses that are meant to be statically assigned. This range is 10.1.1.1 to 10.1.1.20. Example 6-20 shows this work.

Example 6-20 *The DHCP Excluded Addresses Are Corrected*

```
R1#
R1# conf t
Enter configuration commands, one per line. End with CNTL/Z.
R1(config)# no ip dhcp excluded-address 10.1.1.100
R1(config)# ip dhcp excluded-address 10.1.1.1 10.1.1.20
R1(config)#
R1# end
```

To ensure that the users will receive unique addresses from the DHCP server and will not incur any more address conflicts, you must renew IP address leases on all DHCP clients, especially those that have experienced conflicts before.

DHCP Troubleshooting Example: Relay Agent Issue

The final DHCP troubleshooting example is based on the diagram depicted in Figure 6-9. In this case, there is a centrally located DHCP server, represented by R4 in the topology diagram shown in Figure 6-9. The DHCP clients in network segment 10.1.1.0 are unable to obtain IP address and other parameters from the central DHCP server. R2 is a DHCP client that is having trouble acquiring the IP address, and R2 is the router that is supposed to act as a relay agent and forward DHCP messages between local clients and the DHCP server (R4).

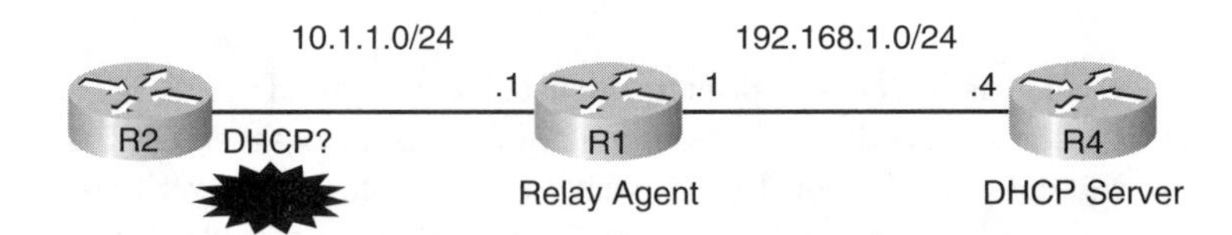

Figure 6-9 *The DHCP Server Is Not Serving the IP Address and Other Parameters to Remote Clients*

Based on the symptom and the network topology, there are several possible causes:

- The clients could be misconfigured or faulty.
- The relay agent could be not configured or misconfigured.

- The server could be misconfigured or exhausted (or faulty/disabled).
- There could be network problems or filtering/security barriers.

Using a structured approach, you should start at the most simple and direct place, where you can start eliminating hypotheses quickly. If you start at the client side, you might need to renew DHCP addresses in multiple clients to prove the point. Because multiple clients are having the same problem, it is possible that they are all misconfigured, but that is not likely. It is simpler to check the relay agent. If you find no problem with the relay agent, you can then check the DHCP server. One of the quickest ways to verify DHCP relay agent operations is using the **debug ip udp** command. You use this debug on R1 and observe the results, as shown in Example 6-21.

Example 6-21 *Result of* **debug ip udp** *on the DHCP Relay Agent (R1)*

```
R1#
R1# debug ip udp
UDP packet debugging is on
R1#
R1#
*Aug 23 19:01:05.303: UDP: rcvd src-0.0.0.0(68), dst=255.255.255.255(67),
  length=584
*Aug 23 19:01:05.303: UDP: broadcast packet dropped, src=0.0.0.0,
  dst=192.168.1.255
*Aug 23 19:01:08.911: UDP: rcvd src-0.0.0.0(68), dst=255.255.255.255(67),
  length=584
*Aug 23 19:01:08.911: UDP: broadcast packet dropped, src=0.0.0.0,
  dst=192.168.1.255
*Aug 23 19:01:12.911: UDP: rcvd src-0.0.0.0(68), dst=255.255.255.255(67),
  length=584
*Aug 23 19:01:12.911: UDP: broadcast packet dropped, src=0.0.0.0,
  dst=192.168.1.255
*Aug 23 19:01:35.795: UDP: rcvd src-0.0.0.0(68), dst=255.255.255.255(67),
  length=584
*Aug 23 19:01:35.795: UDP: broadcast packet dropped, src=0.0.0.0,
  dst=192.168.1.255
*Aug 23 19:01:38.911: UDP: rcvd src-0.0.0.0(68), dst=255.255.255.255(67),
  length=584
*Aug 23 19:01:38.911: UDP: broadcast packet dropped, src=0.0.0.0,
  dst=192.168.1.255
*Aug 23 19:01:42.911: UDP: rcvd src-0.0.0.0(68), dst=255.255.255.255(67),
  length=584
*Aug 23 19:01:42.911: UDP: broadcast packet dropped, src=0.0.0.0,
  dst=192.168.1.255
```

As you can see in the output shown in Example 6-21, R1 is certainly receiving DHCP requests. The UDP/IP packets shown have a source address of 0.0.0.0, destination address of 255.255.255.255 with source UDP port of 68 (DHCP client) and destination UDP port of 67 (DHCP server). The problem could be that the fa0/0 interface facing the DHCP client is missing the **ip helper-address** command pointing to 192.168.1.4. Checking the configuration reveals that this command is indeed missing, so adding this command is the first thing you have to do. Next, you can use the **debug ip udp** command on R4, the DHCP server. Example 6-22 shows the result.

Example 6-22 debug ip udp *on R4 Shows DHCP Requests Are Being Forwarded by R1*

```
R1(config)# int fa0/0
R1(config-if)# ip helper-address 192.168.1.4
R1(config-if)# end

R4#
R4#
R4#
*Aug 23 19:31:39.303: UDP: sent src=0.0.0.0(67), dst=255.255.255.255(68),
  length=308
*Aug 23 19:31:39.303: UDP: rcvd src=0.0.0.0(68), dst=255.255.255.255(67),
  length=584
*Aug 23 19:31:39.303: UDP: sent src=0.0.0.0(67), dst=255.255.255.255(68),
  length=308
*Aug 23 19:31:40.159: UDP: rcvd src=0.0.0.0(68), dst=192.168.1.4(67), length=584
*Aug 23 19:31:44.159: UDP: rcvd src=0.0.0.0(68), dst=192.168.1.4(67), length=584
*Aug 23 19:31:46.307: UDP: rcvd src=10.1.1.11(53470), dst=255.255.255.255(69),
  length=30
*Aug 23 19:31:49.307: UDP: rcvd src=10.1.1.11(53470), dst=255.255.255.255(69),
  length=30
*Aug 23 19:31:53.307: UDP: rcvd src=10.1.1.11(53470), dst=255.255.255.255(69),
  length=30
*Aug 23 19:31:58.307: UDP: rcvd src=10.1.1.11(53470), dst=255.255.255.255(69),
  length=30
*Aug 23 19:32:04.307: UDP: rcvd src=10.1.1.11(53470), dst=255.255.255.255(69),
  length=30
*Aug 23 19:32:11.307: UDP: rcvd src=10.1.1.11(53470), dst=255.255.255.255(69),
  length=30
*Aug 23 19:32:19.307: UDP: rcvd src=10.1.1.11(53470), dst=255.255.255.255(69),
  length=30
*Aug 23 19:32:28.439: UDP: rcvd src=10.1.1.11(53470), dst=255.255.255.255(69),
  length=29
*Aug 23 19:32:31.439: UDP: rcvd src=10.1.1.11(53470), dst=255.255.255.255(69),
  length=29
*Aug 23 19:32:35.439: UDP: rcvd src=10.1.1.11(53470), dst=255.255.255.255(69),
  length=29
*Aug 23 19:32:37.011: UDP: rcvd src=0.0.0.0(68), dst=192.168.1.4(67), length=584
```

Finally, you verify the status of the DHCP clients, such as R2, in the 10.1.1.0 subnet, and see that they are acquiring IP address and other parameters from the DHCP server.

Identify Common IPv6 Routing Issues

This section presents the most commonly found issues in IPv6 networks. This discussion includes issues that affect multiple areas of IPv6 deployments, such as neighbor discovery, routing protocols, and tunneling implementations. The section ends with an IPv6 troubleshooting example.

IPv6 Routing

In IPv6 troubleshooting, you must also identify the problem symptoms and resolve them using a structured troubleshooting approach. IPv6 has many similarities with IPv4, and that makes information gathering and analysis processes similar, too. Network practitioners already have knowledge of IPv4, and comparing the symptoms of malfunctioning IPv6 components and protocols against previous knowledge of similar components and protocols in IPv4 is an intuitive and straightforward task. The similarities between, for example, OSPFv3 or RIPng (RIP Next Generation), with their counterparts in IPv4, make it easier to compare observed behavior against expected behavior. This makes the process of eliminating possible causes also a more direct task. Something as important as choosing the appropriate commands to gather information and document the symptoms becomes an intuitive task: Commands that contain the word *IP* maintain most of their syntax in terms of structure, as you shift from IPv4 to IPv6.

It is important to point out, however, that while IPv6 and IPv4 similarities represent a benefit, their differences might affect the troubleshooting process. This typically results in something being overlooked, or it might simply cause a conceptual misunderstanding of the issues. You need to know your basics; for example, there are no broadcasts in IPv6. Neighbors are discovered through ICMPv6 multicasts and the neighbor discovery (ND) process. The addressing structure is still hierarchical, and classless interdomain routing (CIDR) rules and nomenclature still apply. The subnet mask is still there, it is only potentially longer. You will see /96, or even /128, where before you saw /32 at the most. However, the meaning and semantics are the same, and you can use this knowledge to troubleshoot summarization errors or connectivity problems, such as suboptimal routing, caused by incorrect or poor summarization. OSPFv3 is still a link state protocol, and it behaves as such. You will see some of the major differences that can result in interesting troubleshooting scenarios; however, neighbor sessions, link state advertisements (LSAs), hierarchical areas, and so on, still exist.

The command structure for IPv6 is similar to IPv4, with a few additions and omissions in IPv6. For almost every IPv4 command, you will find an IPv6 counterpart. For example, the **show ip route** command becomes **show ipv6 route**, the **show ip interface** command becomes **show ipv6 interface**, and so on. The testing commands, **ping** and **trace**, the backbone of many troubleshooting tests, are still there and maintain syntax and outcome consistency with their IPv4 counterparts. Although the similarities between IPv4 and

IPv6 will definitely help you in your troubleshooting efforts, the differences between the protocols represent a clear departure from conventional IP thinking. IPv6 is much more than a simple expansion in the address space. It does away with broadcasts, which affects protocols such as DHCP, and the Address Resolution Protocol (ARP) does not exist. Layer 2 addresses are gathered by hosts using the ICMPv6-based neighbor discovery process, which serves other purposes, as well, including duplicate address detection (DAD), stateless autoconfiguration, and other processes. Table 6-5 shows some important differences between IPv4 and IPv6.

Table 6-5 *Some of the Differences Between IPv4 and IPv6*

	IPv4	IPv6
Address Resolution Protocol	Used to find Layer 2 address mappings	Does not exist. ICMPv6 neighbor discovery is used instead.
Secondary IP addresses	Available, but the main IP address is used as packet source	Do not exist. Interfaces can have multiple concurrent IPv6 addresses of different types.
Routing Protocols	Use interface IP address to exchange routing information	Use the link-local address to create neighbor sessions and to assign as the next hop.
Address Assignment	Static or dynamic (dynamic using DHCP)	Static or dynamic (dynamic using DHCP or stateless autoconfiguration).

In IPv6, a standard host or router interface can have multiple IP addresses without using the concept of a secondary address. In fact, interfaces are "expected" to have multiple addresses, and different components of the protocol stack might eventually use the different identifiers for different purposes. One example for that is how routing protocols use the link-local address as a next hop and for protocol adjacencies. This can result in interesting troubleshooting scenarios and even more interesting protocol behaviors, such as the fact that OSPF routers could establish a routing protocol adjacency even when they do *not* belong to the same IP subnet. Many other subtle differences make IPv6 a bit of a challenge for IPv4 practitioners. The last row of Table 6-5 mentions IPv6 stateless autoconfiguration, where routers become DHCP-type providers of IP subnets and default gateways to the local hosts; this is another source of potential issues affecting hosts when misconfigured.

Troubleshooting IPv6 Issues

It is difficult to identify all the possible issues in a full protocol stack such as IPv6. Administrators of IPv6 networks usually have some familiarity with the issues discussed here, especially in specific areas such as stateless autoconfiguration or routing protocols such as OSPF. Examining IPv6 issues reveals that there are many common configuration mistakes. An example for this is a misconfigured autoconfiguration router that is not advertising network information to hosts. Until a problem like this is recognized and corrected, IPv6 hosts cannot establish full connectivity as they lack global unicast addresses.

Other typical problem areas are related to IPv6 routing protocols. There are many similarities between IPv6 routing problems and their IPv4 counterparts. Examples of IPv6 routing problems include suboptimal routing due to improper summarization and parameter mismatches on protocols such as OSPF that negotiate parameters.

For tunnel scenarios, because of the great variety of methods, you might find several instances in which other components such as routing protocols need to change when the specific migration or tunneling method changes. For example, when using 6to4 tunnels, not all interior gateway protocols (IGPs) will function properly, because when multicast addresses are used to establish adjacencies, those addresses are not properly mapped to a tunnel destination.

Identifying the IPv6 issues and failure conditions is not always an easy task, given the complexity of the protocol and especially considering the lack of experienced network practitioners who have used it. The good news is that several Cisco IOS tools and commands can help, including the following:

- **debug ipv6 routing:** Use this command to display debugging messages for IPv6 routing table updates and route cache updates. This command displays messages whenever the routing table changes.
- **debug ipv6 nd:** Use this command to display debugging messages for IPv6 Internet Control Message Protocol (ICMP) ND transactions. During troubleshooting, this command can help determine whether the router is sending or receiving IPv6 ICMP ND messages.
- **debug ipv6 packet:** Use this command to display debugging messages for IPv6 packets. The debugging information includes packets received, generated, and forwarded. Note that fast-switched packets do not generate messages.
- **show ipv6 interface:** Use this command to display the usability status of interfaces configured for IPv6 or to validate the IPv6 status of an interface and its configured addresses. If the interface's hardware is usable, the interface is marked as up. If the interface can provide two-way communication for IPv6, the line protocol is marked as up.
- **show ipv6 routers:** This is an IPv6-specific command (does not have an IPv4 counterpart) you can use to display IPv6 router advertisement (RA) information received from onlink routers.
- **show ipv6 route:** This command displays the contents of the IPv6 routing table.
- **show ipv6 protocols:** This command displays the parameters and current state of the active IPv6 routing protocol processes. The information displayed by this command proves useful in troubleshooting routing operations.

In addition to the commands, an effective troubleshooting method provides a comprehensive end-to-end approach to identifying symptoms and isolating problems. For example, consider the output of the **debug ipv6 nd** command, and how helpful it can be in identifying neighbor discovery, duplicate addresses, autoconfiguration, and other conditions. The output of this command is critical not only in understanding the ND process and the role of ICMPv6, but also for identifying and isolating IPv6 failure conditions.

IPv6 Troubleshooting Example: Stateless Autoconfiguration Issue

This example is based on the network diagram shown in Figure 6-10. You are informed that recent changes in the network have rendered router R3 isolated and with no connectivity outside the Fast Ethernet segment connected to R1. You verify this by performing a ping from R3 to a remote destination (24::24:2), and it does not succeed. When you inspect the change log you notice that the changes were aimed at providing automatic IP address assignment and configuration to certain devices. After the change, R3 lost connectivity to the rest of the network. You will apply a troubleshooting method to resolve this problem. This particular scenario follows a bottom-up approach, starting at R3.

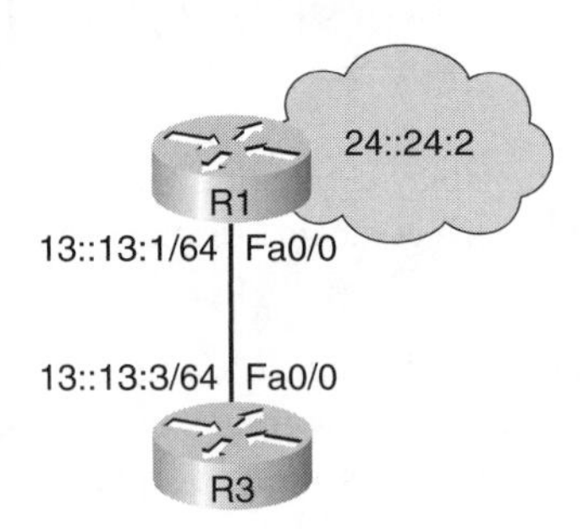

Figure 6-10 *IPv6 Troubleshooting Example Network Diagram: R3 Has Lost Some Connectivity*

In following the bottom-up approach, the first order of business is to determine the status of the interface on R3, and start gathering information. The choice of commands is important because some commands will give you information on multiple layers, an important feature for the more experienced troubleshooter. In this example, you will use the **show ipv6 interface** command and refer to the Fast Ethernet 0/0 interface. Example 6-23 shows the results. You'll notice that the interface is up at both Layers 1 and 2. So, you can start eliminating hypotheses here; there seems to be physical connectivity at this point. You also notice that the interface has a global unicast address configured, on network 13::/64, and a link-local address.

Example 6-23 show ipv6 interface fa0/0 *Command Output on Router R3*

```
R3# show ipv6 interface f0/0
FastEthernet0/0 is up, line protocol is up
  IPv6 is enabled, link-local address is FE80::219:55FF:FEF0:B7D0
  Global unicast address(es):
    13::13:3, subnet is 13::/64
  Joined group address(es):
    FF02::1
```

```
    FF02::2
    FF02::1:FF13:3
    FF02::1:FFF0:B7D0
  MTU is 1500 bytes
  ICMP error messages limited to one every 100 milliseconds
  ICMP redirects are enabled
  ND DAD is enabled, number of DAD attempts: 1
  ND reachable time is 30000 milliseconds
  ND advertised reachable time is 0 milliseconds
  ND advertised retransmit interval is 0 milliseconds
  ND router advertisements are sent every 200 seconds
  ND router advertisements live for 1800 seconds
  Hosts use stateless autoconfig for addresses.
R3#
```

Addressing does not seem to be a problem, but because you notice the last line specifying **Hosts use stateless autoconfig for addresses**, it is good to check the configuration of the fa0/0 interface using the **show run interface fa 0/0** command. The result is shown in Example 6-24. The interface fa0/0 is configured to automatically obtain prefix and other information.

Example 6-24 *The Interface fa0/0 Section of R3's Running-Config*

```
R3# show run int f0/0
Building configuration...

Current configuration : 111 bytes
!
Interface FastEthernet0/0
 no ip address
 duplex auto
 speed auto
 ipv6 address autoconfig
 ipv6 enable
end

R3#
```

Now, looking at R3's routing table using the **show ipv6 route** command as demonstrated in the output in Example 6-25, only the connected/local networks are listed.

Example 6-25 *IPv6 Routing Table Is Displayed Using the* **show ipv6 route** *Command*

```
R3# show ipv6 route
IPv6 Routing Table - 6 entries
Codes: C - Connected, L - Local, S - Static, R - RIP, B - BGP
       U - Per-user Static Route
       I1 - ISIS L1, I2 - ISIS L2, IA - ISIS interarea, IS - ISIS summary
       O - OSPF intra, OI - OSPF inter, OE1 - OSPF ext 1, OE2 - OSPF ext 2
       ON1 - OSPF NSSA ext 1, ON2 - OSPF NSSA ext 2
C    13::/64 [0/0]
      via ::, Fast Ethernet0/0
L    13:219:55FF;FEF0:B7D0/128 [0/0]
      via ::, FastEthernet0/0
C    103::/64 [0/0]
      via ::, Loopback0
L    103::3/128 [0/0]
      via ::, Loopback0
L    FE80::/10 [0/0]
      via ::, Null0
L    FF00::/8 [0/0]
      via ::, Null0
R3#
```

At this point, your line of thinking is that R3 has an IP address, but no default route. The router is configured for stateless autoconfiguration on that interface, so it should be obtaining a default router through autoconfiguration. You know that the autoconfiguration process is ruled by ICMPv6 as part of the ND set of features. The best tool to understand this process is the **debug ipv6 nd** command. Shut down the interface and enable it again to see neighbor discovery. The results are shown in Example 6-26, where you can see that the router solicitation messages go out, but you do not see any replies! It looks as if the autoconfiguration router, which is R1 in the network topology, is misconfigured or unreachable.

Example 6-26 *The* **debug ipv6 nd** *Results on R3 Show No Respond for Its Solicitation*

```
R3# debug ipv6 nd
ICMP Neighbor Dicovery events debugging is on
R3#
R3#
R3# conf t
Enter configuration commands, one per line. End with CNTL/Z.
R3(config)# int f0/0
R3(config-if)# sh
R3(config-if)# no shu
R3(config-if)#
*Aug 23 21:44:18.491: ICMPv6-ND: Sending Final RA on FastEthernet0/0
```

```
*Aug 23 21:44:18.491: ICMPv6-ND: Address FE80::219:55FF:FEF0:B7D0/10 is down on
FastEthernet0/0
*Aug 23 21:44:20.491: %LINK-3-UPDOWN: Interface FastEthernet0/0, changed state to
up
*Aug 23 21:44:20.971: ICMPv6-ND: Sending NS for FE80::219:55FF:FEF0:B7D0 on
FastEthernet0/0
*Aug 23 21:44:21.971: ICMPv6-ND: DAD: FE80::219:55FF:FEF0:B7D0 is unique
*Aug 23 21:44:21.971: ICMPv6-ND: Sending NA for FE80::219:55FF:FEF0:B7D0 on
FastEthernet0/0
*Aug 23 21:44:21.971: ICMPv6-ND: Address FE80::219:55FF:FEF0:B7D0 is up on
FastEthernet0/0
*Aug 23 21:44:23.971: ICMPv6-ND: Sending RS on FastEthernet0/0
*Aug 23 21:44:27.971: ICMPv6-ND: Sending RS on FastEthernet0/0
*Aug 23 21:44:31.971: ICMPv6-ND: Sending RS on FastEthernet0/0
```

At this point, you would shift your troubleshooting effort to R1 and look at the interface connecting to R3 first. Interfaces must be active and have a valid IPv6 address to advertise prefix and autoconfiguration information using ICMPv6. So, you type **show running-config int fa0/0** and verify that the interface is properly configured with theIPv6 address 13::13:1/64. Looking at the status of the interface, using the **show ipv6 interface fa0/0** command, you would notice that it is up at both physical and data link layers. Example 6-27 shows the results.

Example 6-27 *Checking the Configuration and Status of the fa0/0 Interface on R1*

```
R1#
R1# show running-config interface f0/0
Building configuration...

Current configuration : 112 bytes
!
interface FastEthernet0/0
 no ip address
 duplex auto
 speed auto
 ipv6 address 13::13:1/64

 ipv6 enable
end


R1#
R1#
R1# show ipv6 interface f0/0
```

```
FastEthernet0/0 is up, line protocol is up
  IPv6 is enabled, link-local address is FE80::219:56FF:FE2C:9856
  Global unicast address(es):
    13::13:1, subnet is 13::/64

  Joined group address(es):
   FF02::1
   FF02::2
   FF02::1:FF13:1
   FF02::1:FF2C:9856
  MTU is 1500 bytes
  ICMP error messages limited to one every 100 milliseconds
  ICMP redirects are enabled
  ND DAD is enabled, number of DAD attempts: 1
  ND reachable time is 30000 milliseconds
  Default router is FE80::219:55F:FEF0:B7D0 on FastEthernet0/0
R1#
```

You must answer the following questions:

- What else does R1 need to become a proper autoconfiguration router?
- How can it be that R3 has a working IPv6 address if the autoconfiguration process is not working?
- Why is it that R3 cannot access the rest of the network, even with a working IPv6 address and no noticeable physical issues?

On R1, you must verify one of the requirements for autoconfiguration, which is having IPv6 unicast routing explicitly enabled, using the **show run | include unicast-routing** command. From the resulting output, you learn that you do not have IPv6 unicast-routing enabled on this router. You enable **ipv6 unicast-routing** on R1, and enter the **debug ipv6 nd** command to observe the results. See the output shown in Example 6-28. The router advertisements go out and it looks as if the autoconfiguration router is back on track.

Example 6-28 *Checking If IPv6 Unicast-Routing Is Enabled on R1*

```
R1# show run | inc unicast-routing
R1#
R1#
R1#
R1#
R1# debug ipv6 nd
ICMP Neighbor Discovery events debugging is on
```

```
R1#
R1#
R1# conf t
Enter configuration commands, one per line. End with CNTL/A.
R1(config)# ipv6 unicast-routing
R1(config)# end
R1#
*Aug 23 22:01:45.175: ICMPv6-ND: Sending RA to FF02::1 on FastEthernet0/0
*Aug 23 22:01:45.175: ICMPv6-ND: MTU = 1500
*Aug 23 22:01:45.175: ICMPv6-ND: prefix = 13::/64 onlink autoconfig
*Aug 23 22:01:45.175: ICMPv6-ND: 2592000/604800 (valid/preferred)
R1#
```

Now you can go back to R3 and see the result of enabling **ipv6 unicast-routing** on R1. On R3, you turn on ND debug using the **debug ipv6 nd** command, and **shutdown** and **no shut** on the fa0/0 interface. You see messages going out and responses coming in. Example 6-29 shows the results. The debug results illustrate that R3 is receiving the route advertisements and that the address has been configured on fa0/0.

Example 6-29 *The* **debug ipv6 nd** *Output on R3 Upon Enabling IPv6 Routing on R1*

```
R3# debug ipv6 nd
ICMP Neighbor Dicovery events debugging is on
R3#
R3#
R3# conf t
Enter configuration commands, one per line. End with CNTL/Z.
R3(config)# int f0/0
R3(config-if)# sh
R3(config-if)# no shu
R3(config-if)#
R3(config-if)# end
*Aug 23 21:57:47.547: ICMPv6-ND: Sending Final RA on FastEthernet0/0
*Aug 23 21:57:47.547: ICMPv6-ND: Address 13::219:55FF:FEF0:B7D0/64 is down on
FastEthernet0/0
*Aug 23 21:57:47.547: ICMPv6-ND: Address FE80::219:55FF:FEF0:B7D0/10 is down on
FastEthernet0/0
R3#
*Aug 23 21:57:48.003: %SYS-5-CONFIG_I: Configured from console by console
*Aug 23 21:57:53.279: ICMPv6-ND: Sending NS for FE80::219:55FF:FEF0:B7D0 on
FastEthernet0/0
*Aug 23 21:57:54.279: ICMPv6-ND: DAD: FE80::219:55FF:FEF0:B7D0 is unique
*Aug 23 21:57:54.279: ICMPv6-ND: Sending NA for FE80::219:55FF:FEF0:B7D0 on
FastEthernet0/0
```

```
*Aug 23 21:57:56.279: ICMPv6-ND: Sending RS on FastEthernet0/0
*Aug 23 21:57:56.279: ICMPv6-ND: Received RA from FE80::219:56FF:FE2C:9856 on
FastEthernet0/0
*Aug 23 21:57:56.279: ICMPv6-ND: Sending NS for 13::219:55FF:FEF0:B7D0 on
FastEthernet0/0
*Aug 23 21:57:56.279: ICMPv6-ND: Autoconfiguring 13::219:55FF:FEF0:B7D0 on
FastEthernet0/0
*Aug 23 21:57:57.279: ICMPv6-ND: DAD: 13::219:55FF:FEF0:B7D0 is unique
*Aug 23 21:57:57.279: ICMPv6-ND: Sending NA for 13::219:55FF:FEF0:B7D0 on
FastEthernet0/0
*Aug 23 21:57:57.279: ICMPv6-ND: Address 13::219:55FF:FEF0:B7D0 is up on
FastEthernet0/0
```

Now you can re-examine R3's IPv6 address on fa0/0 and see what changed as demonstrated in Example 6-30. Notice that R3's fa0/0 interface previously had a valid IPv6 address (see Example 6-23), but no valid lifetime for the IPv6 address. Now you notice that the valid lifetime and preferred lifetime parameters are present (see Example 6-30).

Example 6-30 show ip ipv6 int fa0/0 *Command Output on R3, Upon Enabling IPv6 Routing on R1*

```
R1# sh ipv6 int f0/0
FastEthernet0/0 is up, line protocol is up
  IPv6 is enabled, link-local address is FE80::219:55FF:FEF0:B7D0
  Global unicast address(es):
    13::219:55FF:FEF0:B7D0, subnet is 13::/64 [PRE]
      Valid lifetime 2591941 preferred lifetime 604741
  Joined group address(es):
   FF02::1
   FF02::2
   FF02::1:FFF0:B7D0
  MTU is 1500 bytes
  ICMP error messages limited to one every 100 milliseconds
  ICMP redirects are enabled
  ND DAD is enabled, number of DAD attempts: 1
  ND reachable time is 0 milliseconds
  ND advertised reachable time is 0 milliseconds
  ND advertised retransmit interval is 0 milliseconds
  ND router advertisements are sent every 200 seconds
  ND router advertisements live for 1800 seconds
  Hosts use stateless autoconfig for addresses
R1#
```

You can conclude why R3 had a valid address: At some point R3 was receiving network information from R1 through ICMPv6, so it obtained the IPv6 address. You need to remember that autoconfiguration addresses remains in effect for a specific valid lifetime, even if the device does not hear from the autoconfiguration router during that span. To ensure R3's IPv6 connectivity, you ping remote destinations, and as shown in Example 6-31, the ping succeeds.

Example 6-31 *Ping Result on R3 After Enabling IPv6 Routing on R1*

```
R3# ping 24::24:2

Type escape sequence to abort
Sending 5, 100-byte ICMP Echos to 24::24:2, timeout is 2 seconds:
!!!!!
Success reate is 100 percent (5/5), round-trip min/avg/max = 0/0/0 ms
R3#
```

IPv6 Troubleshooting Example: Redistribution Issue

The second troubleshooting example is based on the topology shown in Figure 6-11. R1 and R2 have two connections: one through the 6to4 tunnel, and a main link over a Frame Relay network. There are two RIPng processes running: one between R3 and R1 and then across the tunnel, and the second process running between R4 and R2 and across the Frame Relay virtual circuit. A recent change ticket performed two-way redistribution between the two RIP processes on R2. However, R4 has lost reachability to R3, specifically the loopback interface on R3.

Based on the network topology, one of the methods to provide connectivity between R3 and R4 is to perform redistribution between the two RIPng routing processes. You have been told that redistribution has been configured on R2, but R1 and R2 do not have connectivity. There seem to be a routing problem, so you begin our troubleshooting halfway through the OSI model, at the network layer. You start by looking at the routing table on R4 using the **show ipv6 route rip** command as demonstrated in Example 6-32. Network 103::/64, which is the loopback of R3, is present in R4's routing table, but a ping from R4 to R3's loopback fails.

Example 6-32 show ipv6 route *Command Output Displays R3's Loopback Present in R4's Routing Table*

```
R4# show ipv6 route
IPv6 Routing Table - 6 entries
Codes: C - Connected, L - Local, S - Static, R - RIP, B - BGP
       U - Per-user Static Route
       I1 - ISIS L1, I2 - ISIS L2, IA - ISIS interarea, IS - ISIS summary
       O - OSPF intra, OI - OSPF inter, OE1 - OSPF ext 1, OE2 - OSPF ext 2
       ON1 - OSPF NSSA ext 1, ON2 - OSPF NSSA ext 2
```

```
R      12::/64 [120/2]
        via FE80::219:55FF:FE92:A442, Fast Ethernet0/0
R      103:::/64 [120/7]
        via FE80::219:55FF:FE92:A442, Fast Ethernet0/0
R4#ping 103::3

Type escape sequence to abort.
Sending 5, 100-byte ICMP Echos to 103::3, timeout is 2 seconds:
.....
Success rate is 0 percent (0/5)
R4#
```

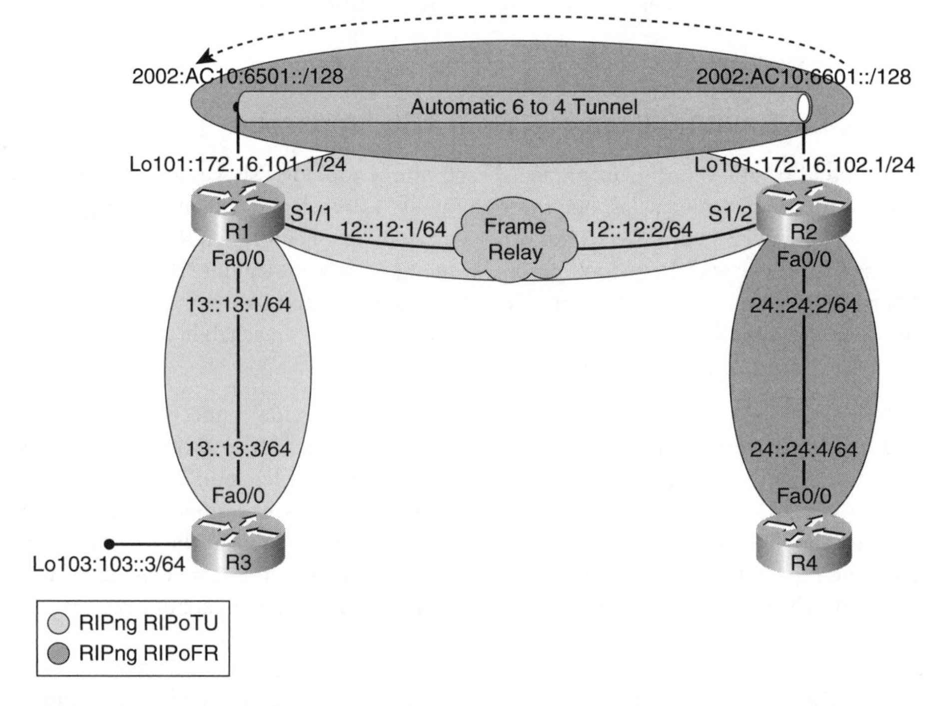

Figure 6-11 *Network Topology for the Second Troubleshooting Example*

The next logical step is to move to the downstream router R2 and check how redistribution was configured there by using the **show ipv6 protocols** command as demonstrated in Example 6-33.

Example 6-33 *Gathering Information About IPv6 Protocol Redistribution on R2*

```
R2# show ipv6 protocols
IPv6 Routing Protocol is "connected"
IPv6 Routing Protocol is "static"
IPv6 Routing Protocol is "rip RIPoFR"
  Interfaces:
    FastEthernet0/0
    Serial0/0/0
  Redistribution:
    Redistributing protocol rip RIPoTU with metric 5
IPv6 Routing Protocol is "rip RIPoTU"
  Interfaces:
    Loopback101
    Tunnel0
  Redistribution:
    Redistributing protocol rip RIPoFR with metric 15
R2#
```

Notice that redistribution on R2 is bidirectional, from RIPoTU to RIPoFR, and vice versa. Technically, R2 should be redistributing RIPoTU into RIPoFR so that it can advertise R3's Ethernet and loopback network addresses, learned through RIPoTU, to R4 through RIPoFR. Performing redistribution of RIPoFR to RIPoTU is better on R1 so that R3 learns about R4's Ethernet and loopback network addresses. Regardless, someone decided to do both redistributions on R2. However, different metrics were used in the two redistributions, perhaps to manipulate path selection or to prevent routing loops. When redistributing into RIPoTU, the networks are being injected with the metric of 15 (the maximum metric value in RIPng). Now, using the **show ipv6 route** command on R1 (see Example 6-34), look at R1's routing table to see whether R4 networks, specifically the 24::/64 network, are present. As the output reveals, the 24::/64 network is not present in R1's IPv6 routing table.

Example 6-34 *R1's IPv6 Routing Table Is Missing Networks (For Example, 24::/64)*

```
R1# show ipv6 route
IPv6 Routing Table - 6 entries
Codes: C - Connected, L - Local, S - Static, R - RIP, B - BGP
       U - Per-user Static Route
       I1 - ISIS L1, I2 - ISIS L2, IA - ISIS interarea, IS - ISIS summary
       O - OSPF intra, OI - OSPF inter, OE1 - OSPF ext 1, OE2 - OSPF ext 2
       ON1 - OSPF NSSA ext 1, ON2 - OSPF NSSA ext 2
S    ::/0 [1/0]
      via ::, Tunnel0
C    12::/64 [0/0]
      via ::, Serial0/0/0
L    12::12:1/128 [0/0]
      via ::, Serial0/0/0
```

```
C     13::/64 [0/0]
       via ::, FastEthernet0/0
L     13::13:1/128 [0/0]
       via ::, FastEthernet0/0
R     103::/64 {120/2]
       via FE80::219:55FF:FEF0:B7D0, FastEthernet0/0
LC    2002:AC10:6501::1/128 [0/0]
       Via ::, Tunnel0
L     FE80::/10 [0/0]
       via ::, Null0
L     FF00::/8 [0/0]
       via ::, Null0
R1#
```

Assuming that redistribution on R2 is causing the problem, you fix the redistribution metric on R2 and modify the **redistribute** command to still have a high metric, such as 10, but not 15, as shown in Example 6-35.

Example 6-35 *Correcting the Redistribution Metric in R2 from 15 to 10*

```
R2# conf t
Enter configuration commands, one per line.  End with CNTL/Z.
R2(config)# ipv6 router rip RIPoTU
R2(config-rtr)# redistribute rip RIPoFR metric 10
R2(config-rtr)#
R2(config-rtr)# end
R2#
```

Now, go back to R1, and check its IPv6 routing table again. Strangely, you don't see the Frame Relay network. R1 is not receiving any routes through the Frame Relay network (the serial interface). You should verify that IPv6 RIP is properly configured in router R1. One of the most useful commands to obtain a complete snapshot of IPv6 RIP in a Cisco router, including the interfaces where the protocol is enabled, is the **show ipv6 rip** command. You use this command on R1 and see the results shown in Example 6-36.

Example 6-36 *The result of the* **show ipv6 rip** *Command on R1*

```
R1# show ipv6 rip
RIP process "RIPoTU", port 521, multicast-grop FF02::9, pid 178
     Administrative distance is 120. Maximum paths is 16
     Updates every 30 seconds, expire after 180
     Holddown lasts 0 seconds, garbage collection after 120
     Split horizon is on; poison reverse is off
     Default routes are not generated
```

```
      Periodic updates 201, trigger updates 13
   Interfaces:
     Tunnel0
     FastEthernet0/0
   Redistribution:
     None
RIP process "RIPoFR", port 521, multicast-group FF02::9, pid 179
      Administrative distance is 120. Maximum paths is 16
      Updates every 30 seconds, expire after 180
      Holddown lasts 0 seconds, garbage collection after 120
      Split horizon is on; poison reverse is off
      Default routes are not generated
      Periodic updates 197, trigger updates 6
   Interfaces:
     None
   Redistribution:
     Redistributing protocol rip RIPoTU with metric 5
R1#
```

The RIPoFR process has no interfaces enabled and that is one reason R1 is not receiving routes through the Frame Relay link. On R1, you enable the RIPoFR process on the serial interface, and observe the results (shown in Example 6-37) using the **debug ipv6 routing** command.

Example 6-37 *The* **debug ipv6 routing** *Results on R1 After Enabling RIPoFR on S0/0/0*

```
R1#
R1# debug ipv6 routing
IPv6 routing table events debugging is on
R1#
R1#
R1#
R1#conf t
Enter configuration commands, one per line. End with CNTL/Z.
R1(config)# int s0/0/0
R1(config-if)# ipv6 rip RIPoFR enable
R1(config-if)#
R1(config-if)# end
R1#
R1#
*Aug 24 00:42:47.250: IPV6RTO: Event: 11::/64, Mod, owner connected, previous None
*Aug 24 00:42:47.250: IPV6RTO: Event: 12::/64, Mod, owner connected, previous None
*Aug 24 00:42:47.538: %SYS-5-CONFIG_I: Configured from console by console
*Aug 24 00:42:49.206: IPV6RTO: rip RIPoFR, Route add 24::/64 [new]
```

```
*Aug 24 00:42:49.206: IPv6RTO: rip RIPoFR, Add 24::/64 to table
*Aug 24 00:42:49.206: IPv6RTO: rip RIPoFR, Adding next-hop
FE80::219::55FF:FE92:A442 over Serial 0/0/0 for 24::/64, [120/2]
*Aug 24 00:42:49.206: IPv6RTO: rip RIPoFR, Added backup for 12::/64, distance 120
*Aug 24 00:42:49.206: IPv6RTO: rip RIPoFR, Added backup for 11::/64, distance 120
*Aug 24 00:42:49.206: IPv6RTO: Event: 24::/64, Add, owner rip, previous None
```

The **debug** output shows the missing routes being added to the routing table. You now use the **show ipv6 route** command on R1 and see that the routes through the Frame Relay network are present. R1's new routing table is shown in Example 6-38. Note that the paths through Frame Relay are preferred because of the lower metric.

Example 6-38 *R1' IPv6 Routing Table, After Enabling RIPoFR on Its Serial Interface*

```
R4# show ipv6 route
IPv6 Routing Table - 17 entries
Codes: C - Connected, L - Local, S - Static, R - RIP, B - BGP
       U - Per-user Static Route
       I1 - ISIS L1, I2 - ISIS L2, IA - ISIS interarea, IS - ISIS summary
       O - OSPF intra, OI - OSPF inter, OE1 - OSPF ext 1, OE2 - OSPF ext 2
       ON1 - OSPF NSSA ext 1, ON2 - OSPF NSSA ext 2
S    ::/0 [1/0]
      via ::, Tunnel0
C    11::/64 [0/0]
      via ::, Serial0/0/0
L    11::11:1/128 [0/0]
      via ::, Serial0/0/0
C    12::/64 [0/0]
      via ::, Serial0/0/0
L    12::12:1/128 [0/0]
      via ::, Serial0/0/0
C    13::/64 [0/0]
      via ::, FastEthernet0/0
L    13::13:1/128 [0/0]
      via ::, FastEthernet0/0
R    24::/64 [120/2]
      via FE80::219:55FF:FE92:A442, Serial0/0/0
R    103::/64 [120/2]
      via FE80::219:55FF:FEF0:B7D0, FastEthernet0/0
C    2001:AC10:6501::/64 [0/0]
      via ::, Tunnel0
L    2001:AC10:6501::1/128 [0/0]
      via ::, Tunnel0
R    2001:AC10:6601::/64 [120/2]
```

```
     via FE80::219:55FF:FE92:A442, Serial0/0/0
S    2002::/16 [1/0]
     via Tunnel0
LC   2002:AC10:6501::1/128 [0/0]
     via ::, Tunnel0
R    2002:AC10:6601::2/128 [120/2]
     via FE80::219:55FF:FE92:A442, Serial0/0/0
L    FE80::/10 [0/0]
     via ::, Null0
L    FF00::/8 [0/0]
     via ::, Null0
R1#
```

Now it is best to go to R3 and see whether it is receiving R4's Ethernet network address (24::/64) from R1. You could use the **show ipv6 route** command, but you can use this opportunity to use the helpful **debug ipv6 packet** command. This command is dangerous, however, because it can cause the router to crash due to the amount of output that it generates and displays on the console. So, you should filter the output with an access list called FILTER, which will display only packets with the destination address matching 24::/64. Example 6-39 shows the FILTER access list as entered with the **show ipv6 access-list** command. Now, use the **debug ipv6 packet access-list FILTER** command on R3 and try to ping R2. The **debug** output shown in Example 6-39, among other messages, displays **Route not found** for the packet destined to 24::24:2 (R2's fa0/0 address). This means that R3 still doesn't have a valid path to R2 (indeed, to the Fast Ethernet link between R2 and R4).

Example 6-39 debug IPv6 packet *Command Output on R3*

```
R3# sh ipv6 access-list
IPv6 access list FILTER
    Permit ipv6 any 24::/64 (5 matches) sequence 10
R3#
R3# debug ipv6 packet access-list FILTER
IPv6 packet debuggin in on for access list FILTER
R3#
*Aug 24 11:25:11.748  IPv6: Sending on Loopback103
*Aug 24 11:25:11.748  IPv6: Sending on FastEthernet0/0
*Aug 24 11:25:39.812: IPv6: Sending on Loopback103
*Aug 24 11:25:39.812: IPv6: Sending on FastEthernet0/0
R3# ping 24::24:2

Type escape sequence to abort.
Sending 5, 100-byte ICMP Echos to 24::24:2, timeout is 2 seconds
```

```
*Aug 24 11:25:51.332:  IPv6: SAS picked source 13::13:3 for 24::24:2
*Aug 24 11:25:51.332:  IPv6: source 13::13:3 (local)
*Aug 24 11:25:51.332:        dest 24::24:2
*Aug 24 11:25:51.332:        traffic class 0, flow 0x0, len 100+0, prot 58, hops
64, Route not found
```

You know that R1 had a route to R4's Ethernet address (24::/64). You also know that R2 is redistributing the Frame Relay routes into RIPoTU and sending them to R1. R1 receives R4's Ethernet address (24::/64) through RIPoFR and RIPoTU, but it ignores the latter because of its large metric. You need to make sure R1 advertises R4's Ethernet address to R3, so you need to return to R1 and fix that. One way to fix this problem is to redistribute RIPoFR into RIPoTU on R1 so that R1 advertises R4's Ethernet to R3. First you should check what redistributions, if any, are done on R1, using the **show ipv6 protocols** command, as demonstrated in Example 6-40.

Example 6-40 *Checking Redistribution on R1 Using the* **show ipv6 protocols** *Command*

```
R1# show ipv6 prot
IPv6 Routing Protocol is "connected"
IPv6 Routing Protocol is "static"
IPv6 Routing Protocol is "rip RIPoTU"
  Interfaces:
    Tunnel0
    FastEthernet0/0
  Redistribution:
    None
IPv6 Routing Protocol is "rip RIPoFR"
  Interfaces:
    Serial0/0/0
  Redistribution:
    Redistributing protocol rip RIPoTU with metric 5
R1#
```

As you can see in the output of Example 6-40, R1 is redistributing RIPoTU into RIPoFR, which is not really necessary here. On the other hand, R1 is not redistributing RIPoFR into RIPoTU, which is necessary, because you want R4's Ethernet address to be advertised to R3. Fixing this is easy. On R1, you go into the RIPoTU process using the **ipv6 router rip RIPoTU** command and perform redistribution using the **redistribute rip RIPoFR include-connected** command, as shown in Example 6-41. Next, to see the outcome, you would go to R3 and ping R4. The ping result is 100 percent success, as you can see in Example 6-41. Next, check to make sure that R4 can now ping R3, too, and that is also successful.

Example 6-41 *After Redistributing RIPoFR into RIPoTU, R3 Has an IPv6 Path to R4*

```
R1# conf t
Enter configuration commands, one per line. End with CNTL/Z.
R1(config)#
R1(config)# ipv6 router rip RIPoTU
R1(config-rtr)# redistribute rip RIPoFR include-connected metric 5
R1(config-rtr)#
R1(config)#

R3# ping 24::24:4

Type escape sequence to abort.
Sending 5, 100-byte ICMP Echos to 24::24:2, timeout is 2 seconds
!!!!!
Success rate is 100 percent (5/5), round-trip min/avg/max = 0/0/4 ms
```

The problem is solved, and it required a lot of effort. There were two main causes:

- On R1, IPv6 RIP was not active on its Frame Relay interface.
- On R1, the RIPoFR process was not redistributed into the RIPoTU process.

IPv6 Troubleshooting Example: OSPFv3 Configuration Errors

The third IPv6 troubleshooting example is based on the network diagram shown in Figure 6-12. In this case, you have OSPFv3 running throughout the network, with the backbone area 0 (including routers R1 and R2), running over the Frame Relay network, and stub area 1 (including R1 and R3) and stub area 2 (including R2 and R4) over Fast Ethernet networks on the far ends of the diagram. It has been reported that a recent power outage might have caused some of the routers to restart. The network administrators are not completely certain that configurations were properly saved before the incident. End-to-end connectivity has been lost in this network ever since.

The best way to start is to perform some testing. You should try to verify that the symptoms were well documented and true. Also, you should try to identify the scope of the problem. Loss of end-to-end connectivity could have several meanings in different contexts. So you start with a ping in the stub routers of each area, to verify interarea connectivity. From R4, you ping the loopback on R3, and the ping fails; then you try it from R2, and the ping fails again. These results are shown in Example 6-42. Next, you ping from R1 and it fails again! Good troubleshooting practices call for pinging more than one address (or interface), in case one is down but the others are not. Therefore, you ping from R1 to R3's fa0/0 interface, which is directly connected to R1, and this one fortunately succeeds, but the same test from R2 does not.

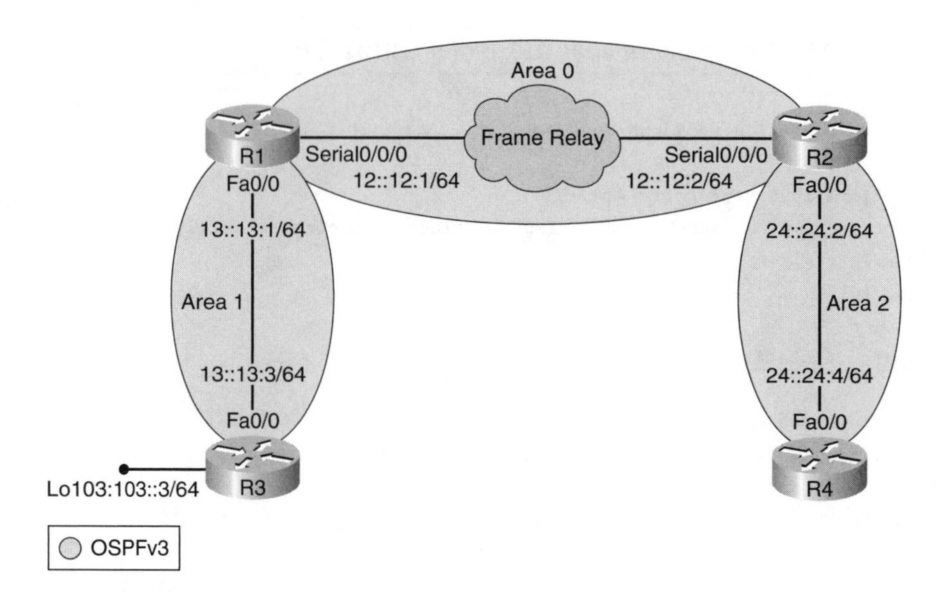

Figure 6-12 *The Network Diagram for the Third IPv6 Troubleshooting Example*

Example 6-42 *Initial Ping Tests from R4 and R2 to R3's Loopback Interface Fail*

```
R4# ping 103::3

Type escape sequence to abort.
Sending 5, 100-byte ICMP Echos to 103::3, timeout is 2 seconds:
..
R2# ping 103::3

Type escape sequence to abort.
Sending 5, 100-byte ICMP Echos to 103::3, timeout is 2 seconds:
..
R1# ping 103::3

Type escape sequence to abort.
Sending 5, 100-byte ICMP Echos to 103::3, timeout is 2 seconds:
.....
Success rate is 0 percent (0/5)
R1# ping 13::13:3

Type escape sequence to abort.
Sending 5, 100-byte ICMP Echos to 13::13:3, timeout is 2 seconds:
!!!!!
Success rate is 100 percent (5/5), round-trip min/avg/max = 0/0/0 ms
R1#
```

```
R2# ping 103::3

Type escape sequence to abort.
Sending 5, 100-byte ICMP Echos to 103::3, timeout is 2 seconds:
.....
Success rate is 0 percent (0/5)
R2# ping 13::13:3

Type escape sequence to abort.
Sending 5, 100-byte ICMP Echos to 13::13:3, timeout is 2 seconds:
.....
Success rate is 0 percent (0/5)
R2#
```

You can fix the problems by starting on R1 and moving your way to the right. This is sometimes a good approach because it helps to isolate problems in specific sections of the network and helps to incrementally build connectivity. As you move to the right fixing problems, devices on those sections of the network can function normally and users can do their work. Starting at R1, you can actually use a bottom-up approach in that specific router. It is helpful to use a command that shows us multiple layers, so that you can see the status of physical, data link, and network layers. The **show ipv6 ospf interface** command shows the status of Layers 1 and 2, and also OSPF information, as demonstrated in Example 6-43. Notice how in R1 you can see that the Frame Relay interface (serial 0/0/0) is a nonbroadcast interface. You can also verify the proper area configuration on each interface, backbone for the Frame Relay interface, and area 1 for the LAN interface. On both interfaces of R1, the OSPF neighbor count is 0. This is also verified using the **show ipv6 ospf neighbor** command (see the bottom of Example 6-43).

Example 6-43 **show ipv6 ospf interface** *Is a Valuable Information-Gathering Command*

```
R1# show ipv6 ospf interface
Serial0/0/0 is up, line protocol is up
  Link Local Address FE80::219:56FF:FE2C:9856, Interface ID 5
  Area 0, Process ID 1, Instance ID 0, Router ID 172.16.101.1
  Network Type POINT_TO_POINT, Cost: 64
  Transmit Delay is 1 sec, State POINT_TO_POINT
  Timer intervals configured, Hello 10, Dead 40, Wait 40, Retransmit 5
    Hello due in 00:00:01
  Index 1/1/2, flood queue length 0
  Next 0x0(0)/0x0(0)/0x0(0)
  Last flood scan length is 1, maximum is 2
  Last flood scan time is 0 msec, maximum is 0 msec
```

```
  Neighbor Count is 0, Adjacent neighbor count is 0
  Suppress hello for 0 neighbor(s)
FastEthernet0/0 is up, line protocol is up
  Link Local Address FE80::219:56FF:FE2C:9856, Interface ID 3
  Area 1, Process ID 1, Instance ID 0, Router ID 172.16.101.1
  Network Type BROADCAST, Cost: 1
  Transmit Delay is 1 sec, State DR, Priority 1
  Designated Router (ID) 172.16.101.1, local address FE80::219:56FF:FE2C:9856
  No backup designated router on this network
  Timer intervals configured, Hello 10, Dead 40, Wait 40, Retransmit 5
    Hello due in 00:00:01
  Index 1/1/1, flood queue length 0
  Next 0x0(0)/0x0(0)/0x0(0)
  Last flood scan length is 0, maximum is 0
  Last flood scan time is 0 msec, maximum is 0 msec
  Neighbor Count is 0, Adjacent neighbor count is 0
  Suppress hello for 0 neighbor(s)
R1#
R1# show ipv6 ospf neighbor

R1#
```

Now you would use the **debug ipv6 ospf hello** command to see any potential mismatches, as demonstrated in Example 6-44. On LAN interfaces, Hello messages occur every 10 seconds.

Example 6-44 debug ipv6 ospf hello *Shows Mismatched Stub/Transit Area*

```
R1# debug ipv6 ospf hello
  OSPFv3 hello events debugging is on
R1#
R1#
*Aug 24 13:19:49.751: OSPFv3: Rcv hello from 103.103.103.103 area 1 from
FastEthernet0/0 FE80::219:55FF:FEF0:B7D0 interface ID 3
*Aug 24 13:19:49.751: OSPFv3: Hello from FE80::219:55FF:FEF0:B7D0 with mismatched
Stub/Transit area option bit
*Aug 24 13:19:56.087: OSPFv3: Send hello to FF02::5 area 1 on FastEthernet0/0 from
FE80::219:56FF:FE2C:9856 interface ID 3
*Aug 24 13:19:59.751: OSPFv3: Rcv hello from 103.103.103.103 area 1 from
FastEthernet0/0 FE80::219:55FF:FEF0:B7D0 interface ID 3
*Aug 24 13:19:59.751: OSPFv3: Hello from FE80::219:55FF:FEF0:B7D0 with mismatched
Stub/Transit area option bit
```

The **mismatched Stub/Transit area option bit** that the **debug** output shows indicates that either R1 is calling the area a stub and R3 does not, or R3 is calling the area a stub and R1 does not. The best way to see the area configuration is to use the **show ipv6 ospf** command. The result, shown in Example 6-45, indicates that on R1 area 1 is configured as a totally stubby area (it is a stub area, no summary LSA in this area); however, the same command on R3 shows area 1 as a normal area. That needs to be fixed. Note that no Hellos to/from the serial 0/0/0 interface can be seen in the output shown in Example 6-44. This is addressed later.

Example 6-45 **show ipv6 ospf** *Command Output on R1 Indicates Area 1 Is Totally Stubby*

```
R1# show ipv6 ospf
 Routing Process "ospfv3 1" with ID 172.16.101.1
 It is an area border router
 SPF schedule delay 5 secs, Hold time between two SPFs 10 secs
 Minimum LSA interval 5 secs. Minimum LSA arrival 1 secs
 LSA group pacing timer 240 secs
 Interface flood pacing timer 33 msecs
 Retransmission pacing timer 66 msecs
 Number of external LSA 0. Checksum Sum 0x000000
 Number of areas in this router is 2. 1 normal 1 stub 0 nssa
 Reference bandwidth unit is 100 mbps
    Area BACKBONE(0) (Inactive)
       Number of interfaces in this area is 1
       SPF algorithm executed 3 times
       Number of LSA 4. Checksum Sum 0x01F36B
       Number of DCbitless LSA 0
       Number of indication LSA 0
       Number of DoNotAge LSA 0
       Flood list length 0
    Area 1
       Number of interfaces in this area is 1
       It is a stub area, no summary LSA in this area
         Generates stub default route with cost 1
       SPF algorithm executed 5 times
       Number of LSA 4. Checksum Sum 0x016293
       Number of DCbitless LSA 0
       Number of indication LSA 0
       Number of DoNotAge LSA 0
       Flood list length 0
R3# show ipv6 ospf
 Routing Process "ospfv3 1" with ID 103.103.103.103
SPF schedule delay 5 secs, Hold time between two SPFs 10 secs
```

```
 Minimum LSA interval 5 secs. Minimum LSA arrival 1 secs
 LSA group pacing timer 240 secs
 Interface flood pacing timer 33 msecs
 Retransmission pacing timer 66 msecs
 Number of external LSA 0. Checksum Sum 0x000000
 Number of areas in this router is 1. 1 normal 0 stub 0 nssa
 Reference bandwidth unit is 100 mbps
    Area 1
        Number of interfaces in this area is 1
        SPF algorithm executed 1 times
        Number of LSA 3. Checksum Sum 0x02286D
        Number of DCbitless LSA 0
        Number of indication LSA 0
        Number of DoNotAge LSA 0
        Flood list length 0
R3#
```

You go into the OSPF routing process with the **ipv6 router ospf 1** command and enter the **area 1 stub** command on router R3. Shown in Example 6-46, the adjacency forms almost immediately when the parameter mismatch is gone. Next, you ping R3's loopback address from R1, and it is successful.

Example 6-46 *Once Area 1 Is Configured as Stub on R3, the Adjacency with R1 Forms*

```
R3#
R3# conf t
Enter configuration commands, one per line. End with CNTL/Z.
R3(config)#
R3(config)#
R3(config)# ipv6 router ospf 1
R3(config-rtr)#
R3(config-rtr)# area 1 stub
R3(config-rtr)# end
R3#
R3#
R3#
Sep 27 20:17:38.367:  %SYS-5-CONFIG_I: Configured from console by console
Sep 27 20:17:38.747:  %OSPFv3-5-ADJCHG: Process 1, Nbr 172.16.101.1 on
FastEthernet0/0 from LOADING to FULL. Loading Done

R1# ping 103::3

Type escape sequence to abort.
```

```
Sending 5, 100-byte ICMP Echos to 103::3, timeout is 2 seconds:
!!!!!
Success rate is 100 percent (5/5), round-trip min/avg/max = 0/0/0 ms
R1#
```

Now focus on the area 0 backbone over the Frame Relay network, because you are still not seeing Hello messages received on that link. Starting with R1, you check to see the mapping between IPv6 addresses and data-link connection identifiers (DLCIs) using the **show frame-relay map** command (see Example 6-47). The global unicast addresses are there, mapped to a DLCI. But that is not what OSPFv3 uses to send Hello messages. Routing protocols use the link-local address to send routing information to neighbors. The link-local addresses do not have a mapping to DLCIs, so the Hellos are not going across the nonbroadcast multiaccess (NBMA) network. On R2, you would use the **show ipv6 interface brief** command to obtain its link-local address. It starts with FE80, as usual. Copy this address to the Clipboard, go to the serial interface of R1, and use the **frame-relay map ipv6** command, followed by the link-local address, followed by the DLCI number. You must use the **broadcast** keyword if you want routing protocols to operate by exchanging multicast packets. You need to do the same on R2; first, copy the link-local address of R1, and on R2 issue the **frame-relay map ipv6** command with that address. You can see the OSPF adjacencies starting to pop up into full state. This work is shown on Example 6-47. Now ping R3 from R2, and as you can see, the ping is successful.

Example 6-47 *Adding the Frame Relay Maps on R2 and R1 for Link-Local Addresses*

```
R1# show frame-relay map
Serial0/0/0 (up): ipv6 12::12:2 dlci 122(0x7A, 0x1CA0), static
              broadcast
              CISCO, status defined, active
R1#
-------------------------------------------------------
R2# show ipv6 interface brief
FastEthernet0/0              [up/up]
    FE80::219:55FF:FE92:A442
    24::24:2
Serial0/0/0                  [up/up]
    FE80::219:55FF:FE92:A442
    11::1:2
    12::12:2
Loopback101                  [up/up]
    FE80::219:55FF:FE92:A442
R2#
-------------------------------------------------------
```

```
R1# conf t
Enter configuration commands, one per line. End with CNTL/Z
R1(config)# int s0/0/0
R1(config-if)# fram map ipv6 FE80::219:55FF:FE92:A442 122 broadcast
R1(config-if)# end
R1# show ipv6 interface brief
FastEthernet0/0                [up/up]
    FE80::219:56FF:FE2C:9856
    13::13:1
Serial0/0/0                    [up/up]
    FE80::219:56FF:FE2C:9856
    11::1:1
    12::12:1
Loopback101                    [up/up]
    FE80::219:56FF:FE2C:9856
R1#
- - - - - - - - - - - - - - - - - - - - - - - - - - - - - - - - - - - - - - - -
R2#
R2# conf t
Enter configuration commands, one per line. End with CNTL/A.
R2(config)# int s0/0/0
R2(config-if)# fram map ipv6 FE80::219:56FF:Fe2C:9856 221 br
R2(config-if)# end
R2#
*Aug 24 13:55:00.459: %SYS-5-CONFIG_I: Configured from console by console
*Aug 24 13:56:59.175: %OSPFv3-5-ADJCHG: Process 1, Nbr 172.16.101.1 on Serial0/0/0
from LOADING to FULL, Loading Done
R2#
R2# ping13::13:3
Type escape sequence to abort.
Sending 5, 100-byte ICMP Echos to 13::13:3, timeout is 2 seconds:
!!!!!
```

Now you need to fix the problem at the R2-to-R4 segment. You must first determine whether OSPF is configured on the interfaces with the **show ipv6 ospf interface** command. The results for both R2 and R4 are shown in Example 6-48. On R2, OSPFv3 is enabled on the fa0/0 interface in area 2, but R4, which also has OSPFv3 enabled on its fa0/0 interface, has it in area 0. This is an error. In OSPF, interfaces drop all OSPFv3 packets that do not have a matching OSPFv3 area ID in the packet header.

Example 6-48 *Checking OSPFv3 Interfaces on R2 and R4*

```
R2# show ipv6 ospf interface
FastEthernet0/0 is up, line protocol is up
  Link Local Address FE80::219:55FF:FE92:A442, Interface ID 3
  Area 2, Process ID 1, Instance ID 0, Router ID 172.16.102.1
  Network Type BROADCAST, Cost: 1
  Transmit Delay is 1 sec, State DR, Priority 1
  Designated Router (ID) 172.16.102.1, local address FE80::219:55FF:FE92:A442
  No backup designated router on this network
  Timer intervals configured, Hello 10, Dead 40, Wait 40, Retransmit 5
    Hello due in 00:00:04
  Index 1/1/2, flood queue length 0
  Next 0x0(0)/0x0(0)/0x0(0)
  Last flood scan length is 0, maximum is 0
  Last flood scan time is 0 msec, maximum is 0 msec
  Neighbor Count is 0, Adjacent neighbor count is 0
  Suppress hello for 0 neighbor(s)
Serial0/0/0 is up, line protocol is up
  Link Local Address FE80::219:55FF:FE92:A442, Interface ID 6
  Area 0, Process ID 1, Instance ID 0, Router ID 172.16.102.1
  Network Type POINT_TO_POINT, Cost: 64
  Transmit Delay is 1 sec, State POINT_TO_POINT
  Timer intervals configured, Hello 10, Dead 40, Wait 40, Retransmit 5
    Hello due in 00:00:01
  Index 1/1/1, flood queue length 0
  Next 0x0(0)/0x0(0)/0x0(0)
  Last flood scan length is 1, maximum is 2
  Last flood scan time is 0 msec, maximum is 0 msec
  Neighbor Count is 1, Adjacent neighbor count is 1
    Adjacent with neighbor 172.16.101.1
  Suppress hello for 0 neighbor(s)
- - - - - - - - - - - - - - - - - - - - - - - - - - - - - - - - - - - - - - -
R4# show ipv6 ospf interface
FastEthernet0/0 is up, line protocol is up
  Link Local Address FE80::219:55FF:FEE0:F04, Interface ID 3
  Area 0, Process ID 1, Instance ID 0, Router ID 104.104.104.104
  Network Type BROADCAST, Cost: 1
  Transmit Delay is 1 sec, State WAITING, Priority 1
  No designated router on this network
  No backup designated router on this network
  Timer intervals configured, Hello 10, Dead 40, Wait 40, Retransmit 5
    Hello due in 00:00:03
    Wait time before Designated router selection 00:00:13
  Index 1/1/1, flood queue length 0
  Next 0x0(0)/0x0(0)/0x0(0)
```

```
  Last flood scan length is 0, maximum is 0
  Last flood scan time is 0 msec, maximum is 0 msec
  Neighbor Count is 0, Adjacent neighbor count is 0
  Suppress hello for 0 neighbor(s)
R4#
```

The next step is to fix the area number on R4 and test end-to-end connectivity by pinging R3's looback interface from R4 once again. As seen in Example 6-49, after the correction was made, the ping is successful. This example demonstrates how a divide-and-conquer approach can prove helpful: Isolate problems in sections of the network along the troubleshooting path, starting at a point that is close to your estimated point of failure. Then, work your way backward, trying to fix the specific issues in each section. This will help you not only to focus on isolated problems, but also to make the network operational section by section, incrementally.

Example 6-49 *Incorrect Area Number on R4 Is Fixed, and Connectivity Is Restored*

```
R4# conf t
Enter configuration commands, one per line. End with CNTRL/Z.
R4(config)# int f0/0
R4(config-if)# ipv6 ospf 1 area 2
R4(config-if)# end
R4#

R4# ping 13::13:3

Type escape sequence to abort.
Sending 5, 100-byte ICMP Echos to 13::13:3, timeout is 2 seconds:
!!!!!
Success rate is 100 percent (5/5), round-trip min/avg/max = 56/58/60 ms
R4#
```

IPv6 Troubleshooting Example: OSPFv3 over 6to4 Tunnel

The fourth and final IPv6 troubleshooting example is based on the diagram shown in Figure 6-13. Two islands of RIPng are connected through an OSPFv3 domain across the 6to4 tunnel. After a readdressing exercise, some traffic cannot traverse the tunnel.

In the topology diagram you can see that routers R1 and R2 are edge/border routers and they are also the tunnel endpoints; you start troubleshooting on these routers. A useful command for this scenario is **debug tunnel**. Example 6-50 shows the **debug** output on R1 as you ping R2 (2002:AC10:6601::2), the other side of the tunnel. You can see the **ping** command succeeds, and the **debug** output shows the encapsulation and decapsulation messages.

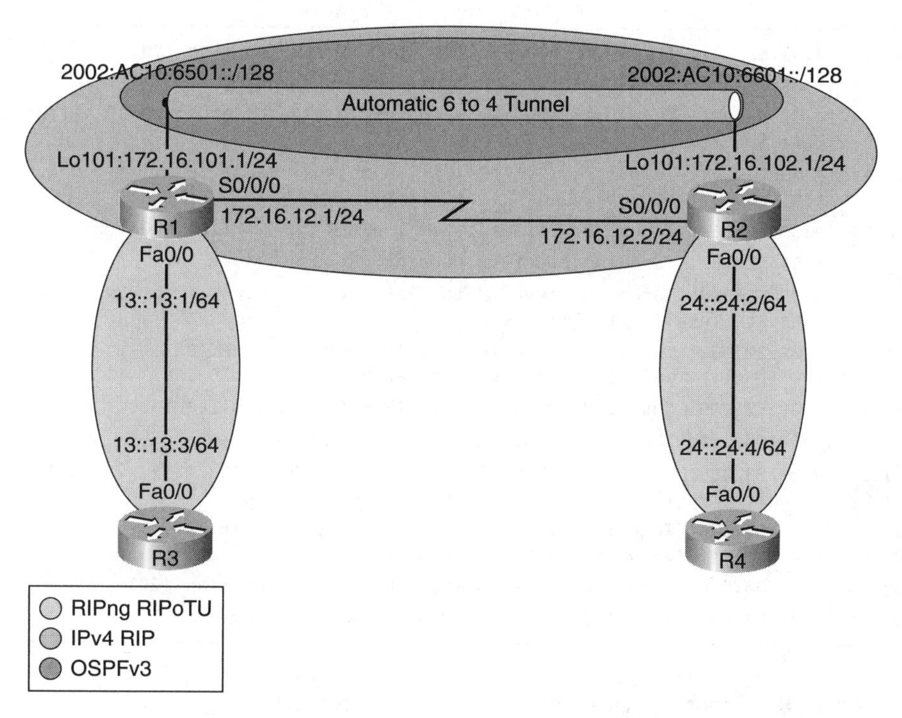

Figure 6-13 *Network Diagram for the Fourth IPv6 Troubleshooting Example*

Example 6-50 *Ping R2 from R1 Is Successful and the Results from the* **debug tunnel** *Command*

```
R1#
R1# ping 2002:AC10:6601::2

Type escape sequence to abort.
Sending 5, 100-byte ICMP Echos to 2002:AC10:6601::2, timeout is 2 seconds:
!!!!!
Success rate is 100 percent (5/5), round-trip min/avg/max = 32/33/36 ms
R1#
*Aug 24 14:39:52.863: Tunnel 0: count tx, adding 20 encap bytes
*Aug 24 14:39:52.895: Tunnel 0: IPv6/IP to classify 172.16.102.1 -> 172.16.101.1
(tbl=0, "default" len=120 ttl=254 tos=0x0)
*Aug 24 14:39:52.895: Tunnel 0: IPv6/IP (PS) to decaps 172.16.102.1 ->
172.16.101.1 (tbl=0, "default" len=120 ttl=254)
*Aug 24 14:39:52.895: Tunnel 0: decapsulated IPv6/IP packet (len 120)
*Aug 24 14:39:52.895: Tunnel 0 count tx, adding 20 encap bytes
*Aug 24 14:39:52.931: Tunnel 0: IPv6/IP to classify 172.16.102.1 -> 172.16.101.1
(tbl=0, "default" len=120 ttl=254 tos=0x0)
*Aug 24 14:39:52.931: Tunnel 0: IPv6/IP (PS) to decaps 172.16.102.1 ->
172.16.101.1 (tbl=0, "default" len=120 ttl=254)
```

```
*Aug 24 14:39:52.931: Tunnel 0: decapsulated IPv6/IP packet (len 120)
*Aug 24 14:39:52.931: Tunnel 0 count tx, adding 20 encap bytes
*Aug 24 14:39:52.963: Tunnel 0: IPv6/IP to classify 172.16.102.1 -> 172.16.101.1
(tbl=0, "default" len=120 ttl=254 tos=0x0)
*Aug 24 14:39:52.967: Tunnel 0: IPv6/IP (PS) to decaps 172.16.102.1 ->
172.16.101.1 (tbl=0, "default" len=120 ttl=254)
*Aug 24 14:39:52.967: Tunnel 0: decapsulated IPv6/IP packet (len 120)
*Aug 24 14:39:52.967: Tunnel 0 count tx, adding 20 encap bytes
*Aug 24 14:39:52.999: Tunnel 0: IPv6/IP to classify 172.16.102.1 -> 172.16.101.1
(tbl=0, "default" len=120 ttl=254 tos=0x0)
*Aug 24 14:39:52.999: Tunnel 0: IPv6/IP (PS) to decaps 172.16.102.1 ->
172.16.101.1 (tbl=0, "default" len=120 ttl=254)
*Aug 24 14:39:52.999: Tunnel 0: decapsulated IPv6/IP packet (len 120)
*Aug 24 14:39:52.003: Tunnel 0 count tx, adding 20 encap bytes
*Aug 24 14:39:53.035: Tunnel 0: IPv6/IP to classify 172.16.102.1 -> 172.16.101.1
(tbl=0, "default" len=120 ttl=254 tos=0x0)
*Aug 24 14:39:53.035: Tunnel 0: IPv6/IP (PS) to decaps 172.16.102.1 ->
172.16.101.1 (tbl=0, "default" len=120 ttl=254)
*Aug 24 14:39:53.035: Tunnel 0: decapsulated IPv6/IP packet (len 120)
*Aug 24 14:39:54.899: Tunnel 0 count tx, adding 20 encap bytes
```

However, R1 cannot ping beyond R2. For example, from R1 a ping to 24::24:4, which is R4's fa0/0 IPv6 address, fails, as shown in Example 6-51.

Example 6-51 *R1 Cannot Ping R4's fa0/0 IPv6 Address 24::24:2*

```
R1# ping 24::24:4

Type escape sequence to abort.
Sending 5, 100-byte ICMP Echos to 24::24:4, timeout is 2 seconds:

*Aug 24 14:41:12.927: Tunnel0 count tx, adding 20 encap bytes.
*Aug 24 14:41:14.899: Tunnel0 count tx, adding 20 encap bytes.
*Aug 24 14:41:14.927: Tunnel0 count tx, adding 20 encap bytes.
*Aug 24 14:41:16.927: Tunnel0 count tx, adding 20 encap bytes.
*Aug 24 14:41:18.927: Tunnel0 count tx, adding 20 encap bytes.
*Aug 24 14:41:20.927: Tunnel0 count tx, adding 20 encap bytes.
Success rate is 0 percent
```

Using the **show ipv6 route** command, you display R1's IPv6 routing table, as shown in Example 6-52. Network 24::/64 is not present in R1's IPv6 routing table, but there is a static route for 2002:AC10:6610::1 pointing to tunnel0 interface and a default route (gateway of last resort) also pointing to the tunnel0 interface. You have to examine validity of the static route for the 6to4 tunnel. You also have to find out why a static default was configured on R1, rather than just using OSPF.

Example 6-52 *R1's IPv6 Routing Table Shows Only Connected and Static Routes*

```
R1# show ipv6 route
IPv6 Routing Table - 17 entries
Codes: C - Connected, L - Local, S - Static, R - RIP, B - BGP
       U - Per-user Static Route
       I1 - ISIS L1, I2 - ISIS L2, IA - ISIS interarea, IS - ISIS summary
       O - OSPF intra, OI - OSPF inter, OE1 - OSPF ext 1, OE2 - OSPF ext 2
       ON1 - OSPF NSSA ext 1, ON2 - OSPF NSSA ext 2
S   ::/0 [1/0]
     via ::, Tunnel0
C   11::/64 [0/0]
     via ::, Serial0/0/0
L   11::11:1/128 [0/0]
     via ::, Serial0/0/0
C   12::/64 [0/0]
     via ::, Serial0/0/0
L   12::12:1/128 [0/0]
     via ::, Serial0/0/0
C   13::/64 [0/0]
     via ::, FastEthernet0/0
L   13::13:1/128 [0/0]
     via ::, FastEthernet0/0
LC  2002:AC10:6501::1/128 [1/0]
     via ::, Tunnel0
S   2002:AC10:6610::1/128 [1/0]
     via Tunnel0
L   FE80::/10 [0/0]
     via ::, Null0
L   FF00::/8 [0/0]
     via ::, Null0
R1#
```

You need to refresh your understanding of 6to4 tunnels. For traffic to go through the tunnel, there must be a valid mapping between the IPv6 destination and the IPv4 next-hop address. In fact, that IPv4 next hop must be embedded in the IPv6 address. You know that someone has changed the addressing scheme recently. It seems that some changes were not made or mistakes have happened. Looking at that static entry a bit more closely, you know that it must point to the IPv6 address of the tunnel endpoint as the next hop, but it does not. The mapping is incorrect, and the packets are not forwarded through the tunnel. You need to change the static entry. On R1, you remove the static entry with the **no ipv6 route** command, and insert a new entry pointing to the correct IPv6 address, the address of the other side of the tunnel. But the ping to R2's fa0/0 IPv6 address fails again. This work is shown in Example 6-53.

Example 6-53 *The Invalid IPv6 Static Route for the 6to4 Tunnel Is Corrected*

```
R1# conf 6
Enter configuration commands, one per line. End with CNTL/Z.
R1(config)#
R1(config)# no ipv6 route 2002:AC10:6610::1/128 tun0
R1(config)#
R1(config)#
R1(config)# ipv6 route 2002:AC10:6601::2/128 tun0
R1(config)#
R1(config)# end
R1#
R1# ping 24::24:4

Type escape sequence to abort.
Sending 5, 100-byte ICMP Echos to 24::24:24, timeout is 2 seconds:
.....
Success rate is 0 percent (0/5)
R1#
```

You must check whether OSPF is working properly on R1. The **show ipv6 protocols** command shows OSPFv3 is active on the tunnel interface (see Example 6-54), but the **show ipv6 neighbor** command shows no neighbors. Using the **debug ipv6 ospf hello** shows that R1 is sending Hellos on the tunnel interface (also shown in Example 6-54), but it is not receiving Hello messages. Using **debug ipv6 ospf hello** on R2 shows that it is sending Hello messages. However, R2 is using its link-local address as the source. Two things are significant here: First, remember that OSPF uses the link-local addresses to exchange Hello packets and establish adjacencies; and furthermore, Hello messages are sent to multicast addresses. Second, those link-local addresses and multicasts do not comply with the rules of a 6to4 tunnel. 6to4 tunnels do not forward multicast messages that OSPF uses to establish adjacencies: There is no IPv4 address embedded in them to serve as a tunnel destination for automatic tunnel establishment.

Example 6-54 *Checking OSPFv3 Configuration on R1*

```
R1# show ipv6 prot
IPv6 Routing Protocol is "connected"
IPv6 Routing Protocol is "static"
IPv6 Routing Protocol is "rip RIPoTU"
  Interfaces:
    FastEthernet0/0
  Redistribution:
    None
IPv6 Routing Protocol is "ospf 1"
```

```
  Interfaces (Area 0):
    Tunnel0
  Redistribution:
    None
R1#
R1#show ipv6 os nei

R1#
R1# debug ipv6 os hello
OSPFv3 hello events debugging is on
R1#
R1#
R1#
*Aug 24 14:59:53.247: OSPFv3: Send hello to FF02::5 area 0 on Tunnel0 from
FE80::AC10:6501 interface ID 13
-------------------------------------------------------------------------
R2# debug ipv6 os hello
OSPFv3 hello events debugging is on
R2#
*Aug 24 15:07:04.635: OSPFv3: Send hello to FE80::219:56FF:FE2C:9856 area 0 on
Serial0/0/0 from FE80::219:55FF:FE92:A442 interface ID 5
*Aug 24 15:07:04.755: OSPFv3: Send hello to FE80::219:56FF:FE2C:9856 area 0 on
Serial0/0/0 from FE80::219:55FF:FE92:A442 interface ID 5
*Aug 24 15:07:04.875: OSPFv3: Send hello to FE80::219:56FF:FE2C:9856 area 0 on
Serial0/0/0 from FE80::219:55FF:FE92:A442 interface ID 5
*Aug 24 15:07:04.995: OSPFv3: send hello to FF02::5 area 0 on Tunnel0 from
FE80::AC10:6601 interface ID 13
*Aug 24 15:07:04.995: OSPFv3: Send hello to FE80::219:56FF:FE2C:9856 area 0 on
Serial0/0/0 from FE80::219:55FF:FE92:A442 interface ID 5
*Aug 24 15:07:05.115: OSPFv3: Send hello to FE80::219:56FF:FE2C:9856 area 0 on
Serial0/0/0 from FE80::219:55FF:FE92:A442 interface ID 5
```

This means that perhaps this network is poorly designed because OSPF (or other traditional IGPs, for that matter) cannot exchange routes across the 6to4 tunnel; however, OSPF allows explicit neighbor configuration using the **neighbor** command, which causes communication between neighbors to become unicast based. The unicast address could be the IPv6 address at the other end of the tunnel. This address complies with 6to4 tunnels, and therefore the Hello messages should flow through. Unfortunately, when you go into interface configuration mode for the tunnel interface, and try to specify the other end of the tunnel as a neighbor, you receive an error message (see Example 6-55). The **neighbor** command is allowed only on NMBA and point-to-multipoint networks.

Example 6-55 *The OSPF* **neighbor** *Command Is Not Allowed on the Tunnel Interface*

```
R1# conf t
Enter configuration commands, one per line. End with CNTL/Z.
R1(config)# int tun 0
R1(config-if)# ipv6 os neigh FE80::AC10:6601
R1(config-if)# end
R1#
R1#
*Aug 24 15:19:16.219: %OSPFv3-4-CFG_NBR_INVAL_NET_TYPE: Can not use configured
neighbor: neighbor command is allowed only on NBMA and point-to-multipoint networks
*Aug 24 15:19:16.343: %SYS-5-CONFIG_I: Configured from console by console
```

If using a dynamic routing protocol between routers R1 and R2 is mandatory, the only option is BGP. BGP establishes peering based on TCP sessions that use unicasts. Those unicasts can be the 6to4 IPv6 address of the other side of the tunnel. If you choose *not* to use BGP, the only way to make this work is with static routes. You saw earlier that R1 had a faulty static route, which you fixed, and a static default. If you also add a proper static route on R2, you'll restore connectivity across the network. In this example, the tunnel was configured correctly, and it was operational; however, it was routing through the tunnel that was failing. When troubleshooting, you should always think of temporary solutions that other troubleshooters left behind. In this example, OSPF was supposed to be running across the tunnel; however, it was not, and it seems that other troubleshooters tried static default routes to make it work. Static routes were indeed the correct option, and only BGP would have worked in this scenario for dynamic routing across the 6to4 tunnel.

Summary

The three main NAT categories are as follows:

- Static NAT
- Dynamic NAT
- NAT with overloading (or PAT)

The advantages of NAT include the following:

- Conserves registered addresses
- Hides the actual address of internal hosts and services
- Increases flexibility when connecting to Internet
- Eliminates address renumbering as the network changes from one ISP to another

The disadvantages of NAT are these:

- Translation introduces processing delays.

- Loss of end-to-end IP reachability.
- Certain applications will not function with NAT enabled.
- Considerations are needed when working with VPNs.

Examples of NAT sensitive protocols include the following:

- IPsec
- ICMP
- SIP

Some of the useful NAT troubleshooting commands are as follows:

- **clear ip nat translation**
- **show ip nat translations**
- **show ip nat statistics**
- **debug ip nat**
- **debug ip packet** [*access-list*]
- **debug condition interface** *interface*
- **show debug condition**

The main DHCP packets used during the address acquisition process are as follows:

- DHCP discover
- DHCP offer
- DHCP request
- DHCP ack

Other packet types involved in DHCP transactions include the following:

- DHCP decline
- DHCP nack
- DHCP release
- DHCP inform

With respect to DHCP, a router may play one of these roles:

- DHCP server
- DHCP client
- DHCP relay agent

Enabling a router interface with the **ip helper-address** command makes the interface forward UDP broadcasts for six protocols (not just DHCP) to the IP address configured using the **ip helper-address** command. Those protocols are as follows:

- TFTP (port 69)
- DNS (port 53)
- Time Service (port 37)
- NetBIOS Name Service and Datagram Service (ports 137 and 138)
- TACACS (port 49)
- DHCP/BOOTP Client and Server (ports 67 and 68)

The main DHCP options are these:

- 1: Subnet mask (Specifies the subnet mask for the client to use)
- 3: Router (The list of routers the client can use)
- 6: Domain Name Server (The list of DNS servers the client can use)
- 35: ARP cache timeout (Specifies the timeout, in seconds, for ARP cache entries)
- 51: IP address lease time (Specifies the period over which the IP address is leased for)
- 82: Relay agent information (Information about the port from which the DHCP request originates)
- 150: TFTP server IP address (Typically used by devices such as IP phones to download their configuration files)

Common troubleshooting issues related to DHCP snooping include the following:

- Improper configuration of the DHCP snooping trust boundaries
- Failure to configure DHCP snooping on certain VLANs
- Improper configuration of the DHCP snooping rate limits
- Performance degradation

The following Cisco IOS commands can prove helpful for DHCP troubleshooting:

- **show ip dhcp server**
- **show ip dhcp binding**
- **show ip dhcp conflict**
- **show ip dhcp database**
- **show ip dhcp pool**
- **show ip socket** (or **show sockets**)

- **debug ip udp**
- **debug dhcp detail**
- **debug ip dhcp server** [**packet** | **event**]
- **clear ip dhcp binding**
- **clear ip dhcp conflict**

Useful Cisco IOS IPv6 troubleshooting commands include the following:

- **debug ipv6 routing**
- **debug ipv6 nd**
- **debug tunnel**
- **debug ipv6 packet**
- **show ipv6 interface**
- **show ipv6 routers**
- **show ipv6 route**
- **show ipv6 protocols**

Review Questions

Use the questions here to review what you learned in this chapter. The correct answers are found in Appendix A, "Answers to Chapter Review Questions."

1. Which of the following is not a main NAT category?
   a. Static NAT
   b. Dynamic NAT
   c. Controlled NAT
   d. NAT overloading
2. Which of the following is not an advantage of NAT?
   a. Conserves private IP addresses
   b. Hides the actual address of internal hosts and services
   c. Increases flexibility when connecting to Internet
   d. Eliminates address renumbering as the network changes from one ISP to another

3. Which of the following are disadvantages of NAT? (Choose three.)

a. Translation introduces processing delays.

b. Loss of end-to-end IP reachability.

c. Certain applications will not function with NAT enabled.

d. Hides the address of the internal hosts.

4. Which two of the following are NAT-sensitive protocols?

a. IPsec

b. Telnet

c. SMTP

d. SIP

5. For outbound traffic, address translation occurs before output access lists are evaluated. True or False?

a. True

b. False

6. Which of the following correctly describes the effect of **debug condition interface serial 0/0**?

a. **debug** output is generated only when interface serial 0/0 goes down.

b. **debug** output is generated only when interface serial 0/0 goes up.

c. **debug** output is generated when interface serial 0/0 goes up or down.

d. **debug** output will only be limited to interface serial 0/0.

7. Which of the following commands displays the NAT table content?

a. **show ip nat translations**

b. **show ip nat statistics**

c. **show ip nat**

d. **show ip nat pool**

9. Which of the following commands configures a router interface with the relay agent functionality?

a. **ip helper-address**

b. **ip relay-agent**

c. **ip server-address**

d. **ip helper-server**

10. What is the proper order of DHCP messages going between a client and a server?

   a. DHCP offer, DHCP discover, DHCP request, DHCP ack

   b. DHCP discover, DHCP request, DHCP offer, DHCP ack

   c. DHCP discover, DHCP offer, DHCP request, DHCP ack

   d. DHCP request, DHCP discover, DHCP offer, DHCP ack

11. Which of the following is not a DHCP packet (message)?

   a. DHCP ack

   b. DHCP reject

   c. DHCP release

   d. DHCP inform

12. Which of following is *not* among the default ports (protocols) for the **ip forward-protocol udp** command?

   a. TFTP (port 69)

   b. DNS (port 53)

   c. Network Time Service (port 123)

   d. NetBIOS Name Service and Datagram Service (ports 137 and 138)

   e. TACACS (port 49)

13. Option code 82 is related to which of the following DHCP options?

   a. ARP cache timeout

   b. IP address lease time

   c. Relay agent information

   d. TFTP server IP address

14. Option code 150 is related to which of the following DHCP options?

   a. ARP cache timeout

   b. IP address lease time

   c. Relay agent information

   d. TFTP server IP address

15. Which of the following protocols has been eliminated from the IPv6 protocol suite?

a. ICMP

b. ARP

c. DHCP

d. OSPF

16. What type of communication is not supported by IPv6?

a. Unicast

b. Multicast

c. Anycast

d. Broadcast

Chapter 7

Troubleshooting Network Performance Issues

This chapter covers the following topics:

- Troubleshooting network applications services
- Troubleshooting performance issues on switches
- Troubleshooting performance issues on routers

This chapter consists of three main sections. The first section provides an overview of Cisco Network Application Services and provides troubleshooting tips and examples for NetFlow, IP service level agreement (SLA), and AutoQoS. The second and third sections discuss troubleshooting performance issues on Cisco LAN switches and routers.

Troubleshooting Network Applications Services

Cisco Application Networking Services (ANS) is a comprehensive portfolio of application networking solutions and technologies that enable successful and secure delivery of applications within data centers to local, remote, and branch-office users. Using technology to accelerate, secure, and increase availability of both application traffic and computing resources, Cisco ANS provides a comprehensive and application-adaptive set of solutions for meeting the core application challenges related to the network. Unlike application delivery point products that are focused on specific IT issues or places in the network, Cisco ANS consists of a broad portfolio of application networking platforms coupled with application fluency integrated into existing devices throughout the network, resulting in a truly end-to-end application delivery network. The topic of application-enabled networks is wide and includes everything from application acceleration services such as Wide Area Application Services (WAAS), to server load-balancing products such as Application Control Engine (ACE), and to monitoring and quality of service (QoS) mechanisms. Figure 7-1 shows the main categories of applications services.

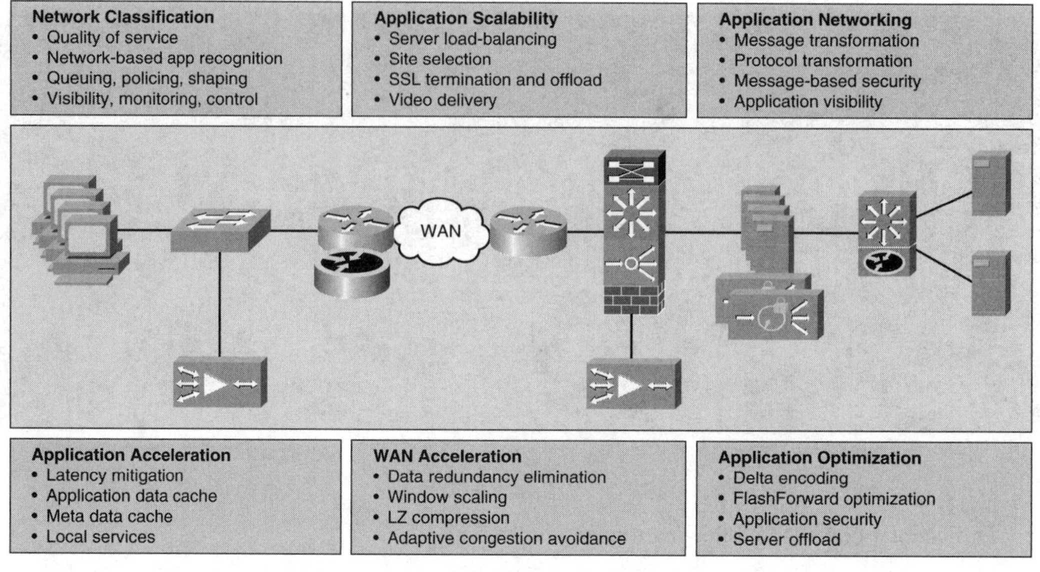

Figure 7-1 *The Main Categories of Application Services*

The focus of this section is on Cisco IOS application services, and on network infrastructure services aimed at optimizing application traffic as it uses that infrastructure. This section also discusses some of the common issues with Cisco IOS application services, and it concludes with a troubleshooting example related to this topic.

Network Application Services

The recipe to application optimization is a four-step cycle that incrementally increases your understanding of network applications and enables you to progressively deploy measurable improvements and adjustments as required; those steps are as follows:

Step 1. **Baseline application traffic:** Profile network activity by establishing a reference from which service quality and application delivery effectiveness can be measured. You must understand the basic traffic, application flows, and network performance.

Step 2. **Optimize the network:** Apply optimization or control techniques to enhance application performance. Products and technologies such as WAAS, ACE, and others, are beyond the scope for this book, but applying Cisco IOS tools such as QoS to reduce congestion and prioritize traffic is discussed.

Step 3. **Measure, adjust, and verify:** Assess the effectiveness of each successive optimization initiative such as a QoS configuration effort. This includes continuously monitoring and collecting information about the network and application behavior, and comparing the behavior before and after the optimization and QoS initiatives.

Step 4. **Deploy new applications:** Deploy new applications and updates to existing applications to meet changing business needs. As new applications are deployed or changes are made, new baselines need to be established. The application optimization cycle must start all over again.

Figure 7-2 shows the four-step application optimization cycle with the relevant Cisco IOS tools mentioned beside each step.

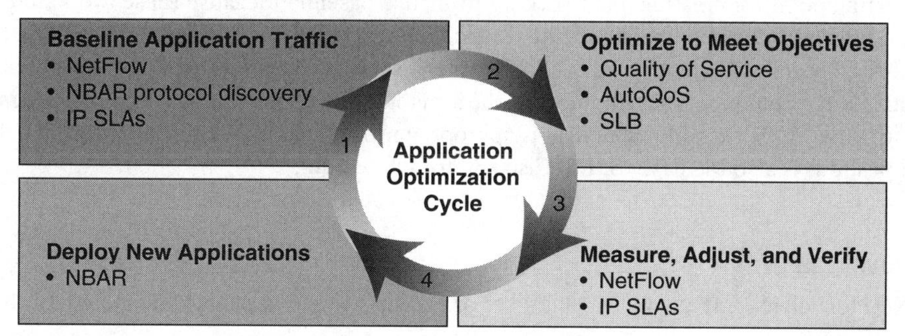

Figure 7-2 *Application Optimization and Cisco IOS Technologies*

The focus of this section is on Cisco IOS tools that mostly serve the purpose of baselining application traffic. The profile of a network describes the traffic patterns and resource bottlenecks of a network, and it identifies the links and protocols that are the best candidates for optimization. Through profiling, a network engineer can focus on only those network components whose optimization will help improve network performance. This way, baselines become performance benchmarks. Baselining is also the establishment of acceptable network behavior, which includes the following:

- Understanding available bandwidth
- Identifying a normal pattern of network behavior such as network delays and what applications are running on the network
- Understanding the behavior (and requirements) of each application on the network
- Measuring application response times

Network administrators need to know the acceptable range for network performance before they can make reliable conclusions about possible performance degradation. With proper baselining, administrators can differentiate between consistent network behavior and anomalous network behavior.

The sections that follow provide a brief discussion on the following Cisco IOS application optimization tools:

- NetFlow accounting
- IP SLAs

- Network-Based Application Recognition (NBAR) packet inspection
- Server load balancing (SLB)
- QoS and AutoQoS

Some of them, such as NetFlow, IP SLAs, and NBAR packet inspection, provide a good starting point for creating a network performance baseline. Because these tools are capable of classifying and characterizing traffic, you can use them to also measure the effect of the optimization technologies. Some others, such as Cisco IOS SLB, are actual optimization techniques that will improve the scalability of applications. Given its integration into Cisco IOS, the SLB capability is appropriate for scenarios with smaller traffic volumes; this is also the case for the Cisco AutoQoS feature.

NetFlow

NetFlow efficiently provides a vital set of services for IP applications, including the following:

- Network traffic accounting
- Usage-based network billing
- Network planning
- Security denial-of-service monitoring
- Overall network monitoring

Designed by Cisco, NetFlow is now in its ninth version, which is now on the IETF standards track to become an industrywide standard. Similar to what is shown on Figure 7-3, NetFlow works by creating a NetFlow cache that will hold information for all active flows.

A flow is a unidirectional stream of packets, between a given source and a destination, that have several components in common. The seven fields that need to match for packets to be considered part of the same flow are as follows:

- Source IP Address
- Destination IP Address
- Source Port (protocol dependent)
- Destination Port (protocol dependent)
- Protocol (Layer 3 or 4)
- Type of Service (ToS) Value (differentiated services code point [DSCP])
- Input interface

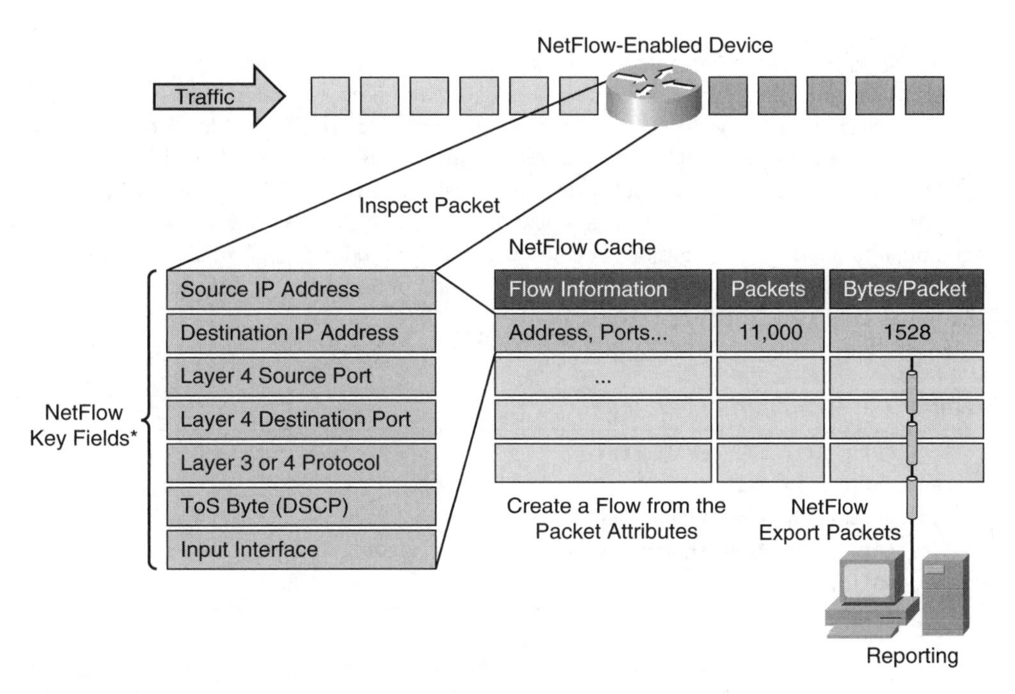

Figure 7-3 *A Router with NetFlow Enabled (Notice the NetFlow Key Fields for Each Entry)*

The NetFlow cache will eventually grow so large that it could exhaust the resources of the router; however, you can push information periodically to a NetFlow Collector, effectively exporting the information and allowing for offline analysis. Therefore, the NetFlow cache entries can simply expire and be removed from the router, which in turn can gather more flow information and fill up the table again.

Configuring NetFlow is straightforward. The first thing you need to do is enable it on a per-interface basis using the command **ip flow ingress**. This command actually enables NetFlow accounting on that interface for ingress traffic. If you want to export the NetFlow cache entries to an external collector, you must define the version and the destination IP address and the UDP port number as demonstrated in Example 7-1. Optionally, you can also configure cache timeouts and size, and how you want to aggregate the data.

Note NetFlow Version 1 format was the initially released version, and Version 5 is a later enhancement to add Border Gateway Protocol (BGP) autonomous system information and flow sequence numbers. Versions 2 through 4 were not released. The Version 6 enhancement is not used in the new IOS releases. Version 7, which is not compatible with Cisco routers, is an enhancement that exclusively supports NetFlow with Cisco Catalyst 5000 series switches equipped with a NetFlow feature card (NFFC). Version 8 is an enhancement that adds router-based aggregation schemes, and finally, Version 9 is an enhancement to support technologies such as multicast, Internet Protocol Security (IPsec), and Multiprotocol Label Switching (MPLS).

Example 7-1 *Configuring NetFlow*

```
Router(config-if)# ip flow ingress
Router(config-if)# exit
Router(config)# ip flow-export version 9
Router(config)# ip flow-export destination 1.1.1.1 9991
Router(config)# end
```

You can display the NetFlow statistics with the **show ip cache flow** command, as demonstrated in Example 7-2. You can see information on packet size distribution, which is important in baselining your network traffic, and see summary information regarding the number of flows, aging timers, and other statistics such as packet rates.

Example 7-2 *Displaying NetFlow Statistics Using the* **show ip cache flow** *Command*

```
router_A# sh ip cache flow
IP packet size distribution (85435 total packets):
! Packet Sizes
  1-32   64   96   128   160   192   224   256   288   320   352   384   416   448   480
  .000 .000 .000 .000  000 .000 .000  .000 .000 .000 .000 .000  .000 .000 .000

      512  544  576  1024  1536  2048  2560  3072  3584  4096  4608
     .000 .000 .000  .000  1.00  .000  .000  .000  .000  .000  .000

IP Flow Switching Cache, 278544 bytes
  ! Number of Active Flows
  2728 active, 1638 inactive, 85310 added
  463824 ager polls, 0 flow alloc failures
  Active flows timeout in 30 minutes
  Inactive flows timeout in 15 seconds
  last clearing of statistics never
! Rates and Duration
Protocol      Total   Flows   Packets   Bytes  Packets   Active (Sec)  Idle (Sec)
----          Flows   /Sec    /Flow     /Pkt   /Sec        /Flow          /Flow
```

```
TCP-X              2   0.0          1       1440     11.2          0.0            9.5
TCP-other      82580   11.2         1       1440     11.2          0.0           12.0
Total          82582   11.2         1       1440     11.2          0.0           12.0

! Flow Details Cache
SrcIF         SrcIPaddress     DstIf            DstIPaddress      Pr   SrcP  DstP   Pkts
Et0/0         132.122.25.60    Se0/0            192.168.1.1       06   9AEE  0007      1
Et0/0         139.57.220.28    Se0/0            192.168.1.1       06   708D  0007      1
Et0/0         165.172.153.65   Se0/0            192.168.1.1       06   CB46  0007      1
```

Arguably, the most important part of the **show ip cache flow** command output is the actual flow information. Notice that you can not only see the main flow parameters, such as source and destination IP addresses and ports, but you can also see volume and performance information such as total number of flows, flows per second, bytes and packets per second, and so on. In the flow collector, you can aggregate this data, manipulate it and graph it, and build effective baseline information for your network.

Cisco IP SLA

The IP SLA feature of Cisco IOS Software enables you to configure a router to send synthetic (generated) traffic to a host computer or router that has been configured to respond. One-way or return travel times and packet loss data are gathered and certain measurements allow jitter data to be collected, too. You can run multiple IP SLA probes at the same time, and customize the nature of the probe by selecting ports and traffic characteristics, packet sizes, frequency and timeouts for the probe, and many other parameters. Figure 7-4 shows an IOS router that has IP SLA enabled, performing hop-by-hop analysis, end-to-end measurements, and proactive notification (Simple Network Management Protocol [SNMP] traps) when rising and falling thresholds are crossed.

IP SLA is useful for performance measurement, monitoring, and network baselining. You can tie the results of the IP SLA operations to other features of your router, and trigger action based on the results of the probe. For example, you can enable a path to a specific destination to be inserted into the routing table only if the IP SLA probe succeeds in reaching a host in that destination on a specific port. You can use IP SLA operations to monitor the performance of any area in the network without deploying a physical probe. An IP SLA operation uses generated traffic to measure network performance between two networking devices.

Figure 7-4 shows that a device sends a generated packet to the destination device, which is configured as a responder. After the destination device receives the packet, depending on the type of IP SLA operation, it responds with time-stamp information for the source to make the calculation on performance metrics. An IP SLA operation performs a network measurement from the source device to a destination in the network using a specific protocol such as User Datagram Protocol (UDP). When you configure an IP SLA operation, you must schedule the operation to begin capturing statistics and collecting error

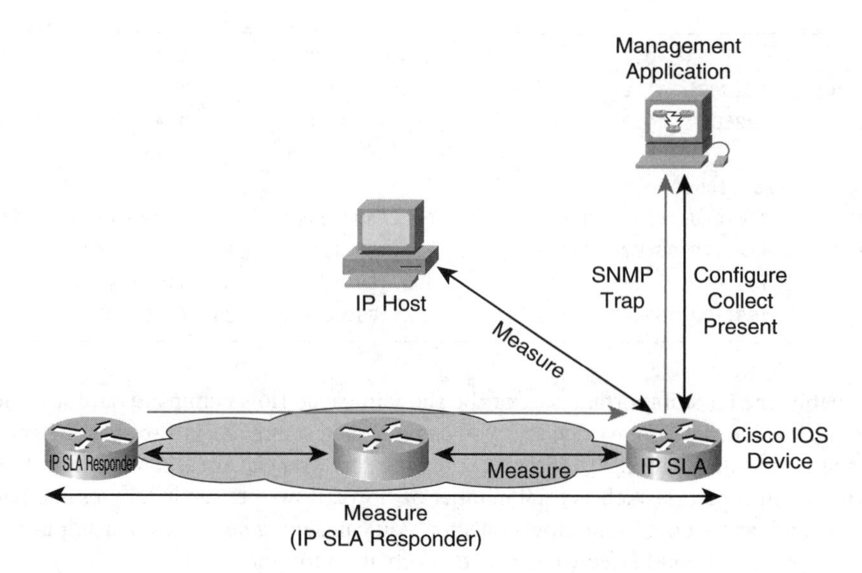

Figure 7-4 *IP SLA Enabled Cisco IOS Device Performs SLA Probes and Notifications*

information. You can schedule an operation to start immediately or to start at a certain month, day, and hour. To implement IP SLA network performance measurement, you need to perform the following tasks:

- Enable the IP SLA responder, if required.
- Configure the required IP SLA operation type.
- Configure any options available for the specified operation type.
- Configure threshold conditions, if required.
- Schedule the operation to run, and then let the operation run for a period of time to gather statistics.
- Display and interpret the results of the operation using the Cisco IOS command-line interface (CLI) or a network management system (NMS) with SNMP

Example 7-3 shows an IP SLA configuration on a router. The first thing you do is define the operation identifier; in the example, the SLA monitor operation identifier is 1. Then you enter the IP SLA configuration mode and define the type of operation. There are several operation types available, a few examples of which are **dhcp**, **dns**, **echo**, **framerelay**, **ftp**, **http**, **path-echo**, **path-jitter**, **slm**, **tcp-connect**, **udp-echo**, and **voip**. There are several rich options, from basic echo operations to more complex application layer probes that let you define the type of application layer information you want to send such as HTTP URLs, TCP and UDP ports, and others. Example 7-3 uses **echo protocol ipIcmpEcho** to address 10.32.130.2. This example also defines the frequency to be every 120 seconds and the value of ToS to be 32 (32 is 00100000 in binary and equivalent to IP precedence 1 or DSCP CS1). The configuration in Example 7-3 schedules IP SLA to run forever, starting now. You can also configure specific dates and times and a specific duration of the probe.

Example 7-3 *IP SLA Configuration Example*

```
Router> enable
Router# configure terminal
Router(config)# ip sla monitor 1
Router(config-sla-monitor)# type echo protocol ipIcmpEcho 10.32.130.2
Router(config-sla-monitor-echo)# frequency 120
Router(config-sla-monitor-echo)# tos 32
Router(config-sla-monitor-echo)# exit
Router(config)# ip sla monitor schedule 1 start-time now life forever
Router(config)# exit
```

Depending on the type of probe you set up, you might or might not need to configure an IP SLA responder. For example, if you are setting up a simple echo probe, you do not need a responder. If the echo packet comes back, it means success. The echo packet targets an IP address. Success means that the IP address is live in the network and is able to respond. It also means that there is reachability to it.

The Cisco IOS IP SLA Responder is a component embedded in the destination Cisco routing device that allows the system to anticipate and respond to Cisco IOS IP SLAs request packets. The Cisco IOS IP SLA Responder provides an enormous advantage with accurate measurements without the need for dedicated probes and additional statistics not available via standard ICMP-based measurements. The patented Cisco IOS IP SLA Control Protocol is used by the Cisco IOS IP SLA Responder, providing a mechanism through which the responder can be notified on which port it should listen and respond. Only a Cisco IOS device can be a source for a destination IP SLA Responder. The Cisco IOS IP SLA Responder listens on a specific port for control protocol messages sent by a Cisco IOS IP SLA's operation. Upon receipt of the control message, the responder will enable the specified UDP or TCP port for the specified duration. During this time, the responder accepts the requests and responds to them. The responder disables the port after it responds to the Cisco IOS IP SLA's packet, or when the specified time expires. For added security, Message Digest 5 (MD5) authentication for control messages is available.

If you need to configure IP SLA responder, you must use the **ip sla responder** command and specify the IP address and port that will be used to respond. The complete syntax of that command is as follows:

```
ip sla responder {tcp-connect | udp-echo} ipaddress ip-address port port-number
```

After an IP SLA responder is also configured, you can use the **show ip sla responder** command to display information about recent sources of IP SLA control messages, such as who has sent recent control messages and who has sent invalid control messages.

NBAR

Network-Based Application Recognition (NBAR) is another important tool for baselining and traffic-classification purposes. NBAR is a classification engine that recognizes a wide variety of applications, including web-based and other difficult-to-classify protocols that use dynamic TCP/UDP port assignments. If an application is recognized and classified by NBAR, the network can invoke services for that specific application. NBAR can be used to ensure that network bandwidth is used efficiently by classifying packets, and then applying QoS to the classified traffic. NBAR can also be used to identify malicious or unwanted traffic and block or filter it. When you use the **match protocol** command inside a route map, you are identifying the application using NBAR. If a packet matches a particular application, you can then do things like mark those packets with particular DSCP values, rate-limit those packets, or simply drop them.

There is a long list of applications identified by NBAR. At one point, the number of applications and protocols supported by NBAR exceeded 90. Those applications and protocols include those that use static ports, those that use dynamic ports, and even the non-UDP and non-TCP-based ones. Traditionally, routers have not been able to recognize many applications by just inspecting the Layer 3 and Layer 4 headers. NBAR performs deep packet inspection up to the application layer for traffic classification. When enabled, NBAR reads into the payload of the packet and can identify application layer components, such as negotiated ports.

Note For more information about the protocols/applications that NBAR supports, see the Cisco.com article "Network-Based Application Recognition," which you can find at http://tinyurl.com/yezz8pd.

The simplest use of NBAR is baselining through protocol discovery. Use the interface configuration command **ip nbar protocol-discovery** to gather information about the applications known to NBAR that are transiting an interface. NBAR can also be used to plan your QoS deployment or simply to understand the type of traffic lurking around your network. Using NBAR protocol discovery is simple: After your enable it on an interface, you can use the **show ip nbar protocol-discovery** command to look at application statistics at any point during your analysis. Example 7-4 demonstrates sample output from this command. The packet count, byte count, and bit rate statistics for both input and output traffic for each application are displayed. These are useful variables in capacity planning, security, and QoS design.

Example 7-4 *Viewing Application Statistics with the* **show ip nbar protocol-discovery** *Command*

```
Router# show ip nbar protocol-discovery interface FastEthernet 6/0

FastEthernet6/0
                  Input                            Output
```

```
  Protocol          Packet Count               Packet Count
                    Byte Count                 Byte Count
                    5 minute bit rate (bps)    5 minute bit rate (bps)
 --------           -------------              -------------
  RTP               279538                     14644
! Packet Count
                    319106191                  673624
! Byte Count
                    0                          0

...
Total               17203819                   151684936
                    19161397327                50967034611
                    4179000                    6620000
```

Because NBAR depends on Cisco Express Forwarding (CEF), it does not cause huge performance degradation on the routers; however, NBAR can only be used to classify packets of known applications. Therefore, there is a finite list of supported applications that NBAR knows and can analyze. To be able to match more protocols and applications that the base IOS NBAR feature supports, you need to upload Packet Description Language Modules (PDLMs). PDLMs allow NBAR to recognize new protocols without requiring a new Cisco IOS image or a router reload. PDLMs contain the rules that are used by NBAR to recognize an application and can be used to bring new or changed functionality to NBAR. You can load an external PDLM at runtime to extend the NBAR list of recognized protocols and enhance NBAR's existing protocol recognition capability. After you copy a PDLM from Cisco.com into your router's flash memory, you can load it using this command: **ip nbar pdlm flash://***pdlm-name*. Currently available PDLMs support Citrix ICA (Independent Computing Architecture) and peer-to-peer file-sharing applications such as KaZaa2, Gnutella, BitTorrent, eDonkey2000, and WinMX.

Note To find out more about using the Custom PDLM feature of NBAR to match on unclassified traffic or traffic that is not specifically supported as a match protocol statement, refer to Cisco.com document "Determining the Traffic Not Recognized by NBAR," available at http://tinyurl.com/rotrf.

SLB

The Cisco IOS server load balancing (SLB) feature allows you to define a virtual server that represents a cluster of real servers, known as a server farm. When a client initiates a connection to the virtual server, the Cisco IOS SLB load balances the connection to a chosen real server based on the configured load-balance algorithm or predictor. Clients initiate their connections to a virtual IP address (VIP), which is configured at the load balancer and represents the servers of the server farm (see Figure 7-5).

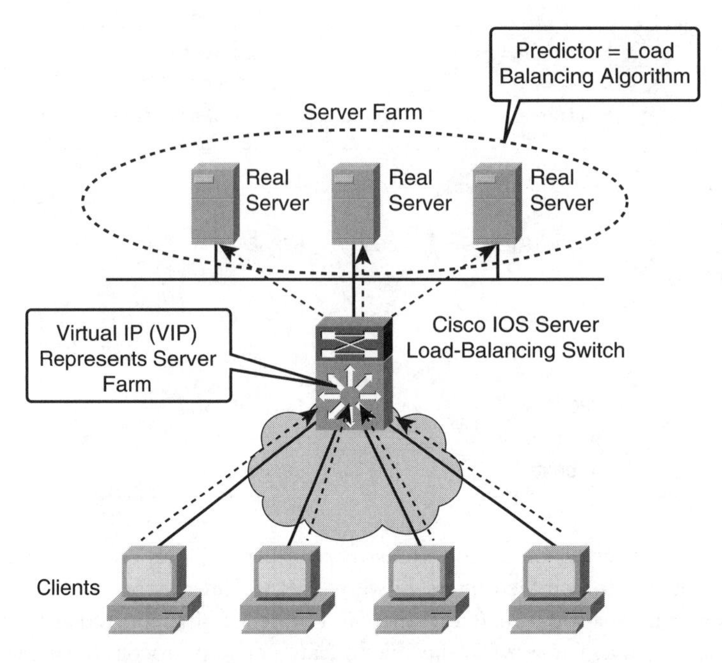

Figure 7-5 *SLB Overview*

This solution not only adds optimization by balancing the load across multiple servers, but it also provides scalability. If you need more capacity, you just add more servers, and the solution remains transparent to clients. They will still point to the VIP to reach the server farm. This results in operational efficiencies, too. If you need to remove a server or put it out of rotation for maintenance purposes, you simply remove it from the server farm, and transparency is still maintained. Clients will still point to the VIP; what happens inside the server farm is transparent to them.

QoS and AutoQoS

One of the building blocks of QoS is traffic classification and NBAR is an excellent traffic-classification tool. Within the framework of QoS, each traffic class is treated differently by the network, with different methods of congestion management, congestion avoidance, policing, and other policies. Cisco AutoQoS is an automation tool for deploying QoS policies. The newer versions of Cisco AutoQoS have two phases. In the first phase, information is gathered and traffic is baselined to define traffic classes and volumes; this is called autodiscovery. You enter the **auto discovery qos** command in the interface configuration mode. You must let discovery run for a period of time appropriate for your baselining or monitoring needs, with 3 days to 2 weeks being the usual range. The router collects information on traffic metrics, using NBAR to classify and identify the traffic at the application layer. During the process, you can view the data collection in progress using the **show auto discovery qos** command. Figure 7-6 demonstrates sample output from this command. In the second phase you enter the **auto qos** command, which is also an interface configuration mode command. This command uses the information gathered by autodiscovery in phase one to apply QoS policies accordingly. The autodiscovery phase generates templates on the basis of the data collected. These templates are then used to create QoS policies. It is in the second phase that these policies are installed by AutoQoS on the interface.

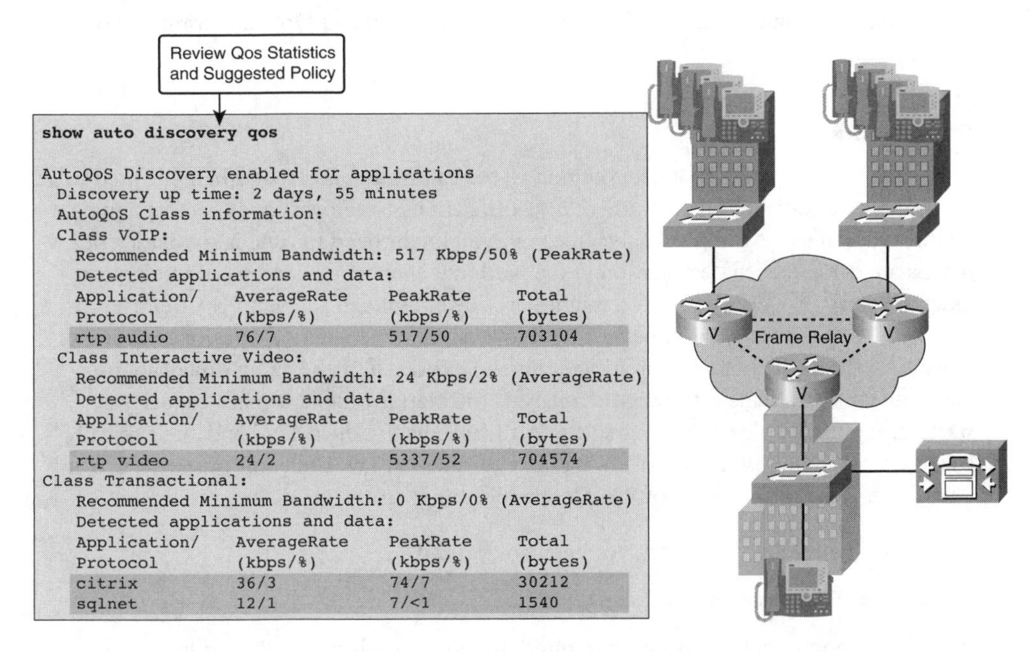

Figure 7-6 *Sample Output of the QoS Autodiscovery Tool*

In the output of the discovery phase, as you can see in Figure 7-6, traffic is defined into traffic classes. An interesting discovery is the VoIP traffic class and the Real-Time Transport Protocol (RTP). According to traffic volumes, a full definition of bandwidth reservation and queuing is also shown. Note that this definition of policy is applied only when you actually deploy Cisco AutoQoS during the second phase. You can display the AutoQoS generated commands using **show auto qos**. Be sure to back up your router configuration before you implement AutoQoS, and be ready to escalate to a QoS specialist for advanced troubleshooting. For Cisco AutoQoS to work, routers must meet the following requirements:

- CEF must be enabled on the interface.
- The interface (or subinterface) must have an IP address configured.
- For serial interfaces (or subinterfaces), the appropriate bandwidth must be configured.
- On point-to-point serial interfaces, both sides must have AutoQos configured.
- The interface should not have any prior QoS configurations.

Common Issues with Network Application Services

This section briefly presents the main issues with the network application services discussed in the previous section, namely NetFlow, IP SLA, NBAR, SLB, QoS, and AutoQoS. Some of these tools, such as NBAR, NetFlow, and IP SLA, are used for baselining and monitoring, and some of them, such as SLB and QoS, are optimization techniques.

Common NetFlow Issues

In the case of NetFlow, the most common issues can be categorized as being related to performance and the exporting process. As efficient as NetFlow is in exporting aggregated information to a NetFlow Analyzer server, you might need to tune it so that it does not create performance degradation in the NetFlow-enabled device by consuming too much memory or CPU cycles. You might have to set limits to the number of entries in the cache, or tune the aging timers of NetFlow. Aging timers define how long a flow remains in the cache before being timed out and exported. If the aging timers are too high, the table can remain full continuously. If the NetFlow table reaches capacity, it starts dropping the oldest flows first. Export problems, on the other hand, are typically based on configuration errors or reachability to the NetFlow Collector or server. The following are some of the common NetFlow export culprits:

- A destination IP address has not been configured.
- A source interface has not been configured.
- A source interface has been configured, but does not have an IPv4 address.
- A source interface has been configured, but it is not in the up state.
- The subnet of the destination is unreachable.

Common IP SLA Issues

IP SLAs require readiness on the sender side, the responder side, and the network. Issues related to performance are common because probes will cause a burden if overscheduled, if multiple senders overwhelm one receiver, or if the device is already a bottleneck and its CPU utilization is high. Senders generally suffer more from the overscheduling and frequency of probes. Probe scheduling can be problematic if the clock on the device is out of sync; that is the reason synchronizing through Network Time Protocol (NTP) is highly recommended. For example, if you schedule for December 31 at 23:59, but the sender clock is set to last year, the probe will not go out when you expect it to. Network readiness is also essential; when using IP SLAs for troubleshooting purposes, the very same reason that prevents a certain application from working on the network will prevent the probe from working. Typically, it is the firewalls and access control mechanisms that filter or block traffic.

Common NBAR Issues

NBAR is a traffic-classification mechanism that allows you to classify based on application-layer components. What can be done with the resulting traffic classes varies. You can apply a QoS mechanism to a traffic class or block traffic that matches a traffic class, assuming it is conducting a malicious attack. NBAR does not detect traffic that uses non-standard ports. A typical example would be running HTTP on port 8080 or other non-standard ports for security reasons. At any time you can check the current NBAR port map using the command **show ip nbar port-map**. NBAR allows you to map any port you wish and even map multiple ports simultaneously to a single application or protocol, using the following command:

```
ip nbar port-map protocol-name [tcp ¦ udp] port-number
```

Yet another issue that affects most NBAR deployments is application support. Traffic going unnoticed by NBAR and not being classified will have important implications, especially if you were using NBAR for critical functions such as security. The solution to this problem is to load a PDLM. PDLMs, which are readily available at Cisco.com for users with proper permissions, will upgrade the application definition for NBAR in your router. This is similar to upgrading antivirus software with a new virus definition file.

Common AutoQoS Issues

Many of the common Cisco AutoQoS issues relate directly to its requirements and limitations, such as not having CEF enabled. Cisco AutoQoS requires CEF to be enabled on the interface, and the interface must be configured with an IP address and a specific (proper) bandwidth. Note that the bandwidth on a serial interface is not autosensed. Cisco AutoQoS uses the configured interface bandwidth to enable or disable certain QoS features such as compression and fragmentation. Another common AutoQoS problem cause is mismatched parameters on the two sides of a serial link. If the configured bandwidths differ, for example, Cisco AutoQoS might enable certain features on one side while disabling them on the other side of the same link. This can cause Layer 2 issues and bring the interface down. Modifying the Cisco AutoQoS configuration after the feature has been enabled can prove problematic, too. For example, if you disable AutoQoS on an interface using the **no auto qos** command, all Cisco AutoQoS generated commands are removed with the exception of those that have been changed/modified. If you do not remove those commands manually, they might cause errors or performance problems. Finally, you must know that AutoQoS does not work on an interface if it already has a policy applied to it. Before you apply AutoQoS, confirm that the interface has an IP address, has proper bandwidth configured, has CEF enabled, and has no policies applied to it already.

Troubleshooting Example: Network Application Services Problem

This section presents three troubleshooting examples related to NetFlow, IP SLA, and AutoQoS. Table 7-1 presents some the useful troubleshooting commands related to these technologies. Most of these commands are referenced during the troubleshooting examples.

Table 7-1 *Useful Network Application Services Troubleshooting Commands*

Network Application Service	Cisco IOS Troubleshooting Command
NetFlow	**show ip cache flow** **show ip flow export** **show ip flow interface** **debug ip flow export**
IP SLA	**show ip sla monitor statistics** **show ip sla monitor collection-statistics** **show ip sla monitor configuration** **debug ip sla monitor trace**
NBAR	**show ip nbar port-map** **show ip nbar protocol-discovery** **debug ip nbar unclassified-port-stats**
AutoQoS	**show auto qos interface** **show auto discovery qos**

NetFlow Troubleshooting Example

The first troubleshooting example is based on Figure 7-7. NetFlow is used for traffic metering and baselining, and a NetFlow Collector server with the IP address 10.1.1.10 is used to collect and aggregate NetFlow data. The reported problem is that the NetFlow Collector is not receiving data from router R1, one of the NetFlow-enabled routers. Start this troubleshooting exercise by testing connectivity between R1 and the NetFlow Collector and checking the NetFlow-specific configuration (to verify the configured parameters). Using the **ping** command, you can confirm IP connectivity between R1 and NetFlow Collector, and through some fact gathering, you can discover that the NetFlow Collector's address is 10.1.1.10, the NetFlow port number is 9991, and the server is configured to receive NetFlow data only from devices on subnet 10.254.0.0/24. Furthermore, the **show ip flow interface** command verifies that on router R1, NetFlow is active on interface serial 0/0 for ingress traffic.

To check whether R1 is actually exporting NetFlow and if there are any flows to export, you use the **show ip cache flow** command on R1. As you can see in the output shown in Example 7-5, R1 is collecting plenty of data. Next, you check if R1 is exporting the NetFlow data to the correct server using the **show ip flow export** command. Based on the output (also shown on Example 7-5), there are a fair number of exported flows, but the IP address of the NetFlow Collector and the source interface are incorrect. The NetFlow Collector's address is 10.1.152.1 instead of 10.1.1.10, and the source interface is FastEthernet0/0 rather than Loopback0.

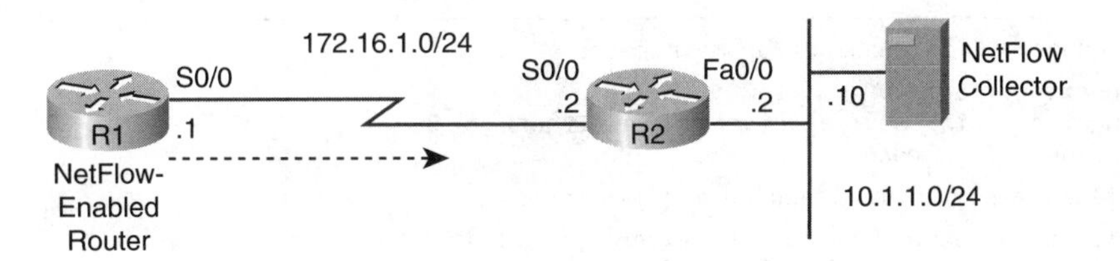

Figure 7-7 *The Network Diagram for NetFlow Troubleshooting Example*

Example 7-5 **show ip cache flow** *and* **show ip flow export** *Command Output on R1*

```
R1# show ip cache flow
IP packet size distribution
  1-32   64   96  128  160  192  224  256  288  320  352  384  416  448  480
  .000 .687 .000 .312 .000 .000 .000 .000 .000 .000 .000 .000 .000 .000 .000

    512  544  576 1024 1536 2048 2560 3072 3584 4096 4608
   .000 .000 .000 .000 .000 .000 .000 .000 .000 .000 .000
IP Flow Switching Cache, 278544 bytes
  0 active, 4096 inactive, 12 added
  192 ager polls, 0 flow alloc failures
  Active flows timeout in 30 minutes
  Inactive flows timeout in 15 seconds
IP Sub Flow Cache, 21640 bytes
  0 active, 1024 inactive, 12 added, 12 added to flow
  0 alloc failures, 0 force free
  1 chunk, 1 chunk added
  last clearing of statistics never
Protocol         Total    Flows   Packets  Bytes  Packets  Active (Sec)  Idle (Sec)
--------         Flows     /Sec     /Flow   /Pkt     /Sec         /Flow       /Flow
UDP-other           11      0.0         1     52      0.0           0.0        15.6
ICMP                 1      0.0         5    100      0.0           0.1        15.6
Total               12      0.0         1     67      0.0           0.0        15.6

SrcIF         SrcIPaddress    DstIf         DstIPaddress    Pr SrcP DstP  Pkts
Se0/0         172.16.1.2      Local         172.16.1.1      01 0000 0301     1
Se0/0         172.16.1.2      Null          255.255.255.255 11 0208 0208     1
R1#

R1# show ip flow export
```

```
Flow export v5 is enabled for main cache
  Exporting flows to 10.1.152.1 (9991)
  Exporting using source interface FastEthernet0/0
  Version 5 flow records
  5 flows exported in 3 udp datagrams
  0 flows failed due to lack of export packet
  0 export packets were sent up to process level
  0 export packets were dropped due to no fib
  0 export packets were dropped due to adjacency issues
  0 export packets were dropped due to fragmentation failures
  0 export packets were dropped due to encapsulation fixup failures
R1#
```

You correct the two mistakes you have found, namely the NetFlow Collector's address and IP NetFlow's source interface. Next, verify your work using the **show ip flow export** command once again, as shown in Example 7-6.

Example 7-6 *The NetFlow Collector's Address Is Corrected*

```
R1# conf t
Enter configuration commands, one per line.  End with CNTL/Z.
R1(config)# no ip flow-ex destination 10.1.152.1 9991
R1(config)#
R1(config)#
R1(config)# ip flow-ex destination 10.1.1.10 9991
R1(config)#
R1(config)# end
R1#
R1#
R1# conf t
Enter configuration commands, one per line.  End with CNTL/Z.
R1(config)# no ip flow-export source f0/0
R1(config)# ip flow-export source lo0
R1(config)#
R1(config)# end
R1#
R1#
R1# show ip flow export
Flow export v5 is enabled for main cache
  Exporting flows to 10.1.1.10 (9991)
  Exporting using source interface Loopback0
  version 5 flow records
  29 flows exported in 22 udp datagrams
```

```
   0 flows failed due to lack of export packet
   5 export packets were sent up to process level
   0 export packets were dropped due to no fib
   0 export packets were dropped due to adjacency issues
   0 export packets were dropped due to fragmentation failures
   0 export packets were dropped due to encapsulation fixup failures
R1#
```

NetFlow Collector is now receiving the NetFlow exports; the problem is solved.

IP SLA Troubleshooting Example

The IP SLA troubleshooting example is based on the diagram shown in Figure 7-8. In this case, to measure delay, a TCP connection probe (entry 1) is sent on port 2002 from R1 to R2 every 10 minutes, and SNMP traps are sent to an SNMP console if a certain threshold is surpassed. The problem is that the probe does not start and it does not report any statistics. To start this troubleshooting exercise, first check to see whether the SLA sender is sending and if the SLA receiver is receiving.

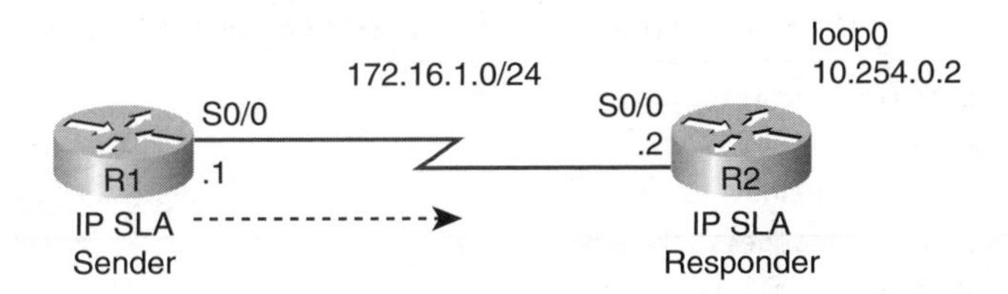

Figure 7-8 *The Network Diagram for IP SLA Troubleshooting Example*

The first thing to do is use the **show ip sla monitor configuration** command on R1, the SLA sender. The output, as shown in Example 7-7, displays correct information about probe number 1.

Example 7-7 **show ip sla monitor configuration** *Command Output on R1 Shows No Errors*

```
R1# show ip sla monitor configuration
SA Agent, Infrastructure Engine-II
Entry number: 1
Owner:
Tag:
Type of operation to perform: tcpConnect
Target address: 10.254.0.2
Source address: 0.0.0.0
Target port: 2002
Source port: 0
```

```
Operation timeout (milliseconds): 60000
Type of service parameters: 0x0
Control packets: enabled
Operation frequency (seconds): 600
Next Scheduled Start Time: 23:59:00
Group Scheduled: FALSE
Life (seconds): Forever
Entry Ageout (seconds): never
Recurring (Starting Everyday): FALSE
Status of entry (SNMP RowStatus): Active
Threshold (milliseconds): 5000
Number of statistic hours kept: 2
Number of statistic distribution buckets kept: 1
Statistic distribution interval (milliseconds): 20
--More--
```

Next, use the **show ip sla monitor statistics**, and notice in the output (see Example 7-8) that no results are reported for probe 1 whatsoever (they are all unknown).

Example 7-8 show ip sla monitor statistics *Command Output Reports No Results on R1*

```
R1# show ip sla monitor statistics
Round trip time (RTT)  Index 1
        Latest RTT: Unknown
Latest operation return code: Unknown
Latest operation start time: Unknown
Number of successes: 0
Number of failures: 0
Operation time to live: Forever
```

Next, look at the SLA configuration on R1 (shown in Example 7-9), using the **show run | section ip sla** command. Notice that the probe was supposed to start at 23:59, and even though it is past that time, it has not started. Ensure that R1's clock is synchronized with the NTP server.

Example 7-9 *The IP SLA Configuration on R1*

```
R1# show run ¦ section ip sla
ip sla monitor 1
 type tcpConnect dest-ipaddr 10.254.0.2 dest-port 2002
 frequency 600
ip sla monitor schedule 1 life forever start-time 23:59:00 Sep 10
ip sla monitor 2
 type echo protocol ipIcmpEcho 10.9.9.21 source-interface FastEhternet0/0
```

```
ip sla monitor schedule 2 life forever start-time now
ip sla monitor 3
 type udpEcho dest-ipaddr 10.1.1.100 dest-port 5247
ip sla monitor schedule 3 life forever start-time now
R1#
```

When you check the NTP status on R1, you notice that it is not synchronized with the NTP server (see Example 7-10). The phrase **no reference clock** in the output indicates that the NTP server, which is R2's address 10.254.0.2, is unavailable. On R2, enter the **ntp master 1** command and check R1's NTP status again (also shown in Example 7-10). Now the clock on R1 is synchronized with the NTP master (10.254.0.2).

Example 7-10 *NTP Status on R1 Indicates the NTP Server Was Unavailable*

```
R1# show ntp status
Clock is unsynchronized, stratum 16, no reference clock
nominal freq is 250.0000 Hz, actual freq is 250.0000 Hz, precision is 2**18
reference time is CE3D3F49.C3932713 (16:33:13.763 UTC Mon Aug 24 2009)
clock offset is 1.2491 msec, root delay is 22.99 msec
root dispersion is 1.68 msec, peer dispersion is 0.41 msec
R1#

R2# conf t
Enter configuration commands, one per line. End with CNTL/Z.
R2(config)# ntp master 1
R2(config)#
R2(config)# end
R2#

R1# show ntp status
Clock is synchronized, stratum 2, reference is 10.254.0.2
nominal freq is 250.0000 Hz, actual freq is 250.0000 Hz, precision is 2**18
reference time is CE54DCFD.19C87A09 (14:28:13.100 UTC Fri Sep 11 2009)
clock offset is 0.4728 msec, root delay is 22.87 msec
root dispersion is 7875.56 msec, peer dispersion is 7875.08 msec
R1#
```

At this point, you can return to the original problem, namely IP SLA, and see whether the monitor (probe) on R1 has successfully started. On R1, use the **show ip sla monitor statistics**; the results (shown in Example 7-11) look great: SLA monitor 1 has started with the return code of **Ok** and there has been one success and no failures. The IP SLA problem has been solved.

Example 7-11 *IP SLA Statistics on R1 Indicate Success After Fixing R1's Clock*

```
R1# sh ip sla monitor statistics
Round trip time (RTT)  Index 1
        Latest RTT: 20 ms
Latest operation start time: 14:31:17.083 UTC Fri Sep 11 2009
Latest operation return code: Ok
Number of successes: 1
Number of failures: 0
Operation time to live: Forever

Round trip time (RTT)  Index 2
        Latest RTT: NoConnection/Busy/Timeout
Latest operation start time: 14:31:41.239 UTC Fri Sep 11 2009
Latest operation return code: No connection
Number of successes: 0
Number of failures: 24
Operation time to live: Forever

Round trip time (RTT)  Index 3
        Latest RTT: NoConnection/Busy/Timeout
Latest operation start time: 14:31:47.659 UTC Fri Sep 11 2009
Latest operation return code: No connection
Number of successes: 0
Number of failures: 24
```

AutoQoS Troubleshooting Example

The third troubleshooting example is based on the diagram in Figure 7-9. The connection between routers R1 and R2 is down; however, the service provider maintains that the backbone service is fully operational.

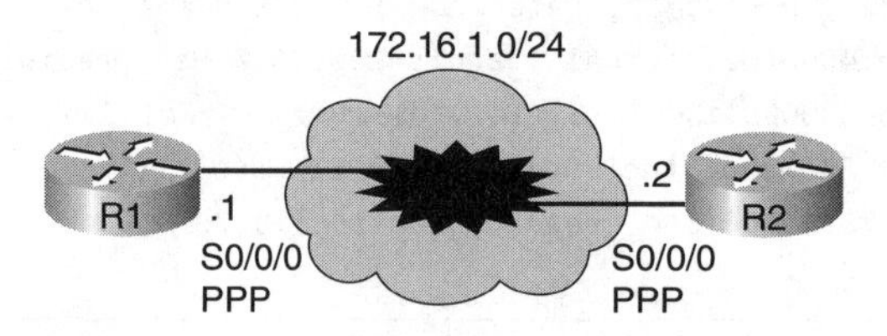

Figure 7-9 *Network Diagram for the AutoQoS Troubleshooting Example*

First, you want to check the status of the IP interfaces on R1, using the **show ip interfaces brief** command, and see that serial 0/0/0 is up, but the line protocol is down (see the output shown in Example 7-12). Using the **show interfaces** command, you will notice that serial 0/0/0 is configured for High-Level Data Link Control (HDLC) encapsulation.

The documentation, however, indicates that this serial interface must be configured for PPP encapsulation.

Example 7-12 *The Line Protocol of the Serial 0/0/0 Interface Is Down*

```
R1# show ip interfaces brief
Interface            IP-Address     OK?  Method  Status                    Protocol
FastEthernet0/0      unassigned     YES  unset   up                        up
FastEthernet0/1      unassigned     YES  unset   administratively down     down
Serial0/0/0          172.16.1.1     YES  unset   up                        down
R1#
```

On R1, you fix the encapsulation problem by going into interface configuration mode for the interface s0/0/0 and changing the encapsulation to PPP. As you can see in the output shown in Example 7-13, the interface serial 0/0/0's line protocol status changes to up, and a ping from R1 to R2 (to ensure end-to-end connectivity) is successful.

Example 7-13 *With PPP Encapsulation, the Line Protocol on Serial 0/0/0 Goes Up*

```
R1# conf t
Enter configuration commands, one per line. End with CNTL/Z.
R1(config)# int s0/0/0
R1(config-if)# encap ppp
R1(config-if)# shut
R1(config-if)# no shut
Sep 11 14:44:28.164: %LINK-%-CHANGED: Interface Serial0/0/0, changed state to
administratively down
R1(config-if)# end
R1#
Sep 11 14:44:30.984:  %SYS-5-CONFIG_I: Configured from console by console
Sep 11 14:44:32.356:  %LINK-3-UPDOWN: Interface Serial0/0/0, changed state to up
Sep 11 14:44:33.364:  %LINEPROTO-5-UPDOWN: Line protocol on Interface Serial0/0/0,
changed state to up
R1#
R1# ping 172.16.1.2

Type escape sequence to abort.
Sending 5, 100-byte ICMP Echos to 172.16.1.2, timeout is 2 seconds:
!!!!!
Success rate is 100 percent (5/5), round-trip min/avg/max = 28/28/28 ms
R1#
```

It seems strange that the encapsulation on serial 0/0/0 was changed from PPP to HDLC. Through some investigation and fact gathering, you learn that the problem was reported after someone tried to enable AutoQoS on this interface. Apparently, after encountering errors, that person removed AutoQoS, but the circuit remained down. What that person did not know is that when AutoQoS was removed, the interface encapsulation was changed back to serial interface default encapsulation, which is HDLC. All that was needed was to set the encapsulation to PPP, as done in Example 7-13; however, the issue that remains is that you need to make use of AutoQoS on this interface. AutoQoS (enterprise) has two phases. In the first phase, you need to enable "autodiscovery" on the interface for a while (minimum of 3 days is recommended). In the second phase, you actually enable AutoQoS, which will generate templates and policies based on the discovery enabled in phase one. Example 7-14 shows this work, but notice that the interface went down soon after we entered the **auto qos** command on serial 0/0/0. It seems that AutoQoS attempted to set the multilink feature on serial 0/0/0 and that failed.

Example 7-14 *Enabling AutoQoS on R1's Serial 0/0/0 Interface*

```
R1# conf t
Enter configuration commands, one per line. End with CNTL/Z
R1(config)# int s0/0/0
R1(config-if)# auto discovery qos

! Recommended practice dictates letting auto discovery run for some time,
  preferably 3-5 days

R1(config-if)# auto qos
R1(config-if)#
Sep 11 14:52:54.141: %LINK-3-UPDOWN: Interface Multilink2001100115, changed
  state to down
Sep 11 14:52:55.273: %RMON-5-FALLINGTRAP: Falling trap is generated because
  the value of cbQosCMDropBitRate.1317.1319 has fallen below the
  falling-threshold value 0
```

AutoQoS attempts the multilink feature for fragmentation purposes, on low bandwidth interfaces. You need to find out what is the configured bandwidth for the serial 0/0/0 interface. R1's running configuration reveals that the bandwidth on serial 0/0/0 is set to 200 (kbps) rather than 2000 (see Example 7-15). This tells you why AutoQoS considered this interface a slow bandwidth interface and attempted the multilink feature on it.

Example 7-15 *Serial0/0/0's Bandwidth Is Mistakenly Set to 200 kbps Instead of 2 Mbps*

```
R1# sh run int s0/0/0
Building configuration...

Current configuration : 277 bytes
!
interface Serial0/0/0
```

```
 bandwidth 200
 ip address 172.16.1.1 255.255.255.0
 ip nbar protocol-discovery
 ip flow ingress
 encapsulation ppp
 auto qos
 auto discovery qos
 no fair-queue
 ppp multilink
 ppp multilink group 2001100115
 service-policy input TEST
 service-policy output TEST
end

R1#
R1#
```

The next logical step is to fix the bandwidth configuration on R1's serial 0/0/0 interface and reapply the AutoQoS feature; however, you need to remove AutoQoS first. When you remove the AutoQoS feature, an error occurs and a message indicates that all policies have not been removed. Therefore, when you retry the AutoQoS feature, you receive yet another error message that indicates because there is a policy on the interface, AutoQoS cannot be applied. This is shown in Example 7-16.

Example 7-16 *After Fixing the Bandwidth, Reapplying AutoQoS Is Still Unsuccessful*

```
R1# conf t
Enter configuration commands, one per line. End with CNTL/Z
R1(config)# int s0/0/0
R1(config-if)# no auto qos
% Cannot disable multilink on a multilink group interface
% Not all config may be removed and may reappear after reactivating the
   Logical-interface/sub-interfaces
R1(config-if)# bandwidth 2000
R1(config-if)# auto qos
 Policy map TEST is already attached
AutoQoS Error: the following command was not properly applied:
service-policy output AutoQoS-Policy-UnTrust
R1(config-if)# end
R1#
R1#
R1#
Sep 11 14:56:49.329: %LINK-3-CHANGED: Interface Multilink2001100115, changed
  state to administratively down
Sep 11 14:56:50.205: %SYS-5-CONFIG_I: Configured from console by console
```

The running configuration shown in Example 7-15 shows a service policy called TEST is applied to serial 0/0/0 interface for both inbound and outbound traffic. You must remove those lines, reset encapsulation back to PPP, and then reapply AutoQoS. This time AutoQoS succeeds, and the interface stays up. Test the connection between R1 and R2 with a ping to ensure success (see the output shown in Example 7-17). It is important to keep in mind that you can only remove policies after verifying they are not necessary. In this case, as the name implies, the TEST policy was put in place for testing purposes but it was not removed upon test completion.

Example 7-17 *Successful Ping from R1 to R2 Proves the Problem Is Now Solved*

```
R1# ping 172.16.1.2
Type escape sequence to abort.
Sending 5, 100-byte ICMP Echos to 172.16.1.2, timeout is 2 seconds:
!!!!!
Success rate is 100 percent (5/5), round-trip min/avg/max = 28/28/32 ms
R1#
```

Troubleshooting Performance Issues on Switches

It is also important for a support engineer to be able to identify and possibly resolve the cause of an observed difference between the expected performance and the actual performance of the network as a whole, and of a specific device such as a LAN switch. This section provides information useful for diagnosing performance problems on Catalyst LAN switches. You will learn the Cisco IOS commands to perform the following tasks:

- Diagnose physical and data link layer problems on switch ports.
- Analyze ternary content-addressable memory (TCAM) utilization on switches to determine the root cause of TCAM-allocation failures.
- Determine the root cause of high CPU usage on a switch.

Identifying Performance Issues on Switches

A network performance problem can be defined as a situation where the observed traffic handling of the network does not meet certain expected standards. Because performance problems are defined in terms of "expected behavior," which is subjective to a certain extent, they are considered hard to troubleshoot by many people. One would wonder if such a problem is caused by devices that are not performing according to predefined requirements or whether the problem is just a matter of mismatched perceptions and expectations. In other words, it has to become clear if the problem is at the business level or at the technical level. As you can imagine, cases involving something simply "not working" are straightforward. In those scenarios, all you need to ask yourself is if according to the requirements and design of the network, the application or functionality is expected/supposed to work (for that particular user and at that particular time). If the answer to that question is yes (and things are not working), the problem is clearly a technical one. The point is that performance problems are defined in terms of expectations and requirements by different entities:

- User expectations and requirements
- Business expectations and requirements
- Technical expectations and requirements

As an example to illustrate the role of expectations in performance problems, suppose that a switch serves 20 users, each connected to a 100-Mbps port. There is a file server connected to the same switch on a 1-Gbps port. Users access the file server at different times, transferring files of various sizes. As long as not more than half of them are transferring files at the same time, they will experience transfer rates of up to the full 100 Mbps that is available to each user. Imagine that at the exact same moment, all users need to transfer a file from the server. Because the server has a total bandwidth of only 1 Gbps, the average transfer rate of the users will be 50 Mbps, while they are all transferring files. If users have come to expect transfer rates of 100 Mbps, they will perceive this as a performance problem; however, from a technical standpoint, the network performance is as expected. On the other hand, if one of the users never gets transfer rates higher than 50 Mbps, even if he is the only person transferring files, from a technical standpoint, this is a performance problem. Note that in the latter case the user might not even perceive this as a performance problem, because he has not come to expect transfer rates higher than 50 Mbps. In general, troubleshooting performance problems is a three-step process:

Step 1. **Assessing whether the problem is technical in nature:** Evaluate whether the behavior experienced by the user matches the technical expectations. If it turns out that the performance is technically within the boundaries of what can be expected of the network (as specified by the design and requirements), but the user still experiences it as a problem, this is not a technical problem. The business requirements might need to be reevaluated. Eventually, this could result in a change of the technical requirements and the network design.

Step 2. **Isolating the performance problem to a device, link, or component:** If it is determined that the observed behavior is not within the boundaries of what should be expected from a technical standpoint, the problem will need to be isolated to a particular device, link, or component. A common approach to eliminate components from the chain of links and devices between the endpoints is comparing the behavior of different devices along different segments of the network path and spotting the differences or similarities in the behavior.

Step 3. **Diagnosing and resolving the performance degradation at the component level:** After you have determined that a particular component is likely to be the limiting factor in the chain between the endpoints, you have to investigate that component for symptoms that confirm that this component is causing the performance problems. Once this has been confirmed, the next step is to diagnose the underlying cause and, if possible, resolve the problem. The focus of this lesson is on this step: diagnosing and resolving performance problems using IOS tools on a switch, after you have determined that a switch or a link connected to a switch could be the cause of performance degradation on the network.

Although there are differences between the hardware architectures among various Catalyst switch families, all switches include the following components:

- **Interfaces:** These are used to receive and transmit frames.
- **Forwarding hardware:** This consists of two elements: Hardware that implements the decision-making logic that is necessary to rewrite a frame and forward it to the correct interface; and a backplane to carry frames from the ingress interface to the egress interface.
- **Control plane hardware:** These execute the processes that are part of the operating system.

Traffic flowing through a switch enters on an ingress interface, is forwarded by the forwarding hardware, and leaves through the egress interface. The performance of these components directly influences switch overall performance. The control plane CPU and memory are not involved in switching traffic. Therefore, the control plane hardware does not have a direct impact on switch performance. However, the control plane is responsible for updating the information in the forwarding hardware. Therefore, the control plane has an indirect effect on the forwarding capability of the platform. If the control plane is consistently running at a high load, this could eventually affect the forwarding behavior of the device. Moreover, the control plane hardware handles any traffic that cannot be handled by the forwarding hardware. A high load on the control plane hardware could therefore be an indication that the forwarding hardware has reached its maximum capacity or is not handling traffic as it should. As Figure 7-10 shows, components of both the control plane (memory and CPU) and the data plane (ingress interface, forwarding hardware, and the egress interface) contribute to the overall switch performance.

Troubleshooting Switch Interface Performance Problems

In case of suspected performance problems, interfaces are among the first to be inspected. If the physical cabling is bad, this will cause packet loss, and packet loss can cause various performance problems. TCP-based applications can survive a certain amount of packet loss because that protocol has retransmission capabilities that allow it to recover lost packets. However, TCP also has flow control mechanisms. TCP slows down its transmission rate based on packet loss, because the most common cause of packet loss is (temporary) congestion. Consequently, packet loss caused by bad cables or interfaces

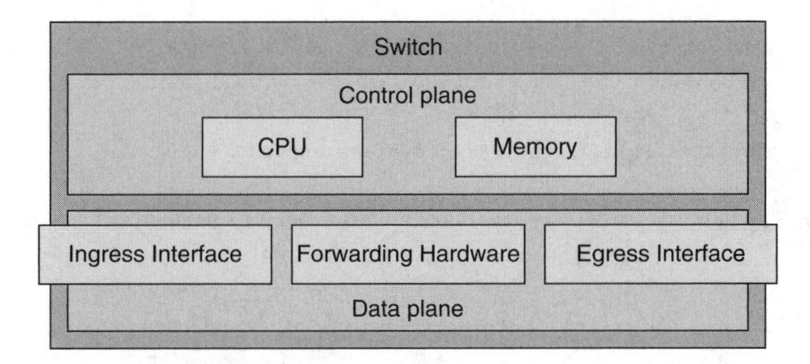

Figure 7-10 *Switch Performance Depends on Control Plane and Data Plane Components*

usually results in slow TCP-based connections across an interface. UDP does not have inherent retransmission mechanisms, and therefore the result of packet loss on UDP-based applications depends on the way that the application deals with packet loss. For real-time traffic, such as voice or video, a high percentage of packet loss has a direct and negative affect on the quality of the voice or video communications.

When you find indications of packet loss on a switch, the first place to look is usually the output of the **show interface** command. This output shows packet statistics including various error counters. On switches, two additional command options are supported that are not available on routers:

- **show interfaces** *interface* **counters:** This command displays the total numbers of input and output unicast, multicast, and broadcast packets and the total input and output byte counts.
- **show interfaces** *interface* **counters errors:** This command displays the error statistics for each interface. Table 7-2 lists the parameters reported by this command output.

It is important to relate any error statistics to the total number of received frames in case of receive errors (such as FCS errors) or the total number of transmitted frames in case of transmit errors (such as collisions). For example, in Example 7-18, you can see that there are 12618 FCS errors on a total of 499128 + 4305 + 0 = 503433 received frames, which translates to 2.5 percent of the received traffic on the interface. In general, more than one FCS error in a million frames (0.0001 percent) is reason to investigate.

Example 7-18 *Checking for Interface Errors*

```
ASW1# show interfaces FastEthernet 0/1 counters

Port          InOctets      InUcastPkts         InMcastPkts       InBcastPkts
Fa0/1        647140108           499128                4305                 0
```

```
Port          OutOctets     OutUcastPkts       OutMcastPkts      OutBcastPkts
Fa0/1          28533484           319996                 52                 3

ASW1# show interfaces FastEthernet 0/1 counters errors

Port      Align-Err    FCS-Err     Xmit-Err      Rcv-Err   UnderSize   OutDiscards
Fa0/1             0      12618            0        12662           0             0

Port    Single-Col    Multi-Col  Late-Col  Excess-Col  Carri-Sen  Runts    Giants
Fa0/1            0            0         0           0          0      0        44
```

Table 7-2 *The Parameters Reported by* **show interfaces** *interface* **counters errors**

Reported Parameter	Description
Align-Err	This is the number of frames with alignment errors, which are frames that do not end with an even number of octets and have a bad cyclic redundancy check (CRC), received on the port. These usually indicate a physical problem, for example, cabling, a bad port, or a bad network interface card (NIC), but can also indicate a duplex mismatch. When the cable is first connected to the port, some of these errors can occur. Also, if there is a hub connected to the port, collisions between other devices on the hub can cause these errors.
FCS-Err	The number of valid size frames with frame check sequence (FCS) errors, but no framing errors. This is typically a physical issue (for example, cabling, a bad port, or a bad NIC), but can also indicate a duplex mismatch.
Xmit-Err and Rcv-Err	This indicates that the internal port transmit (Tx) or receive (Rx) buffers are full. A common cause of Xmit-Err is traffic from a high-bandwidth link that is switched to a lower-bandwidth link, or traffic from multiple inbound links that is switched to a single outbound link. For example, if a large amount of bursty traffic comes in on a Gigabit port and is switched out to a 100-Mbps port, the Xmit-Err field might increment on the 100-Mbps port. This is because the port output buffer is overwhelmed by the excess traffic because of the speed mismatch between the incoming and outgoing bandwidths.
Undersize	The frames received that are smaller than the minimum IEEE 802.3 frame size of 64 bytes long (which excludes framing bits, but includes FCS octets) that are otherwise well formed, so it has a valid CRC. Check the device that sends out these frames.
Single-Col	The number of times one collision occurs before the port transmits a frame to the media successfully. Collisions are normal for ports operating in half-duplex mode, but should not be seen on ports operating in full-duplex mode. If collisions are increasing dramatically, this indicates a highly utilized link or possibly a duplex mismatch with the attached device.

Table 7-2 *The Parameters Reported by* **show interfaces** *interface* **counters errors**

Reported Parameter	Description
Multi-Col	This is the number of times multiple collisions occur before the port transmits a frame to the media successfully. Collisions are normal for ports operating in half-duplex mode, but should not be seen on ports operating in full-duplex mode. If collisions increase dramatically, this indicates a highly utilized link or possibly a duplex mismatch with the attached device.
Late-Col	This is the number of times that a collision is detected on a particular port late in the transmission process. For a 10-Mbps port, this is later than 512 bit-times into the transmission of a packet. Five hundred and twelve bit-times corresponds to 51.2 microseconds on a 10-Mbps system. This error can indicate a duplex mismatch among other things. For the duplex mismatch scenario, the late collision is seen on the half-duplex side. As the half-duplex side transmits, the full-duplex side does not wait its turn and transmits simultaneously, which causes a late collision. Late collisions can also indicate an Ethernet cable or segment that is too long. Collisions should not be seen on ports configured as full-duplex.
Excess-Col	This is a count of frames transmitted on a particular port, which fail due to excessive collisions. An excessive collision occurs when a packet has a collision 16 times in a row. The packet is then dropped. Excessive collisions are typically an indication that the load on the segment needs to be split across multiple segments, but can also point to a duplex mismatch with the attached device. Collisions should not be seen on ports configured as full duplex.
Carri-Sen	This occurs every time an Ethernet controller wants to send data on a half-duplex connection. The controller senses the wire and checks whether it is not busy before transmitting. This is normal on a half-duplex Ethernet segment.
Runts	The frames received are smaller than the minimum IEEE 802.3 frame size (64 bytes for Ethernet) and have a bad CRC. This can be caused by a duplex mismatch and physical problems, such as a bad cable, port, or NIC on the attached device.
Giants	These are frames that exceed the maximum IEEE 802.3 frame size (1518 bytes for nonjumbo Ethernet), and have a bad FCS. Try to find the offending device and remove it from the network. In many cases, it is the result of a bad NIC.

A common cause for interface errors is a mismatched duplex mode between two ends of an Ethernet link. In many Ethernet-based networks, point-to-point connections are now the norm and the use of hubs and the associated half-duplex operation is not common. This means that most modern Ethernet links operate in full-duplex mode, and although collisions were seen as normal for an Ethernet link in the past, today, collisions often indicate that duplex negotiation has failed and the link is not operating in the correct duplex mode. The IEEE 802.3ab Gigabit Ethernet standard mandates the use of autonegotiation for speed and duplex. In addition, although it is not strictly mandatory, practically all Fast Ethernet NICs also use auto negotiation by default. The use of autonegotiation for speed and duplex is the current recommended practice at the network edge; however, if duplex negotiation fails for some reason, it might be necessary to set the speed and duplex manually on both ends. Typically, in this situation the duplex mode is set to full duplex on both ends of the connection; if that doesn't work, setting half duplex on both ends of a connection is naturally preferred over a duplex mismatch!

Switch Port/Interface Issues

Some problems are caused by physical issues related to cabling or switch ports. Checking the cable and both sides of a given connection, particularly when you are using a bottom-up approach, is strongly advised. The LEDs on switches can provide valuable information. With the information gathered from the LEDs, you can determine what corrective action might be needed. Common interface and wiring problems and their corresponding remedies include the following:

- **No cable connected:** Connect the cable from the switch to a known good device.
- **Wrong port:** Make sure that both ends of the cable are plugged into the correct ports.
- **Device has no power:** Ensure that both devices have power.
- **Wrong cable type:** Verify that the correct type of cable is being used.
- **Bad cable:** Swap the suspect cable with a known good cable. Look for broken or missing pins on connectors.
- **Loose connections:** Check for loose connections. Sometimes a cable appears to be seated in the jack, but it is not. Unplug the cable and reinsert it.
- **Patch panels:** Eliminate faulty patch panel connections. Bypass the patch panel if possible to rule it out as the problem.
- **Media converters:** Eliminate faulty media converters. Bypass the media converter, if possible, to rule it out as the problem.
- **Bad or wrong gigabit interface converter (GBIC):** Swap the suspect GBIC with a known good GBIC. Verify hardware and software support for the GBIC.

Some other issues are related to configuration problems that can result in performance degradation. The most common ones are duplex negotiations, speed negotiation, and EtherChannel configurations.

Troubleshooting Example: Duplex Problem

This example is based on the network diagram shown in Figure 7-11. The user on PC1 has complained that transferring large files to SRV1 takes hours. First, you need to verify whether this is really a technical problem or if the performance is within expected boundaries. Assume that after determining the traffic path between the client and the server, the maximum throughput that this user can expect is 100 Mbps. Transfer of 1 GB (gigabyte) of data at the rate of 100 Mbps takes approximately 80 seconds, not taking any overhead into account. However, it is clear that even with added overhead the transfer should still only take minutes, not hours. There can be two potential explanations: Either congestion on the network causes this user to get only a small portion of the available bandwidth (100 Mbps), or this is caused by underperforming hardware or software on the client, network, or server. When you verify the load on the links in the path using the performance management system, you notice that the average load has not been higher than 50 percent over the past few hours. Ruling out congestion as the cause, you could run comparative tests from several different points in the network, but decide to first verify the physical path between the client and server to see whether the network is causing this problem.

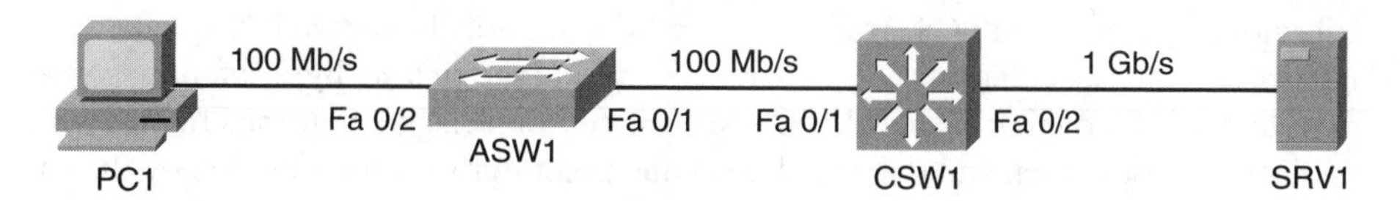

Figure 7-11 *Performance Problems Caused by Duplex Mismatch*

As shown in Example 7-19, interface FastEthernet 0/2 on ASW1, which leads to the client, does not show a significant number of errors. However, when you verify interface FastEthernet 0/1, which leads to CSW1, you notice a high percentage of FCS errors. Although FCS errors can have various other causes, such as bad cabling or bad interface hardware, they are also a symptom associated with a duplex mismatch. If one side of an Ethernet link is running in full-duplex mode and the other side is running in half-duplex mode, on the side of the connection that is running in full-duplex mode, you will see FCS errors rapidly increasing. This happens because a NIC that is operating in full-duplex mode will not listen for carrier, and it simply transmits whenever it has a frame to send. If the other side happens to be transmitting at that same moment, it will sense the transmission coming in, detect the collision, and will immediately stop its own transmission. This, in turn, causes only a partial frame to be received by the full-duplex side of the connection, which is recorded as an FCS error.

Example 7-19 *Results of Duplex Mismatch on the Full-Duplex Side*

```
ASW1# show interface FastEthernet 0/1 ¦ include duplex
  Full-duplex, 100Mb/s, media type is 10/100Base TX

ASW1# show interfaces FastEthernet 0/1 counters errors

Port      Align-Err   FCS-Err    Xmit-Err     Rcv-Err   UnderSize   OutDiscards
Fa0/1             0     12618           0       12662           0             0

Port    Single-Col    Multi-Col  Late-Col  Excess-Col  Carri-Sen  Runts    Giants
Fa0/1            0            0         0           0          0      0        44
```

When you connect to switch CSW1 and verify the same connection on that side. As Example 7-20 shows, a high numbers of collisions occur, specifically late collisions. This is an important clue because collisions only happen on links that run in half-duplex mode. The fact that you see high numbers of collisions on this side and no collisions on the other side tells you that this side is running in half-duplex mode and the other side in full-duplex mode. Even if you did not have access to switch ASW1, the counters for interface FastEthernet 0/1 on CSW1 strongly suggest a duplex problem. If this link is supposed to run in half-duplex mode, a certain number of collisions is considered normal. However, late collisions should not happen and always indicate a problem. The reason that you see late collisions on the half-duplex side of a duplex mismatch is the same behavior that causes the FCS errors on the full-duplex side. In normal half-duplex Ethernet operation, collisions will only happen during the first 64 bytes of a transmission. In case of a duplex mismatch, however, the full-duplex side transmits frames without listening for carrier, and this might be at any point during a transmission by the half-duplex side.

Example 7-20 *Results of Duplex Mismatch on the Half-Duplex Side*

```
CSW1# show interface FastEthernet 0/1 ¦ include duplex
  Full-duplex, 100Mb/s, media type is 10/100Base TX

CSW1# show interfaces FastEthernet 0/1 counters errors

Port      Align-Err   FCS-Err    Xmit-Err     Rcv-Err   UnderSize   OutDiscards
Fa0/1             0         0           0           0           0             0

Port    Single-Col    Multi-Col  Late-Col  Excess-Col  Carri-Sen  Runts    Giants
Fa0/1          664          124     12697           0          0      0        44
```

After considering all the symptoms, you conclude that the duplex mismatch is likely the cause of the performance problem. You verify the settings on both switches, and it turns out that somehow a mismatched manual speed and duplex configuration has caused this mismatch. You configure both sides for autonegotiation, clear the counters, and confirm that the negotiation results in full duplex. Together with the user, you perform a test by transferring some files. The transfers now only take a few minutes. You verify on the switches that the FCS and collision counters do not increase. Finally, you make a backup of the configuration and document the change.

Auto-MDIX

Automatic medium-dependent interface crossover (auto-MDIX) is a feature supported on many switches and NICs. This feature automatically detects the required cable connection type (straight-through or crossover) for a connection. As long as one of the two sides of a connection supports auto-MDIX, you can use a crossover or a straight-through Ethernet cable and the connection will work. However, this feature depends on the speed and duplex autonegotiation feature, and disabling speed and duplex negotiation will also disable auto-MDIX for an interface. The default setting for auto-MDIX was changed from disabled to enabled starting from Cisco IOS Software Release 12.2(20)SE. Therefore, auto-MDIX does not specifically have to be enabled on most switches. However, if you have a switch that supports auto-MDIX, but is running older software, you can enable this feature manually using the **mdix auto** command (see Example 7-21). Be aware that this command enables auto-MDIX only if speed and duplex autonegotiation are enabled, too.

Example 7-21 *Configuring Auto-MDIX*

```
Switch(config)# interface FastEthernet 0/10
Switch(config-if)# shutdown
Switch(config-if)# speed auto
Switch(config-if)# duplex auto
Switch(config-if)# mdix auto
Switch(config-if)# no shutdown
Switch(config-if)# end
Switch#
!
```

To verify the status of auto-MDIX, speed, and duplex for an interface, you can use the **show interface transceiver properties** command, as demonstrated in Example 7-22.

Example 7-22 show interface transceiver properties *Command Output*

```
CSW1# show interface FastEthernet 0/10 transceiver properties
Diagnostic Monitoring is not implemented
Name : Fa0/10
Administrative Speed: auto
Administrative Duplex: auto
Administrative Auto-MDIX: on
Administrative Power Inline: N/A
```

```
Operational Speed: 100
Operational Duplex: full
Operational Auto-MDIX: on
Media Type: 10/100BaseTX
```

The Forwarding Hardware

After considering the impact of ingress and egress interfaces on switch performance, this topic looks at the components of the forwarding hardware involved in switching the frames from the ingress interface to the egress interface and the impact that they have on the performance of the switch. Essentially, the forwarding hardware always consists of two major components:

- **Backplane:** The backplane carries traffic between interfaces. There are many different types of backplane architectures. The hardware of a switch backplane can be based on a ring, bus, shared memory, crossbar fabric, or a combination of these elements.
- **Decision-making logic:** For each incoming frame, the decision-making logic makes the decision to either forward the frame or discard it; this is also called performing Layer 2 and Layer 3 switching actions. For forwarded frames, the decision-making logic provides the information necessary to rewrite and forward the frame and may take other actions such as the processing of access lists or quality of service (QoS) features.

The impact of the backplane on switch performance is limited. The backplane of a switch is designed for very high switching capacity. In most cases, the limiting factor in throughput on a switched network is the capacity of the links between the devices, not the capacity of the backplanes of the switches. Still, in certain specific cases the backplane might become a bottleneck and needs to be taken into account to correctly compute the maximum total throughput between a number of devices. For instance, a number of ports might share a certain amount of bandwidth to the switch backplane. If that shared bandwidth is lower than the total bandwidth of all the ports combined, the ports are oversubscribed. This situation is similar to the situation where you have an access switch with 24 Fast Ethernet ports and a single 1-Gbps uplink. The total aggregate bandwidth for the 24 Fast Ethernet ports is 2.4 Gbps, and if they all need to send at full speed across the uplink, congestion will occur and frames will be dropped. However, in most cases, the 24 ports will not be transmitting at full speed at the same time, and their combined load will easily fit the 1-Gbps uplink.

Troubleshooting TCAM Problems

The decision-making logic of a switch has a significant impact on its performance. The decision-making logic consists of specialized high performance lookup memory, the ternary content-addressable memory (TCAM). The control plane information necessary to make forwarding decisions, such as MAC address tables, routing information, access list information, and QoS information, build the content of the TCAM. The TCAM then takes all the necessary forwarding decisions for a frame at speeds that are high enough and it utilizes full capacity of the switch backplane. TCAM's decision-making process does not impede or limit the forwarding performance of the switch. However, if for some reason frames cannot be forwarded by the TCAM, they will be handed off (punted) to the CPU for processing. Because the CPU is also used to execute the control plane processes, it can only forward traffic at certain rate. Consequently, if a large amount of traffic is punted to the CPU, the throughput for the traffic concerned will descend, and an adverse affect on the control plane processes will also be observed.

TCAM will punt any frames to the CPU for forwarding that it cannot forward itself. This does not include frames that are explicitly dropped (for example, by an access list) because the inbound port is in the spanning-tree Blocking state or because a VLAN is not allowed on a trunk. Traffic might be punted or handled by the CPU for many reasons, some main examples of which are as follows:

- Packets destined for any of the switch IP addresses. Examples of such packets include Telnet, Secure Shell (SSH), or Simple Network Management Protocol (SNMP) packets destined for one of the switch IP addresses.
- Multicasts and broadcasts from control plane protocols such as the Spanning Tree Protocol (STP) or routing protocols. Routing protocol broadcasts and multicasts are processed by the CPU in addition to being flooded to all ports within the VLAN that the frame was received in, as usual.
- Packets that cannot be forwarded by the TCAM because a feature is not supported in hardware. For example, generic routing encapsulation (GRE) tunnels can be configured on a Catalyst 3560 switch, but because this is not a TCAM-supported feature on this switch, the GRE packets will be punted.
- Packets that cannot be forwarded in hardware because the TCAM could not hold the necessary information. The TCAM has a limited capacity, and when entries cannot be programmed into the TCAM, the packets associated to those entries will have to be punted to the CPU to be forwarded. If you have too many IP routes or too many access list entries, some of them might not be installed in the TCAM, and associated packets cannot be forwarded in hardware. This item is the most likely to cause performance problems on a switch. The CPU always handles control plane packets in software, and the volume of this type is relatively low. However, the volume of traffic that flows through a switch is substantial, and if even a fraction of this traffic is handed off to the CPU, it will quickly cause performance degradation. The traffic itself might be dropped or forwarded slowly. Furthermore, the control plane processes will suffer because the packet-switching process consumes a large share of the available CPU cycles.

Note The commands to verify TCAM utilization are platform dependent. The examples shown here apply to Catalyst 3560 and 3750 switches. Consult the documentation of the platforms that you are working on to find the relevant commands to troubleshoot TCAM problems.

To discover how close the current TCAM utilization is to the platform limits, use the **show platform tcam utilization** command. The TCAM is carved into separate areas that contain entries associated with a particular usage. Each of these areas has its associated limits. On the Catalyst 3560 and 3750 series switches, the allocation of TCAM space for specific uses is based on a switch database manager (SDM) template. Templates other than the default can be selected to change the allocation of TCAM resources to better fit the role of the switch in the network. For more information, consult the SDM section of the configuration guide for the Catalyst 3560 or 3750 series switches.

Example 7-23 shows the maximum number of masks and values that can be assigned to IP Version 4 not directly connected routes are 272 and 2176, respectively. Currently, 30 masks and 175 values are in use. This means that this switch is still far from reaching its maximum capacity. As the output of the **show** command states (on the bottom), the exact algorithm to allocate TCAM entries for a particular feature is complex and you cannot simply tell how many IPv4 routes can be added to the routing table before the TCAM will reach its maximum. However, when you see the values in the Used column getting close to the values in the Max column, you might start experiencing extra load on the CPU because failed allocation of TCAM resources.

Example 7-23 **show platform tcam utilization** *Command Output*

```
CSW1# show platform tcam utilization

CAM Utilization for ASIC# 0                      Max              Used
                                             Masks/Values      Masks/Values

Unicast mac addresses:                         784/6272           23/99
IPv4 IGMP groups + multicast routes:           144/1152            6/26
IPv4 unicast directly-connected routes:        784/6272           23/99
IPv4 unicast indirectly-connected routes:      272/2176           30/175
IPv4 policy based routing aces:                  0/0              30/175
IPv4 qos aces:                                 768/768           260/260
IPv4 security aces:                           1024/1024           27/27

Note: Allocation of TCAM entries per feature uses
A complex algorithm. The above information is meant
To provide an abstract view of the current TCAM utilization
```

For some types of TCAM entries, it is possible to see whether any TCAM-allocation failures have occurred. For example, the output of the **show platform ip unicast counts** command, displayed in Example 7-24, shows if any TCAM-allocation failures were experienced for IP Version 4 prefixes. In general, TCAM-allocation failures are rare because switches have more than enough TCAM capacity for the roles that they are designed and positioned for. However, all networks are different, so be aware of the fact that TCAM-allocation failures can be a possible cause of performance problems. Even though it is more of a security-related topic, it is still related to this discussion to caution you about MAC attacks which fill up the CAM/TCAM, leading to performance degradation.

Example 7-24 show platform ip unicast counts *Command Output*

```
CSW1# show platform ip unicast counts
# of HL3U fibs 141
# of HL3U adjs 9
# of HL3U mpaths 2
# of HL3U covering-fibs 0
# of HL3U fibs with adj failures 0
Fibs of Prefix length 0, with TCAM fails: 0
Fibs of Prefix length 1, with TCAM fails: 0
Fibs of Prefix length 2, with TCAM fails: 0
Fibs of Prefix length 3, with TCAM fails: 0
Fibs of Prefix length 4, with TCAM fails: 0
Fibs of Prefix length 5, with TCAM fails: 0
Fibs of Prefix length 6, with TCAM fails: 0
<... further output omitted ...>
```

Another way to spot potential TCAM-allocation failures is by observing traffic being punted to the CPU for forwarding. The command **show controllers cpu-interface** (shown in Example 7-25) displays packet counts for packets that are forwarded to the CPU. If the retrieved packet counter in the **sw forwarding** row is rapidly increasing when you execute this command multiple times in a row, traffic is being switched in software by the CPU rather than in hardware by the TCAM. An increased CPU load usually accompanies this behavior.

Example 7-25 show controllers cpu-interface *Command Output*

```
CSW1# sh controllers cpu-interface
ASIC     Rxbiterr   Rxunder    Fwdctfix   Txbuflos   Rxbufloc   Rxbufdrain
-------------------------------------------------------------------------
ASIC0       0          0          0          0          0          0


cpu-queue-frames  retrieved  dropped    invalid    hol-block  stray
----------------- ---------- ---------- ---------- ---------- ----------
rpc               1          0          0          0          0
stp               853663     0          0          0          0
ipc               0          0          0          0          0
routing protocol  1580429    0          0          0          0
```

```
L2 protocol        22004      0          0          0          0
remote console     0          0          0          0          0
sw forwarding      1380174    0          0          0          0
<... further output omitted ...>
```

You can conclude that it is important to recognize that TCAM resources are limited and that TCAM-allocation problems can lead to packets being switched by the CPU rather than the TCAM. This might overload the CPU and lead to dropping or slowdown of the CPU-forwarded traffic. In addition, a negative impact on control plane processes will be experienced. Whenever you observe performance problems for traffic passing through a switch and the CPU of that switch is consistently running at a very high load, you should find out whether the CPU is handling a significant amount of traffic forwarding, and if the latter is caused by exhaustion of TCAM resources.

One remedy to the TCAM utilization and exhaustion problem is reducing the amount of information that the control plane feeds into the TCAM. For example, you can make use of techniques such as route summarization, route filtering, and access list (prefix list) optimization. Generally, TCAM is not upgradeable, so either the information that needs to be programmed into the TCAM needs to be reduced or you will have to upgrade to a higher-level switch, which can handle more TCAM entries. On some switches, such as the Catalyst 3560 and 3750 series of switches, the allocation of TCAM space among the different features can be changed. For example, if you are deploying a switch where it is almost exclusively involved in Layer 3 switching and next to no Layer 2 switching, you can choose a different template that sacrifices TCAM space for MAC address entries in favor of IP route entries. The TCAM allocation on the 3560 and 3750 series of switches is managed by the switch database manager (SDM). For more information, consult the SDM section of the configuration guide for the Catalyst 3560 or 3750 series switches at Cisco.com.

Control Plane: Troubleshooting High CPU Load on Switches

On a switch, the CPU load is directly related to the traffic load. Because the bulk of the traffic is switched in hardware by the TCAM, the load of the CPU is often low even when the switch is forwarding a large amount of traffic. This behavior is not similar in routers: Low- to mid-range routers use the same CPU for packet forwarding that is also used for control plane functions, and therefore an increase in the traffic volume handled by the router can result in a proportional increase in CPU load. On switches, this direct relationship between CPU load and traffic load does not exist. The command to display the switch CPU load is **show processes cpu**, which is the same command used in routers. However, because of the difference in implementation of packet-switching process in routers and switches, the conclusions drawn from the output of this command usually differ. Example 7-26 shows sample output from this command.

Example 7-26 show processes cpu *Command Output on a LAN Switch*

```
CSW1# show processes cpu sorted
CPU utilization for five seconds: 23%/18%; one minute: 24%; five minutes: 17%
! 23%, 24%, and 17% indicate total CPU spent on processes and interrupts
  (packet switching). 18% indicates CPU spent on interrupts (packet switching)
PID  Runtime(ms)  Invoked      uSecs   5Sec    1Min    5Min   TTY  Process
170       384912  1632941        235   0.47%   0.35%   0.23%    0  IP Input
 63         8462  5449551          1   0.31%   0.52%   0.33%    0  HLFM address lea
274       101766  1410665         72   0.15%   0.07%   0.04%    0  HSRP IPv4
  4       156599    21649       7233   0.00%   0.07%   0.05%    0  Check heaps
! Output omitted for brevity
```

Example 7-26 shows a scenario where over the past 5 seconds, the switch consumed 23 percent of the available CPU cycles. Of those, 18 percent of CPU cycles were spent on interrupt processing, while only 5 percent was spent on the handling of control plane processes. For a router, this is perfectly acceptable and no reason for alarm. The CPU is forwarding packets and using the CPU to do so, and the total CPU usage is not high enough to warrant further investigation. Of course, this also depends on the normal baseline level of the CPU. However, on a switch, this same output is a reason to investigate. A switch should not spend a significant amount of CPU time on interrupt processing, because the TCAM should forward the bulk of the traffic and the CPU should not be involved. A percentage between 0 percent and 5 percent of CPU load spent on interrupts is considered normal, and a percentage between 5 percent and 10 percent is deemed acceptable, but when CPU time spent in interrupt mode is above 10 percent, you should start to investigate what might be the cause. If the CPU time spent in interrupt mode is high, this means that the switch is forwarding part of the traffic in software instead of the TCAM handling it. The most likely reason for this is TCAM-allocation failures or configuration of unsupported features that cannot be handled in hardware. To troubleshoot CPU problems effectively, it is important to have the baseline measurements for comparison purposes. In general, an average CPU load of 50 percent is not problematic, and temporary bursts to 100 percent are not problematic as long as there is a reasonable explanation for the observed peaks. The following events cause spikes in the CPU utilization:

- **Processor intensive Cisco IOS commands:** Commands such as **show tech-support** or debugs, or even **show running-configuration**, **copy running-config startup-config**, and **write memory** are examples of CPU-intensive commands.
- **Routing protocol update processing:** If the switch is acting as a Layer 3 switch and participating in a routing protocol, it might experience peaks in CPU usage when many routing updates are received at the same time.
- **SNMP polling:** During SNMP discoveries or other bulk transfers of SNMP information by a network management system, the CPU can temporarily peak to 100 percent. If the SNMP process is constantly utilizing a high percentage of the available CPU cycles on a switch, investigate the settings on the network management station that is

polling the device. The device might be polled too often, it might be polled for too much information, or both.

If you are observing CPU spikes that cannot be explained by known events or if you are seeing that the CPU load is high for long periods, further investigation is warranted. First, you have to decide whether the load is caused by interrupts or by processes. If the load is mainly caused by interrupts, investigate the packet-switching behavior of the switch and look for possible TCAM-allocation problems. If the high load is mainly caused by processes, identify the responsible process or processes and see how these can be explained. Example 7-27 shows a case where the IP Input process is responsible for most of the CPU load. The IP Input process is responsible for all IP traffic that is not handled by the TCAM or forwarded in interrupt mode. This includes the transmission of ICMP messages such as unreachable or echo reply packets. Other processes that can be responsible for high CPU load are the following:

- **IP ARP:** This process handles Address Resolutions Protocol (ARP) requests.
- **SNMP Engine:** This process is responsible for answering SNMP requests.
- **IGMPSN:** This process is responsible for Internet Group Management Protocol (IGMP) snooping and processes IGMP packets.

Example 7-27 *A Case of IP Input Process Being Responsible for Most of the CPU Load*

```
CSW1# show processes cpu sorted 5min
CPU utilization for five seconds: 32%/4%; one minute: 32%; five minutes: 26%
PID  Runtime(ms)   Invoked      uSecs     5Sec     1Min     5Min    TTY   Process
170       492557   1723695        285   22.52%   20.57%   15.49%      0   IP Input
 95         7809       693      11268    0.00%    0.00%    0.41%      0   Exec
274       101766   1410665         72    0.15%    0.15%    0.09%      0   HSRP IPv4
  4       158998     21932       7249    0.00%    0.06%    0.05%      0   Check heaps
! Output omitted for brevity
```

A high CPU load due to control plane protocols, such as routing protocols, first-hop redundancy protocols, ARP, and others might be caused by a broadcast storm in the underlying Layer 2 network. In that case, the routing protocols are not the root cause of the problem, but their behavior is a symptom of the underlying problem. This type of scenario is usually dealt with in two stages. For example, assume that a switch is running at 100 percent CPU, because protocols such as the Hot Standby Router Protocol (HSRP), Open Shortest Path First (OSPF), ARP, and the IEEE Spanning Tree Protocol (STP) are all using many CPU cycles as a result of a broadcast storm in the switched network. In this case, consider implementing broadcast and multicast storm control to limit the impact of the excessive broadcasts and multicasts generated by the broadcast storm. However, this is only a workaround, which will help you make the switch more manageable, but it does not solve the underlying problem. The problem could be due to a topological loop, unidirectional link, or a spanning-tree misconfiguration, for example. After implementing this workaround, you must diagnose and resolve the underlying problem that caused the broadcast storm.

DHCP Issues

Dynamic Host Configuration Protocol (DHCP) is commonly used in LAN environments, and sometimes the multilayer switch is configured as a DHCP server. Many issues related to DHCP can result in performance degradation. For example, as shown in Figure 7-12, interface GigabitEthernet0/1 on the switch will forward the broadcasted DHCPDISCOVER of the client to 192.168.2.2.

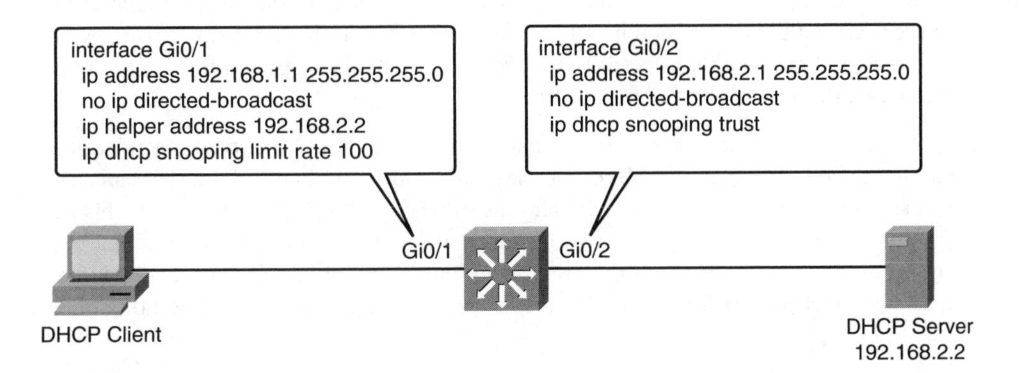

Figure 7-12 *The Gi0/1 Interface Is Configured as a DHCP Relay Agent*

The **limit rate** command on the G0/1 interface will limit the number of DHCP messages that an interface can receive per second, and can have an impact on switch performance if set incorrectly. This issue is related to misconfiguration, and even though the network is to blame in terms of the apparent source of the issue, the actual problem is related to poor planning and baselining of the network and improper tuning of a feature such as DHCP snooping.

Other sources of DHCP issues that can have performance impact can be subject to abuse by nonmalicious and malicious users. In the case of malicious attacks, many exploit tools are readily available and are easy to use. An example of those tools is Gobbler, a public domain hacking tool that performs automated DHCP starvation attacks. DHCP starvation can be purely a denial-of-service (DoS) mechanism or can be used in conjunction with a malicious rogue server attack to redirect traffic to a malicious computer ready to intercept traffic. This method effectively performs DoS attacks using DHCP leases. Gobbler looks at the entire DHCP pool and tries to lease all the DHCP addresses available in the DHCP scope. Several security controls, such as port security, DHCP snooping, and DHCP rate limits, are available to mitigate this type of attack. However, you must consider security vulnerabilities and threats when isolating the problem from a troubleshooting perspective.

Spanning-Tree Issues

STP is a common source of switch performance degradation. An ill-behaving instance of STP might slow down the network and the switch. The impact is that the switch might drop bridge protocol data units (BPDUs), and as a result go into Listening state. This problem causes unneeded reconvergence phases that lead to even more congestion and performance degradation. STP issues can also cause topology loops. If one or more switches no longer receive or process BPDUs, they will not be able to discover the network topology. Without knowledge of the correct topology, the switch cannot block the loops. Therefore, the flooded traffic will circulate over the looped topology, consume bandwidth, and result in high CPU utilization. Other STP situations include issues related to capacity planning. Per-VLAN Spanning Tree Plus (PVST+) creates an instance of the protocol for each VLAN. When many VLANs exist, each additional instance represents a burden. The CPU time utilized by STP varies depending on the number of spanning-tree instances and the number of active interfaces. The more instances and the more active interfaces, the greater the CPU utilization.

STP might also impact on network and bandwidth utilization. Most recommendations call for a deterministic approach to selecting root bridges. In Figure 7-13, there are two roots: one for VLANs 10, 30, and 50; and the other for VLANs 20, 40, and 60. This way, the designated or blocked ports are selected in such a way that allows for load sharing across the infrastructure. If, on the other hand, only one root is selected, there will be only one blocked port for all VLANs, preventing a more balanced utilization of all links.

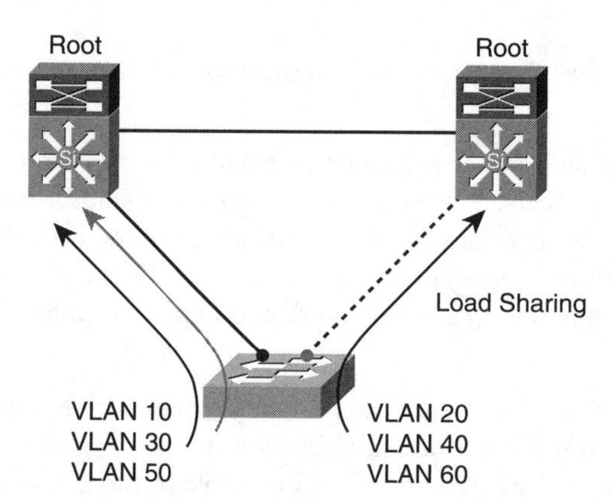

Figure 7-13 *PVST and MST Allow for Load Sharing Through the Selection of Multiple Root Devices*

Finally, by just having poor control over the selection of root bridges, you could be causing severe traffic performance problems. For example, if an access switch is selected as the root, a high-bandwidth link between switches might go into Blocking state, or the simple access switch might become a transit point and be flooded and overwhelmed.

HSRP

Hot Standby Router Protocol (HSRP) is another common function implemented in switches. Because of the nature of HSRP, specific network problems can lead to HSRP instability and to performance degradation. Several HSRP-related problems are not true HSRP issues. Instead, they are network problems that affect the behavior of HSRP. Common HSRP-specific issues include the following:

- **Duplicate HSRP standby IP addresses:** This problem typically occurs when both switches in the HSRP group go into the active state. A variety of problems can cause this behavior, including momentary STP loops, EtherChannel configuration issues, or duplicated frames.
- **Constant HSRP state changes:** These changes cause network performance problems, application timeouts, and connectivity disruption. Poor selection of HSRP timers, such as hello and hold time, in the presence of flapping links or hardware issues, can cause the state changes.
- **Missing HSRP peers:** If an HSRP peer is missing, the fault tolerance offered by HSRP is at stake. The peer may only appear as missing because of network problems.
- **Switch error messages that relate to HSRP:** These messages might indicate issues such as duplicate addresses that need to be addressed.

Switch Performance Troubleshooting Example: Speed and Duplex Settings

The first switch performance troubleshooting example is a case of a user complaining about speed issues when downloading large files from a file server. This user has been using his PC for several months and never noticed a problem before. The problem occurred after a maintenance window over the weekend. Although the user can access the file server, the speed, when downloading large files, is unacceptable. You must determine whether there has been any degradation in network performance over the weekend and restore the connectivity to its original performance levels. You need to decide on a troubleshooting method. The difficulty in this kind of case is that it revolves around performance issues, and performance is something that can be very subjective. Determining a baseline is a critical part of analyzing this troubleshooting task. If you have a baseline and can compare current performance against pervious performance, you can determine if there is in fact degradation in network performance. After establishing that, you can look for places in the network where this degradation may occur. In this case, we have a simple scenario with one switch one PC and one file server, as shown in Figure 7-14. If there is degradation of performance, it has to be occurring between the PC and the switch, within the switch, or between the switch and the file server. The fact that no other users are complaining about download speed might lead you to believe that this problem is between the PC and the switch.

A call to the maintenance team tells you that the maintenance over the weekend involved reorganizing the switch's connectivity to the network. In other words, port configurations

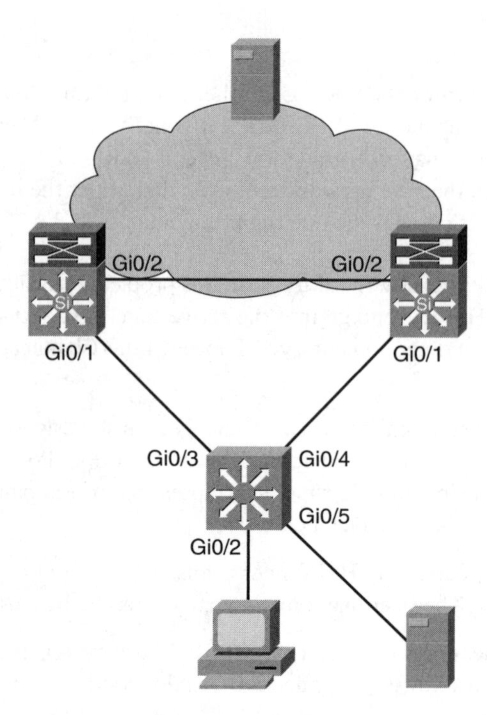

Figure 7-14 *Network Diagram for the First Switch Performance Troubleshooting Example*

were changed, and PCs were connected to different ports over the weekend. This points to a problem with the port to which the PC connects. The fact that the PC and the file server are in the same VLAN makes it unlikely that the issue comes from the switch itself. Because both devices are in the same VLAN, switching occurs in hardware, and should be very fast. To be thorough, confirm the PC connection to the switch and the file server connection to the switch. The first task is to confirm the interfaces with the **show interfaces** command, as demonstrated in Example 7-28. The output confirms that the interface connecting to the PC is up and line protocol is up. So, everything seems to be normal on that side. Using the same command for the file server interface shows the same status. So, there is no problem with the connection itself. If the user can connect to the Internet and the network and download files from the file server, the issue is not about connectivity, it is about performance.

Example 7-28 *Checking the Status of the Interfaces Connecting to the PC and to the Server*

```
Switch# show interfaces Gi 0/2
GigabitEthernet0/2 is up, line protocol is up (connected)
  Hardware is Gigabit Ethernet, address is 0023.5d08.5682 (bia 0023.5d08.5682)
  Description: to new PC
```

```
! Output omitted for brevity

Switch# show interfaces Gi 0/5
GigabitEthernet0/5 is up, line protocol is up (connected)
  Hardware is Gigabit Ethernet, address is 0023.5d08.5685 (bia 0023.5d08.5685)
  Description: to file server
! Output omitted for brevity
```

You now use **the show controller utilization** command to check the bandwidth utilization on the ports connecting to the server (port G0/5) and the client (port G0/2). This can help you verify that you indeed have a performance issue as demonstrated in Example 7-29. The large discrepancy in the receive and transmit utilization on the user port is due to the fact that the traffic is mostly file downloads. The user is receiving much more than he is sending.

Example 7-29 *Utilization Results on the Ports Connecting to the Server and Client*

```
Switch# sh controller g0/5 utilization
Receive Bandwidth Percentage Utilization      : 0
Transmit Bandwidth Percentage Utilization     : 0

Switch# sh controller g0/2 utilization
Receive Bandwidth Percentage Utilization      : 2
Transmit Bandwidth Percentage Utilization     : 76

Switch#
```

Next, you ask the user to start a download so that you can monitor the performance of the connection, but first you clear the counters for the user interface. While the download runs, there are useful commands to monitor activity on the interface. The first command is **show interface accounting**, which shows you what kind of traffic is going through the interface. The output (as shown in Example 7-30) shows some STP packets, Cisco Discovery Protocol (CDP) packets, and other packets. There is not a lot of activity, so you do not expect a loop or spanning-tree issue. The traffic bottleneck must come from data itself.

Example 7-30 *The Output Does Not Show a Lot of Activity on the User Port*

```
Switch# clear counters g0/2
Clear "show interface" counters on this interface [confirm]
Switch#
Switch# sh int g0/2 accounting
GigabitEthernet0/2 to new PC
                 Protocol     Pkts In   Chars In   Pkts Out   Chars Out
```

```
                    Other          0          0          6        360
            Spanning Tree          0          0         32       1920
                      CDP          0          0          1        397
Switch#
```

To find out why the user application is slow, use the **show interface g0/2 stats** command as demonstrated in Example 7-31. Of course, the values here do not mean much without a baseline for comparison; however, considering the switch model and the overall traffic on the network, it is safe to assume that these values are within the normal range. So, the switch itself is performing normally. Immediately, you try the **show interface counters errors** command to have a closer look at the interface error counters. As shown in Example 7-31, the single-collision and multiple-collision counters report the number of times a collision occurred before the interface transmitted a frame onto the media successfully. In other words, the switch tried to transmit a frame to the PC, but a collision occurred, and the frame could not be transmitted. When the frame could not be sent the first time and succeeded the second time, you see the single-collision counter increment. If the same frame suffers a number of collisions, the multiple-collision counters increase. This output shows a lot of single collisions and quite a few multiple collisions. The OutDiscards counter is also noteworthy. This counter shows the number of outbound frames discarded even though no error has been detected. In other words, the switch needed to send these frames, but ended up discarding them without sending them at all, possibly to free up buffer space. In other words, the speed of the link is so slow that the switch cannot send the frame in a reasonable time and has to discard it.

Example 7-31 *The Results of the* **show interface g0/2 stats** *Command Look Normal*

```
Switch# show int g0/2 stats
GigabitEthernet0/2
          Switching path    Pkts In   Chars In   Pkts Out   Chars Out
               Processor          0          0        156       11332
             Route cache          0          0          0           0
                   Total          0          0        156       11332
Switch#
Switch#show int g0/2 counters errors

Port      Align-Err    FCS-Err    Xmit-Err     Rcv-Err   UnderSize   OutDiscards
Gi0/2             0          0           0           0           0          3495

Port   Single-Col   Multi-Col  Late-Col  Excess-Col  Carri-Sen   Runts    Giants
Gi0/2      126243       37823         0           0          0       0         0
Switch#
```

The PCs are new enough to support full duplex, so there should not be any collisions. You verify the switch interface for parameters such as speed and duplex setting. The results shown in Example 7-32 reveal that the interface is set to half duplex and 10 Mbps. This could be a configuration mistake or due to autonegotiation with the PC.

Example 7-32 *The Switch Port Is Operating at 10 Mbps and Half Duplex*

```
Switch# show int g0/2 | include duplex
  Half-duplex, 10Mb/s, media type is 10/100/1000BaseTX
Switch#
```

The running configuration for the switch interface, shown in Example 7-33, reveals that it is manually configured. You know that PCs were moved over the weekend. Perhaps the device that was once connected to this port required half duplex and 10 Mbps. Therefore, you reconfigure the interface to auto speed and duplex settings and confirm with the user that this has resolved the issue.

Example 7-33 *Auto Speed and Duplex Settings on the Switch Port Solve the Problem*

```
Switch# show running-config int g0/2
Building configuration...

Current configuration : 166 bytes
!
interface GigabitEthernet0/2
 description to new PC
 switchport access vlan 50
 switchport mode access
 speed 10
 duplex half
 mls qos trust cos
 no mdix auto
end

Switch#

Switch# configure terminal
Enter configuration commands, one per line. End with CNTL/Z.
Switch(config)# int g0/2
Switch(config-if)# speed auto

% Speed autonegotiation subset must not contain 1Gbps when duplex is set to half

Switch(config-if)# duplex auto
Switch(config-if)# end
Switch#
```

Switch Performance Troubleshooting Example: Excessive Broadcasts

The second switch performance troubleshooting example concerns a user with complaints about connectivity issues. The user reports that sometimes he cannot connect to the network at all, and his PC will not even get an IP address. Other times, he is able to connect, but the connection is of poor quality (experiencing slow downloads and connection timeouts). The issue seems to have started a few days ago and is not consistently occurring all day long. Because several other users have also reported the issue and they all connect to the same switch, the most logical approach is "follow the path." The place to start is with one PC's connectivity to the switch and then verifying the switch itself. Next, you'll verify the uplink from the switch to the rest of the network. You start troubleshooting at port GigabitEthernet0/2 where the user the PC is connected to, by checking the speed and duplex setting, controller utilization, and interface errors. The results are shown in Example 7-34. The port is operating at full duplex and 1000 Mbps, and the **show controllers g0/2 utilization** displays a near 0 port utilization. You need to verify that the PC is actually connected. The **show interfaces** command reveals that the interface is up and line protocol is up, and the statistics near the bottom of the output seem normal.

Example 7-34 *Investigating the User's Port Shows No Problem at Port Level*

```
Switch# show int g0/2 | include duplex
  Full-duplex, 1000Mb/s, media type is 10/100/1000BaseTX
Switch#
Switch# show controllers g0/2 utilization
Receive Bandwidth Percentage utilization      : 0
Transmit Bandwidth Percentage utilization     : 0

Switch# show int g0/2
GigabitEthernet0/2 is up, line protocol is up (connected)
  Hardware is Gigabit Ethernet, address is 0023.5d08.5682 (bia 0023.5d08.5682)
  Description: to new PC
  MTU 1504 bytes, BW 1000000 Kbit, DLY 10 usec,
     reliability 255/255, txload 4/255, rxload 1/255
  Encapsulation ARPA, loopback not set
  Keepalive set (10 sec)
  Full-duplex, 1000Mb/s, media type is 10/100/1000BaseTX
  input flow-control is off, output flow-control is unsupported
  ARP type: ARPA, ARP Timeout 04:00:00
  Last input never, output 00:00:00, output hang never
  Last clearing of "show interface" counters 01:01:23
  Input Queue: 0/75/0/0 (size/max/drops/flushes); Total output drops: 74855
  Queueing strategy: fifo
  Output queue: 0/40 (size/max)
  5 minute input rate 128000 bits/sec, 261 packets/sec
  5 minute output rate 17019000 bits/sec, 6559 packets/sec
```

```
     400082 packets input, 26803863 bytes, 0 no buffer
     Received 174 broadcasts (21 multicasts)
     0 runts, 0 giants, 0 throttles
     0 input errores, 0 CRC, 0 frame, 0 overrun, 0 ignored
     0 watchdog, 21 multicast, 0 pause input
     0 input packets with dribble condition detected
     10277284 packets output, 2907407121 bytes, 0 underruns
     0 output errors, 207597 collisions, 2 interface resets
     0 babbles, 0 late collision, 0 deferred
     0 lost carrier, 0 no carrier, 0 PAUSE output
     0 output buffer failures, 0 output buffers swapped out
Switch#
```

Because there is no communication problem between the switch and the PC, the problem might be within the switch itself. Check to see whether the switch is overloaded using the **show processes cpu** command, as demonstrated in Example 7-35. The output displays that CPU utilization is 98 percent over 5 seconds, 94 percent over 1 minute, and 92 percent over 5 minutes! That is very high: the switch is definitely overloaded, and you need to find out why.

Example 7-35 *CPU Utilization Is Alarmingly High*

```
Switch# show processes cpu
CPU utilization for five seconds: 98%/18%; one minute: 94%; five minutes 92%

PID  Runtime(ms)   Invoked   usecs    5Sec    1Min    5Min   TTY   Process
1            0        15        0   0.00%   0.00%   0.00%     0   Chunk Manager
2           24      1517       15   0.00%   0.00%   0.00%     0   Load Meter
3            0         1        0   0.00%   0.00%   0.00%     0   CEF RP IPC Backg
4        16496      1206    13678   0.00%   0.00%   0.00%     0   Check heaps
5            0         1        0   0.00%   0.00%   0.00%     0   Pool Manager
6            0         2        0   0.00%   0.00%   0.00%     0   Timers
7            0         1        0   0.00%   0.00%   0.00%     0   Image Licensing
8            0         2        0   0.00%   0.00%   0.00%     0   License Client N
9         2293        26   115115   0.00%   0.00%   0.00%     0   Licensing Auto U
10           0         1        0   0.00%   0.00%   0.00%     0   Crash writer
11     3330507    521208     6389  44.08%  37.34%  33.94%     0   ARP Input
12           0         1        0   0.00%   0.00%   0.00%     0   CEF MIB API
13           0         1        0   0.00%   0.00%   0.00%     0   AAA_SERVER_DEADT
14           0         2        0   0.00%   0.00%   0.00%     0   AAA high-capacit
15           0         1        0   0.00%   0.00%   0.00%     0   Policy Manager
16           0         5     1800   0.00%   0.00%   0.00%     0   Entity MIB API
17           0         1        0   0.00%   0.00%   0.00%     0   IFS Agent Manage
18           0       128        0   0.00%   0.00%   0.00%     0   IPC Dynamic Cach
--More--
```

Next, use the **show processes cpu sorted** command, which classifies the processes by task and CPU consumption, to discover the processes that use up most of the CPU cycles. The results shown in Example 7-36 reveal that ARP is consuming half of the resources on this switch. That is definitely not normal. Having a certain amount of ARP processing is normal, but not to the point where it is consuming more than 40 percent of the resources. Using the command **show interfaces accounting**, you discover that vlan10 is the where the excessive ARP packets are located (also shown in Example 7-36).

Example 7-36 show processes cpu *Reveals 42 Percent of CPU Utilization Is Due to ARP*

```
Switch# show processes cpu sorted
CPU utilization for five seconds: 94%/19%; one minute: 97%; five minutes: 94%
PID   Runtime(ms)   Invoked   usecs    5Sec    1Min    5Min  TTY  Process
 11       3384474    529325    6393  42.97%  41.59%  36.35%    0  ARP Input
178       2260178    569064    2971  15.01%  17.25%  21.34%    0  IP Input
205         31442     26263    1197   5.43%   6.31%   4.38%    0  DHCPD Receive
124        341457    215879    1581   2.71%   3.02%   2.91%    0  Hulc LED Process
 89        289092    180034    1605   2.55%   2.77%   2.70%    0  hpm main process
 92         80558      7535   10691   0.63%   0.79%   0.83%    0  hpm counter proc
183          1872      1379    1357   0.15%   0.08%   0.03%    1  virtual Exec
 31          2004      4898     409   0.15%   0.02%   0.00%    0  Net Background
184          5004     19263     259   0.15%   0.04%   0.02%    0  Spanning Tree
132         19307      1549   12464   0.15%   0.17%   0.16%    0  HQM Stack Proces
 72         26070    209264     124   0.15%   0.13%   0.15%    0  HLFM address lea
 56         31258    115660     270   0.15%   0.29%   0.27%    0  RedEarth Tx Mana
112          6672     37587     177   0.15%   0.07%   0.04%    0  Hulc Storm Contr
 13             0         1       0   0.00%   0.00%   0.00%    0  AAA_SERVER_DEADT
 15             0         1       0   0.00%   0.00%   0.00%    0  Policy Manager
 14             0         2       0   0.00%   0.00%   0.00%    0  AAA high-capacit
 12             0         1       0   0.00%   0.00%   0.00%    0  CEF MIB API
 18             0       129       0   0.00%   0.00%   0.00%    0  IPC Dynamic Cach
--More--
Switch# show interfaces accounting
vlan1
                   Protocol    Pkts In   Chars In   Pkts Out   Chars Out
                         IP         35       4038          2         684
                        ARP         13        780         15         900
vlan6
                   Protocol    Pkts In   Chars In   Pkts Out   Chars Out
                        ARP          0          0         14         840
```

```
vlan8
                Protocol    Pkts In   Chars In   Pkts Out   Chars Out
                     ARP          0          0         14         840
vlan10
                Protocol    Pkts In   Chars In   Pkts Out   Chars Out
                      IP   16705943 1727686324      77739    26586738
                     ARP   10594397  635663820        484       29040

Vlan12
                Protocol    Pkts In   Chars In   Pkts Out   Chars Out
                     ARP          0          0         14         840
--More--
```

The **show vlan** command (not shown) reveals that Gi 0/2, 9, 11, 12, 13, and 22 are in vlan10.

To find out which of these ports is the source of the excessive ARP packets, use the **show interfaces** *interface* **controller include broadcasts** command. This command, with the **include broadcasts** parameter, displays the broadcast section of the output only. The results, shown in Example 7-37, point to g0/11 and g0/13 ports, to which the wireless access points (WAPs) are connected. You now know that these are the broadcasts from the wireless clients, and because the WAPs act like hubs, they forward all their client broadcasts to the switch.

Example 7-37 *The* **show controller** *Command Output Displays an Excessive Number of Broadcasts*

```
Switch# show interfaces g0/2 controller ¦ inc broadcast
     Received 236 broadcasts (28 multicasts)
Switch# show interfaces g0/9 controller ¦ inc broadcast
     Received 0 broadcasts (0 multicasts)
Switch# show interfaces g0/11 controller ¦ inc broadcast
     Received 2829685 broadcasts (2638882 multicasts)
Switch# show interfaces g0/13 controller ¦ inc broadcast
     Received 41685559 broadcasts (145888 multicasts)
Switch# show interfaces g0/22 controller ¦ inc broadcast
     Received 0 broadcasts (0 multicasts)
Switch#
```

To reduce the impact of the wireless broadcast on the wired network, you can limit the amount of broadcasts the switch accepts from those ports. As demonstrated in Example 7-38, you use the **storm-control** command on g0/11 and g0/13 interfaces to limit broadcasts (because ARP requests are broadcasts) to three packets per second. Next, you observe the positive results on the output of the **show processes cpu sorted** command. You confirm with the users that they are no longer experiencing any problems and document your work.

Example 7-38 *The* storm-control *Command on the Interface Solves the Problem*

```
Switch# conf t
Enter configuration commands, one per line. End with CNTL/Z.
Switch(config)# int g0/11
Switch(config-if)# storm-control broadcast level pps 3
Switch(config-if)# int g0/13
Switch(config-if)# storm-control broadcast level pps 3
Switch(config-if)# end
Switch#
Switch# sh process cpu sorted
PID  Runtime(ms)   Invoked    usecs    5Sec    1Min    5Min   TTY  Process
 11      3770480    607472     6206  11.50%   3.65%   4.94%     0  ARP Input
  4        19773      1472    13432   0.31%   0.11%   0.11%     0  Check heaps
144         7650      9228      828   0.15%   0.11%   0.13%     0  PI MATM Aging Pr
183         2559      2062     1241   0.15%   0.03%   0.00%     1  Virtual Exec
214         9467     20611      459   0.15%   0.01%   0.00%     0  Marvell wk-a Pow
 92        91428      9224     9911   0.15%   0.23%   0.30%     0  hpm counter proc
 89       316788    218111     1452   0.15%   0.24%   0.39%     0  hpm main process
  7            0         1        0   0.00%   0.00%   0.00%     0  Image Licensing
  6            0         2        0   0.00%   0.00%   0.00%     0  Timers
  5            0         1        0   0.00%   0.00%   0.00%     0  Pool Manager
  8            0         2        0   0.00%   0.00%   0.00%     0  License Client N
  9         3714        32   116062   0.00%   0.01%   0.00%     0  Licensing Auto U
 13            0         1        0   0.00%   0.00%   0.00%     0  AAA_SERVER_DEADT
 10            0         1        0   0.00%   0.00%   0.00%     0  Crash writer
  2           24      1878       12   0.00%   0.00%   0.00%     0  Load Meter
 16            9         5     1800   0.00%   0.00%   0.00%     0  Entity MIB API
 17            0         1        0   0.00%   0.00%   0.00%     0  IFS Agent Manage
 12            0         1        0   0.00%   0.00%   0.00%     0  CEF MIB API
--More--
```

Switch Performance Troubleshooting Example: Excessive Security

The third and final switch performance troubleshooting example is about a case where users connecting to a specific switch have connectivity issues and say that while working with their PCs a window sometimes pops up indicating that their network cable is unplugged. At other times, the PC reports that the cable is plugged in, but the connection is very bad. Many of the user workstations cannot even obtain an IP address from the DHCP server. Those who do receive IP addresses find the network unusable. Almost all users connected to this switch experience the same problem. When you look at the maintenance log for this network, you see that a security update occurred on this switch.

When security is involved, a common approach is divide and conquer, starting at Layer 4, and determine whether the problem is above or below this layer. Often when security is involved, Layer 3 or Layer 4 security policies are blocking the traffic. However, you cannot ignore the PC message that says the cable is unplugged. That cannot be a security configuration, and you need to investigate.

Use a bottom-up approach for this example, starting at one of the PCs, which is connected to the switch Gi0/2 interface. You first confirm that the PC is connected using the **show interfaces** command, and see that it is up/up (see the results in Example 7-39). You must remember that the user reported that the connection is intermittent, so although it might be connected now, it might have been disconnected a moment ago. Therefore, you reset the counters on the interface.

Example 7-39 *Cisco IOS IPS CLI Configuration*

```
Switch# sh int g0/2
GigabitEthernet0/2 is up, line protocol is up (connected)
  Hardware is Gigabit Ethernet, address is 0023.5d08.5682 (bia 0023.5d08.5682)
  Description: to new PC
  MTU 1504 bytes, BW 1000000 Kbit, DLY 10 usec,
     reliability 255/255, txload 1/255, rxload 1/255
  Encapsulation ARPA, loopback not set
  Keepalive set (10 sec)
  Full-duplex, 1000Mb/s, media type is 10/100/1000BaseTX
  input flow-control is off, output flow-control is unsupported
  ARP type: ARPA, ARP Timeout 04:00:00
  Last input never, output 00:00:00, output hang never
  Last clearing of "show interface" counters 03:55:56
  Input Queue: 0/75/0/0 (size/max/drops/flushes); Total output drops: 74855
  Queueing strategy: fifo
  Output queue: 0/40 (size/max)
  5 minute input rate 107000 bits/sec, 9 packets/sec
  5 minute output rate 1233000 bits/sec, 2411 packets/sec
     439536 packets input, 85060088 bytes, 0 no buffer
     Received 343 broadcasts (28 multicasts)
     0 runts, 0 giants, 0 throttles
     0 input errores, 0 CRC, 0 frame, 0 overrun, 0 ignored
     0 watchdog, 28 multicast, 0 pause input
     0 input packets with dribble condition detected
--More--

Switch# clear counters
Clear "show interface" counters on all interfaces [confirm]
Switch#
```

Next, you contact the user and ask whether the problem is occurring. The user reports that the problem is occurring right at that moment. You use the **show interface** command again and see that the counters increase, meaning that some packets are being sent and received. You tend to think about a cabling issue, but it is not likely that all users all of a sudden have bad cables. Just to be sure, you replace the cable, but the problem remains, as expected.

The problems were reported after a security update, although the problem is intermittent; however, a problem caused by security policy would be consistent. After eliminating Layer 1 as a possible problem cause, you move on to Layer 2 and continue researching by checking the user's VLAN using the **show vlan** command, as demonstrated in Example 7-40. The user is in VLAN 10.

Example 7-40 *The Access Port to Which the User Is Connected Is in VLAN 10*

```
Switch# show vlan
VLAN   Name                             Status     Ports
--     ----------------                 -----      ----------------
1      default                          active     Gi0/1, Gi0/4, Gi0/6, Gi0/7
                                                   Gi0/8, Gi0/10, Gi0/18, Gi0/24
                                                   Gi0/25, Gi0/26, Gi0/27, Gi0/28
3      VLAN0003                         active
6      VLAN0006                         active
8      VLAN0008                         active
9      VLAN0009                         active
10     VLAN0010                         active     Gi0/2, Gi0/9, Gi0/11, Gi0/12
                                                   Gi0/13, Gi0/22
11     VLAN0011                         active
12     VLAN0012                         active
14     VLAN0014                         active
20     VLAN0020                         active     Gi0/21
34     VLAN0034                         active
50     VLAN0050                         act/unsup  Gi0/3, Gi0/5, Gi0/17, Gi0/19
                                                   Gi0/20, Gi0/23
63     VLAN0063                         active
99     VLAN0099                         active
543    VLAN0543                         active
1002   fddi-default                     active

Switch#
```

Next, knowing that security policies can be implemented at Layer 2 using VLAN filters, you check if a VLAN filter is applied to VLAN 10. The **show vlan filter vlan 10** command output (shown in Example 7-41) reveals that a filter called VLAN10_OUT is applied to VLAN 10. Naturally, you display this filter using the **show vlan access-map VLAN10_OUT** command, so you can analyze it.

Example 7-41 *Discovering and Inspecting a Filter Applied to VLAN 10*

```
Switch# sh vlan filter vlan 10
vlan 10 has filter VLAN10_OUT
Switch#
Switch# sh vlan access-map VLAN10_OUT
Vlan access-map "VLAN10_OUT" 10
 Match clauses:
   ip address: VLAN10_OUT
 Action:
   forward
Vlan access-map "VLAN10_OUT" 20
 Match clauses:
   ip address: VLAN11_OUT
 Action:
   forward
Vlan access-map "VLAN10_OUT" 30
 Match clauses:
   ip address: VLAN12_OUT  VLAN13_OUT  VLAN14_OUT  VLAN15_OUT
 Action:
   forward
Switch#
```

You can see that all of the access maps match on IP address, so this would not have an effect on Layer 1 or 2. To be sure, display one of these access lists (see Example 7-42). You get overwhelmed to see that the access list has more than 400 entries! The situation is made worse by the fact that several access lists are referenced for the packets going into or out of this VLAN.

Example 7-42 *Access List VLAN10_OUT Is Very Large*

```
Switch# sh access-list VLAN10_OUT
Extended IP access list VLAN10_OUT
    2 permit tcp 10.1.20.0 0.0.0.255 host 10.10.50.124 eq domain
    10 permit tcp 10.1.1.0 0.0.0.255 host 10.10.150.24 eq www
    11 permit tcp 10.1.1.0 0.0.0.255 host 10.10.151.24 eq www
    20 permit tcp 10.1.1.0 0.0.0.255 host 10.10.150.24 eq 22
    21 permit tcp 10.1.1.0 0.0.0.255 host 10.10.151.24 eq 22
    30 permit tcp 10.1.1.0 0.0.0.255 host 10.10.150.24 eq telnet
    31 permit tcp 10.1.1.0 0.0.0.255 host 10.10.151.24 eq telnet
    40 permit tcp 10.1.1.0 0.0.0.255 host 10.10.150.24 eq 443
    41 permit tcp 10.1.1.0 0.0.0.255 host 10.10.151.24 eq 443
    50 permit udp 10.1.1.0 0.0.0.255 host 10.10.150.24 eq snmp
    51 permit udp 10.1.1.0 0.0.0.255 host 10.10.151.24 eq snmp
    60 permit udp 10.1.1.0 0.0.0.255 host 10.10.150.24 eq snmptrap
```

```
    61 permit udp 10.1.1.0 0.0.0.255 host 10.10.151.24 eq snmptrap
    70 permit tcp 10.1.1.0 0.0.0.255 host 10.10.150.24 eq ftp
    71 permit tcp 10.1.1.0 0.0.0.255 host 10.10.151.24 eq ftp
    80 permit tcp 10.1.1.0 0.0.0.255 host 10.10.150.24 eq ftp-data
    81 permit tcp 10.1.1.0 0.0.0.255 host 10.10.151.24 eq ftp-data
    90 permit tcp 10.1.1.0 0.0.0.255 host 10.10.150.24 eq domain
    91 permit tcp 10.1.1.0 0.0.0.255 host 10.10.151.24 eq domain
    100 permit tcp 10.1.1.0 0.0.0.255 host 10.10.150.99 eq domain
! Output omitted for brevity
    3920 permit tcp 10.1.40.0 0.0.0.255 host 10.10.50.99 eq 90
    3930 permit udp 10.1.40.0 0.0.0.255 host 10.10.50.99 eq snmp
    3940 permit udp 10.1.40.0 0.0.0.255 host 10.10.50.99 eq snmptrap
    3950 permit tcp 10.1.40.0 0.0.0.255 host 10.10.50.99 eq ftp
    3960 permit tcp 10.1.40.0 0.0.0.255 host 10.10.50.99 eq ftp-data
    3961 permit tcp any host 10.10.50.100 eq ftp-data
    3962 permit tcp any host 10.10.50.100 eq ftp (730 matches
Switch#
```

Next, check to see whether an IP access list is applied to the VLAN 10 interface, using the command **show ip interface vlan 10**. The output, shown in Example 7-43, reveals both an outgoing and an inbound access list VLAN10 applied to the VLAN 10 interface.

Example 7-43 *An Outgoing and an Incoming Access List Is Applied to Interface VLAN 10*

```
Switch# sh ip int vlan 10
Vlan10 is up, line protocol is up
  Internet address is 10.1.1.1/24
  Broadcast address is 255.255.255.255
  Address determined by nonvolatile memory
  MTU is 1500 bytes
  Helper address is not set
  Directed broadcast forwarding is disabled
  Outgoing access list is VLAN10
  Inbound access list is VLAN10
  Proxy ARP is enabled
  Local Proxy ARP is disabled
  Security level is default
  Split horizon is enabled
  ICMP redirects are always sent
  ICMP unreachables are always sent
  ICMP mask replies are never sent
  IP fast switching is enabled
  IP CEF switching is enabled
  IP CEF switching turbo vector
```

```
  IP Null turbo vector
  IP multicast fast switching is enabled
  IP multicast distributed fast switching is disabled
  IP route-cache flags are Fast, CEF
--More--
```

When you display access list VLAN 10, you observe a huge output similar to the output when you displayed access list VLAN10_OUT (see Example 7-44). You cannot help but to wonder if this access list is affecting switch performance so badly that users cannot connect.

Example 7-44 *Access List VLAN 10 Also Has Too Many Lines*

```
Switch# sh access-li VLAN10
Extended IP access list VLAN10_OUT
     10 permit tcp 10.1.1.0 0.0.0.255 host 10.10.50.24 eq www
     11 permit tcp 10.1.1.0 0.0.0.255 host 10.10.151.24 eq www
     20 permit tcp 10.1.1.0 0.0.0.255 host 10.10.50.24 eq 22
     21 permit tcp 10.1.1.0 0.0.0.255 host 10.10.151.24 eq 22
     30 permit tcp 10.1.1.0 0.0.0.255 host 10.10.50.24 eq telnet
     31 permit tcp 10.1.1.0 0.0.0.255 host 10.10.151.24 eq telnet
     40 permit tcp 10.1.1.0 0.0.0.255 host 10.10.50.24 eq 443
     41 permit tcp 10.1.1.0 0.0.0.255 host 10.10.151.24 eq 443
     50 permit udp 10.1.1.0 0.0.0.255 host 10.10.50.24 eq snmp
     51 permit udp 10.1.1.0 0.0.0.255 host 10.10.151.24 eq snmp
     60 permit udp 10.1.1.0 0.0.0.255 host 10.10.50.24 eq snmptrap
     61 permit udp 10.1.1.0 0.0.0.255 host 10.10.151.24 eq snmptrap
     70 permit tcp 10.1.1.0 0.0.0.255 host 10.10.50.24 eq ftp
     71 permit tcp 10.1.1.0 0.0.0.255 host 10.10.151.24 eq ftp
     80 permit tcp 10.1.1.0 0.0.0.255 host 10.10.50.24 eq ftp-data
     81 permit tcp 10.1.1.0 0.0.0.255 host 10.10.151.24 eq ftp-data
     90 permit tcp 10.1.1.0 0.0.0.255 host 10.10.50.24 eq domain
     91 permit tcp 10.1.1.0 0.0.0.255 host 10.10.151.24 eq domain
     100 permit tcp 10.1.1.0 0.0.0.255 host 10.10.50.99 eq domain
     101 permit tcp 10.1.1.0 0.0.0.255 host 10.10.151.99 eq domain
     110 permit tcp 10.1.1.0 0.0.0.255 host 10.10.50.99 eq 3389
     111 permit tcp 10.1.1.0 0.0.0.255 host 10.10.151.99 eq 33894
     120 permit tcp 10.1.1.0 0.0.0.255 host 10.10.50.99 eq 3114
     121 permit tcp 10.1.1.0 0.0.0.255 host 10.10.151.99 eq 3114
     130 permit tcp 10.1.1.0 0.0.0.255 host 10.10.50.99 eq 10000
     131 permit tcp 10.1.1.0 0.0.0.255 host 10.10.151.99 eq 10000
     140 permit tcp 10.1.1.0 0.0.0.255 host 10.10.50.99 eq 3124
     141 permit tcp 10.1.1.0 0.0.0.255 host 10.10.151.99 eq 3124
     150 permit tcp 10.1.1.0 0.0.0.255 host 10.10.50.99 eq www
```

```
    151 permit tcp 10.1.1.0 0.0.0.255 host 10.10.151.99 eq www
    160 permit tcp 10.1.1.0 0.0.0.255 host 10.10.50.99 eq 22
    161 permit tcp 10.1.1.0 0.0.0.255 host 10.10.151.99 eq 22
    170 permit tcp 10.1.1.0 0.0.0.255 host 10.10.50.99 eq telnet
    171 permit tcp 10.1.1.0 0.0.0.255 host 10.10.151.99 eq telnet
    180 permit tcp 10.1.1.0 0.0.0.255 host 10.10.50.99 eq 443
    181 permit tcp 10.1.1.0 0.0.0.255 host 10.10.151.99 eq 443
    190 permit udp 10.1.1.0 0.0.0.255 host 10.10.50.9
! Output omitted for brevity
```

You know that access lists are managed by the TCAM. So, access list entries should not be managed by the CPU. However, if the TCAM is full, packets will be sent to the CPU for processing (punt). You can verify this using the **show platform tcam utilization** command. The results in Example 7-45 display the TCAM entries and utilization of these entries.

Example 7-45 *IP Security Access Lines Are Near the Maximum Values*

```
Switch# show platform tcam utilization

CAM utilization for ASIC# 0                          Max               Used
                                                 Masks/Values      Masks/Values
Unicast mac addresses:                            6364/6364           29/29
IPv4 IGMP groups + multicast routes:              1120/1120            1/1
IPv4 unicast directly-connected routes:           6144/6144            5/5
IPv4 unicast indirectly-connected routes:         2048/2048           39/39
IPv4 policy based routing aces:                    452/452            12/12
IPv4 qos aces:                                     512/512             8/8
IPv4 security aces:                                964/964           790/790


Note: Allocation of TCAM entries per feature uses
A complex algorithm. The above information is meant
To provide an abstract view of the current TCAM utilization

Switch#
```

The IPv4 security access line is eye-catching. There are 964 slots, and 790 slots are in use. Checking the CPU utilization next, you find that it is very high (see Example 7-46). This indicates that the TCAM is sending packets to the CPU for processing, overloading the CPU as a result.

Example 7-46 *CPU Utilization Is High*

```
Switch# show process cpu
CPU utilization for five seconds: 98%/17%; one minute: 72%; five minutes: 30%
PID  Runtime(ms)    Invoked    usecs    5Sec    1Min    5Min    TTY   Process
1            34        813       41   0.00%   0.00%   0.00%      0   Chunk Manager
2            32       4387        7   0.00%   0.00%   0.00%      0   Load Meter
3             0          1        0   0.00%   0.00%   0.00%      0   CEF RP IPC Backg
4         39508       3210    12307   1.75%   0.24%   0.14%      0   Check heaps
5            73        106      688   0.00%   0.00%   0.00%      0   Pool Manager
6             0          2        0   0.00%   0.00%   0.00%      0   Timers
7             0          1        0   0.00%   0.00%   0.00%      0   Image Licensing
8             0          2        0   0.00%   0.00%   0.00%      0   License Client N
9          8756         74   118324   0.00%   0.03%   0.02%      0   Licensing Auto U
10            0          1        0   0.00%   0.00%   0.00%      0   Crash writer
11      4158258     862519     4821  15.65%  14.81%   4.33%      0   ARP Input
12            0          1        0   0.00%   0.00%   0.00%      0   CEF MIB API
13            0          1        0   0.00%   0.00%   0.00%      0   AAA_SERVER_DEADT
14            0          2        0   0.00%   0.00%   0.00%      0   AAA high-capacit
15            0          1        0   0.00%   0.00%   0.00%      0   Policy Manager
16            0          6     1500   0.00%   0.00%   0.00%      0   Entity MIB API
17            0          1        0   0.00%   0.00%   0.00%      0   IFS Agent Manage
18            0        367        0   0.00%   0.00%   0.00%      0   IPC Dynamic Cach
19            0          1        0   0.00%   0.00%   0.00%      0   IPC Zone Manager
20          381      21700       17   0.00%   0.00%   0.00%      0   IPC Periodic Tim
```

You have found the problem and its source. The solution, noting that this is an extreme example, is that you need to rewrite and simplify the access lists. Also, you need to verify whether the same VLAN access lists at both the VLAN level and the interface level are necessary. If the access lists cannot be simplified, it might be time to invest in a dedicated platform for security filtering of this network.

Troubleshooting Performance Issues on Routers

Diagnosing and resolving router performance problems is an important skill set for network support engineers. Common causes for performance problems on routers are high CPU utilization and memory-allocation problems. Therefore, it is important to be able to recognize the typical symptoms associated with CPU or memory issues and to know the typically causes of these types of issues. This section prepares you to diagnose problems caused by high CPU utilization on routers using the Cisco IOS CLI, explains the typical symptoms and possible causes of memory-allocation failures, and offers guidelines for troubleshooting memory problems.

Troubleshooting High CPU Usage Issues on Routers

The CPU on a router performs two major tasks: forwarding packets and executing management and control plane processes. The CPU can become too busy when the CPU either has many packets to forward or when a system process consumes a large amount of the CPU time. For example, if the CPU is receiving many SNMP packets because of intensive network monitoring, it can become so busy processing all those packets that the other system processes cannot get access to CPU resources.

It is very to understand when high CPU utilization is at a problematic level and when it is considered to be normal. In some cases, high CPU utilization is normal and does not cause network problems. If CPU utilization is high for a short period of time, it does not necessarily cause a problem, as it is merely due to a short burst of network management requests or expected peaks of network traffic. If CPU utilization is consistently very high and packet forwarding or process performance on the router performance degrades, however, it is usually considered to be a problem and needs to be investigated.

When the router CPU is too busy to forward all packets as they arrive, the router might start to buffer packets, increasing latency, or even drop packets. This affects the application traffic passing through the router, and as a result, network performance will suffer. Also, because the CPU is spending most of its time on packet forwarding, control plane processes may not be able to get sufficient access to the CPU, which could lead to further disruptions because of failing routing or other control plane protocols.

Common symptoms of a router CPU that is too busy is that the router fails to respond to certain service requests. In those situations, the router might exhibit the following behaviors:

- Slow response to Telnet requests or to the commands that are issued in active Telnet sessions
- Slow response to commands issued on the console
- High latency on ping responses or too many ping timeouts
- Failure to send routing protocol packets to other routers

The following are some of the most common router processes that could cause high CPU utilization:

- **ARP Input:** High CPU utilization by the ARP Input process occurs if the router has to originate an excessive number of ARP requests. Multiple ARP requests for the same IP address are rate-limited to one request every 2 seconds, so excessive numbers of ARP requests can only occur if the router needs to originate ARP requests for many different IP addresses. This can happen if an IP route has been configured pointing to a broadcast interface. This causes the router to generate an ARP request for each IP address that is not reachable through a more specific route. An excessive amount of ARP requests can also be caused by malicious network traffic. An indication of such traffic is the presence of a high number of incomplete ARP entries in the ARP table, similar to the one shown in Example 7-47.

Example 7-47 *The Output of* **show arp** *Has Several Incomplete Entries*

```
Router# show arp
Protocol   Address           Age (min)  Hardware Addr   Type   Interface
Internet   10.10.10.1               -   0013.1918.caae  ARPA   FastEthernet0/0
Internet   10.16.243.249            0   Incomplete      ARPA
Internet   10.16.243.250            0   Incomplete      ARPA
Internet   10.16.243.251            0   Incomplete      ARPA
Internet   10.16.243.252            0   Incomplete      ARPA
Internet   10.16.243.253            0   Incomplete      ARPA
Internet   10.16.243.254            0   Incomplete      ARPA
```

- **Net Background:** The Net Background process runs whenever a buffer is required but is not available to a process or an interface. It uses the main buffer pool to provide the requested buffers. Net Background also manages the memory used by each process and cleans up freed-up memory. The symptoms of high CPU are increases in throttles, ignores, overruns, and resets on an interface; you can see these in the output of the **show interfaces** command.
- **TCP Timer:** The TCP Timer process is responsible for TCP sessions running on the router. When the TCP timer process uses a lot of CPU resources, this indicates that there are too many TCP peers (such as Border Gateway Protocol [BGP] peers). The **show tcp statistics** command (a sample is shown in Example 7-48) displays detailed TCP information.

Example 7-48 *The Output of* **show tcp statistics** *Displays Detailed TCP-Related Information*

```
Router# show tcp statistics
Rcvd: 22771 Total, 152 no port
      0 checksum error, 0 bad offset, 0 too short
      4661 packets (357163 bytes) in sequence
      7 dup packets (860 bytes)
      0 partially dup packets (0 bytes)
      0 out-of-order packets (0 bytes)
      0 packets (0 bytes) with data after window
      0 packets after close
      0 window probe packets, 0 window update packets
      4 dup ack packets, 0 ack packets with unsend data
      4228 ack packets (383828 bytes)
Sent: 22490 Total, 0 urgent packets
      16278 control packets (including 17 retransmitted)
      5058 data packets (383831 bytes)
      7 data packets (630 bytes) retransmitted
      0 data packets (0 bytes) fastretransmitted
```

```
     1146 ack only packets (818 delayed)
     0 window probe packets, 1 window update packets
8 Connections initiated, 82 connections accepted, 65 connections established
32046 Connections closed (including 27 dropped, 15979 embryonic dropped)
24 total rxmt timeout, 0 connections dropped in rxmt timeout
0 Keepalive timeout, 0 keepalive probe, 0 Connections dropped in keepalive
```

- **IP Background:** This process is responsible for encapsulation type changes on an interface, the move of an interface to a new state (up or down), and change of IP address on an interface. The IP Background process modifies the routing table in accordance with the status of the interfaces and notifies all routing protocols of the status change of each IP interface.

To determine the CPU utilization on a router, issue the **show processes cpu** command. The output of this command shows how busy the CPU has been in the past 5 seconds, the past 1 minute, and the past 5 minutes. The output also shows the percentage of the available CPU time that each system process has used during these periods. In the output shown in Example 7-49, the CPU utilization for the last 5 seconds was 72 percent. Out of this total of 72 percent, 23 percent of the CPU time was spent in interrupt mode, which corresponds to switching of packets. On the same line of output, you can also see the average utilization for the last 1 minute (74 percent in this example), and the average utilization for the past 5 minutes (71 percent in this example).

Example 7-49 *The* **show processes cpu** *Command Displays the Overall CPU Utilization and the CPU Utilization Due to Each Individual Process*

```
Router# show processes cpu sorted
CPU utilizatin for five seconds: 72%/23%; one minute: 74%; five minutes: 71%
! 72%, 74%, and 71% indicate total CPU spent on processes and interrupts
  (packet switching). 23% indicates CPU spent on interrupts (packet switching)
PID  Runtime(ms)    Invoked      uSecs    5Sec    1Min    5Min  TTY  Process
 62   3218415936  162259897       8149  65.08%  72.01%  68.00%    0  IP Input
183        47280   35989616          1   0.16%   0.08%   0.08%    0  RADIUS
 47          432        223       2385   0.24%   0.03%   0.06%    0  SSH Process
  2         9864     232359         42   0.08%   0.00%   0.00%    0  Load Meter
 61         6752     139374         48   0.08%   0.00%   0.00%    0  CDP Protocol
 33        14736    1161808         12   0.08%   0.01%   0.00%    0  Per-Second Jobs
 73        12200    4538259          2   0.08%   0.01%   0.00%    0  SSS Feature Time
! Output omitted for brevity
```

Issue the **show processes cpu history** command to see the CPU utilization for the last 60 seconds, 60 minutes, and 72 hours. The command output for this command provides

ASCII graphical views of how busy the CPU has been. You can see if the CPU has been constantly busy or whether utilization has been spiking. CPU utilization spikes caused by a known network event or activity do not indicate problems, but if you see prolonged spikes that do not seem to correspond to any known network activity, you must definitely investigate.

Troubleshooting Switching Paths

To understand the different switching options and how they work, it is necessary to understand that there are different types of router platforms and that each of these platforms has its own behavior. For example, 2800 series routers are based on a single CPU, and all functions of the router can be executed by the Cisco IOS Software running on the main CPU. However, many of the functions can be offloaded to separate network modules that can be installed into these routers. 7600 series routers are based on special hardware that is responsible for all packet-forwarding actions, which means that the main CPU is not involved in processing of most packets. The task of packet forwarding (data plane) consists of two steps:

Step 1. **Making a routing decision:** The routing decision is made based on network topology information and all the configured policies. Information about network destinations, gathered by a routing protocol, and possible restrictions like access lists or policy-based routing (PBR) are used to decide where to send each packet.

Step 2. **Switching the packet:** Switching packets on a router (not to be confused with Layer 2 switching) involves moving a packet from an input buffer to an output buffer and rewriting the data link layer header of the frame to forward the packet to the next hop toward the final destination.

The data link layer addresses necessary to rewrite the frame are stored in different tables such as the ARP table, which lists the MAC addresses for known IP devices reachable via Ethernet interfaces. Usually routers discover the data link layer addresses to be used for a destination through an address resolution process that matches the Layer 3 address to the Layer 2 address of a next hop device.

There are three types of packet switching modes supported by Cisco routers:

- Process switching
- Fast switching
- CEF

The newest switching mode is CEF, and it is the default, preferred, and recommended switching mode. It is important to remember that the switching method used affects the router's performance. To successfully troubleshoot problems related to the switching path it is essential to understand which method is used and how it works. The switching method might be altered globally or per interface for several reasons:

- During troubleshooting, to verify if the observed behavior is caused by the switching method
- During debugging, to direct all packets to CPU for processing
- Because some IOS features require a specific switching method

Process Switching

Process switching is the oldest mode. When using process switching to forward packets, the router strips the Layer 2 header from an incoming frame, looks up the Layer 3 network address in the routing table for the packet, and then sends the frame with a rewritten Layer 2 header, including a newly computed cyclical redundancy check (CRC) to the outgoing interface. All these operations are performed for each individual frame by the IP Input process that is running on the central CPU. Process switching is configured on an interface by disabling fast switching (and CEF) on that interface. Process switching is the most CPU-intensive method available on Cisco routers. It greatly degrades performance figures such as throughput, jitter, latency, and so on. This method should be used only temporarily as a last resort during troubleshooting.

Note To use process switching, fast switching must be disabled using this command:

```
Router(config-if)# no ip route-cache
```

Fast Switching

After performing a routing table lookup for the first packet destined for particular IP network, the router also initializes the fast-switching cache that is used by the fast-switching process. When subsequent frames to that same destination arrive, a cache lookup is performed and the destination is found in the fast-switching cache. Then the frame is rewritten with the corresponding data link layer header that was stored in the cache, and the frame is sent to the outgoing interface. The interface processor computes the CRC for the frame. Because the cache is destination based, fast switching can provide load sharing on a per-destination basis. Fast switching is less processor intensive than process switching because it uses a cache entry created by the first packet sent to a particular destination. The CPU utilization can go high even when the fast switching method is used, in a situation that there are a high number of new flows per second. This can happen when a network attack generates too many new flows rapidly.

Note Fast switching is enabled using the following command:

```
Router(config-if)# ip route-cache
```

Cisco Express Forwarding

Cisco Express Forwarding (CEF) is the default switching mode on Cisco routers. CEF is less CPU-intensive than fast switching or process switching. CEF is a highly scalable and resilient switching technique. When CEF is enabled, information used for packet forwarding purposes resides in the following two tables:

- **CEF Forwarding Information Base (FIB):** A router that has CEF enabled uses the FIB to make IP destination prefix-based switching decisions. This table is updated after each network change, but only once, and contains all known routes. There is no need to build a route cache by first using process switching for some of the packets. Each change in the IP routing table triggers a similar change in FIB table because it contains all next-hop addresses associated with all network destinations.
- **CEF adjacency table:** The adjacency table contains Layer 2 frame headers for all next hops used by the FIB. These addresses are used to rewrite frame headers for packets that are forwarded by a router.

Both tables are built independently, and a change in one table does not lead to change in the other. CEF is an efficient mechanism for traffic load balancing. In this case, both the FIB and the adjacency table contain multiple entries for a single network destination to reflect the multiple network paths toward it. It is important to note that there are several Cisco IOS features that require CEF to be enabled for their operation because they rely on the data structures that are built and maintained by Cisco operation. Some of those features are as follows:

- Network-Based Application Recognition (NBAR)
- AutoQoS and Modular QoS CLI (MQC)
- Frame Relay traffic shaping
- Multiprotocol Label Switching (MPLS)
- Class-based weighted random early detection

Note CEF can be enabled and disabled globally using the command:

```
Router(config)# [no] ip cef
```

You can also enable or disable CEF on each interface individually using the command:

```
Router(config-if)# [no] ip route-cache cef
```

Generally, if CEF is disabled globally, it cannot be enabled on an interface, but if it is enabled globally, it can be disabled on a single interface.

Troubleshooting Process and Fast Switching

Example 7-50 shows sample output from the **show ip interface** command after disabling the default CEF packet-switching mode using the **no ip cef** command. In the output, you can see that fast switching is enabled for all packets (except for packets that are sent back to the same interface that they came in on), but CEF switching is disabled.

Example 7-50 **show ip interface** *Command Output Shows That CEF Has Been Disabled*

```
Router# show ip interface GigabitEthernet 0/0
GigabitEthernet0/0 is up, line protocol is up
<...output omitted...>
IP fast switching is enabled
IP fast switching on the same interface is disabled
IP Flow switching is disabled
IP CEF switching is disabled
IP Fast switching turbo vector
IP multicast fast switching is enabled
IP multicast distributed fast switching is disabled
IP route-cache flags are Fast
! Output omitted for brevity
```

If you turn fast switching off, too, using the command **no ip route-cache**, and repeat the **show ip interface** command, the output will look similar to the one shown in Example 7-51. As you can see, however, multicast fast switching is still enabled. This is because IP multicast routing is configured entirely separate from IP unicast routing and there are separate configuration statements related to unicast and multicast operations. The **no ip route-cache** command only applies to unicast packets. To disable fast switching for multicast packets, the **no ip mroute-cache** command is used.

Example 7-51 **show ip interface** *Command Output Reveals That Fast Switching Is Disabled*

```
Router# show ip interface GigabitEthernet 0/0
GigabitEthernet0/0 is up, line protocol is up
<... output omitted ...>
  IP fast switching is disabled
  IP fast switching on the same interface is disabled
  IP Flow switching is disabled
  IP CEF switching is disabled
  IP Fast switching turbo vector
  IP multicast fast switching is enabled
  IP multicast distributed fast switching is disabled
  IP route-cache flags are Fast
! Output omitted for brevity
```

Disabling fast switching increases the load on the system CPU because every packet is processed by the IP Input process on the router CPU. In some situations however, disabling fast switching might be necessary (for example, during troubleshooting of connectivity problems) to eliminate the use of the fast-switching cache and to allow processing of all packets by the router CPU.

The **show ip cache** command displays the content of the fast-switching cache, as shown in Example 7-52. If fast switching is disabled on a particular interface, this cache will not have any network entries for that interface. The route cache is periodically cleared to remove stale entries and make room for new entries. This command is useful when troubleshooting because it shows that the fast-switching cache is initialized and populated with information for different network prefixes and associated outgoing interfaces.

Example 7-52 show ip cache *Displays the Current Content of the Fast-Switching Cache*

```
Router# show ip cache
IP routing cache 4 entries, 784 bytes
   5 adds, 1 invalidates, 0 refcounts
Minimum invalidation interval 2 seconds, maximum interval 5 seconds,
   quiet interval 3 seconds, threshold 0 requests
Invalidation rate 0 in last second, 0 in last 3 seconds
Last full cache invalidation occurred 00:11:31 ago

Prefix/Length     Age       Interface         Next Hop
10.1.1.1/32       00:07:20  FastEthernet0/0   10.1.1.1
10.2.1.1/32       00:04:18  FastEthernet0/1   10.2.1.1
10.10.1.0/24      00:01:06  FastEthernet0/0   10.1.1.1
10.11.1.0/24      00:01:20  FastEthernet0/1   10.2.1.1
```

Troubleshooting CEF

CEF builds two main data structures for its operation: the FIB and the adjacency table. When troubleshooting CEF, you have to check both tables and correlate entries between them. The items that you should check and verify when troubleshooting CEF are as follows:

- Is CEF enabled globally and per interface?
- Is there a FIB entry for a given network destination?
- Is there a next hop associated with this entry?
- Is there an adjacency entry for this next hop?

To find out whether CEF is enabled on a particular interface, issue the **show ip interface** command. As you can see in Example 7-53, the output clearly states whether CEF switching is enabled.

Example 7-53 *To Check Whether CEF Is Enabled on an Interface, Use the* **show ip interface** *Command*

```
Router# show ip interface GigabitEthernet 0/0
GigabitEthernet0/0 is up, line protocol is up
<... output omitted ...>
  IP fast switching is enabled
  IP fast switching on the same interface is disabled
  IP Flow switching is disabled
  IP CEF switching is disabled
  IP Fast switching turbo vector
  IP multicast fast switching is enabled
  IP multicast distributed fast switching is disabled
  IP route-cache flags are Fast
! Output omitted for brevity
```

If CEF is enabled on the router, you will see output similar to that shown in Example 7-54 after issuing the **show ip cef** command. This command displays the content of the FIB table, but you also discover if CEF is globally enabled or disabled on the router. All directly connected networks in the output are marked as **attached** in the Next Hop field. Network prefixes that are local to the router are marked as **receive.** The **show ip cef** command does not display the interfaces on which CEF is explicitly disabled.

Example 7-54 *Use the* **show ip cef** *Command to Display the FIB*

```
Router# show ip cef
Prefix              Next Hop                       Interface
0.0.0.0/0           10.14.14.19                    GigabitEthernet0/0
0.0.0.0/32          receive
10.14.14.0/24       attached                       GigabitEthernet0/0
10.14.14.0/32       receive
! Output omitted for brevity
10.14.14.252/32     receive
224.0.0.0/4         drop
224.0.0.0/24        receive
255.255.255.255/32  receive
```

In Example 7-54, the output shows that the router uses output interface GigabitEthernet0/0 and next hop 10.14.14.19/32 to reach 0.0.0.0/0 (the default route). You can also see what other destinations are associated with this interface/next-hop pair, using the **show ip cef adjacency** command for this interface and next-hop value, as shown in Example 7-55. This specific combination of output interface and next hop is used to reach two network destinations: the default route and a specific host destination (10.14.14.19/32), in this example.

Example 7-55 *Checking the Adjacency Table for Gi0/0 and Next Hop 10.14.14.19*

```
Router# show ip cef adjacency GigabitEthernet0/0 10.14.14.19 detail
IP CEF with switching (Table Version 24), flags=0x0
  23 routes, 0 reresolve, 0 unresolved (0 old, 0 new), peak 0
  2 instant recursive resolutions, 0 used background process
  28 leaves, 22 nodes, 26516 bytes, 79 inserts, 51 invalidations
  0 load sharing elements, 0 bytes, 0 references
  universal per-destination load sharing algorithm, id 56F4BAB5
  4(1) CEF resets, 2 revisions of existing leaves
  Resolution Timer: Exponential (currently 1s, peak 1s)
  1 in-place/0 aborted modifications
  refcounts:  6223 leaf, 6144 node
  Table epoch: 0 (23 entries at this epoch)
Adjacency Table has 13 adjacencies
0.0.0.0/0, version 22, epoch 0, cached adjacency 10.14.14.19
0 packets, 0 bytes
  via 10.14.14.19, 0 dependencies, recursive
    next hop 10.14.14.19, GigabitEthernet0/0 via 10.14.14.19/32
    valid cached adjacency
10.14.14.19/32, version 11, epoch 0, cached adjacency 10.14.14.19
0 packets, 0 bytes
  via 10.14.14.19, GigabitEthernet0/0, 1 dependency
    next hop 10.14.14.19, GigabitEthernet0/0
    valid cached adjacency
```

To see the adjacency table entries for this next hop, you use the **show adjacency** command. Note the difference that there is no **ip** in this command. The output of the **show adjacency** command for the Gi0/0 interface, beginning with the next-hop value of 10.14.14.19, is shown in Example 7-56. In this entry, you can see the full Layer 2 frame header associated with this next hop, which has been built through ARP. The Layer 2 MAC address for this next-hop IP address can also be checked in the ARP cache using the **show ip arp** command for the specific 10.14.14.19 address (also shown in Example 7-56).

Example 7-56 show adjacency *Command Output*

```
Router# show adjacency GigabitEthernet 0/0 detail | begin 10.14.14.19
Protocol Interface                 Address
IP       GigabitEthernet0/0        10.14.14.9(5)
                                   0 packets, 0 bytes
                                   001200A2BC41001BD5F9E7C00800
                                   ARP          03:19:39
                                   Epoch: 0
[...]
Router# show ip arp 10.14.14.19
```

```
Protocol  Address          Age (min)  Hardware Addr   Type   Interface
Internet  10.14.14.19              4  0012.009a.0c42  ARPA   GigabitEthernet0/0
```

You must know that the CPU might process some packets, even if CEF is enabled. This can happen for reasons such as an incomplete adjacency table or when processing packets that need special handling by the main processor. You can gather information about the packets that are not switched with CEF by using the **show cef not-cef-switched** command, as shown in Example 7-57.

Example 7-57 *Gathering Information About the Non-CEF-Switched Packets*

```
Router# show cef not-cef-switched
CEF Packets passed on to next switching layer
Slot   No_adj No_encap Unsupp'ted Redirect  Receive  Options    Access     Frag
RP     424260        0    5227416    67416  2746773        9     15620        0
```

IOS Tools to Analyze Packet Forwarding

Cisco IOS Software is a powerful operating system that has an embedded set of tools to assist in troubleshooting various networking problems. These tools enable network administrators to quickly and effectively find, isolate, and repair IP communication problems. The following series of steps shows you an example of a troubleshooting process that could be used to find problems related to the switching path used by a router. The example is based on the network shown in Figure 7-15. Be aware that the actual routers used for command outputs in this example do not have any problems. The aim is to show the Cisco IOS commands in action.

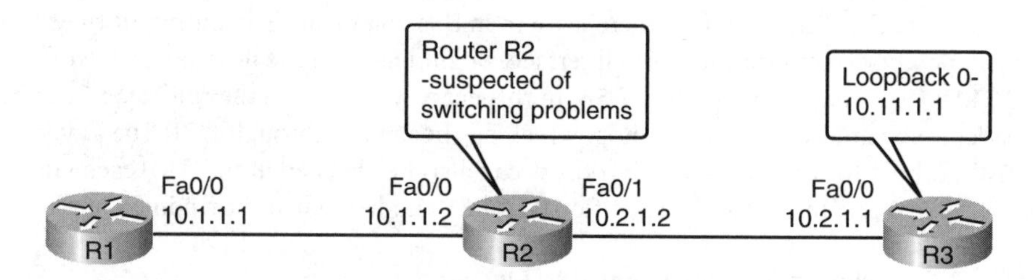

Figure 7-15 *Network Diagram for the Step-by-Step CEF Troubleshooting Example*

Step 1. First try to find the problematic router along the path with the **traceroute** utility as demonstrated in Example 7-58. Although the output seems normal, suppose that the **traceroute** command would have shown a much higher delay or packet loss on router R2 compared to router R3. Such symptoms can lead you to suspect problems in router R2.

Example 7-58 *Make Use of the* **traceroute** *Command to Find the Problematic Router*

```
R1# traceroute 10.11.1.1
Type escape sequence to abort.
Tracing the route to 10.11.1.1
  1 10.1.1.2 72 msec 56 msec 64 msec
  2 10.2.1.1 76 msec 104 msec *
```

Step 2. Check the CPU utilization on router R2 for load due to packet processing, using the **show processes cpu** command, as shown in Example 7-59. In this example, there are no problems related to packet processing.

Example 7-59 *Checking the CPU Utilization on R2*

```
R2# show processes cpu ¦ exclude 0.00
CPU utilization for five seconds: 4%/0%; one minute: 1%; five minutes: 1%
 PID Runtime(ms)   Invoked      uSecs    5Sec   1Min   5Min TTY Process
   2        3396       650       5224  0.08%  0.07%  0.10%   0 Load Meter
   3       11048       474      23308  3.27%  0.51%  0.37%   0 Exec
  99       13964      6458       2162  0.90%  0.66%  0.71%   0 DHCPD Receive
 154         348       437        796  0.08%  0.09%  0.08%   0 CEF process
```

Step 3. Check the routing table for the corresponding destination prefix (in this example, 10.11.1.1), as shown in Example 7-60. In this example, the routing information is present.

Example 7-60 *Display the Routing Table Entry for the Destination Under Investigation*

```
R2# show ip route 10.11.1.1
Routing entry for 10.11.1.1/32
  Known via "ospf 1", distance 110, metric 11, type intra area
  Last update from 10.2.1.1 on FastEthernet0/1, 00:29:20 ago
  Routing Descriptor Blocks:
  * 10.2.1.1, from 10.11.1.1, 00:29:20 ago, via FastEthernet0/1
      Route metric is 11, traffic share count is 1
```

Step 4. Find which switching mode is used by the router and on the interfaces involved in packet forwarding. Using **show ip cef**, find out if CEF is enabled, for the destination under investigation, discover the egress interface, and use the **show ip interface** for that interface to see what type of switching is operational on it. This work is shown in Example 7-61 for the current example. In this example, CEF is enabled globally, and all involved interfaces are enabled for CEF switching.

Example 7-61 *Find Out the Type of Switching Used on the Router and the Interfaces*

```
R2# show ip cef
Prefix              Next Hop             Interface
0.0.0.0/0           drop                 Null0 (default route handler entry)
0.0.0.0/32          receive
10.1.1.0/24         attached             FastEthernet0/0
10.1.1.0/32         receive
10.1.1.1/32         10.1.1.1             FastEthernet0/0
10.1.1.2/32         receive
10.1.1.255/32       receive
10.2.1.0/24         attached             FastEthernet0/1
10.2.1.0/32         receive
10.2.1.1/32         10.2.1.1             FastEthernet0/1
10.2.1.2/32         receive
10.2.1.255/32       receive
10.10.1.1/32        10.1.1.1             FastEthernet0/0
10.11.1.1/32        10.2.1.1             FastEthernet0/1
224.0.0.0/4         drop
224.0.0.0/24        receive
255.255.255.255/32  receive

R2# show ip interface FastEthernet 0/0 | include CEF
  IP CEF switching is enabled
  IP CEF Fast switching turbo vector
  IP route-cache flags are Fast, CEF

R2# show ip interface FastEthernet 0/1 | include CEF
  IP CEF switching is enabled
  IP CEF Fast switching turbo vector
  IP route-cache flags are Fast, CEF
```

Step 5. Check the FIB entry for the routing information under investigation (in this case, 10.11.1.1), as shown in Example 7-62. The related adjacency entry shows interface FastEthernet0/1 with next hop 10.2.1.1.

Example 7-62 *Display the FIB Entry for the Destination Under Investigation*

```
R2# show ip cef 10.11.1.1 255.255.255.255
10.11.1.1/32, version 13, epoch 0, cached adjacency 10.2.1.1
0 packets, 0 bytes
  via 10.2.1.1, FastEthernet0/1, 0 dependencies
    next hop 10.2.1.1, FastEthernet0/1
    valid cached adjacency
```

Step 6. Check the adjacency table for the next-hop value of the destination you are investigating, as shown in Example 7-63. In this case, the relevant adjacency is built using ARP.

Example 7-63 *Use* **show adjacency** *to Discover the Layer 2 Value for Your Next Hop*

```
R2# show adjacency FastEthernet0/1 detail
Protocol Interface                 Address
IP       FastEthernet0/1           10.2.1.1(7)
                                   203 packets, 307342 bytes
                                   C40202640000C4010F5C00010800
                                   ARP         02:57:43
                                   Epoch: 0
```

Step 7. Check the ARP cache entry for the next hop, as shown in Example 7-64. You see that the MAC address information is present in the router. Based on this verification process, you can conclude that the routers in this example do not have any switching-related problems.

Example 7-64 *Display the ARP Cache and Look for the Next-Hop Value*

```
R2# show ip arp
Protocol  Address          Age (min)  Hardware Addr   Type   Interface
Internet  10.2.1.1                67  c402.0264.0000  ARPA   FastEthernet0/1
Internet  10.1.1.2                 -  c401.0f5c.0000  ARPA   FastEthernet0/0
Internet  10.1.1.1                67  c400.0fe4.0000  ARPA   FastEthernet0/0
Internet  10.2.1.2                 -  c401.0f5c.0001  ARPA   FastEthernet0/1
```

The steps shown can be used as generic procedure for finding issues with CEF switching.

Troubleshooting Router Memory Issues

Memory-allocation failure is the most common router memory issue. Memory-allocation failures happen when the router has used all available memory (temporarily or permanently), or the memory has been fragmented into such small pieces that the router cannot find a usable available block. This can happen to the processor memory, which is used by Cisco IOS Software, or to the packet memory, which is used to buffer incoming and outgoing packets. Symptoms of memory allocation failures include the following:

- Messages such as **%SYS–2–MALLOCFAIL: Memory allocation of 1028 bytes failed from 0x6015EC84, Pool Processor, alignment 0** display in the router logs.
- **show** commands generate no output.
- Receiving **Low on memory** messages.

- Receiving the message **Unable to create EXEC – no memory or too many processes** on the console.

When a router is low on memory, in some instances it is not even possible to use Telnet to connect to the router. When you get to this point, you need to get access to the console port to collect data for troubleshooting. When connecting to the console port, however, you might see the **Unable to create EXEC – no memory or too many processes** message. If you see this message, there is not even enough available memory to allow for a console connection.

Some of the main reasons for memory problems are as follows:

- **Memory size does not support the Cisco IOS Software image:** First, check the Release Notes (available to registered customers only) or the IOS Upgrade Planner (available to registered customers only) for the minimum memory size for the Cisco IOS Software feature set and version that you are running. Make sure that you have sufficient memory in your router to support the software image. The actual memory requirements will vary based on protocols used, routing tables, and traffic patterns on the network.
- **Memory-leak bug:** A memory leak occurs when a process requests or allocates memory and then forgets to free (de-allocate) the memory when it is finished with that task. As a result, the memory block stays reserved until the router is reloaded. The **show memory allocating-process totals** command will help you to identify how much memory is used and is free, and the per-process memory utilization of the router. Example 7-65 shows sample output from this command. Memory leaks are caused by bugs in the Cisco IOS code, and the only solution is to upgrade Cisco IOS Software on the device to a version that fixes the issue.

Example 7-65 **show memory allocating-process totals** *Command Output*

```
Router# show memory allocating-process totals
             Head        Total (b)    Used(b)    Free(b)     Lowest(b)  Largest(b)
Processor   62A2B2D0    183323952   26507580  156816372   155132764  154650100
      I/O   ED900000     40894464    4957092   35937372    35887920    3590524
Allocator PC Summary for: Processor
    PC           Total    Count  Name
0x6136A5A8     5234828        1  Init
0x608E2208     3576048      812  TTY data
0x6053ECEC     1557568      184  Process Stack
0x61356928     1365448       99  Init
! Output omitted for brevity
```

- **Security-related problems:** MALLOCFAIL errors can also be caused by a security issue, such as a worm or virus operating in your network. This is likely the cause, especially if there have not been any recent changes to the network, such as router IOS upgrades or configuration changes. You can often mitigate the effect of this type of problem by adding a number of configuration statements to your router, such as an access list that drops the traffic generated by the worm or virus. The Cisco Product Security Advisories and Notices page contains information on detection of the most likely causes and specific workarounds.

- **Memory-allocation failure at process = interrupt level:** The error message identifies the cause. If the process is listed as <interrupt level>, as shown in the message that follows, the memory-allocation failure is being caused by a software problem:

```
%SYS-2-MALLOCFAIL: Memory allocation of 68 bytes failed from
0x604CEF48, pool Processor, alignment 0-Process= <interrupt level>,
ipl= 3
```

  You can use the Bug Toolkit to search for a matching software bug ID (unique bug identification) for this issue. After you have identified the software bug, upgrade to a Cisco IOS Software version that contains the fix to resolve the problem.

- **Buffer-leak bug:** When a process is finished using a buffer, the process should free the buffer. A buffer leak occurs when the code forgets to free it. As a result, the buffer pool continues to grow as more and more packets are stuck in the buffers.

The **show interfaces** command displays statistics for all interfaces configured on the router. Figure 7-66 displays sample output from this command. The output indicates that the interface input queue is wedged, which is a symptom of buffer leak. The full input queue (76/75) warns of a buffer leak. Here, the values 76 and 75 represent the number of packets in the input queue, and the maximum size of the input queue, respectively: The number of packets in the input queue is larger than the queue depth! This is called a *wedged interface*. When the input queue of an interface is wedged, the router no longer forwards traffic that enters the affected interface.

Example 7-66 **show interfaces** *Command Output Displays a Full Input Queue, a Sign of Buffer Leak*

```
Router# show interfaces
<...output omitted...>
ARP type: ARPA, ARP Timeout 04:00:00
  Last input 00:00:58, output never, output hang never
  Last clearing of "show interface" counters never
  input queue 76/75, 1250 drops
  Output queue 0/40, 0 drops;
! Output omitted for brevity
```

The **show buffers** command displays statistics for the buffer pools on the router. The output in Example 7-67 reveals a buffer leak in the middle buffers pool. There are a total of 17602 middle buffers in the router, and only 11 are in the free list. This implies that some process takes all the buffers, but does not return them. Other symptoms of this type of buffer leak are **%SYS–2–MALLOCFAIL** error messages for the pool "processor" or "input/output (I/O)," based on the platform. Similar to a generic memory leak, a buffer leak is caused by a software bug, and the only solution is to upgrade Cisco IOS Software on the device to a version that fixes the issue.

Example 7-67 show buffers *Command Output Indicates Buffer Leak*

```
Router# show buffers
<...output omitted...>
Middle buffers, 600 bytes (total 17602, permanent 170):
     11 in free list (10 min, 400 max allowed)
     498598 hits, 148 misses, 671 trims, 657 created
     0 failures (0 no memory)
! Output omitted for brevity
```

BGP Memory Use

Cisco IOS has three main processes used by the Border Gateway Protocol (BGP):

- **BGP I/O:** This process handles reading, writing, and executing of all BGP messages. This process is also the interface between TCP and BGP.
- **BGP router:** This process is responsible for initiation of a BGP process, session maintenance, processing of incoming updates, sending of BGP updates, and updating the IP RIB (Routing Information Base) with BGP entries.
- **BGP scanner:** This process performs periodic scans of the BGP RIB to update it as necessary, and it scans the IP RIB to ensure that all BGP next hops are valid.

The BGP router process consumes the majority of the memory used by BGP. The BGP router process uses memory to store the BGP RIB, IP RIB for BGP prefixes, and IP switching data structures for BGP prefixes. If you do not have enough memory to store this information, BGP cannot operate in a stable manner, and network reliability will be compromised. If you are using chassis-based routers, which distribute routing information to the line cards, you should not only check the memory availability for the route processor, but also the memory availability on the line cards. The **show diag** command displays the different types of cards present in your router and their respective amounts of memory, as demonstrated in Example 7-68. This command is useful to identify a lack of memory on the line cards when the router runs BGP.

Example 7-68 show diag *Command Output*

```
Router# show diag ¦ I (DRAM¦SLOT)
SLOT 0    (RP/LC 0 ): 1 Port SONET based SRP OC-12c/STM-4 Single Mode
  DRAM size: 268435456 bytes
  FrFab SDRAM size: 134217728 bytes, SDRAM pagesize: 8192 bytes
  ToFab SDRAM size: 134217728 bytes, SDRAM pagesize: 8192 bytes
SLOT 2    (RP/LC 2 ): 12 Port Packet over E3
  DRAM size: 67108864 bytes
  FrFab SDRAM size: 67108864 bytes
```

```
  ToFab SDRAM size: 67108864 bytes
SLOT 3   (RP/LC 3 ): 1 Port Gigabit Ethernet
  DRAM size: 134217728 bytes
  FrFab SDRAM size: 134217728 bytes, SDRAM pagesize: 8192 bytes
  ToFab SDRAM size: 134217728 bytes, SDRAM pagesize: 8192 bytes
SLOT 5   (RP/LC 5 ): Route Processor
  DRAM size: 268435456 bytes
```

Summary

The main categories of application services are as follows:

- Network classification
- Application scalability
- Application networking
- Application acceleration
- WAN acceleration
- Application optimization

The recipe to application optimization is a four-step cycle that incrementally increases your understanding of network applications and allows you to progressively deploy measurable improvements and adjustments as required, as follows:

Step 1. Baseline application traffic.

Step 2. Optimize the network.

Step 3. Measure, adjust, and verify.

Step 4. Deploy new applications.

NetFlow efficiently provides a vital set of services for IP applications, including network traffic accounting, usage-based network billing, network planning, security DoS monitoring, and overall network monitoring. A flow is a unidirectional stream of packets, between a given source and a destination, that have several components in common. The seven fields that need to match for packets to be considered part of the same flow are as follows:

- Source IP Address
- Destination IP Address
- Source Port (protocol dependent)
- Destination Port (protocol dependent)
- Protocol (Layer 3 or 4)
- Type of Service (ToS) Value (differentiated services code point [DSCP])

- Input Interface

IP SLA is useful for performance measurement, monitoring, and network baselining. You can tie the results of the IP SLA operations to other features of your router, and trigger action based on the results of the probe. To implement IP SLA network performance measurement, you need to perform the following tasks:

- Enable the IP SLA responder, if required.
- Configure the required IP SLA operation type.
- Configure any options available for the specified operation type.
- Configure threshold conditions, if required.
- Schedule the operation to run, and then let the operation run for a period of time to gather statistics.
- Display and interpret the results of the operation using the Cisco IOS CLI or an NMS, with SNMP.

NBAR is another important tool for baselining and traffic classification purposes. NBAR is a classification engine that recognizes a wide variety of applications, including web-based and other difficult-to-classify protocols that utilize dynamic TCP/UDP port assignments. The simplest use of NBAR is baselining through protocol discovery.

The Cisco IOS SLB feature is a Cisco IOS-based solution that provides server load balancing. This feature allows you to define a virtual server that represents a cluster of real servers, known as a server farm. When a client initiates a connection to the virtual server, the Cisco IOS SLB load balances the connection to a chosen real server based on the configured load-balance algorithm or predictor.

Cisco AutoQoS is an automation tool for deploying QoS policies. The newer versions of Cisco AutoQoS have two phases. In the first phase, information is gathered and traffic is baselined to define traffic classes and volumes; this is called autodiscovery. The command **auto discovery qos** is entered at the interface configuration mode. You must let discovery run for a period of time that is appropriate for your baselining or monitoring needs. The **auto qos** command, which is also an interface configuration mode command, uses the information gathered by autodiscovery to apply QoS policies accordingly. The autodiscovery phase generates templates on the basis of the data collected. These templates are then used to create QoS policies. Finally, the policies are installed by AutoQoS on the interface.

For Cisco AutoQoS to work certain requirements must be met, as follows:

- CEF must be enable on the interface.
- The interface (or subinterface) must have an IP address configured.
- For serial interfaces (or subinterfaces) configure the appropriate bandwidth.
- On point-to-point serial interfaces, both sides must be configured AutoQoS.

Some useful NetFlow troubleshooting commands are the following:

- **show ip cache flow**
- **show ip flow export**
- **show ip flow interface**
- **debug ip flow export**

Useful IP SLA troubleshooting commands include the following:

- **show ip sla monitor statistics**
- **show ip sla monitor collection-statistics**
- **show ip sla monitor configuration**
- **debug ip sla monitor trace**

Some useful NBAR troubleshooting commands are these:

- **show ip nbar port-map**
- **show ip nbar protocol-discovery**
- **debug ip nbar unclassified-port-stats**

Some of the useful AutoQoS troubleshooting commands are as follows:

- **show auto qos interface**
- **show auto discovery qos**

Troubleshooting performance problems is a three-step process:

Step 1. Assessing whether the problem is technical in nature

Step 2. Isolating the performance problem to a device, link, or component

Step 3. Diagnosing and resolving the performance degradation at the component level

The following events cause spikes in the CPU utilization:

- Processor-intensive Cisco IOS commands
- Routing protocol update processing
- SNMP polling

Some common interface and wiring problems are as follows:

- No cable connected
- Wrong port

- Device has no power
- Wrong cable type
- Bad cable
- Loose connections
- Patch panels
- Faulty media converters
- Bad or wrong GBIC

Common symptoms of a router CPU that is too busy is that the router fails to respond to certain service requests. In those situations, the router might exhibit the following behaviors:

- Slow response to Telnet requests or to the commands issued in active Telnet sessions
- Slow response to commands issued on the console
- High latency on ping responses or too many ping timeouts
- Failure to send routing protocol packets to other routers

When troubleshooting CEF, you always want to check and verify the following:

- Is CEF enabled globally and per interface?
- Is there a FIB entry for a given network destination?
- Is there a next hop associated with this entry?
- Is there an adjacency entry for this next hop?

Symptoms of memory-allocation failures include the following:

- Messages such as **%SYS-2-MALLOCFAIL: Memory allocation of 1028 bytes failed from 0x6015EC84, Pool Processor, alignment 0** display in the router logs.
- Not getting any output from **show** commands.
- Receiving **Low on memory** messages.
- Receiving the message **Unable to create EXEC – no memory or too many processes** on the console.

Some of the main reasons for memory problems are as follows:

- Memory size does not support the Cisco IOS Software image
- Memory-leak bug

- Security-related problems
- Memory-allocation failure at process = interrupt level error message
- Buffer-leak bug

Review Questions

Use the questions here to review what you learned in this chapter. The correct answers are found in Appendix A, "Answers to Chapter Review Questions."

1. Match the following application optimization cycle elements with the definitions provided.

   a. Baseline application traffic

   b. Optimize the network

   c. Measure, adjust, and verify

   d. Deploy new applications

   Understand the basic traffic and application flows and network performance.

   Roll out new applications and observe the effects on existing applications.

   Apply QoS to reduce congestion, prioritize specific traffic, select best paths, and so on.

   Find out the effect of QoS on your network, and understand performance using IOS features.

2. Which of the following is not used to baseline application traffic?

   a. NetFlow

   b. SLB

   c. NBAR Protocol Discovery

   d. IP SLAs

3. Which of the following is not a NetFlow key field?

   a. Source IP Address

   b. Layer 4 Source Port

   c. ToS Byte (DSCP)

   d. TTL

   e. Input Interface

4. Which of the following commands displays the NetFlow statistics?
   - a. **show ip cache flow**
   - b. **show ip flow ingress**
   - c. **show netflow stats**
   - d. **show ip netflow statistics**
5. Place the letter corresponding to each IP SLA configuration task in front of the task number, according to the order the task must be performed.

   1: __ 2:__ 3:__ 4:__ 5:__
   - a. Configure the required IP SLA operation type and any options available.
   - b. Configure threshold conditions, if required.
   - c. Display and interpret the results of the operation.
   - d. Schedule the operation to run.
   - e. Enable the IP SLA responder, if required.
6. Based on the output of the commands displayed in Example 7-69, which of the following statements is true?

Example 7-69 **show interface counters** *and* **show interface counters errors** *Command Output*

```
ASW1# show interfaces FastEthernet 0/1 counters

Port          InOctets     InUcastPkts    InMcastPkts    InBcastPkts
Fa0/1        647140108          499128           4305              0

Port          OutOctets     OutUcastPkts    OutMcastPkts    OutBcastPkts
Fa0/1          28533484           319996              52               3

ASW1# show interfaces FastEthernet 0/1 counters errors

Port          Align-Err     FCS-Err  Xmit-Err    Rcv-Err  Undersize   OutDiscards
Fa0/1                 0       12618         0      12662          0             0

Port     Single-Col  Multi-Col  Late-Col  Excess-Col  Carri-Sen  Runts  Giants
Fa0/1             0          0         0           0          0      0      44
```

   - a. There is a problem because the number of FCS errors in relation to the number of input packets is too high.
   - b. There is a problem because the number of FCS errors in relation to the number of output packets is too high.
   - c. You cannot tell whether there is a problem without knowing the duplex mode. FCS errors are normal on half-duplex Ethernet.

d. You cannot tell whether there is a problem without knowing when the counters were cleared.

e. There is no problem. The number of FCS errors is within acceptable boundaries.

7. You have connected a switch that supports automatic media-dependent interface crossover (auto-MDIX) to another switch that supports auto-MDIX, too. A straight-through cable has been used to connect the switches, and both switches are configured for 100-Mbps full duplex. The link should come up and work without problems. True or False?

a. True

b. False

8. Which two of the following hardware components can affect the switch packet forwarding performance?

a. DRAM

b. FLASH

c. TCAM

d. Console

e. Interface hardware

9. Which three of the following types of information can be programmed into a switch TCAM?

a. IP Version 4 unicast routes

b. Access lists

c. IPS signatures

d. IP Version 4 multicast routes

e. NAT rules

10. Based on the output of the commands displayed in Example 7-70, which of the following statements is true?

Example 7-70 show processes cpu sorted *Command Output*

```
CSW1# show processes cpu sorted
CPU utilization for five seconds: 23%/18%; one minute: 24%; five minutes: 17%
PID  Runtime(ms)   Invoked   usecs   5Sec   1Min   5Min  TTY  Process
170       384912   1632941     235  0.47%  0.35%  0.23%    0  IP Input
 63         8462   5449551       1  0.31%  0.52%  0.33%    0  HLFM address lea
274       101766   1410665      72  0.15%  0.07%  0.04%    0  HSRP IPv4
  4       156599     21649    7233  0.00%  0.07%  0.05%    0  Check heaps
<...further output omitted...>
```

a. There is a potential problem on this switch because the 1-minute average should not be above 20 percent.

b. There is a potential problem on this switch because the IP Input process is ranked the highest when the processes are sorted.

c. There is a potential problem on this switch because the second value in the 5-second average is higher than 10 percent.

d. You cannot determine whether there is a problem on this switch because the baseline values are unknown.

e. There is no indication of problems on this switch.

11. Which three of following events could cause spikes in the CPU load of a switch?

a. An engineer executes the show tech-support command.

b. A network management station polls the switch using SNMP to obtain the content of the routing table.

c. The switch startup configuration is copied from NVRAM to a TFTP server.

d. The OSPF process executes its SPF algorithm.

e. An engineer logs in to the switch using Telnet.

12. Which two of the following are common symptoms of high CPU utilization?

a. Slow performance

b. Many errors on the input interface

c. Routing update problems

d. Low percentages in the show processes CPU command output

13. Which two of the following are common causes of high CPU utilization?

a. High CPU utilization caused by different processes

b. High CPU utilization caused by interface flaps

c. High CPU utilization caused by a security issue

d. Lack of an active routing protocol

14. Which of the following is a Cisco IOS tool for troubleshooting high CPU utilization?

    a. **show processes cpu**

    b. **show version**

    c. **show buffers**

    d. **show controllers**

15. Which two of the following are memory-allocation failure symptoms?

    a. Refused Telnet sessions

    b. Too many log messages

    c. No output from the **show** commands

    d. Slow performance in packet processing

16. Which three of the following are common memory problems?

    a. Buffer-leak bug

    b. Memory-leak bug

    c. Routing problems

    d. Slow IGP convergence

    e. Security-related memory problems

17. Which of the following is a symptom of a buffer-leak problem?

    a. Route processor buffer leaks

    b. Wedged interface

    c. System buffer leak

    d. SVI buffer leaks

18. Which two of the following should you check if you suspect issues with CEF switching?

    a. ARP table and routing table

    b. Adjacency table and FIB table

    c. CLNS table and ARP table

    d. FIB table and GBRC table

19. What command should you use if you suspect performance problems related to IP switching?

a. **show processes memory**

b. **show processes cpu**

c. **show processes switching**

d. **show ip switching**

20. Which three of the following are symptoms of buffer leak?

a. **%SYS-2-MALLOCFAIL** error messages.

b. Packet drops on the router interfaces.

c. Frequently router reload.

d. **show buffer** command output indicates a buffer leak in some of the buffer pools.

Chapter 8

Troubleshooting Converged Networks

This chapter covers the following topics:

- Troubleshooting converged networks to support wireless operations
- Troubleshooting unified communications issues in a converged network
- Troubleshooting video issues in a converged network

This chapter consists of three sections. The first section focuses on network issues that affect the wireless LAN components and their operation. It is important to distinguish that troubleshooting actual wireless LAN components is not intended here. Those topics are covered in wireless-specific books and courses. In the second section, troubleshooting network issues that affect unified communications (VoIP, IP telephony, and so on) are the target. Finally, in the third section, troubleshooting issues that affect video applications are discussed. Again, note that these sections do not provide any technical coverage of unified communications or video applications. (You can find books and courses especially designed to discuss topics such as troubleshooting unified communications and so on.) Throughout this chapter, several troubleshooting examples are presented so that you become familiar with how certain misconfigurations manifest themselves as network problems and how you can go about isolating those issues and solve them with systematic troubleshooting skills.

Troubleshooting Converged Networks to Support Wireless Operations

This section's focus is on the readiness of the wired network to support wireless deployments. This subject includes network services such as Power over Ethernet (PoE), Dynamic Host Configuration Protocol (DHCP), quality of service (QoS), and security. The impact of wireless traffic and services on the rest of the network shall also be discussed.

Note This section does not cover troubleshooting wireless technologies.

The Cisco Unified Wireless Network is composed of five interconnected elements that work together to deliver a unified enterprise-class wireless solution, as follows:

- Client devices
- Access points
- Network unification
- World-class network management
- Mobility services

Common Wireless Integration Issues

Designing (and troubleshooting) a wireless network that integrates into a campus network, requires several considerations, including the following matters:

- Is the wireless network based on the autonomous model or will it be based on its counterpart, the split MAC model (using lightweight access points and wireless controllers)?
- What are the switch capabilities and requirements in terms of PoE, trunking, wireless local-area network (WLAN)-to-VLAN mapping, security, and QoS?
- How will the Lightweight Access Point Protocol (LWAPP) be handled?
- What type of roaming will the network support?

In a standalone or autonomous solution, autonomous access points (APs) provide all the wireless services. Deployment is based on those APs functioning as critical wireless devices, with the rest of the network providing services such as PoE, security, and QoS. Network servers, such as the Cisco Secure Access Control Server (ACS), are used for security and implement protocols such as RADIUS and TACACS+.

The controller-based architecture splits the processing of the IEEE 802.11 protocol between two devices: the AP and a centralized Cisco wireless LAN controller (WLC). The processing of the 802.11 data and management protocols and the AP functionality is also divided between the two devices. This approach is called *split MAC* or *lightweight*. Communications between the devices (lightweight APs and the WLCs) are implemented through LWAPP tunnels, as illustrated in Figure 8-1.

Understanding the autonomous and split MAC models is important because the model used defines where and how to troubleshoot potential problems when you integrate the wireless infrastructure into a campus LAN. For example, in both models, the role of the switch and other wired network elements is very important. The location of power source equipment, the configuration of trunks, and the mapping between WLANs and VLANs become important items in gathering information for your troubleshooting process. The security surrounding the wireless solution plays an important role in the proper transport

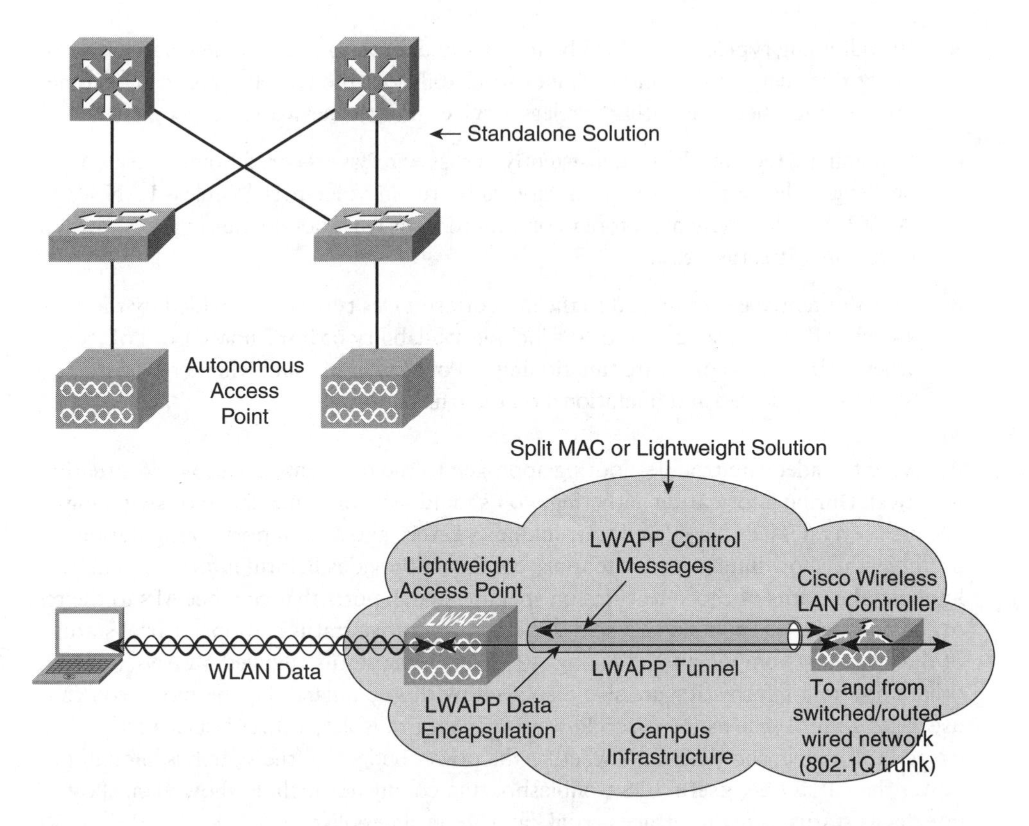

Figure 8-1 *Autonomous Versus Lightweight (Split MAC) Wireless LAN Solutions*

of protocols such as LWAPP across the wired network. Firewalls and access control lists (ACLs) must allow the protocol between APs and Cisco WLCs. Some of the common wireless integration issues are as follows:

- Even if there is radio frequency (RF) connectivity between the AP and the client, there can still be a problem at the side where traffic flows from the client, through the AP, to the rest of the network. In a controller-based solution, the boundary between the wireless and the wired network is the Cisco WLC because traffic is tunneled between the AP and the WLC. The WLC is an important point of troubleshooting.
- If any filters are configured on either the Ethernet side or the radio side of the AP, disable them temporarily, until you resolve connectivity issues. Disabling the filters helps you to determine whether the filters are contributing to the problem. If the filters are long or complex, reintroduce them in phases so that you can isolate what is causing the problem. The filters might be blocking critical traffic, such as those related to LWAPP tunnels, or perhaps related to wireless security (IEEE 802.1x, Extensible Authentication Protocol [EAP], or RADIUS).

- IP addressing typically needs to be investigated, especially in roaming scenarios. You might find that static IP addressing or reachability of the DHCP server can become problematic when integrating wireless services into the network.
- Maintaining QoS markings consistently across wireless-to-wired boundaries is a challenge. The necessity of this is especially true in Voice over Wireless LAN (VoWLAN) deployments. Proper configuration of trust boundaries in access switches requires attention, too.
- Other potential issues related to the network services typically provided by the switches that are connected to APs include availability of PoE, amount of PoE, whether the access ports are functioning in PortFast mode, and whether proper VLANs are allowed and operational on the trunks.

Applying the adequate troubleshooting approach to the different scenarios and situations is critical. During information gathering, you should use your knowledge of switching because several issues are related to trunking, VLANs, and switch port configuration. For example, the **show interfaces switchport** command provides helpful information in knowing the status of those features on specific switch ports that connect APs to the rest of the network. This command displays the administrative status and operational status of the switching components. Trunking, VLAN pruning status, allowed VLANs, and other important information are also displayed by this command. Furthermore, you can use a design tool such as the Cisco Power Calculator to isolate power issues, verify capacity planning, and determine whether the power budget on the switch is enough to power the APs. Other useful IOS troubleshooting commands include **show vlan**, **show interfaces status**, **show interfaces trunk**, and **show access-lists**.

WLAN Connectivity Troubleshooting Example: Misconfigured Trunk

This troubleshooting example is based on the network diagram/topology shown in Figure 8-2. The physical topology is shown on the left, with a lightweight AP, a WLC, and a wireless client, and the logical diagram is shown on the right side. Wireless services have suddenly stopped; clients are not able to associate to the AP. Even from the wired PCs that are used for troubleshooting, it is not possible to connect to the AP or the WLC, using either Secure Shell (SSH) or HTTP-Secure (HTTPS).

Using a bottom-up approach, you start with the access switch and look at the interfaces, looking for clues at the physical and data link layers. You can start with the **show cdp neighbors** command to try to identify on the switch which ports are connected to the controller and which are connected to the access point. Based on the results shown in Example 8-1, WLC connects to interface Gi 0/36 and the AP connects to interface Gi 0/37.

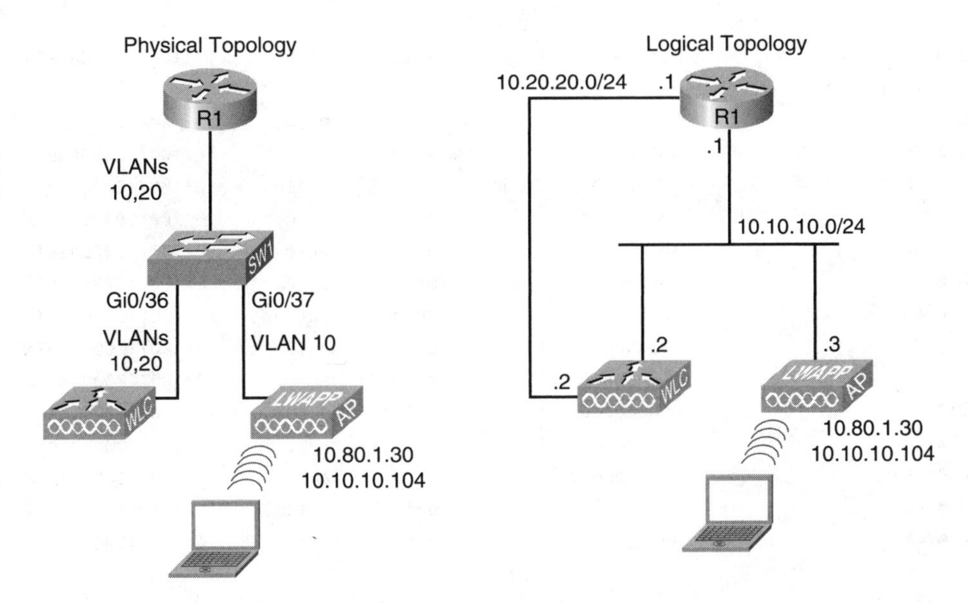

Figure 8-2 *Network Diagram for the First Wireless Troubleshooting Example*

Example 8-1 *The Output Displays the Interfaces to Which the AP and WLC Are Connected*

```
SW1# show cdp neighbors
Capability Codes:   R - Router, T - Trans Bridge, B - Source Route Bridge
                    S - Switch, H - Host, I - IGMP, r - Repeater, P - Phone

Device ID       Local Intrfce  Holdtme  Capability   Platform     Port ID
ap              Gig 0/37       128           T I     AIR-LAP125Gig  0
521-8           Gig 0/39       135                   AIR-LAP521Fas  0
521-7           Gig 0/34       122                   AIR-LAP521Fas  0
Cisco_9a:8c:e0  Gig 0/36       175            H      AIR-WLC210Unit - 0 Slot - 0
Port - 1
SW1#
```

Next, examine the status of the interfaces with the **show interface status** command, as demonstrated in Example 8-2. The Gi 0/37 interface connected to the AP is associated to VLAN 10, and the Gi 0/36 interface connected to the WLC is configured as trunk.

Example 8-2 **show interface status** *Output Confirms That the Gi 0/36 Interface Is Set Up as a Trunk*

```
SW# show interface status

Port       Name          Status      vlan      Duplex  Speed    Type
Gi0/1                    notconnect  1           auto  auto     10/100/1000BaseTX
```

```
Gi0/2                   notconnect  1        auto      auto      10/100/1000BaseTX
! output omitted for brevity
Gi0/34                  connected   1        a-full    a-100     10/100/1000BaseTX
Gi0/35                  notconnect  1        auto      auto      10/100/1000BaseTX
Gi0/36                  connected   trunk    a-full    a-100     10/100/1000BaseTX
Gi0/37                  connected   10       a-full    a-1000    10/100/1000BaseTX
Gi0/38                  notconnect  1        auto      auto      10/100/1000BaseTX
Gi0/39                  connected   1        a-full    a-100     10/100/1000BaseTX
Gi0/40                  notconnect  1        auto      auto      10/100/1000BaseTX
Gi0/41                  notconnect  1        auto      auto      10/100/1000BaseTX
Gi0/42                  notconnect  1        auto      auto      10/100/1000BaseTX
Gi0/43                  connected   1        a-full    a-100     10/100/1000BaseTX
Gi0/44                  connected   1        a-full    a-1000    10/100/1000BaseTX
Gi0/45                  notconnect  1        auto      auto      10/100/1000BaseTX
Gi0/46                  connected   1        a-full    a-1000    10/100/1000BaseTX
Gi0/47                  notconnect  1        auto      auto      10/100/1000BaseTX

--More--
```

You need to find out which VLANs are used for AP to WLC communication, which VLAN is used for client traffic, and whether the access point is operational and registering to the WLC using LWAPP or Control and Provisioning of Wireless Access Points (CAPWAP). The wireless administrator informs us that the AP has a static IP address and that the WLC and the AP should be on the same VLAN, but the WLC is not seeing registration requests from the AP. The static IP address on the AP enables you to rule out DHCP preventing the AP from initiating a LWAPP request. The Layer 1 and Layer 2 status of the interfaces are operational, and the wireless team tells you that it looks the same on their side, for both the AP and the WLC. You should therefore pursue the AP to WLC registration process; if the AP cannot register with the WLC, it will not be able to service client requests. Using the **debug ip packet** command on the switch, you can observe AP's registration process. Because **debug** might produce too much output, you would filter it to see only the traffic related to LWAPP using access list 100. LWAPP uses UDP port 12223 for control messages. Example 8-3 shows this output. The AP's request originating from interface Gi 0/37, which is associated to VLAN 10, is present (see **rcvd** at the end of the **debug** output lines shown in Example 8-3), but this traffic is not forwarded to the trunk on the Gi 0/36 interface. That is probably why there is no response from the WLC.

Example 8-3 *Filtered* **debug** *Output Shows Requests from the AP, but No Response from the WLC*

```
SW1# conf t
Enter configuration commands, one per line. End with CNTL/Z.
SW1(config)# access-list 100 permit udp any any eq 12223
SW1(config)# end
SW1# debug ip packet 100
IP packet debugging is on for access list 100
SW1#
5d13h: %SYS-5-CONFIG_I: Configured from console by console
SW1#
5d13h: IP: s=10.80.1.30 (vlan10), d=255.255.255.255, len 123, rcvd 1
5d13h: IP: s=10.10.10.104 (vlan10), d=255.255.255.255, len 123, rcvd 1
5d13h: IP: s=10.10.10.104 (vlan10), d=255.255.255.255, len 123, rcvd 1
```

To verify that VLAN 10 is allowed on the trunk interface (Gi 0/36), you use the **show interfaces switchport** command. The output shown in Example 8-4 reveals that only VLAN1 is enabled (allowed) on the trunk; in other words, other VLANs such as VLAN 10 are not allowed on the trunk. This is definitely wrong.

Example 8-4 *The* **show interface switchport** *Command Reveals That VLAN 10 Is Not Allowed on the Trunk Between the Switch and the WLC*

```
SW1# show interfaces switchport ¦ begin 0/36
Name: Gi0/36
Switchport: Enabled
Administrative Mode: trunk
Operational Mode: trunk
Administrative Trunking Encapsulation: dot1q
Operational Trunking Encapsulation: dot1q
Negotiation of Trunking: On
Access Mode VLAN: 1 (default)
Trunking Native Mode VLAN: 99 (Inactive)
Administrative Native VLAN tagging: enabled
Voice VLAN: none
Administrative private-vlan host-association: none
Administrative private-vlan mapping: none
Administrative private-vlan native VLAN: none
Administrative private-vlan Native VLAN tagging: enabled
Administrative private-vlan trunk encapsulation: dot1q
```

```
Administrative private-vlan trunk normal VLANs: none
Administrative private-vlan trunk private VLANs: none
Operational private-vlan: none
Trunking VLANs Enabled: 1
Pruning VLANs Enabled: 2-1001
Capture Mode Disabled
Capture VLANs Allowed: All
--More--
```

You should add the appropriate VLANs to the list of allowed VLANs on the trunk interface. The wireless team tells you that the client VLAN is 10, and that the management VLAN is 20. As demonstrated in Example 8-5, use the **switchport trunk allowed vlan add 10,20** command so that VLANs 10 and 20 are allowed on the trunk interface Gi 0/36.

Example 8-5 *VLANs 10 and 20 Are Added as Allowed VLANs on the Trunk Interface*

```
SW1# conf t
Enter configuration commands, one per line. End with CNTL/Z.
SW1(config)# int g0/36
SW1(config-if)# switchport trunk allowed vlan add 10,20
SW1(config-if)# end
SW1#
```

Based on your responsibilities and authorities, you cannot test wireless connectivity or LWAPP operations, but after a few minutes the wireless team tells you that the problem is solved. The AP is registering again to the WLC, and wireless connectivity has been restored.

WLAN Connectivity Troubleshooting Example: Duplex and Trust Issues

This wireless troubleshooting example is based on the network topology shown in Figure 8-3. The wireless operations team complains about the reliability and performance of wireless traffic. The symptom they observe is that the AP interface pointing to the wired network goes up and down intermittently, and when the port is operational, there is a substantial slowdown on Voice over WLAN.

The first thing to do is display the log and look for any clues about the interface (Gi 0/34) that apparently goes up and down intermittently. Example 8-6 shows output from the **show logging | include 0/34** command, which provides the interface identifier for the port connecting the AP.

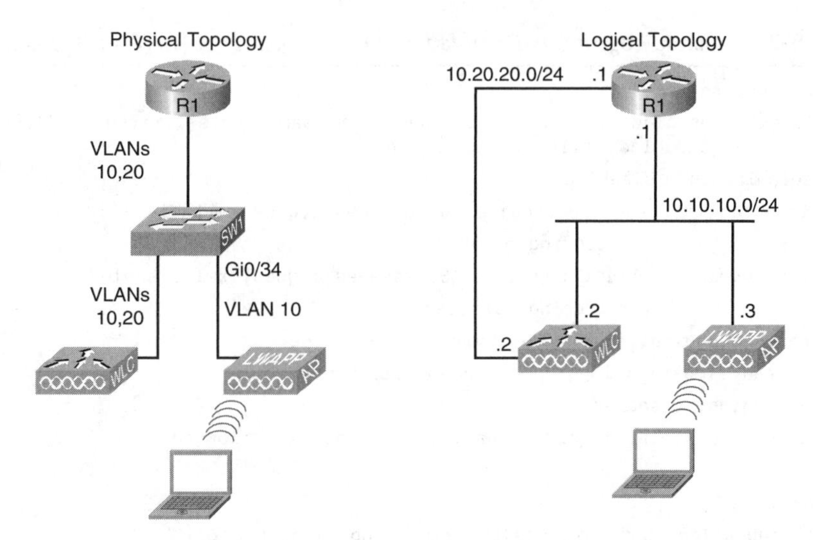

Figure 8-3 *Network Topology for the Second Wireless Troubleshooting Example*

Example 8-6 *The Log Shows a Duplex Mismatch Problem*

```
SW1# show logging ¦ include 0/34
00:12:00: %CDP-4-DUPLEX_MISMATCH: duplex mismatch discovered on
GigabitEthernet0/34 (not half duplex), with 521-7 FastEthernet0 (half duplex)
00:13:00: %CDP-4-DUPLEX_MISMATCH: duplex mismatch discovered on
GigabitEthernet0/34 (not half duplex), with 521-7 FastEthernet0 (half duplex)
00:14:00: %CDP-4-DUPLEX_MISMATCH: duplex mismatch discovered on
GigabitEthernet0/34 (not half duplex), with 521-7 FastEthernet0 (half duplex)
00:15:00: %CDP-4-DUPLEX_MISMATCH: duplex mismatch discovered on
GigabitEthernet0/34 (not half duplex), with 521-7 FastEthernet0 (half duplex)
00:16:00: %CDP-4-DUPLEX_MISMATCH: duplex mismatch discovered on
GigabitEthernet0/34 (not half duplex), with 521-7 FastEthernet0 (half duplex)
00:17:00: %CDP-4-DUPLEX_MISMATCH: duplex mismatch discovered on
GigabitEthernet0/34 (not half duplex), with 521-7 FastEthernet0 (half duplex)
00:18:19: %SYS-5-CONFIG_I: Configured from console by console
00:19:00: %CDP-4-DUPLEX_MISMATCH: duplex mismatch discovered on
GigabitEthernet0/34 (not half duplex), with 521-7 FastEthernet0 (half duplex)
00:20:00: %CDP-4-DUPLEX_MISMATCH: duplex mismatch discovered on
GigabitEthernet0/34 (not half duplex), with 521-7 FastEthernet0 (half duplex)
SW1#
```

There is a duplex mismatch, but you should see the duplex mismatch messages on the console, too. A plain **show logging** command tells you that the console logging is disabled, which makes a lot of sense in a production switch. If you enable it, you will see the duplex mismatch messages. Example 8-7 demonstrates how to fix the duplex problem by configuring the interface for full-duplex 100 Mbps. Note that it is a good practice to find out why the duplex was set to half to begin with.

Example 8-7 *Console Logging Is Disabled, but the Duplex Problem Can Be Fixed*

```
SW1# show logging
Syslog logging: enabled (0 messages dropped, 1 messages rate-limited, 0 flushes,
0 overruns, xml disabled, filtering disabled
    Console logging: disabled
    Monitor logging: level debugging, 0 messages logged, xml disabled,
                     filtering disabled
    Buffer logging: level debugging, 48 messages logged, xml disabled,
                     filtering disabled
    Exception Logging: size (4096 bytes)
    Count and timestamp logging messages: disabled
    File logging: disabled
    Trap logging: level informational, 51 message lines logged
--More--
SW1# conf t
Enter configuration commands, one per line. End with CNTL/Z.
SW1(config)# int g0/34
SW1(config-if)# duplex full
SW1(config-if)# speed 100
SW1(config-if)# end
SW1#
```

Next, you call the wireless team, and they inform you that the AP comes up and does not go down again, but they are still experiencing performance issues, especially for VoIP traffic coming from the wireless network. High CPU utilization could be an issue, so you need to investigate that using the **show processes cpu** command, the output of which shows a relatively low level of utilization at this point, as demonstrated in Example 8-8. When you look at the available baseline for this device, provided by the team as additional documentation, you realize that these values are not too far from the baseline.

Example 8-8 *The CPU Utilization Seems Normal*

```
SW# show processes CPU
CPU utilization for five seconds: 4%/0%; one minute: 6%, five minutes: 5%
PID  Runtime(ms)  Invoked   uSecs    5Sec     1Min    5Min    TTY    Process
1            0          5       0   0.00%    0.00%   0.00%      0    Chunk Manager
2            0        275       0   0.00%    0.00%   0.00%      0    Load Meter
3            0         33       0   0.00%    0.00%   0.00%      0    SpanTree Helper
4         1019        149    6838   0.00%    0.07%   0.05%      0    Check heaps
5            0          1       0   0.00%    0.00%   0.00%      0    Pool Manager
6            0          2       0   0.00%    0.00%   0.00%      0    Timers
7          118        845     139   0.00%    0.00%   0.00%      0    ARP Input
8            0          1       0   0.00%    0.00%   0.00%      0    AAA_SERVER_DEADT
9            0          2       0   0.00%    0.00%   0.00%      0    AAA high-capacit
```

```
10              0        1       0  0.00%  0.00%  0.00%    0  Policy Manager
11             26        3    8666  0.00%  0.00%  0.00%    0  Entity MIB API
12              0        1       0  0.00%  0.00%  0.00%    0  IFS Agent Manage
13              0       25       0  0.00%  0.00%  0.00%    0  IPC Dynamic Cach
14              0        1       0  0.00%  0.00%  0.00%    0  IPC Zone Manager
15              0     1412       0  0.00%  0.00%  0.00%    0  IPC Periodic Tim
16              0     1412       0  0.00%  0.00%  0.00%    0  IPC Deferred Por
17              0       94       0  0.00%  0.00%  0.00%    0  IPC Seat Manager
18              0      345       0  0.00%  0.00%  0.00%    0  HC Counter Timer
19              0        1       0  0.00%  0.00%  0.00%    0  Net Input
20              9     1412       6  0.00%  0.00%  0.00%    0  Dynamic ARP Insp
21              0        1       0  0.00%  0.00%  0.00%    0  ARP Snoop
22              9        2    4500  0.00%  0.00%  0.00%    0  XML Proxy Client
23              0        1       0  0.00%  0.00%  0.00%    0  Critical Bkgnd
--More--
```

Next, you consider possible QoS configuration errors. This sounds likely as a possibility; perhaps wireless voice traffic is not being properly prioritized when entering the network. In other words, the voice traffic may not be tagged with proper QoS priorities. In the case of a LWAPP deployment, if the AP is tagging packets with values, it is the differentiated services code point (DSCP) field that gets used. You should check to see whether the switch port is honoring that. At the switch, use the **show mls qos int gi0/34** command to display the trust boundary settings. A trust boundary is the point within the network where QoS markings such as DSCP are first accepted. By default, switch ports will reset DSCP values unless you explicitly tell the port to trust those values. The output of **show mls qos** (shown in Example 8-9) indicates that the switch does not trust anything coming from the AP. This could be a real issue; voice traffic is being prioritized on the wireless network, but it is losing its priority when crossing over to the wired network.

Example 8-9 *The Interface is Shown as Configured Not to Trust the QoS (DSCP) Setting*

```
SW1# show mls qos int g0/34
GigabitEthernet0/34
trust state: not trusted
trust mode: not trusted
trust enabled flag: ena
COS override: dis
default COS: 0
DSCP Mutation Map: Default DSCP Mutation Map
Trust device: None
qos mode: port-based

SW1#
```

You must set the switch port to trust DSCP values (following best practices and guidelines) using the **mls qos trust dscp** command, which is entered at the interface configuration mode. After entering the command, you inspect the configuration with the **show mls qos** command. The output indicates that the switch is now trusting DSCP values. Example 8-10 shows the necessary configuration and verification. After a while, the wireless network support staff confirm that performance issues are alleviated for VoWLAN traffic. The problem is solved.

Example 8-10 *The Interface Is Configured to Trust the QoS (DSCP) Setting*

```
SW1# conf t
Enter configuration commands, one per line. End with CNTL/Z.
SW1(config)# int g0/34
SW1(config-if)# mls qos trust dscp
SW1(config-if)# end
SW1# end
SW1#
SW1# show mls qos int g0/34
GigabitEthernet0/34
trust state: trust dscp
trust mode: trust dscp
trust enabled flag: ena
COS override: dis
default COS: 0
DSCP Mutation Map: Default DSCP Mutation Map
Trust device: None
qos mode: port-based

SW1#
```

WLAN Connectivity Troubleshooting Example: LWAPP Denied by New Security Implementations

The third wireless troubleshooting example is based on the topology shown in Figure 8-4. The wireless team tells you that wireless operations have stopped and that none of the APs are able to register to the WLC. This problem has been expected, because a security auditor recently performed a security assessment and recommended a few improvements to the network policy. In taking all the necessary precautions, all configurations have been reverted to their pre-audit state, except for the LAN switch shown in Figure 8-4.

After investigating the recent change in security policy, you find that Cisco IOS firewall services were installed in some switches that are critical to the network. The auditor recommended hardening network devices at locations subject to higher levels of risk. Having studied the security implications and considerations on a wireless network, you know that the wireless-to-wired edge is a likely candidate to have a firewall deployed. This line of thinking allows you to focus on the Cisco IOS firewall, without discarding the

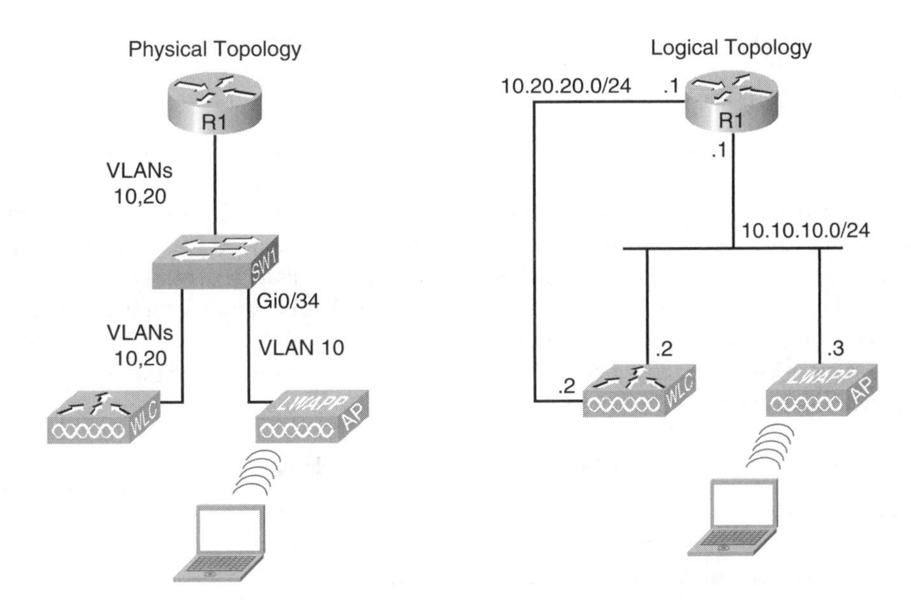

Figure 8-4 *Network Topology for the Third Wireless Troubleshooting Example*

possibility of other issues. Therefore, instead of focusing on a bottom-up or top-down approach, you start at the firewall level and analyze the implications of it in the wireless infrastructure. The reported symptom, wireless APs not being able to register to the WLC, provides another hint as to what to look for: LWAPP traffic may be denied by the firewall. This is a valid hypothesis with a good likelihood of being accurate, and you need to verify it. While gathering information about the Cisco IOS firewall, you must remember that Cisco IOS Software allows the firewall to be configured using one of two methods:

- The classical Cisco IOS firewall, which uses ACLs exclusively on interfaces
- The zone-based firewall, more widely used and more flexible for a comprehensive deployment of firewall rules

You check the zone-based policy first, but after entering the **show zone-pair security** command you receive an error message, effectively informing you that no zone-based policies are configured on this router. The **show zone-pair security** command is normally used to display the policy attached to zone-pairs. Next, you consider interface ACLs on the switch using the **show ip interface** command for the interface connected to the access point. The result, shown in Example 8-11, reveals that there is an ACL called FIREWALL applied inbound to the Gi 0/34 interface.

Example 8-11 *The* **show interface** *Command Reveals an Inbound ACL on Gi 0/34*

```
R1# show ip interface g0/34
```

```
GigabitEthernet0/34 is up, line protocol is up
  Inbound access list is FIREWALL
R1#
```

You display the access list (see Example 8-12) and notice that it allows routing protocols and management protocols such as SSH. If you think in the context of a controller-based wireless architecture, you'll notice one important thing is missing: permission for the LWAPP ports. Both control (the traffic between AP and WLC) and user traffic traverse through the LWAPP tunnel; however, the firewall is blocking those ports. This proves how important it is that the designers of the security policy be aware of the services and applications running on the network.

Example 8-12 *The Access List Does Not Permit LWAPP Traffic*

```
R1# sh access-list
Extended IP access list 100
    10 permit udp 10.10.10.0 0.0.0.255 any eq 12223
    20 permit udp any any eq 12223
Extended IP access list FIREWALL
    10 permit icmp any any echo-reply
    20 permit tcp any any eq www
    30 permit tcp any any eq ftp
    40 permit tcp any any eq ftp-data
    50 permit tcp any any eq telnet
    60 permit tcp any anyeq smtp
    70 permit tcp any any eq pop3
    80 permit eigrp any any
    90 permit udp any any eq rip
R1#
```

It looks like you have found the problem, and you can verify it by changing the access list. Following best practices, you add a line to the ACL, and a remark indicating why this line was added. You need to permit UDP 12222 for user data traffic, and UDP 12223 for AP-to-WLC control messages. This work is shown in Example 8-13. The wireless team reports that this fix seems to have solved the problem. You changed the security policy by changing the firewall rules. You should carefully monitor the accuracy of the change and the potential implications it might have. A simple **show access-lists** command displays the number of packets matching each ACL line. You can closely monitor the ACL matches under different traffic loads and profiles to determine the implications of the recent change.

Example 8-13 *The ACL Is Modified to Permit LWAPP Traffic*

```
R1# conf t
Enter configuration commands, one per line. End with CNTL/Z.
R1(config)# ip access-list extended FIREWALL
R1(config-ext-nacl)# remark ---allowing LWAPP control and data ports---
R1(config-ext-nacl)# permit udp any any range 12222 12223
R1(config-ext-nacl)# end
R1#
```

WLAN Connectivity Troubleshooting Example: DHCP Issues

The fourth and final wireless troubleshooting example is based on the network topology shown in Figure 8-5. In this case, the AP and the WLC are in different VLANs, and the R1 router is performing inter-VLAN routing and also acts as the DHCP server for the APs. You have received a call from the wireless team stating that none of the APs can register to the WLC. All APs are DHCP clients but are not able to obtain their IP address from the DHCP server (which is R1 at address 10.50.50.100). The wireless group is blaming this problem on the wired network, so it is your job to find the problem and fix it.

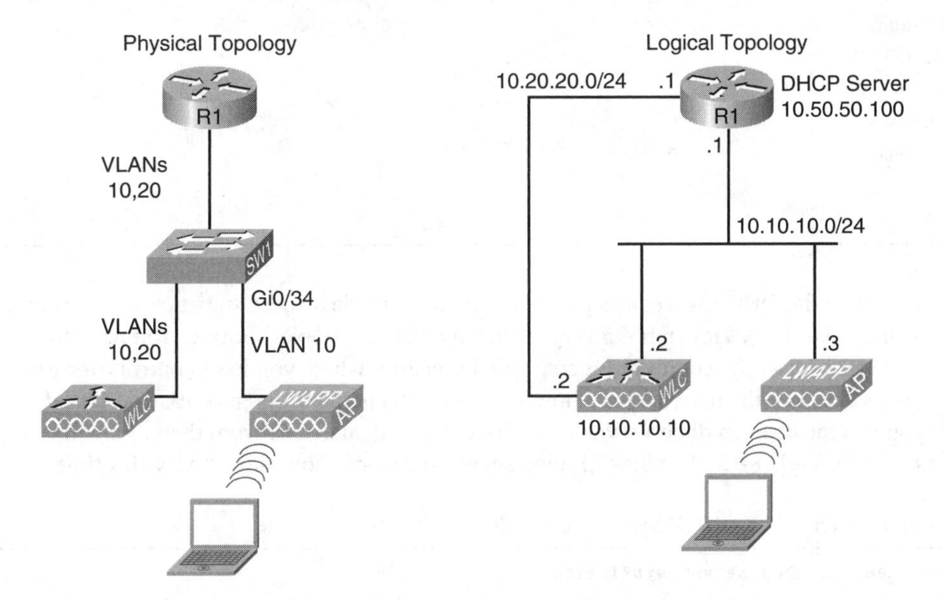

Figure 8-5 *The Network Topology Diagram for the Fourth Wireless Troubleshooting Example*

Several things could be wrong here. One of them is the process that the APs go through to obtain an IP address lease from the DHCP server. After the APs have obtained an IP address, they register with the WLC. You will look at both processes to isolate the problem. So, you will start with the DHCP server. You switch to the console of the router acting as the DHCP server and enter the **show ip dhcp server statistics** command, the output from which is shown in Example 8-14.

Example 8-14 *DHCP Server Statistics Do Not Reveal Any Conclusions*

```
R1# show ip dhcp server statistics
Memory usage             5317
Address pools            1
Database agents          0
Automatic bindings       2
Manual bindings          0
Expired bindings         0
Malformed messages       0

Message                  Received
BOOTREQUEST              0
DHCPDISCOVER             9
DHCPREQUEST              6
DHCPDECLINE              0
DHCPRELEASE              12
DHCPINFORM               0

Message                  Sent
BOOTREPLY                0
DHCPOFFER                9
DHCPPACK                 6
DHCPNAK                  0

R1#
```

To isolate the DHCP server as a problem, you need to clear these statistics and start monitoring from there. This step is a very important step in troubleshooting. You need to analyze statistics in the context of a controlled scenario, where you have control over when test traffic is in the network, and how your test affects the different statistics. Therefore, you use the **clear ip dhcp server statistics** command, and start from there. As you can see in Example 8-15, the **show ip dhcp server statistics** shows no activity this time.

Example 8-15 *The DHCP Server Shows No Activity*

```
R1# clear ip dhcp server statistics
R1#
R1#
R1# show ip dhcp server statistics
Memory usage             5317
Address pools            1
Database agents          0
Automatic bindings       2
Manual bindings          0
```

```
Expired bindings        0
Malformed messages      0

Message                 Received
BOOTREQUEST             0
DHCPDISCOVER            0
DHCPREQUEST             0
DHCPDECLINE             0
DHCPRELEASE             0
DHCPINFORM              0

Message                 Sent
BOOTREPLY               0
DHCPOFFER               0
DHCPPACK                0
DHCPNAK                 0

R1#
```

Next, you will use the **debug ip udp** command to monitor for any DHCP client activity such as DHCP discover messages, but see no reference to UDP port 67 (DHCP client). Because the DHCP clients are in a subnet different than that of the DHCP server, you might be missing the DHCP relay agent. This will have to be configured in the switch connecting the AP to the rest of the network. You use the **show running interface command**, selecting the gi0/34 port that points to the APs, but notice that the command **ip-helper address** is missing. This is a switchport interface associated to VLAN 10, so you must inspect interface VLAN 10 instead. See the results in Example 8-16. There is no **ip-helper address** configured there either.

Example 8-16 *Neither the Interface Nor the Access VLAN Show a Helper Address Configuration*

```
SW1# show running-config interface g0/34
Building configuration...

Current configuration : 108 bytes
!
interface GigabitEthernet0/34
 switchport access vlan 10
 switchport mode access
 mls qos trust dscp
end

SW1#
```

```
SW1# show running-config interface vlan 10
Building configuration...

Current configuration : 61 bytes
!
interface vlan10
 ip address 10.10.10.1 255.255.255.0
end

SW1#
```

As Example 8-17 shows, the **show running | include helper** command reveals that one IP helper address is configured on the switch, but it is pointing to an old address of the DHCP server, and it is obviously not on the right interface. So, you need to fix that issue. You go into the interface VLAN 10 and enter the correct IP helper address (after proper investigation, you might have to delete the old/erroneous command).

Example 8-17 *We Correcting the Helper Address Configuration*

```
SW1# show running-config ¦ include helper
 ip helper-address 10.100.100.100
SW1#

SW1# conf t
Enter configuration commands, one per line. End with CNTL/Z.
SW1(config)# int vlan 10
SW1(config-if)# ip helper-address 10.50.50.100
SW1(config-if)# end
SW1#
```

Back at the DHCP server, now the **debug** results show UDP packets finally arriving at the DHCP server, as shown in Example 8-18.

Example 8-18 *Client DHCP Requests Show Up at the Server (Router)*

```
02:13:57: UDP: rcvd src=0.0.0.0(68), dst=255.255.255.255(67), length=584
02:13:58: DHCPD: assigned IP address 10.10.10.115 to client 0100.1bd5.1324.42.
02:13:58: UDP: sent src=0.0.0.0(67), dst=255.255.255.255(68), length=308
02:13:58: UDP: sent src=0.0.0.0(67), dst=255.255.255.255(68), length=308
02:13:58: UDP: rcvd src=0.0.0.0(68), dst=255.255.255.255(67), length=584
02:14:00: UDP: rcvd src=0.0.0.0(68), dst=255.255.255.255(67), length=584
02:14:01: UDP: rcvd src=0.0.0.0(68), dst=255.255.255.255(67), length=584
02:14:03: UDP: rcvd src=0.0.0.0(68), dst=255.255.255.255(67), length=584
```

```
02:14:05: DHCPD: assigned IP address 10.10.10.116 to client 0100.2290.0bc1.02.
02:14:05: UDP: sent src=0.0.0.0(67), dst=255.255.255.255(68), length=308
02:14:05: UDP: sent src=0.0.0.0(67), dst=255.255.255.255(68), length=308
02:14:05: UDP: sent src=0.0.0.0(67), dst=255.255.255.255(68), length=308
02:14:05: UDP: sent src=0.0.0.0(67), dst=255.255.255.255(68), length=308
02:14:05: UDP: sent src=0.0.0.0(67), dst=255.255.255.255(68), length=308
02:14:05: UDP: sent src=0.0.0.0(67), dst=255.255.255.255(68), length=308
02:14:05: UDP: sent src=0.0.0.0(67), dst=255.255.255.255(68), length=308
02:14:09: UDP: rcvd src=10.10.10.105(61019), dst=255.255.255.255(12223),
length=103
02:14:09: UDP: rcvd src=10.10.10.115(68), dst=10.10.10.1(67), length=584
02:14:09: UDP: sent src=10.10.10.1(67), dst=10.10.10.115(68), length=308
02:14:09: UDP: rcvd src=10.10.10.104(61121), dst=255.255.255.255(12223),
length=103
```

A few minutes later, you speak to the wireless support team and they verify the successful IP address assignment; however, there is still no registration into the WLC. The wireless operations team tells you to check the configuration of option 43 on the DHCP server. On the DHCP server, you display the details of the address pool using the **show ip dhcp pool** command and see nothing there. The **show running | section ip dhcp pool** displays no option 43 either (see Example 8-19).

Example 8-19 *The DHCP Pool Shows No Option 43 Configuration*

```
R1# show running-config ¦ section ip dhcp pool
ip dhcp pool vlan10
   network 10.10.10.0 255.255.255.0
   default-router 10.10.10.1
!
```

Option 43 is used to notify the DHCP client the AP-management IP address of the WLC. Therefore, you need to go into the DHCP pool configuration mode using the **ip dhcp pool** command, and enter the AP-management IP address of the WLC as part of option 43. For that, you will use the command **option 43**, followed by the right IP address in hexadecimal format, as shown in Example 8-20. The hex string is assembled by concatenating Type, Length, and Value. Type is always f1 (hex), Length is the number of controller management IP addresses times 4 in hex, and Value is the IP address of the controller listed sequentially in hex. If there is only one WLC management address, the Length is 04 (hex), and in this case the WLC management IP address is 10.10.10.10, which is 0a0a0a0a (hex).

Example 8-20 *Adding the Option 43 Configuration to the DHCP Configuration*

```
R1# conf t
Enter configuration commands, one per line. End with CNTL/Z.
R1(config)# ip dhcp pool vlan10
R1(dhcp-config)# option 43 hex f1040a0a0a0a
R1(dhcp-config)# end
R1#
```

The wireless operations team notifies you that the problem is now fully solved.

Troubleshooting Unified Communications Issues in a Converged Network

This section discusses convergence, which over the past decade has become an integral part of most networks. Note that this section is not a lesson on unified communications or IP telephony. Instead, it deals with the readiness of a campus network to support those converged services. This section concludes with a number of troubleshooting examples that deal with the impact of converged traffic in a campus and potential changes in the traditional network that result in very interesting troubleshooting scenarios.

Common Unified Communications Integration Issues

IP telephony services are often provided over the campus infrastructure. To have data and voice application traffic coexist in harmony, certain mechanisms are necessary to differentiate types of traffic and to offer priority processing to voice traffic, which is sensitive to delay. QoS policies mark and qualify traffic as it traverses the campus switch blocks. Specific VLANs keep voice traffic separate from other data to ensure that it is carried through the network with special handling and with minimal delay. Specific design and implementation considerations should be made at all campus switches supporting VoIP. These considerations result in a wide variety of scenarios to deal with in troubleshooting converged networks. The underlying routing and switching infrastructure will be responsible for providing a reliable, efficient, and secure transport for signaling traffic from IP phones to the call-processing engine. The infrastructure is also responsible for the gateway-to-gateway traffic needed to forward calls to the public switched telephone network (PSTN) or WAN destinations. Figure 8-6 illustrates a sample converged network with the main elements such as voice gateway, Cisco Unified Communications Manager (CUCM), Cisco Unity (for voice mail), telephony endpoints (IP phones, conference units), LAN router and switches, WAN, and PSTN.

Unified communications endpoints rely on a series of network services for their proper operation. Those services are the focus of this section. As already mentioned, this lesson does not troubleshoot IP telephony components such as the CUCM or voice gateways; it intends to cover troubleshooting the campus network to facilitate the work of those IP telephony components. The following list summarizes the design considerations of integrating unified communications into a campus. All of the items in the list result in challenging troubleshooting scenarios that increasingly involve multiple components of the network,

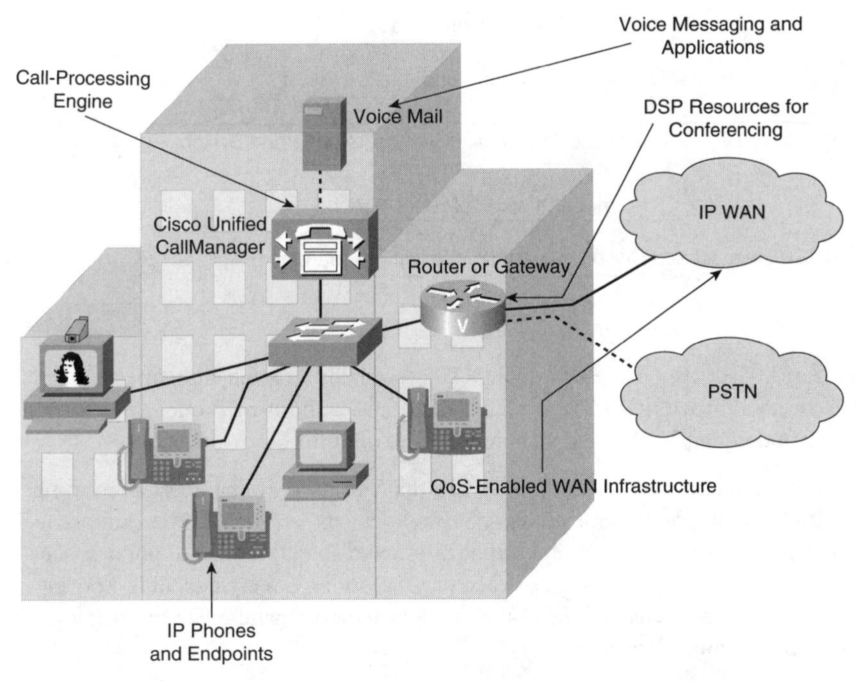

Figure 8-6 *A Sample Converged Network and Its Main Elements*

multiple layers of the Open Systems Interconnection (OSI) model, multiple integrated technologies, and potentially multiple operations and support teams within an organization:

- **Quality of service:** Bandwidth, delay, jitter, packet loss, network QoS readiness, trust boundaries, switch QoS
- **High availability:** STP/RSTP, HSRP/GLBP/VRRP
- **Security:** Traffic segregation (voice versus data VLANs), firewalling/filtering
- **Provisioning and management:** PoE, DHCP, TFTP, NTP, CDP, trunking, VLANs

QoS is an important requirement of network infrastructures supporting converged applications and traffic. The goal here will be to understand the high-level components of a QoS architecture and to be able to determine whether that architecture is the source of network issues. You need to be familiar with the problems that occur when trust boundaries are not set or are improperly set. We also need to know how to monitor network elements, such as routers, to make sure QoS is operational.

Other considerations are related to security, not only in terms of how to protect unified communications traffic, but also in terms of how existing security controls might affect that traffic in a negative way. Multiple issues result from segregating voice and data traffic in different VLANs. You need to consider the effect of firewalls filtering not only voice traffic, but also critical control and signaling protocols.

In terms of readiness, the unified communications network requires specific components that might become additional sources of problems. Power (PoE) must be readily available to endpoints. Repositories of firmware and configuration files through TFTP, time

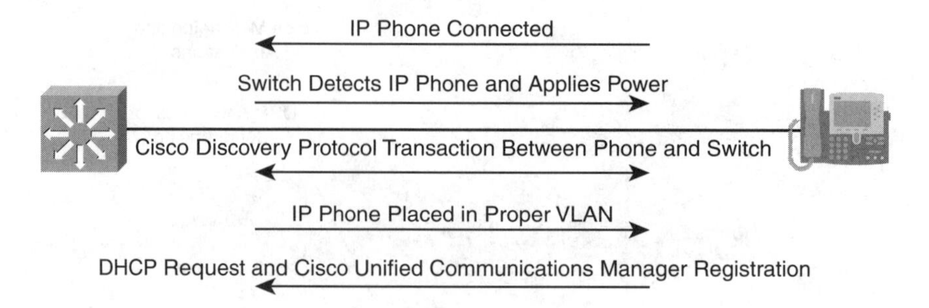

Figure 8-7 *IP Phone Boot Process*

synchronization (Network Time Protocol [NTP]) for cryptographic authentication, and Cisco Discovery Protocol (CDP) to facilitate the IP phone booting process are all services that use the underlying VLAN and switching infrastructure.

One of the important processes in the network that the support engineers need to be familiar with is the IP phone boot process. Several devices, services, and protocols need to work in harmony for the successful initialization and startup of the IP phones (see Figure 8-7). Knowing the process is critical to laying out an effective troubleshooting method and making good use of the available tools and commands. The following is a list of IP phone boot process steps:

Step 1. The IP phone powers on.

Step 2. The phone performs a power-on self-test, or POST.

Step 3. The phone boots.

Step 4. The phone uses CDP to learn the voice VLAN.

Step 5. The phone initializes the IP stack.

Step 6. The IP phone sends DHCP broadcasts.

Step 7. The DHCP server selects a free IP address from the pool and sends it, along with the other parameters, including option 150.

Step 8. The IP phone initializes, applying the IP configuration to the IP stack.

Step 9. The IP phone requests a configuration file from the TFTP server defined in Option 150.

Note that prior to IP phone power on in Step 1, the LAN switch to which it connects must detect the phone's power requirement and apply power (PoE) to the appropriate port accordingly. Furthermore, after the phone copies its configuration file from the TFTP server in Step 9, it registers with the CUCM that the configuration file specifies.

The VLAN architecture is very important, and knowing the voice and data VLANs is crucial. Also, knowing how voice and data traffic is carried across switch ports help in troubleshooting efforts. Figure 8-8 shows that the voice VLAN uses IEEE 802.1Q encapsulation, while data traffic remains untagged and uses the native VLAN. The switch port where the IP phone connects is configured as an access port, but it supports an auxiliary VLAN called the voice VLAN.

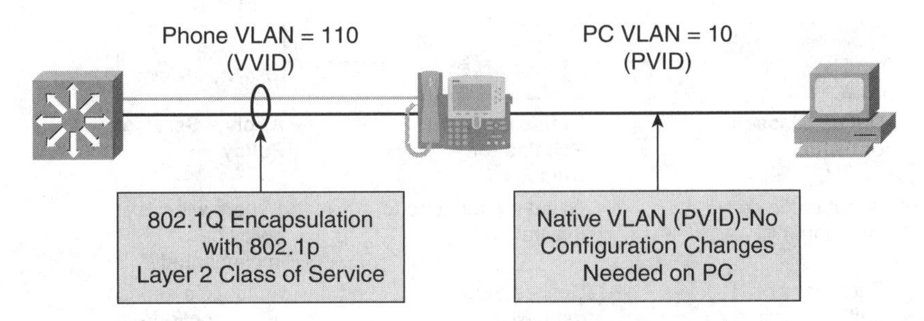

Figure 8-8 *Voice (Auxiliary) and Data VLANs Are Carried over the Same Port*

The design considerations can result in scenarios that need troubleshooting. If the services that the network infrastructure needs to provide are not available, are misconfigured, or are simply not reachable, IP phones might become out of sync in terms of digital certificate verification, or they might not obtain the right amount of power, if CDP is missing. Furthermore, a misconfigured DHCP server might prevent IP phones from obtaining their configuration files if option 150 is not enabled.

Even if the network services are operational and provide the required support infrastructure, QoS architectures might render voice traffic useless. Furthermore, security controls might interfere with control protocols such as DHCP. They could also filter required signaling protocols, crucial in VoIP operations. It is important to understand the protocols and ports involved in standard IP telephony deployments. Examples of those protocols are Real-Time Transport Protocol (RTP) and its UDP port ranges, Session Initiation Protocol (SIP) on TCP port 5060, or H323 on TCP port 1720.

On most Cisco IOS devices, you use what is known as Modular QoS CLI (MQC) to configure QoS. MQC offers the configuration objects that implement QoS in a modular fashion, so that you can configure policies once and apply them to multiple interfaces, even different devices (because MQC syntax is not platform specific). It is also modular because it decouples the traffic classification components from the policy components, so that you can apply the same policy to different traffic classes without having to create it multiple times.

QoS configuration in summary, is assigning different treatments to different types of traffic, according to the traffic or application requirements. Figure 8-9 displays the process of configuring a QoS policy using Cisco IOS MQC, which has three main components:

- **Class maps:** Class maps are used to create classification templates that are later used in policy maps in which QoS mechanisms are bound to classes. Examples include voice, video, bulk data transfers, and transactional traffic.

- **Policy maps:** Policy maps are used to create a traffic policy. The purpose of a traffic policy is to configure the QoS features that should be associated with the traffic that has been classified in a user-specified traffic class or classes. Examples of policies applied to specific traffic classes are rate-limit video traffic, reserve bandwidth for voice traffic, and always drop bulk transfers first at moments of heavy congestion.

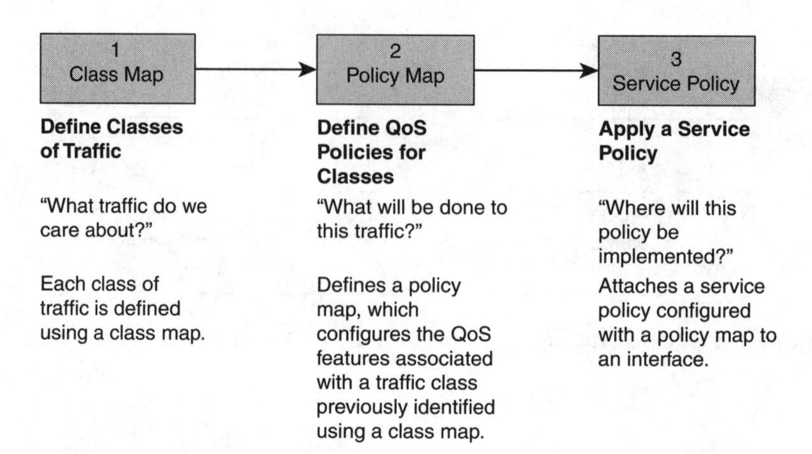

Figure 8-9 *QoS Configuration Using MQC*

- **Service policy:** The **service-policy** command is used to assign a policy map to an interface or VC with respect to incoming or outgoing traffic. A service policy can also be applied to a class within a policy map, which results in a nested or hierarchical policy.

When the class maps, policy maps, and service policies are configured on the device interfaces and enforce the built QoS policies, the main command used for troubleshooting is the **show policy-map interface** command, which you will see in action later in Example 8-30.

Troubleshooting converged networks requires the gathering-information stage to include QoS and network services information. The **show policy-map interface** command is used in the routers, and the **show mls qos** command is used on the switches, to summarize the status of the QoS components. You much also make use of the appropriate show and debug commands to examine the more traditional services such as DHCP and CDP. Analyzing the potential hypotheses requires an integrated effort. In converged networks, we have to consider issues related to PoE, followed by CDP, followed by DHCP, followed by TFTP, because that is the sequence of events and protocols that allow IP phones to be connected to the network and become operational. You also need to understand that the LAN services that are used to support unified communications are being used in other capacities, too. For example, the DHCP server probably assigns IP addresses to devices other than the IP phones, too, and the NTP service will also be synchronizing router clocks to enable SSH communications. Every time we change any of these services to fix VoIP issues, we might be affecting another protocol or application's operation.

Table 8-1 shows a list of useful commands used for troubleshooting converged networks. As usual, using the appropriate **debug** command is crucial. For example, **debug ip dhcp server events** enables you to look at all DHCP transactions and perform specific troubleshooting for the DHCP protocol. On a router that is acting as a DHCP server, this debug displays all stages of DHCP (discover, offer, request, and acknowledgment) that lead to a client obtaining an IP lease. The **debug ephone** command is also very informative; it shows the detail of IP phone registration process, including IP phones obtaining power (PoE), IP addresses, and configuration files.

Unified Communications Troubleshooting Example: Port Security and Voice VLAN Issues

The first troubleshooting example is based on the network topology diagram shown in Figure 8-10. The problem here is that the IP phones will not boot and initialize. They have no access to the IP network. We are having this problem in multiple areas of the network, but not all of them. The issue seems to be permanent, and not intermittent. In those switches where the problem IP phones are connected, it is not clear whether all IP phones have the same problem.

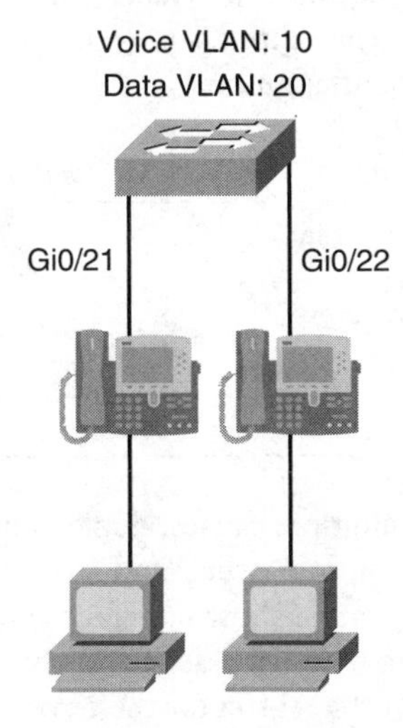

Figure 8-10 *The Network Topology Diagram for the First Unified Communications Troubleshooting Example*

Table 8-1 *Useful Converged Network Troubleshooting Commands*

Focus	Command
Switching	**show interfaces trunk** **show interfaces switchport** **show vlan** **show errdisable recovery**
Auto-QoS	**show auto qos** **show auto discovery qos**
IP services	**show ip dhcp pool** **show ip dhcp server** **show ntp status**
IP communications	**debug ephone**
Security	**show crypto engine connections active**

Knowing from the reported symptoms that this issue seems to be a network-wide problem, the support team decided to identify the wiring closets where the symptoms were detected and try to find a common recent change, upgrade, or incident recently happening. The change logs for the affected wiring closets show a recent change on VLAN Trunking Protocol (VTP) domains and configuration. The support team decided to check the status of the ports for the failing IP phones. In the past, changes such as the VTP change have resulted in unwanted or unneeded configuration changes that fail to get documented.

You begin at the switch, with the **show interfaces status** command for the interface where the phone is connected. The output, shown in Example 8-21, provides an overall view of port status and basic configuration.

Example 8-21 *The Output Shows the Gi0/21 Interface in Err-Disabled Status*

```
Switch# show interfaces g0/21 status

Port      Name                  Status          Vlan   Duplex   Speed   Type
Gi0/21    to phone number one   err-disabled    20     auto     auto    10/100/1000BaseTX
Switch#
```

The err-disable state can have multiple causes: duplex mismatches, late collisions, EtherChannel problems, spanning-tree issues, and so on. You now try the command that complements **show interfaces status: show interface status err-disabled.** This command lists the ports in this state along with the reasons for this state. Looking at the output on Example 8-22, you can see that the reason for the error is a port security violation.

Example 8-22 *Port Secure Violation Caused the Port to Go into Err-Disabled State*

```
Switch# show interface status err-disabled

Port      Name                  Status          Reason                  Err-disabled vlans
Gi0/21    to phone number one   err-disabled    psecure-violation
Switch#
```

You must use the port security commands to determine the configuration, and inquire about the need for this feature and the possibility that this configuration was a mistake. If you look at the output of the **show port-security interface** command in Example 8-23, you see that the maximum allowed MAC addresses setting on the port is set to 1.

Example 8-23 *The Port Security Feature Allows a Maximum of One MAC Address*

```
Switch# show port-security interface g0/21
Port Security                              : Enabled
Port Status                                : Secure-shutdown
Violation Mode                             : Shutdown
Aging Time                                 : 0 mins
Aging Type                                 : Absolute
```

```
SecureStatic Address Aging          : Disabled
Maximum MAC Addresses               : 1
Total MAC Addresses                 : 1
Configured MAC Addresses            : 1
Sticky MAC Addresses                : 0
Last Source Address:vlan            : 0021.7098.30ab:20
Security Violation Count            : 1

Switch#
```

That setting is probably why the problem has occurred. A maximum of one MAC address is allowed in the interface, yet some of the phones have PCs connected to them, and both the phone and the PC send packets. This means that two MAC addresses will be reported on the port, which is beyond the maximum allowed. After investigation, those who were investigating whether the port security feature was needed inform you that this setting is not needed on IP phone switch ports, so you proceed to remove the configuration from all the ports in this switch. To remove the port security configuration, you need to run not just the **no switchport port-security** command, but also all commands related to port security. You first use the **show running interface** command to display the whole configuration for the interfaces, and then remove all port security commands as shown in Example 8-24. After the corrections are made, you must reset the interface by entering **shutdown** before removing the erroneous commands, and entering the **no shutdown** command after-wards (as shown in Example 8-24). Finally, you check the status of the interface and the status shows as connected.

Example 8-24 *Displaying the Configuration and Removing the Port Security Commands*

```
Switch# sh run int g0/21
Building configuration...

Current configuration : 200 bytes
!
Interface GigabitEthernet0/21
 description to phone number one
 switchport access vlan 20
 switchport mode access
 switchport port-security
 switchport port-security mac-address 000b.8572.1810
end

Switch#
Switch#
Switch# conf t
Enter configuration commands, one per line. End with CNTL/Z.
```

```
Switch(config)# int g0/21
Switch(config-if)# shutdown
Switch(config-if)# no switchport port-security
Switch(config-if)# no switchport port-security mac-address 000b.8572.1810
Switch(config-if)# no shutdown
Switch(config-if)#end
Switch# sh int g0/21 status

Port      Name               Status       Vlan  Duplex  Speed   Type
Gi0/21    to phone number on connected    20    a-full  a-1000  10/100/1000BaseTX
Switch#
```

You hear back from the IP telephony support personnel, and they state that their IP phones are still down. So, you must continue troubleshooting. Scrolling back through the running configuration of the interface, you notice that voice VLAN is not configured for the port. At this point, the support team has provided you with the configuration template for switch ports connecting IP phones to the network. You notice that the interfaces are missing the trust boundary settings and have no voice VLAN configuration, as per the template. Therefore, you should restore interface configurations according to the configuration template. You do that only on one interface to test and verify the changes as shown in Example 8-25: set the voice VLAN using **switchport voice vlan 10** and trust IP phone markings using **mls qos trust cos** and **mls qos trust device ip-phone** commands. This last command configures CDP so that it can detect whether a Cisco IP phone is attached to the port. If CDP detects a Cisco IP phone, the interface applies the configured **mls qos trust cos** command. If CDP does not detect a Cisco IP phone, QoS ignores any configured non-default trust state. The configuration work is then checked using the **show interfaces switchport** command.

Example 8-25 *Voice VLAN and Trust Configurations Are Added to the Interface*

```
Switch# conf t
Enter configuration commands, one per line. End with CNTL/Z.
Switch(config)# int g0/21
Switch(config-if)# switchport voice vlan 10
Switch(config-if)# mls qos trust cos
Switch(config-if)# mls qos trust device cisco-phone
Switch(config-if)#

Switch# show interface switchport g0/21
Name: Gi0/21
Switchport: Enabled
Administrative Mode: static access
Operational Mode: static access
```

```
Administrative Trunking Encapsulation: negotiate
Operational Trunking Encapsulation: native
Negotiation of Trunking: Off
Access Mode VLAN: 20 (VLAN0020)
Trunking Native Mode VLAN: 1 (default)
Administrative Native VLAN tagging: enabled
Voice VLAN: 10 (VLAN0010)
Administrative private-vlan host association: none
Administrative private-vlan mapping: none
Administrative private-vlan trunk native VLAN: none
Administrative private-vlan trunk Native VLAN tagging: enabled
Administrative private-vlan trunk encapsulation: dot1q
Administrative private-vlan trunk normal VLANs: none
Administrative private-vlan trunk associations: none
Administrative private-vlan trunk mappings: none
Operational private-vlan: none
Trunking VLANs Enabled: ALL
Pruning VLANs Enabled: 2-1001
Capture Mode Disabled
Capture VLANs Allowed: ALL

Protected: false
Unknown unicast blocked: disabled
Unknown multicast blocked: disabled
Appliance trust: none
Switch#
```

You hear from the support team that the phone has initialized successfully and is now operational, so your job here has been completed. You now proceed with replicating the change to other affected interfaces, and you do similar verifications for those ports.

Note When an IP phone and a PC share a switchport, if port security is mandatory, the maximum number of MAC addresses should be set to 2 or 3, based on the platform.

Unified Communications Troubleshooting Example: Invalid Marking of VoIP Packets

The second troubleshooting example of this section is based on the network topology shown in Figure 8-11. In this case, users from one building complain about their experience with voice calls and claim that it is choppy, they lose connections frequently, and at some point voice conversations are intermittent. A cause for the issue has not been documented, and the problem is worse for branch-to-branch calls. Your task is to determine whether the network is to blame, and if it is, locate where the problem is occurring.

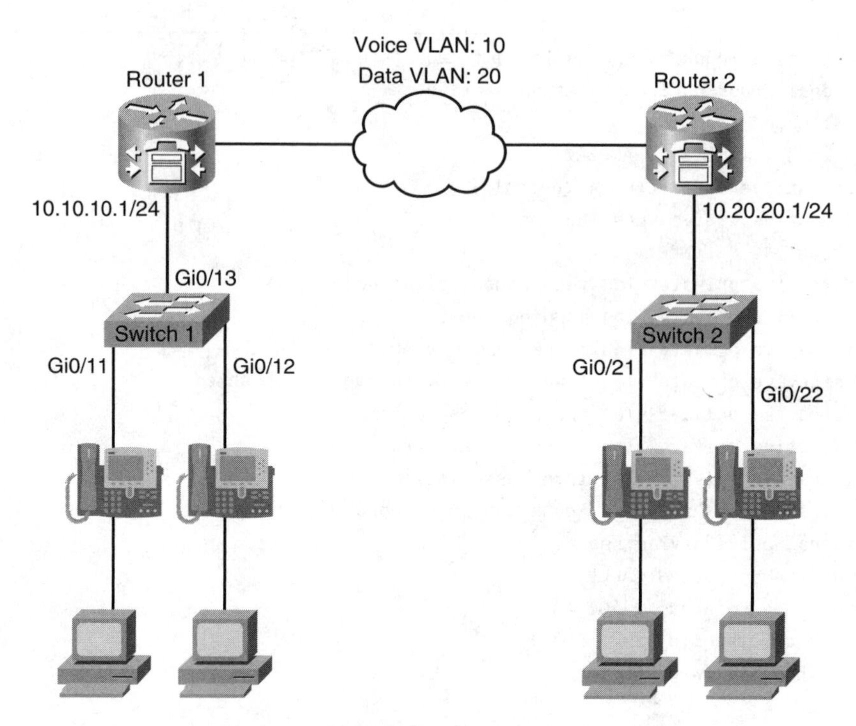

Figure 8-11 *Network Topology Diagram for the Second Unified Communications Troubleshooting Example*

The information you have is definitely vague. Part of your job in gathering information is to obtain measurable information. While gathering information, you need to ask the following questions:

- How often do you observe the reported symptoms?
- Is there a particular time of the day in which they commonly occur?
- Is the perceived quality the same when calling internal extension numbers and as it is when calling outside numbers?
- How often are you unable to obtain a dial tone? For how long does this condition remain?
- Which locations of the network are experiencing the problem (building/branch)?
- Are the problematic devices connected to the same wiring closet?

With these answers, you can reduce the scope of our search and make an effective approach to solving the problem. You have enough information to suspect a certain wiring closet where the devices in our diagram are located. All symptoms (intermittent connections, choppy voice, disconnections) seem to be related to QoS. You have obtained baseline numbers for some QoS metrics, and have determined that in fact end-to-end delay for voice traffic has doubled across the campus. Packet-loss percentages are a bit higher than 1 percent, which is around the baseline. The latency numbers are definitely showing that a QoS issue exists. Knowing that the policy trend in this campus is to push QoS settings toward the distribution and access layers, you start at the lower layers and work your way up. This means you will check the access switch first, and then move your way up to the distribution layer switch or router, trying to confirm the QoS settings. This is a *follow-the-path* strategy.

Because the switch itself could be a bottleneck, you start by checking global switch settings that might affect QoS, in the hopes of finding the problem there, so that you will not have to check each phone. One of the possible issues is high CPU utilization at the switch level. You use the **show processes CPU** command (see Example 8-26) and observe that the 5-minute averages go to around 25 percent utilization. This percentage is not bad, especially when compared to a baseline of 34 percent at peak hours. Because you have the QoS baseline, you can compare all the numbers you gather.

Example 8-26 *The CPU Utilization Is Not Alarming*

```
Switch1# show processes cpu
CPU utilization for five seconds: 99%/22%; one minute: 58%, five minutes: 25%
PID  Runtime(ms)   Invoked    uSecs     5Sec    1Min    5Min    TTY   Process
1            0          15        0    0.00%   0.00%   0.00%     0    Chunk Manager
2            9        1131        7    0.00%   0.00%   0.00%     0    Load Meter
3            0           1        0    0.00%   0.00%   0.00%     0    CEF RP IPC Backg
4         8308         772    10761    0.00%   0.13%   0.11%     0    Check heaps
5            0           1        0    0.00%   0.00%   0.00%     0    Pool Manager
6            0           2        0    0.00%   0.00%   0.00%     0    Timers
7            0           1        0    0.00%   0.00%   0.00%     0    Image Licensing
8            0           2        0    0.00%   0.00%   0.00%     0    License Client N
9         2088          20   104400    2.39%   0.19%   0.04%     0    Licensing Auto U
10           0           1        0    0.00%   0.00%   0.00%     0    Crash writer
11       67769       15394     4402   56.70%  32.81%  12.60%     0    ARP Input
12           0           1        0    0.00%   0.00%   0.00%     0    CEF MIB API
13           0           1        0    0.00%   0.00%   0.00%     0    AAA_SERVER_DEADT
14           0           2        0    0.00%   0.00%   0.00%     0    AAA high-capacit
15           0           1        0    0.00%   0.00%   0.00%     0    Policy Manager
16           8           5     1600    0.00%   0.00%   0.00%     0    Entity MIB API
17           0           1        0    0.00%   0.00%   0.00%     0    IFS Agent Manage
18          96         345        0    0.00%   0.00%   0.00%     0    IPC Dynamic Cach
```

The next step is a port-by-port analysis. The interface Gi0/11 has a phone attached to it. Therefore, you use the **show interface** command and inspect its bandwidth utilization averages, and as shown in Example 8-27, they are at around 1.5 percent of the total interface bandwidth (15 Mbps/1 Gbps). The other reported numbers on this output do not look bad either.

Example 8-27 *The Numbers for the Access Port (Interface Gi0/11) Look Normal*

```
Switch1# show interfaces gi0/11
5 minute input rate 729000 bits/sec, 847 packets/sec
5 minute output rate 14150000 bits/sec, 1129 packets/sec
   104911 packets input, 13035040 bytes, 0 no buffer
   Received 22020 broadcasts (110 multicasts)
   0 runts, 0 giants, 0 throttles
   0 input errors, 0 CRC, 0 frame, 0 overrun, 0 ignored
   0 watchdog, 114 multicast, 0 pause input
   0 input packets with dribble condition detected
   225001 packets output, 41332141 bytes, 0 underruns
   0 output errors, 0 collisions, 0 interface resets
   0 babbles, 0 late collision, 0 deferred
   0 lost carrier, 0 no carrier, 0 PAUSE output
   0 output buffer failures, 0 output buffers swapped out
```

The next things you need to investigate are the trunks, which aggregate traffic uplink to the distribution layer. Therefore, you use the **show interface** command for the uplink trunk interfaces, too, and discover that utilization is naturally higher, but it is consistent with the numbers recorded in the baseline (see Example 8-28).

Example 8-28 *The Numbers for the Trunk Uplink Port (Interface Gi0/13) Look Normal*

```
Switch1# show interfaces g0/13
GigabitEthernet0/13 is up, line protocol is up (connected)
  Hardware is Gigabit Ethernet, address is 0023.5d08.568d (bia 0023.5908.568d)
  Description: to Cisco phone
  MTU 1504 bytes, BW 100000 Kbit, DLY 100 usec,
     reliability 255/255, txload 5/255, rxload 6/255
  Encapsulation ARPA, loopback not set
  Keepalive set (10 sec)
  Full-duplex, 100Mb/s, media type is 10/100/1000BaseTX
  input flow-control is off, output flow-control is unsupported
  ARP type:ARPA, ARP Timeout 04:00:00
  Last input 00:00:10, output 00:00:00, output hang never
  Last clearing of "show interface" counters 00:10:45
  Input queue: 0/75/0/0 (size/max/drops/flushes); Total output drops: 0
  Queueing strategy: fifo
  Output queue: 0/40 (size/max)
  5 minute input rate 2478000 bits/sec, 1642 packets/sec
  5 minute output rate 2194000 bits/sec, 690 packets/sec
     917323 packets input, 171833916 bytes, 0 no buffer
     Received 913155 broadcasts (26001 multicasts)
     0 runts, 0 giants, 0 throttles
--More--
```

You should now shift your focus to QoS. QoS is about managing business and technical priorities, to prioritize critical traffic and provide appropriate levels of service to it. At peak congestion times, if all traffic is treated equally, all traffic classes will probably suffer. Therefore, typically you assign priorities to different traffic classes. You should check and see whether the QoS classes, and their corresponding markings, are being enforced in the network. From the documentation, you learn that IP phones represent the trust boundary, and that the DSCP markings are being used throughout the network. Phones are allowed to tag their own packets with high priorities, in this instance DSCP value EF (Expedited Forwarding). You should check and see whether the switch ports are maintaining those tags, and not resetting them. Using the command **show mls qos interface** on one of the ports pointing to the phones reveals that the port is indeed trusted and that DSCP values are being maintained and not reset, as shown in Example 8-29.

Example 8-29 *The Access Interface Gi0/11 Is Set Up to Trust DSCP*

```
Switch1# show mls qos int g0/11
GigabitEthernet0/11
trust state: trust dscp
trust mode: trust dscp
trust enabled flag: ena
COS override: dis
Default COS: 0
DSCP Mutation Map: Default DSCP Mutation Map
Trust device: none
qos mode: port-based

Switch1#
```

You can conclude that the access switch is configured properly. Next, you move up along the path of the traffic. The distribution layer in this network is collapsed at the branch router level. That will be the next focus and you will verify QoS settings on that device, the router. You use the **show policy-map interface** command on the router and observe the results as shown in Example 8-30.

Example 8-30 *The Output Shows That the Policy "Reclassify" Is Applied to Fa0/0*

```
Router1# show policy-map interface
 FastEthernet0/0

Service-policy input: reclassify

    Class-map: signaling (match-any)
     0 packets, 0 bytes
     5 minute offered rate 0 bps, drop rate 0 bps
     Match: protocol h323
```

```
          0 packets, 0 bytes
          5 minute rate 0 bps
        Match: protocol sip
          0 packets, 0 bytes
          5 minute rate 0 bps
        Match: protocol mgcp
          0 packets, 0 bytes
          5 minute rate 0 bps
        QoS set
          dscp af11
            Packets marked 0

Class-map: voice (match-all)
    0 packets, 0 bytes
    5 minute offered rate 0 bps, drop rate 0 bps
    Match: protocol rtp audio
    QoS Set
      dscp af31
        Packets marked 0

Class-map: management (match-all)
    0 packets, 0 bytes
    5 minute offered rate 0 bps, drop rate 0 bps
    Match: telnet
    Match: snmp
    Match: ssh
    QoS Set
      dscp cs2
        Packets marked 0

Class-map: class-default (match-any)
    12 packets, 1516 bytes
    5 minute offered rate 0 bps, drop rate 0 bps
    Match: any
    QoS Set
      dscp default
        Packets marked 12
```

There is a policy called **reclassify** attached to the router fa0/0 interface. The name suits the purpose; it looks like people are trying to reclassify and re-mark packets coming into this interface. That makes sense because this device is the WAN edge device, and the service provider may require a different marking to maintain QoS policies in their network.

However, the "QoS Set" section within the VOICE class tells us that VOICE is being reclassified and tagged with the DSCP value AF31. This value is strange; voice traffic is typically classified with DSCP value EF, the highest priority. In this instance, it looks like the voice traffic class is being reclassified into a lower priority. When you verify this fact with the QoS team, they confirm your suspicion. Voice is being incorrectly marked down (toaf31). The impact of this improper remarking is that QoS policies such as bandwidth reservation, priority queuing, and preferred path selection shall not be enforced. Voice traffic is suffering because of the identified voice remarking mistake. Once this error is fixed, you are notified that the problems are now all solved.

Note For more information about traffic classification with DSCP values, see the Cisco.com document "Classifying VoIP Signaling and Media with DSCP for QoS," at http://tinyurl.com/4m9ojm.

Unified Communications Troubleshooting Example: ACL and Trunk Issues

The third troubleshooting example is based on the network topology shown in Figure 8-12. A recent security audit has resulted in new security policies being put in place. The network team failed previous audits, so this time they are committed to enforcing security end to end. This enforcement seems to have affected our branch, because now the IP phones are not able to initialize and obtain their base configuration. Those settings are obtained from configuration files stored in the TFTP server, which is the local branch router. The local branch router is also serving as a call agent, performing call routing, Call Admission Control (CAC), and other IP telephony functions. In applying a troubleshooting method, you have perhaps more information to work with than with the previous examples. Investigating the recent change in security policy, you find that Cisco IOS firewall services were installed in some key routers of the network. The auditor recommended network locations with higher levels of risk. This recommendation included certain power branches that were deemed vulnerable because of their recent history of being the source of worm outbreaks. This line of thinking allows you to focus on the Cisco IOS firewall, without discarding the possibility of other issues. Therefore, instead of focusing on a bottom-up or top-down approach, you start at the firewall level and analyze the implications of it on the unified communications infrastructure.

The reported symptom is that the IP phones cannot initialize and obtain their settings, or make calls. While gathering information about the Cisco IOS firewall, you must remember that Cisco IOS Software allows the firewall configuration using two methods:

- The classical Cisco IOS firewall, which uses ACLs exclusively on interfaces
- The zone-based firewall, which is more widely used and it is more flexible for a comprehensive deployment of firewall rules

You could check both of them starting at the access switch (Switch1). Using the **show zone-pair security** command will tell you whether the zone-based firewall is configured. You can see in the output shown in Example 8-31 that there are no policies of this kind,

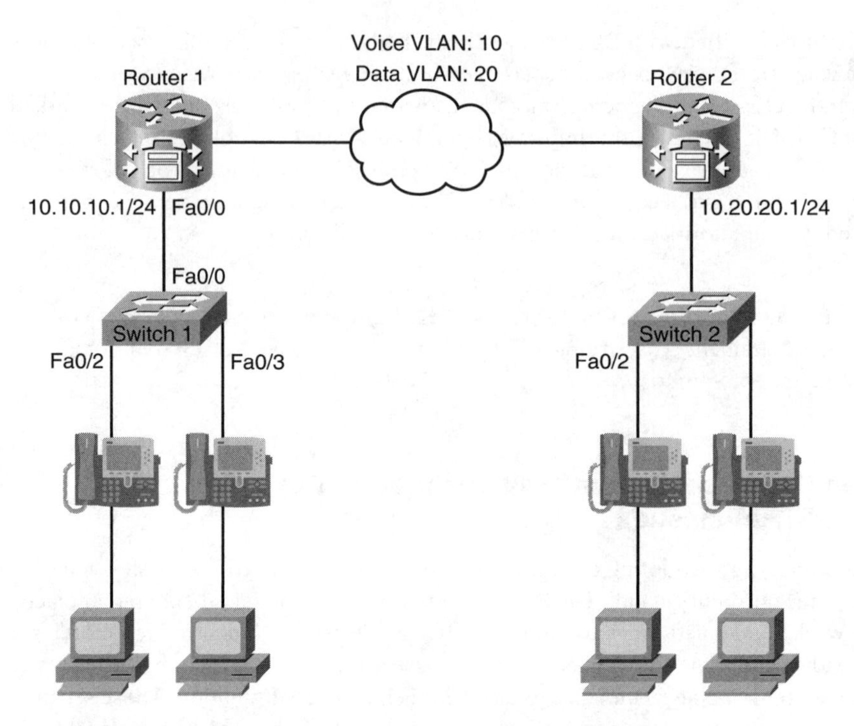

Figure 8-12 *Network Topology Diagram for the Third Unified Communications Troubleshooting Example*

so this firewall is probably a classic firewall. Using the **show access-lists** command on the switch reveals that no ACLs are configured there.

Example 8-31 *No Firewall Features Are Configured on the Switch*

```
Switch1# show zone-pair security
                ^
%Invalid input detected at '^' marker.

Switch1# show access-lists

Switch1#
```

You move on to the router (Router1) and do the same verification. On this particular router, the **show zone-pair security** command is also not supported. You use the **show ip interfaces** command, which displays the access lists that are applied to each interface and the direction in which they are applied as shown in Example 8-32. An ACL called FIRE-WALL is applied to the fa0/0 interface. This interface is the interface that points to the access switch and the IP phones.

Example 8-32 *The Output Shows That the FIREWALL ACL Is Applied to Fa0/0 (Inbound)*

```
Router1# show ip interfaces
FastEthernet0/0 is up, line protocol is up
  Internet address is 10.10.10.1/24
  Broadcast address is 255.255.255.255
  Address determined by non-volatile memory
  MTU is 1500 bytes
  Helper address is not set
  Directed broadcast forwarding is disabled
  Outgoing access list is not set
  Inbound access list is FIREWALL
  Proxy ARP is enabled
  Local Proxy ARP is disabled
  Security level is default
  Split horizon is enabled
  ICMP redirects are always sent
  ICMP unreachables are always sent
  ICMP mask replies are never sent
  IP fast switching is enabled
  IP fast switching on the same interface is disabled
  IP Flow switching is disabled
--More--
```

Now you display the access list itself (shown in Example 8-33). The ACL looks simple, yet comprehensive, allowing traditional traffic such as HTTP and FTP, and management protocols such as SSH. The ACL looks like a closed policy: Allow what you need, deny everything else. That might point to the problem; whoever designed the security policy was not fully aware of the legitimate services and applications running on the network.

Example 8-33 *The FIREWALL ACL Permits Traffic for Only Four Applications*

```
Router1# show access-list
Standard IP access list 23
    10 permit 10.10.10.0, wildcard bits 0.0.0.7
    20 permit 172.29.128.128, wildcard bits 0.0.0.31
    30 permit 10.10.50.0, wildcard bits 0.0.0.255 (2 matches)
    40 permit 10.10.60.0, wildcard bits 0.0.0.255
Extended IP access list FIREWALL
    10 permit tcp any any eq telnet (500 matches)
    20 permit tcp any any eq 22
    30 permit tcp any host 10.10.60.60 eq www
    40 permit tcp any host 10.10.60.60 eq 443
    50 permit udp any any
Router1#
```

At this point, you must confirm with the IP telephony support team the exact process that an IP phone follows to become operational. The IP phone registers to the router using Skinny Client Control Protocol (SCCP), which is also referred to as "Skinny." SCCP runs over TCP and uses port 2000. This issue is one of the culprits you are facing. You need to change the access list to allow the SCCP traffic. You simply add a **permit** line at the end allowing TCP 2000, as shown in Example 8-34

Example 8-34 *A Line Is Added to the FIREWALL ACL to Permit SCCP*

```
Router1# conf t
Enter configuration commands, one per line. End with CNTL/Z.
Router1(config)# ip access-list extended FIREWALL
Router1(config-ext-nacl)# permit tcp any any eq 2000
Router1(config-ext-nacl)# end
Router1#
```

For testing, you initiate one of the IP phones and see whether it is able to make calls. Here, you can make use of the **debug ephone register** command that belongs to the Cisco Unified Communications Manager Express product, the software on the router that performs call routing and other IP telephony capabilities. The output of the **debug ephone register** helps you determine whether phones are at least trying to register and obtain their settings from Cisco Unified Communications Manager Express. You initialize the phone and the debug displays no output (see Example 8-35). The phones are still not registering.

Example 8-35 *The* **debug ephone register** *shows no activity*

```
Router1# debug ephone register
EPHONE registration debugging is enabled
Router1#
```

You now follow the link along the voice traffic path. The next step in the troubleshooting process should be to determine whether the trunk between the access switch and the router is allowing SCCP traffic. You need to make sure that the voice VLAN is allowed across the trunk from the switch to the router, and you use the **show interfaces trunk** command to discover this information, as demonstrated in Example 8-36. You can see that the voice VLAN10 is not allowed across the trunk. That is why voice traffic is not going through it. You can easily fix the problem by going into the trunk interface and entering the **switchport trunk allowed vlan add 10** command (also shown in Example 8-36).

Example 8-36 *The Trunk Between the Switch and Router Does Not Allow the Voice VLAN*

```
Switch1# show interface trunk

Port          Mode              Encapsulation    Status        Native vlan
Fa0/0         on                802.1q            trunking      50

Port          Vlans allowed on trunk
Fa0/0         1,50,60

Port          Vlans allowed and active in management domain
Fa0/0         1,50,60

Port          Vlans in spanning tree forwarding state and not pruned
Fa0/0         1,50,60

Switch1# conf t
Enter configuration commands, one per line. End with CNTL/Z.
Switch1(config)# int Fa0/0
Switch1(config-if)# switchport trunk allowed vlan add 10
Switch1(config-if)# end
Switch1#
```

The best way to know if you fixed the problem is to see the telephone registering to the router and obtaining its IP telephony settings. You switch back to the router console, and the **debug ephone register** is still enabled. Example 8-37 shows the results. You clearly see the phone activity messages that indicate the phone has successfully registered. The problem is now solved.

Example 8-37 *The* **debug** *Output Displays Successful Phone Registration*

```
*Sep 1 17:22:37.155: ephone-1[0/1][SEP0023331B9090]:ButtonTemplate buttonCount=2
totalButtonCount=2 buttonOffset=0
*Sep 1 17:22:37.155: ephone-1[0/1][SEP0023331B9090]:Configured 0 speed dial buttons
*Sep 1 17:22:37.159: ephone-1[0/1]:StationSoftKeyTemplateReqMessage
*Sep 1 17:22:37.159: ephone-1[0/1]:StationSoftKeyTemplateReqMessage
*Sep 1 17:22:37.171: ephone-1[0/1]:StationSoftKeySetReqMessage
*Sep 1 17:22:37.171: ephone-1[0/1]:StationSoftKeySetReqMessage
*Sep 1 17:22:37.175: ephone-1[0/1][SEP0023331B9090]:StationLineStatReqMessage from
ephone line 2
*Sep 1 17:22:37.175: ephone-1[0/1][SEP0023331B9090]:StationLineStatReqMessage from
ephone line 2 Invalid DN -1
*Sep 1 17:22:37.175: ephone-1[0/1][SEP0023331B9090]:StationLineStatResMessage sent
to ephone (1 of 2)
*Sep 1 17:22:37.175: ephone-1[0/1][SEP0023331B9090]:StationLineStatReqMessage from
ephone line 1
*Sep 1 17:22:37.179: ephone-1[0/1]:StationLineStatReqMessage ephone line 1 DN 1 =
1000 desc = 1000 label =
```

```
*Sep 1 17:22:37.179: ephone-1[0/1]:StationLineStatResMessage sent to ephone (2 of 2)
*Sep 1 17:22:37.179: ephone-1[0/1]:SkinnyCompleteRegistration
*Sep 1 17:22:37.195: ephone-1[0/1][SEP0023331B9090]:Skinny Available Lines 2 set
for socket [1]
*Sep 1 17:22:37.195: ephone-1[0/1]:Already done SkinnyCompleteRegistration
```

Troubleshooting Video Issues in a Converged Network

The growth of video and rich media in enterprises not only strains networks, it also fundamentally changes them. Current IP networks must evolve to better handle rich media in its many forms and formats. Traditional IP networks struggle with interactive and real-time requirements, make delivery and quality of media unpredictable, and increase complexity for the network operators and managers.

This section addresses the challenge of troubleshooting the network infrastructure supporting video and rich media traffic. This section has two parts: The first part outlines the considerations, requirements, and the common issues; the second part demonstrates troubleshooting methods that can be used to approach some of the potential problems you may face in your video-ready network.

Common Video-Integration Issues

Enterprises understand the need and significant benefit of adopting the various media-rich applications because they dramatically improve productivity, increase collaboration, and reduce cost. They also can help enterprises meet the challenge of globalization while simplifying and optimizing business processes and operations. Several different media-rich applications that can positively affect business are available for enterprises. High-definition room-based interactive video such as Cisco TelePresence and standard-definition desktop collaboration applications such as Cisco Unified Videoconferencing Systems are examples of such applications. There are also various streaming and broadcast types of video applications such as digital signage, video on demand (VoD), and video surveillance (see Figure 8-13).

All of these types of video applications have different characteristics: Some of them are less interactive, and some of them are more interactive. Some of them are more massive than the others, in terms of network traffic volume, reaching bigger audiences in the enterprise. All of these types of video applications impose strict requirements on the underlying network infrastructure and services.

This growing use of video on networks requires a better and intelligent network. Delivering new video experiences will place additional demands on IP networks in terms of performance, adaptability, and manageability. Networks will need to scale and deliver an optimized quality of experience (QoE), introducing additional complexity. Networks that were designed for an era of best-effort delivery, low bandwidth, and high latency do

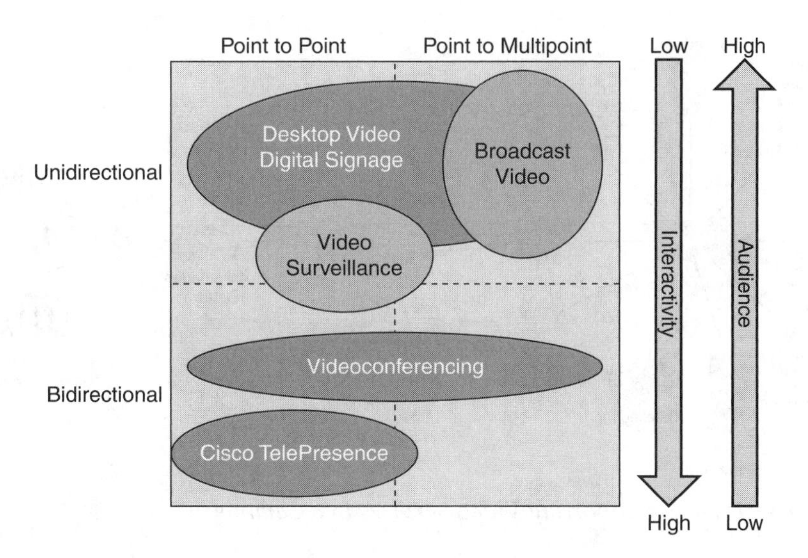

Figure 8-13 *Types of Video Applications*

not work for video. Because video is the most demanding media type, a network optimized for interactive video will support many other rich-media types.

Converging video with data and voice is more complex than converging data and voice: It demands more considerations, and it imposes stricter requirements on the underlying IP network. As you look at the Figure 8-14, you notice the similarities of this diagram and its components with a voice-enabled network. In fact, the good news is that several components and infrastructure services are shared between video and voice applications. Sometimes the endpoints are the same, or at least integrated. Some of the critical protocols, such as SIP, are going to be the same too. SIP is a signaling protocol that is used to initiate, manage, and terminate voice calls but also video sessions. The end user is going to experience an integrated service (for example, IP phones and video solutions such as Cisco Unified Video Advantage coordinating a person-to-person videoconference transparently).

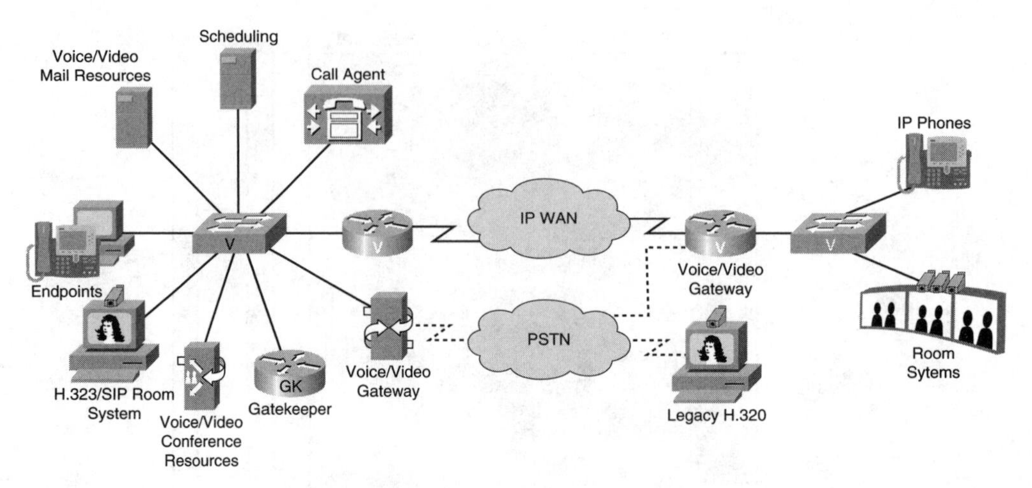

Figure 8-14 *Devices Supporting Video Services in a Campus*

As you review the challenges of enabling video applications in the network, you will see the similarities with voice requirements, and also the differences. Both need end-to-end QoS; however, converging video into an IP network is much more complex than converging VoIP because video is much more bandwidth intensive and very bursty. A high-definition stream could require more than 20-Mbps bandwidth for delivery over the network. Packet sizes are much larger, and there are several different types of video applications, such as live and on-demand high-definition streaming video, high-definition video surveillance, desktop videoconferencing, and high-definition virtual-presence interactive video. Each type of video application has unique requirements and characteristics and requires a networkwide strategy to help ensure a high-quality user experience. Table 8-2 outlines the QoS requirements for some of the main video applications.

In terms of high availability, video applications require millisecond-level network service recovery because video traffic cannot accept unpredictable or large network recovery timeouts. Therefore, convergence targets will be higher, and packet loss due to network

Table 8-2 *Video Application QoS Requirements*

Metric	Video Collaboration	Cisco TelePresence	Video Surveillance
Latency	200 ms	150 ms	500 ms
Jitter	10 ms	10 ms	10 ms
Loss	0.05%	0.05%	0.5%

outage must be minimal. This makes redundancy design and the convergence of routing protocols and spanning tree extremely critical.

Building a multicast-aware network is another important consideration. This lesson does not intend to be a multicast primer, and it will not detail multicast operations; however, it will try to identify the multicast components and explain the tools needed to verify their configuration and existence in routers and switches.

Finally, security is also a major matter for consideration. It is important to know how existing security controls affect video traffic. In simple terms, access control and threat management mechanisms need to consider the various protocols and traffic flows that result from a video-enabled network, and allow them to exist in a controlled manner. Similar to the voice deployments, the protocols that might need to be permitted are SIP, H.323, SCCP (Skinny), RTP, RTCP, and perhaps some others.

Multicast traffic is used to send the same data packets to multiple receivers efficiently. If you were to transport video across the network using unicast, the transmitter would send multiple copies of data, one copy for each receiver. Multicast transmission sends a single copy of data to multiple receivers (see Figure 8-15). The way multicast works is that the sender sends only one copy of a single data packet, but addressed to a group of receivers called a multicast group. Multicast groups are nothing more than IP

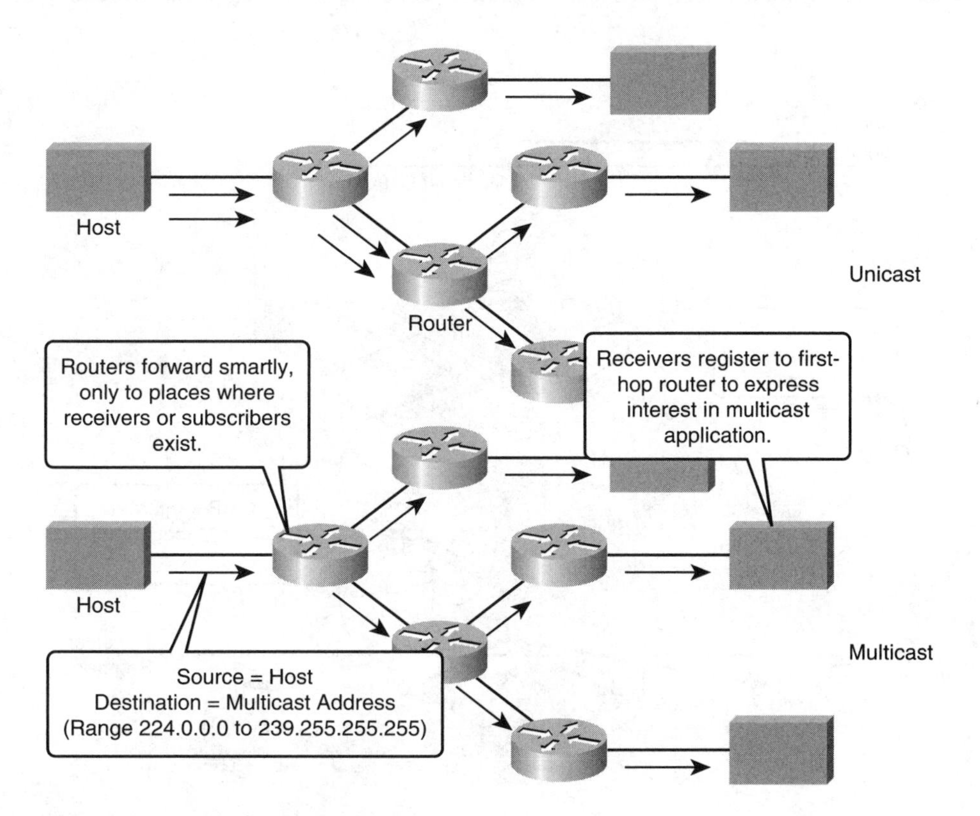

Figure 8-15 *Multicast Operation*

addresses that use the Class D address space. Class D addresses are denoted by the high-order 4 bits of the address set to 1110. This results in the range of addresses 224.0.0.0 through 239.255.255.255. Downstream multicast routers replicate and forward the data packet to all those branches where receivers (might) exist. They do it intelligently; traffic will be forwarded only to those "branches" of the network where there are "subscribers" to the group. Receivers express their interest in multicast traffic by registering at their first-hop router.

This model and resulting protocols make video deployments more efficient, protecting bandwidth resources, saving in resource utilization on routers and switches and improving QoS and the user experience overall. There are two main protocols involved. In the multicast network, routers will run a multicast routing protocol, typically Protocol Independent Multicast (PIM) whose main role is to advertise the location of multicast receivers, by indicating which interfaces of each router "point" to receivers, and therefore should forward multicast streams. The second main component is the way receivers subscribe to groups, and announce themselves as members of the group. As illustrated in Figure 8-16, this is done in the LAN, typically using Internet Group Management Protocol (IGMP).

IGMP is a highly dynamic protocol. It will run on first-hop routers and LAN switches. Using this protocol is a requirement in multicast networks because it is the protocol that

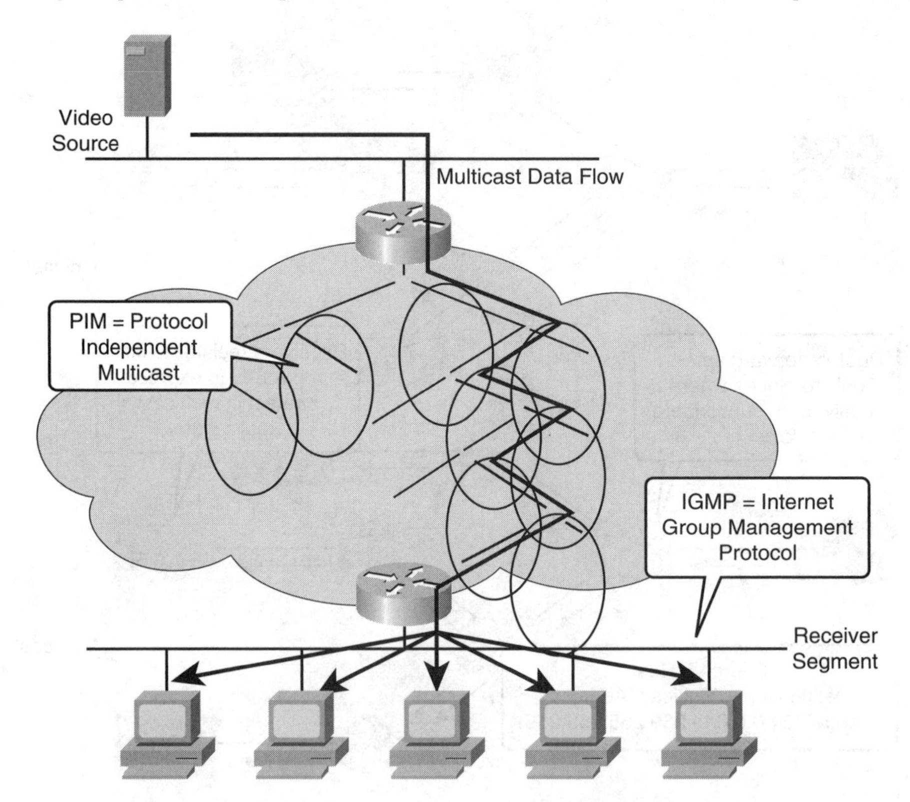

Figure 8-16 *Multicast Conceptual Model and Protocols*

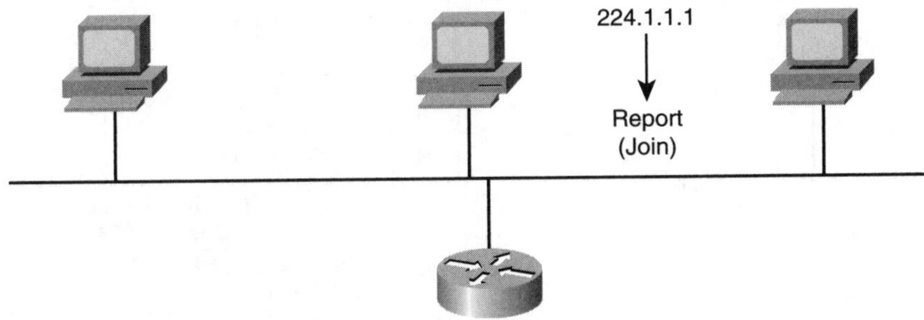

Figure 8-17 *A Multicast Client Joining a Multicast Group Using IGMP Report (Join)*

allows hosts to become members of multicast groups, maintain their membership, receive multicast traffic, and then leave their group and stop receiving multicast traffic. Figure 8-17 illustrates the process of a multicast client joining a multicast group using IGMP. Members joining a multicast group do not have to wait for a Membership Query from a router to join; they send an unsolicited report indicating their interest. This action reduces join latency for the end system joining if no other members are present. Once the Membership Report is received by the router, it starts advertising the news to the rest of the network. Multicast sources will forward traffic directed to the group to this router because there are members of the group that have joined it.

The multicast group will remain active and is advertised by the router as long as there are members in the group within that network segment. As long as there is at least one member, the group will remain active (see Figure 8-18).

At some point, users terminate their multicast based application and when they do, their applications send "leave" messages to the router. The router then sends a query, just to verify whether there are still members of the group in the segment. If a device replies, the group remains active and the router advertises it. If no reports are received, it means that there are no more members of the group in the segment. At that point, the router stops advertising the group to the rest of the network (see Figure 8-19).

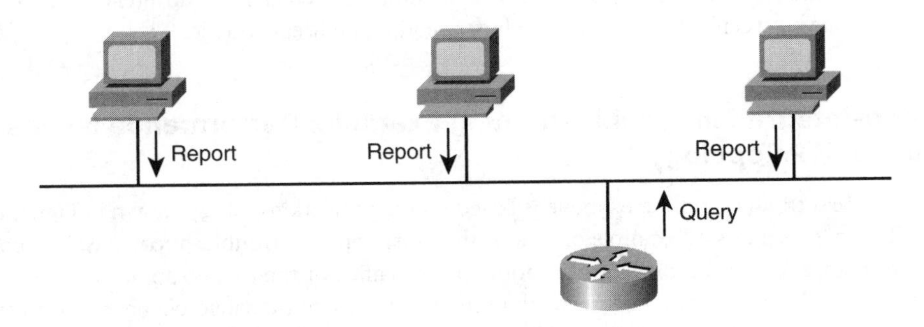

Figure 8-18 *Multicast Router Performs Group Maintenance*

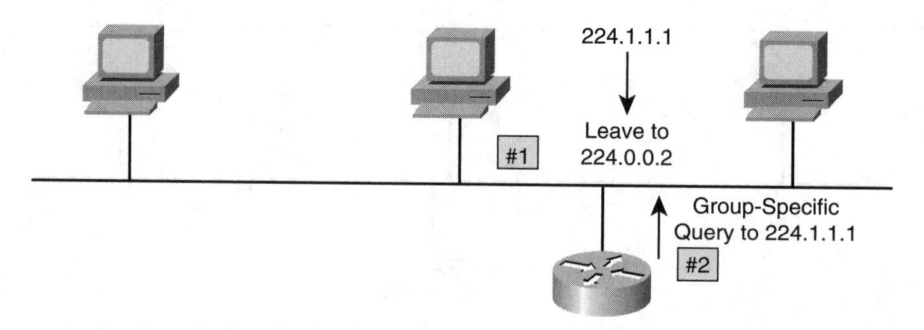

Figure 8-19 *Router Stops Advertising the Groups Presence After the Last Member Leaves*

Common video-integration issues include the following:

- Excessive bandwidth utilization
- Lack of control
- Poor quality (lack of QoS)
- Security issues (filtering of key protocols, and stateful requirements)
- Multicast issues

The bursty nature of video traffic, along with its packet sizes and massive deployment, makes QoS a common problem. Video traffic tends to monopolize the available bandwidth, and at the same time it is a delay-sensitive application that must be protected and prioritized, to the detriment of other traffic classes. Your network security might also interfere with video traffic. Firewalls, ACLs, and other security controls can get in the way of protocols such as RTP, RTCP, SIP, H.323, and others. All of these protocols are critical to video traffic. You need to consider all these factors because you might have to change your security policies to allow video traffic in the network. Multicast configuration, if enabled in the network, is always a source of potential issues. In terms of IGMP, the only multicast protocol that was briefly explained here, common problems are related to group filtering, where routers might not accept join request from certain multicast group addresses. Another potential issue in multicast is related to differences in IGMP versions between the router and the hosts sending multicast traffic.

Video-Integration Troubleshooting Example: Performance Issues Due to STP Topology

The first troubleshooting example is based on the network topology shown in Figure 8-20. This case is a classic example of one of the most complex troubleshooting issues: performance. Users complain about "poor" performance of their video application. The scenario includes the switched network in the figure, where the video clients reside in two VLANS, 10 and 20, implemented in the access switch. The access switch is serviced by two distribution switches that connect the clients to the campus network, where the video server resides. The distribution switches have recently been upgraded to a new version of Cisco IOS Software. After the change, users started complaining about the poor performance.

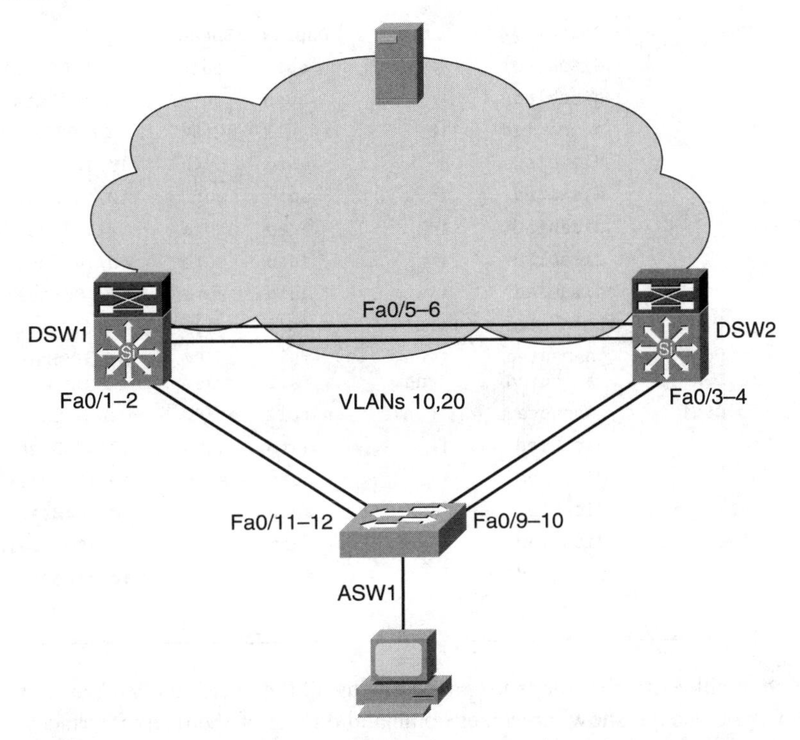

Figure 8-20 *Network Topology for the First Video-Integration Troubleshooting Example*

Using a structured troubleshooting method, the first thing you need to do is to clarify what users mean by the "poor performance" of their application. You must translate the quality of user experience with the application into something tangible you can measure, such as delay, jitter, or packet loss. You should also try to determine the scope of the problem by finding out if the performance degradation occurring for all video applications, for all server destinations, or for all clients. After some information gathering, you have determined that the server location is inside the campus, and that the issue occurred after the change on the distribution switches. The exact symptom, as told by the users of the application is choppy video, long download and buffering times, and that streaming video stops every few seconds for the application to buffer video frames.

You will use a follow-the-path troubleshooting approach and start with the access switch, as it is the first device in the path between the clients and the server. At each device, you will use a bottom-up troubleshooting approach, checking the physical layer, and move up layer by layer according to the OSI model. On the access switch, you enter the **show interfaces status** command to see some Layer 1 and Layer 2 status information about all interfaces, as demonstrated in Example 8-38. The four trunks connecting this switch to the distribution layer switches show as connected and trunking.

Example 8-38 *The Output of the* **show interfaces status** *on the Access Switch*

```
ASW1# show interfaces status

Port      Name       Status       vlan       Duplex  Speed   Type
Fa0/1                disabled     1            auto   auto   10/100BaseTX
Fa0/2                disabled     1            auto   auto   10/100BaseTX
Fa0/3                connected    10         a-full  a-100   10/100BaseTX
Fa0/4                disabled     1            auto   auto   10/100BaseTX
Fa0/5                disabled     1            auto   auto   10/100BaseTX
Fa0/6                disabled     1            auto   auto   10/100BaseTX
Fa0/7                disabled     1            auto   auto   10/100BaseTX
Fa0/8                disabled     1            auto   auto   10/100BaseTX
Fa0/9     To DSW2    connected    trunk      a-full  a-100   10/100BaseTX
Fa0/10    To DSW2    connected    trunk      a-full  a-100   10/100BaseTX
Fa0/11    To DSW1    connected    trunk      a-full  a-100   10/100BaseTX
Fa0/12    To DSW1    connected    trunk      a-full  a-100   10/100BaseTX
Fa0/13               disabled     1            auto   auto   10/100BaseTX
Fa0/14               disabled     1            auto   auto   10/100BaseTX
Fa0/15               disabled     1            auto   auto   10/100BaseTX
Fa0/16               disabled     1            auto   auto   10/100BaseTX
Fa0/17               disabled     1            auto   auto   10/100BaseTX
--More--
```

Next, you will verify that the trunks are allowing all the necessary VLANs. For that verification, you use the **show interfaces** command on one of the trunk interfaces, Fa 0/9 for example, and include the **switchport** keyword. As shown in Example 8-39, all VLANs are allowed on this trunk interface, and the interface is enabled and active. However, you also notice that this trunk is a member of a bundle, port channel 1. This indicates that the documentation is not complete, because its diagram does not specify EtherChannel connections between the switches.

Example 8-39 *The Output Shows That All VLANs Are Allowed on the Trunk Interface*

```
ASW1# show interfaces fa0/9 switchport
Name: Fa0/9
Switchport: Enabled
Administrative Mode: trunk
Operational Mode: trunk (member of bundle Po1)
Administrative Trunking Encapsulation: dot1q
Operational Trunking Encapsulation: dot1q
Negotiation of Trunking: on
Access Mode VLAN: 1 (default)
Trunking Native Mode VLAN: 1 (default)
Trunking Native Mode VLAN: 1 (default)
Administrative Native VLAN tagging: enabled
```

```
Voice VLAN: none
Administrative private-vlan host association: none
Administrative private-vlan mapping: none
Administrative private-vlan trunk native VLAN: none
Administrative private-vlan trunk Native VLAN tagging: enabled
Administrative private-vlan trunk encapsulation: dot1q
Administrative private-vlan trunk normal VLANs: none
Administrative private-vlan trunk associations: none
Administrative private-vlan trunk mappings: none
Operational private-vlan: none
Trunking VLANs Enabled: ALL
Pruning VLANs Enabled: 2-1001
Capture Mode Disabled
Capture VLANs Allowed: ALL

--More--
```

You use the **show etherchannel summary** command to see a snapshot of the EtherChannel configuration, and see how these bundles are configured, as demonstrated in Example 8-40. The output shows two bundles, one for each of the distribution layer switches. It is a good practice to examine the traffic and utilization levels on these connections, so you immediately display the statistics for port channel 1 (physical interfaces Fa 0/9 and Fa 0/10) using the **show interfaces po1** command.

Example 8-40 *Cisco IOS IPS CLI Configuration*

```
ASW1# show etherchannel summary
Flags:  D - down        P - in port-channel
        I - stand-alone s - suspended
        H - Hot-standby (LACP only)
        R - Layer3      S - Layer2
        U - in use      f - failed to allocate aggregator
        w - waiting to be aggregated
        d - default port


Number of channel-groups in use: 2
Number of aggregators:           2

Group  Port-channel  Protocol    Ports
------+-------------+-----------+-----------------------------------------------
1      Po1(SU)           -        Fa0/9(P)    Fa0/10(P)
2      Po2(SU)           -        Fa0/11(P)   Fa0/12(P)
```

```
ASW1#
ASW1# show interfaces po1
Port-channel1 is up, line protocol is up (connected)
  Hardware is EtherChannel, address is 001b.0c91.7f8a (bia 001b.0c91.7f8a)
  Description: TO DSW2
  MTU 1500 bytes, BW 200000 Kbit, DLY 100 usec,
     reliability 255/255, txload 1/255, rxload 1/255
  Encapsulation ARPA, loopback not set
  Full-duplex, 100Mb/s, link type is auto, media type is unknown
  input flow-control is off, output flow-control is unsupported
  Members in this channel: Fa0/9 Fa0/10
  ARP type: ARPA, ARP Timeout 04:00:00
  Last input 00:00:01, output 02:34:07, output hang never
  Last clearing of "show interface" counters 01:16:51
  Input queue: 0/75/0/0 (size/max/drops/flushes); Total output drops: 0
  Queueing strategy: fifo
  Output queue: 0/40 (size/max)
  5 minute input rate 619000 bits/sec, 59 packets/sec
  5 minute output rate 616000 bits/sec, 54 packets/sec
     275043 packets input, 354702160 bytes, 0 no buffer
     Received 23141 broadcasts (0 multicast)
--More--
```

The indicators related to load are low (almost none), but you wonder if this is because the network is merely not congested at this moment. Therefore, you look at other indicators in the output, such as the 5-minute input/output rates, but those numbers are very low, too. Next, we look at the other port channel and compare the two. The numbers themselves might not be important, but differences in the numbers are. The output for the Po2 is shown in Example 8-41, and you can see marked differences between the two uplinks. In fact, there is 0 packet output rate over the past 5 minutes on the second uplink.

Example 8-41 *The Po2 Interface Shows No Output Over the Past 5 Minutes*

```
ASW1# show interfaces po2
Port-channel1 is up, line protocol is up (connected)
  Hardware is EtherChannel, address is 001b.0c91.7f8a (bia 001b.0c91.7f8a)
  Description: TO DSW1
  MTU 1500 bytes, BW 200000 Kbit, DLY 100 usec,
     reliability 255/255, txload 1/255, rxload 1/255
  Encapsulation ARPA, loopback not set
  Full-duplex, 100Mb/s, link type is auto, media type is unknown
  input flow-control is off, output flow-control is unsupported
  Members in this channel: Fa0/11 Fa0/12
  ARP type: ARPA, ARP Timeout 04:00:00
```

```
  Last input 00:00:00, output 02:35:01, output hang never
  Last clearing of "show interface" counters 01:17:38
  Input queue: 0/75/0/0 (size/max/drops/flushes); Total output drops: 0
  Queueing strategy: fifo
  Output queue: 0/40 (size/max)
  5 minute input rate 2000 bits/sec, 4 packets/sec
  5 minute output rate 0 bits/sec, 0 packets/sec
     24200 packets input, 1796256 bytes, 0 no buffer
     Received 23272 broadcasts (0 multicast)
--More--
```

Even though both EtherChannel trunk uplinks from the access switch to the distribution switches are connected and active, one carries much more traffic than the other. To find the reason, you use the **show interfaces trunk** command, and as you can see in Example 8-42, Po2 is not carrying traffic from any of the VLANs. These VLANs are not in spanning-tree Forwarding state; in other words, the port is in Blocking state for those VLANs. There is redundancy built in the network, but it is not set up correctly. You are only using one of the two uplinks.

Example 8-42 *Po2 Trunk Allows All VLANs, but None Are in Forwarding State*

```
ASW1# show int trunk

Port          Mode            Encapsulation  Status     Native vlan
Po1           on              802.1q          trunking  1
Po2           on              802.1q          trunking  1

Port          vlans allowed on trunk
Po1           1-4094
Po2           1-4094

Port          vlans allowed and active in management domain
Po1           1, 10, 20, 30, 40, 50, 60
Po2           1, 10, 20, 30, 40, 50, 60

Port          vlans in spanning tree forwarding state and not pruned
Po1           1, 10, 20, 30, 40, 50, 60
Po2           none
ASW1#
```

Ideally, you would like to share the load across both trunks. Redundancy and load sharing are achieved by proper setup of physical links and proper configuration of spanning tree.

The ideal command for this situation is **show spanning-tree blockedports.** This command displays the ports that are in the Blocking state. The output shown in Example 8-43 confirms that all VLANs are blocking on port channel 2.

Example 8-43 *All the VLANs Show as Blocking on the Po2 Interface*

```
ASW1# show spanning-tree blockedports

Name                 Blocked Interfaces List
-----------          ---------------------
VLAN0001             Po2
VLAN0010             Po2
VLAN0020             Po2
VLAN0030             Po2
VLAN0040             Po2
VLAN0050             Po2
VLAN0060             Po2

Number of blocked ports (segments) in the system : 7

ASW1#
```

Note Common Spanning Tree (CST) uses only one instance of spanning tree for all VLANs. This means that in a situation similar to the example, one of the uplink ports will go into blocking for all VLANs while the other ports goes into forwarding for all the VLANs. Cisco Systems designed Per-VLAN Spanning Tree Plus (PVST+), which will run one instance of STP per VLAN. With that ability, and careful selection and placement of the root bridge per STP instance, different ports would be blocked for different VLANs, allowing traffic to utilize multiple links. Multiple Spanning Tree (MST) creates one instance of spanning tree per group of VLANs, allowing you to distribute the load according to traffic volume analysis for all of your VLANs. Ports would be blocked per instance of STP again, but this time each instance would include traffic from multiple VLANs.

You can discover which type of STP is configured on the switch via the **show spanning-tree summary** command. As shown in Example 8-44, the switch spanning-tree mode is Rapid PVST. You need to find out why the switch is choosing to block all VLANs on Po2.

Example 8-44 *The Switch Spanning Tree Is in Rapid-PVST Mode*

```
ASW1# show spanning-tree summary
Switch is in rapid-pvst mode
Root bridge for: none
Extended system ID           is enabled
Portfast Default             is disabled
```

```
PortFast BPDU Guard Default  is disabled
Portfast BPDU Filter Default is disabled
Loopguard Default            is disabled
EtherChannel misconfig guard is enabled
UplinkFast                   is disabled
BackboneFast                 is disabled
Configured Pathcost method used is short

Name                 Blocking Listening Learning Forwarding STP Active
-------------------- -------- --------- -------- ---------- ----------
VLAN0001                    1         0        0          1          2
VLAN0010                    1         0        0          2          3
VLAN0020                    1         0        0          1          2
VLAN0030                    1         0        0          1          2
VLAN0040                    1         0        0          1          2
--More--
```

You must verify if the problem is the selection of the root; the root might be the same for all VLANs. Using the **show spanning-tree root** command, as shown in Example 8-45, you see the root ID is the same for all VLANs. That is the problem. You are not using the redundancy in the network effectively. You can tell from the output that the root port on the switch is the port channel 1 interface. That means port channel 2 is the alternate port for all VLANs, explaining why it is blocking for all VLANs.

Example 8-45 *Po1 Is the Selected Root Port for All VLANs*

```
ASW1# show spanning-tree root

                                        Root    Hello Max Fwd
vlan                  Root ID           Cost    Time  Age Dly  Root Port
---------------- -------------------- --------- ----- --- ---  ----------
VLAN0001         32769 0012.7f4b.ba80        12     2  20  15  Po1
VLAN0010         32769 0012.7f4b.ba80        12     2  20  15  Po1
VLAN0020         32769 0012.7f4b.ba80        12     2  20  15  Po1
VLAN0030         32769 0012.7f4b.ba80        12     2  20  15  Po1
VLAN0040         32769 0012.7f4b.ba80        12     2  20  15  Po1
ASW1#
```

Now you confirm that DSW1 is actually the root, using the **show spanning-tree root** command on DSW1. As Example 8-46 shows, the Root Port column is empty. DSW1 is indeed the root for all VLANs.

Example 8-46 *DSW1 Has No Root Port for Any VLAN; It Is the Root for All VLANs*

```
DSW1# show spanning-tree root

                                        Root    Hello Max  Fwd  Root Port
vlan                 Root ID            Cost    Time  Age  Dly
----------------   ----------------   ------  ----- ---  ---  ---------
VLAN0001           32769 0012.7f4b.ba80      0      2   20   15
VLAN0010           32769 0012.7f4b.ba80      0      2   20   15
VLAN0020           32769 0012.7f4b.ba80      0      2   20   15
VLAN0030           32769 0012.7f4b.ba80      0      2   20   15
VLAN0040           32769 0012.7f4b.ba80      0      2   20   15
VLAN0050           32769 0012.7f4b.ba80      0      2   20   15
VLAN0060           32769 0012.7f4b.ba80      0      2   20   15
DSW1#
```

To fix this problem, you can designate DSW1 as the root for VLANs 10, 30, and 50, and DSW2 as the root for VLANs 20, 40, and 60. In a production network, traffic for VLANs would be analyzed and distributed based on volume; arbitrary division as we did here may not distribute the load in balance. There is an IOS macro that allows you to specify the switch to be the primary or the back up root for one or more VLANs. You will use that macro to make DSW1 the primary root for VLANs 10, 20, and 30, and to make it secondary root for VLANs 20, 40, and 60. You do the opposite on the DSW2 switch. This work is shown in Example 8-47.

Example 8-47 *Using the Root Primary and Root Secondary Macros on DSW1 and DSW2*

```
DSW1(config)# spanning-tree vlan 10,30,50 root primary
DSW1(config)# spanning-tree vlan 20,40,60 root secondary
DSW1(config)#
================================================================================
DSW2(config)# spanning-tree vlan 10,30,50 root secondary
DSW2(config)# spanning-tree vlan 20,40,60 root primary
DSW2(config)#
```

Now you go back to the access switch and look at the blocked ports again. You might have to wait a few seconds to allow STP to converge to a consistent state. You type the **show spanning-tree blockedports** command again and see the result shown in Example 8-48. Now you see that spanning tree is blocking for VLANs 1, 10, 30, and 50 on Po2 and it is blocking for VLANs 20, 40, and 60 on Po1. The output of the **show spanning-tree root** command demonstrates the same results.

Example 8-48 *Po1 and Po2 Are Now Sharing the Blocking for Different VLANs*

```
ASW1# show spanning-tree blockedports

Name                 Blocked Interfaces List
-------------------- ------------------------------------
VLAN0001             Po2
VLAN0010             Po2
VLAN0020             Po1
VLAN0030             Po2
VLAN0040             Po1
VLAN0050             Po2
VLAN0060             Po1

Number of blocked ports (segments) in the system : 7

ASW1#

ASW1# show spanning-tree root

                                        Root    Hello Max Fwd  Root Port
vlan                 Root ID            Cost    Time  Age Dly
-------------------- -------------------- --------- ----- --- ---  ------------
VLAN0001         32769 0012.7f4b.ba80       12     2    20  15   Po1
VLAN0010         32769 0012.7f4b.ba80       12     2    20  15   Po1
VLAN0020         32769 0012.7f4b.ba80       12     2    20  15   Po2
VLAN0030         32769 0012.7f4b.ba80       12     2    20  15   Po1
VLAN0040         32769 0012.7f4b.ba80       12     2    20  15   Po2
VLAN0050         32769 0012.7f4b.ba80       12     2    20  15   Po1
VLAN0060         32769 0012.7f4b.ba80       12     2    20  15   Po2
ASW1#
```

Going back to check traffic statistics on Po1 and Po2, you see that both links are now being used somewhat evenly, as shown in Example 8-49.

Example 8-49 *Traffic Statistics Show Even Distribution Between Po1 and Po2*

```
ASW1# show int po1 | include rate
  Queueing strategy: fifo
  5 minute input rate 1443000 bits/sec, 143 packets/sec
  5 minute output rate 1501000 bits/sec, 272 packets/sec
ASW1# show int po2 | include rate
  Queueing strategy: fifo
  5 minute input rate 1163000 bits/sec, 107 packets/sec
  5 minute output rate 1162000 bits/sec, 103 packets/sec
ASW1#
```

Because you do not want to sacrifice reliability, you need to make sure that the network is resilient to a failure on these links (one at the time). To test that, you shut down both ports in the port channel 1 EtherChannel. Spanning tree should be fast enough so that in the event of a network outage, applications do not time out. Spanning tree should reconverge and unblock ports. The output from the **show spanning-tree blockedports** command shows that no ports are blocked after the link failure. This is critical for sensitive traffic such as video. These results are shown in Example 8-50. The problem is solved.

Example 8-50 *Cisco IOS IPS CLI Configuration*

```
ASW1(config)# int range fa0/9-10
ASW1(config-if-range)#shut
ASW1(config-if-range)#
%LINEPROTO-5-UPDOWN: Line protocol on Interface Port-channel1, changed state to
down
%LINK-5-CHANGED: Interface FastEthernet0/9, changed state to administratively down
%LINK-5-CHANGED: Interface FastEthernet0/10, changed state to administratively down
%LINK-3-UPDOWN: Interface Port-channel1, changed state to down^Z
ASW1#

ASW1# show spanning-tree blockedports

Name                 Blocked Interfaces List
-------------------- ------------------------------------

Number of blocked ports (segments) in the system : 0

ASW1#
```

Video-Integration Troubleshooting Example: IP Multicast Configuration Error

The second troubleshooting example for this section is based on the network topology shown in Figure 8-21. This network is simulating an IGMP network, with R1 acting as an IGMP client, similar to a PC running a video application and joining multicast groups. R2 will act as the first-hop router, listening to IGMP join and leave transactions. And R3 will act as the video server, pushing multicast traffic downstream. The video server is simulated by the loopback interface with the IP address 100.100.100.100 on R3. R2 and R3 are preconfigured to communicate multicast group information through Protocol Independent Multicast (PIM). R1 and R2 are preconfigured to use IGMP to allow R1 to join multicast groups. The problem here is that users in the R1 LAN are not able to watch the video stream; they are able to connect to the server and request the video, but the video stream is not reaching them after that. The application team has verified that the software is installed correctly and the server is configured properly, and they suspect the network is to blame.

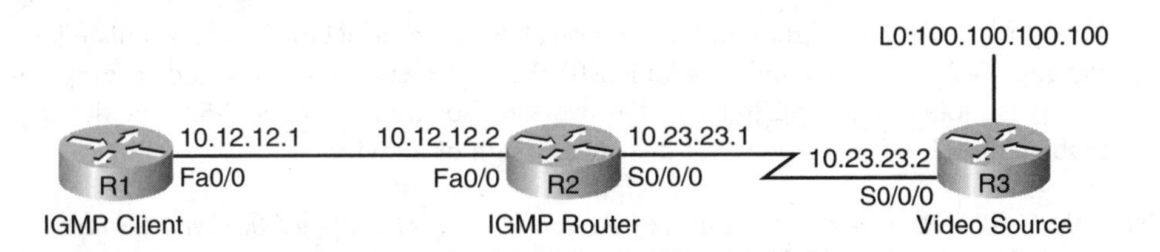

Figure 8-21 *Network Topology for the Second Video-Integration Troubleshooting Example*

Because the video application is the only one that is not working, you can discard IP reachability and routing issues as the problem, except of course for the networks that are related to the video application. Because you are dealing with a multicast issue, keep in mind that end devices must join a multicast group before they can receive traffic directed to that group. So, you get on R2 to see the multicast groups the hosts in this LAN have joined. Use the **show ip igmp groups** command; the result is shown in Example 8-51. R1 is not joining any group. The group that you see on the example output is on the serial 0/0/0 interface, while R1 is on the LAN interface Fa 0/0. The **show ip igmp membership** command, which shows all members of all groups, does not list the IP address of R1 (10.12.12.1) anywhere.

Example 8-51 *Cisco IOS IPS CLI Configuration*

```
R2# show ip igmp group
IGMP Connected Group Membership
Group Address   Interface        Uptime    Expires  Last Reporter   Group Accounted
224.0.1.40      Serial0/0/0      00:08:48  Stopped  10.23.23.2
R2#

R2# show ip igmp membership
Flags: A - aggregate, T - tracked
       L - Local, S - static, V - virtual, R - Reported through v3
       I - v3lite, U - Urd, M - SSM (S,G) channel
       1,2,3 - The version of IGMP the group is in
Channel/Group-Flags:
        / - Filtering entry (Exclude mode (S,G), Include mode (*,G)
Reporter:
        <mac-or-ip-address> - last reporter if group is not explicitly tracked
        <n>/<m>      - <n> reporter in include mode, <m> reporter in exclude

Channel/Group                  Reporter         Uptime    Exp   Flags  Interface
*.224.0.1.40                   10.23.23.2       00:09:24  stop  2LA    Se0/0/0
R2#
```

Now you try **debug ip igmp** on R2, but you also will go to R1 and try to simulate joining a group. Because R1 is simulating an IGMP client, you enter the command **ip igmp join-group** and join the group 224.8.8.8. This work is shown on Example 8-52. The debug you enabled on R2, however, does not display any sign of activity.

Example 8-52 *R2 Does Not Show Any Activity After R1 Joins a Multicast Group*

```
R2# debug ip igmp
IGMP debugging is on
R2#

R1# config t
Enter configuration commands, one per line. End with CNTL/Z.
R1(config)# int fa0/0
R1(config-if)# ip igmp joi
R1(config-if)# ip igmp join-group 224.8.8.8
R1(config-if)#
```

The first step you must take to further isolate the problem is to determine whether IGMP is actually running on router R2. So, you use the **show ip igmp interface** command on R2. The result is shown on Example 8-53. There is only one interface enabled for IGMP in this router and that is serial 0/0/0. Because IGMP is not enabled on the R2's Fa 0/0 interface, R1 could not join the multicast group, and that is why multicast connectivity is not working.

Example 8-53 *On R2, the Only Interface Where IGMP Is Enabled Is Serial 0/0/0*

```
R2# show ip igmp interface
Serial0/0/0 is up, line protocol is up
  Internet address is 10.23.23.2/24
  IGMP is enabled on interface
  Current IGMP host version is 2
  Current IGMP router version is 2
  IGMP query interval is 60 seconds
  IGMP querier timeout is 120 seconds
  IGMP max query response time is 10 seconds
  Last member query count is 2
  Last member query response interval is 1000 ms
  Inbound IGMP access group is not set
  IGMP activity: 1 joins, 0 leaves
  Multicast routing is enabled on interface
  Multicast TTL threshold is 0
  IGMP querying router is 0.0.0.0 (this system)
  Multicast groups joined by this system (number of users):
      224.0.1.40(1)
R2#
```

You will configure IGMP on router R2's Fa 0/0 interface by enabling PIM on this interface, using the command **ip pim sparse-dense** (see Example 8-54). The **debug** output shows R2 sending IGMP Version 2 query and receiving a report from R1 (10.12.12.1 joining the multicast group 224.8.8.8).

Example 8-54 *Upon Enabling PIM on R2's Fa 0/0, Multicast Query and Reports Begin*

```
R1# config t
Enter configuration commands, one per line. End with CNTL/Z.
R1(config)# int fa0/0
R1(config-if)# ip pim
R1(config-if)# ip pim sp
R1(config-if)# ip pim sparse-d
R1(config-if)# ip pim sparse-dense-mode
R1(config-if)#
IGMP(0): Send v2 init  Query on FastEthernet0/0
%PIM-5-DRCHG: Dr change from neighbor 0.0.0.0 to 10.12.12.2 on interface
FastEthernet0/0
IGMP(0): Received v2 Report on FastEthernet0/0 from 10.12.12.1 for 224.8.8.8
IGMP(0): Received Group record for group 224.8.8.8, mode 2 from 10.12.12.1 for 0
sources
IGMP(0): WAVL Insert group: 224.8.8.8 interface: FastEthernet0/0Successful
IGMP(0): Switching to EXCLUDE mode for 224.8.8.8 on FastEthernet0/0
IGMP(0): Updating EXLUDE group timer for 224.8.8.8
IGMP(0): MRT Add/Update FastEthernet0/0 for (*,224.8.8.8) by 0
```

The **show ip igmp interface** command output now informs you that IGMP Version 2 is enabled on interface Fa 0/0 (see Example 8-55). It is important to notice and verify that the IGMP versions used by the hosts and the router are compatible. You enter the **show ip igmp groups** command next, and discover that 224.8.8.8 is now known on Fa 0/0 with last reporter as R1 (10.12.12.1).

Example 8-55 *IGMP Is Now Enabled on Both Serial 0/0/0 and FastEthernet 0/0 Interfaces*

```
R2# show ip igmp interface
Serial0/0/0 is up, line protocol is up
  Internet address is 10.23.23.2/24
  IGMP is enabled on interface
  Current IGMP host version is 2
  Current IGMP router version is 2
  IGMP query interval is 60 seconds
```

```
  IGMP querier timeout is 120 seconds
  IGMP max query response time is 10 seconds
  Last member query count is 2
  Last member query response interval is 1000 ms
  Inbound IGMP access group is not set
  IGMP activity: 1 joins, 0 leaves
  Multicast routing is enabled on interface
  Multicast TTL threshold is 0
  IGMP querying router is 0.0.0.0 (this system)
  Multicast groups joined by this system (number of users):
      224.0.1.40(1)
FastEthernet0/0 is up
  Internet address is 10.12.12.2/24
  IGMP is enabled on interface
  Current IGMP host version is 2
  Current IGMP router version is 2
  IGMP query interval is 60 seconds
 --More--

R2#
R2# show ip igmp group
IGMP Connected Group Membership
Group       Interface          Uptime     Expires    Last Reporter  Group Accounted
Address
224.8.8.8   FastEthernet0/0/0  00:08:48   00:02:51   10.12.12.1
224.0.1.40  Serial0/0/0        00:19:43   stopped    10.23.23.2
R2#
```

Finally, you need to verify that multicast connectivity is working end to end. You go to the video server, R3 in this example, and ping 224.8.8.8. This action simulates multicast traffic originating from the multicast server (R3), which must reach the members of the multicast group 224.8.8.8. In just a few moments a reply is received from R1 (see Example 8-56). This result simulates the situation that the multicast server is pushing video, and the client is able to receive it and watch it. The problem is fixed.

Example 8-56 *Ping to the Multicast Address 224.8.8.8 from R3 Receives Reply from R1*

```
R3# ping 224.8.8.8

Type escape sequence to abort.
Sending 1, 100-byte ICMP Echos to 224.8.8.8, timeout is 2 seconds:

Reply to request 0 from 10.12.12.1, 1 mss
R3#
```

Summary

Troubleshooting a wireless network requires the following considerations:

- Is the wireless network based on the autonomous model or the split MAC (lightweight) model?
- What are the switch capabilities and requirements in terms of Power over Ethernet (PoE), trunking, WLAN-to-VLAN mapping, security, and quality of service (QoS)?
- How will the Lightweight Access Point Protocol (LWAPP) be handled?
- What type of roaming will the network support?

Common wireless integration issues include the following:

- **Problems at the wireless to wired boundary:** In case of the autonomous model, the AP has a wired connection to a switch and this connection must be in working condition. In case of the split MAC model, the lightweight AP (LWAP) sends and receives control and data to the wireless LAN controller (WLC) using LWAPP. This communication must be in working condition.
- **Filters might be blocking traffic:** In addition to the switches, the radio and Ethernet side of the APs must be checked for filters that might be blocking legitimate traffic such as LWAPP or security/authentication. LWAPP control uses UDP port 12223, and LWAPP data uses UDP port 12222.
- **Wireless QoS and wired QoS mapping might be incorrect:** QoS markings must be maintained and remain consistent across wireless-to-wired boundaries.
- **PoE issues:** The AP might need PoE on the switch port it connects to, and power amount must be appropriate.
- **Trunk issues:** All trunks must be checked to make sure they allow appropriate VLANs.

Some useful switch troubleshooting commands to support wireless LANS are as follows:

- **show interfaces switchport**
- **show interfaces status**
- **show interfaces trunk**
- **show interface** *interface* **switchport**
- **show access-lists**

The design and troubleshooting considerations of integrating unified communications into a campus LAN are as follows:

- **QoS:** Adequate trust boundaries, plus proper router and switch QoS configurations.
- **High availability:** Usage of resilient technologies such as RSTP and HSRP.

- **Security:** Implementation of voice VLAN(s) and accurate filters and firewall configurations.
- **Availability and correct provisioning of other services:** PoE, DHCP, TFTP, NTP, CDP, and so on.

The IP phone boot process consists of the following main steps:

Step 1. The IP phone powers on.

Step 2. The phone performs a power-on self-test (POST).

Step 3. The phone boots.

Step 4. The phone uses CDP to learn the voice VLAN.

Step 5. The phone initializes the IP stack.

Step 6. The IP phone sends DHCP requests to obtain an IP address.

Step 7. The DHCP server selects a free IP address from the pool and sends it, along with the other parameters, including option 150 (TFTP server).

Step 8. The IP phone initializes, applying the IP configuration to the IP stack.

Step 9. The IP phone requests a configuration file from the TFTP server defined in option 150.

Useful converged network troubleshooting commands include the following:

- **show interface trunk**
- **show interfaces switchport**
- **show vlan**
- **show errdisable recovery**
- **show auto qos**
- **show auto discovery qos**
- **show ip dhcp pool**
- **show ip dhcp server**
- **show ntp status**
- **debug ephone**
- **show crypto engine connections active**

Video-integration considerations and requirements are as follows:

- **Quality of service:** QoS considerations for video are not quite the same as VoIP; video requires more bandwidth and can be bursty.
- **High availability:** Video applications require millisecond-level network service recovery because video traffic cannot withstand unpredictable or large network recovery timeouts.
- **Multicast:** Improper router and switch multicast (PIM, IGMP, and so on) configurations impede operation of multicast-based video applications.
- **Security:** Access control and threat management mechanisms must consider the various protocols and traffic flows that result from a video-enabled network and allow them in the network in a controlled manner.

Common video-integration issues include the following:

- Excessive bandwidth utilization
- Lack of control
- Poor quality (lack of QoS)
- Security issues (filtering of key protocols, and stateful requirements)
- Multicast issues

Review Questions

Use the questions here to review what you learned in this chapter. The correct answers are found in Appendix A, "Answers to Chapter Review Questions."

1. What are the two main wireless LAN implementation models?
2. Name at least three switch readiness areas with respect to wireless integration.
3. Which UDP ports does LWAPP use?
4. What does the output of the command **show zone-pair security** display?
5. Which DHCP option is for AP-management IP address of the WLC?
6. Specify at least two unified communications integration considerations.
7. Name at least two services that are usually used with unified communications.

8. Put the IP phone initialization/boot sequence in order.

   ____ The IP phone initializes, applying the IP configuration to the IP stack.

   ____ The phone attempts to obtain an IP address through DHCP.

   ____ The IP phone powers on, performs POST, and boots.

   ____ The DHCP server offers an IP address (with option 150) to the IP phone.

   ____ The phone uses Cisco Discovery Protocol to learn the voice VLAN.

9. What is the output of the **show interfaces status err-disabled** command?

10. Which TCP port number does Skinny Client Control Protocol (SCCP) use?

11. Which command is used to display the multicast groups with receivers that are directly connected to the router and that were learned through Internet Group Management Protocol?

Chapter 9

Maintaining and Troubleshooting Network Security Implementations

This chapter covers the following topics:

- Troubleshooting challenges in secure networks
- Troubleshooting management plane security
- Troubleshooting control plane security
- Troubleshooting data plane security
- Troubleshooting branch office and remote worker connectivity

Networks need to be secured, and the level of security that is needed and the features that must be deployed are dependent on the organization and its security policies. However, in any network, at least a basic level of security needs to be implemented. Access to network infrastructure devices themselves needs to be secured to prevent tampering and unauthorized activities, and the control plane of the network devices needs to be hardened to prevent infrastructure denial of service. Routers and switches can participate in securing user traffic through implementation of packet filtering, virtual private network (VPN), and intrusion prevention system (IPS) features. Deployment of security features on routers and switches adds an extra layer of complexity to network troubleshooting. Because most security features aim to restrict connectivity by nature, their implementation adds many potential problem causes that need to be eliminated during the troubleshooting process. Also, reported problems and possible solutions need to be validated against the organization's security policy.

Troubleshooting Secure Networks

To troubleshoot effectively and efficiently in a secure infrastructure, it is important to understand which features are deployed and how they operate. Most security features operate at the transport layer and above. Therefore, it is important to be familiar with the generic principles of troubleshooting Layer 4 connectivity. Using a generic troubleshooting process can help to determine whether the problems are likely to be related to security features or caused by underlying Layer 1, 2, or 3 connectivity issues. After you have determined that the problem must be related to a security feature, you need to have detailed knowledge of the specific feature to diagnose and resolve the issue. Depending on your organization, you might need to escalate the issue to a security specialist once you arrive at this point in the troubleshooting process.

Troubleshooting Challenges in Secured Networks

The objective of building a network infrastructure is to enable connectivity between devices or between different parts of a network. The objective of security, however, is the complete opposite. Security features usually aim to restrict connectivity and only allow traffic that is specifically permitted by the security policy to support the organization's business processes. This adds another dimension to network troubleshooting. In a network that is completely open and has been designed to enable connectivity from any point to any point in the network, it is easy to validate a reported problem. If there is no connectivity between any two hosts or applications, there is definitely a problem. In that case, you initiate a troubleshooting process to isolate the problem, find the point where connectivity is failing, and restore the connectivity by implementing the necessary changes.

In a secured environment, a reported connectivity problem does not automatically translate to a valid problem that needs to be resolved. First, you need to determine whether the reported lack of connectivity actually concerns authorized traffic according to the security policy of your organization. If this is not the case, the problem is not a technical problem, but should be resolved at the business level. If there is a valid reason for a user who is currently not allowed to have access/connectivity to some resource to be granted access/connectivity to that resource, the security policy may need to be reevaluated and changed. Eventually, changes in the policy should result in changes in the implementation, such as the addition of a new firewall rule. After you have validated the problem and determined that the reported lack of connectivity concerns traffic that should be allowed (according to the policy), the implemented security features complicate the troubleshooting process, because they add more potential problem causes that need to be eliminated to diagnose the problem. Therefore, it is vital that you know which security features have been implemented at each point in your network, because that will help you to quickly assess whether a misconfigured security feature might be a potential cause of the problem.

Once you have partially diagnosed a problem and you want to establish whether the problem is caused by a security feature, a useful diagnostic technique is to temporarily disable the security feature and see whether that fixes the problem. However, you should realize that by doing so, you are creating a situation that is not compliant with the security policy, and therefore, you are taking a risk of opening the network to an attack. Therefore, always consider the potential risk of the change and balance that against the criticality of the problem that you are troubleshooting. For example, imagine that you are troubleshooting a network problem caused by the fact that two Open Shortest Path First (OSPF) Protocol routers do not establish an OSPF adjacency, and the security policy states that message digest 5 (MD5) authentication should be used between OSPF routers. You might consider authentication as a possible cause of the problem. In that case, it might be permissible to temporarily remove the OSPF authentication between the two routers to confirm or eliminate OSPF authentication as the source of the problem. The criticality and urgency of the problem is high, and the risk of an actual security incident if you remove OSPF authentication for a few minutes is low. Now imagine that you are troubleshooting a connectivity problem of a user who cannot reach a particular site on the Internet. You suspect that this might be caused by an access list on the perimeter router. In this case, it might not be safe to temporarily remove the access list to verify that is indeed the cause of the problem.

In conclusion, if you realize that disabling a security feature restores connectivity, you cannot consider it as an actual solution to the problem. Even though it is beneficial to establish that the security feature is causing the problem, if the solution is not compliant with the security policy, it is not an acceptable solution; it is a workaround at best. In those situations, you must roll back the change and continue your troubleshooting process until you find a solution compliant with the security policy.

Security Features Review

In the past, network security was often implemented as an additional layer on top of the network infrastructure. Special devices, such as firewalls, VPN concentrators, and intrusion detection systems (IDS) were added to the network to implement specific security features, while the routers and switches would provide the basic network connectivity and not be involved in the security aspects of the network. A common approach was to design and implement a network infrastructure to provide connectivity and then design and implement a security solution on top of that. Over the years, it was realized that a more holistic approach to security is necessary to build secure networks. A system is as secure as its weakest component, and therefore, the security risks and vulnerabilities of each component and layer of the network should be evaluated and addressed. In addition to using specialized security devices, such as firewalls, intrusion prevention systems (IPS), and VPN concentrators, network devices such as routers and switches and the protocols that are used between these devices should be secured. If the network infrastructure itself is compromised, the entire system can be compromised. In addition, in smaller networks, the router might have a dual role, functioning as both a router and as a security device by providing firewall, IPS, or VPN services. Finally, infrastructure devices such as routers and switches can function as a component in a distributed security system.

The implementation of security features can affect router and switch operation on different planes. On a network device, there are three fundamental categories of functionality, also called functional planes. These planes and their corresponding types of traffic must be secured. The three main functional planes are as follows:

- **Management plane:** The management plane represents all the functions and protocols involved in managing the device. This includes accessing information about the device configuration, device operation, and statistics. It also includes changing the device configuration to alter its behavior. Securing this plane is vital to the overall security of the device. If the management plane is compromised, the other planes are also exposed.

- **Control plane:** The control plane represents all the functions and protocols that are used between network devices to control the operation of the network, such as routing protocols, the Spanning Tree Protocol (STP), or other signaling and control protocols. Because the control plane affects the behavior of the data plane, the control plane protocols need to be secured. If unauthorized devices are allowed to participate in the control plane protocols, this opens up possibilities for an attacker to block or divert traffic.
- **Data plane:** The data plane represents all the functions involved in forwarding traffic through the device. Routers and switches can inspect and filter traffic as part of the implementation of a security policy. It is important to note that all management and control plane traffic flow through the data plane, too. Consequently, security features on the data plane can be used to secure the management and control planes, too. This implies that failures on the management and control plane may be caused by the implementation of security features on the data plane.

Troubleshooting Management Plane Security

The management functions of a router or switch are commonly accessed using three different methods:

- The Cisco IOS command-line interface (CLI)
- Web-based device management
- A network management platform based on Simple Network Management Protocol (SNMP)

All these methods must be used in the most secure way, based on the device type, its operating system capabilities (IOS), and the security policies of the organization.

The Management Plane

The CLI that is part of Cisco IOS Software is the most common and most powerful method to manage routers and switches. Commands can be entered directly through a serial connection to the console of the device, or remotely through Telnet or Secure Shell (SSH). For all these methods, at the very least, some form of authentication should be implemented to ensure that only authorized personnel can access and configure the network devices. Furthermore it is recommended to restrict the network locations that these devices can be accessed from. Moreover, because of its more secure operation, SSH should be used as the access method rather than Telnet when possible. Telnet transmissions contain unencrypted data (including the password), whereas SSH uses encryption to secure its transmission. If it is not possible to use SSH to the devices themselves and Telnet is the only option, additional precautions need to be taken to secure the management traffic. For example, Telnet access could be restricted to a secure part of the network that is used only for management and access to this network itself is secured through use of VPN techniques or SSH using a bastion host (possibly exposed, but hardened to withstand attacks). Finally, you should be aware that physical security of the device itself is also vital to the security of the management plane. The CLI can always be accessed through the serial console of the device itself, and therefore having physical access to the device implies having access to the command line. Again, authentication can limit access, but you have to be aware that if someone has access to the console of the device and the ability to power cycle the device, that person can perform the password recovery procedure and gain control of the device.

Note On some devices, the impact of a successful password recovery procedure can be limited by use of the **no service password-recovery** command. By enabling this command, the original configuration and passwords of the device cannot be recovered using the password recovery procedure. However, the device configuration can still be erased causing the device to be reset to factory defaults. If no additional control plane and data plane security measures have been implemented and the attacker has sufficient knowledge of the network, it may be possible to rebuild the configuration and gain access to the network.

An alternative method to manage routers and switches is by use of a web-based device manager such as the Cisco Configuration Professional (CCP) or the Security Device Manager (SDM), which is either installed on the device itself or on a PC. The protocol used by these web-based device managers is either HTTP or HTTPS. HTTPS is more secure than HTTP because it uses encryption to secure its transmissions, while HTTP transmits unencrypted data. Similar arguments that are used in the discussion about the use of Telnet versus SSH can be applied to the use of HTTP versus HTTPS. Authentication should be implemented to restrict web-based access to authorized users only, and it is safer to restrict the locations that these devices can be accessed from.

A third method to access the management functions of the device is by use of a network management platform using SNMP. Most commonly, this method is only used to access operational parameters and statistics of the device, not to change the configuration. In that case, devices are only configured for read-access, and the configuration cannot be changed. From a security standpoint, this means that the associated security risk is generally lower. If the devices have been configured for read-write access, the configuration can be changed, and the same level of security should be applied that is also applied for command-line or web-based access.

Authentication, authorization, and accounting (AAA) is a major component of the network security of the organization. AAA is the basis for providing secure remote access to the network and remote management of network devices. Network devices can use a centralized security server containing all of the security polices that define the list of users and what they are allowed to do. TACACS+ and RADIUS are the commonly used protocols to communicate with a centralized (AAA) security server such as Cisco Secure Access Control Server (ACS). The following are some of the main characteristics of these protocols:

- RADIUS combines authentication and authorization. The access-accept packets sent by the RADIUS server to the client contain authorization information. This makes it difficult to decouple authentication and authorization. On the other hand, TACACS+ uses the AAA architecture, which decouples authentication and authorization.

- RADIUS uses UDP, whereas TACACS+ uses TCP (port 49). RADIUS uses UDP port 1812 (or 1645) for authentication, and UDP port 1813 (or 1646) for accounting messages.
- RADIUS encrypts only the password in the access-request packet, from the client to the server. The remainder of the packet is unencrypted. Other information, such as username, authorized services, and accounting, can be captured by a third party. TACACS+ encrypts the entire body of the packet but leaves a standard TACACS+ header. Within this header, a field indicates whether the body is encrypted. For debugging purposes, it is useful to have the body of the packets unencrypted; however, during normal operation, the body of the packet is fully encrypted for more secure communications.
- RADIUS does not allow specification (or enforcement) of which commands can be and which commands cannot be executed on a router on a per user basis. Therefore, RADIUS is not as useful for router management or as flexible for terminal services. TACACS+ provides two methods to control the authorization of router commands on a per-user or per-group basis:
  - Assign privilege levels to commands and have the router verify with the TACACS+ server whether the user is authorized at the specified privilege level
  - Explicitly specify in the TACACS+ server, on a per-user or per-group basis, the commands that are allowed
- RADIUS has extensive accounting capabilities, whereas TACACS+ has limited accounting capabilities.
- RADIUS is based on an open standard (RFC 2865); TACACS+ was developed by Cisco Systems.

Securing the Management Plane

There are two common techniques to secure management access to network devices. First, access to the management plane can be restricted using packet or session filters. Second, access can be allowed from only specific source IP addresses or networks. This can be implemented in several ways. Because all access to the management plane goes through the data plane, generic access lists can be applied to the interfaces of the device to restrict the access to the management IP addresses and interfaces of the device. If packet filtering using access lists or the Cisco IOS firewall feature has already been implemented, this is just a small addition to the existing filtering policies. If packet filtering or firewalling has not been configured yet, this might not be the best way to secure the management plane because it will also affect the forwarding of all data plane traffic. All the management protocols, such as Telnet, SSH, HTTP, HTTPS, and SNMP, allow access lists to be specifically applied to the sessions directed to these management plane applications. Incoming access requests are evaluated against an access list and permitted or denied based on the source of the session. The advantage of this method is that only management plane traffic is affected and the forwarding of data plane traffic is unaffected.

After a management session is established from an authorized source IP address, it is necessary to authenticate the user that is attempting to access the device. This can be done through a simple password authentication or an authentication based on a username and password combination. These usernames and passwords can be stored locally on the device itself or, for a more scalable solution, they can be stored in a central database. The router or switch can verify these credentials against the central database through use of the TACACS+ or RADIUS protocols. In addition to centralized authentication, the use of a TACACS+ or RADIUS server also allows for added authorization and accounting capabilities. Furthermore, the use of a TACACS+ or RADIUS server also opens up the possible use of more sophisticated and secure authentication methods such as token card services.

From a troubleshooting standpoint, it is important to know the answer to the following questions:

- What security policies have been implemented for management access to the devices?
- From which IP addresses or networks can the network devices be accessed?
- What type of authentication, authorization, and accounting is used on the network?
- If centralized AAA services are deployed, what happens when these servers fail or become unreachable?
- Are there any backdoors or fallback mechanisms to access the devices?

Clearly, the more restrictive the policy is, the more secure the network will be. On the other hand, you have to be careful to not create a situation where devices cannot be accessed during a network outage. In those cases a very dangerous, "catch-22" situation can be created: A network problem causes you to lose management access to the devices. To diagnose and resolve the problem, you first need access to the devices. However, to access the devices, you first need to solve the problem. However, to solve the problem, you first need access to the network devices. Eventually, you might not have another option other than hoping that you can get physical access to the device to perform a password recovery procedure and gain access to the command line of the device.

Cisco Secure ACS offers centralized command and control for all user authentication, authorization, and accounting from a web-based, graphical interface (see Figure 9-1).

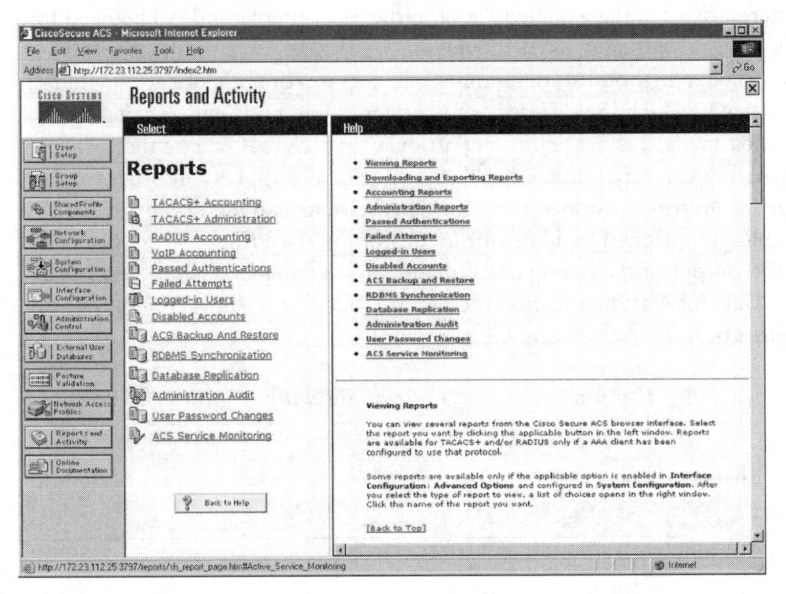

Figure 9-1 *Cisco Secure Access Control Server Reports and Activity Options*

Under Reports and Activity option, Cisco Secure ACS provides the following mechanisms to troubleshoot AAA-related problems:

- **Accounting Reports:** The TACACS+ and the RADIUS, accounting reports contain a record of all successful authentications during the period covered by the report. Information captured includes time, date, username, type of connection, amount of time logged in, and bytes transferred.
- **Administration Reports:** This report contains all TACACS+ commands requested during the period covered by the report. This is typically used when Cisco Secure ACS is being used to manage access to routers.
- **Passed Authentications:** This report lists successful authentications during the period covered by the report.
- **Failed Attempts:** This report contains a record of all unsuccessful authentications during the period covered by the report for both TACACS+ and RADIUS. The reports capture the username attempted, time, date, and cause of failure.
- **Logged-in Users:** This report shows all users currently logged in, grouped by AAA client.
- **Disabled Accounts:** This list contains accounts that have been disabled. They might have been manually disabled or disabled automatically based on the aging information defined under User Setup.

Troubleshooting Security Implementations in the Management Plane

Authentication provides a method for identifying users based on credentials such as a username and password. Access to network devices or network services should only be granted after the user's identity has been verified. AAA authentication on routers and switches is configured by defining a named list of authentication methods to be used for a specific service, such as logging in to the device or connecting to an interface using PPP. The list, also called a method list, determines which types of authentication will be used and the sequence in which the different authentication methods will be tried. If a default authentication method is defined for a particular service that will be the authentication method used unless a different method list is specifically applied. In other words, the default list can be overruled by specifying an alternative named method list, which should then be explicitly assigned to a line (for logins) or interface (for network-based authentication). The output of the **debug aaa authentication** command can be very useful for troubleshooting AAA authentication problems. Example 9-1 shows the output of **debug aaa authentication** for a successful login attempt.

Example 9-1 debug aaa authentication *Command Output Showing a Successful Login*

```
Router# debug tacacs
Router# debug aaa authentication
13:21:20: AAA/AUTHEN: create_user user='' ruser='' port='tty6'
```

```
                rem_addr='10.0.0.32' authen_type=1 service=1 priv=1
13:21:20: AAA/AUTHEN/START (0): port= 'tty6' list='' action=LOGIN service=LOGIN
13:21:20: AAA/AUTHEN/START (0):  using "default" list
13:21:20: AAA/AUTHEN/START (70215483): Method=TACACS+
13:21:20: TAC+ (70215483): received authen response status = GETUSER
13:21:20: AAA/AUTHEN (70215483): status = GETUSER
13:21:23: AAA/AUTHEN/CONT (70215483): continue_login
13:21:23: AAA/AUTHEN (70215483): status = GETUSER
13:21:23: AAA/AUTHEN (70215483): Method=TACACS+
13:21:23: TAC+ : send AUTHEN/CONT packet
13:21:23: TAC+ (70215483): received authen response status = GETPASS
13:21:23: AAA/AUTHEN (70215483): status = GETPASS
13:21:27: AAA/AUTHEN/CONT (70215483): continue_login
13:21:27: AAA/AUTHEN (70215483): status = GETPASS
13:21:27: AAA/AUTHEN (70215483): Method=TACACS+
13:21:27: TAC+ : send AUTHEN/CONT packet
13:21:27: TAC+ (70215483): received authen response status = PASS
13:21:27: AAA/AUTHEN (70215483): status = PASS
```

The **debug aaa authentication** output captured in Example 9-1 shows the following events:

- A remote user with the IP address 10.0.0.32 attempts to log in to the router.
- The router checks to see whether AAA authentication for the LOGIN service is enabled (and it is).
- Because no other authentication method list is applied, the router applies the default method, and the first method defined by the default method list is TACACS+.
- The authentication process then prompts the user for a username and password, and upon receiving these credentials, they are sent to the TACACS+ server for verification.
- The TACACS+ server checks the credentials against its database and responds with a PASS status as a sign of successful authentication.

Note In Example 9-1, the lines in the output that are preceded by AAA are generated by the **debug aaa authentication** command, while the lines preceded by TAC+ are originated by the **debug tacacs** command.

Authorization determines what resources the user has access to (on the router, for example). In other words, AAA authorization assembles a set of attributes that describe what tasks the user is authorized to perform. These attributes are compared to the information contained in a database for a given user, and the result is returned to AAA to determine the user's actual capabilities and restrictions. The database can be located locally on the device or it can be hosted remotely on a RADIUS or TACACS+ security server.

As with authentication, you configure AAA authorization by defining a named list of authorization methods, and then applying that list to various interfaces. As demonstrated in Example 9-2, the output of the **debug aaa authorization** command can prove quite useful to troubleshoot AAA authorization problems.

Example 9-2 **debug aaa authorization** *Command Output Showing a Denied Authorization*

```
Router# debug aaa authorization
2:23:21: AAA/AUTHOR (0): user= 'admin1'
2:23:21: AAA/AUTHOR (0): send AV service=shell
2:23:21: AAA/AUTHOR (0): send AV cmd*
2:23:21: AAA/AUTHOR (342885561): Method=TACACS+
2:23:21: AAA/AUTHOR/TAC+ (342885561): user=admin1
2:23:21: AAA/AUTHOR/TAC+ (342885561): send AV service=shell
2:23:21: AAA/AUTHOR/TAC+ (342885561): send AV cmd*
2:23:21: AAA/AUTHOR (342885561): Post authorization status = FAIL
```

The **debug aaa authorization** output captured in Example 9-2 shows the following events:

- The user (admin1) is attempting to do something that requires authorization (in Example 9-2, the user attempts to gain an EXEC shell service).
- The **cmd** parameter specifies a command that the user is trying to execute. If * is listed, it refers to plain EXEC access.
- The method used to authorize this access is TACACS+.
- The router sends the necessary information (user credentials) through TACACS+ to the security server.
- The security server verifies the authorization, determines that the user is not authorized to perform this function, and sends back a FAIL status response.

Accounting provides a method for collecting and sending information about user activities to the security server for billing, auditing, and reporting purposes. This information includes user identities, start and stop times, executed commands (such as PPP), and the number of packets and bytes sent and received. When AAA accounting is activated, the network access server reports user activity to the RADIUS or TACACS+ security server in the form of accounting records. This data can then be analyzed for network management, client billing, or for auditing purposes. All accounting methods must be defined through AAA. As with authentication and authorization, you configure AAA accounting by defining a named list of accounting methods, and applying that list to various interfaces. As demonstrated in Example 9-3, the output of the **debug aaa accounting** command is very informative; hence, this debug can help you troubleshoot AAA accounting problems.

Example 9-3 debug aaa accounting *Command Output*

```
Router# debug aaa accounting
May 10 14:48:33.011: AAA/ACCT/EXEC(00000005): Pick method list 'default'
May 10 14:48:33.011: AAA/ACCT/SETMLIST(00000005): Handle 0, mlist 81CA79CC,
Name default
May 10 14:48:33.011: Getting session id for EXEC (00000005): db=82099258
May 10 14:48:33.011: AAA/ACCT/EXEC(00000005): add, count 2
May 10 14:48:33.011: AAA/ACCT/EVENT(00000005): EXEC UP
```

The **debug aaa accounting** output captured in Example 9-3 shows a scenario where the default method was used, and that a user successfully gained access to the router's EXEC shell.

There are a number of common TACACS+ failures, including the following:

- A TACACS+ server goes down or a device (TACACS client) cannot connect to the server. To be ready for a situation like this, you may want to configure the network device to use the local database for authenticating critical users.
- A device (client) shared key and the server's shared key do not match.
- User credentials (username, password, or both) getting rejected by the server.

Example 9-4 shows TACACS messages regarding these common cases.

Example 9-4 *Common TACACS+ Failures*

```
Router# debug tacacs
Router# debug aaa authentication
! The TACACS+ server is down or the device has no connectivity to the server:
TAC+: TCP/IP open to 171.68.118.101/49 failed-
Connection refused by remote host
AAA/AUTHEN (2546660185): status = ERROR
AAA/AUTHEN/START (2546660185): Method=LOCAL
AAA/AUTHEN (2546660185): status = FAIL
As1 CHAP: Unable to validate response. Username chapuser: Authentication failure

! The key on the device and TACACS+ server do not match:
TAC+: received bad AUTHEN packet: length = 68, expected 67857
TAC+: Invalid AUTHEN/START packet (check keys)
AAA/AUTHEN (1771887965): status = ERROR
```

```
! Bad user name, bad password, or both:
AAA/AUTHEN: free_user (0x170940) user= 'chapuser' ruser= ''
Port= 'Async1' rem_addr= 'async' authen_type=CHAP service=PPP priv=1
TAC+: Closing TCP/IP 0x16EF4C connection to 171.68.118.101/49
AAA/AUTHEN (2082151566): status = FAIL
As1 CHAP: Unable to validate Response. Username papuser: Authentication failure
```

Note In Example 9-4, both the **debug tacacs** and the **debug aaa authentication** commands have been enabled. The lines in the output that are preceded by **AAA** are generated by the **debug aaa authentication** command, while the lines preceded by **TAC+** are originated by the **debug tacacs** command.

The common RADIUS problems are similar to the common TACACS+ problems. Example 9-5 shows cases of RADIUS server's failure or loss of network connectivity, mismatch of the shared key between the RADIUS server and the network device (RADIUS client), user authorization failure, and finally, a case of bad username, password, or both.

Example 9-5 *Common RADIUS Failures*

```
Router# debug radius
Router# debug aaa authentication
! The RADIUS server is down or the device has no connectivity to the server:
As1 CHAP: I RESPONSE id 12 len 28 from "chapadd"
RADIUS: id 15, requestor hung up.
RADIUS: No response for id 15
RADIUS: No response from server
AAA/AUTHEN (1866705040): status = ERROR
AAA/AUTHEN/START (1866705040): Method=LOCAL
AAA/AUTHEN (1866705040): status = FAIL
As1 CHAP: Unable to validate Response. Username chapadd: Authentication failure
As1 CHAP: 0 FAILURE id 13 len 26 msg is "Authentication failure"

! The key on the device and RADIUS server do not match:
RADIUS: received from id 21 171.68.118.101:1645, Access-Reject, len 20
RADIUS: Reply for 21 fails decrypt
```

```
NT client sends 'DOMAIN\user' and Radius server expects 'user':
RADIUS: received from id 16 171.68.118.101:1645, Access-Reject, len 20
AAA/AUTHEN (2974782384): status = FAIL
As1 CHAP: Unable to validate Response. Username CISCO\chapadd: Authentication
failure
As1 CHAP: 0 FAILURE id 13 len 26 msg is "Authentication failure"

! Username and password are correct, but authorization failed:
RADIUS: received from id 19 171.68.118.101:1645, Access-Accept, len 20
RADIUS: no appropriate authorization type for user
AAA/AUTHOR (2370106832): Post authorization status = FAIL
AAA/AUTHOR/LCP As1: Denied

! Bad username, bad password, or both:
RADIUS: received from id 17 171.68.118.101:1645, Access-Reject, len 20
AAA/AUTHEN (3898168391): status = FAIL
As1 CHAP: Unable to validate Response. Username ddunlap: Authentication failure
As1 CHAP: 0 FIALURE id 14 len 26 msg is "Authentication failure"
As1 PPP: Phase is TERMINATING
```

If a user is trying to get service for which he or she is not authorized, an authorization status failed message appears in the log. Misconfiguration of the RADIUS server must be investigated, as it is a common mistake. Misconfiguring usernames, passwords, or both, as is the case in Example 9-5, is likewise common.

Troubleshooting Control Plane Security

Even though the majority of the packets going to a router/switch are forwarded by the data plane, some of the packets must be handled by the system's route processor. A few examples of those types of traffic, formally referred to as control plane traffic, are routing protocols, keepalives, and spanning tree. Packet overloads on a router's control plane can slow down routing processes and, as a result, degrade network service levels and user productivity. Packets that traverse the control plane are those destined for that router's CPU, as opposed to network endpoints. All packets entering the control plane are redirected by the data (forwarding) plane. One cause for an overburdened router control plane is denial-of-service (DoS) attacks on the control plane.

Control plane protocols such as routing protocols, Spanning Tree Protocol (STP), and Address Resolution Protocol (ARP) influence or feed the data structures that are used by the data plane to forward frames or packets. Therefore, any device that participates in these protocols can affect the forwarding behavior of the network. By manipulating routing tables, ARP caches, or the spanning-tree topology, packets/frames can be diverted or dropped. Similarly, first-hop redundancy protocols (FHRP), Dynamic Host Configuration Protocol (DHCP), and ARP can be used to influence the forwarding behavior between hosts and routers. Therefore, unauthorized participation in any of these protocols should be prevented to secure the network.

Securing the Control Plane

Most routing protocols support neighbor authentication based on MD5 hashes, only allowing a router that is in possession of a shared key to become a neighbor. A similar mechanism is supported by first-hop redundancy protocols, such as the Hot Standby Router Protocol (HSRP), Virtual Router Redundancy Protocol (VRRP), and Gateway Load Balancing Protocol (GLBP). Using an authentication mechanism prevents unauthorized devices from participating in these important control plane protocols and misdirecting or black-holing application traffic.

The IEEE 802.1D STP does not have an authentication mechanism. Therefore, other mechanisms must be used to prevent unauthorized interaction with the Spanning Tree Protocol. To facilitate this, Cisco switches support the BPDU Guard feature, which shuts down a port if bridge protocol data units (BPDUs) are detected on a port. Cisco switches also support the Root Guard feature, which allows a neighboring switch to participate in the spanning tree protocol but shuts down the port if it sends superior BPDUs. A superior BPDU leads to election of a new device as the spanning-tree root. Other features such as BPDU filtering are also available to protect STP.

The DHCP and ARP protocols can be secured by enabling the DHCP snooping and dynamic ARP inspection (DAI) features. These features inspect DHCP and ARP packets to detect malicious DHCP requests, DHCP replies, and ARP replies. They allow only legitimate ARP and DHCP traffic, and block malicious traffic that aim to redirect user traffic by manipulating the ARP and DHCP tables.

Finally, the control plane policing and control plane protection features can be implemented to protect the CPU of infrastructure devices (routers and switches) from being overloaded by unwanted control plane traffic. Control plane and control plane protection use the Cisco Modular QoS CLI (MQC) to protect the infrastructure from DoS attacks.

Troubleshooting Security Implementations in the Control Plane

It is important to know which control plane security features have been implemented in your network and where (on which devices) they have been implemented. Control plane security features restrict which devices can participate in the control plane protocols. If these features are misconfigured, they may cause the operation of a control plane protocol between devices to fail. A checklist similar to the following could be used by support engineers to troubleshoot control plane security implementations:

- Are routing protocols or FHRPs set up for authentication properly?
- Are STP security features such as BPDU Guard, BDPU Filter, Loop Guard, or Root Guard enabled correctly?
- Is DHCP snooping configured properly?
- Is the configuration of DAI correct?
- Are the configurations for control plane policing or control plane protection done appropriately?

Troubleshooting Data Plane Security

Routers and switches can play an important role in protecting the hosts on the network and securing the exchange of traffic on the network. Because routers and switches are involved in processing and forwarding network traffic, they can play an effective role in inspecting and filtering traffic as it flows through the network.

Securing The Data Plane

The Cisco IOS firewall software provides enhanced security functions for the data plane. There are two types of Cisco IOS firewall:

- Classic Cisco IOS firewall (stateful packet inspection)
- Zone-based policy firewall

Securing the Data Plane Using IOS Stateful Packet Inspection

Cisco IOS stateful packet inspection (formerly context-based access control) is a component of the Cisco IOS firewall. Cisco IOS stateful packet inspection allows certain incoming flows by first inspecting and recording flows initiated from the trusted network. IOS stateful packet inspection is able to inspect all the way to the application layer, taking into consideration characteristics of a flow on a per-protocol basis (context). IOS stateful packet inspection offers interface-based stateful inspection. The combination of the inspection policy and the ACL-based policy defines the overall firewall policy. For example, assume that you want to protect a trusted (internal) network from an untrusted (external) network using a router with two interfaces. The router must be placed between the two networks, and there will be four logical points at which the router can inspect traffic:

- Inbound on the internal interface
- Outbound on the external interface
- Inbound on the external interface
- Outbound on the internal interface

Cisco IOS stateful packet inspection is configured per interface, and it operates by dynamically modifying access list entries facing one direction based on the traffic it sees flowing in the opposite direction. As an example, assume that you are allowing all traffic traversing the router from the internal LAN (192.168.0.0/24) to the Internet (10.0.0.0/8), and denying all traffic flowing from the Internet toward the LAN (see Figure 9-2). To do this, you apply a simple access list to deny all IP traffic on the inbound direction of the external interface (Fa 0/0). Example 9-6 shows this work.

Example 9-6 *An ACL Denying All Inbound Traffic Is Created and Applied to Fa 0/0*

```
Router(config)# ip access-list extended DENY_ALL
Router(config-ext-nacl)# deny ip any any
Router(config-ext-nacl)# exit
Router(config)# interface f0/0
Router(config-if)# ip access-group DENY_ALL in
Router(config-if)# exit
```

To allow web access initiated from the internal network, you must permit the response to the web request to return. Cisco IOS stateful packet inspection allows you to define an inspection rule for each protocol you want to monitor, and permit its respond. In this case, you want to track HTTP sessions. To create an inspection rule (called **inshttp**) to monitor HTTP, you would enter the following command:

```
Router(config)# ip inspect name inshttp http
```

The inspection rule has to be applied on the interface in a particular direction. In this example, the direction has to be outbound on the external interface (Fa 0/0), because the router inspects traffic originating from the trusted network, and dynamically adjusts the ACL restricting traffic inbound on the external interface. Example 9-7 shows the inspect rule (called **inshttp**) being applied to the external interface (Fa 0/0) in the out direction.

Example 9-7 *Applying the Inspect Rule to the Fa 0/0 Interface in the Outbound Direction*

```
Router(config)# ip inspect name inshttp http
Router(config)# interface f0/0
Router(config-if)# ip inspect inshttp out
Router(config-if)# end
Router#
```

Now, the Cisco IOS stateful packet inspection is enabled in one direction for HTTP traffic on interface Fa 0/0. Outbound traffic (going toward the Internet) is tracked in the state table by session, and the DENY_ALL extended ACL restricting inbound traffic is automatically modified to accommodate legitimate return traffic. From the output of **show ip inspect sessions** illustrated in Figure 9-2, you can see that the trusted host 192.168.0.2

has opened an HTTP connection to 10.0.0.2. Cisco IOS stateful packet inspection will continue to track this session until it is closed by either end or when the idle timer expires.

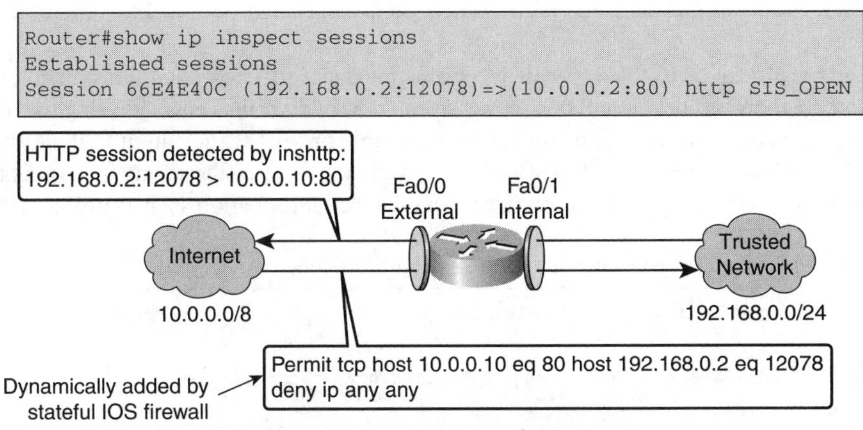

Figure 9-2 show ip inspect sessions *Command Output*

To display Cisco IOS stateful packet inspection configuration and session information, use the **show ip inspect all** command in privileged EXEC mode, as demonstrated in Example 9-8. Cisco has an added ACL bypass functionality so that a packet can avoid redundant ACL checks. This is done by allowing the firewall to permit the packet on the basis of existing inspection sessions rather than dynamic ACLs. Because input and output dynamic ACLs have been eliminated from the firewall configuration, the **show ip inspect session detail** command output no longer shows dynamic ACLs. Instead, the output displays the matching inspection session for each packet that is permitted through the firewall.

Example 9-8 show ip inspect all *Command Output*

```
Router# show ip inpsect all
Session audit trail is enabled
Session alert is enabled
<...output omitted...>
Inspection Rule Configuration
 Inspection name inshttp
    http alert is on audit-trail is on timeout 3600
    https alert is on audit-trail is on timeout 3600
Interface Configuration
 Interface FastEthernet0/0
  Inbound inspection rule is not set
  Outgoing inspection rule is inshttp
    http alert is on audit-trail is on timeout 3600
    https alert is on audit-trail is on timeout 3600
```

```
  Inbound access list is DENY_ALL
  Outing access list is not set
! Output omitted for brevity
```

Audit trails can be enabled to generate syslog messages for each stateful inspection session creation and deletion. Example 9-9 shows how audit trail is enabled using the **ip inspect audit-trail** command. You can see a sample firewall session audit trail message in the figure output. Example 9-9 also shows a sample output of the **debug ip inspect** command that has been entered to observe more detailed information such as object creation.

Example 9-9 *Enabling IP Inspect Audit Trail and Debug*

```
Router(config)# ip inspect audit-trail
Router(config)#
%FW-6-SESS_AUDIT_TRAIL_START: Start http session: initiator
(192.168.0.2:10032) -- responder (10.0.0.10:80)

Router# debug ip inspect
Object-creation INSPECT Object Creations debugging is on
Router#
CBAC* OBJ_CREATE: Pak 6621F7A0 sis 66E4E154 initiator_addr
(192.168.0.2:10032) responder_addr (10.0.0.10:80) initiator_alt_addr
(192.168.0.2:10032) responder_alt_addr (10.0.0.2:80)
CBAC OBJ-CREATE: sid 66E684B0 acl DENY_ALL Prot: tcp
Src 10.0.0.10 Port [80:80]
Dst 192.168.0.2 Port [10032:10032]
CBAC OBJ_CREATE: create host entry 66E568DC addr 10.0.0.10 bucket 8
(vrf 0:0) insp_cb 0x66B61C0C
```

Securing the Data Plane Using the Zone-Based Policy Firewall

The zone-based policy firewall (ZPF) offers an easy-to-understand configuration model. Figure 9-3 shows a pictorial presentation of implementing ZPF. ZPF allows grouping of physical and virtual interfaces.

Firewall policies are configured on traffic moving between zones. ZPF simplifies firewall policy troubleshooting by applying explicit policy on interzone traffic. Firewall policy configuration is very flexible. Varying policies can be applied to different host groups, based on ACL configuration.

ZPF supports the following functionalities:

- Stateful inspection
- Application inspection: IM, POP, IMAP, SMTP/ESMTP, HTTP
- URL filtering

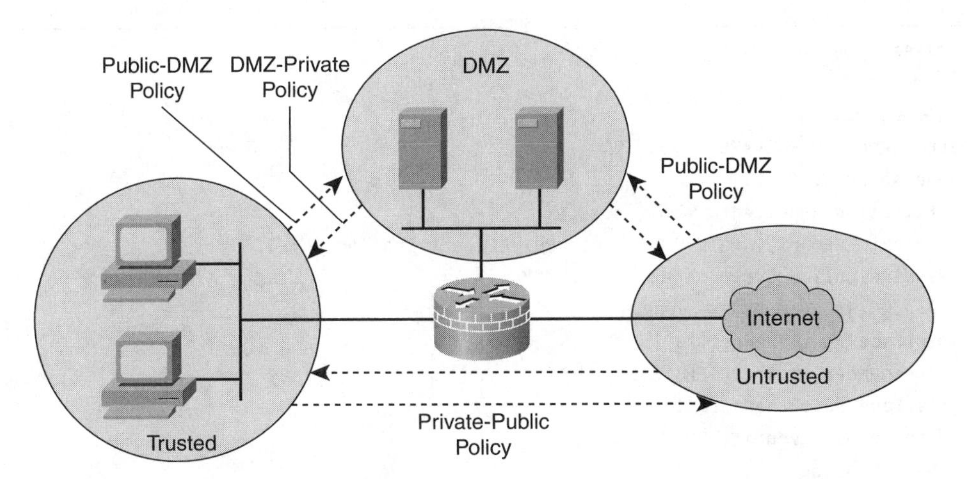

Figure 9-3 *A Pictorial Presentation of Zone-Based Policy Firewall Configuration*

- Per-policy parameter
- Transparent firewall
- Virtual Routing and Forwarding (VRF)-aware firewall

Example 9-10 demonstrates a simple ZPF configuration. First, the inspect class map called MY-CLASS is defined as all TCP-based traffic that also match access list 102 (Telnet, SMTP, FTP, and HTTP). Next, the policy map MY-POLICY defines which action to perform on the traffic matching the class map MY-CLASS. In this example, the action is to inspect the traffic to create dynamic inspection objects. Before applying this policy to the traffic, you need to define security zones. A corresponding zone pair is then created to represent the direction of the traffic to which the policy will be applied. Finally, the zones need to be assigned to the appropriate interfaces. In this example, there are two zones: PRIVATE and PUBLIC. Interface FastEthernet 0/0 is in zone PRIVATE, and interface FastEthernet 0/1 is in the zone PUBLIC. Zone pair PRIV-PUB states that all traffic sourced from zone PRIVATE and destined for zone PUBLIC will be processed according to policy map MY-POLICY.

Example 9-10 *ZPF Configuration Example*

```
! Define inspect class-maps:
class-map type inspect match-any TCP
 match protocol tcp
class-map type inpsect match-all MY-CLASS
 match access-group 102
 match class-map TCP
! Define inspect policy-map:
policy-map type inspect MY-POLICY
```

```
 class type inspect MY-CLASS
  inspect
! Define zones:
zone security PRIVATE
zone security PUBLIC
! Establish zone pair, apply policy:
zone-pair security PRIV-PUB source PRIVATE destination PUBLIC
 service-policy type inspect MY-POLICY
! Assign interfaces to zones:
interface FastEthernet0/0
 zone-member security PRIVATE
interface FastEthernet0/1
 zone-member security PUBLIC
! Define ACLs
access-list 102 permit tcp any any eq telnet
access-list 102 permit tcp any any eq smtp
access-list 102 permit tcp any any eq ftp
access-list 102 permit tcp any any eq www
```

Other Methods of Securing the Data Plane

Unauthorized or unwanted traffic can be blocked by implementing traffic-filtering features such as ACLs and VLAN access maps (on LAN switches) and Cisco IOS firewall and IPS features. The Unicast Reverse Path Forwarding (uRPF) feature can be deployed as an antispoofing mechanism by filtering packets that enter a router or switch through an interface that is not on the best path back to the source IP address of the packet. Routers (and Adaptive Security Appliances) can also protect network traffic using IP Security (IPsec). IPsec encryption and authentication techniques guarantee the integrity and confidentially of traffic that needs to be tunneled across an unsecure network.

Another category of features that can be used to secure the data plane are those that allow controlled access to interfaces on switches and, to a lesser extent, routers. For example, technologies such as 802.1X and Network Admission Control (NAC) can be used to allow network access through a switch port only if certain criteria are met. In case of 802.1X, a device is allowed access to the network only after the user has been successfully authenticated. 802.1X authentication is performed using the RADIUS protocol by a server that references its own local database or an external database. In the case of NAC, the criteria for successful admission to the network can be more sophisticated. For example, a device is allowed access only if it has a specific patch level for its operating system or a minimum version of antivirus software.

Troubleshooting Security Implementations in the Data Plane

It is vital that you know which security features are implemented at which points in the network. Misconfigured security features can cause valid traffic to be dropped. Therefore, security features should always be considered as a possible cause of network connectivity problems. When your troubleshooting process indicates that there is network layer connectivity between two hosts, but upper layers are not working as expected, you should consider whether any form of packet filtering might be implemented between those two hosts.

In addition, when you are observing problems on the management plane or control plane of a network device, always keep in mind that management and control traffic also passes through the data plane and that data plane security features could be the cause of the failure.

The troubleshooting tools for the ZPF are similar to the tools used for classic Cisco IOS firewall:

- When audit trails are enabled, syslog messages are generated for each stateful inspection session.
- Debugging can be used to obtain more detailed information.

Example 9-11 shows a sample of syslog messages generated due to stateful inspection.

Example 9-11 *Syslog Messages for IP Stateful Inspect*

```
May 31 18:02:34.739 UTC: %FW-6-SESS_AUDIT_TRAIL_START: (target:class)-
publicPrivateOut:myClassMap:Start http session: initiator (10.1.1.100:3372)
-- responder (172.16.1.100:80)
May 31 18:02:34.907 UTC: %APPFW-4-HTTP_JAVA_APPLET: HTTP Java Applet
detected - resetting session 172.16.1.100:80 10.1.1.100:3372 on zone-pair
publicPrivateOut class myClassMap appl-class HttpAic
May 31 18:02:34.919 UTC: %FW-6_SESS_AUDIT_TRAIL: (target:class)-
(publicPrivateOut:myClassMap):Stop http session: initiator
(10.1.1.100:3372) sent 297 bytes -- responder (172.16.1.100:80) sent 0 bytes
```

As a demonstration of how useful syslog messages can be, let us assume that a user complains that he is unable to browse to a web server with the IP address 172.16.1.100. An administrator searches the syslog for the string 172.16.1.100, and from the search results shown in Example 9-11, the administrator realizes that a Java applet reset option was configured on the ZPF. The class map is myClassMap, and the appl-class is HttpAic. The administrator corrects this problem by allowing the embedded Java applet to the server in the HTTP AIC policy (HttpAic). Syslog is the most effective troubleshooting tool available for ZPF. It captures alert, audit trail, and **debug** command output.

There are several useful **show** commands for performing ZPF troubleshooting and verification:

- **show zone security:** This command displays information for all the zones configured on the router and the corresponding member interfaces. With this command, you can verify zones configuration and their assignment.
- **show zone-pair security:** This command provides important information about how zones are paired, the zone-pair direction (with respect to the traffic flow), and the policy applied to the zone-pair traffic, as demonstrated in Example 9-12.
- **show policy-map type inspect:** This command shows the relevant information for the policy, what traffic is matched to which class, and what action is applied to each class of traffic. This command also displays the dynamically created session objects.

Example 9-12 show zone-pair security *Command Output*

```
Router# show zone-pair security source PRIVATE destination PUBLIC
Zone-pair name PRIV-PUB
    Source-Zone PRIVATE Destination-Zone Public
    Service-policy MY-POLICY
```

Troubleshooting Branch Office and Remote Worker Connectivity

This section discusses issues related to remote-access connectivity both for branch offices and for remote workers. The focus of the discussion remains on the impact of the overall solution in routing and switching and on the underlying requirements to support branch and remote worker connectivity.

Branch Office and Remote Worker Connectivity

Branch office connectivity involves multiple topics and technologies, including WAN connectivity through VPN and generic routing encapsulation (GRE) tunnels, routing, LAN services, security, and other topics (see Figure 9-4).

VPN connectivity is a major method used for modern branch office and remote-access connectivity. In many cases routing protocols are run over the VPN connection. VPN connectivity is often used as a WAN backup solution. Support services, such as Dynamic Host Configuration Protocol (DHCP), Network Address Translation (NAT), and Hot Standby Router Protocol (HSRP), provide the necessary infrastructure for VPN traffic to be successfully routed end to end. Security is an important part of remote connectivity. Cisco IOS firewalls and other security controls are becoming increasingly popular in branch deployments. That is also true for advanced services such as Cisco Unified Communications and WAN optimization. The end result is a series of functions that are not only integrated in your router devices, but also have a clear impact in, and are affected by, routing.

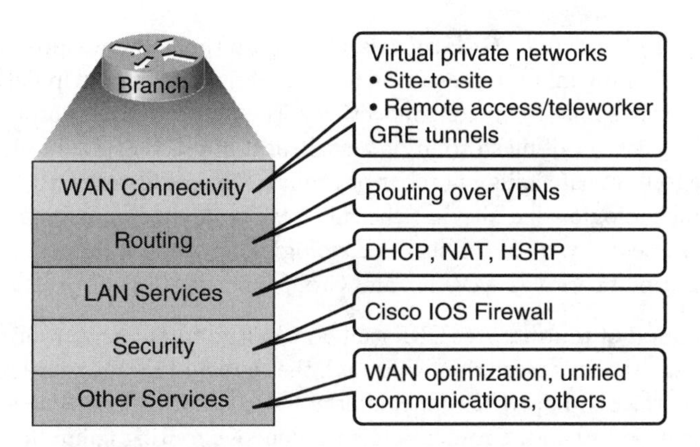

Figure 9-4 *Topics and Technologies Related to Branch Office Remote Connectivity*

Identifying Issues with Branch Office and Remote Worker Connectivity

With respect to VPN connectivity, configuration errors are the typical cause of parameter mismatches on the VPN-termination routers. In the case of GRE tunnels, for example, misconfiguring tunnel source and tunnel destination causes routing issues that prevent the tunnel from forming and becoming active. In many situations, it is not even the VPN that is the cause of the problem. An example is the case of overlapping IP subnets on the opposite sides of the tunnel: NAT is needed to artificially make the subnets nonoverlapping. For remote-access VPNs, given that connections are typically initiated from a remote host, usually a PC or laptop, potential issues relate to host readiness. For example, endpoint security such as antivirus software filters essential traffic and prevents connectivity. User authentication and authorization is also a critical function; if users are not recognized or their permissions are not properly set, they will not be able to connect as teleworkers.

GRE tunnels deserve special consideration because they are typically used to transport routing protocols across IPsec VPNs. A common issue is related to maximum transmission unit (MTU) and fragmentation. Routing protocol packets are first encapsulated in GRE packets. It is those GRE packets that in turn get encapsulated within IPsec tunnel packets. The remote end needs to do two decapsulations when terminating the tunnel. This architecture can cause many performance issues such as extra work at the router level because of double encapsulation, packet sizes, MTU, and fragmentation. Problems related to GRE tunnel establishment are usually due to configurations of tunnel sources and tunnel destinations, along with improper routing of loopbacks. Network readiness is also important because firewalls and traffic filters may block the IPsec traffic that carries the GRE tunnels. Multiple GRE point-to-point tunnels can saturate the physical link with routing information if the bandwidth is not adequately provisioned or configured on the tunnel interface.

The point-to-point nature of GRE tunnels, along with the hub-and-spoke nature of the typical GRE solution, might represent an issue, in terms of round-trip delay for latency-sensitive traffic in spoke-to-spoke connectivity. The point-to-point nature of traditional GRE tunnels makes a full-mesh solution a challenge, in terms of the burden that all routers have to terminate a high number of tunnels. This is the motivation behind introduction of technologies that alleviate the full-mesh requirement, making it dynamic, automatic, and efficient. Examples of such technologies are Virtual Tunnel Interface (VTI), Dynamic Multipoint VPN (DMVPN), and Group-Encrypted Transport VPN (GET VPN).

Misconfiguration of routing over GRE tunnels can lead to recursive routing. When the best path to the tunnel destination is through the tunnel itself, recursive routing causes the tunnel interface to flap. The tunnel interface status depends on IP reachability to the tunnel destination. When the router detects a recursive routing failure for the tunnel destination, it shuts the tunnel interface down for a few minutes so that the situation causing the problem can resolve itself as the routing protocol converges. If the problem is caused by misconfiguration, the link might flap indefinitely. In normal situations, this might occur by just enabling a routing protocol such as Enhanced Interior Gateway Routing Protocol (EIGRP) over the tunnel. In the example shown in Figure 9-5, the GRE tunnel is terminated at the loopback interfaces of the routers at each end. Those loopback interfaces are also injected into EIGRP, and they are advertised across the tunnel to the other side, from R3 to R1 and vice versa. The routing tables will show that the best path to the loopbacks, the source of the tunnel, is the tunnel itself. This causes the inconsistent routing that leads to the recursive routing problem.

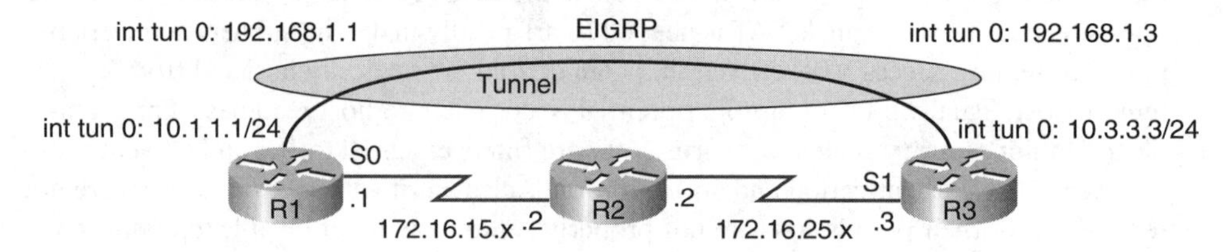

Figure 9-5 *Recursive Routing Caused by Misconfigured Routing over a GRE Tunnel*

A number of other considerations with respect to troubleshooting branch connectivity relate to network readiness, including the following:

- Are there firewalls or access lists blocking the VPN traffic?
- Are there overlapping subnets at the opposite ends of the tunnel?
- Is asymmetric routing causing VPN tunnels to fail?
- Do we have HSRP aligned with VPN high-availability functions? (When an HSRP failover happens, does the new HSRP active router have or set up a VPN connection to the remote site so that the operations can carry on?)

All these issues deal with the routing, addressing, and high-availability infrastructures present in the network. They are necessary for branch connectivity and require additional configuration, and therefore require additional troubleshooting when they fail.

Dealing with the issues such as those mentioned, a structured troubleshooting approach is necessary, in conjunction with knowledge of the building block technologies. For example, gathering information on symptoms and existing configurations requires a multidimensional approach: The IP addressing scheme at the branch office and the central location must be determined, the type of VPN must be recognized, the networks to be advertised by the routing protocol must be known, and the MTU values (per interface and path-long maximum) must be identified. These questions touch many areas and building-block technologies. Similarly, our analysis needs to have an integrated approach, and the same multidimensional, integrated approach is needed when suggesting hypotheses for the problem.

Because branch connectivity touches so many areas, your tool box for troubleshooting its deployments include **show** and **debug** commands in many areas. On the one hand, you need some basic knowledge of IPsec troubleshooting. On the other hand, you need some GRE troubleshooting tools.

Table 9-1 lists a simple set of **show** and **debug** commands that examine and display the status of VPN and GRE tunnels, IP routing table and protocols, and some IP services such as DHCP, NAT, and HSRP.

Table 9-1 *A Small Set of Remote Connectivity Troubleshooting Commands*

Focus	Command
IPsec	**show crypto ipsec sa** **show crypto engine connections active** **show crypto map**
GRE	**show interfaces tunnel** **debug tunnel**
IP routing	**show ip route** **show ip protocols** **debug ip routing**
IP services	**show ip dhcp pool** **show ip dhcp bindings** **show ip nat statistics** **show ip nat translations** **show standby** **show standby brief**

Branch Office/Remote Worker Troubleshooting Example: Address Translation Error

The troubleshooting examples presented in this section are all based on the network topology diagram shown in Figure 9-6, with changes to accommodate for different scenarios. Any changes to addressing or routing will be noted appropriately. The diagram shows a private WAN and an Internet option for branch connectivity. There is also a remote-access service for mobile users and traveling users.

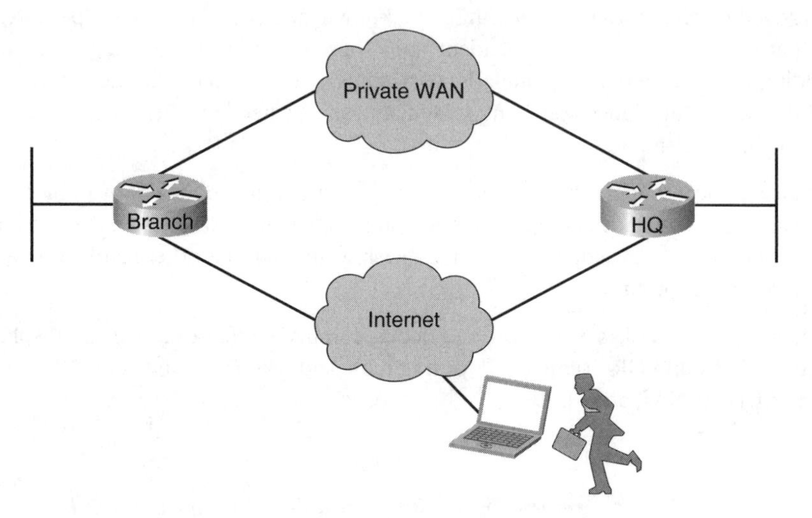

Figure 9-6 *Main Network Diagram for Branch Office Remote Connectivity Troubleshooting*

The first troubleshooting example is a common case. The Branch router is using an IPsec tunnel to provide connectivity to headquarters for its LAN users. This deployment has been working for a while, but a recent change in NAT configuration has caused the tunnel to go down and to not get reestablished, and VPN connectivity to fail. Regular Internet access, however, has been restored, and users are able to connect to websites normally. Figure 9-7 shows the diagram specific to this case.

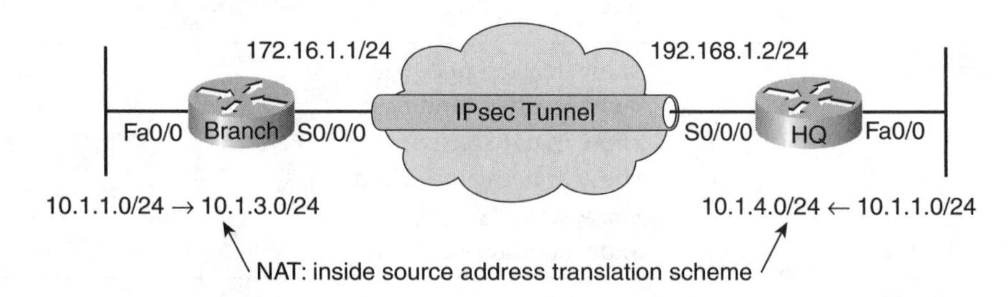

Figure 9-7 *Network Diagram for the First Troubleshooting Example*

The first step in a structured approach is to gather information. A good initial question to ask is how many branches are experiencing the same problem. If all branches are experiencing the same problem, the central hub router is the best candidate to be analyzed first. In this example, the trouble report clearly states that this is the only branch experiencing the problem. Given that NAT was recently changed, you can try a "shoot-from-the-hip" approach. This means that you will use your experience and try to solve the problem quickly by considering alternatives that are apparent: It seems reasonable to look at the NAT changes and start from there. On the Branch router, you use the **show ip nat statistics** command to display NAT information (see Example 9-13).

Example 9-13 **show ip nat statistics** *Command Output on the Branch Router*

```
BRANCH# sh ip nat statistics
Total active translations: 1 (1 static, 0 dynamic, 0 extended)
Outside interfaces:
  Serial0/0/0
Inside interfaces:
  FastEthernet0/0
Hits: 0  Misses: 0
CEF Translated packets: 0, CEF Punted packets: 0
Expired translations: 0
Dynamic mappings:
-- Inside Source
[Id: 1] access-list 150 pool PUBLIC refcount 0
 pool PUBLIC: netmask 255.255.255.0
        start 172.16.1.100 end 172.16.1.200
        type generic, total addresses 101, allocated 0 (0%), misses 0
[Id: 2] access-list VPN pool VPN_NAT refcount 0
        start 10.1.10.10 end 10.1.10.200
        type generic, total addresses 191, allocated 0 (0%), misses 0
Queued Packets: 0
BRANCH#
```

From the output in Example 9-13, you can see that the VPN traffic is exempted from "public" translation because it remains private as it goes through the tunnel. Based on the network topology diagram, there is a culprit, however: The subnets on the opposite sides of the VPN are both using address 10.1.1.0/24 (overlapping)! Because of this overlap, NAT is needed to translate VPN traffic into something other than 10.1.1.0/24 on both sides. According to the output of the valuable **show ip nat statistics** command, traffic matching the VPN access list is being statically translated into an address from the range 10.1.10.10 to 10.1.10.200. This does not seem correct. Based on the information on the diagram (Figure 9-7), traffic leaving the branch toward the headquarters (destination subnet 10.1.4.0/24), should have its source address translate to an address from the 10.1.3.0/24 subnet. The traffic leaving the headquarters network should have its source address translated to an address from the 10.1.4.0/24 subnet.

Note A complex problem with overlapping addresses not discussed here has to do with the destination address. As a device on either end attempts to initiate communication with the other party at the opposite end, it must refer to destination device's translated address, not its real address. This implies that NAT must be static in this situation. While you study this example, assume that these issues (related to destination address) are taken care of.

It seems that the translation done for the VPN traffic at the branch office is incorrect. The branch traffic's source address is being translated to 10.1.10.x rather than 10.1.3.x. At first glance, you might think that does not matter as long as the branch traffic's source address translates into something other than 10.1.1.x. That is not true. The VPN traffic you are translating will eventually go to the WAN interface to be tunneled through the IPsec VPN. The translated address must match the crypto access list; otherwise, it will not go through the VPN tunnel. You can verify this information using the **show crypto map** command as demonstrated in Example 9-14. As mentioned previously, the crypto map contains a crypto ACL that defines the traffic that it will accept to the VPN tunnel.

Example 9-14 **show crypto map** *Command Output at the Branch Router*

```
BRANCH# show crypto map
Crypto Map "map1" 10 ipsec-isakmp
        Peer = 192.168.1.2
        Extended IP access list 106
            access-list 106 permit ip 10.1.3.0 0.0.0.255 10.1.4.0 0.0.0.255
        Current peer: 192.168.1.2
        Security association lifetime: 4608000 kilobytes/3600 seconds
        PFS (Y/N): N
        Transform sets={
                Ts1,
        }
        Interfaces using crypto map map1:
                Serial0/0/0
```

The output of the **show crypto map** shows that the access list used is ACL 106 and it only matches traffic with source address of 10.1.3.x and destination address of 10.1.4.x. Therefore, if the source address of the traffic from the branch translates to anything other than 10.1.3.x, it will not go through the VPN tunnel. You are now sure that the NAT configuration is inconsistent with the crypto map (VPN) configuration, and fixing that might solve our problem. You correct the VPN_NAT pool by removing the old definition and adding the new definition, as shown in Example 9-15. To test that the problem is solved, you ping an address from the 10.1.4.0 pool (headquarters) and notice that now the ping is successful and the issue is indeed taken care of.

Example 9-15 *Correcting the Translation Problem and Testing the Result*

```
BRANCH# conf t
Enter configuration commands, one per line. End with CNTL/Z
BRANCH(config)# no ip nat pool VPN_NAT 10.1.10.10 10.1.10.200 netmask
255.255.255.0
BRANCH(config)#
BRANCH(config)# ip nat pool VPN_NAT 10.1.3.10 10.1.3.200 netmask 255.255.255.0
BRANCH(config)#
BRANCH(config)# end
BRANCH#
BRANCH#
%SYS-5-CONFIG_I: Configured from console by console
BRANCH#

BRANCH# ping 10.1.4.1 source f0/0

Type escape sequence to abort.
Sending 5, 100-byte ICMP Echos to 10.1.4.1, timeout is 2 seconds:
Packet sent with a source address of 10.1.1.1
!!!!!
Success rate is 100 percent (5/5), round-trip min/avg/max - 56/57/60 ms
BRANCH#
```

Branch Office/Remote Worker Troubleshooting Example: Crypto Map ACL Error

The second troubleshooting example is based on the same topology as the first example (shown in Figure 9-8). However, this time there is no subnet overlapping between the branch and headquarters networks. The symptoms of this troubleshooting example are similar to the last one: The VPN connection is down, but the Internet connection is working well. This time, however, there have not been any recent documented configuration changes, and no other information is provided.

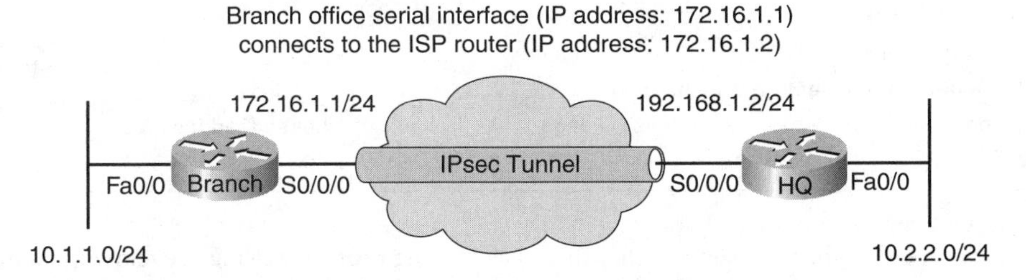

Figure 9-8 *Network Diagram for the Second Troubleshooting Example*

You need to keep in mind that you are troubleshooting end to end and that multiple components and technologies are involved. The culprit could be anything from incorrect

DHCP pools to routing issues and VPN configurations. For this reason, a follow-the-path approach is more appropriate in this case. As you analyze each function along the path, you should be able to discard potential issues and eventually isolate the problem. Taking this approach requires that you understand the order of processing of the various functions within the router.

This Branch router is providing DHCP services to LAN hosts, so you can start there and use a bottom-up approach for each phase or step along the path. First, using the **show ip interfaces brief** command, you check the Layer 1 and Layer 2 status of the Branch router's interfaces. As shown in Example 9-16, both the LAN and WAN interfaces are up.

Example 9-16 *The Status of the Branch Router Interfaces*

```
BRANCH# sh ip int brief
Interface            IP-Address     OK?  Method    Status                   Protocol
FastEthernet0/0      10.1.1.1       YES  manual    up                       up

FastEthernet0/1      unassigned     YES  unset     administratively down    down
Serial0/0/0          172.16.1.1     YES  manual    up                       up
NVIO                 unassigned     NO   unset     up                       up
BRANCH#
```

Now you can check whether hosts are obtaining IP address and related parameters through DHCP. The **show ip dhcp pool** command on the Branch router confirms that the address space 10.1.1.0/24 is being served to hosts through DHCP (see Example 9-17).

Example 9-17 **show ip dhcp pool** *Command Output on the Branch Router*

```
BRANCH# show ip dhcp pool

Pool LAN :
 Utilization mark (high/low)    : 100 / 0
 Subnet size (first/next)       : 0 / 0
 Total addresses                : 254
 Leased addresses               : 6
 Pending event                  : none
 1 subnet is currently in the pool :
Current index        IP address range                    Leased addresses
10.1.1.1             10.1.1.1        - 10.1.1.254        6
```

Now you can check to see whether there is a routing problem. Using the **show ip route** command as demonstrated in Example 9-18, you see what is expected for a small branch office (a static default pointing to a next hop on the WAN interface).

Example 9-18 *Branch Router's Routing Table Shows Static Default Pointing to HQ*

```
BRANCH# show ip route
Codes: C - connected, S - static, R - RIP, M - mobile, B - BGP
       D - EIGRP, EX - EIGRP external, O - OSPF, IA - OSPF inter area
       N1 - OSPF NSSA external tyupe 1, N2 - OSPF NSSA external type 2
       E1 - OSPF external type 1, E2 - OSPF external type 2
       I - IS-IS, SU - IS-IS summary, L1 - IS-IS level-1, L2 - IS-IS level-2
       ia - IS-IS inter area, * - candidate default, U - per-user static route
       o - ODR, P - periodic downloaded static route

Gateway of last resort is 172.16.1.2 to network 0.0.0.0

     172.16.0.0 255.255.255.0 is subnetted, 1 subnets
C       172.16.1.0 is directly connected, Serial0/0/0
     10.0.0.0 255.255.255.0 is subnetted, 3 subnets
C       10.1.1.0 is directly connected, FastEthernet0/0
S*   0.0.0.0 0.0.0.0 [1/0] via 172.16.1.2
BRANCH#
```

Next, you should check NAT. A basic rule of VPN connectivity is that VPN traffic should not use NAT, except for the overlapping network scenario, which is not the case here, as demonstrated in Example 9-19 with the **show ip nat statistics** command. The output reveals that traffic matching ACL 107 will be translated. So, you display ACL 107 to see its content (also shown in Example 9-19). ACL 107 looks correct because it denies traffic going from branch to headquarters, and that means the traffic going from branch to headquarters will not be subjected to NAT.

Example 9-19 *Checking NAT Stat on the Branch Router*

```
BRANCH# show ip nat statistics
Total active translations: 1 (1 static, 0 dynamic, 0 extended)
Outside interfaces:
  Serial0/0/0
Inside interfaces:
  FastEthernet0/0
Hits: 60  Misses: 0
CEF Translated packets: 10, CEF Punted packets: 30
Expired translations: 7
Dynamic mappings:
-- Inside Source
[Id: 3] access-list 107 pool PUBLIC refcount 0
 pool PUBLIC: netmask 255.255.255.0
        start 172.16.1.100 end 172.16.1.200
        type generic, total addresses 101, allocated 0 (0%), misses 0
Queued Packets: 0
```

```
BRANCH#

BRANCH# show access-list 107
Extended IP access list 107
    10 deny ip 10.1.1.0 0.0.0.255 10.2.2.0 0.0.0.255
    20 permit ip 10.1.1.0 0.0.0.255 any
BRANCH#
```

Next, check the VPN configuration using the **show crypto map** on the Branch router as demonstrated in Example 9-20. ACL 106 used in the crypto map states that only the traffic with source address 10.1.3.x and destination address 10.2.2.y will go through the VPN tunnel. That is incorrect, however, because the traffic from the branch going to the headquarters (which is not subject to NAT) will have source address of 10.1.1.x, which is furnished by the DHCP server.

Example 9-20 *The Crypto Map on the Branch Router Shows an Incorrect Crypto ACL*

```
BRANCH# show crypto map
Crypto Map "map1" 10 ipsec-isakmp
        Peer = 192.168.1.2
        Extended IP access list 106
            access-list 106 permit ip 10.1.3.0 0.0.0.255 10.2.2.0 0.0.0.255
        Current peer: 192.168.1.2
        Security association lifetime: 4608000 kilobytes/3600 seconds
        PFS (Y/N): N
        Transform sets={
                ts1,
        }
        Interfaces using crypto map map1:
                Serial0/0/0

BRANCH#
```

It seems that you have found the problem cause: The source IP addresses of the packets from the branch office are not matching the crypto ACL. You can test this hypothesis just by changing the crypto ACL 106 and using the **ping** command to verify connectivity, as demonstrated in Example 9-21. The ping from branch to the headquarters is successful, and the problem is fixed.

Example 9-21 *Correcting the Crypto ACL Number 106 and Using Ping to Verify*

```
BRANCH# conf t
Enter configuration commands, one per line. End with CNTL/Z
BRANCH(config)# no access-list 106
```

```
BRANCH(config)#
BRANCH(config)# access-list 106 permit ip 10.1.1.0 0.0.0.255 10.2.2.0 0.0.0.255
BRANCH(config)#
BRANCH(config)# end
BRANCH#
%SYS-5-CONFIG_I: Configured from console by console
BRANCH#

BRANCH# ping 10.2.2.1 source f0/0

Type escape sequence to abort.
Sending 5, 100-byte ICMP Echos to 10.2.2.1, timeout is 2 seconds:
Packet sent with a source address of 10.1.1.1
!!!!!
Success rate is 100 percent (5/5), round-trip min/avg/max - 88/89/92 ms
BRANCH#
```

Branch Office/Remote Worker Troubleshooting Example: GRE Configuration Error

The third troubleshooting example is based on the network topology shown in Figure 9-9. In this example, you are routing EIGRP across an IPsec VPN tunnel, using GRE. The GRE tunnel is sourced at the loopback interfaces on each router: 10.100.100.1 on the Branch router, and 10.200.200.2 on the Headquarters router. EIGRP is used to advertise internal networks, the networks on the 10.0.0.0 address space, for branch-to-headquarters connectivity. This time the problem is that traffic is not reaching the headquarters network, which hosts multiple mission-critical servers. At this point, the support team does not have many details, just that connectivity is lost. In dealing with this type of issue, it is best to apply a structured, follow-the-path approach.

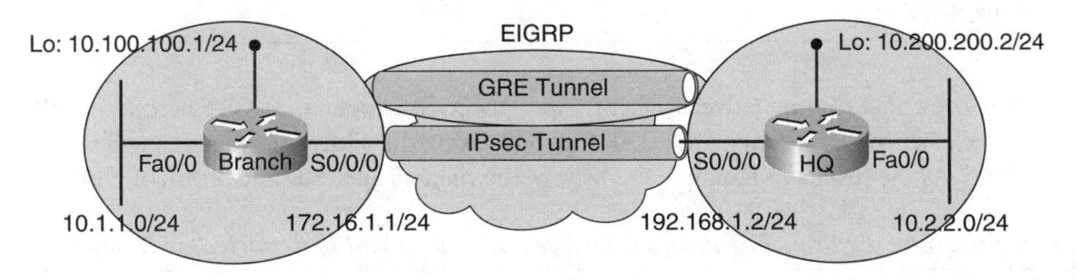

Figure 9-9 *Network Diagram for the Third Troubleshooting Example*

Starting with the Headquarters router, check for the status of the VPN tunnel and look for the IP address of the Branch router as a destination using the **show crypto isakmp sa** command, as demonstrated in Example 9-22. The status of the tunnel to branch at 172.16.1.1 is ACTIVE. The same command at the Branch router shows an ACTIVE status, too.

Example 9-22 *The Security Association to the Branch Router Is Shown as ACTIVE*

```
HQ# sh crypto isakmp sa
IPv4 Crypto ISAKMP SA
dst             src             state          conn-id  slot  status
172.16.1.1      192.168.1.2     QM_IDLE           1002     0  ACTIVE

IPv6 Crypto ISAKMP SA

HQ#

BRANCH# sh crypto isakmp sa
IPv4 Crypto ISAKMP SA
dst             src             state          conn-id  slot  status
192.168.1.2     172.16.1.1      QM_IDLE           1001     0  ACTIVE

IPv6 Crypto ISAKMP SA

BRANCH#
```

Because the VPN tunnel is reported as active from both ends, the next cause you can think of, going bottom up, is a routing issue. The next step is to determine whether the headquarters destinations can be found in the Branch router's routing table. Use the **show ip route** command and search for network 10.2.2.0/24. As the results in Example 9-23 show, this subnet is not in there.

Example 9-23 *Headquarters 10.2.2.0 Is Not Found in Branch Router's Routing Table*

```
BRANCH# sh ip route 10.2.2.0
% Subnet not in table
BRANCH#
BRANCH#
```

You know that routing (advertisement) is supposed to happen over GRE across the VPN tunnel. Hence, you examine the GRE (tunnel0) using the **show interfaces tunnel 0** command. As the results in Example 9-24 show, the tunnel is up, but line protocol is down.

Example 9-24 *At Branch, Tunnel0 Interface's Line Protocol Is Reported as Down*

```
BRANCH# show interfaces tunnel 0
Tunnel0 is up, line protocol is down
  Hardware is Tunnel
  Internet address is 10.1.3.2 255.255.255.0
  MTU 1514 bytes, BW 9 Kbit, DLY 500000 usec,
     Reliability 255/255, txload 1/255, rxload 1/255
```

```
  Encapsulation TUNNEL, loopback not set
  Keepalive not set
  Tunnel source 10.100.100.1 (Loopback101), destination 10.200.200.22
  Tunnel protocol/transport GRE/IP
    Key disabled, sequencing disabled
    Checksumming of packets disabled
  Tunnel TTL 255
  Fast tunneling enabled
  Tunnel transmit bandwidth 8000 (kbps)
  Tunnel receive bandwidth 8000 (kbps)
  Last input 00:19:31, output 00:18:58, output hang never
  Last clearing of "show interface" counters never
  Input queue: 0/75/0/0 (size/max/drops/flushes); Total output drops: 0
  Queueing strategy: fifo
  Output queue: 0/0 (size/max)
  5 minute input rate 0 bits/sec, 0 packets/sec
  5 minute output rate 0 bits/sec, 0 packets/sec
     56 packets input, 5662 bytes, 0 no buffer
     Received 0 broadcasts, 0 runts, 0 giants, 0 throttles
     0 input errors, 0 CRC, 0 frame, 0 overrun, 0 ignored, 0 abort
     120 packets output, 17158 bytes, 0 underruns
     0 output errors, 0 collisions, 0 interface resets
     0 output buffer failures, 0 output buffers swapped out
BRANCH#
```

The **show interfaces tunnel 0** command shows the traditional interface parameters, plus tunnel interface parameters. As shown in Example 9-24, the tunnel source at BRANCH is 10.100.100.1 (loopback101), and the tunnel destination is 10.200.200.22. You must check the Headquarters router and see whether address 10.200.200.22 is a valid destination for this tunnel. First, try the **show interfaces tunnel 0** command on the HQ router. As shown in Example 9-25, the tunnel source at HQ is loopback101 with the IP address 10.200.200.2, not 10.200.200.22. It looks like a typing error has happened at the Branch router, but notice that the tunnel interface at HQ is administratively down and that needs to be fixed, too.

Example 9-25 *Checking the Status of the GRE (Tunnel) Interface at the HQ Router*

```
HQ# show interfaces tunnel 0
Tunnel0 is administratively down, line protocol is down
  Hardware is Tunnel
  Internet address is 10.1.3.1 255.255.255.0
  MTU 1514 bytes, BW 9 Kbit, DLY 500000 usec,
    Reliability 255/255, txload 1/255, rxload 1/255
  Encapsulation TUNNEL, loopback not set
```

```
  Keepalive not set
  Tunnel source 10.200.200.2 (Loopback101), destination 10.100.100.1
  Tunnel protocol/transport GRE/IP
    Key disabled, sequencing disabled
    Checksumming of packets disabled
  Tunnel TTL 255
  Fast tunneling enabled
  Tunnel transmit bandwidth 8000 (kbps)
  Tunnel receive bandwidth 8000 (kbps)
  Last input 00:21:56, output 00:21:58, output hang never
  Last clearing of "show interface" counters never
  Input queue: 0/75/0/0 (size/max/drops/flushes); Total output drops: 17
  Queueing strategy: fifo
  Output queue: 0/0 (size/max)
  5 minute input rate 0 bits/sec, 0 packets/sec
  5 minute output rate 0 bits/sec, 0 packets/sec
     49 packets input, 7090 bytes, 0 no buffer
--More--
```

You return to the Branch router to fix the tunnel destination address error. You first enter the **debug ip routing** command to see the EIGRP routes popping up in the routing table as a result of repairing the tunnel. Next, you go into the interface configuration mode for the tunnel0 interface, remove the incorrect tunnel destination address, and enter the correct tunnel destination address (10.200.200.2). This work is shown in Example 9-26.

Example 9-26 *Tunnel Destination Address Error Is Corrected at the Branch Router*

```
BRANCH#
BRANCH# debug ip routing
IP routing debugging is on
BRANCH#

BRANCH# conf t
Enter configuration commands, one per line. End with CNTL/Z
BRANCH(config)# int tunnel0
BRANCH(config-if)# no tunnel destination 10.200.200.22
BRANCH(config-if)# tunnel destination 10.200.200.2
BRANCH(config-if)# end
BRANCH#
```

In just a few seconds, you can see the EIGRP neighbor session going up, and almost immediately you see the routing table being populated across the tunnel. To confirm end-to-end connectivity, you then try an extended ping from the Branch router using its

Fa 0/0 interface as the source, to the address 10.2.2.1, which resides at the headquarters. Example 9-27 shows the results, which are 100 percent successful. The problem is solved.

Example 9-27 debug *Output Shows the Tunnel Going Up, and the Ping Succeeds, Too*

```
BRANCH#
%SYS-5-CONFIG_I: Configured console by console
%DUAL-5-NBRCHANGE: IP-EIGRP(0) 1: Neighbor 10.1.3.1 (Tunnel0) is up: new adjacency
BRANCH#
%LINK-3-UPDOWN: Interface Tunnel0, changed state to up
%LINEPROTO-5-UPDOWN: Line protocol on Interface Tunnel0, changed state to up
BRANCH#

BRANCH# ping 10.2.2.1 source f0/0

Type escape sequence to abort.
Sending 5 100-byte ICMP Echos to 10.2.2.1, timeout is 2 seconds:
Packet sent with a source address of 10.1.1.1
!!!!!
Success rate is 100 percent (5/5), round-trip min/avg/max = 88/91/92 ms
BRANCH#
```

Branch Office/Remote Worker Troubleshooting Example: Recursive Routing Problem

The fourth troubleshooting example is based on the network topology shown in Figure 9-10. In this example, we are told that the IPsec tunnel was established and tested, and it was carrying user traffic with no problem. Then suddenly tunnel interface went down and EIGRP was no longer able to advertise routes. Level 1 operators claim that they have tried resetting the interfaces, but that did not help. Tunnels get established, only to go down after a few seconds every time.

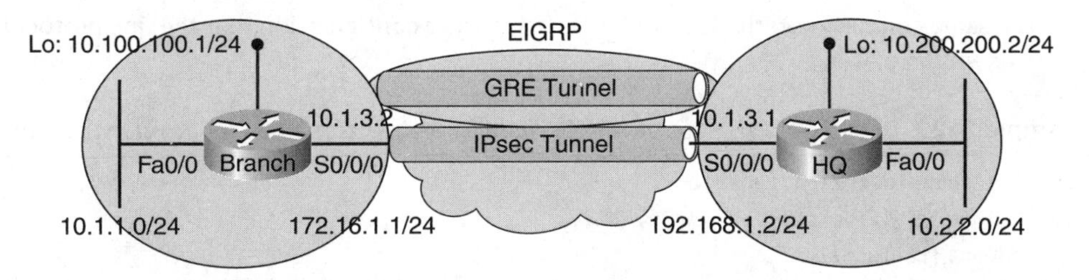

Figure 9-10 *Network Diagram for the Fourth Troubleshooting Example*

You will gather some more information before deciding the course of action for resolving this problem. You are using GRE to carry EIGRP advertisements across the VPN. So, you will first verify the EIGRP configuration and learn the autonomous system number and the networks that belong to this routing process. The **show ip protocols** command provides all that information. The output is shown in Example 9-28, and it looks correct.

Example 9-28 show ip protocols *Command Output on Branch Router Looks Correct*

```
BRANCH# show ip protocols
Routing Protocol is "eigrp 1"
  Outgoing update filter list for all interfaces is not set
  Incoming update filter list for all interfaces is not set
  Default networks flagged in outgoing updates
  Default networks accepted from incoming updates
  EIGRP metric weight K1 =1, K2 = 0, K3 = 1, K4 = 0, K5 = 0
  EIGRP maximum hopcount 100
  EIGRP maximum metric variance 1
  Redistributing: eigrp 1
  EIGRP NSF-aware route hold timer is 240s
  Automatic network summarization is not in effect
  Maximum path: 4
  Routing for Networks:
    10.0.0.0
  Routing Information Sources:
    Gateway         Distance      Last Update
    (this router)         90      00:38:11
  Distance: internal 90 external 170

BRANCH#
```

It is now a good idea to check the status of the GRE tunnel interface using the **show interfaces tunnel** command, as demonstrated in Example 9-29. The results show that interface tunnel0's line protocol is down; however, the source and destination of the tunnel, based on the network diagram, are correct. No tunnel configuration error is apparent. The same command on the HQ router shows correct configuration, but the line protocol is down there, too.

Example 9-29 *The Line Protocol of the Tunnel0 Interface at the Branch Router Is Down*

```
BRANCH# show interface tunnel0
Tunnel0 is up, line protocol is down
  Hardware is Tunnel
  Internet address is 10.1.3.2 255.255.255.0
  MTU 1514 bytes, BW 9 Kbit, DLY 500000 usec,
    Reliability 255/255, txload 1/255, rxload 1/255
  Encapsulation TUNNEL, loopback not set
  Keepalive not set
```

```
 Tunnel source 10.100.100.1 (Loopback101), destination 10.200.200.2
 Tunnel protocol/transport GRE/IP
   Key disabled, sequencing disabled
   Checksumming of packets disabled
 Tunnel TTL 255
 Fast tunneling enabled
 Tunnel transmit bandwidth 8000 (kbps)
 Tunnel receive bandwidth 8000 (kbps)
 Last input 00:07:30, output 00:07:31, output hang never
 Last clearing of "show interface" counters never
 Input queue: 0/75/0/0 (size/max/drops/flushes); Total output drops: 5
 Queueing strategy: fifo
 Output queue: 0/0 (size/max)
 5 minute input rate 0 bits/sec, 0 packets/sec
 5 minute output rate 0 bits/sec, 0 packets/sec
    169 packets input, 15866 bytes, 0 no buffer
--More--
```

In a scenario such as this, it is sometimes beneficial to replicate the symptoms and the problem itself. If dynamic components are causing the interface to go down, a good way to see those dynamic components is by replicating the whole scenario. This can be somewhat challenging in some cases, but it is simple in this example: You just shut down the interfaces and bring them back up. That should initiate the establishment of the tunnel. On HQ, you go into the tunnel0 interface configuration mode and use the **shutdown** and the **no shutdown** commands in sequence. You see some informational message; a new adjacency with neighbor 10.1.3.2 (BRANCH) across tunnel0 is reported. Unfortunately, however, after a few seconds you see a message: "Tunnel0 temporarily disabled due to recursive routing." After that, the line protocol on interface tunnel0 changes state to down, and so does the neighbor 10.1.3.2 as the results in Example 9-30 indicate. Recursive routing over a tunnel happens when the best path to the tunnel destination turns out to be through the tunnel itself. That causes the tunnel interface to flap. Therefore, this is a routing problem. It is important to look up and research messages like this one; it helps you to focus on and isolate the problem.

Example 9-30 *Resetting the Tunnel Interface Allows You to See a Useful Log Message*

```
HQ# conf t
Enter configuration commands, one per line. End with CNTL/Z.
HQ(config)# int tunnel0
HQ(config-if)# shutdown
HQ(config-if)# no shutdown
HQ(config-if)# end
HQ#
%SYS-5-CONFIG_I: Configured from console by console
```

```
HQ#
%DUAL-5-NBRCHANGE: IP-EIGRP(0) 1: Neighbor 10.1.3.2 (Tunnel0) is up: new
adjacency
HQ#
%TUN-5-RECURDOWN: Tunnel0 temporarily disabled due to recursive routing
%LINEPROTO-5-UPDOWN: Line protocol on Interface Tunnel0, changed state to down
%DUAL-5-NBRCHANGE: IP-EIGRP(0) 1: Neighbor 10.1.3.2 (Tunnel0) is down: interface
  down
HQ#
```

One way to fix this issue is to make sure that there is always a path to the tunnel destination and that path is better than the one through the tunnel itself. A static route is a solid way to do this. The default administrative distance of a static route is better than all dynamic routing protocols. On HQ, shut down the tunnel interface, and then enter the static route command **ip route 10.100.100.1 255.255.255.255 172.16.1.1**, as demonstrated in Example 9-31. You then enter a similar command on the Branch router mirroring the one entered at the HQ router, and enable the tunnel interfaces (no shut) at both ends (see Example 9-31). Note that the next hop for the static route entered at the BRANCH router must be 192.168.1.2. Furthermore, you must keep in mind that the BRANCH address 172,16.1.1 (assumed to be a public address in this example) is considered to be the address the ISP has assigned to the BRANCH router, and that the HQ address 192.168.1.2 (assumed to be a public address in this example) is considered to be the address that HQ's ISP has assigned to the HQ router. The tunnel interface goes up and neighbor adjacency is established, but you have seen this before. So, you need to wait to see whether they go back down again.

Example 9-31 *Entering a Static Route to a Tunnel Destination Using a Nontunnel Path*

```
HQ# configure terminal
Enter configuration commands, one per line. End with CNTL/Z.
HQ(config)# interface tunnel0
HQ(config-if)# shutdown
HQ(config-if)#exit
HQ(config)# ip route 10.100.100.1 255.255.255.255 172.16.1.1
HQ(config)# end
HQ#
%SYS-5-CONFIG_I: Configured from console by console
HQ#
HQ# configure terminal
Enter configuration commands, one per line. End with CNTL/Z.
HQ(config)# interface tunnel0
HQ(config-if)# no shutdown
HQ(config-if)# end
HQ#
```

```
%SYS-5-CONFIG_I: Configured from console by console
HQ#
%LINK-3-UPDOWN: Interface Tunnel0, changed state to up
%LINEPROTO-5-UPDOWN: Line protocol on Interface Tunnel0, changed state to up
HQ#
%DUAL-5-NBRCHANGE: IP-EIGRP(0) 1: Neighbor 10.1.3.2 (Tunnel0) is up: new
  Adjacency

HQ#
```

Meanwhile, look at HQ's routing table using the **show ip route** command. As shown in Example 9-32, the routing table includes three paths to the tunnel0 destination (10.100.100.1):

- The first one is using the gateway of last resort (0.0.0.0/0) through 192.168.1.1 (the ISP's IP address at HQ, not shown in Figure 9-10).
- The second one is using the EIGRP route 10.100.100.0/24 through the tunnel0 interface.
- The third one is using the static route we entered to 10.100.100.1/32 through 172.16.1.1.

Obviously, the EIGRP recursive route is back (the second path), but among the three options, the static route is the most specific one (with a 32-bit match), and that is the one that will be used to reach the tunnel end, not the other two. This explains why the tunnel is now staying up. The problem, which was caused by recursive routing, is solved. However, note that this problem could also be fixed by using a filter stopping EIGRP to advertise the tunnel end address through the tunnel interface.

Example 9-32 *HQ's Routing Table Shows a Converged and Stable Set of IP Paths*

```
HQ# show ip route
Codes: C - connected, S - static, R - RIP, M - mobile, B - BGP
       D - EIGRP, EX - EIGRP external, O - OSPF, IA - OSPF inter area
       N1 - OSPF NSSA external tyupe 1, N2 - OSPF NSSA external type 2
       E1 - OSPF external type 1, E2 - OSPF external type 2
       I - IS-IS, SU - IS-IS summary, L1 - IS-IS level-1, L2 - IS-IS level-2
       ia - IS-IS inter area, * - candidate default, U - per-user static route
       o - ODR, P - periodic downloaded static route

Gateway of last resort is 192.168.1.1 to network 0.0.0.0

     10.0.0.0 255.0.0.0 is variably subnetted, 8 subnets, 2 masks
C       10.1.3.0 255.255.255.0 is directly connected, Tunnel0
C       10.200.200.0 255.255.255.0 is directly connected, Loopback101
```

```
D        10.100.100.0 255.255.255.0
            [90/297372416] via 10.1.3.2, 00:00:07, Tunnel0
C        10.2.2.0 255.255.255.0 is directly connected, FastEthernet0/0
D        10.1.1.0 255.255.255.0 [90/297372416] via 10.1.3.2, 00:00:07, Tunnel0
S        10.100.100.1 255.255.255.255 [1/0] via 172.16.1.1

C      192.168.1.0 255.255.255.0 is directly connected, serial0/0/0
S*    0.0.0.0 0.0.0.0 [1/0] via 192.168.1.1

HQ#
```

Branch Office/Remote Worker Troubleshooting Example: ACL Denies IPsec Protocols

The fifth and last troubleshooting example is based on the network diagram shown in Figure 9-11. A security auditor recently performed a security assessment and recommended a few improvements to the network policy. After the change, IPsec tunnels do not work and never get established. VPN connectivity is critical for branch services. In taking all the necessary precautions, all configurations have been reverted to their pre-audit state, except for the Branch router.

Figure 9-11 *Network Diagram for the Fifth Troubleshooting Example*

Investigating the recent change in security policy, you find that the Cisco IOS firewall services were installed in some important routers of the network. Therefore, instead of taking a bottom-up or top-down approach, you will start at the firewall level. The reported symptom, an IPsec VPN tunnel failing to establish a security association, provides another hint as to what to look for: IPsec traffic might be denied by the firewall. It seems like you have reached a valid hypothesis, but you must verify its validity and correct the problem.

While gathering information about the Cisco IOS firewall, you must remember that Cisco IOS allows you to configure the firewall using one of two methods:

- The classic Cisco IOS firewall, which applies ACLs on interfaces
- The ZPF, which is more widely used and is more flexible for a comprehensive deployment

By trying the **show zone-pair security** command on the Branch router, you notice that ZPF is not configured on this router. Therefore, you must check to see whether a classic firewall is configured in this router. Entering the **show ip interfaces** command displays if ACLs are applied to any interface. As the results in Example 9-33 show, an ACL called FIREWALL-INBOUND is applied to the s0/0/0 interface in the inbound direction. This interface is the one that terminates the IPsec tunnel. Next, you display the ACL.

Example 9-33 *An ACL Is Applied to s0/0/0 in the Inbound Direction*

```
BRANCH# show ip interface s0/0/0
Serial0/0/0 is up, line protocol is up
  Internet address is 172.16.1.1 255.255.255.0
  Broadcast address is 255.255.255.255
  Address determined by setup command
  MTU is 1500 bytes
  Helper address is not set
  Directed broadcast forwarding is disabled
  Outgoing access list is not set
  Inbound access list is FIREWALL-INBOUND
  Proxy ARP is enabled
  Local Proxy ARP is disabled
  Security level is default
  Split horizon is enabled
  ICMP redirects are always sent
  ICMP unreachables are always sent
  ICMP mask replies are never sent
  IP fast switching is enabled
  IP fast switching on the same interface is enabled
  IP Flow switching is disabled
  IP CEF switching is enabled
  IP CEF Feature Fast Switching turbo vector
  IP multicast fast switching is enabled
  IP multicast distributed fast switching is disabled
--More--

BRANCH# show access-list FIREWALL-INBOUND
Extended IP access list FIREWALL-INBOUND
    10 permit tcp any 192.168.250.16 0.0.0.15 established
    20 permit tcp any host 192.168.250.16 eq www
    30 permit tcp any any eq 22
    40 permit tcp any any eq telnet
    50 permit tcp any host 192.168.250.16 eq ftp
    60 permit icmp any any
    70 permit eigrp any any (120 matches)
BRANCH#
```

The access list FIREWALL-INBOUND that is applied to Branch router's serial interface is allowing routing protocols and management protocols such as SSH. If you think in the context of IPsec, the access list is missing the statements that permit IPsec protocols and ISAKMP. IPsec requires ESP/AH (protocols 50/51) and ISAKMP (UDP Port 500) to be allowed by access lists. However, the access list FIREWALL-INBOUND is not permitting (therefore, it is blocking) those ports. This proves how important it is for security policy designers to be fully aware of the services and applications running on the network.

You might have found the problem cause, but you must verify it by changing the ACL. Following best practices, add the required lines to the ACL, and also add a remark indicating why you are making this change using the **access-list remark** command. You must add three lines to allow the required protocols: ESP, AHP, and ISAKMP. Example 9-34 demonstrates these modifications.

Example 9-34 *Modifying the FIREWALL-INBOUND ACL to Permit IPsec Protocols*

```
BRANCH# configure terminal
Enter configuration commands, one per line. End with CNTL/Z
BRANCH(config)# ip access-list extended FIREWALL-INBOUND
BRANCH(config-ext-nacl)# remark --additions for IPSEC ---
BRANCH(config-ext-nacl)# permit udp any any eq 500
BRANCH(config-ext-nacl)# permit esp any any
BRANCH(config-ext-nacl)# permit ahp any any
BRANCH(config-ext-nacl)# end
BRANCH#
```

After modifying the access list, you can successfully ping the HQ router (loopback interface), which is learned through the tunnel, from the Branch router. The problem is solved.

You altered the security policy by changing the firewall rules, so you must carefully test the accuracy of the change and the potential implications it might have. A simple **show access-lists** displays the number of packets matching each ACL line, and this is a simple way to make sure that changes did not affect the rest of the network. You can closely monitor the ACL matches under different traffic loads and profiles, to determine the implications of our recent change. This example was short, but it reinforces the importance of network readiness toward branch connectivity. The problem was simple: IPsec protocols/ports were not permitted by the ACL (the firewall was not allowing them).

Summary

In a secured environment, a reported connectivity problem does not automatically translate to a valid problem that needs to be resolved. First, you need to determine whether the reported lack of connectivity actually concerns authorized traffic according to the security policy of your organization. It is vital that you know which security features have been implemented at each point in your network, because that will help you to quickly assess whether a misconfigured security feature may be a potential cause of the problem.

In addition to using specialized security devices, such as firewalls, IPSs, and VPN concentrators, network devices such as routers and switches and the protocols that are used between these devices should be secured. If the network infrastructure itself is compromised, the entire system can be compromised. In smaller networks, the router may have a dual role, functioning as both a router and as a security device by providing firewall, IPS, or VPN services.

The three main functional planes are as follows:

- **Management plane:** The management plane represents all the functions and protocols involved in managing and configuring the device. Securing this plane is vital to the overall security of the device. If the management plane is compromised, the other planes are also exposed.
- **Control plane:** The control plane represents all the functions and protocols that are used between network devices to control the operation of the network, such as routing protocols, the STP, or other signaling and control protocols. Because the control plane affects the behavior of the data plane, the control plane protocols need to be secured.
- **Data Plane:** The data plane represents all the functions involved in forwarding traffic through the device. Routers and switches can inspect and filter traffic as part of the implementation of a security policy. It is important to note that all management and control plane traffic flow through the data plane, too. Consequently, security features on the data plane can be used to secure the management and control planes too.

The management functions of a router or switch are commonly accessed using three different methods: the Cisco IOS CLI, web-based device management, or a network management platform that is based on SNMP. All these methods must be used in the most secure way, based on the device type, its operating system (IOS) capabilities, and the security policies of the organization.

There are two common techniques to secure management access to network devices. First, access to the management plane can be restricted using packet or session filters: Access is allowed only from specific source IP addresses. Second, it is necessary to authenticate the user who is attempting to access the device. This can be done using simple password authentication, local username and password authentication, or using a centralized authentication server. The **debug aaa authentication** command is useful for troubleshooting AAA authentication problems. Authorization determines what resources the user has access to. AAA authorization can also happen locally or centrally using a AAA server such as Cisco Secure Access Control Server. The **debug aaa authorization** command can be useful for troubleshooting AAA authorization problems. With AAA accounting, the network access server reports user activity to a security server (RADIUS or TACACS+) in the form of accounting records. This data can then be analyzed for network management, client billing, or for auditing purposes. The **debug aaa accounting** command can be useful to troubleshoot AAA accounting problems. The most common problem occurring when centralized security servers are used is the server going down or becoming unreachable.

When troubleshooting control plane issues, you must first discover what protocols and features are enabled on the network devices. Next, for those protocols and features, you must consider possible configuration errors. Misconfiguration of any of the following can lead to control plane failures:

- Routing protocol or FHRP authentication
- STP options such as BPDU Guard, BPDU Filter, Root Guard, and Loop Guard
- DHCP snooping
- DAI
- Control plane policing and control plane protection

The Cisco IOS firewall software provides enhanced security functions for the data plane. There are two types of Cisco IOS firewall:

- Classic Cisco IOS firewall
- ZPF

The **show ip inspect** commands, audit trails to generate syslog messages (using **ip inspect audit-trail** command), and **debug ip inspect** commands are useful tools for troubleshooting IP firewall (CBAC) configurations. The troubleshooting tools for the ZPF are similar to the tools used to troubleshoot the classic Cisco IOS firewall. There are several useful **show** commands for performing ZPF troubleshooting and verification, including **show zone security**, **show zone-pair security**, **show policy-map type inspect**.

Data plane security is accomplished using a variety of router and switch options such as uRPF, IPsec, NAC, 802.1X port authentication, and so on.

The main considerations with respect to troubleshooting branch connectivity relate to network readiness and include the following:

- Are firewalls or ACLs blocking crucial VPN traffic?
- Are there overlapping subnets at the opposite ends of the tunnel?
- Is asymmetric routing causing VPN tunnels to fail?
- Do we have HSRP aligned with VPN high-availability functions?

Review Questions

Use the questions here to review what you learned in this chapter. The correct answers are found in Appendix A, "Answers to Chapter Review Questions."

1. Which three of the following security services can be provided by routers and switches?
   a. IPS
   b. TACACS+ services

c. VPN
d. Packet filtering and firewall functionality
e. Antivirus updates
f. Spam filtering

2. Which two of the following security mechanisms can be used to protect the management plane of a router or switch?
   a. Unicast Reverse Path Forwarding (uRPF)
   b. Bridge Protocol Data Unit (BPDU) Guard
   c. Authentication, authorization, and accounting (AAA)
   d. Generic packet filtering

3. Which two of the following security mechanisms can be used to protect the control plane of a router or switch?
   a. Root Guard
   b. Routing protocol authentication
   c. Secure Shell (SSH)
   d. Network Admission Control (NAC)

4. Which three of the following security mechanisms can be used to protect the data plane of a router or switch?
   a. Root Guard
   b. Routing protocol authentication
   c. Unicast Reverse Path Forwarding (uRPF)
   d. Secure Shell (SSH)
   e. Virtual private networks (VPN)
   f. Intrusion prevention system (IPS)

5. Which statement best describes Cisco IOS stateful inspection?
   a. Allow certain incoming flows by first inspecting and recording flows initiated from the trusted network
   b. Can inspect only Layer 4 information of the session
   c. Statically define all entries in the access list of the outside interface to allow bidirectional communication between the trusted and untrusted networks

6. Which command enables you to apply an inbound inspection rule named WEB on the interface?

   a. router# **ip inspect WEB in**

   b. router (config)# **ip inspect WEB in**

   c. router(config)# **inspect WEB in**

   d. router (config-if)# **ip inspect WEB in**

   e. router(config-if)# **inspect WEB in**

7. Which two commands display configuration and session information for the stateful inspection feature?

   a. **show ip inspect all**

   b. **show ip access-list**

   c. **show running-config**

   d. **show ip inspec**

   e. **show inspec all**

8. Which three of the following are components of AAA?

   a. Authentication

   b. Administration

   c. Authorization

   d. Accounting

   e. Activation

9. What does the term *authorization* mean?

   a. Determining which resources the user can access on the network

   b. Providing accounting records for billing purposes

   c. Providing a username and password prompt when somebody uses Telnet to connect to the router

   d. Authorizing network equipment to communicate with the security server

10. What is the purpose of the RADIUS and TACACS+ protocols?

    a. Provide comprehensive tools for network device monitoring.

    b. Transport user-related information between two routers.

    c. Transport user-related information between network device and centralized security server.

    d. They are obsolete and not in use.

11. What are three differences between RADIUS and TACACS+?

a. RADIUS uses TCP, and TACACS+ uses UDP.

b. RADIUS uses UDP, and TACACS+ uses TCP.

c. RADIUS offers limited accounting, and TACACS+ provides extensive accounting.

d. TACACS+ offers limited accounting, and RADIUS provides extensive accounting.

e. RADIUS encrypts the whole packet while TACACS+ encrypts only the password.

f. TACACS+ encrypts the whole packet; RADIUS encrypts only the password.

Chapter 10

Review and Preparation for Troubleshooting Complex Enterprise Networks

This chapter covers the following topics:

- Review of key maintenance and troubleshooting concepts and tools
- Applying maintenance and troubleshooting concepts and tools

Today's networks incorporate many different technologies, protocols, devices, and features. To maintain and troubleshoot these complex, integrated enterprise networks efficiently and effectively, you need to acquire broad knowledge and a wide range of skills. In addition to detailed knowledge of individual technologies, protocols, devices, and features, you need to understand how these components interact and depend on each other.

You need to have a sound understanding of the methods that you could use to isolate problems to a particular device, protocol, or feature, and have the ability to plan a troubleshooting process and adjust your plan based on the results of the process. You also need to know how to find the documentation for technologies, protocols, or features that you are not familiar with. In addition, you must be familiar with the tools that are available to support network maintenance and troubleshooting processes and know how to use those tools. Finally, you need to be able to plan, communicate, document, and execute structured network maintenance and troubleshooting processes.

Practicing these skills in a noncritical environment is an important tool to assess whether you have understood and incorporated your acquired knowledge, and to further improve your troubleshooting expertise.

Review of Key Maintenance and Troubleshooting Concepts and Tools

In Chapter 1, "Planning Maintenance for Complex Networks," you learned about the advantages of structured network maintenance over interrupt-driven network maintenance, and you were introduced to some examples of structured network maintenance methodologies. Network maintenance planning includes scheduling maintenance, change-control procedures, network documentation, effective communication, defining templates/procedures/conventions, and disaster recovery.

In Chapter 2, "Troubleshooting Processes for Complex Enterprise Networks," you learned that the fundamental elements of a troubleshooting process are gathering information and symptoms, analyzing information, eliminating possible causes, formulating a hypothesis, and testing the hypothesis. You also learned that the commonly used troubleshooting approaches are top down, bottom up, divide and conquer, follow the path, spot the differences, and move the problem. Communication is an essential part of the troubleshooting process, and it happens in all the following stages of troubleshooting:

Step 1. Reporting the problem

Step 2. Gathering information

Step 3. Analyzing and eliminate

Step 4. Proposing and test a hypothesis

Step 5. Solving the problem.

Chapter 3, "Using Maintenance and Troubleshooting Tools and Applications," showed you how to use the Cisco IOS commands to selectively gather information in support of basic diagnostic processes. It also introduced you to the tools commonly used for specific maintenance and troubleshooting processes and preparing the infrastructure for their use.

Chapter 4, "Maintaining and Troubleshooting Campus Switched Solutions," reviewed important LAN switching topics and presented you with useful skills and commands to troubleshoot VLANs, Spanning Tree Protocol, inter-VLAN routing, and first-hop redundancy protocols.

Chapter 5, "Maintaining and Troubleshooting Routing Solutions," discussed network layer connectivity and in-depth troubleshooting of Enhanced Interior Gateway Protocol (EIGRP), Open Shortest Path First (OSPF) Protocol, Border Gateway Protocol (BGP), and route redistribution.

Chapter 6, "Troubleshooting Addressing Services," analyzed common IPv4 addressing issues related to address translation (NAT), Dynamic Host Configuration Protocol (DHCP) and common IPv6 routing issues.

In Chapter 7, "Troubleshooting Network Performance Issues," you learned that the main categories of application services are as follows:

- Network classification
- Application scalability
- Application networking
- Application acceleration
- WAN acceleration
- Application optimization

You also learned that the recipe to application optimization is a four-step cycle that incrementally increases your understanding of network applications and allows you to progressively deploy measurable improvements and adjustments as required. Those steps are as following:

Step 1. Baseline application traffic.

Step 2. Optimize the network.

Step 3. Measure, adjust, and verify.

Step 4. Deploy new applications.

Chapter 7 also provided you with some knowledge and skills to troubleshoot network applications services, switch performance issues, and router performance issues.

In Chapter 8, "Troubleshooting Converged Networks," you learned that common wireless integration issues include the following:

- Problems at the wireless to wired boundary
- Filters that might be blocking traffic
- Wireless quality of service (QoS) and wired QoS mapping might be incorrect
- Power over Ethernet (PoE) issues
- Trunk issues

You also learned that the design and troubleshooting considerations of integrating unified communications (VoIP and IP Telephony, for example) into a campus LAN are as follows:

- QoS (bandwidth, delay, jitter, packet loss, network QoS readiness, trust boundaries)
- High availability (Spanning Tree Protocol / Rapid Spanning Tree Protocol (STP/RSTP), Hot Standby Router Protocol / Gateway Load Balancing Protocol / Virtual Router Redundancy Protocol (HSRP/GLBP/VRRP)
- Security (traffic segregation, firewalling/filtering)
- Availability and correct provisioning of other services (Power over Ethernet (PoE), Dynamic Host Control Protocol (DHCP), Trivial File Transfer Protocol (TFTP), Network Time Protocol (NTP), Cisco Discovery Protocol (CDP), trunking, VLANs)

In the final part of Chapter 8 you learned some of the common video integration issues:

- Excessive bandwidth utilization
- Lack of control
- Poor quality (lack of QoS)
- Security issues (filtering of key protocols, and stateful requirements)
- Multicast issues

In Chapter 9, "Maintaining and Troubleshooting Network Security Implementations," you learned about the three main functional planes:

- Management plane
- Control plane
- Data plane

The management functions of a router or switch are commonly accessed using three different methods:

- Cisco IOS command-line interface (CLI)
- Web-based device management
- A network management platform that is based on Simple Network Management Protocol (SNMP)

All of these methods must be used in the most secure way, based on the device type, its operating system (IOS) capabilities, and the security policies of the organization. There are two common techniques to secure management access to network devices. First, access to the management plane can be restricted using packet or session filters: Access is allowed only from specific source IP addresses. Second, it is necessary to authenticate the user that is attempting to access the device. Misconfiguration of any of the following can lead to control plane failures:

- Routing protocol or first-hop redundancy protocol authentication
- STP options such as BPDU Guard, BPDU filter, Root Guard, and Loop Guard
- DHCP snooping
- Dynamic ARP inspection
- Control plane policing or protection

Data plane security is accomplished using a variety of router and switch options such as Unicast Reverse Path Forwarding (Unicast RPF), IPsec, Network Admission Control, and 802.1x port authentication.

Applying Maintenance and Troubleshooting Concepts and Tools

In complex integrated networks, a combination of many different protocols and technologies deliver network services that support the enterprise applications. These protocols and technologies interact with each other: Some processes merely interact with each other, some depend on other processes, and yet other processes perform their functions in parallel (see Figure 10-1). If one of the elements fails or does not perform as expected, it impacts the system as a whole. At some point, symptoms will become noticeable at the application level, and a user will report a problem. A diagnostic process starts to find the elements that are causing the problem and eliminates the problem by implementing a solution or workaround.

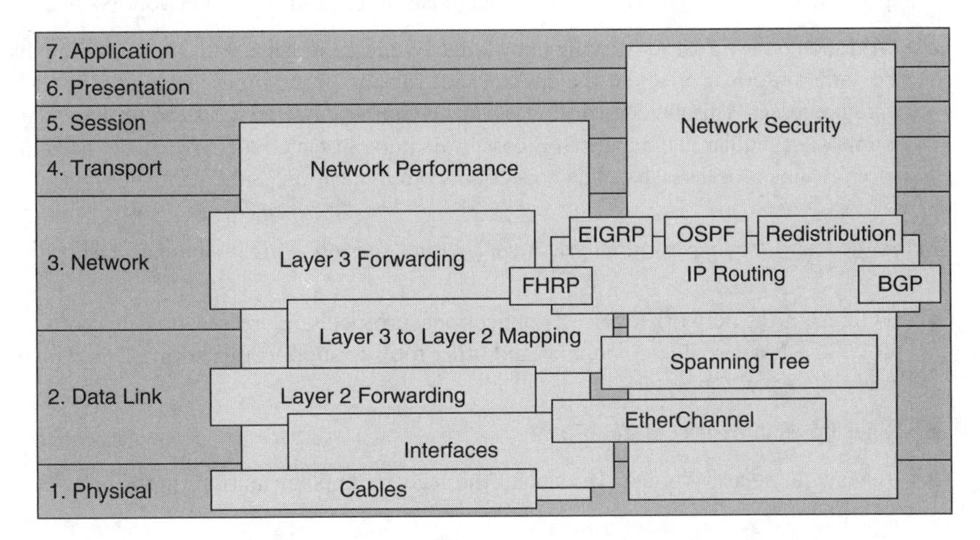

Figure 10-1 *Network Elements Are Interrelated, or Dependent on Each Other, or Run in Parallel*

To be able to troubleshoot a complex network in an effective and efficient manner, the following aspects are important:

- You should have a good understanding of each of the individual technologies, protocols, and features used in your network. At the minimum, you should have a high-level overview of the functionality offered by each of the technologies, protocols, and features. You might not need to have specialist knowledge about each particular technology, but if this is not the case, you should know how to obtain the required background knowledge, documentation, or expert support in your organization.
- You should have a good understanding of the interactions and dependencies between the different technologies, protocols, and features in your network. If a problem symptom is noticed in one of the elements, this does not necessarily mean that the root cause of the problem exists in that element itself. The root cause might be in another element, upon which the element that you are investigating, depends or interacts with. For example, a routing protocol failure might be caused by an underlying Layer 2 problem.
- You should have a good understanding of the way control plane processes influence data plane processes. Problem symptoms are usually noticed and reported on the

data plane, while the root cause in many cases is in the control plane, where the solutions or workarounds must be implemented. Knowing how control plane data structures are used in data plane forwarding, and knowing how these data structures are populated, is essential for successful diagnosis and resolution of network problems.

- You should have a good working knowledge of and experience with the tools available to gather information about the operation of various technologies, protocols, features, and processes. This includes both specialized troubleshooting tools and tools used in support of regular maintenance processes. Examples of such tools are those that support change processes, baseline collection, communication, and documentation.

Before you start troubleshooting, you must perform the following preliminary tasks:

- Document the network (devices, connections, protocols, addresses, routing protocols, VLANs). Use IOS commands and other tools to support this effort. Create physical and logical topologies.
- Back up all current configurations.
- Review the security policy. Document the security implementations in the network.

As you troubleshoot different cases, keep in mind that different approaches might suit different cases. Therefore, depending on the case, the approach you take might be top down, bottom up, follow the path, or a hybrid method. The key is to have an approach and follow through, documenting all discoveries or changes. No matter which method is used, the basic elements should include the following, the workflow for which is illustrated in Figure 10-2:

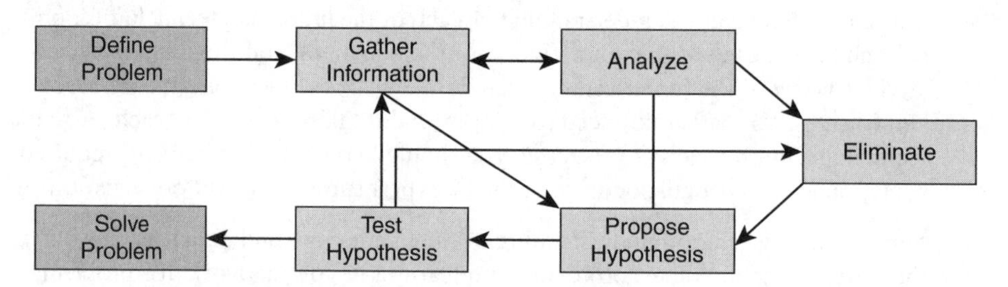

Figure 10-2 *Troubleshooting Approach Workflow*

Step 1. Define the problem.

Step 2. Gather information. Document any issues.

Step 3. Analyze the information.

Step 4. Eliminate possible causes.

Step 5. Formulate and propose a hypothesis. Document possible solutions.

Step 6. Implement and test hypothesis. Always circle back to the security policy to ensure any changes meet the policy requirements.

Step 7. Solve problem and document changes.

Summary

Previous chapters reviewed many of the individual technologies commonly used in complex, integrated enterprise networks. Furthermore, these chapters demonstrated the use of tools and structured methods with many troubleshooting examples, and important lessons and best practices derived from these experiences.

If you need to master network troubleshooting, you must get a lot of hands-on experience with the networking devices. This can be done using the in-house lab of your employer, by using rental remote labs, setting up your own small lab, or by using network simulators. Also, the Cisco Networking Academy and Cisco Learning Partners offer Cisco official curriculum courses, most of which include extensive hands-on labs.

Finally, if you are interested in becoming a Cisco Certified Network Professional, and need other books to prepare you for the troubleshooting examination, you should consider the Cisco Press *CCNP Troubleshooting Exam Certification Guide.*

Appendix A

Answer to Review Questions

This appendix provides an answer key to the Review Questions found at the end of Chapters 1 through 9. Compare the answer key to your answers and follow up with any needed remediation within each chapter to ensure that you have mastered your understanding of the topics and concepts covered throughout the book.

Chapter 1

1. a, c, d
2. a, b, d
3. a, d
4. b, c
5. Risk, impact, and resources should be balanced against urgency, necessity, and business needs.
6. a, d, e
7. a.
8. a, b, c, e, f
9. c
10. **archive config**
11. b
12. **logging 10.1.1.1**
13. d
14. c, d

Chapter 2

1. a, b, d
2. a, b, c, e
3. a, b, f
4. e
5. Existence of consistent templates for configurations and a baseline of network behavior under normal circumstances
6. d
7. a, b
8. a, b, c, e
9. a, b, e
10. c
11. c

Chapter 3

1. d
2. c
3. a
4. a
5. b
6. b
7. b, e
8. b, e
9. d
10. a, d
11. b.
12. d, e
13. a
14. c
15. d
16. b

Chapter 4

1. a
2. b, c
3. a, b, d
4. **show interfaces switchport**
5. MAC address table
6. c, a, b
7. b, d
8. c
9. a, b, e
10. Physically remove redundant links until all loops are eliminated from the topology.
11. d
12. a, d
13. d
14. b.
15. a, c
16. c
17. c
18. c
19. b
20. b

Chapter 5

1. b, c
2. d
3. a.
4. a, d
5. e
6. **show ip cef exact-route** *source destination*
7. **show adjacency detail**

8. b, d, f
9. b.
10. c
11. a, d
12. d
13. a, d, f
14. d
15. a, c, e
16. Nine type 3 LSAs: four in the area 0 database, and five in the area 2 database
17. Which of the following statements best describes the subsequent stages of the establishment of an OSPF adjacency? Fill in the blanks with: init, 2-way, ex-start, loading
    a. Ex-start
    b. Init
    c. Loading
    d. 2-way
18. a, c, d, e
19. **debug ip ospf adj**
20. c
21. c
22. c
23. b
24. a, d
25. **debug ip routing**
26. b, d
27. c, g
28. a. True
29. b. False
30. a, c
31. a
32. c

Chapter 6

1. c

2. a

3. a, b, c

4. a, d

5. a.

6. d

7. a

9. a

10. c

11. b

12. c

13. c

14. d

15. b

16. d

Chapter 7

1. **a.** Understand the basic traffic and application flows and network performance.

d. Roll out new applications and observe the effects on existing applications.

b. Apply QoS to reduce congestion, prioritize specific traffic, select best paths, and so on.

c. Find out the effect of QoS on your network, and understand performance using IOS features.

2. b

3. d

4. a

5. 1: _e_ 2: _a_ 3: _b_ 4: _d_ 5: _c_

6. b

7. b.

8. c, e
9. a, b, d
10. c
11. a, b, d
12. a, b
13. a, c
14. a
15. a, c
16. a, b, e
17. b
18. a, b
19. b
20. a, b, d

Chapter 8

1. The autonomous model and the split MAC (lightweight) model
2. PoE, trunking, WLAN-to-VLAN mapping, security, QoS
3. 12223 for control and 12222 for data
4. It displays the policy attached to the zone-pair specified.
5. Option 43
6. QoS, high availability, security, PoE
7. DHCP, TFTP, NTP, CDP
8. 5. The IP phone initializes, applying the IP configuration to the IP stack.

   3. The phone attempts to obtain an IP address through DHCP.

   1. The IP phone powers on, performs POST, and boots.

   4. The DHCP server offers an IP address (with option 150) to the IP phone.

   2. The phone uses Cisco Discovery Protocol to learn the voice VLAN.
9. This command lists the ports in the disabled state along with the reasons for why they are disabled.
10. Port number 2000
11. **show ip igmp groups**

Chapter 9

1. a, c, d
2. c, d
3. a, b
4. c, e, f
5. a
6. d
7. a, c
8. a, c, d
9. a
10. c
11. b, d, f

Index

SYMBOLS

A

B

C

D

E

F

G

H

J

K

L

M

N

O

P

Q

R

T

U

V

W

Z

GO FURTHER, FASTER.
BECOME CERTIFIED.
Stop thinking about your potential. Realize it. Take your training, skills and knowledge to the next level. Get Cisco Certified through Pearson VUE.
Take your Cisco Career Certification exam at one of more than 4,400 conveniently located Pearson VUE® Authorized Test Centers worldwide to experience a no-hassle test experience. To register at a test center near you, simply visit PearsonVUE.com/Cisco.
PEARSON
VUE
Copyright © 2009 Pearson Education, Inc. or its affiliate(s). All rights reserved. PearsonVUE.com